EL SALVADOR:

CENTRAL AMERICA IN THE NEW COLD WAR

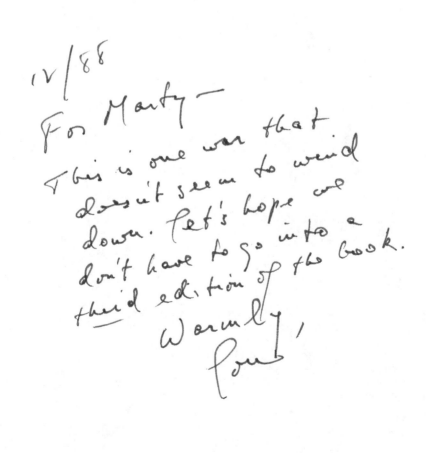

iv/88

For Marty —
This is one war that
doesn't seem to wind
down. Let's hope we
don't have to go into a
third edition of the book.
Warmly,
Paul

EL SALVADOR:

CENTRAL AMERICA IN THE NEW COLD WAR *Revised and Updated*

EDITED BY

Marvin E. Gettleman
Patrick Lacefield
Louis Menashe
David Mermelstein

GROVE PRESS
New York

Published by Grove Press, Inc.
920 Broadway
New York, N.Y. 10010

Library of Congress Cataloging-in-Publication Data

El Salvador : Central America in the Cold War.

   1. El Salvador—Politics and government—1979–
2. Communism—El Salvador—History—20th century.
3. El Salvador—Foreign relations—United States.
4. United States—Foreign relations—El Salvador.
I. Gettleman, Marvin E.
F1488.3.E4 1987 972.84′053 86-33499
ISBN 0-394-55557-0
ISBN 0-394-62345-2 (pbk.)

Designed by Irving Perkins Associates
Manufactured in the United States of America
First Edition 1987

10 9 8 7 6 5 4 3 2 1

"U.S. Interests in Central America," by Ronald Reagan. "Dictatorships and Double Standards," by Jeane T. Kirkpatrick, reprinted from *Commentary,* November, 1979, by permission, all rights reserved. "Totalitarianism vs. Authoritarianism," by Michael Walzer, reprinted by permission of *The New Republic,* © 1981, The New Republic, Inc. "Reagan's Latin America," by Tom J. Farer, reprinted with permission from *The New York Review of Books.* Copyright © 1981 by Nyrev, Inc. "El Salvador: A Political Chronology," by the editors. "Class Struggle and Civil War in El Salvador," by Harald Jung, reprinted with permission from *New Left Review.* "Roots of the Salvadoran Right: Origins of the Death Squads," by Craig Pyes, © 1986, reprinted by permission of the Albuquerque Journal Publishing Co. "El Salvador's Divided Military," by Shirley Christian, reprinted from *The Atlantic Monthly,* © Shirley Christian 1983. "The Roman Catholic Church in El Salvador: The Early Years," by the staff of CARIN, copyright © 1982. "The Ideology of Salvadoran Christian Democracy," by Stephen Webre, reprinted by permission of Louisiana State University Press, from *José Napoleón Duarte and the Christian Democratic Party in Salvadoran Politics: 1960–1972,* copyright © 1979. "The Rebirth of the Christian Militancy in El Salvador," by the staff of CARIN. "Oscar Romero, Archbishop of the Poor," by Patrick Lacefield, reprinted with permission from the November, 1979, *Fellowship,* the magazine of the Fellowship of Reconcilliation, Box 271, Nyack, N.Y. "Avoiding Bloodshed: A Letter to President Jimmy Carter," by Archbishop Oscar Romero. "The Option for Life: Challenge to the Church in El Salvador," by Jon Sobrino, reprinted with permission of the Universidad Centroamericana, José Simeon Cañas, San Salvador, El Salvador, © 1984. "The Protestant Challenge in El Salvador," by Marlise Simons, reprinted with permission from "El Salvador is Fertile Ground for

To the memory of
Benjamin Ernest Linder

Acknowledgments
to the First Edition

In the course of putting this book together, we received advice and help for which we are grateful. First of all, we thank our editor at Grove Press, Lisa Rosset, whose enthusiasm for our project from the very start has been heartening. We are also appreciative of the efforts of our literary agent, Betty Anne Clarke.

Special thanks go to Cynthia Arnson, John Dinges and Michael Parenti, all of whom are affiliated with the Institute for Policy Studies in Washington, D.C., an organization recently much maligned by the political right wing in the United States; and to Anne Nelson, who helped us select from among her many moving photographs those most appropriate and who also assisted in designing their layout.

In addition, we wish to acknowledge the assistance of the following: Zena Jacobs, Vera Marek and Hana Stranska of the Spicer Library, Polytechnic Institute of New York; the helpful if anonymous librarians at the Herbert H. Lehman Library, Columbia University, and the Government Documents Division, New York Public Library; Deborah Levenson and Marilyn Young, both of New York University; Nancy Lieber, Institute for Democratic Socialism; Walter LaFeber, Cornell University; Cindy Hounsell, Ellen Schrecker and Allis Wolfe, all of Manhattan; Hobart A. Spalding, Jr., Brooklyn College, City University of New York; Robert Armstrong and Stephen Volk, North American Congress on Latin America; Fred Siegel, Jan Rosenberg, Sheila Menashe, Claudia Menashe, Daniel Radosh, Laura Radosh, Linnea Capps Lacefield and Rachel Fruchter, all of Brooklyn, New York; Penny Schantz, Democratic Socialist Organizing Committee; Rick Kunnes, New American Movement; John A. Womack, Jr., Harvard University; I. Leonard Leeb and Frederick C.

Kreiling, Department of Social Sciences, Polytechnic Institute of New York; Hermione McLemore and Darline Vincent, office of the Department of Social Sciences, Polytechnic Institute of New York; Albert L. Brusakos, the Polytechnic Institute of New York print shop; Pete Seeger; David Curzon and Gonzalo Martner, of the office of Planning, Programming and Evaluation of the United Nations; Michael Barry, Dot Gregory, Tom Bleha, Carl Matthews, Peter Knecht and David Simcox, all of the U.S. Department of State; Victoria Rideout, office of Congressman Gerry Studds; Mark Pinsky, office of Congressman Ted Weiss; Julius Topol, District Council 37, Municipal Employees Legal Services Plan, New York; Marvin Ciporen, Amalgamated Clothing and Textile Workers' Union, New York; Richard E. Feinberg, Woodrow Wilson International Center for Scholars; and Carlos Torres, a Salvadoran student at the Polytechnic Institute of New York. Finally, a special note of gratitude to a Salvadoran friend who was of invaluable assistance to Patrick Lacefield during a visit to El Salvador in 1979.

Acknowledgments
to the Revised Edition

This second edition is a thoroughly revised book, and we have accumulated a fresh set of obligations in putting it together. Special mention must again be made of Mrs. Hermione McLemore, secretary of the Social Sciences Department, Polytechnic University. The skilled librarians at the Spicer Library of Polytechnic—especially Zena Jacobs and Liliana Middleton—again rendered us invaluable service in supplying essential data. For assistance in making use of the rich resources of the North American Congress on Latin America library, we wish to thank the knowledgeable, helpful NACLA staff. Joanne Kenen of Reuters made many useful suggestions and helped with the translations. Professor Susan Besse of the City College of New York assisted on the bibliography. Professor Barton Meyers of Brooklyn College contributed in more ways than one. At Grove Press the editorial assistance of Lisa Rosset, Walter Bode and Paul Busby was exemplary.

Marv Gettleman, in particular, wishes to thank Professor Arnon Hadar of Dominican College (California) and the Rev. Chester Wickwire of Johns Hopkins University who in 1985 facilitated travel and data collection in Central America through FACHRES (Faculty Committee on Human Rights in El Salvador). Traveling companions *extraordinaire* in El Salvador and elsewhere in Central America included Professor Piero Gleijeses of the School of Advanced International Studies, Johns Hopkins, Professor William Harris of Wheelock College, Professor Angela Delli Santi of the University of New Mexico, Dr. Jane Halpern of Towson State College, Dr. Wafaa El Sadr of New York University, and Professor Joseph Straley of the University of North Carolina.

In El Salvador, Maria Julia Hernández of the Tutela Legal office of the Archbishopric of San Salvador supplied information on human rights. Julio Cesar Portillo of ANDES (the teachers union) provided insight into the problems of popular organizations. From a different political perspective, Johnny Maldonado and Carlos Castenneda of the San Salvador Chamber of Commerce presented the viewpoint of the Salvadoran business community. Also, several faculty members at the University of El Salvador and the Central American University were helpful, as were many other Salvadorans who will here remain anonymous.

Chris Norton, Central American correspondent for *In These Times* (a Chicago weekly) was helpful, as was James LeMoyne, *New York Times* bureau chief in San Salvador. Professor William M. LeoGrande of American University was kind enough to share with us his immense knowledge of materials pertaining to U.S. policy and Central America. We would also like to thank John Dinges of National Public Radio. Marc Cooper, free-lance journalist and official of the (U.S.) National Writers Union, shared with us his considerable expertise on El Salvador in the era of José Napoleón Duarte.

M.E.G.
P.L.
L.M.
D.M.
(November, 1986)

Contents

General Introduction

Coffee growers should not anguish over the situation in El Salvador today; there was a similar one in 1932, and if it was solved then it can be now.
—Representative of the Frente Unido Cafetalero (coffee plantation owners)
March, 1980

WHEN the first edition of this book appeared, the tiny Central American nation of El Salvador was in the throes of a civil war that already displayed ominous regional and international overtones. The conflict continues, and dangers that it will intensify and spread are, if anything, more serious now, a half decade later. Why?

The answers must be sought not only in the present situation but in a history extending back to the fateful *matanza* (massacre) of 1932 referred to by the oligarch quoted in the epigraph above, and even to the sixteenth-century Spanish conquest. By 1524 Pedro de Alvarado, one of the cruelest of the *Conquistadores,* had subdued the indigenous population of Central America with legendary brutality. Under Spanish colonial domination, El Salvador was part of the Captaincy-General of Guatemala, and for some time after independence it continued to be part of a federated Republic of Central America.[1] Although this union dissolved in factional struggles among the post-independence local tyrants, these indigenous leaders could occasionally unite in response to a common situation, as in 1855–56, when Central American armed forces came together temporarily to defeat the U.S. *filibustero* William Walker.[2] For the remainder of the nineteenth century and into the twentieth, El Salvador was plagued by frequent interference by the dictators of neighboring countries, as well as the depredations of its own dictators. The most

[1] Fred Rippy, *Latin America: A Modern History* (Rev. ed., Ann Arbor, Mich., 1968), chapter 15.

[2] Alastair White, *El Salvador* (London, 1973), 76–77.

notorious modern dictator, whose name has been adopted by a leading right-wing "death squad,"[3] was General Maximiliano Hernández Martínez. Believer in the esoteric doctrines of Theosophy, as well as in the tenets of fascism, Martínez (as he was universally called in El Salvador) took over the state by a *coup d'état* in 1931,[4] just as the full force of world depression was reaching Central America, dramatically affecting the already vulnerable economies of the region.

Introduced in the early nineteenth century, coffee rapidly came to dominate not only the economy but the social structure of El Salvador. The coffee plantations that flourished on the country's fertile volcanic soil depended upon a fluctuating world market and demanded intensive mobilization of the labor force. Thus, there developed both a coffee growers' oligarchy, virtually a state within a state, and a rapidly growing rural proletariat.[5] (Already the most densely populated country in Central America, El Salvador experiences the staggering population growth rate of 3 percent per year.) Leftist organizations and propaganda began to appear by the 1920s, appealing not only to the landless workers but to segments of the middle class as well. The major figure in the Salvadoran left in this period was Augustín Farabundo Martí, scion of one of the leading oligarchic families, who, when the international price for coffee dropped and the growers attempted to pass on at least part of their losses to the peasants, organized resistance in the rural areas. In January 1932, just as El Salvador's major volcano, Izalco, erupted, the peasants in many regions attacked villages and cities, aiming at the local oligarchs, military outposts, and telegraph stations. This has been called the first Communist revolution in Latin America.[6] Accounts of it, and of the massacre carried out by General Martínez, may be found in a major work of scholarship by the U.S. historian Thomas P. Anderson. According to Professor Anderson, the heritage of military dictatorship and "Indeed, the whole [subsequent] political labyrinth of El Salvador can be explained only in reference to the traumatic experience of the uprising and the *Matanza.*"[7]

Dealt a crushing blow in 1932, the left in El Salvador has risen again in response to the persistence of misused oligarchic power and military brutality. The leading insurgent organization has taken the name of the martyred leader of the 1932 uprising while a right-wing death squad took the name of the dictator who ordered his execution. The current contest of such forces as the Hernández Martínez death squad against the Farabundo Martí National Lib-

[3.] See Reading 16.

[4.] David Lena, "Análisis de una Dictadura Fascista Latin-Americana: Maximiliano Hernández Martínez," *La Universidad,* 94 (Sept.–Oct. 1969); Thomas P. Anderson, *Matanza: El Salvador's Communist Revolt of 1932* (Lincoln, Neb., 1971), chapters 3 and 4.

[5.] David Browning, *El Salvador: Landscape and Society* (London, 1971), 155–73, 222–23; Alejandro D. Marroquin, *Latin America and the Caribbean* (Belfast, 1968), 188ff.

[6.] Anderson, *Matanza,* 2 and passim.

[7.] Anderson, *Matanza,* 159.

eration Front illustrates the importance of historical factors in shaping the present-day confrontation in El Salvador.

This book is being offered in the hope of stimulating informed debate and careful consideration of policy options, some of which go far beyond the alternatives now being considered in official circles. Even before Ronald Reagan won the presidency in 1980, Washington exhibited an alarming tendency to view upheavals and insurgencies in such places as Central America (despite much contrary evidence and the views of knowledgeable scholars) as exercises in externally directed "Communist expansion."

We have included in this book a rich selection of readings expressing this orthodox if contested point of view, including in its entirety Jeane Kirkpatrick's now-famous 1979 *Commentary* essay "Dictatorships and Double Standards" (Reading 2), which anticipated the Reagan administration's outlook so well that it earned its author a high government position. We have also presented several official U.S. government policy pronouncements, briefing reports, and "white papers," in as full and complete versions as space allowed (although in some readings we had to eliminate or condense footnotes).

We also offer other points of view, as well as those emanating from official Washington, including the position of the U.S.-backed Salvadoran government and its antagonists, the guerrillas of the Farabundo Martí National Liberation Front (FMLN).[8] Allowed in these pages to speak in their own voices, the actual participants in the Salvadoran conflict—rebels and oligarchs, military brass and church workers, President Duarte and his opponents—can bring readers as close as many of them will ever come to the struggle in Central America—unless, of course, deepening U.S. involvement should lead to the introduction of increasing numbers of North American combat troops. But that is precisely what the editors of this volume are trying to avoid. By presenting developments, reports, viewpoints, and perspectives little known by the general public, we hope to promote wider knowledge and thus help prevent the tacit or active support for further bloodshed in that country named for a peaceful savior.

—The Editors

[8.] Here we wish to clarify a linguistic point. The Spanish word *guerrilla* does not refer to apes; it is the diminutive of *guerra* (war) and was first used to refer to the actions of Spanish irregular partisans battling Napoleon's invading French army in the 1809–14 Peninsular War with ambushes, traps, and other unconventional tactics. Of course, the practice of *guerrilla* warfare is much older than the Spanish name, having been practiced in ancient and modern China, during the American Revolution, in the anti-Nazi struggle, and of course during the Vietnam War. In Spanish, *guerrillero* is someone fighting a "little war" *(guerrilla)*. In Latin American usage *gorila* (gorilla in English) refers to military or policy tyrants and their oligarchic sponsors. For a general treatment, see Eric Hobsbawm, *Revolutionaries* (New York, 1973), chapter 17.

EL SALVADOR:

CENTRAL AMERICA IN THE
NEW COLD WAR

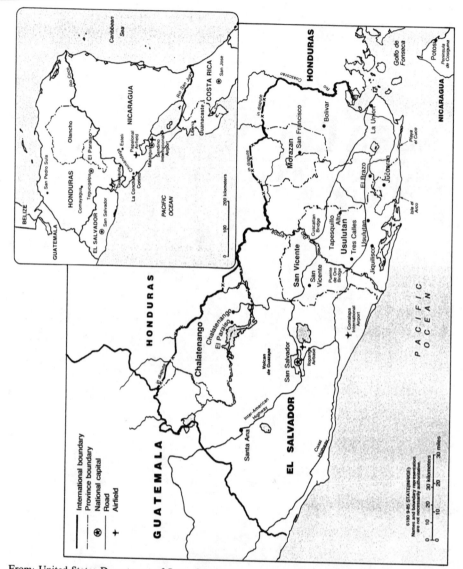

From: United States Department of State, Special Report No. 132, September 1985.

El Salvador in Brief

El Salvador ("The Savior") was conquered in 1525 by Pedro de Alvarado, a lieutenant of Cortés. Along with other Central American territories, El Salvador declared independence from Spain in 1821. With the dissolution of the United Provinces of Central American states in 1838, El Salvador became a republic.

GEOGRAPHY:

Area: 8,124 square miles (the size of Massachusetts). Contiguous neighbors: Honduras (43,277 square miles) to the east and north; Guatemala (42,042 square miles) to the west and north; Nicaragua (57,143 square miles) across the Gulf of Fonseca.

The Pacific and the mountains form the natural boundaries of El Salvador, the smallest mainland nation in the western hemisphere. The country is about 160 miles long, from east to west, and about 60 miles wide, from the ocean to Honduras. A hot Pacific coastal plain in the south rises to a cooler plateau and valley region about 2,000 feet high. The mountainous north holds many volcanoes and crater lakes. There are no jungles.

POPULATION:

Total population (1983): 4,685,000.
Annual rate of population increase, 1970–81: 3 percent (urban 3.3 percent; rural 2.8 percent).
Density: 570 per square mile (the most densely populated in the region but somewhat less so than Massachusetts or Connecticut).
Age distribution: 0–14 years, 45.2 percent; 15–59 years, 48.4 percent; 60 years and above, 5.4 percent.

Capital: San Salvador, population (1982 estimate) 440,000.
Second largest city: Santa Ana, population (1982 estimate) 175,000.
Ethnicity: Mestizos, 89 percent; Indians, 10 percent; Caucasians, 1 percent.
Language: Spanish (and, among some Indians, Nahuatl).
Religion: Roman Catholicism prevails but Protestantism is gaining adherents.

ECONOMY:

Overview

Monetary unit: colon. Official rate (spring 1985) 2.50 colons for U.S. $1;
   black-market rate: 4.15–5.00.
Gross national product (1980): $2.7 billion; gross domestic product (GDP;
   1982): $2.9 billion.
Per-capita income (1983): $470.
Average annual growth of GNP (1970–79): 1.4 percent.
1979–83: GNP down 25 percent; average per-capita income down 29 percent;
   capital outflow: $1 billion.

AGRICULTURE AND LAND:

Percentage of GDP from agriculture (1982): 26 percent.
Agricultural exports as percent of total (1980): 59 percent.
Land: 60 percent engaged in agriculture; 1.9 percent of population owns 57
   percent of land.
Agricultural production (1978 = 100)
   Agriculture (1980) 107.4; (1984 preliminary) 91.7
   Cattle (1980) 88.3; (1984 preliminary) 67.2

AGRICULTURAL PRODUCTION

(1,000s of tons)	1980	1982	1984 *(preliminary)*
Coffee	186	172	152
Cotton	61	40	28
Sugar cane	2,564	2,372	3,402

Since 1979, the production of coffee, accounting for 60 percent of all foreign-exchange earnings, has dropped 20 percent.

EXPORTS AND IMPORTS:

Value of exports (in millions) 1982, $626 (1981, $700; 1980, $874; 1979, $998).

Value of imports (in millions) 1982, $741 (1981, $843; 1980, $911; 1979, $1147).

Value of exports, by crop (1984 preliminary): coffee, $473 million; sugar, $30 million; shrimp, $17 million; cotton, $9 million.

INVESTMENT AND DEBT:

U.S. share of foreign investment: approximately 56 percent.

Value of American investment (1980): $103 million.

Foreign debt (1982): $2.3 billion (private and public).

Deficit on current account (1983): $204 million.

Interest and capital payments on foreign debt (1985 approximate): $250 million; as a percentage of the value of exports: 40 percent.

Interest and capital payments on foreign debt plus petroleum imports, as a percentage of the value of exports (1985 approximate): 60 percent.

U.S. aid, U.S. fiscal years 1981–85: $1.7 billion (75 percent is war related).

INFLATION AND UNEMPLOYMENT:

Inflation rate (1983): 13.1 percent.

Unemployment (1983): 30 percent (40 percent in countryside), up from 6.7 percent in 1979; unemployment plus underemployment, 60 percent.

SOCIAL:

Literacy rate (1978): urban, 50 percent; rural, 30 percent.

Life expectancy at birth (1980): males, 56.7; females, 59.7.

Infant mortality (1979): 60 per 1,000 live births (of total deaths of natural causes in rural El Salvador, 47 percent are children under five who starve).

Physicians per 100,000 (1977): 27 (about one-seventh the number in the United States, same year).

Durables in use (1981): TV sets, 300,000; radios, 1.5 million; telephones, 75,920; passenger motor vehicles, 77,300; commercial vehicles, 63,000.

Electrification: percentage of total population, 18 percent.

World Economic-Social Standing (1978): average rank (criteria include GNP per capita, education, health, nutrition, safe water) El Salvador 84th (United States 7th, Canada 14th, Cuba 36th, Panama 48th, Costa Rica 50th, Nicaragua 74th, Guatemala 85th, Honduras 91st, Haiti 122nd).

Cold War Cartography

JACK HUBERMAN

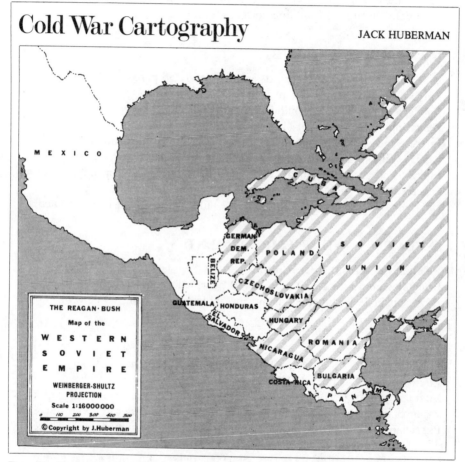

From *The Nation,* June 15, 1985

CHAPTER I

Seeing Red:
The Reagan Administration
Looks at the World

Editors' Introduction

Ronald Reagan brought to the presidency a fundamentalist anti-Communism and a hostility to the Soviet Union that recalled the mood and rhetoric of the early cold war. Reagan and his first Secretary of State, Alexander Haig, spoke the language of Harry Truman and John Foster Dulles.

At his first press conference in 1981, President Reagan accused Soviet leaders of "reserv[ing] unto themselves the right to commit any crime; to lie; to cheat . . ." Later, he would describe the Soviet Union as an "evil empire," with Moscow as the "focus of evil in the modern world." Secretary Haig, in his first public speech in office, denounced Moscow as "the greatest source of international insecurity today" and charged that "Soviet promotion of violence as the instrument of change constitutes the greatest danger to world peace."[1]

[1.] Haig's statements appear in his address to the American Society of Newspaper Editors, April 24, 1981 (United States Department of State, *Current Policy*, No. 275, April 1981). Reagan's "evil empire" remarks were made in a speech to the National Association of Evangelicals, March 8, 1983 (*New York Times*, March 9, 1985). His press-conference remarks were made on January 29, 1981 (*New York Times*, January 30, 1981). Haig resigned as Secretary of State on June 25, 1982, after many disputes with other administration officials, often over managerial style. He was replaced by George P. Shultz, whose public pronouncements have been markedly more temperate than Haig's. See chapter 9.

This rhetoric helped justify a new escalation of arms production. Adding another aperture to the vocabulary of strategic metaphors arising from U.S.-Soviet rivalry—remember earlier talk of the "bomber gap" and the "missile gap"—President Reagan warned of the existence of a "window of vulnerability." This signified a purported disproportion between U.S. and Soviet nuclear arsenals that could allow Moscow to launch an incapacitating first strike. In 1981, accordingly, the Reagan administration programmed new generations of intercontinental weapons systems—MX missiles, B-1 bombers, and Trident submarines. In 1983, the United States deployed updated intermediate-range missiles, the ground-launched Cruises and Pershing IIs, in several NATO countries to offset what was perceived as the threat from Soviet SS-20s based in European Russia. The same year, President Reagan announced his commitment to research and development of an antimissile shield in space, what he called the strategic defense initiative, popularly known as Star Wars. In so doing, the President had unlocked a new, potent destabilizing force in the nuclear balance of terror.

If the 1970s were the decade of détente, of relaxing Soviet-American tension, the 1980s inaugurated a revival of international friction and confrontation, with the boundaries possibly extended into space.[2]

Yet, as during other periods of the cold war, propitious circumstances could generate dramatic reversals. The rabid anti-Communist Richard Nixon and his Secretary of State, Henry Kissinger, orchestrated U.S. foreign policy along themes of accommodation with the Soviet Union. They concentrated on improving relations and building mutual trust through arms treaties and cultural, scientific, and economic exchanges. The Soviet invasion of Afghanistan in 1979, together with what were described by Washington as threatening projections of Soviet power in other regions of the world (in Africa, for example, with Cuban assistance), helped unravel détente even before the tough anti-Soviet posture of the new Reagan administration.[3]

[2] For good introductions, from different ideological perspectives, on U.S.-Soviet relations and Soviet military capabilities, see Adam B. Ulam, *Dangerous Relations: The Soviet Union in World Politics, 1970–1982* (New York, 1983), and Andrew Cockburn, *The Threat: Inside the Soviet Military Machine* (New York, 1983).

[3] Among other things, the Carter administration allowed the results of SALT II (the second set of strategic-arms-limitation talks) to go unratified by the Senate; a "rapid deployment force" was established for quick military action in the Third World; and arms shipments were resumed to the Salvadoran military-civilian junta. As George Kennan warned, a climate of war hysteria settled over Washington in the wake of the Soviet invasion of Afghanistan: "Never since World War II has there been so far-reaching a militarization of thought and discourse in the capital. An unsuspecting stranger, plunged into its midst, could only conclude that the last hope of peaceful, nonmilitary solutions had been exhausted—that from now on only weapons, however used, could count" (*New York Times,* February 1, 1980). Kennan's words carry a special kind of weight: a former ambassador to Moscow, he was also one of the architects of the original containment policy and his "The Sources of Soviet Conduct," signed "X," was a basic document of the cold war. See *Foreign Affairs,* 25 (July 1947), 566–82.

Gradually, however, even Reagan began modulating his anti-Soviet rhetoric and started exploring policy alternatives. One sign of this came late in 1983, when his administration concluded the largest grain sale in history to the Soviets. Most remarkably, in November 1985, Reagan went to Geneva to meet the new Soviet leader, Mikhail S. Gorbachev, for the first summit encounter between the superpowers since Carter and Brezhnev met in 1979. No major breakthroughs in the outstanding area of arms control took place at Geneva, but at least the two leaders were talking to one another, often cordially. The process has continued. Reagan and Gorbachev met again in the early fall of 1986 in the so-called "pre-summit" in Reykjavik, Iceland. If in the end this meeting ended in ambiguous disarray, it should nonetheless be noted that daring proposals to end the arms race were negotiated in apparent seriousness. With another summit meeting yet promised, it appears the curtain of total antagonism has been partially lifted. Perhaps the new cold war was making way, painfully, with measured steps, toward a new détente, or at least a thaw in U.S.-Soviet relations.

It was no longer entirely accurate, therefore, to characterize Reagan's foreign policy as animated by the single spring of simple anti-Sovietism.[4] Global strategic, economic, and political realities, especially the nightmare prospect of nuclear conflict are apparent enough to impress even the most hardened anti-Sovieteer like President Reagan with the need to negotiate with, rather than confront, the Soviet Union. Has speaking more softly to the Soviet Union meant that the big stick is now less an instrument of U.S. policy abroad? With respect to the Third World, the answer is, unfortunately, no. The amicable spirit of Geneva was still in the air when President Reagan startled the press with his announcement of support for covert military assistance to the South African-supported forces fighting the left-wing government of Angola.[5] The revelations about arms sales to Iran and subsequent diversion of funds to the contras late in 1986 showed the lengths, including possibly illegal ones, the Reagan White House was willing to pursue to supply arms to the anti-Sandinista forces based in Honduras.

In Central America and the Caribbean, historically zones of North American influence and hegemony, the temptation for Washington to employ direct or indirect force against the left is very nearly irresistible. One does not have to reach back to the era of McKinley and Teddy Roosevelt for examples of this historic trend; it is evident from a glance at the recent record. In 1954 the Eisenhower administration engineered, with CIA direction, the destruction of the left-leaning Arbenz government in Guatemala, leading to decades

---

4. This was the assessment of the new Reagan administration by, for example, the political commentator Ronald Steel: "The Reagan administration's foreign policy is simple and direct. Anti-Sovietism is its name" (*The New Republic,* April 11, 1981, 15–17).

5. *New York Times,* November 23, 1985. President Reagan made his remarks to editors and columnists in Washington during an interview covering the Geneva summit.

of military rule, opposition, and violent repression in that country. In 1961, under the new leadership of John F. Kennedy, an earlier plan to invade revolutionary Cuba, using anti-Castro exiles under CIA control, was put into motion and failed—the inglorious landing at the Bay of Pigs. In 1965 President Johnson sent airborne troops and the Marines into the Dominican Republic to ensure that leftist officers did not take power in the aftermath of a coup. Most recently, in 1983, President Reagan ordered the Marines into the tiny commonwealth island republic of Grenada, ostensibly to protect U.S. citizens, in order to crush a new leftist regime.[6]

Clearly, the status of Soviet-American relations has little bearing on U.S. determination to settle things its way in Central America and the Caribbean.[7] Reasons of geography, together with traditional patterns of trade, tourism, military assistance, and emigration, explain the fate that has bound the small nations of the region to the will of the colossal neighbor to the north. Late in the nineteenth century and into the first decades of the twentieth, the U.S. desire for stability and protection of economic investments dictated policies that resulted in periodic military interventions. With the cold war, the powerful ideological lubricants of preventing the spread of Communism or of Soviet influence (often the two are mistakenly conflated) were added to the machinery of diplomacy and security strategies for the region.

The Reagan administration contributed still another impetus for asserting U.S. global strength: a resolution to overcome what were decried as the foreign-policy doldrums of the Carter years. Vietnam had shown that U.S. power, even massively applied, had limits. Ultimately, despite tremendous costs to themselves and their land, the Vietnamese achieved national unity and independence according to their own lights despite Washington's initiatives to prevent this. This was a sobering lesson in the limits of superpower control over the Third World and its nationalist and revolutionary turbulence. (The Soviets might be taught a similar lesson in Afghanistan. Earlier, they were rudely evicted from Egypt and Somalia, two countries in which they once boasted enormous diplomatic and military influence.)

[6.] A good account of U.S. "globalism" in general is Stephen E. Ambrose, *Rise to Globalism: American Foreign Policy Since 1938* (4th revised edition, New York, 1985). Walter LaFeber covers Central America in particular in his *Inevitable Revolutions: The United States in Central America* (New York, 1984). For the Caribbean, see Lester D. Langley, *Struggle for the American Mediterranean . . . 1776–1904* (Athens, Ga., 1976), and *The United States and the Caribbean, 1900–1970* (Athens, Ga., 1980). An in-depth case study is provided by the anthology *Guatemala in Rebellion: Unfinished History*, edited by Jonathan L. Fried, Marvin E. Gettleman, Deborah T. Levenson, and Nancy Peckenham (New York, 1984).

[7.] An even more forceful parallel to U.S. behavior is Soviet activity in eastern Europe. Seeking peaceful relations with the United States, the Soviet Union will nonetheless resort to armed intervention, as in Czechoslovakia in 1968, or the threat of it, as in Poland in 1981, to ensure the safety of reliably pro-Soviet regimes. Afghanistan, a country bordering the Soviet Union, belongs —at present, at least—to eastern Europe in this political sense.

But what was a lesson for some in the United States was a sense of national humiliation for others.[8] When the Iranian revolution of 1979 exploded against a regime long considered comfortably in the American orbit, another chapter was added to the lesson. But the sense of humiliation was enlarged as well, especially when Iranians subjected the U.S. Embassy staff to a harrowing confinement lasting more than a year. In 1978, the Panama Canal, long the great symbol of U.S. sway in Central America, was turned over by treaty to full Panamanian sovereignty. In the last half of the Carter presidency, leftist revolutionaries of uncertain ideological orientation, the Sandinistas, overthrew the pro-U.S. dictatorship of the Somoza family in Nicaragua. In El Salvador, a military-civilian junta fell apart and a guerrilla campaign, led by leftist groups, took shape in the countryside.

All these events were mourned as foreign-policy reversals either engendered by weak-willed Carter policies or having effects that the Carter administration was powerless to manage. Ronald Reagan, seeing red, resolute about overcoming the "Vietnam syndrome" of defeat and humiliation, prepared the United States for a mission to regain lost prestige and reassert former influence. In the Caribbean region and Central America, there were several targets of opportunity. One of them was El Salvador.

1. U.S. Interests in Central America*

BY RONALD REAGAN

In referring to Reagan administration efforts to topple the Sandinista government of Nicaragua, an anonymous "White House official" argued: "If the Soviet Union metaphysically is equated to an ancient evil empire, then to the extent we can, we ought to attack it by going at the colonies. We don't do it well now. Central America is the first opportunity to do it right" (New York Times, August 9, 1985). In such a view of the world, a victorious insurgency, dominated by Marxist-Leninists, would convert El Salvador, like Cuba and Nicaragua, into a Soviet "colony." Although President Reagan has stopped calling the Soviet Union an evil empire in public, his framework for explaining U.S. policy in Central America, and in El Salvador in particular, is consistent with the remarks of the unnamed official.

IN the last 15 years the growth of Soviet military power has meant a radical change in the nature of the world we live in. This does not mean, as some

---

[8.] See Reading 52 below for an analysis of recent debates about the Vietnam war and their relevance to Central America.

* Excerpts from President Reagan's televised address to the nation, Washington, D.C., May 9, 1984, United States Department of State, *Current Policy*, No. 576.

would have us believe, that we're in imminent danger of nuclear war. We're not.

As long as we maintain the strategic balance and make it more stable by reducing the level of weapons on both sides, then we can count on the basic prudence of the Soviet leaders to avoid that kind of challenge to us. They are presently challenging us with a different kind of weapon: subversion and the use of surrogate forces—Cubans, for example. We've seen it intensifying during the last 10 years as the Soviet Union and its surrogates moved to establish control over Vietnam, Laos, Kampuchea, Angola, Ethiopia, South Yemen, Afghanistan, and recently, closer to home in Nicaragua and now El Salvador. . . .

The issue is our effort to promote democracy and economic well-being in the face of Cuban and Nicaraguan aggression, aided and abetted by the Soviet Union. It is definitely not about plans to send American troops into combat in Central America. Each year, the Soviet Union provides Cuba with $4 billion in assistance; and it sends tons of weapons to foment revolution here in our hemisphere. . . .

Central America is a region of great importance to the United States. And it is so close—San Salvador is closer to Houston, Texas, than Houston is to Washington, D.C. Central America is America; it's at our doorstep. And it has become the stage for a bold attempt by the Soviet Union, Cuba, and Nicaragua to install communism by force throughout the hemisphere.

When half of our shipping tonnage and imported oil passes through Caribbean shipping lanes, and nearly half of all our foreign trade passes through the Panama Canal and Caribbean waters, America's economy and well-being are at stake.

Right now in El Salvador, Cuban-supported aggression has forced more than 400,000 men, women, and children to flee their homes. And in all of Central America, more than 800,000 have fled, many, if not most, living in unbelievable hardship. Concerns about the prospect of hundreds of thousands of refugees fleeing communist oppression to seek entry into our country are well founded.

What we see in El Salvador is an attempt to destabilize the entire region and eventually move chaos and anarchy toward the American border.

As the National Bipartisan Commission on Central America,[1] chaired by Henry Kissinger, agreed, if we do nothing or if we continue to provide too little help, our choice will be a communist Central America with additional communist military bases on the mainland of this hemisphere and communist subversion spreading southward and northward. This communist subversion poses the threat that 100 million people from Panama to the open border on our south could come under the control of pro-Soviet regimes. . . .

[1.] See Reading 48.

If the communists can start war against the people of El Salvador, then El Salvador and its friends are surely justified in defending themselves by blocking the flow of arms. If the Soviet Union can aid and abet subversion in our hemisphere, then the United States has a legal right and a moral duty to help resist it. This is not only in our strategic interest; it is morally right. It would be profoundly immoral to let peace-loving friends depending on our help be overwhelmed by brute force if we have any capacity to prevent it.

If our political process pulls together, Soviet- and Cuban-supported aggression can be defeated. On this, the centennial anniversary of President Harry Truman's birth, it's fitting to recall his words spoken to a joint session of the Congress in a similar situation: "The free peoples of the world look to us for support in maintaining their freedoms. If we falter . . . we may endanger the peace of the world, and we shall surely endanger the welfare of this nation."[2]

The speech was given in 1947. The problem then was 2 years of Soviet-supported indirect aggression against Greece. The communists were close to victory. President Truman called on the Congress to provide decisive aid to the Greek Government. Both parties rallied behind President Truman's call. Democratic forces succeeded and Greece became a parliamentary democracy. . . .

The simple questions are: will we support freedom in this hemisphere or not? Will we defend our vital interests in this hemisphere or not? Will we stop the spread of communism in this hemisphere or not? Will we act while there is still time?

There are those in this country who would yield to the temptation to do nothing. They are the new isolationists, very much like the isolationists of the late 1930s, who knew what was happening in Europe but chose not to face the terrible challenge history had given them. They preferred a policy of wishful thinking that if they only gave up one more country, allowed just one more international transgression, then surely, sooner or later, the aggressor's appetite would be satisfied.

Well, they didn't stop the aggressors; they emboldened them. They didn't prevent war; they assured it. . . .

It's up to all of us, the Administration, you as citizens, and your representatives in the Congress. The people of Central America can succeed if we provide the assistance I have proposed. We Americans should be proud of what we're trying to do in Central America, and proud of what, together with our friends, we can do in Central America, to support democracy, human rights, and

---

[2.] Truman's address was delivered on March 12, 1947, and was the basis for what became known as the Truman Doctrine—"that it must be the policy of the United States to support free peoples who are resisting attempted subjugation by armed minorities or by outside pressures." This is at least the second time President Reagan invoked the Truman Doctrine in defending his Central America policies: See his address to a joint session of Congress, April 27, 1983, United States Department of State, *Current Policy,* No. 482.

economic growth, while preserving peace so close to home. Let us show the world that we want no hostile, communist colonies here in the Americas: South, Central, or North.

2. *Dictatorships and Double Standards**

BY JEANE KIRKPATRICK

Jeane Kirkpatrick was Leavey Professor of Political Science at Georgetown University and a resident scholar at the American Enterprise Institute when this article was published. Her arguments so impressed Ronald Reagan that he brought her into his Cabinet as U.S. Ambassador to the United Nations, a post she held until March 1985.

THE failure of the Carter administration's foreign policy is now clear to everyone except its architects, and even they must entertain private doubts, from time to time, about a policy whose crowning achievement has been to lay the groundwork for a transfer of the Panama Canal from the United States to a swaggering Latin dictator of Castroite bent [the late Brig. Gen. Omar Torrijos Herrera—Eds.]. In the thirty-odd months since the inauguration of Jimmy Carter as President there has occurred a dramatic Soviet military buildup, matched by the stagnation of American armed forces, and a dramatic extension of Soviet influence in the Horn of Africa, Afghanistan, Southern Africa, and the Caribbean, matched by a declining American position in all these areas. The U.S. has never tried so hard and failed so utterly to make and keep friends in the Third World.

As if this were not bad enough, in the current year [1979] the United States has suffered two other major blows—in Iran and Nicaragua—of large and strategic significance. In each country, the Carter administration not only failed to prevent the undesired outcome, it actively collaborated in the replacement of moderate autocrats friendly to American interests with less friendly autocrats of extremist persuasion. It is too soon to be certain about what kind of regime will ultimately emerge in either Iran or Nicaragua, but accumulating evidence suggests that things are as likely to get worse as to get better in both countries. The Sandinistas in Nicaragua appear to be as skillful in consolidating power as the Ayatollah Khomeini is inept, and leaders of both revolutions display an intolerance and arrogance that do not bode well for the peaceful sharing of power or the establishment of constitutional governments, especially since those leaders have made clear that they have no intention of seeking either.

---

* *Commentary*, 68, No. 5 (November 1979), 34–45.

It is at least possible that the SALT debate may stimulate new scrutiny of the nation's strategic position and defense policy, but there are no signs that anyone is giving serious attention to this nation's role in Iranian and Nicaraguan developments—despite clear warnings that the U.S. is confronted with similar situations and options in El Salvador, Guatemala, Morocco, Zaïre, and elsewhere. Yet no problem of American foreign policy is more urgent than that of formulating a morally and strategically acceptable, and politically realistic, program for dealing with non-democratic governments who are threatened by Soviet-sponsored subversion. In the absence of such a policy, we can expect that the same reflexes that guided Washington in Iran and Nicaragua will be permitted to determine American actions from Korea to Mexico—with the same disastrous effects on the U.S. strategic position. (That the administration has not called its policies in Iran and Nicaragua a failure—and probably does not consider them such—complicates the problem without changing its nature.)

There were, of course, significant differences in the relations between the United States and each of these countries during the past two or three decades. Oil, size, and proximity to the Soviet Union gave Iran greater economic and strategic import than any Central American "republic," and closer relations were cultivated with the Shah, his counselors, and family than with President Somoza, his advisers, and family. Relations with the Shah were probably also enhanced by our approval of his manifest determination to modernize Iran regardless of the effects of modernization on traditional social and cultural patterns (including those which enhanced his own authority and legitimacy). And, of course, the Shah was much better-looking and altogether more dashing than Somoza; his private life was much more romantic, more interesting to the media, popular and otherwise. Therefore, more Americans were more aware of the Shah than of the equally tenacious Somoza.

But even though Iran was rich, blessed with a product the U.S. and its allies needed badly, and led by a handsome king, while Nicaragua was poor and rocked along under a long-tenure president of less striking aspect, there were many similarities between the two countries and our relations with them. Both these small nations were led by men who had not been selected by free elections, who recognized no duty to submit themselves to searching tests of popular acceptability. Both did tolerate limited opposition, including opposition newspapers and political parties, but both were also confronted by radical, violent opponents bent on social and political revolution. Both rulers, therefore, sometimes invoked martial law to arrest, imprison, exile, and occasionally, it was alleged, torture their opponents. Both relied for public order on police forces whose personnel were said to be too harsh, too arbitrary, and too powerful. Each had what the American press termed "private armies," which is to say, armies pledging their allegiance to the ruler rather than the "constitution" or the "nation" or some other impersonal entity.

In short, both Somoza and the Shah were, in central ways, traditional rulers of semi-traditional societies. Although the Shah very badly wanted to create a technologically modern and powerful nation and Somoza tried hard to introduce modern agricultural methods, neither sought to reform his society in the light of any abstract idea of social justice or political virtue. Neither attempted to alter significantly the distribution of goods, status, or power (though the democratization of education and skills that accompanied modernization in Iran did result in some redistribution of money and power there).

Both Somoza and the Shah enjoyed long tenure, large personal fortunes (much of which were no doubt appropriated from general revenues), and good relations with the United States. The Shah and Somoza were not only anti-Communist, they were positively friendly to the U.S., sending their sons and others to be educated in our universities, voting with us in the United Nations, and regularly supporting American interests and positions even when these entailed personal and political cost. The embassies of both governments were active in Washington social life, and were frequented by powerful Americans who occupied major roles in this nation's diplomatic, military, and political life. And the Shah and Somoza themselves were both welcome in Washington, and had many American friends.

Though each of the rulers was from time to time criticized by American officials for violating civil and human rights, the fact that the people of Iran and Nicaragua only intermittently enjoyed the rights accorded to citizens in the Western democracies did not prevent successive administrations from granting—with the necessary approval of successive Congresses—both military and economic aid. In the case of both Iran and Nicaragua, tangible and intangible tokens of U.S. support continued until the regime became the object of a major attack by forces explicitly hostile to the United States.

But once an attack was launched by opponents bent on destruction, everything changed. The rise of serious, violent opposition in Iran and Nicaragua set in motion a succession of events which bore a suggestive resemblance to one another and a suggestive similarity to our behavior in China before the fall of Chiang Kai-shek, in Cuba before the triumph of Castro, in certain crucial periods of the Vietnamese war, and, more recently, in Angola. In each of these countries, the American effort to impose liberalization and democratization on a government confronted with violent internal opposition not only failed, but actually assisted the coming to power of new regimes in which ordinary people enjoy fewer freedoms and less personal security than under the previous autocracy—regimes, moreover, hostile to American interests and policies.

The pattern is familiar enough: an established autocracy with a record of friendship with the U.S. is attacked by insurgents, some of whose leaders have long ties to the Communist movement, and most of whose arms are of Soviet, Chinese, or Czechoslovak origin. The "Marxist" presence is ignored and/or minimized by American officials and by the elite media on the ground that U.S. support for the dictator gives the rebels little choice but to seek aid "elsewhere." Violence spreads and American officials wonder aloud about the viability of a regime that "lacks the support of its own people." The absence of an opposition party is deplored and civil-rights violations are reviewed. Liberal columnists question the morality of continuing aid to a "rightist dicta-torship" and provide assurances concerning the essential moderation of some insurgent leaders who "hope" for some sign that the U.S. will remember its own revolutionary origins. Requests for help from the beleaguered autocrat go unheeded, and the argument is increasingly voiced that ties should be estab-lished with rebel leaders "before it is too late." The President, delaying U.S. aid, appoints a special emissary who confirms the deterioration of the govern-ment position and its diminished capacity to control the situation and recom-mends various measures for "strengthening" and "liberalizing" the regime, all of which involve diluting its power.

The emissary's recommendations are presented in the context of a growing clamor for American disengagement on grounds that continued involvement confirms our status as an agent of imperialism, racism, and reaction; is incon-sistent with support for human rights; alienates us from the "forces of democ-racy"; and threatens to put the U.S. once more on the side of history's "losers." This chorus is supplemented daily by interviews with returning missionaries and "reasonable" rebels.

As the situation worsens, the President assures the world that the U.S. desires only that the "people choose their own form of government"; he blocks delivery of all arms to the government and undertakes negotiations to establish a "broadly based" coalition headed by a "moderate" critic of the regime who, once elevated, will move quickly to seek a "political" settlement to the conflict. Should the incumbent autocrat prove resistant to American demands that he step aside, he will be readily overwhelmed by the military strength of his opponents, whose patrons will have continued to provide sophisticated arms and advisers at the same time the U.S. cuts off military sales. Should the incumbent be so demoralized as to agree to yield power, he will be replaced by a "moderate" of American selection. Only after the insurgents have refused the proffered political solution and anarchy has spread throughout the nation will it be noticed that the new head of government has no significant following, no experience at governing, and no talent for leadership. By then, military commanders, no longer bound by loyalty to the chief of state, will depose the faltering "moderate" in favor of a fanatic of their own choosing.

In either case, the U.S. will have been led by its own misunderstanding of the situation to assist actively in deposing an erstwhile friend and ally and installing a government hostile to American interests and policies in the world. At best we will have lost access to friendly territory. At worst the Soviets will have gained a new base. And everywhere our friends will have noted that the U.S. cannot be counted on in times of difficulty and our enemies will have observed that American support provides no security against the forward march of history.

No particular crisis conforms exactly with the sequence of events described above; there are always variations on the theme. In Iran, for example, the Carter administration—and the President himself—offered the ruler support for a longer time, though by December 1978 the President was acknowledging that he did not know if the Shah would survive, adding that the U.S. would not get "directly involved." Neither did the U.S. ever call publicly for the Shah's resignation. However, the President's special emissary, George Ball, "reportedly concluded that the Shah cannot hope to maintain total power and must now bargain with a moderate segment of the opposition . . ." and was "known to have discussed various alternatives that would effectively ease the Shah out of total power" (*Washington Post,* December 15, 1978). There is, furthermore, not much doubt that the U.S. assisted the Shah's departure and helped arrange the succession of Bakhtiar. In Iran, the Carter administration's commitment to nonintervention proved stronger than strategic considerations or national pride. What the rest of the world regarded as a stinging American defeat, the U.S. government saw as a matter to be settled by Iranians. "We personally prefer that the Shah maintain a major role in the government," the President acknowledged, "but that is a decision for the Iranian people to make."

Events in Nicaragua also departed from the scenario presented above both because the Cuban and Soviet roles were clearer and because U.S. officials were more intensively and publicly working against Somoza. After the Somoza regime had defeated the first wave of Sandinista violence, the U.S. ceased aid, imposed sanctions, and took other steps which undermined the status and the credibility of the government in domestic and foreign affairs. Between the murder of ABC correspondent Bill Stewart by a National Guardsman in early June and the Sandinista victory in late July, the U.S. State Department assigned a new ambassador who refused to submit his credentials to Somoza even though Somoza was still chief of state, and called for replacing the government with a "broadly based provisional government that would include representatives of Sandinista guerrillas." Americans were assured by Assistant Secretary of State Viron Vaky that "Nicaraguans and our democratic friends in Latin America have no intention of seeing Nicaragua turned into a second Cuba," even though the State Department knew that the top Sandinista leaders had close personal ties and were in continuing contact with Havana, and, more specifically, that a Cuban secret-police official, Julian López, was frequently present in the Sandinista headquarters and that Cuban military advisers were present in Sandinista ranks.[1]

In a manner uncharacteristic of the Carter administration, which generally seems willing to negotiate anything with anyone anywhere, the U.S. govern-

---

[1.] For Vaky's views on Central America after the Sandinista victory in Nicaragua, see his statement before the Subcommittee on Inter-American Affairs of the House Committee on Foreign Affairs at hearings on *Central America at the Crossroads,* September 11, 1979, Washington, D.C.: U.S. Government Printing Office, 1979.—Eds.

ment adopted an oddly uncompromising posture in dealing with Somoza. "No end to the crisis is possible," said Vaky, "that does not start with the departure of Somoza from power and the end of his regime. No negotiation, mediation, or compromise can be achieved any longer with a Somoza government. The solution can only begin with a sharp break from the past." Trying hard, we not only banned all American arms sales to the government of Nicaragua but pressured Israel, Guatemala, and others to do likewise—all in the name of insuring a "democratic" outcome. Finally, as the Sandinista leaders consolidated control over weapons and communications, banned opposition, and took off for Cuba, President Carter warned us against attributing this "evolutionary change" to "Cuban machinations" and assured the world that the U.S. desired only to "let the people of Nicaragua choose their own form of government."

Yet despite all the variations, the Carter administration brought to the crises in Iran and Nicaragua several common assumptions, each of which played a major role in hastening the victory of even more repressive dictatorships than had been in place before. These were, first, the belief that there existed at the moment of crisis a democratic alternative to the incumbent government; second, the belief that the continuation of the status quo was not possible; third, the belief that any change, including the establishment of a government headed by self-styled Marxist revolutionaries, was preferable to the present government. Each of these beliefs was (and is) widely shared in the liberal community generally. Not one of them can withstand close scrutiny.

Although most governments in the world are, as they always have been, autocracies of one kind or another, no idea holds greater sway in the mind of educated Americans than the belief that it is possible to democratize governments, anytime, anywhere, under any circumstances. This notion is belied by an enormous body of evidence based on the experience of dozens of countries which have attempted with more or less (usually less) success to move from autocratic to democratic government. Many of the wisest political scientists of this and previous centuries agree that democratic institutions are especially difficult to establish and maintain—because they make heavy demands on all portions of a population and because they depend on complex social, cultural, and economic conditions.

Two or three decades ago, when Marxism enjoyed its greatest prestige among American intellectuals, it was the economic prerequisites of democracy that were emphasized by social scientists. Democracy, they argued, could function only in relatively rich societies with an advanced economy, a substantial middle class, and a literate population, but it could be expected to emerge more or less automatically whenever these conditions prevailed. Today, this picture seems grossly oversimplified. While it surely helps to have an economy strong enough to provide decent levels of well-being for all, and "open" enough to provide mobility and encourage achievement, a pluralistic society and the right kind of political culture—and time—are even more essential.

In his essay on *Representative Government,* John Stuart Mill identified three fundamental conditions which the Carter administration would do well to ponder. These are: "One, that the people should be willing to receive it [representative government]; two, that they should be willing and able to do what is necessary for its preservation; three, that they should be willing and able to fulfill the duties and discharge the functions which it imposes on them."

Fulfilling the duties and discharging the functions of representative government make heavy demands of leaders and citizens, demands for participation and restraint, for consensus and compromise. It is not necessary for all citizens to be avidly interested in politics or well-informed about public affairs— although far more widespread interest and mobilization are needed than in autocracies. What *is* necessary is that a substantial number of citizens think of themselves as participants in society's decision-making and not simply as subjects bound by its laws. Moreover, leaders of all major sectors of the society must agree to pursue power only by legal means, must eschew (at least in principle) violence, theft, and fraud, and must accept defeat when necessary. They must also be skilled at finding and creating common ground among diverse points of view and interests, and correlatively willing to compromise on all but the most basic values.

In addition to an appropriate political culture, democratic government requires institutions strong enough to channel and contain conflict. Voluntary, non-official institutions are needed to articulate and aggregate diverse interests and opinions present in the society. Otherwise, the formal governmental institutions will not be able to translate popular demands into public policy.

In the relatively few places where they exist, democratic governments have come into being slowly, after extended prior experience with more limited forms of participation during which leaders have reluctantly grown accustomed to tolerating dissent and opposition, opponents have accepted the notion that they may defeat but not destroy incumbents, and people have become aware of government's effects on their lives and of their own possible effects on government. Decades, if not centuries, are normally required for people to acquire the necessary disciplines and habits. In Britain, the road from the Magna Carta to the Act of Settlement, to the great Reform Bills of 1832, 1867, and 1885, took seven centuries to traverse. American history gives no better grounds for believing that democracy comes easily, quickly, or for the asking. A war of independence, an unsuccessful constitution, a civil war, a long process of gradual enfranchisement marked our progress toward constitutional democratic government. The French path was still more difficult. Terror, dictatorship, monarchy, instability, and incompetence followed on the revolution that was to usher in a millennium of brotherhood. Only in the twentieth century did the democratic principle finally gain wide acceptance in France and not until after World War II were the principles of order and democracy, popular sovereignty and authority finally reconciled in institutions strong enough to contain conflicting currents of public opinion.

Although there is no instance of a revolutionary "socialist" or Communist society being democratized, right-wing autocracies do sometimes evolve into democracies—given time, propitious economic, social and political circumstances, talented leaders, and a strong indigenous demand for representative government. Something of the kind is in progress on the Iberian peninsula and the first steps have been taken in Brazil. Something similar could conceivably have also occurred in Iran and Nicaragua if contestation and participation had been more gradually expanded.

But it seems clear that the architects of contemporary American foreign policy have little idea of how to go about encouraging the liberalization of an autocracy. In neither Nicaragua nor Iran did they realize that the only likely result of an effort to replace an incumbent autocrat with one of his moderate critics or a "broad-based coalition" would be to sap the foundations of the existing regime without moving the nation any closer to democracy. Yet this outcome was entirely predictable. Authority in traditional autocracies is transmitted through personal relations: from the ruler to his close associates (relatives, household members, personal friends) and from them to people to whom the associates are related by personal ties resembling their own relation to the ruler. The fabric of authority unravels quickly when the power and status of the man at the top are undermined or eliminated. The longer the autocrat has held power, and the more pervasive his personal influence, the more dependent a nation's institutions will be on him. Without him, the organized life of the society will collapse, like an arch from which the keystone has been removed. The blend of qualities that bound the Iranian army to the Shah or the national guard to Somoza is typical of the relationships—personal, hierarchical, non-transferable—that support a traditional autocracy. The speed with which armies collapse, bureaucracies abdicate, and social structures dissolve once the autocrat is removed frequently surprises American policy-makers and journalists accustomed to public institutions based on universalistic norms rather than particularistic relations.

The failure to understand these relations is one source of the failure of U.S. policy in this and previous administrations. There are others. In Iran and Nicaragua (as previously in Vietnam, Cuba, and China) Washington overestimated the political diversity of the opposition—especially the strength of "moderates" and "democrats" in the opposition movement; underestimated the strength and intransigence of radicals in the movement; and misestimated the nature and extent of American influence on both the government and the opposition.

Confusion concerning the character of the opposition, especially its intransigence and will to power, leads regularly to downplaying the amount of force required to counteract its violence. In neither Iran nor Nicaragua did the U.S.

adequately appreciate the government's problem in maintaining order in a society confronted with an ideologically extreme opposition. Yet the presence of such groups was well known. The State Department's 1977 report on human rights described an Iran confronted

> with a small number of extreme rightist and leftist terrorists operating within the country. There is evidence that they have received substantial foreign support and training . . . [and] have been responsible for the murder of Iranian government officials and Americans. . . .

The same report characterized Somoza's opponents in the following terms:

> A guerrilla organization known as the Sandinista National Liberation Front (FSLN) seeks the violent overthrow of the government, and has received limited suport from Cuba. The FSLN carried out an operation in Managua in December 1974, killing four people, taking several officials hostage . . . since then, it continues to challenge civil authority in certain isolated regions.

In 1978, the State Department's report said that Sandinista violence was continuing—after the state of siege had been lifted by the Somoza government.

When U.S. policy-makers and large portions of the liberal press interpret insurgency as evidence of widespread popular discontent and a will to democracy, the scene is set for disaster. For if civil strife reflects a popular demand for democracy, it follows that a "liberalized" government will be more acceptable to "public opinion."

Thus, in the hope of strengthening a government, U.S. policy-makers are led, mistake after mistake, to impose measures almost certain to weaken its authority. Hurried efforts to force complex and unfamiliar political practices on societies lacking the requisite political culture, tradition, and social structures not only fail to produce desired outcomes; if they are undertaken at a time when the traditional regime is under attack, they actually facilitate the job of the insurgents.

Vietnam presumably taught us that the United States could not serve as the world's policeman; it should also have taught us the dangers of trying to be the world's midwife to democracy when the birth is scheduled to take place under conditions of guerrilla war.

If the administration's actions in Iran and Nicaragua reflect the pervasive and mistaken assumption that one can easily locate and impose democratic alternatives to incumbent autocracies, they also reflect the equally pervasive and equally flawed belief that change *per se* in such autocracies is inevitable, desirable, and in the American interest. It is this belief which induces the Carter administration to participate actively in the toppling of non-Communist autocracies while remaining passive in the face of Communist expansion.

At the time the Carter administration came into office it was widely reported that the President had assembled a team who shared a new approach to foreign policy and a new conception of the national interest. The principal elements of this new approach were said to be two: the conviction that the cold war was over, and the conviction that, this being the case, the U.S. should give priority to North-South problems and help less developed nations achieve their own destiny.

More is involved in these changes than originally meets the eye. For, unlikely as it may seem, the foreign policy of the Carter administration is guided by a relatively full-blown philosophy of history which includes, as philosophies of history always do, a theory of social change, or, as it is currently called, a doctrine of modernization. Like most other philosophies of history that have appeared in the West since the 18th century, the Carter administration's doctrine predicts progress (in the form of modernization for all societies) and a happy ending (in the form of a world community of developed, autonomous nations).

The administration's approach to foreign affairs was clearly foreshadowed in [Carter's National Security Adviser] Zbigniew Brzezinski's 1970 book on the U.S. role in the "technetronic era," *Between Two Ages*. In that book, Brzezinski showed that he had the imagination to look beyond the cold war to a brave new world of global politics and interdependence. To deal with that new world a new approach was said to be "evolving," which Brzezinski designated "rational humanism." In the new approach, the "preoccupation" with "national supremacy" would give way to "global" perspectives, and international problems would be viewed as "human issues" rather than as "political confrontations." The traditional intellectual framework for dealing with foreign policy would have to be scrapped:

> Today, the old framework of international politics . . . with their spheres of influence, military alliances between nation states, the fiction of sovereignty, doctrinal conflicts arising from 19th-century crisis—is clearly no longer compatible with reality.[2]

Only the "delayed development" of the Soviet Union, "an archaic religious community that experiences modernity existentially but not quite yet normatively," prevented wider realization of the fact that the end of ideology was already here. For the U.S., Brzezinski recommended "a great deal of patience," a more detached attitude toward world revolutionary processes, and a less anxious preoccupation with the Soviet Union. Instead of engaging in

[2] Concerning Latin America, Brzezinski observed: "Latin American nationalism, more and more radical as it widens its popular base, will be directed with increasing animosity against the United States unless the United States rapidly shifts its own posture. Accordingly, it would be wise for the United States to make an explicit move to abandon the Monroe Doctrine and to concede that in the new global age geographic or hemispheric contiguity no longer need be politically decisive. Nothing could be healthier for Pan-American relations than for the United States to place them on the same level as its relations with the rest of the world, confining itself to emphasis on cultural-political affinities (as it does with Western Europe) and economic-social obligations (as it does with less developed countries)." [Footnote in original.]

ancient diplomatic pastimes, we should make "a broader effort to contain the global tendencies toward chaos," while assisting the processes of change that will move the world toward the "community of developed nations."

The central concern of Brzezinski's book, as of the Carter administration's foreign policy, is with the modernization of the Third World. From the beginning, the administration has manifested a special, intense interest in the problems of the so-called Third World. But instead of viewing international developments in terms of the American national interest, as national interest is historically conceived, the architects of administration policy have viewed them in terms of a contemporary version of the same idea of progress that has traumatized Western imaginations since the Enlightenment.

In its current form, the concept of modernization involves more than industrialization, more than "political development" (whatever that is). It is used instead to designate ". . . the process through which a traditional or pretechnological society passes as it is transformed into a society characterized by machine technology, rational and secular attitudes, and highly differentiated social structures." Condorcet, Comte, Hegel, Marx, and Weber are all present in this view of history as the working out of the idea of modernity.

The crucial elements of the modernization concept have been clearly explicated by Samuel P. Huntington (who, despite a period at the National Security Council, was assuredly not the architect of the administration's policy). The modernization paradigm, Huntington has observed, postulates an ongoing process of change: complex, because it involves all dimensions of human life in society; systemic, because its elements interact in predictable, necessary ways; global, because all societies will, necessarily, pass through the transition from traditional to modern; lengthy, because time is required to modernize economic and social organization, character, and culture; phased, because each modernizing society must pass through essentially the same stages; homogenizing, because it tends toward the convergence and interdependence of societies; irreversible, because the direction of change is "given" in the relation of the elements of the process; progressive, in the sense that it is desirable, and in the long run provides significant benefits to the affiliated people.

Although the modernization paradigm has proved a sometimes useful as well as influential tool in social science, it has become the object of searching critiques that have challenged one after another of its central assumptions. Its shortcomings as an analytical tool pale, however, when compared to its inadequacies as a framework for thinking about foreign policy, where its principal effects are to encourage the view that events are manifestations of deep historical forces which cannot be controlled and that the best any government can do is to serve as a "midwife" to history, helping events to move where they are already headed.

This perspective on contemporary events is optimistic in the sense that it foresees continuing human progress; deterministic in the sense that it perceives events as fixed by processes over which persons and policies can have but little influence; moralistic in the sense that it perceives history and U.S. policy as having moral ends; cosmopolitan in the sense that it attempts to view the world not from the perspective of American interests or intentions but from the perspective of the modernizing nation and the "end" of history. It identifies modernization with both revolution and morality, and U.S. policy with all three.

The idea that it is "forces" rather than people which shape events recurs each time an administration spokesman articulates or explains policy. The President, for example, assured us in February of this year:

> The revolution in Iran is a product of deep social, political, religious, and economic factors growing out of the history of Iran itself.

And of Asia he said:

> At this moment there is turmoil or change in various countries from one end of the Indian Ocean to the other; some turmoil as in Indo-China is the product of age-old enmities, inflamed by rivalries for influence by conflicting forces. Stability in some other countries is being shaken by the process of modernization, the search for national significance, or the desire to fulfill legitimate human hopes and human aspirations.

Harold Saunders, Assistant Secretary for Near Eastern and South Asian Affairs, commenting on "instability" in Iran and the Horn of Africa, states:

> We, of course, recognize that fundamental changes are taking place across this area of western Asia and northeastern Africa—economic modernization, social change, a revival of religion, resurgent nationalism, demands for broader popular participation in the political process. These changes are generated by forces within each country.

Or here is Anthony Lake, chief of the State Department's Policy Planning staff, on South Africa:

> Change will come in South Africa. The welfare of the people there, and American interest, will be profoundly affected by the way in which it comes. The question is whether it will be peaceful or not.

Brzezinski makes the point still clearer. Speaking as chief of the National Security council, he has assured us that the struggles for power in Asia and Africa are really only incidents along the route to modernization:

> . . . all the developing countries in the area from northeast Asia to southern Africa continue to search for viable forms of government capable of managing the process of modernization.

No matter that the invasions, coups, civil wars, and political struggles of less violent kinds that one sees all around do not *seem* to be incidents in a global personnel search for someone to manage the modernization process. Neither

Brzezinski nor anyone else seems bothered by the fact that the political partici-pants in that arc from northeast Asia to southern Africa do not *know* that they are "searching for viable forms of government capable of managing the process of modernization." The motives and intentions of real persons are no more relevant to the modernization paradigm than they are to the Marxist view of history. Viewed from this level of abstraction, it is the "forces" rather than the people that count.

So what if the "deep historical forces" at work in such diverse places as Iran, the Horn of Africa, southeast Asia, Central America, and the United Nations look a lot like Russians or Cubans? Having moved past what the President calls our "inordinate fear of Communism," identified by him with the cold war, we should, we are told, now be capable of distinguishing Soviet and Cuban "machinations," which any way exist mainly in the minds of cold warriors and others guilty of oversimplifying the world, from evolutionary changes, which seem to be the only kind that actually occur.

What can a U.S. President faced with such complicated, inexorable, imper-sonal processes *do?* The answer, offered again and again by the President and his top officials, is, not much. Since events are not caused by human decisions, they cannot be stopped or altered by them. Brzezinski, for example, has said: "We recognize that the world is changing under the influence of forces no government can control. . . ." And [Carter's first Secretary of State] Cyrus Vance has cautioned: "The fact is that we can no more stop change than Canute could still the waters."

The Carter administration's essentially deterministic and apolitical view of contemporary events discourages an active American response and encourages passivity. The American inability to influence events in Iran became the Presi-dent's theme song:

> Those who argue that the U.S. should *or could* intervene directly to thwart [the revolution in Iran] are wrong about the realities of Iran. . . . We have encouraged *to the limited extent of our own ability* the public support for the Bakhtiar govern-ment. . . . How long [the Shah] will be out of Iran, we have no way to determine. Further events and his own desires will determine that. . . . It is impossible for anyone to anticipate all future political events. . . . Even if we had been able to anticipate events that were going to take place in Iran or in other countries, obviously our ability to determine those events is very limited [emphasis in original].

Vance made the same point:

> In Iran our policy throughout the current crisis has been based on the fact that only Iranians can resolve the fundamental political issues which they now confront.

Where once upon a time an American President might have sent Marines to assure the protection of American strategic interests, there is no room for force in this world of progress and self-determination. Force, the President told us at Notre Dame, does not work; that is the lesson he extracted from Vietnam. It offers only "superficial" solutions. Concerning Iran, he said:

> Certainly we have no desire or ability to intrude massive forces into Iran or any other country to determine the outcome of domestic political issues. This is something that we have no intention of ever doing in another country. We've tried this once in Vietnam. It didn't work, as you well know.

There was nothing unique about Iran. In Nicaragua, the climate and language were different but the "historical forces" and the U.S. response were the same. Military intervention was out of the question. Assistant Secretary of State Viron Vaky described as "unthinkable" the "use of U.S. military power to intervene in the internal affairs of another American republic." Vance provided parallel assurances for Africa, asserting that we would not try to match Cuban and Soviet activities there.

What *is* the function of foreign policy under these conditions? It is to understand the processes of change and then, like Marxists, to align ourselves with history, hoping to contribute a bit of stability along the way. And this, administration spokesmen assure us, is precisely what we are doing. The Carter administration has defined the U.S. national interest in the Third World as identical with the putative end of the modernization process. Vance put this with characteristic candor in a recent statement when he explained that U.S. policy vis-à-vis the Third World is "grounded in the conviction that we best serve our interest there by supporting the efforts of developing nations to advance their economic well-being and preserve their political independence." Our "commitment to the promotion of constructive change worldwide" (Brzezinski's words) has been vouchsafed in every conceivable context.

But there is a problem. The conceivable contexts turn out to be mainly those in which non-Communist autocracies are under pressure from revolutionary guerrillas. Since Moscow is the aggressive, expansionist power today, it is more often than not insurgents, encouraged and armed by the Soviet Union, who challenge the status quo. The American commitment to "change" in the abstract ends up by aligning us tacitly with Soviet clients and irresponsible extremists like the Ayatollah Khomeini [in Iran] or, in the end, Yasir Arafat [head of the Palestine Liberation Organization].

So far, assisting "change" has not led the Carter administration to undertake the destabilization of a *Communist* country. The principles of self-determination and nonintervention are thus both selectively applied. We seem to accept the status quo in Communist nations (in the name of "diversity" and national autonomy), but not in nations ruled by "right-wing" dictators or white oligarchies. Concerning China, for example, Brzezinski has observed: "We recognize that the [People's Republic of China] and we have different ideologies and economic and political systems. . . . We harbor neither the hope nor the desire that through extensive contacts with China we can remake that nation into the

American image. Indeed, we accept our differences." Of Southeast Asia, the President noted in February:

> Our interest is to promote peace and the withdrawal of outside forces and not to become embroiled in the conflict among Asian nations. And, in general, our interest is to promote the health and the development of individual societies, not to a pattern cut exactly like ours in the United States but tailored rather to the hopes and the needs and desires of the peoples involved.

But the administration's position shifts sharply when South Africa is discussed. For example, Anthony Lake asserted in late 1978:

> . . . We have indicated to South Africa the fact that if it does not make significant progress toward racial equality, its relations with the international community, including the United States, are bound to deteriorate.
>
> Over the years, we have tried through a series of progressive steps to demonstrate that the U.S. cannot and will not be associated with the continued practice of apartheid.

As to Nicaragua, [State Department spokesman] Hodding Carter III said in February 1979:

> The unwillingness of the Nicaraguan government to accept the [OAS] group's proposal, the resulting prospects for renewal and polarization, and the human-rights situation in Nicaragua . . . unavoidably affect the kind of relationship we can maintain with that government. . . .

And Carter commented on Latin American autocracies:

> My government will not be deterred from protecting human rights, including economic and social rights, in whatever ways we can. We prefer to take actions that are positive, but where nations persist in serious violations of human rights, we will continue to demonstrate that there are costs to the flagrant disregard of international standards.

Something very odd is going on here. How does an administration that desires to let people work out their own destinies get involved in determined efforts at reform in South Africa, Zaïre, Nicaragua, El Salvador, and elsewhere? How can an administration committed to nonintervention in Cambodia and Vietnam announce that it "will not be deterred" from righting wrongs in South Africa? What should be made of an administration that sees the U.S. interest as identical with economic modernization and political independence and yet heedlessly endangers the political independence of Taiwan, a country whose success in economic modernization and egalitarian distribution of wealth is unequaled in Asia? The contrast is as striking as that between the administration's frenzied speed in recognizing the new dictatorship in Nicaragua and its continuing refusal to recognize the elected government of Zimbabwe Rhodesia [the former white minority regime of Ian Smith.—Eds.], or its refusal to maintain any presence in Zimbabwe Rhodesia while staffing a U.S. Information Office in Cuba. Not only are there ideology and a double standard at work here, the ideology neither fits nor explains reality, and the double standard involves the administration in the wholesale contradiction of its own principles.

Inconsistencies are a familiar part of politics in most societies. Usually, however, governments behave hypocritically when their principles conflict with the national interest. What makes the inconsistencies of the Carter administration noteworthy are, first, the administration's moralism—which renders it especially vulnerable to charges of hypocrisy; and, second, the administration's predilection for policies that violate the strategic and economic interests of the United States. The administration's conception of national interest borders on doublethink: it finds friendly powers to be guilty representatives of the status quo and views the triumph of unfriendly groups as beneficial to America's "true interests."

This logic is quite obviously reinforced by the prejudices and preferences of many administration officials. Traditional autocracies are, in general and in their very nature, deeply offensive to modern American sensibilities. The notion that public affairs should be ordered on the basis of kinship, friendship, and other personal relations rather than on the basis of objective "rational" standards violates our conception of justice and efficiency. The preference for stability rather than change is also disturbing to Americans whose whole national experience rests on the principles of change, growth, and progress. The extremes of wealth and poverty characteristic of traditional societies also offend us, the more so since the poor are usually *very* poor and bound to their squalor by a hereditary allocation of role. Moreover, the relative lack of concern of rich, comfortable rulers for the poverty, ignorance, and disease of "their" people is likely to be interpreted by Americans as moral dereliction pure and simple. The truth is that Americans can hardly bear such societies and such rulers. Confronted with them, our vaunted cultural relativism evaporates and we become as censorious as Cotton Mather confronting sin in New England.

But if the politics of traditional and semi-traditional autocracy is nearly antithetical to our own—at both the symbolic and the operational level—the rhetoric of progressive revolutionaries sounds much better to us; their symbols are much more acceptable. One reason that some modern Americans prefer "socialist" to traditional autocracies is that the former have embraced modernity and have adopted modern modes and perspectives, including an instrumental, manipulative, functional orientation toward most social, cultural, and personal affairs; a profession of universalistic norms; an emphasis on reason, science, education, and progress; a de-emphasis of the sacred; and "rational," bureaucratic organizations. They speak our language.

Because socialism of the Soviet/Chinese/Cuban variety is an ideology rooted in a version of the same values that sparked the Enlightenment and the democratic revolutions of the 18th century; because it is modern and not traditional; because it postulates goals that appeal to Christian as well as to secular values (brotherhood of man, elimination of power as a mode of human relations), it is highly congenial to many Americans at the symbolic level. Marxist revolutionaries speak the language of a hopeful future while traditional autocrats speak the language of an unattractive past. Because left-wing revolutionaries invoke the symbols and values of democracy—emphasizing egalitarianism rather than hierarchy and privilege, liberty rather than order, activity rather than passivity—they are again and again accepted as partisans in the cause of freedom and democracy.

Nowhere is the affinity of liberalism, Christianity, and Marxist socialism more apparent than among liberals who are "duped" time after time into supporting "liberators" who turn out to be totalitarians, and among Left-leaning clerics whose attraction to a secular style of "redemptive community" is stronger than their outrage at the hostility of socialist regimes to religion. In Jimmy Carter—egalitarian, optimist, liberal, Christian—the tendency to be repelled by frankly non-democratic rulers and hierarchical societies is almost as strong as the tendency to be attracted to the idea of popular revolution, liberation, and progress. Carter is, *par excellence,* the kind of liberal most likely to confound revolution with idealism, change with progress, optimism with virtue.

Where concern about "socialist encirclement," Soviet expansion, and traditional conceptions of the national interest inoculated his predecessors against such easy equations, Carter's doctrine of national interest and modernization encourages support for all change that takes place in the name of "the people," regardless of its "superficial" Marxist or anti-American content. Any lingering doubt about whether the U.S. should, in case of conflict, support a "tested friend" such as the Shah or a friendly power such as Zimbabwe Rhodesia against an opponent who despises us is resolved by reference to our "true," our "long-range" interests.

Stephen Rosenfeld of the *Washington Post* described the commitment of the Carter administration to this sort of "progressive liberalism":

> The Carter administration came to power, after all, committed precisely to reducing the centrality of strategic competition with Moscow in American foreign policy, and to extending the United States' association with what it was prepared to accept as legitimate wave-of-the-future popular movements around the world—first of all with the victorious movement in Vietnam.
>
> . . . Indochina was supposed to be the state on which Americans could demonstrate their "post-Vietnam" intent to come to terms with the progressive popular element that Kissinger, the villain, had denied.

In other words, the Carter administration, Rosenfeld tells us, came to power resolved not to assess international developments in the light of "cold-war" perspectives but to accept at face value the claim of revolutionary groups to represent "popular" aspirations and "progressive" forces—regardless of the ties of these revolutionaries to the Soviet Union. To this end, overtures were made looking to the "normalization" of relations with Vietnam, Cuba, and the Chinese People's Republic, and steps were taken to cool relations with South Korea, South Africa, Nicaragua, the Philippines, and others. These moves followed naturally from the conviction that the U.S. had, as our enemies said, been on the wrong side of history in supporting the status quo and opposing revolution.

One might have thought that this perspective would have been undermined by events in Southeast Asia since the triumph of "progressive" forces there over the "agents of reaction." To cite Rosenfeld again:

> In this administration's time, Vietnam has been transformed, for much of American public opinion, from a country wronged by the U.S. to one revealing a brutal essence of its own.
> This has been a quiet but major trauma to the Carter people (as to all liberals), scarring their self-confidence and their claim on public trust alike.

Presumably, however, the barbarity of the "progressive" governments in Cambodia and Vietnam has been less traumatic for the President and his chief advisers than for Rosenfeld, since there is little evidence of changed predispositions at crucial levels of the White House and the State Department. The President continues to behave as before—not like a man who abhors autocrats but like one who abhors only right-wing autocrats.

In fact, high officials in the Carter administration understand better than they seem to the aggressive, expansionist character of contemporary Soviet behavior in Africa, the Middle East, Southeast Asia, the Indian Ocean, Central America, and the Caribbean. But although the Soviet/Cuban role in Grenada, Nicaragua, and El Salvador (plus the transfer of MIG-23's to Cuba) had already prompted resumption of surveillance of Cuba (which in turn confirmed the presence of a Soviet combat brigade), the President's eagerness not to "heat up" the climate of public opinion remains stronger than his commitment to speak the truth to the American people. His statement on Nicaragua clearly reflects these priorities:

> It's a mistake for Americans to assume or to claim that every time an evolutionary change takes place in this hemisphere that somehow it's a result of secret, massive Cuban intervention. The fact in Nicaragua is that the Somoza regime lost the confidence of the people. To bring about an orderly transition there, our effort was to let the people of Nicaragua ultimately make the decision on who would be their leader—what form of government they should have.

This statement, which presumably represents the President's best thinking on the matter, is illuminating. Carter's effort to dismiss concern about military events in this specific country as a manifestation of a national proclivity for seeing "Cuban machinations" under every bed constitutes a shocking effort to falsify reality. There was no question in Nicaragua of "evolutionary change" or of attributing such change to Castro's agents. There was only a question about the appropriate U.S. response to a military struggle in a country whose location gives it strategic importance out of proportion to its size or strength.

But that is not all. The rest of the President's statement graphically illustrates the blinding power of ideology on his interpretation of events. When he says that "the Somoza regime lost the confidence of the people," the President implies that the regime had previously rested on the confidence of "the people," but that the situation had now changed. In fact, the Somoza regime had never rested on popular will (but instead on manipulation, force, and habit), and was not being ousted by it. It was instead succumbing to arms and soldiers. However, the assumption that the armed conflict of Sandinistas and Somocistas was the military equivalent of a national referendum enabled the President to imagine that it could be, and should be, settled by the people of Nicaragua. For this pious sentiment even to seem true the President would have had to be unaware that insurgents were receiving a great many arms from other non-Nicaraguans; and that the U.S. had played a significant role in disarming the Somoza regime.

The President's mistakes and distortions are all fashionable ones. His assumptions are those of people who want badly to be on the progressive side in conflicts between "rightist" autocracy and "leftist" challenges, and to prefer the latter, almost regardless of the probable consequences.

To be sure, neither the President, nor Vance, nor Brzezinski *desires* the proliferation of Soviet-supported regimes. Each has asserted his disapproval of Soviet "interference" in the modernization process. But each, nevertheless, remains willing to "destablize" friendly or neutral autocracies without any assurance that they will not be replaced by reactionary totalitarian theocracies, totalitarian Soviet client states, or worst of all, by murderous fanatics of the Pol Pot variety [in Cambodia].

The foreign policy of the Carter administration fails not for lack of good intentions but for lack of realism about the nature of traditional versus revolutionary autocracies and the relation of each to the American national interest. Only intellectual fashion and the tyranny of Right/Left thinking prevent intelligent men of good will from perceiving the *facts* that traditional authoritarian governments are less repressive than revolutionary autocracies, that they are more susceptible of liberalization and that they are more compatible with U.S. interests. The evidence on all these points is clear enough.

Surely it is now beyond reasonable doubt that the present governments of Vietnam, Cambodia, Laos are much more repressive than those of the despised previous rulers; that the government of the People's Republic of China is more repressive than that of Taiwan, that North Korea is more repressive than South Korea, and so forth. This is the most important lesson of Vietnam and Cambodia. It is not new but it is a gruesome reminder of harsh facts.

From time to time a truly bestial ruler can come to power in either type of autocracy—Idi Amin [Uganda], Papa Doc Duvalier [Haiti], Joseph Stalin, Pol Pot are examples—but neither type regularly produces such moral monsters (though democracy regularly prevents their accession to power). There are, however, *systemic* differences between traditional and revolutionary autocracies that have a predictable effect on their degree of repressiveness. Generally speaking, traditional autocrats tolerate social inequities, brutality, and poverty while revolutionary autocracies create them.

Traditional autocrats leave in place existing allocations of wealth, power, status, and other resources which in most traditional societies favor an affluent few and maintain masses in poverty. But they worship traditional gods and observe traditional taboos. They do not disturb the habitual rhythms of work and leisure, habitual places of residence, habitual patterns of family and personal relations. Because the miseries of traditional life are familiar, they are bearable to ordinary people who, growing up in the society, learn to cope, as children born to untouchables in India acquire the skills and attitudes necessary for survival in the miserable roles they are destined to fill. Such societies create no refugees.

Precisely the opposite is true of revolutionary Communist regimes. They create refugees by the million because they claim jurisdiction over the whole life of the society and make demands for change that so violate internalized values and habits that inhabitants flee by the tens of thousands in the remarkable expectation that their attitudes, values, and goals will "fit" better in a foreign country than in their native land.

The former deputy chairman of Vietnam's National Assembly from 1976 to his defection early in August 1979, Hoang Van Hoan, described recently the impact of Vietnam's ongoing revolution on that country's more than one million Chinese inhabitants:

> They have been expelled from places they have lived in for generations. They have been dispossessed of virtually all possessions—their lands, their houses. They have been driven into areas called new economic zones, but they have not been given any aid.
>
> How can they eke out a living in such conditions reclaiming new land? They gradually die for a number of reasons—diseases, the hard life. They also die of humiliation.

It is not only the Chinese who have suffered in Southeast Asia since the "liberation," and it is not only in Vietnam that the Chinese suffer. By the end of 1978 more than six million refugees had fled countries ruled by Marxist governments. In spite of walls, fences, guns, and sharks, the steady stream of people fleeing revolutionary utopias continues.

There is a damning contrast between the number of refugees created by

Marxist regimes and those created by other autocracies: more than a million Cubans have left their homeland since Castro's rise (one refugee for every nine inhabitants) as compared to about 35,000 each from Argentina, Brazil, and Chile. In Africa more than five times as many refugees have fled Guinea and Guinea Bissau as have left Zimbabwe Rhodesia, suggesting that civil war and racial discrimination are easier for most people to bear than Marxist-style liberation.

Moreover, the history of this century provides no grounds for expecting that radical totalitarian regimes will transform themselves. At the moment there is a far greater likelihood of progressive liberalization and democratization in the governments of Brazil, Argentina, and Chile than in the government of Cuba; in Taiwan than in the People's Republic of China; in South Korea than in North Korea; in Zaïre than in Angola; and so forth.

Since many traditional autocracies permit limited contestation and participation, it is not impossible that U.S. policy could effectively encourage this process of liberalization and democratization, provided that the effort is not made at a time when the incumbent government is fighting for its life against violent adversaries, and that proposed reforms are aimed at producing gradual change rather than perfect democracy overnight. To accomplish this, policy-makers are needed who understand how actual democracies have actually come into being. History is a better guide than good intentions.

A realistic policy which aims at protecting our own interest and assisting the capacities for self-determination of less developed nations will need to face the unpleasant fact that, if victorious, violent insurgency headed by Marxist revolutionaries is unlikely to lead to anything but totalitarian tyranny. Armed intellectuals citing Marx and supported by Soviet-bloc arms and advisers will almost surely not turn out to be agrarian reformers, or simple nationalists, or democratic socialists. However incomprehensible it may be to some, Marxist revolutionaries are not contemporary embodiments of the Americans who wrote the Declaration of Independence, and they will not be content with establishing a broad-based coalition in which they have only one voice among many.

It may not always be easy to distinguish between democratic and totalitarian agents of change, but it is also not too difficult. Authentic democratic revolutionaries aim at securing governments based on the consent of the governed and believe that ordinary men are capable of using freedom, knowing their own interest, choosing rulers. They do not, like the current leaders in Nicaragua, assume that it will be necessary to postpone elections for three to five years during which time they can "cure" the false consciousness of almost everyone.

If, moreover, revolutionary leaders describe the United States as the scourge of the twentieth century, the enemy of freedom-loving people, the perpetrator of imperialism, racism, colonialism, genocide, war, then they are not authentic democrats or, to put it mildly, friends. Groups which define themselves as enemies should be treated as enemies. The United States is not in fact a racist, colonial power, it does not practice genocide, it does not threaten world peace with expansionist activities. In the last decade especially we have practiced remarkable forbearance everywhere and undertaken the "unilateral restraints on defense spending" recommended by Brzezinski as appropriate for the technetronic era. We have also moved further, faster, in eliminating domestic racism than any multiracial society in the world or in history.

For these reasons and more, a posture of continuous self-abasement and apology vis-à-vis the Third World is neither morally necessary nor politically appropriate. No more is it necessary or appropriate to support vocal enemies of the United States because they invoke the rhetoric of popular liberation. It is not even necessary or appropriate for our leaders to forswear unilaterally the use of military force to counter military force. Liberal idealism need not be identical with masochism, and need not be incompatible with the defense of freedom and the national interest.[3]

3. Totalitarianism vs. Authoritarianism*

By Michael Walzer

Michael Walzer taught at Brandeis, Princeton, and Harvard universities before taking his current position as permanent fellow of the Institute for Advanced Studies in Princeton, N.J. He is coeditor of Dissent *magazine, and his many books include* The Revolution of the Saints *(1965);* Just and Unjust Wars *(1977); and* Exodus and Revolution *(1984).*

CONSIDER . . . the two major moral/political arguments of the new cold warriors. I'll take them from Jeane Kirkpatrick's *Commentary* article, a particularly good example of contemporary ideology, even if it isn't, or just because it isn't, a particularly good article. The first of these is an argument about political possibility. Communist totalitarianism brings with it a long, dark night. "There is no instance of a revolutionary 'socialist' or Communist society being democratized," writes Kirkpatrick. Our own tyrants, by contrast, are sometimes replaced by democratic regimes—though it is always important for the stability of the new democracy that the replacement take place *very slowly.* Kirkpatrick doesn't discuss what might be called the reverse replacement rate. In fact, I'm afraid, the decline of democracy in the free world

[3.] For a Latin American update on Kirkpatrick's views, see her "U.S. Security & Latin America," *Commentary,* 71, No. 1, January 1981, 29–40.—Eds.

* *The New Republic,* 185, Nos. 1 and 2 (July 4 and 11, 1981), 21–25.

is rather more noticeable than its slow advance. In any case, this is a false distinction. Hungary, Czechoslovakia, and Poland probably would be democratic states today were it not for the Red Army. The Red Army is a threat to human freedom, but communism, in these states at least, is an ugly but not a powerful political system. There is nothing in its internal mechanics that rules out a democratic transformation. Assuming that the Russians don't intervene—an unlikely but analytically necessary assumption—the prospects for democracy are probably better, certainly no worse, in much of Eastern Europe than, to cite some of Kirkpatrick's odder examples, in Argentina, Brazil, South Korea, and Zaïre. In all these cases, social structure and political culture are far more important than the current regime in shaping the long-term evolution.

The second argument is about relative brutality. Old-fashioned tyrannies, according to Kirkpatrick, because they don't set out to transform their societies, do much less damage to them. They tolerate existing patterns of misery and injustice, but at least they don't create new ones. And their subjects are accustomed to the old patterns, have long ago adjusted to them and learned how to survive. Hence "such societies create no refugees." This is the "damning contrast" between Communist regimes and "other autocracies." The massive refugee population of the modern world is largely a creation of Communist totalitarianism. It would be nice—not for the refugees but for the ideological peace of mind of the rest of us—if this were true. But it isn't true. The refugees who fled Hungary in 1956 or Afghanistan in 1980 were fleeing the Red Army, not domestic oppression. The million Cubans who have reached our shores since the 1960s probably could be matched by a million Haitians, were the latter given a comparable welcome. And the largest single group of refugees since World War II was produced by Pakistani repression in East Bengal, which was nothing if not old-fashioned. Certainly there are Communist states that fit Kirkpatrick's account. East Germany and Cambodia are different but equally clear-cut examples. But the line she draws is a fabrication.

The contrast between totalitarian and authoritarian regimes is a conceptual contrast, not a practical one. It doesn't conform to, nor does it justify, our actual alliances. It doesn't make Kissinger's Pakistani "tilt" of 1971 smell any better. It doesn't rule out economic (or even military) cooperation with Communist China. One can't pull politics or morality out of a theoretical hat. That sort of thing is always a trick. Theory, *once we have it right,* does nothing more than shape our perceptions, guide our understanding; within the framework it provides, choices still have to be made.

The hardest choice, and the one for the sake of which the new cold war ideology has been worked out, is simply this: an authoritarian regime, old-fashioned, brutal, repressive, allied to the West, is threatened by a revolutionary movement some of whose leaders have totalitarian ambitions and/or Russian connections. What should we do? The claim of the new cold warriors is that the liberal impulse in all such cases is to support the revolutionaries or at least to desert at the first opportunity the authoritarian regime. And what they want instead is the opposite policy, a steadfast commitment to the regime, because totalitarianism is the greater danger, the irreversible transformation, and so on.

But this is to turn policy into a reflex of ideology (disguised as theory). There just isn't going to be one answer in cases like the one I've described, and to act as if there is one answer—we get it right or wrong, we win or lose—is the beginning of political disaster. Often we can't do anything at all. Or rather, our choice is the same choice that the Russians have faced again and again in Eastern Europe: send in the troops or let the local conflict take its course. But let's assume that there is room, some limited room, for political maneuver (economic aid, military supply, diplomatic pressure, and so on). Then, obviously, the direction of our maneuvers will have to be determined by the shape of the terrain. How much popular support does the regime have? How much capacity for change? Who are the rebels and what is their "cause"? What sorts of alliances have they already made and how stable are those alliances? What are our own strategic interests in the area? That last question is generally taken to mean we should align ourselves with the established regime. In fact, however, if there really are strategic interests, and if we take them seriously, then it would seem to follow that we should line up as early as possible with the side most likely to win, so long as there is a real chance of keeping the winners out of the Russian camp. It is characteristic of the new cold warriors that they would support authoritarian governments both when it is in our interests to do so and also when it isn't—so that one is led to suspect that they just support authoritarian governments. In any case, there probably are such governments that we ought on balance to help. Otherwise, we could hardly have any relations at all with third world states. And there probably are oppositionists and revolutionaries whom we ought on balance to help too.

Rarely, however, in any part of the third world, are there going to be old or new regimes, governments, or movements to which we should be ideologically committed. We don't have to become apologists for the internal policies of our allies. What we owe them at most is critical support. Foreign policy is always a double business: we have to pursue our interests and we have to defend our values. In the long run, we hope that these two efforts come together, but at any given moment there are conflicts and contradictions. Maybe it is in our interest to support, say, the present South Korean regime. But we must also, for the sake of our values, maintain some critical distance from it. And that kind of argument doesn't work only for right-wing regimes. After 1960, it was in our interest that Cuban communism develop in, say, a Yugoslav rather than a Bulgarian direction, and we might have accomplished that, or at least assisted in it, through some sort of economic cooperation. But cooperation would have been no excuse for a failure to criticize Castro's dictatorship, the repression of dissidents, the campaign against homosexuals, and so on.

A policy of this kind assumes that there is no long, dark night, no thousand-year Reich, no totalitarian transformation that is proof against political opposition and social change. That has to be, I think, the working assumption of any sane diplomacy. The new cold warriors exploit what we might think of as the apocalyptic features of the theory of totalitarianism. And in the 20th century it is difficult to avoid some engagement with, some hard contemplation of, apocalypse. In political terms that means that there have been and will be again regimes so evil that the only moral stand one can adopt toward them is absolute opposition. But what policies follow from that moral stand? Surely Stalin's was one such regime, and yet we fought with Stalin against the Nazis. Even evil has its degrees. We must hope—we can reasonably believe—that it also has its duration.

In the third world, at any rate, there is not likely to be much permanence —no sustained development toward modernity and liberty, but also very few stable or solidly established tyrannies. No doubt many of the tyrants will have totalitarian ambitions; the rhetoric of revolution is now the *lingua franca* of the third world. But that only means that there will be many failed totalitarianisms. Whether these failures will be bloodier than the "other autocracies" is a question unlikely to find a yes or no answer. Some of them will and some won't. For our part, we can and should maintain a steady hostility toward every sort of totalitarian ambition. But that is no reason for supporting the "other autocracies" or excusing their bloodiness. We can make the alliances we have to make on both sides of this shadowy line, and we can condemn when we must the internal policies of our allies. I understand, of course, that there are serious diplomatic difficulties involved in any such policy—much discussed and never overcome during the Carter years. But it is a worse policy to refuse altogether to confront those difficulties. The real danger, *the present danger,* of the new cold war ideology is that it will drive us into alliances that our material defense does not require and rule out the outspokenness that the defense of our values does require. And all this for the sake of a misunderstood and badly applied political theory!

But perhaps I overestimate the power of theory (it is a common professional mistake). One might detect among contemporary cold warriors a sneaking sympathy for "traditional autocrats [who] leave in place existing allocations of wealth, power, status, and other resources. . . ." On the far left, there is often similar sympathy for revolutionaries who upset those allocations, even if they do so only in order to establish a new tyranny—and this view, too, has its theoretical rationale. But I would propose a different sympathy: for the tortured dissidents, the imprisoned oppositionists, the threatened minorities, all the "disappeared" and murdered men and women of all the tyrannies, old and new. And we don't need a political theory to explain why we should keep these people always in the forefront of our consciousness, their names on the tip of our tongues.

4. *Reagan's Latin America**

BY TOM J. FARER

Tom J. Farer has been President of the University of New Mexico, Distinguished Professor at Rutgers-Camden Law School, and President of the Inter-American Commission on Human Rights of the Organization of American States (1980–82). Professor Farer's re-election in June 1981 as head of the Commission—he was the first U.S. citizen to hold elected office in the O.A.S.—was unanimous despite an attack on him by the Chilean government for views expressed in the following article.

SOME of President Reagan's advisers believe that Jimmy Carter had a clear policy for dealing with Third World countries, and that it was wrong, above all in Latin America. Probably the most detailed and influential statement of their view is the article "Dictatorships and Double Standards." The central problem, according to Professor Kirkpatrick, is "that of formulating a morally and strategically acceptable, and politically realistic, program for dealing with non-democratic governments who are threatened by Soviet-sponsored subversion."

Drawing principally on Iran and Nicaragua, she describes what she takes to be a typical "non-democratic" government and the wrong-headed response to it she had come to expect from the Carter administration.

In such a government, a long-established autocrat is supported by a private army—which owes allegiance to him and his family rather than to some abstract idea of the state. The autocrat tolerates "limited opposition, including opposition newspapers and political parties." But because he is "confronted by radical, violent opponents bent on social and political revolution," he must sometimes invoke martial law to arrest, imprison, exile, "and occasionally, it was alleged" (Kirkpatrick says, referring to the specific cases of Iran and Nicaragua) "torture [his] opponents." The autocrat enriches himself in large part by confusing his own resources with those of the state and makes no attempt "to alter significantly the distribution of goods, status, or power."

In the past, this model autocrat was a good friend of the United States and successive American administrations gave him tangible and intangible support. But then came Jimmy Carter. . . .

* *The New York Review of Books,* 28, No. 4 (March 19, 1981), 10–16. For convenience, some of the author's footnotes have been bracketed into the text by the editors.

Kirkpatrick's remedies follow ineluctably from her diagnosis of Carter's errors. The United States must not undermine friendly authoritarian governments. It may encourage a "process of liberalization and democratization, provided that the effort is not made at a time when the incumbent government is fighting for its life against violent adversaries, and that proposed reforms are aimed at producing gradual change rather than perfect democracy overnight." When Marxists or other enemies of the United States seek violently to overthrow the traditional order, the United States should send aid, not excluding the Marines.

Of this proposal, it may be said, first, that it rests on an almost demented parody of Latin American [and Caribbean] political realities as well as on a grave misperception of Carter's policies and achievements. On the most elementary facts Kirkpatrick is misinformed, for example when she claims that Carter "disarmed" Somoza. Before the last round of the Nicaraguan conflict, Somoza's National Guard bristled with weapons supplied by Argentina and Israel. Passing to more important misconceptions, dictatorial regimes of the Somoza type are far less common today than they were twenty or thirty years ago when Kirkpatrick's views seem to have been formed. A few relics survive: Duvalier, Jr., in Haiti, Stroessner in Paraguay. But in number, population, resources, and strategic importance, such countries are inconsequential compared to the Hemisphere's other nondemocratic, anticommunist governments, including those in Argentina, Bolivia, Brazil, El Salvador, and Uruguay. Nor, despite his success in eliminating all personal rivals, does her model apply to Pinochet's Chile.

In these authoritarian countries, the names at the top can and generally do change without any shifts in the pattern of wealth and political power. Formidable institutions are in control, usually the armed forces, a notable exception being Mexico's dominant political party [the Institutional Revolutionary Party], and the huge state bureaucracy dependent on it. And these institutions work within a complicated setting of interest groups—including various sectors of the national business community, multinational corporations, the Catholic Church, professionals' guilds, the state bureaucracy, and occasionally (and in most cases marginally) trade unions—all struggling to influence the regime's economic and social policies. It is a political world very different from the one conjured up by Kirkpatrick. [Even outside Latin America, Kirkpatrick's model fits reality poorly. While it covers the little states of the Persian Gulf and Saudi Arabia, and a few African states like Zaïre and the Ivory Coast, it does not apply to such "Free World" allies as Indonesia, Thailand, and South Korea.]

While the eccentricity of Kirkpatrick's account may raise doubts about her competence for public service, what matters more is the effect her account is likely to have on policy makers who confuse it with reality. Any political order sustained by little more than the force of a single autocrat's or family's prestige is bound to be precarious, especially where that prestige is linked to the ruler's bestial behavior or his special relationship with a feared or admired great power. Regarding such cases as the norm, Kirkpatrick not surprisingly demands we form a circle of fire around our protégés as soon as reformers of any kind appear armed in the street. What would she do about those missionaries (nuns?) and other "activists" as she calls them who get in the way of hard-nosed policy? One possible hint appears in an interview Kirkpatrick gave after the election. Commenting on the torture, mutilation, and summary execution of the civilian leaders of El Salvador's left-wing coalition, she said that "people who choose to live by the sword can expect to die by it" [*New York Times*, December 7, 1980]. So apparently any form of association with rebels makes one fair game.

If we turn from Kirkpatrick's model to the real world, we find instead of the old-style caudillos, regimes of a very different character. Roughly half the members of the Organization of American States are recognizable democracies, including, for example, Venezuela, Colombia, Costa Rica, Peru, the Dominican Republic, and most of the Anglophonic states of the Caribbean. Kirkpatrick has little to say about democracy in such Third World countries other than to doubt its existence when it elects leaders who practice socialism, criticize the United States, and talk with Castro. While castigating Carter for tolerating the Manley regime in Jamaica, she refers to it as a "so-called democracy." One wonders whether the recent transfer of power there has shaken her implied assumption that socialism is totalitarianism aching to be born. For her, the heart of our Third World problem is the regime that is anticommunist, but authoritarian, brutal, poor, corrupt, and hence unloved by the liberals.

One redeeming feature of Kirkpatrick's essay is its demonstration of how a distinction that could be useful, between authoritarian and totalitarian regimes, is being subverted by dogmatists who assign practically all rulers professing capitalism and trying to liquidate leftists to the category of "merely authoritarian" while coincidentally expelling every revolutionary government and movement into the outer darkness of totalitarianism. In this way the distinction has become simply a polemical weapon, useful for attacking Carter's human rights policy and for countering criticism of regimes that brutally crush proponents of reform, liberals, socialists, and Marxists alike.

In order to maintain their Manichaean vision, former liberals like Kirkpatrick must practice a heroic indifference to detail. The revolutionary who haunts their hysterical prose never acquires a face. Neoconservatives ask no questions about the particulars of time and place and program, about why a man or woman has assumed the awful peril of rebellion; they never ask because, for their crabbed purposes, they have all the necessary answers. Having taken up arms—some of them Cuban or Russian or otherwise tainted

—against an anticommunist government, the revolutionary is either a totalitarian communist or a foolish tool, not to mention a "terrorist."

You find an equivalent coarseness of thought in the pages of *Pravda,* where the Soviet counterparts of our intellectual thugs ask not, "Who is Lech Walesa?" but rather, "Whom does Walesa consciously or unconsciously serve?" Since his opponent is a loyal communist government, for *Pravda* the only possible answer is "U.S. Imperialism."

Kirkpatrick herself admits that absolute monsters such as Hitler and Stalin or Pol Pot and Papa Doc Duvalier will occasionally appear at both ends of the imagined political spectrum. What concerns her, however, are the

> *systemic* differences between traditional and revolutionary autocracies that have a predictable effect on their degree of repressiveness. Generally speaking, traditional autocrats tolerate social inequities, brutality, and poverty while revolutionary autocracies create them.
>
> Traditional autocrats . . . do not disturb the habitual rhythms of work and leisure, habitual places of residence, habitual patterns of family and personal relations. Because the miseries of traditional life are familiar, they are bearable to ordinary people who, growing up in the society, learn to cope, as children born to untouchables in India acquire the skills and attitudes necessary for survival in the miserable roles they are destined to fill.

The other presumed moral advantage of anticommunist autocracies is their capacity for evolution toward more humane societies.

Nothing so well illustrates the stupefying power of dogma than this attribution of permanence to revolutionary regimes and of an always latent fluidity to most conservative ones. In any fair test of durability, the latter make an impressive showing. The Somoza family, for example, lasted forty-five years. By monopolizing so much of the nation's economy, it had, by the time of its overthrow, actually reduced the possibility of democratic evolution.

Military rule in El Salvador, to take another current example, has endured since Franklin Delano Roosevelt's first election. If we use a measure more relevant to human rights and equate the "regime" with a very rigid structure of power and wealth and opportunity, then El Salvador had a stable autocracy from its independence in the early nineteenth century at least until the armed forces coup of 1979. What was characteristic of this period was not "evolution" toward democracy but prevention of that evolution. In Peru, one hundred and fifty years of oligarchic control ended in 1968 not through democratic evolution but by means of reforms imposed by the armed forces.

Authoritarian governments of every ideological hue extend their jurisdiction as far as necessary to achieve their ends. They tolerate autonomous activity outside the formal state structure only when it is harmless or when it is informally but effectively integrated with the regime. In El Salvador before 1979, the military government and a small group of capitalists ("the fourteen families") consciously shared virtually the same interests and acted together. Though the press was nominally free, mass circulation newspapers in San Salvador conformed to the policies of the ruling groups.

"Preserving the existing distribution of wealth and power and poverty" is a deceptive summary of the goals of Kirkpatrick's "traditional autocrats." It is deceptive in that it implies that Latin American nations exist in a state of muscular placidity, as if society were ruled by a group of not necessarily good-natured but decidedly unambitious thugs who have no serious ambition beyond retaining control of their privileges and extorting protection money and are willing to live and let live. When threatened by violent assault, of course they will actively hurt people—the violent malcontents and their sympathizers. But once the problem is liquidated, the "ordinary people" who want only to be left alone will come out of the cellar, where they have been hiding to avoid getting caught in the cross-fire, and docilely resume their "habitual rhythms."

This image is unreal because it misses the dynamic character of contemporary Latin American societies. When the masses are quiet, unambitious rulers can be placid. Today their serenity is constantly disturbed. All the interconnected tendencies of recent years—urbanization, industrialization, rapid population increase, the vast spread of TV and transistor radios, revolutionary ideas about man and society—have unleashed a torrent of demands that may seem all the more terrifying because they cannot be suppressed by a government's administering exemplary punishment from time to time. Feeling a consequent need for sterner and more sweeping measures, rulers claim that national security requires them to impose comprehensive surveillance and more tightly controlled social institutions by increasing the power and reach of public authority.

This political project is "corporatism," fascism's cousin. As the Yale political scientist Alfred Stepan notes in his penetrating study of Peru's corporatist experiment, it has two poles. At the "inclusionary pole," the state offers working-class groups positive inducements to take part in its political and economic plans, as did the first Perón regime in Argentina, Lázaro Cárdenas in pre-war Mexico, and Peru's military government before it turned to the right in 1975. At the "exclusionary pole," the state elite relies heavily on coercion to break up existing working-class organizations and then to institutionalize docility. Chile under Pinochet is a particularly harsh example.

When the second of the two patterns predominates, as in Brazil and Chile following their respective military coups [Brazil in 1964 and Chile in 1973], it follows that universities are purged, political parties dissolved, unions reorganized, dissidents murdered, the Church harassed, all as part of a huge effort first to demobilize the popular classes, and then to direct and strain their demands through new, purified institutions subject to manipulation by the state. In this effort, which has been analyzed with particular brilliance by the

Argentine social scientist Guillermo O'Donnell, the ruling groups can be said to be following, consciously or not, the example of empires like that of Rome which for several centuries aggressively expanded its domain in a furious effort to liquidate threats to the status quo before they became unmanageable.

Seeking to preserve their own status quo, uncompromising right-wing governments ape the campaigns of classical revolutionary regimes to remove every source of dissent. They call themselves conservative. They are anticommunist. They will say nice thing about the Free World. And contrary to Kirkpatrick's optimistic speculations, they often take society on a road without any democratic exit.

The defense of right-wing authoritarian regimes finds a receptive, uncritical audience among many Americans because deeply ingrained ideological commitments affect their moral sensitivity. Anyone familiar with conditions in Haiti, for example, knows that its desperately hungry people would emigrate en masse if only a country able to provide life's basic needs would open its doors. Although poverty and the nature of the Duvalier regime are linked, since that autocracy is noncommunist the U.S. government presumes that its refugees who reach our shores merely flee economic "conditions" and must therefore be turned back. On the other hand, practically all Cubans who arrive here are presumed to be fleeing political persecution rather than economic privation.

Another case of selective perception: If a revolutionary state commands people to move from one section of a country to another, we naturally condemn this ugly act as violating the right to travel freely and choose one's place of residence. But if the state enforces an absentee landowner's decision to expel sharecroppers, who have tilled the land for generations, and if the landowner's choice was a rational response to market forces, even if those forces were themselves determined by political decisions about subsidies or the tariff on imported farm equipment, many economists will applaud it. Farming will be more efficient, free marketeers will say, and sharecroppers will eventually find employment in more productive and hence better-paying activities. Or at least, it is claimed, they would if only markets could be manipulated to function in accordance with theory.

The account of the Third World provided by Kirkpatrick and those who think like her obscures the realities of life under authoritarian governments—not only the torture and murder of political dissidents but also the more subtle yet often more comprehensively destructive acts carried out through the operation and manipulation of economic forces in societies with vast gaps between the power and education and wealth of relatively few people and the rest of the population, a pattern of inequality often inherited from a precapitalist era. In countries like Brazil and Guatemala, these differences and the statist tradition that goes with them multiply the community-shattering impact of capitalism by placing the state at the service of a relatively few powerful people.

Acting through the state, the few can require proof of land tenure which illiterate peasants cannot produce. They can manipulate the exchange rate to encourage high technology imports at the expense of high employment. They can prohibit strikes and hold wage increases below the rate of inflation. They can subsidize large-scale agriculture and monopolize irrigation, while withholding subsidies for basic consumption goods. They can and do intervene in a thousand ways which have the predictable effect of uprooting whole communities because neither they nor the state apparatus is a neutral arbiter guided by some abstract calculus of national interest. One certainly need not be a Marxist to see this. And one needs only a minimum of candor to admit it.

Quietly and anonymously, economic and social forces unleashed or at least aided by the state can eliminate entire cultures. Sylvia Hewlett notes in her recent study of Brazil that there remained during the 1950s "a major concentration of indigenous tribes (numbering approximately 200,000 people) in the Amazon and central regions . . ." [*The Cruel Dilemmas of Development: Twentieth Century Brazil* (New York, 1979), 171]. As a consequence of the decision to open up these regions through highway building, colonization schemes, and other means, the indigenous population is disappearing. Some Indians will survive disoriented, adrift on the edge of an alien world. As for their "habitual patterns of family and personal relations," soon the world will forget that they ever existed.

Honest scholarship would have to ask what is the difference between a revolutionary state that decides to eliminate a group with bayonets and one that proceeds to do so by indirection. Both claim that they are promoting modernization and advancing national interests as defined by those who rule. Yet one case rightly horrifies us and will command the attention of Walter Cronkite while the other passes almost unnoticed.

Conservatives are properly impressed by Brazil's rapid expansion and the deepening of its industrial base during the era of intense political repression —1968–1973. They tend to be silent about its record in producing equity or welfare. A recent World Bank study using 1977 figures estimates that 65 percent of the Brazilian population age fifteen and above is functionally illiterate; the figure runs close to 90 percent in rural areas ["Brazil: Human Resources Special Report," World Bank Staff Working Paper (Washington, D.C., 1979), pp. 28–31]. Roughly 20 percent of the children in Brazil are in a state of second or third degree malnutrition (body weight 25 percent or more below normal).

According to figures cited by Hewlett, between 1960 and 1973 the rate of infant mortality in São Paulo (the richest part of Brazil) increased 45 percent to a high of ninety-seven deaths per thousand live births.

[This might have something to do with the fact that in the ten years following the coup of 1964, the percentage of national income obtained by the wealthiest 10 percent of the population increased from 39 to 50. Sri Lanka's per capita income is roughly one-eighth of Brazil's, or about the same as that of a town in the rural northeast of Brazil; its infant mortality figure is about half (that) of São Paulo. Life expectancy in Sri Lanka is sixty-eight. See tables in James P. Grant's *Disparity Reduction Rates in Social Indicators,* Overseas Development Council, Monograph No. 11, 1978.] Life expectancy for the middle and upper classes of São Paulo is estimated to be around sixty-seven. The poor in parts of the rural northeast still have a life expectancy of only about forty years. Such misery is no doubt "familiar," as Kirkpatrick claims, but unlike our new ambassador to the U.N., even a minister in the Brazilian government wonders if it is bearable. In a recent interview with *Veja,* Brazil's equivalent of *Newsweek,* the present Minister of Industry and Commerce, João Camilo Penna, said:

> The country possesses today a social stratum with high managerial capacity that has, however, a great debt with 40 million humble Brazilians. A debt that, if it is not paid, will result in these humble people being turned into humiliated people. And after humiliated people, I don't know.

Preoccupied with such games as distinguishing between the "authoritarian" and the "totalitarian," many people concerned with U.S. diplomacy have failed to notice changes in Latin American institutions that have been unfolding in the shadows cast by state and private terrorism. Perhaps the most important of these is the emergence of national human rights movements. Under a variety of names, often supported by the Catholic Church, these movements have united hereditary political enemies in alliances reminiscent of wartime France. In countries where the armed forces agree to return to their barracks, these Latin analogies to the Resistance could emerge as stable, center-to-left political coalitions able to carry out orderly programs of economic and social reform. In most of the Western hemisphere today, moreover —unlike postwar Western Europe—the orthodox Moscow-oriented party is only a fragment of the left, in many countries a trivial one. [Moreover, unlike some leftist groups, the communist party during the past two decades with few exceptions—e.g., recently in El Salvador—has generally sought popular front alliances and opposed armed revolution. For that reason, particularly during the 1960s, romantic followers of Che Guevara despised the orthodox communists. In the El Salvador case, most of the likely participants in a conventional popular front, including the social democrats, had already decided to back an armed struggle for social change.]

The experience of modern authoritarian government has enhanced the prospects for such coalitions. Frustrated in the 1960s by the obduracy of vested interests, their imagination fired by illusions about the Cuban revolution, susceptible to a rigidly Marxist view of norms and political institutions, reformers in such countries as Brazil, Colombia, and Chile tended to see democratic politics only as the means of preserving privilege. They became correspondingly insensitive to the violence lying beneath the accumulated restraints and tolerance of relatively decent social orders.

They have since learned how ferociously competent modern security forces can be and how private leftist terrorism can evoke deep antipathy throughout societies with liberal if not always strictly democratic traditions; the result in such countries as Argentina, Uruguay, and Brazil has been increased support of unrestrained counterterrorism. However, moderates and conservatives who have seen their children ground up in the state's security machine also have had a lesson in the difficulty of stopping violence once it rushes into the streets.

The failure of Cuba's economic model is another factor in the education of the left. Fidel Castro himself has helped to disseminate the bad news and has drawn one of the appropriate conclusions. In conversations with Alfonso Robelo, leader of the political opposition to the present Nicaraguan government, and with Sandinista leaders, Castro emphasized the importance of preserving a significant private business sector. Some Central and South American leftists may still be reluctant to admit it, but they cannot indefinitely evade the fact that a commitment to a private sector is also a commitment to some species of political pluralism.

Advocates of democratic reform face enormous difficulties. In many Latin American countries a demographic explosion is taking place while the economy relies on a capital-intensive technology that was developed in the labor-scarce states of Europe and North America—a combination that usually creates very high levels of unemployment. Also imported from the developed states are consumer appetites that stimulate the greed of the well-to-do. Because international capital is hard to obtain, politicians and businessmen feel they must compete for it by suppressing every sign of social disorder; and modern technology provides an apparatus for official terror beyond the dreams of nineteenth-century rulers. Western stagflation meanwhile threatens export markets and consequently the ability to finance growth of any kind.

The rush to authoritarian governments in the Sixties and early Seventies heightened academic appreciation of these and related obstacles, and encouraged a pessimistic determinism about projects for social and political reform. But the failure of countries like Chile and Uruguay to reproduce the Brazilian economic "miracle" by combining assaults on the working class with an open door to international capital has helped to undermine confidence in the stability of that formula for social order. It received another blow recently when Uruguayan voters rejected a constitution designed by the armed forces to perpetuate their rule. The democratic impulse has not yielded to competing claims to legitimacy.

The great question is whether reform coalitions can increase equity and welfare without sacrificing the long-term growth necessary for peaceful relations between classes. If they can, they should satisfy the demands of the Latin

American military officers who have seized power in order to halt class warfare and the consequent disintegration of all traditional institutions, including the armed forces themselves. Plausible blueprints are available. In the case of Brazil, for instance, a recent confidential study shows how moderate changes in government policy designed substantially to reduce inequality could also do much to relieve the shortages of energy and foreign exchange that threaten the country's future. A more equitable distribution of income would coincidentally benefit domestically controlled private businesses because they enjoy a comparative advantage over multinational corporations in producing basic consumer goods.

Most of Latin America is now open to renewed projects for democratic social reform, or could soon become so. Carter helped to shape this more promising situation by insisting that the way a regime treats its own people has to affect the quality of its relations with the United States. Having initially disarmed himself by forswearing intervention in trade or private capital as a means of defending human rights, he could, however, offer few incentives and he used few convincing threats. By 1977, only a derisory amount of bilateral economic aid was available to reward good behavior.

In a few cases Carter could and did block or delay aid to authoritarian states such as Argentina from international financial institutions; but various, partially self-imposed, constraints made this a rarely used and only marginally threatening weapon. In cautioning authoritarian governments against repression, Carter drew mainly on the accumulated prestige of the United States among Latin American military establishments and the upper classes. His considerable achievements, including fair elections in the Dominican Republic, are partly owing to the weight of American influence, but primarily to the gathering force of human rights as an ideal that cuts across deep divisions of class and ideology in Latin America. That force powerfully multiplied the effect of Carter's efforts.

Simply by acting to demonstrate some continuity in Washington's support for human rights, Ronald Reagan could easily match Carter's achievement. He needs to act quickly. His victory has particularly encouraged the predators in those few remaining social jungles where an alliance of corrupted soldiers, industrialists, and landowners would rather fight to the last worker, peasant, politician, and priest than accept reform.

While campaigning for the presidency, Mr. Reagan allowed certain ideologues who were vindictive toward all critics of traditional capitalist order to speak in his name. Responsible Republicans such as Congressman Jack Kemp should urge the president to reject association of American power with conservatism that relies on vicious repression. They should act because it is the right thing to do; and because it is in the national interest that Latin Americans succeed in establishing capitalism with a human face.

CHAPTER II

Social Forces and Ideologies in the Making of Contemporary El Salvador

Editors' Introduction

> *Coffee was king [in early twentieth-century El Salvador]; it earned the country's foreign exchange, paid for its imports, provided revenue for central and local government, financed the construction of roads, parks and railways, gave employment— permanent or seasonal—to a large part of the population and made the fortunes of a few.*
>
> —David Browning, *El Salvador* (1971)

In his classic description of oligarchy, Aristotle defined this form of government as a corruption of aristocracy, in which presumably the noble and virtuous rule. An oligarchy exists "when men of property have the government in their hands."[1] In the broad sense of rule by the wealthy and powerful, most governments (and often even the leadership of antigovernment insurgent movements[2]) are to some extent oligarchies, whatever other formal

[1.] Aristotle, *Politics,* sections 1279–81.

[2.] One recent critic of the Salvadoran left, the Mexican writer Gabriel Zaid, has charged the leadership of the FMLN/FDR (Farabundo Martí National Liberation Front/Democratic Revolutionary Front) with being the same oligarchs whose ancestors and present relatives traditionally dominate El Salvador. See Zaid, "Enemy Colleagues: A Reading of the Salvadoran Tragedy," *Dissent* (Winter 1982). Phillip Berryman's response (Ibid., Summer 1982) offers a defense of the Salvadoran rebel leadership, but one that fails to address some of the political assumptions of political designation may be applied to them. Although they fit the Aristotelian definition, the clusters of plantation owners, industrialists, and high military officers that make up the traditional oligarchies of Latin and Central America exhibit certain special features.[3] Their historical genealogies may be traced to the early sixteenth-century *Conquistadores* and their decendants, the European colonial elites, whose special privileges under Spanish and Portuguese royal power far exceeded anything comparable in the British colonial settlements farther to the north, out of which the United States eventually emerged.[4]

In the postcolonial period, the Salvadoran oligarchy evolved similarly to other Central American elites, while showing certain unique features as well. The study by Harald Jung (Reading 6) attempts to analyze some of these social forces, concluding that the social structure of El Salvador is highly differentiated, not only with sectors of the oligarchy occasionally pitted against each other, but also with elements of what in that country can only be called the oppressed groups divided from others in ways that prevent sufficient popular mobilization to achieve overthrow of even a tyrannical government. In a Central American context, rivalries between factions of the ruling class, even when they result in armed struggle and overthrow of regimes (*golpes de estado,* the Spanish for the more widely known French phrase *coups d'état*), must be sharply differentiated from revolutions, which involve shifts in power between social classes. Thus the turbulence of political life in such a place as El Salvador, which is skillfully summarized in the early chapters of Tom Buckley's *Violent Neighbors: El Salvador, Central America and the United States* (New York, 1984), tend to be "palace revolts," disputes *within* the oligarchy over who would enjoy the profitable privileges of exploiting the peasant masses.[5] The present struggle is far deeper and may even

Zaid's argument—that upper class involvement somehow vitiates a rebel movement's claim to legitimacy. It is an issue on which Karl Marx and Friedrich Engels (both of whom came from ruling-class backgrounds) had some interesting observations: "[I]n times when class struggle reaches the decisive moment," they wrote in *The Communist Manifesto* (1848), ". . . a small section of the ruling class cuts itself adrift, and joins the revolutionary class, the class that holds the future in its hands."

[3.] There are several studies of the social composition of the Salvadoran oligarchy (sometimes inaccurately called *Los Catorce,* the "fourteen families"—there are probably more than 100 families in the Salvadoran oligarchy). Among the most useful are: Robert T. Audrey, "Entrepreneurial Formation in El Salvador," *Explorations in Entrepreneurial History* (Cambridge, Mass.) 2d ser., VI (1968–69); Italo Lopez Vallecillos, "Fuerzas Sociales y Cambio Social en El Salvador," *ECA* (Central American University, San Salvador), 34, No. 369/370 (July–August 1979); Enrique Baloyra, *El Salvador in Transition* (Chapel Hill, 1982), part I.

[4.] Clarence H. Haring, *The Spanish Empire in America* (New York, 1963), especially 27–28.

[5.] For an older, patronizing scholarly treatment of regional "palace revolts," see also Dana G. Munro, *The Five Republics of Central America* (New York, 1918), chapter 9, and the far more sophisticated interpretation in José Nun, "A Latin American Phenomenon: The Middle Class Military Coup," in *Latin America: Reform or Revolution,* James Petras and Maurice Zeitlin eds. (New York, 1968), 145–85.

strike at the heart of the question whether exploitation itself (at least in its traditional forms) need necessarily exist. Or so the guerrillas seek to frame the question.

The military is also far from a negligible social force in El Salvador, reflecting the general importance of the armed forces in countries where democratic tendencies have been suppressed. Arising not from the upper reaches of the oligarchy, but from the lower middle class, and getting its training at the Gerardo Barrios Military Academy in the capital city, the Salvadoran officer corps has developed intense institutional loyalties and beliefs that include intense anti-Communism, contempt for civilians, an easygoing tolerance for corruption, and a penchant for extralegal violence. According to veteran journalist Raymond Bonner, the armed forces operate with the macho belief that "authority that does not abuse loses its prestige."[6] Thus, the phenomenon the extraordinary number of unpunished brutal killings by the country's armed forces, a phenomenon that immediately strikes even the most casual observer of Salvadoran reality, is no longer a puzzle. In her insightful study of the Salvadoran military, Reading 8, Shirley Christian shows how abuses of authority by the armed forces (to be treated in more detail in subsequent chapters of this book) are part of the institutional fabric of Salvadoran society.

Although the higher levels of the armed forces come from other sectors of society than the oligarchy, military leadership provides opportunities for later entrance into the charmed circles of wealth and political power. This social mobility for military officers reinforces the historic role of the Salvadoran armed forces: to keep "order" in the interests of of the country's economic and political elite. The lower ranks of the army are filled with peasant conscripts and draftees from the urban underclasses, who, of course, have no say in determining how military power is used and many of whom welcome the regular pay and freedom from agricultural toil as a relief from destitution and direct exploitation.[7] Thus, the army served to keep a lid on popular discontent inherent in an system that functioned to enrich the dominant oligarchies and their allies, but by the 1960s social forces that were impossible to contain became manifest.

By the time John F. Kennedy became President of the United States, an enormous population rise, fluctuating markets for Latin American agricultural staples, and political pressures were combining to produce unprecedented levels of popular discontent in the region. The Cuban revolution had suggested one possible reaction to this discontent, one that not only generated

---

[6] Raymond Bonner, *Weakness and Deceit: U.S. Policy and El Salvador* (New York, 1984), 55.

[7] For an analysis of trends in the Latin American military, see Edwin Lieuwen, *Arms and Politics in Latin America* (New York, 1977), and Robert V. Elam, "Appeal to Arms: The Army and Politics in El Salvador, 1931–1964" (unpublished Ph.D. thesis, University of New Mexico, 1968). The editors have also benefited from conversations on this topic with the distinguished Latin American scholar Professor John A. Womack, Jr., of Harvard University.

panic among the oligarchies, but also stimulated cold-war fears among U.S. policy-makers as well. The Kennedy administration launched the Alliance for Progress as a U.S.-aided reform program aimed at diverting burgeoning popular discontent into moderate channels. But this modern reform was too little and too late;[8] by the end of the decade sustained indigenous guerrilla movements had spread through all the countries of Central America, except the lone democracy, Costa Rica.

The local oligarchies used their military forces to put up a fierce campaign of terror against the insurgents. The U.S. government, always more favorable to established, authoritarian regimes of the right than to left-wing insurgents,[9] gave military aid to the oligarchies, but was recently unable to prevent a popular resistance movement from overthrowing the almost half-century-old Nicaraguan dictatorship imposed by the Somoza family and supported by U.S. power.

The 1979 revolution in Nicaragua threatened embattled oligarchies across the borders in Honduras and El Salvador and in nearby Guatemala. One response was for the dominant groups to suppress even more fiercely any dissenting or revolutionary tendencies in their country. In El Salvador, with an unspecified level of support and encouragement from the United States,[10] the response to the challenge of revolutionary upheaval was a coup that brought into power a military junta that displayed what Harald Jung shows (Reading 6) as a significant reformist impulse. But the power of the right-wing oligarchy soon reasserted itself, blunting this initial thrust.

The persistence and staying power of the Salvadoran right cannot be simply credited to the backing it gets from the United States. Massive military and economic aid does in part sustain the right and its military allies, as Craig Pyes shows in Reading 7, a path-breaking exploration of the sources of the leading (but not the only) right-wing grouping in El Salvador—the National Republican Alliance (ARENA). But this sector also enjoys wide popular support, as measured by the electoral success of ARENA and other right-wing parties in the Constituent Assembly elections of 1982. So great was this success, and so embarrassing to Washington policy-makers hesitant at the prospect of backing yet another militaristic dictatorship, that they later threw support to the Christian Democrats and helped bring José Napoleón Duarte to the presidency in 1984.

[8.] Among the many obituaries for the Alianza para el Progreso, one of the most poignant is "The Alliance That Lost Its Way," by Eduardo Frei Montalva (leader of the Chilean Christian Democrats), reprinted in Irving Louis Horowitz, Josué de Castro, and John Gerassi, eds., *Latin American Radicalism* (New York, 1969), 457–68.

[9.] Although this was the de facto policy long before Ronald Reagan arrived in the White House, he and his advisers have made this point an ideological keystone of their policy (see chapter 1).

[10.] On U.S. involvment in the October 1979 coup that overthrew the regime of General Carlos Humberto Romero, see Robert Armstrong and Janet Schenk, *El Salvador: The Face of Revolution* (Boston, 1982), chapter 5.

The left in El Salvador is obviously a significant social force, with a powerful ideological appeal. Because it is rarely allowed legitimate political expression, the left's claim to speak for the overwhelming majority of the Salvadoran people is difficult to verify. Harald Jung explores the circumstances under which, after the military *golpe* of 1979, elements of a divided left came together into a coalition that would eventually call itself the FMLN/FDR (Reading 6). (Subsequent developments bearing on the evolution of the Salvadoran left are reserved for chapter 5.)

The United States is one of the strongest social forces shaping contemporary El Salvador. This theme permeates this chapter, and the rest of the book. One example of this is the substantial U.S. impact on the origins of the Salvadoran right, dealt with in Reading 7. But influence is not always control, and Washington policy-makers have often been hard put to restrain the very rightist groups they helped to create. Thus, North American support for Duarte as a "third force," dealt with in chapter 4, emerged as the main U.S. strategy. But in turn, Duarte's position, squeezed between unreconstructed rightists and an aggressive left, leaves the future of El Salvador uncertain.

5. El Salvador: A Political Chronology

BY THE EDITORS

1821. Independence from Spain.

1823. United Provinces of Central America declared independent from Mexico.

1847. El Salvador declared a sovereign republic.

1879–82. The commercial lands that had been used by peasants to grow food for their own consumption are expropriated by government decree and consolidated into large farms to grow coffee. "Fourteen Families," the core of the emerging El Salvador oligarchy, control the export crops, in particular coffee.

1930. The Salvadoran Communist Party (PCS) is formed, uniting leaders of many of the local unions of the Regional Federation of Salvadoran Workers (FRTS).

1930. May Day, 80,000 workers and peasants march into San Salvador demanding minimum wage for farmworkers and relief centers for the unemployed.

1931. Arturo Araújo is elected president but is deposed by the military led by Vice President General Martínez. The oligarchy gives the mandate to the military to rule El Salvador.

1932. The military government refuses to allow the seating of PCS candidates who win in municipal and legislative elections. Economic conditions are grave. The PCS responds with a call for uprisings simultaneously in cities, countryside, and military garrisons.

Three days before the uprising, Augustín Farabundo Martí and other leaders are arrested. Because of a communications breakdown, Salvadoran peasants and farmworkers nevertheless march into the cities as originally planned. Virtually unarmed, the rebels cannot defend themselves against the military. As a result, 4,000 are killed and the uprising crushed.

As a lesson, the army begins what comes to be known as *"La Matanza,"* the massacre. Within the first few weeks the army and paramilitary forces kill more than 30,000 people. Peasant leaders are hanged in the town square. By the time the *Matanza* is over, 4 percent of the population is killed, the PCS liquidated, the FRTS annihilated, and the Indian population forced to abandon their native dress, language, and cultural activities.

1931–44. Martínez rules for thirteen years, his policies preventing industrialization.

1944. Martínez is forced from power, but the military continues to rule.

Late 1940s. This is a period of major economic transformation. A new coalition is formed of the military technocrats and a tiny industrial bourgeoisie, with part of the coffee oligarchy. Martínez's anti-industrial laws are abolished. U.S. manufacturing investments begin.

1950. Colonel Oscar Osorio becomes president in fraudulent elections. Continued repression is viewed as a necessary complement to reforms, which are intended to induce economic modernization, rationalize an otherwise archaic society, and produce a modest facade of democracy.

1950s. The Revolutionary Party of Democratic Unity (PRUD) is formed as the official party of the coalition of the military and the bourgeoisie who want modernization. Its policies lead to the growth of the Salvadoran economy and the development of small middle and working classes in the cities.

1961. The Central American Common Market is formed with support from the United States, providing a "free trade zone" in El Salvador, Guatemala, Honduras, Nicaragua, and Costa Rica. The United States views the common market as providing the necessary political infrastructure for the investment of U.S. capital.

1962. PRUD is by this point thoroughly discredited because of continued election frauds, the failure to improve living conditions, and uninterrupted repression. The same ruling military oligarchy coalition reconstitutes the party as the Party of National Conciliation (PCN), and Colonel Rivera comes to power. The PCN rules for the next seventeen years.

1962–67. Rivera, the first to have truly contested elections, allows opposition parties for the first time since 1934. Three main opposition parties quickly emerge. The Christian Democratic Party (PDC), supported by European Christian Democracy and by local professionals, quickly becomes the largest opposition party. The National Revolutionary Movement (MNR) is a small party, made up of professionals and intellectuals. The National Democratic Union (UDN) emerges; it includes the PCS, outlawed in 1932.

1969. War breaks out between Honduras and El Salvador, precipitated by Honduras in an effort to expropriate the lands of peasants who had migrated from El Salvador after losing their land to the coffee and cotton plantations. The Central American Common Market collapses. The Christian Democrats, the MNR, and the UDN form a coalition called the National Opposition Union (UNO).

1970–72. The manipulation by the military of the elections of 1970 and the blatant fraud in the 1972 elections announce to many sectors that meaningful reform via elections will not work.

1970–75. Popular armed elements emerge. The Popular Liberation Force (FPL) develops from a split within the PCS. The FPL argues for both armed action and mass organizing. The People's Revolutionary Army (ERP) develops from a split in the left wing of the Christian Democratic Party and focuses primarily on armed struggle. The National Resistance (RN), like the FPL, urges both military action and mass organizing.

1975–80. Thousands of people from the worker, peasant, teacher, student, and church sectors come together in the popular organizations, using civil disobedience and mass protests as their tactic. The popular organizations are linked to the popular armed movements.

1977–79. The PCN selects General Carlos Romero to replace Colonel Molina in the 1977 "elections." Romero represents the far-right, repression-without-reform faction. Under General Romero there is a major escalation of government terror.

June–July 1979. Archbishop Oscar Romero (no relation to General Romero) becomes an outspoken critic of the military's rule and economic injustice. The excesses of General Romero's regime earn the condemnation of Amnesty International and other human-rights organizations. Finally, the government's repression becomes an intolerable embarrassment to the Carter administration and the victory of the Sandinistas in nearby Nicaragua makes the United States fearful of backing an unpopular dictator.

October 15, 1979. The first "revolutionary junta" is formed. A U.S.-backed bloodless coup overthrows General Romero and sets up the Revolutionary Governing Junta of two military persons and three civilians from the center and moderate left. A truce with the popular organizations is worked out. Many members of the UNO coalition join the government in various ministerial and subministerial positions. A proclamation of October 15 calls for nationalization of foreign trade in coffee and sugar, establishment of an investigatory commission on political prisoners and the disappeared, beginning a land-reform program, and mobilization of international support.

By December it becomes clear that none of the measures will be carried out.

January 3, 1980. The civilian members of the junta, virtually all the civilian members of the cabinet, and most civilian subministers resign over the continued repression by the government and paramilitary forces.

January 6, 1980. Archbishop Romero calls on the people to back the popular organizations and "preserve the liberation process."

January 9, 1980. A second governing junta is constituted, again with two military and three civilian members.

January 11, 1980. The popular organizations begin to unify. The People's Revolutionary Bloc (BPR), the United Front for Popular Action (FAPU), the Democratic Nationalist Union (UDN), the February 28 Peoples Leagues (LP-28), and the People's Liberation Movement (MPL) come together to form the Revolutionary Coordinating Committee of the Masses (CRM).

January 22, 1980. 200,000 march in San Salvador to celebrate the popular unity.

February 17, 1980. Archbishop Romero denounces the "unscrupulous military" and calls on Christian Democrats to stop serving the junta as a "cover for repression." In a letter to President Carter, Romero demands that the United States stop military, economic, and diplomatic intervention.

March 3, 1980. The second junta falls and a third is created. Civilian members resign from the second junta to protest continued repression.

March 6, 1980. The new junta announces a land-reform program under the direction of the U.S. State Department and the American Institute for Free Labor Development, an affiliate of the AFL-CIO, which has known links with the CIA. At the same time, a state of siege is imposed as peasants are attacked by the military and paramilitary forces.

March 23, 1980. Archbishop Romero denounces the agrarian reform as "reforms bathed in blood" and calls on military personnel to disobey their commanders.

March 24, 1980. Archbishop Romero is assassinated while celebrating mass by right-wing forces.

April 2, 1980. The United States approves $5.7 million in military aid to El Salvador.

April 18, 1980. Thousands attend ceremony to celebrate the creation of the Democratic Revolutionary Front (FDR), a broad coalition of the CRM, the social democratic party, Christian Democrats fed up with the junta, 80 percent of the trade unions, church people, professionals, students, small-business people, and the National and Catholic universities. It is the largest political movement in El Salvador's history.

May 14, 1980. 600 peasants fleeing rural repression massacred at the Sumpul River by Salvadoran and Honduran troops.

June 24, 1980. Three-day general strike is 90 percent effective. Army occupies National University, killing fifty.

August 12, 1980. Three-day general strike a partial success. Government bombs sections of San Salvador, killing 200.

September 1980. The United States sends $20 million in economic aid to El Salvador to make a total of $90 million for 1980.

October 4, 1980. Army begins military offensive in Morazán region, creating 24,000 refugees and killing 3,000.

November 1980. The Farabundo Martí Front for the National Liberation is formed as the political-military arm of the FDR. It brings together the FPL, the ERP, and the RN, as well as the PCS and the newly formed Central American Revolutionary Workers Party (PRTC).

November 28, 1980. Six leaders of the FDR assassinated by security forces and paramilitary agents.

December 3, 1980. Four U.S. churchwomen assassinated by the National Guard.

December 4, 1980. Carter administration suspends military and economic aid to El Salvador.

December 6, 1980. Acting Archbishop Rivera y Damas denounces U.S. military aid for facilitating "repression against the people and persecution of the church."

December 13, 1980. Third junta dissolves. Fourth junta forms with José Napoleón Duarte as President. The United States reinstates economic aid.

December 15, 1980. U.N. General Assembly passes a resolution condemning the repression in El Salvador, with fifty-five countries abstaining.

December 16, 1980. U.S. government loans $20 million to El Salvador government.

December 18, 1980. U.S. government loans El Salvador government a further $45.5 million, bringing the total aid for 1980 to $150 million.

December 26–27, 1980. FMLN, the political-military arm of the FDR, attacks four major towns in the northern province of Chalatenango, where the Salvadoran government maintains police and military installations.

January 5, 1981. AFL-CIO representatives Michael Hammer and Mark Pearlman, who had been working in El Salvador as advisers on the land-reform program, and José Viera, the president of the Salvadoran Institute for Agrarian Transformation, are murdered by two right-wing hit men.

January 11, 1981. A general offensive of the FMLN begins.

January 13, 1981. The FDR calls for a general strike.

January 14, 1981. The U.S. administration resumes fiscal-year 1981 military assistance to El Salvador. That aid—$5 million in foreign military sales credits and $420,000 in training funds—had been held up on December 5, 1980, after the murder of four U.S. churchwomen. In addition, the United States sends six advisers to El Salvador.

January 15, 1981. About half the shops in San Salvador are closed, in addition to the walkout of 20,000 government workers.

January 17, 1981. U.S. administration invokes special executive powers to send an emergency package of $5 million in military assistance to El Salvador.

January 18, 1981. The United States approves an additional $5 million in military aid, bringing the total for the first three weeks of 1981 to $10 million. The latest aid package includes three military advisory teams.

February 7, 1981. The FDR calls for "a dialogue with the U.S. government." "We want to find a way to end the violence," an FDR spokesperson explains.

February 11, 1981. The Reagan administration drops U.S. insistence on an investigation into the death of the four U.S. churchwomen as a condition for giving economic and military aid to El Salvador.

February 23, 1981. The State Department releases a major "white paper" purporting to show that what is occurring in El Salvador is indirect armed aggression by the Soviet Union, Cuba, North Vietnam, and other Communist-bloc governments. Mexican Foreign Minister José Velasco calls the document an attempt by the United States "to transfer its confrontation with the Soviet Union to Latin America."

March 7, 1981. State Department spokesperson James R. Cheek denies the authenticity of a "dissent paper" from within the government that takes issue with administration policy.

March 1981. Secretary of State Alexander Haig denies on several occasions that the United States would look favorably upon a coup by the rightist oligarchy. The comments come in response to statements by rightist leader Roberto D'Aubuisson in El Salvador.

March 1981. The Salvadoran junta names an electoral committee to pave the way for "free elections" in 1982. Duarte wants a "dialogue" but no negotiations with the FDR. He invites opposition figures back to take part in electoral process but admits he cannot assure their safety should they return.

April and May 1981. The U.S. Congress passes strictures on U.S. aid to El Salvador that require President Reagan to certify that the Salvadoran government is dedicated to assuring human rights and prepared to negotiate.

May 3, 1981. 100,000 Americans rally at the Pentagon in opposition to U.S. involvement in El Salvador.

June 1981. Efforts at pursuing mediation in the Salvadoran conflict by the Socialist International (separate missions by Hans Wischniewski of the West German Social Democratic Party and Ed Broadbent of the Canadian New Democratic Party) end in failure. The Christian Democratic–military junta refuses to negotiate.

June 1981. The Salvadoran Association of Jurists declines to participate in preparations for 1982 elections because of the continuing terror and state of siege.

July 1981. Duarte calls conservative businessmen trying to roll back limited land reform and nationalization of banks "the biggest threat" to the junta. "The private sector," says Duarte, "is in its final offensive."

July 2, 1981. Newly elected French Socialist President François Mitterrand expresses support for the Salvadoran rebellion. "It is a question of people refusing to submit to misery and humiliation," he states. Two days later, the French Socialist Party promises an FDR delegation "all possible support" in the struggle.

July 17, 1981. The Reagan administration declares itself committed to a "political solution" in El Salvador, by which it means support for the 1982 proposed elections rather than, as European and Latin American allies have urged, negotiations with the FDR.

August 28, 1981. A joint French and Mexican declaration gives official recognition to the Salvadoran opposition as a representative political force.

January 1982. Reagan certifies that Salvadoran junta is making progress in curbing violations of human rights; 800 people killed by National Guard at Mozote; FMLN destroys half of Salvadoran Air Force in raid at Ilopango Airport.

February 1982. U.S. adviser sent home for carrying rifle in combat zone; Mexican President José López Portillo announces plan for regional Contadora negotiations.

March 28, 1982. Right-wing coalition of the Nationalist Republican Alliance (ARENA) and the National Conciliation Party (PCN) win a majority of the sixty seats in the Constituent Assembly. Christian Democrats are the largest single party. There is a massive turnout despite sporadic FMLN efforts to halt the balloting.

April 29, 1982. After extraordinary U.S. pressure and at the behest of the Salvadoran military, the Constituent Assembly elects banker Álvaro Magaña rather than Roberto D'Aubuisson as the country's provisional president.

May 1982. Constituent Assembly suspends provisions of the land-reform process.

October 29, 1982. Ambassador Hinton, departing from the Reagan administration's policy of "quiet diplomacy," tells the U.S.-Salvadoran Chamber of Commerce that a "Mafia" that carries out the murder of innocent civilians and American citizens "must be stopped."

November 8, 1982. In a cover story *Newsweek* reveals details about the Reagan administration's so-called secret war against Nicaragua, being fought from Honduras by "counterrevolutionaries" trained and supplied by the United States.

March 1983. Pope John Paul II visits Central America.

April 12, 1983. Guerrilla leader Salvador Cayetano Carpio commits suicide in Managua, Nicaragua, a few days after one of his top aides, Comandante Ana María, is bludgeoned to death, publicly revealing splits within the Salvadoran guerrilla forces.

April 27, 1983. Reagan takes his Central America policy to a joint session of Congress, one of the few times in history that an American President has addressed the joint body on a foreign-policy issue.

May 25, 1983. Lieutenant Commander Albert A. Schaufelberger III assassinated by a guerrilla faction while sitting in his car, waiting for his woman-friend, at the Catholic university in San Salvador.

May 28–29, 1983. Reagan shakes up his Central America team, removing Thomas Enders as assistant secretary of state for Inter-American affairs and Hinton as ambassador to El Salvador.

June 1983. 100 U.S. military advisers begin training Salvadoran troops in Honduras.

July 20, 1983. Reagan names former Secretary of State Henry Kissinger to head a twelve-man National Bipartisan Commission on Central America.

July 20, 1983. Reagan administration certifies for the fourth time that Salvadoran government is making progress on human rights, implementation of land reform, and investigations into the murders of American citizens.

November 30, 1983. President Reagan vetoes a bill that would have continued the certification requirements.

December 30, 1983. Guerrilla forces, in their largest and most successful action of the war, attack military base at El Paraíso, killing at least 100 government soldiers, who are buried in a mass grave.

January 1, 1984. Guerrillas destroy Cuscatlán suspension bridge.

January 11, 1984. Kissinger Commission releases its report.

March 25, 1984. Christian Democrat José Napoleón Duarte wins round one of the Salvadoran presidential elections (goes on to defeat ARENA's Roberto D'Aubuisson by 54 to 46 percent in the run-off on May 6).

April 13, 1984. Reagan uses emergency powers to send an additional $32 million in military aid to El Salvador.

May 24, 1984. Five National Guardsmen convicted of the murder of the four American churchwomen in December 1980, although charges remain of complicity and cover-up on the part of high officials, including the current Defense Minister, Carlos Eugenio Vides Casanova.

September 1984. University of El Salvador reopened after being closed two years; Duarte, in speech before the United Nations, offers to open a dialogue with the opposition (accepted by the FDR/FMLN).

October 15, 1984. FDR/FMLN representatives meet with Duarte and representatives of the armed forces at La Palma under the mediation of the Salvadoran church.

November 30, 1984. Second dialogue meeting is held at Ayagualo, a few miles south of San Salvador.

January 2, 1985. New Year's truce ends as guerrillas dynamite power lines, blacking out parts of San Salvador.

February 12, 1985. United States acknowledges it routinely has 120 soldiers in El Salvador but claims it is not in violation of fifty-five-person congressional limit, since surplus soldiers are handling other duties or are in El Salvador for less than two weeks of temporary duty.

March 23, 1985. Retired rightist general José Alberto Medrano, founder of

ORDEN, slain, an indication guerrillas are moving their fight back to the cities.

March 31, 1985. The Christian Democrats win an upset victory in elections for the Constituent Assembly, gaining thirty-four of the sixty Assembly seats and sweeping most of the country's municipal offices.

April 18, 1985. Guerrilla leader Nidia Díaz captured (announced on April 22) with secret documents purporting to show that (1) rebels attended courses in the Soviet bloc; (2) Nicaragua probably cut off aid after the invasion of Grenada in 1983; (3) Duarte's win was considered a political setback.

April 21, 1985. Government and guerrillas observe undeclared truce, allowing medical teams to vaccinate 250,000 children against five major diseases.

April–May 1985. Guerrillas burn municipal offices and kidnap and kill a number of mayors they say are part of the government's counterinsurgency effort.

May 16, 1985. Duarte meets with President Reagan.

June 2, 1985. Hospitals and clinics, on strike for nearly a month, are stormed by government security forces, who inadvertently kill four of their undercover agents. (Fifteen hundred workers and students march in protest on June 4.)

June 6, 1985. One thousand rebel combatants carry out a spectacular attack —the largest FMLN operation since 1983—on the National Telecommunications Administration installation in Santa Ana.

June 19, 1985. Guerrillas from the Central American Revolutionary Workers Party gun down thirteen people, including four U.S. Marines and two U.S. civilian businessmen, at a sidewalk café in San Salvador.

June 25, 1985. Guerrillas issue warning that the café attack was "only a beginning" and promise to carry war to "Yankee aggressors" wherever they are in El Salvador.

July 31, 1985. Secretary of Defense Caspar Weinberger says the Salvadoran army captured or killed those responsible for the slaying of the Marines, an "action" later "clarified" by the Defense Department as a retaliatory attack on the guerrilla faction that took responsibility for the shootings.

September 4, 1985. Honduran soldiers raid U.N. camp for Salvadoran refugees in Colomoncagua; many injured or killed.

September 10, 1985. Ines Guadalupe Duarte Durán, President Duarte's thirty-five-year-old daughter, kidnapped.

September 16, 1985. Testifying before the World Court, former CIA analyst David MacMichael claims "no credible evidence" of Nicaragua's providing significant arms to Salvadoran guerrillas for at least four years.

September 29, 1985. Roberto D'Aubuisson resigns as head of National Republican Alliance.

October 10, 1985. Guerrillas raid training base near La Unión, killing at least forty and wounding sixty-eight; guerrillas claim their goal was to kill or capture twenty-five American soldiers serving there.

October 14, 1985. Duarte sends three of his daughters and four grandchildren to United States.

October 17, 1985. Series of civil-servant strikes begin, involving 20,000–50,000 workers, mostly on economic matters but partially in protest over the arrest of union members, resulting in concessions by the Christian Democratic government.

October 24, 1985. Duarte's daughter released in exchange for twenty-two of the thirty-four rebel prisoners on the FMLN's list, including Nidia Díaz; also released by the FMLN were twenty-three kidnapped mayors in exchange for about 100 wounded rebels who were given safe conduct out of the country. Two weeks later, guerrillas release tape in which Duarte's daughter praises the rebels. Duarte is criticized by the Salvadoran military for his "emotional" handling of the affair.

November 23, 1985. The guerrilla commanders say they will fight indefinitely if the Salvadoran government ignores their peace plan, reiterated on November 18, which called for a direct sharing of power in a transitional government.

December 21, 1985. Top military leaders of the FMLN say they are trying to unite in a single Marxist-Leninist political party, marking, it is believed, the first time the FMLN has publicly defined itself as a Marxist movement.

January 3, 1986. Rebels end holiday truce with attacks on more than twenty electric power stations in provinces around the capital.

January 12, 1986. Archbishop Arturo Rivera y Damas condemns the Salvadoran military for its indiscriminate bombing of civilians and its destruction of homes and crops in army sweeps of rebel-held areas.

January 18, 1986. Nearly 10,000 march in San Salvador protest against austerity measures planned by the Duarte government (announced by President Duarte on January 22.)

February 13, 1986. Two former National Guardsmen are found guilty of homicide in 1981 deaths of two American land-reform experts and a Salvadoran.

February 21, 1986. Workers march through downtown San Salvador in largest protest to date against the economic policies of Duarte's government.

February 22, 1986. Guerrillas announce they will no longer observe agreement barring kidnapping of relatives of military and Government officials.

February 24, 1986. Claiming that Salvadoran police no longer kill prisoners and face a renewed threat of guerrillas infiltrating the cities, U.S. reportedly begins unrestricted training for all of El Salvador's police forces.

March 15, 1986. 20,000 supporters of President Duarte march in San Salvador in response to a previous demonstration by centrist and leftist union members who had protested economic conditions.

April 29, 1986. Salvadoran government and rebel officials hold low-key talks in Lima, Peru, to explore the possibility of renewed negotiations.

May 1, 1986. May Day march of 15,000 to 25,000 turns into a forum critical of Duarte and the United States as Duarte's inability to end the civil war and his imposition of economic austerity erodes trade union support.

May 19, 1986. Salvadoran soldiers admit they cut off the ears of dead rebels to prove body counts.

June 1, 1986. Addressing the National Assembly, President Duarte proposes a third round of peace talks with the guerrillas, a proposal accepted thereafter by Guillermo Ungo, head of the FDR, and by guerrilla leaders.

June 19, 1986. Five hundred guerrillas attack army garrison in San Miguel, killing or wounding at least fifty soldiers.

July 12, 1986. Rebel peace proposal includes cease-fire during which they will take part in an election after transitional government is formed. Proposal is said to be the first to include an offer to halt fighting.

August 23, 1986. Representatives of Salvadoran government meet rebels in Mexico City and agree to hold third round of peace talks on September 19 in the town of Sesori.

September 14, 1986. Rebels, claiming that Duarte's government has refused to withdraw troops around Sesori, announce they will not attend the talks. Duarte blames rebels for scuttled talks and lavishes money and attention on Sesori to show government is more interested in peace than guerrillas.

October 10, 1986. Major earthquake hits San Salvador causing heavy damage to water supplies, electrical plant and hospitals. Later estimates are that 1,500 were killed and some 200,000 left homeless.

October 11, 1986. State of emergency is declared. Rebels declare unilateral truce which is rejected by the army. Fighting nonetheless slows down as army divisions are pulled into capital to maintain order and clear rubble.

October 12, 1986. Salvadoran government is heavily criticized for its failure to help people of severely damaged Comunidad Modelo rebuild. Archbishop Arturo Rivera y Damas criticizes the Government for its failure to provide relief services to poor neighborhoods.

October 17, 1986. Secretary of State Shultz tours quake area, calls it an economic "catastrophe" of "monumental proportions," and announces $50 million in immediate aid that will ultimately total hundreds of millions of dollars.

October 24, 1986. Guerrillas resume attacks—kill five militiamen and civilians.

November 9, 1986. Salvadoran guerrilla leader defends use of land mines as effective weapon against Government forces but acknowledges that some civilian casualties have occurred.

February 7, 1987. An estimated 50,000 demonstrate in support of Duarte's government to counter the show of force by right wing parties that two weeks earlier had conducted a successful one-day business strike in protest of tax increases.

6. Class Struggle and Civil War in El Salvador*

By Harald Jung

Modern El Salvador took shape in the late nineteenth century when coffee agriculture was introduced and the Indians were driven off the land by the encroaching private plantations. Laws drafted in the interest and at the behest of the coffee oligarchs placed the police agencies at their service in the task of accumulating acreage. [1] *This oppressive apparatus had its first major test in the Communist-led Indian peasant revolt of 1932, and it succeeded only too well in carrying out the massacre* (La Matanza) *described in several of the readings in this book, including this essay by Harald Jung, a former researcher for Fundación IESA (Investigaciones Económicas y Sociales Aplicadas) in Madrid, Spain.*

In contrast to much of the social commentary current in the United States, which focuses on personalities, and to surface chronicles of political events, Jung's essay is an examination of underlying social-class forces at work in El Salvador prior to the golpe of 1979. In short, Jung's work is an exercise in Marxian analysis. For at least a generation, such analysis had been generally excluded from acceptable political and social discourse in the United States. Part of the explanation is the intellectual repression of the 1950s known as McCarthyism. A recent study of the impact of McCarthyism strongly suggests that the exclusion has deprived American society not only of the intellectual products of a marginalized generation of left-wing scholars, but of an entire mode of discourse that might have provided badly needed illumination of such areas as popular social movements in places like Central America and Southeast Asia. [2] *Repression of dissenting scholarship on cold-war issues obviously does not provide anything like a full explanation for American foreign-policy mistakes in the post–World War II era, but it may help suggest why there was so little public opposition to questionable policies. Exposure of a new American generation to the kind of analysis their predecessors lacked is one of the aims of this book; another is the hope that an enlightened public will prevent new cycles of counterrevolutionary interventionism in the future.*

* From *New Left Review* (London), No. 122 (July–August 1980).

[1] Michael McClintock, *The American Connection.* Vol. 1, *State Terror and Popular Resistance in El Salvador* (London: ZED Books, 1985), chapter 6.

[2] Ellen Schrecker, "The Missing Generation: Academics and the Communist Party from the Depression to the Cold War," *Humanities in Society* (University of Southern California), 6 (Spring–Summer 1983); Schrecker, *No Ivory Tower: McCarthyism and the University* (New York: Oxford University Press, 1986).

THE military coup in El Salvador of October 15, 1979, provoked a new and remarkable twist in the bloody social conflicts which have wracked this Central American republic. The former dictator, General Carlos Humberto Romero, was replaced by a junta which proclaimed the need for sweeping reforms and which initially attracted the support of Christian Democrats, Social Democrats and Communists. The most important groups of the armed revolutionary left maintained an attitude of watchful hostility towards the reformist junta, and in the days following the coup there were clashes in several working class districts around the capital between the army and the leftist guerrillas. It quickly became clear that the new government could not carry through its program of reforms in most parts of the country and was unable either to suppress rightist terrorism directed at the popular forces, or even to control its own military and security apparatus. In December the Social Democrats and Communists withdrew support from the junta and in subsequent months some of the Christian Democrats have followed suit. On March 24 Archbishop Oscar Romero was assassinated; on the previous day he had made an impassioned appeal for an end to military repression and had declared that soldiers were not obliged to obey orders that were contrary to their conscience. Between January and June over two thousand people were killed as a result of official or paramilitary violence, while in May the Salvadoran high command declared that two northern provinces, Morazán and Chalatenango, were "military emergency zones." In January and mid-April the oppositional guerrilla forces moved to form a wider united front and to integrate some of those who had formerly supported the reformist Government set up in October 1979. The mounting popular opposition to military repression in El Salvador has often been compared to the last stages of the struggle against Somoza in Nicaragua. Yet, as we will see, El Salvador's particular socio-economic and political development has been different from that of Nicaragua and does not lay the basis for the same type of polarizations. In El Salvador the rightist para-military groups can command some sectional support while the military-sponsored government continues to proclaim the need for reform and to receive the support of some Christian Democrats and the United States.

El Salvador remains as ever an agricultural country. In 1974 agriculture made up 26 percent of the GNP, and in 1977 it provided around four-fifths of revenues from exports. In 1975 more than 60 percent of the population were classed as agricultural. The rural sector is thus of fundamental importance for all political developments.

The division in land utilization between cattle-raising haciendas and villages cultivating maize, which dated from the colonial epoch, was overridden by the introduction of coffee planting. Between 1880 and 1912, the common lands of the villages in the hilly volcanic regions were for the most part sold to urban middle- and upper-class families at giveaway prices, a small portion alone being distributed among the villagers. Since the coffee tree needs five years growth before its first harvest, its cultivation is only possible for persons with a certain amount of capital, and hardly at all for small farmers, for whom the land has to provide their basic foodstuffs. Right from the beginning, therefore, coffee was concentrated pre-eminently in the hands of a small and relatively rich coffee bourgeoisie owning large estates.

At first, these big coffee planters maintained the traditional relations of production that existed on the haciendas. The workers (*colonos*) received a plot of land on which to cultivate food crops in return for their work for the landowner. Since in the coffee-growing regions, however, the land left to the *colonos* could be more profitably used for coffee cultivation, the *colono* system was already replaced by wage labor in the 1920s. The workers no longer received any land for their own use, but only a primitive hut on the estate. During the 1940s and 1950s, with the extension of coffee cultivation (annual receipts from coffee exports rose by a factor of ten), the number of landless rural laborers also rose in proportion to the traditional *colonos*. In the 1950s, modern technology took root in coffee cultivation and made possible a reduction of the permanently employed labor force. In the 1960s, the era of the Alliance for Progress, social legislation and a guaranteed minimum wage was introduced for the permanent employees, so as to forestall the radicalization of the growing (illegal) trade-union organization in the countryside. The coffee bourgeoisie subsequently counteracted the tendencies of the workers to organize, as well as the minimum wage, by seeking to reduce to a minimum the number of permanent employees, replacing labor by capital, so that they only needed to employ a larger number of workers for the short periods of harvesting. A mobile rural proletariat of seasonal workers now grew up, with the chance of finding employment on the coffee estates only between November and March.

This process of replacing permanent employees by seasonal workers, which in coffee cultivation took place only slowly on account of the relatively narrow limits of mechanization imposed by natural conditions, was repeated far more violently in cotton cultivation. The rapidly rising demand for cotton on the world market in the early 1950s opened up the lower lying valleys and coastal areas to agricultural production for export. The land used for cotton was generally leased by the big landlords to capitalist farmers. Fifty-two percent of the cotton fields, at the beginning of the 1970s, were leased in this way, with 83 percent being operated by middle and large enterprises. The *colonos* of the haciendas, who had no legal title to the land that they tilled, had to make way. Since cotton cultivation required still less labor than cattle-raising, and experienced an enormous intensification in the course of the 1950s (the yield per hectare doubling from 1950 to 1960), only a small proportion of the former *colonos* found work in cotton growing, and generally only then during the months of harvest. From *colonos,* they became landless peasants and seasonal workers.

Coffee and cotton remain El Salvador's principal export products. In the late 1970s, coffee comprised between 80 and 90 percent of export revenue, and cotton between 10 and 15 percent. The growth of a mobile rural proletariat, employed only on a seasonal basis, can thus be seen as characteristic for virtually the entire agricultural export sector. At the same time, the mechanization of the agricultural export economy led to a reduction in the number of workers employed in agriculture from 310,097 in 1961 to 267,079 in 1975. The old *colono* system now exists on only a few obsolete haciendas, although in the late 1960s, a middle strata of peasants managed to develop and become quite significant on the basis of sugar cultivation.

The expansion of the agricultural export sector also had its effects on the peasant subsistence economy and the small peasants. In El Salvador 10 hectares is generally taken as the minimum amount of land required to support an average peasant family. In 1971, only 19,951 (5.2 percent) out of 384,540 families engaged in agriculture possessed 10 hectares or more, 15.6 percent cultivated between 2 and 10 hectares, and 245,015 (63.7 percent) less than 1 hectare. Of the peasants with less than 1 hectare, only 24 percent actually owned the land that they tilled, as did only 31 percent of the peasants with between 1 and 2 hectares. The great mass of small peasants are thus directly affected by changes in the conditions of farm leases.

Traditionally, the big landowners leased out portions of their land to small peasants on a sharecropping basis. This pre-capitalist rent in kind was gradually replaced from the 1950s onwards by a variable money rent, with the expansion of the export economy and the emergence of capitalist farmers. The small peasants could not pay the rising land prices and rents, and had to move out.

The rural banking sector controlled by the agricultural bourgeoisie also compelled many peasants to give up their holdings. Between 1961 and 1975 export-oriented undertakings received between 80 and 90 percent of agricultural credits; 87 percent of all these credits, in 1971, went to farms with more than 10 hectares, and only 1 percent to farms with less than 1 hectare. Ninety-five percent of the land belonging to farms with less than 2 hectares was used in 1971 for the production of basic necessities. In the context of an export-oriented agricultural policy, it seemed inopportune to promote this. Many small peasants were therefore forced before harvest time either to borrow from local moneylenders to exorbitant interest rates, or else to sell their crops in advance at cut price, simply so as to feed their families. They thus got into a chronic cycle of unending debt, and had sooner or later to sell their land.

The process of expropriation and expulsion of small peasants, side by side with a simultaneous reduction in employment in the expanding export cultivations, were aggravated in their social consequences because of the limited amount of land available in El Salvador for agriculture, and an annual population growth of 3.1 percent. In 1975, the total population stood at 4.1 million, a density of 192 per square kilometer. A steadily growing number of independent peasants were thus pressed together on a shrinking area. From 1950 to 1961 the number of farms with less than 10 hectares rose in the cotton-growing regions by 72 percent, while the average size of these farms fell by 54 percent. From 1961 to 1975, the number of independent peasants, together with their dependents, rose from 176,051 to 339,601. From 1961 to 1971, the number of peasant families with less than 10 hectares grew by 126,839, out of which the number of families with under 2 hectares grew by 37,194 and the number of completely landless peasant families by 81,657. The number of peasant families with more than 10 hectares grew by only 354.

The big export businesses became ever more concentrated in a few hands. In 1971, 0.5 percent of all agricultural enterprises (those with more than 200 hectares) farmed some 34 percent of the agricultural area, while 52 percent of the peasants (those with less than 2 hectares) farmed only 3.7 percent. Since one family often owns several large agricultural holdings, the real extent of concentration is still higher. In 1971, six families alone possessed as much land as 80 percent of the rural population together.

This situation can be summed up as follows:

1. The agricultural export sector is in the hands of a small number of families.
2. Over the last three decades, permanent workers in the agricultural export cultivations have been increasingly replaced by migrant workers employed only seasonally.
3. The expansion of the export sector is reducing the agricultural land that remains for the small peasants. At the same time, the number of jobs in export cultivations is on the decline, so that a growing agricultural population has to feed itself as peasants off a shrunken area of land. For three decades the size of these peasant farms has been declining, and 95 percent of them do not have sufficient land to guarantee their own subsistence. These small peasants have to compete with the landless seasonal workers for jobs on the big exporting estates.
4. Some 64 percent of rural families are seasonal and migrant workers, with no land or less than 1 hectare. Their number is growing rapidly, particularly the number of completely landless families, even though the number of jobs for wage workers in agriculture is declining. This means a constant rise in underemployment and unemployment in the countryside.

SOCIO-ECONOMIC DEVELOPMENT IN THE TOWNS

The industrial development that has taken place since 1930 and particularly in the 1960s proved unable to absorb the labor power set free in the agricultural sector. Due to the low purchasing power of the mass of the population, and the preference for luxury import goods on the part of those with most money to spend, the local market could only develop a weak demand for locally produced consumption goods. Manufacturing industry, therefore, is not just the further development of traditional handicrafts, but predominantly a capital-intensive export industry concentrated in the hands of a few big bourgeois families. Often the same families accumulated wealth in the agricultural export sector, financed the industrialization boom of the 1960s and subsequently themselves became industrial capitalists. At the present time, the entire economy of El Salvador is dominated by some fourteen families, all involved in agriculture, finance and industry, even if their specializations are somewhat different.

The development of a capital-intensive export industry only created a small number of new industrial jobs. Between 1961 and 1971 the manufacturing sector grew by 24 percent, while the number of people employed in this sector grew by only 6 percent. The number of employees in manufacturing as a proportion of the economically active population fell from around 13 percent in 1961 to some 10 percent in 1971 and 1975. The number of workers in manufacturing industry grew by only 2,500 between 1961 and 1971. The number of wage earners in the sectors of mining, manufacturing, construction and transport, storage and communication (i.e., those that could be described as the classical industrial proletariat) remained virtually constant throughout the 1960s, and only began to increase after 1971, rising by 32,000 to a total of 152,000 in 1975.

In the wake of the industrialization of 1961–1975, the total number of wage earners not employed in agriculture grew by about one-third, from 246,000 to 361,000. The total of self-employed in the non-agricultural sectors, however, almost tripled in the same period, from 68,000 to 193,000. This expresses on the one hand the sharp growth of an independent middle class, on the other a process of marginalization. Out of these 193,000 independently active, 131,000 were involved in commerce and 11,000 in the service sector. Both these categories in statistics for developing countries generally conceal a vast number of shoeshiners, lottery-ticket sellers, street traders, prostitutes, washerwomen, etc. The number of self-employed in commerce grew from 47,000 in 1971 to 131,000 in 1975, but it can hardly be assumed that in these four years El Salvador, with an increase of 122,000 in the total number of economically active, counted 84,000 successful new business people among these. In 1975, 126,000 urban wage earners were employed in the service sector. This total also conceals untold thousands of marginalized people, most of whom have fled into the cities from underemployment and unemployment in the countryside. The capital-intensive export industry could not provide sufficient jobs for these migrants, and compelled them to lead a marginalized existence in the ever growing slum districts in and around San Salvador.

To sum up: Industrialization produced an industrial proletariat that comprises 42 percent of all urban wage earners and 27 percent of all those economically active in the urban sector. Compared with other developing countries, the industrial proletariat is thus relatively well developed in the urban sector. At the same time, the middle class of self-employed and people active in professional services and commerce has expanded. Most of all, however, there has been an explosion in the number of petty retailers and street traders, now running into the tens of thousands. These traders should be classed as marginalized people without adequate income. The surplus of petty traders reduce one another's sales and profit potentials. The number of those marginalized elements who perform personal services and odd jobs should also be estimated in tens of thousands. Among others, this group includes the more than 40 percent of all urban wage earners who in 1974 were receiving less than the legal minimum wage of 28.70 *colones* (about $12) per week. But the economic position of the industrial workers has also deteriorated in the 1970s. While the number of these workers has risen, the index of real industrial wages has fallen by 1975 back to the level of 1965, after rising briefly until 1970–71.

THE POLITICAL IMPLICATIONS OF SOCIAL STRATIFICATION

The political developments in El Salvador must be viewed against this socio-economic background. The expansion of the agricultural export sector did not mean a simple proletarianization of the peasants, a process that would have smoothly transformed the agricultural population into a revolutionary subject. This interpretation, of a kind often met with in the works of left-wing writers, may well be correct in the long run. In a shorter timescale, however—and in El Salvador this has been under way for at least 40 years—the transformation that follows in the wake of the expansion of the agricultural export sector gives rise to a whole range of different groups of peasants and agricultural wage workers, with very different immediate interests based on differing relations of economic dependence. These different immediate interests of small peasants, seasonal workers, worker-peasants, small farmers, permanent plantation workers, etc., time and again serve to impede and destroy the political unification of the agricultural population, even though all these elements are completely subject to a common exploitation by the agricultural oligarchy. This is all the more true for an agricultural population which has to compete for the daily necessities of life on an inadequate land surface and in a hopelessly overfilled labor market. And this competition does not merely determine whether life is more or less comfortable, it also determines the very life or death (from starvation) of individual family members. Political conduct, "good" or "bad," can lead to a peasant having his conditions of existence taken away, it can decide which out of three or four seasonal workers gets the one job, whether a permanently employed agricultural worker continues in his privileged position, etc.

Similar factors destroying the solidarity of the exploited masses also exist in the towns. The wage struggles of the industrial proletariat, to which the urban trade unions confined their activity during the 1960s, can scarcely manage to win the solidarity of those who rarely receive a wage. The masses of marginalized elements, as an industrial reserve army, pose a constant latent threat to unskilled workers. For any worker who is fired, there are ten unemployed who are ready to take his or her place. These marginalized masses are in constant competition for the few irregular jobs in the street markets, in personal services, petty crime, etc. The petty bourgeoisie and the urban middle strata similarly have their own particular interests. "Society is transformed into a conglomerate of people fighting for their survival, without considering or reflecting on who are their true enemies," in the words of a group of Salvadoran social scientists, who characterize their country's society as "disintegrated and organized along alienated lines of battle."

Given an existence of this kind, whether individual and sectoral particular interests end up preventing or dissolving the process of political solidarity and unification of the exploited population is decisively dependent on the extent to which the rulers manage to reinforce these particular interests politically. This is all the more so in that those social sectors that might potentially be united have only a relatively short history, lacking a tradition of struggle that dates back even one generation, such as might be able to harmonize differing immediate interests of particular social groups in the interest of a long-run goal.

POLITICAL DEVELOPMENT UP TO THE 1970S

The El Salvador military regime understood very early the possibilities of this situation for a policy of "divide and rule." Already in January 1932, only a month after seizing power, the military rulers received an important lesson.

In the 1920s groups of working-class activists had risen among the urban artisan population, defining themselves as Communists in the wake of the Russian Revolution. Between 1928 and 1931 coffee prices and the wages of coffee workers fell by more than 50 percent. Against this background, the Communist and revolutionary trade unions in the west of El Salvador succeeded in organizing some 80,000 workers in the coffee plantations and leading major strikes and demonstrations. The relatively free presidential elections of 1930 saw these working-class activists supporting the coffee planter Arturo Araújo, who presented himself as a champion of reform. On assuming office, however, Araújo found himself unable to carry out his promised reforms, owing to the precarious economic situation. The generals accused the President of incompetence, overthrowing him at the end of 1931 and appointing General Martínez as President. In January 1932 Martínez permitted local elections to be held with the participation of the Communists. After the Communists had won the vote in certain coffee-producing districts in the west of the country, the generals refused to allow them to take office. The Communists called for an uprising. On the night of 22nd–23rd January, agricultural workers armed with machetes attacked and occupied public buildings in the western districts. The revolt "was concentrated in the western coffee-growing areas, where coffee had already spread to cover most of the ground in the areas of cultivable altitude, and the rural population was already almost completely dependent on seasonal wage labor on the coffee plantations; there was no space left for them to plant subsistence crops. This process had not gone so far in the eastern coffee-producing zone where there was no revolt." The uprising came to grief due to the division between the pure wage workers and the *colonos* and worker-peasants. The generals butchered between twenty and thirty thousand workers.

Martínez found a *modus vivendi* with the Salvadoran bourgeoisie. The military kept the office of President and the politically important ministries, while the key positions in economic policy were filled by representatives of the bourgeoisie, and in part completely withdrawn from state control. All matters of management and regulation that bore on the cultivation and marketing of coffee were dealt with not by the ministry of agriculture, but by associations and organizations of the coffee bourgeoisie itself. This applied also to the Central Reserve Bank and the Banco Hipótecario, the latter controlling credit to the rural sector. This division of functions between the military and the bourgeoisie continued right through to the 1970s, and emerged intact from all government crises and coups. Political differences within this bourgeois-military alliance, between the reform-oriented forces and those that were exclusively repressive, cut through the bourgeoisie and the military alike.

During the Second World War the Salvadoran economy experienced a recovery which gave an impetus to the democratic forces among the urban workers and artisans, who revolted in 1944 against the extremely repressive regime of the time. These received active support from the students, and even from sections of the bourgeoisie and the military. Even though Martínez was able to suppress the rebellion, the U.S. ambassador in El Salvador declared him "redundant," and he resigned. Following a democratic interlude in summer 1944, the purely repressive faction of the army pushed its way to power again, until it was overthrown in its turn in December 1948 by a new military coup led by Oscar Osorio.

Osorio and his sucessor Lemus (after 1956) aimed to establish a second pillar for the system alongside the bourgeois-military alliance, by reinforcing the division between workers, peasants and the marginalized population. Their policy was to split these sectors along three lines in the following fashion:

1. While the formation of trade unions still remained illegal in the countryside, and the agricultural export economy could expand without government regulation, in the towns a policy of industrialization was pursued, giving the growing industrial working class a certain privilege vis-à-vis the mass of the

population. These workers were granted a relative freedom of trade-union organization, a minimum wage legislation and system of social welfare, as well as a housing program.

2. While the agricultural workers and the small peasants practicing a subsistence economy were prey to the expansion of export cultivation, with no protection from the state, the military sought to create or maintain a stratum of middle peasants, involved in family-based commodity production, by way of state credits and the control of basic grain prices.

3. While moderate demands for reform as well as wage demands were granted to the urban trade unions, revolutionary forces, whether within or outside of the trade unions, were mercilessly persecuted, imprisoned and murdered.

Despite this policy, by 1959–60 the militant left in the towns had so gained in strength that one section of the military and the bourgeoisie saw their only opportunity to stave off crisis in far-reaching reforms. In 1960 they overthrew Lemus, formed a transitional government together with socialist representatives of the working class, and prepared to hold free elections in which the militant left was also permitted to take part. This sharp turn to the left led to a new military coup in 1961 under Julio Rivera. Since the support for the transitional government lay principally in the towns, the mass of the agricultural population being still unorganized and to a large extent uninvolved, any resistance was condemned in advance to failure. For a second time, the divisions between the popular sectors played into the hands of the military in a crisis situation.

Julio Rivera and his successor Fidel Sánchez Rivera (after 1967) understood these lessons well. They refined the divisions and strengthened them organizationally. In the towns a new middle stratum had grown up in the wake of industrialization. The generals permitted this stratum to organize political parties. In the universities the regime permitted the left a certain freedom of debate. The urban working class was allowed to organize trade unions for the purpose of wage demands, while working-class militants, and groups that aimed at any social transformation, were still persecuted and even murdered. In the countryside, trade-union organization continued to be forbidden. At the same time, however, 1965 was set as the date for social and minimum-wage legislation for the permanently employed rural workers, so that these were given a certain privilege over the mass of seasonal workers.

The regime then began to organize the groups and individuals whom it had thus privileged. In the 1950s, already, the ruling circles and their party, the Partido de Conciliación Nacional (PCN) sought to build up trade unions among the urban working class that were friendly towards the regime. They gradually succeeded in establishing the Confederación General de Sindicatos (GGS), which at the beginning of the 1960s had more than 15,000 members, twice as many as the left-wing independent unions. In 1957–58 most of the latter had combined to form the Confederación General de Trabajadores Salvadoreños (CGTS). By a combination of concessions to the industrial working class on the one hand, and brutal suppression of left-wing unionists on the other, the regime forced these independent unions from the mid 1960s onwards to confine their activity to economic demands. This abandonment of political demands and struggles found expression in the replacement of the CGTS by the Federación Unitaria Sindical de El Salvador (FUSS).

In the countryside, any attempt at autonomous organization was brutally suppressed. At the same time, however, the military regime attempted to win certain sections of impoverished peasants behind it. In the early 1960s it began to build up a paramilitary anti-revolutionary organization in the countryside called the Organización Democrática Nacionalista (ORDEN). By 1964–65 ORDEN had already assumed a firm structure. It won its members by helping them to escape the worst poverty. Small peasants who joined the organization could be granted favorable credit terms, while seasonal workers could hope for permanent employment. Privileged members or sympathizers of ORDEN would be engaged for public works in the rural districts. In some cases hospital beds or school places were provided for ORDEN members and their families. For many small peasants, ORDEN provided the only escape from poverty. In return, the ORDEN members supervised the villages in which they lived, reported attempts at subversion, watched over the rest of the agricultural population, and sometimes actually liquidated those who were rebellious. By the early 1970s, ORDEN had covered every village and town with a dense network of informers and collaborators. While the number of armed and military organized members of ORDEN never rose above 10,000, it is estimated to have had up to sixty or a hundred thousand loose or occasional collaborators. If family members are added, we can say that at least one- to two-tenths of the entire rural population were linked up with ORDEN in one way or another. ORDEN directly supported the Guardia Nacional and the president. The generals thus understood how to extract political benefit for their regime from the very poverty of the agricultural population.

THE DEVELOPMENT OF RESISTANCE

The industrialization and political "liberalization" in the towns was accompanied by the development of urban opposition parties and groups. Whereas the bourgeoisie traditionally occupied the key posts in the governing party (PCN) together with the military, during the 1960s a political tendency with the slogan of democratization gained strength even within the fourteen great families of El Salvador. This faction was led by the De Sola family and their Miraflor group of companies, who became consistent opponents of the military regime in the course of the 1970s.

The development of new urban middle strata—either petty bourgeoisie or highly skilled professionals—gave the Partido Demócrata-Cristiano (PDC) its social base. The PDC, formed in 1960, stood for a policy of reform, in which positions of the Chilean Christian-Democrats mingled with social democratic elements. The party demanded freedom of organization for agricultural workers and an economic policy that would accelerate national development by the full use of labor power, rather than the employment of modern machines that had to be paid for by foreign debts. The PDC attracted a steadily growing support in the towns, and in the countryside it organized the first groups of rural workers and peasants out of which the revolutionary people's organizations of the mid 1970s were to emerge.

An older party of liberal opposition, the Partido Acción Renovadora (PAR), also took a turn to the left in the mid 1960s, and adopted left social democrat positions. It called for a fundamental agrarian reform, a far-reaching program of labor procurement by the government, a national cooperative for the marketing and storage of agricultural products, progressive income tax, and a social policy in the interest of the underprivileged sectors.

Once the 1967 elections had shown that the reforming social-democrat positions had found a strong base among the urban working class, the PAR was banned by the military regime. In place of the PAR, there appeared a party of social democrat intellectuals, the Movimiento Nacional Revolucionario (MNR), founded in 1964–65, and the Unión Democrática Nacionalista (UDN), founded in 1968–69, which incorporated former politicians from the left wing of the PAR, and was also strongly influenced by the illegal Partido Comunista Salvadoreño (PCS).

The PCS had increasingly oriented itself after the defeated insurrection of 1932 to trade-union work in the towns, and in the 1960s it confined even this trade-union work to economic demands. Both the Communist-dominated Confederación Unificada de Trabajadores Salvadoreños (CUTS), with some 26,000 members, and the other major urban trade-union grouping, Fesinconstrans, with about 28,000, had stood almost exclusively for economic demands up to the beginning of the 1970s. On the political level, the PCS agitated chiefly for democratic reforms. In the universities it played an important role in organizing Marxist discussion circles, out of which the first beginnings of a guerrilla struggle developed in the course of the 1970s.

It can broadly be said that up to the end of the 1960s the agricultural population was either not organized at all, or was organized in the interest of the regime, while in the towns the middle strata and the working class overwhelmingly followed Christian Democrat and Social Democratic orientations, while the trade unions confined themselves to economic demands. Only in the early 1970s did a broad-based process of radicalization commence, for which the following factors were responsible.

1. The year 1969 saw a war between El Salvador and Honduras, attributable essentially to an ever-growing indebtedness of Honduras towards El Salvador and to the illegal immigration of tens of thousands to Honduras. After the war

the border between the two countries was closed, and Salvadorans driven off the land could no longer move across to the relatively thinly settled Honduras. The number of marginalized and completely landless people rose in the early 1970s by leaps and bounds.

2. The number of industrial workers also underwent a steep rise in the first half of the 1970s. At the same time the real wage level constantly fell. The purely economic policy of the trade unions, which had still been successful in the 1960s, had come up against its limits.

3. The PDC, MNR and UDN had combined for the presidential elections of 1972 into the Unión Nacional de Oposición (UNO), under the leadership of the Christian Democrat Napoleón Duarte. It was only through blatant electoral fraud that the PCN managed to secure the victory of its presidential candidate. A constitutionalist faction in the army made a coup against the illegal government and installed Duarte as president. After a few days, however, Duarte was overthrown by the reactionary majority of the armed forces under Colonel Molina. Molina became president. Duarte was imprisoned and exiled, along with many other politicians from the urban opposition parties. These reform oriented parties were thus thrown into uncompromising opposition to the regime.

4. The regime stepped up its repression against even the reformist left. Numerous intellectuals and trade unionists were imprisoned and expelled from the country. ORDEN and the terrorist organizations of the radical right began a policy of systematic persecution and assassination of trade unionists, peasant leaders and intellectuals. Persecution of the urban and reformist organizations also led to their radicalization and to attempts to bring the reformist forces, whose perspectives had come up against their economic and political limits, together with the revolutionary groups.

In June 1974, the peasant league Federación Católica de Campesinos Salvadoreños (FECCAS), set up in the 1960s by the Christian Democrats and the Catholic church, combined together with the left trade-union organization FUSS, the teachers' union ANDES, and other trade-union organizations, into the Frente de Acción Popular Unificada (FAPU). Representatives of the reform-oriented political parties took part in FAPU as observers. FAPU viewed the Molinas regime as a fascist military dictatorship. In its strategic perspective, the mass organizations of the left, and the revolutionary sectors of workers, peasants, intellectuals and the church, should join together with the democratic and reformist forces into a broad political front (Frente Político Amplio) against the regime. By combining parliamentary and extra-parliamentary struggle, this front should struggle in the first instance against the rising cost of living, and for minimal democratic liberties.

The question of an alliance with the reformist forces, however, led to a split in the FAPU. The peasant league FECCAS, increasingly radicalized in a Marxist direction, split away from the FAPU in 1975. This move was followed by other mass organizations of the left. In the same year, FECCAS joined forces with the left-wing rural workers' Unión de Trabajadores del Campo (UTC) and certain urban trade unions and students' and teachers' organizations, to form the Bloque Popular Revolucionario (BRP). Since FECCAS and UTC, each with 6,000 members, were by far the strongest individual organizations of the militant left, the Bloque was not only the dominant opposition force in the agricultural sector, but the largest revolutionary organization in El Salvador in general. By 1978 the Bloque was estimated to have around 30,000 members.

The Bloque concentrated its activity on mobilizing and organizing the workers and peasants, and aimed to establish a revolutionary people's government (Gobierno Popular Revolucionario) on the basis of a workers' and peasants' alliance under proletarian leadership *("alianza obrero-campesina con hegemonia proletaria")*. FAPU, on the other hand, remained more open to an alliance with the reformist parties and worked together with them on various committees. But FAPU, too, worked in the long run for a "revolutionary people's government of workers and peasants."

In parallel with these mass organizations, the early 1970s saw the development of a guerrilla struggle. The oldest guerrilla group, the Fuerzas Populares de Liberación (FPL), was formed in 1970 from the radical wing of the Communist party and Marxist discussion circles in the universities. The FPL saw its activity as defense and protection against ORDEN and other repressive forces directed against the peasants' and workers' organizations. From 1967–77, the FPL was able to recruit a large number of workers as the repression against the trade unions was intensified.

The Ejército Revolucionario del Pueblo (ERP) was formed in 1972. When one of its leaders, the historian and writer Roque Dalton García, criticized the military activism of the ERP and called for the subordination of armed struggle to political struggle, he was liquidated in 1975 by the militaristic faction of the ERP. This led to a split in the ERP and the foundation of the Fuerzas Armadas de Resistencia Nacional (FARN). The FARN kidnapped several representatives of multinational firms in El Salvador, as well as members of the country's fourteen families, holding them for ransom, and obtaining more than 40 million dollars between 1975 and 1979. Even if the connections between the popular organizations and the guerrilla groups are not visible, it is clear that a part of this sum found its way to the popular organizations.

THE INTENSIFICATION OF THE SITUATION FROM THE MID 1970S

In the mid 1970s, the situation facing the military regime was as follows:

1. Against the background of an economic development locked in crisis, there was a rapid growth in the number of discontented workers, of landless

and unemployed agriculturalists, and, in the slum quarters, of the marginalized population.

2. Revolutionary mass organizations had arisen alongside the mass organizations of the government. And while the lower strata of the population were still divided among themselves, now those that were hostile to the government were also organized.

3. The urban parties and trade unions that in the 1960s had been moderate and oriented to reform were now radicalized.

4. The state's monopoly of violence had been broken. If the security forces of the military and the reactionary bourgeoisie fired on the workers and peasants, then the guerrilla groups also fired on the military and the bourgeoisie.

5. The bourgeoisie was itself split into a reactionary wing and a wing with a democratic orientation. There were even constitutionalist groupings within the military itself, and these had proved strong enough in 1972 to make a coup against the electoral fraud.

In 1975–76 the Molina government sought to defuse this critical situation by a cautious agrarian reform. The rural oligarchy and the association of private businessmen, ANEP, raised a storm against even the first timid reform project; 59,000 hectares in the eastern cotton-growing region was to be distributed to 12,000 peasant families, and the big landowners were to receive the full market price. The proprietors affected organized themselves in the Eastern Region Farmers' Front (FARO), which soon spread right across the country and, together with ANEP, mobilized almost the entire private sector against the reform. This led to a government crisis, with the opponents of reform and the extreme right wing of the PCN and the military under General Romero emerging as victor. This right wing, together with ANEP and FARO, organized the radical right terrorist groups Falange and UGB, who proceeded with murder, torture and terror against both revolutionary and reformist forces in the trade unions, parties, popular organizations and church. By electoral fraud, this right wing under Romero managed to seize the presidency as well in 1977.

Only a few days after Romero's "electoral victory" on 28 December 1977, the military massacred demonstrators in San Salvador. In memory of this massacre, a third left organization, formed in 1978, took the name Liga Popular 28 de Febrero (LP-28). Under Romero, ORDEN and the UGB stepped up their terror. For many reformists, there was no choice left but exile (even many members of the De Sola family left the country), or adhesion to the revolutionary underground. The revolutionaries defended themselves. While the reformist parties and organizations were robbed of their leaders and condemned to inactivity, a particular polarization took place in the rural sector. Every small town and even every village saw a split between the supporters of ORDEN (generally small peasants) and those of the Bloque and the FAPU (mostly rural laborers). ORDEN and the military persecuted every individual suspected of subversion, and 1977 saw bloody attacks upon sectors of the agricultural population. The popular organizations and guerrilla groups resisted bravely. In the rural districts, the beginnings of a civil war developed in the most literal sense of the term, growing still more intense after November 1977, when the "law in defense and guarantee of public order" came into force. It was not just the armed forces that fought against the agricultural population in these regions, but the armed forces together with one section of the rural population who fought against the other section.

In San Salvador, members of the popular organizations occupied foreign embassies and churches, to draw attention to the massacres in the rural districts and compel the release of political prisoners. While the majority of the Catholic clergy supported the moderate opposition forces, a minority, under the leadership of the archbishop of San Salvador, Oscar Romero, in certain cases actually supported the demands of the popular organizations. In both universities, following various massacres of students by the military from 1975 onwards, the guerrilla groups found a pool for recruitment upon which they could draw almost without limit.

At the same time, falling prices for coffee in the world market and a bad harvest in 1978 owing to climatic conditions, as well as a high rate of inflation, led to declining real wages for rural workers and a consequent rise in their combativity. By the late summer of 1978, the domestic political situation in El Salvador had developed into a permanent violent conflict between the extreme right (and its supporters among the agricultural population) and the popular organizations and guerrilla groups of the left. From September 1978 onwards, the U.S., under the direct influence of the popular insurrection in neighboring Nicaragua, sought once again to bring into play the moderate opposition forces and to compel the Romero government to democratic concessions. By now even the Salvadoran private sector, and its ANEP organization, were pressing Romero to make such concessions after resistance by FARN and continuing violent clashes had led to a hectic flight of capital (some 300 million dollars in 1978). The majority of foreign business people had left the country. The Japanese business community, for example, declined from 2,400 to 200 individuals.

At the beginning of March 1979, Romero gave in, repealed the public order law and was immediately faced with strike action by sections of the urban working class, now dominated not by the moderate unions but by the revolutionary popular organizations. It was significant that these strikes included political action in solidarity with the demands of other striking workers.

The workers in the La Constancia and La Tropical bottling plants, a majority of whom were organized in the unions of the Bloque, and a minority in those of the FAPU, went on strike in support of thirty concrete economic and social demands. The army intervened. On 10 March violent clashes took place between demonstrators and the armed forces, with at least seven demonstrators being killed. During the following days, 24 other factories came out on strike in solidarity with the workers of La Constancia and La Tropical. On 19 March the power workers' union, its 1,500 members belonging to FAPU, called a 23-hour sympathy strike, crippling industry and commerce. The power workers locked themselves in the power stations and threatened to blow these up if the military intervened. The armed forces and bosses admitted defeat. Twenty of the thirty demands of the bottling plant workers were conceded.

The right wing made a brutal reply. By the end of April, ORDEN had murdered more than fifty members of the Bloque in the countryside and in the slums. Also in March and April, more than 130 people vanished without trace. At the same time, the Carter administration stepped up its attempt to put together a bloc of the center that could launch a democratic initiative. This bloc was to consist of the Christian Democrats, the De Sola family and a group of parliamentarians including the President of the National Assembly, Leonardo Echevarría. In February, Echevarría had already met Carter for a "working breakfast." The extreme right, for its part, lined up behind the Hill family (one of the fourteen families), and Colonel Eduardo Iraheta, and opted for a decisive violent destruction of the left. General Romero's decline now began.

At the beginning of May the Bloque occupied the embassies of Costa Rica and France, as well as the San Salvador cathedral, demanding the release of five of its leading members. A demonstration in front of the cathedral was fired on by the army. More than 20 demonstrators were killed on the steps of the church (some sources say 40). Archbishop Oscar Romero supported the demands of the Bloque. The Christian Democrat leader, Colonel Ernesto Claramount, living in exile in Costa Rica, called for a coup by the constitutionalist sectors of the army. General Romero, following diplomatic pressure from the U.S., declared himself ready for a "national dialogue" with the moderate opposition parties. The popular organizations, however, were to be excluded from this dialogue. On 22 May the military fired on a demonstration by the Bloque, killing 14 people. Altogether during that month, 188 people died in clashes of this kind.

While these clashes and the guerrilla war in the countryside continued throughout the summer, the U.S. succeeded in wrestling from General Romero the concession that the moderate opposition politicians (Christian Democrats) could return from exile, while seeking to build up Napoleón Duarte as the leading figure of the moderate opposition. These attempts were also supported by Archbishop Oscar Romero, who increasingly distanced himself from the Bloque for its use of violence. The "national dialogue" failed to take place, as General Romero did not accept the preconditions placed by the Christian Democrats and the MNR, demanding the disbanding of ORDEN and the UGB.

THE COUP AND THE NEW JUNTA

The victory of the Sandinistas in Nicaragua was seen by the popular organizations in El Salvador as proof that a dictatorship really could be overthrown by a determined population. In September the unrest in both town and country rapidly intensified, workers supporting the Bloque and the FAPU occupying four factories in San Salvador, and the popular organizations declared 1980 the year of liberation.

The increasing polarization and the failure of attempts at a "national dialogue" left the moderate opposition forces only the solution that the Christian Democrat leaders had already called for in May. On 15 October 1979 a section of the army made a coup, overthrew Romero, disarmed all the officers who had held ministerial posts in Romero's government, dismissed the armed forces' ten generals and prematurely retired many higher and middle-ranking officers. The new junta and cabinet was an alliance between conservatives and left Christian Democrats and Social Democrat forces from the urban sector, intent on "radical reforms" within the capitalist system. Not only were the extreme right excluded; so too were the popular organizations and those forces set on abolishing the capitalist system itself.

FAPU was represented by Jaime Abdul Gutiérrez (a junta member), conservative, from a pro-U.S. faction in the army, which has allowed the overtly fascist elements in the military, implicated in numerous crimes against the population, to go about unpunished. The Defense Minister, Colonel José García, belonged to this same faction. Colonel Adolfo Arnoldo Majano (a junta member) represented a group of young constitutionalist officers, who were suppressed in the army, but gained strength following the coup of 1972 and were held not to have "compromised with imperialism." Mario Andino (a junta member), head of the local Phelps Dodge subsidiary, represented that faction of the fourteen big bourgeois families led by the De Solas, who stood for a democratic initiative and agrarian reform, but could do nothing against the reactionary agrarian oligarchy. The new agriculture minister also belonged to this reform-oriented faction of the fourteen families. He was already minister of agriculture under Molina, subsequently resigning when his land reform projects were rejected. Román Mayorga Quirós (a junta member), rector of the Catholic university UCA, represents a policy oriented towards Catholic social doctrine, pragmatically set on concrete measures to improve the situation of the lower strata of the population. The education minister and the minister for planning also belong to this political tendency. Guillermo Ungo (a junta member) is head of the social-democratic MNR, while the finance minister and the justice minister were both also close to the right wing of that party. The

Christian Democrats provided the foreign minister and the minister-president. The economic ministry was given to a bourgeois technocrat; the ministry of labor to a leading member of the Communist Party.

This composition makes clear that the new government essentially aimed at an effective economy with a strong social component. The junta proclaimed its intention to guarantee freedom of political and trade-union organization without ideological discrimination, as well as freedom of speech, press and assembly. In the junta's program, the prevailing economic and social structures were said to post obstacles to the country's development. Above all, a basic agrarian reform and a reform of the financial system were promised. On the other hand, the program guaranteed private property in its "social function."

Despite this declaration of intent, the junta immediately proclaimed a state of emergency and banned meetings of more than three people. Security forces raided four of the occupied factories and arrested more than 70 workers. The popular organizations accordingly viewed the junta as simply a new form of the familiar Salvadoran military dictatorship, and called for a new popular uprising. This insurrection, however, failed to materialize. By the end of October, several clashes had taken place between demonstrators and security forces, in which more than 100 demonstrators were shot. The junta declared that both the arrest of workers and the murder of demonstrators were the acts of groups in the security forces that were not under its control. In the second week of November, 60 members of the National Guard were discharged, 12 being brought before the courts. After the Bloque had occupied the economic and labor ministries for some two weeks, the junta agreed in principle to the Bloque's demands for higher wages, lower basic food prices, a freeze on bus fares, freedom for political prisoners, the dissolution of ORDEN and a settlement to several labor disputes.

After subsequent dialogues between the popular organizations and the junta, arranged via the Sandinistas, the popular organizations confined their agitation to concrete demands. The Bloque's spokesperson, Juan Chacón, declared: "This is the first Salvadoran government that recognizes the justice of our demands."

THE COLLAPSE OF THE JUNTA AND THE TURN TOWARDS CIVIL WAR

The bourgeois-military junta and its cabinet were in fact a combination of forces whose social base lay only in a minority of the Salvadoran population. To the left, there stood the revolutionary popular organizations with their strong support among the rural workers, sections of the small peasants, industrial workers, marginal population, students and the lower ranks of the clergy. To the extent that the transformation of the rural economy, as depicted above, expelled ever larger sections of the rural population even from the transitional forms between independent work and wage labor, turning them into pure agricultural wage laborers, the socio-economic basis of the split in the agricultural population disappeared and the revolutionary left tended to gain growing influence in the countryside. To the right of the junta, there were the members of ORDEN (even if this organization was formally disbanded), which still had considerable influence among the small peasants and marginal population, and among those who saw themselves faced with the loss of a relative privilege in poverty by the junta's reform policy; groups whose social base (the socio-economic fragmentation of the agricultural population) was becoming ever more narrow—a fact that only intensified their violent readiness for self-defense. Also on the extreme right were to be found the great majority of the bourgeoisie, of the fourteen great families and of the senior military commanders. In the middle stood the government, supported by the reform-oriented urban middle strata, by a small minority of the bourgeoisie proper, by sections of the industrial working class and the army, and the majority of the higher clergy. And this government of the center was itself split into numerous factions, which Lilian Jiménez of the Communist Party saw as stretching from Communist through fascistoid officers, and which can be divided into two major blocs: on the one hand the bloc of the bourgeoisie and military, for whom the intended reforms were only an extreme measure for de-escalating the domestic political situation, and who therefore sought to restrict the reforms to those necessary for this end; on the other hand the young constitutionalist officers, the intellectuals and the politicians of the traditional urban opposition parties, for whom these reforms were only the first step in a series of far-reaching structural measures. This internally divided government was forced by the pressure of the revolutionary popular organizations, as well as by its own supporters among the urban population, to a reform policy that had to be pursued against a right wing prepared to oppose it by all possible means.

Faced with this situation, the government's internal unity inevitably collapsed, with the two blocs pulling increasingly apart. From last November [i.e., of 1979], all proposed reforms were wrecked in the same way. The junta declared a reform measure. The business associations prevented its practical execution and frequently found support for this in the right-wing bloc within the government. This right-wing bloc was led by the defense minister José Guillermo García and included the junta members Colonel Jaime Abdul Gutiérrez and Mario Andino. Workers under the leadership of the popular organizations then sought to compel the reform by mass struggle. The extreme right-wing faction of the armed forces and police brutally repressed the workers, either with support from the right-wing bloc within the government, or in flagrant contravention of the junta's instructions. By the end of 1979, 350 people had been killed by the armed forces since the junta took power. The conflict that led to the collapse of the government also proceeded in the same way. The left demanded wage increases for the coffee workers. In the first half of December, the junta accepted this demand and decreed an increase. The coffee planters ignored the decree. Agricultural workers went on strike and occupied the plantations. Sections of the armed forces evicted the workers with the most brutal violence—not on government orders, but with cover from the right wing in the junta and cabinet. Forty workers were murdered on one farm alone, "El Refugio." In this way, the junta and cabinet lost more and more power to the commanders of the armed forces and the right-wing bloc.

At the end of December nine civilian ministers demanded that the junta take a clear position against the terror campaign abetted by the extreme right wing in the military. They also demanded the resignation of the defense minister and Mario Andino. They demanded, too, that the leadership of the armed forces accept democratization—otherwise they would themselves resign. In the beginning of January [of 1980] the left-wing civilian junta members Róman Mayorga Quirós and Guillermo Ungo stepped down, leaving the big bourgeois Mario Andino as the only remaining civilian. The entire cabinet resigned as well, with the sole exception of the defense minister. The right-wing bloc had won the day, and any reformist solution to El Salvador's problems was now impossible. The officers could only find a right-wing faction of the Christian Democrats to collaborate with them in a new government.

The year 1980, proclaimed by the popular organizations as the "year of liberation," began with the preparation of civil war. The popular organizations and guerrilla groups on the one hand, ORDEN and the business associations on the other, stepped up their efforts to arm their supporters. The traditional parties of the urban opposition and the trade unions overwhelmingly came down on the side of the popular organizations. The clandestine Communist party made known its agreement with the FLP and FARN guerrillas. The three popular organizations and the UDN established coordinating organs at the local and national levels with the aim of achieving the unity of the left. This revolutionary bloc has been working since the middle of January to establish a "Unidad Popular" that would encompass the more progressive sections of the army (loosely organized around the young constitutionalist officers) as well as the traditional urban opposition parties, groups and trade unions. By the end of the month, the university intellectuals of UCA, the MNR and sections of the Catholic clergy under the leadership of Archbishop Romero declared themselves ready to support this Unidad Popular. A further section of the clergy, under the leadership of Bishop Pedro Aparicio, declared a crusade against communism. Rank-and-file priests and monks, for their part, joined the revolutionary organizations by the hundreds.

A deep split also developed within the armed forces. A crucial role in the coup of 15 October 1979 had been played by the "Juventud Militar" group of young constitutionalist officers. This movement can be seen as the successor to the reform-oriented wing of the armed forces of the late 1940s, 1950s and

1960s. In 1968–69 Colonel Adolfo Majano had established a training program in the military academy designed to familiarize competent officers with socio-political problems, so as to form a military cadre able to deploy instruments of social and economic policy, as well as weapons, in dealing with their country's problems. The socio-economic situation rapidly brought home to the officers who experienced this program that El Salvador's problems could only be mastered by radical structural changes. Juventud Militar thus envisaged not only political democratization, in accordance with the Salvadoran constitution, but also the nationalization of foreign trade and the banks, and agrarian reform to promote national economic development.

With this ideological development, Juventud Militar gradually eroded the prevailing consensus between the extreme right wing of the military and the moderate reform wing. Even though these two factions had taken turns in overthrowing one another over the previous four decades, neither had ever sought the other's total elimination. Juventud Militar, however, was repressed as far as possible under the Molina and Romero governments. It sought in turn, after the coup of 15 October 1979, to neutralize the right-wing senior officers by setting up soldiers' councils designed to invigilate recalcitrant commanders. It seems that this experiment backfired in several military zones and strengthened the hand of the Defense Minister, José García, who emerged as the most powerful member of the junta. In early March the Government announced sweeping measures nationalizing the banks and effecting an agrarian reform. The assassination of Archbishop Oscar Romero appears to have been a calculated rightist provocation, aimed at exacerbating tension as well as eliminating an influential opponent. In early May Majano attempted to arrest one of the commanders of the paramilitary forces linked to García, Roberto D'Aubuisson. This attempt met strong resistance within the military hierarchy. García dismissed Majano from his post and appointed Jaime Abdul Gutiérrez as sole Army commander. This marked the eclipse of the "pro-constitutionalist" faction and the imposition of ultra-rightist hegemony within the junta. The U.S. Ambassador, Robert White, was said to have played a "mediating role" in these events.

Meanwhile the military and paramilitary forces passed ahead with their version of the agrarian reform. This entailed not only renewed offensives in the countryside but also a division of some large estates in the interests of the leaders and supporters of ORDEN. In this way the rightists have found a way to exploit the reform program for their own ends, sacrificing the interests only of weaker, or more liberal-minded, land owners. The junta continues to represent a section of the Christian Democrats and to enjoy the support, or toleration, of the bulk of the bourgeoisie. So long as there is no open split in the armed forces the position of the Salvadoran junta remains much stronger than that of Somoza's regime in 1978–79 since the latter had, by this time, lost any significant social base.

7. Roots of the Salvadoran Right: Origins of the Death Squads*

BY CRAIG PYES

There is a perennial debate among social scientists about whether the United States has a ruling class. One group, departing somewhat from the traditional Marxian conception of ruling class, argues that there is a coherent elite that dominates the corporate system, the military, and the government.[1] Another group, more influential academically, maintains that the United States is a "pluralist" society with many groups vying for power, essentially peacefully, with no one of them enjoying hegemony.[2] Obviously, the differences between these schools cannot be resolved here; it is not even possible to review the wide range of issues—substantive and methodological—involved. But on at least one matter both groups agree: Whether or not there is an effective ruling class or power elite, social control in the contemporary United States depends upon popular conceptions of democratic legitimacy rather than upon widespread, regular applications of illegal official and semiofficial terror.[3]

But democratic political practices at home do not preclude support and even encouragement for such antidemocratic practices in such countries as El Salvador, where the United States exercises substantial influence. In its crusade to cripple the revolutionary left in Central America, the U.S. government has often abetted brutality and terror by local security forces it sustains. In Honduras, for example, the CIA has recently aided local security forces responsible for the systematic killing and disappearance of as many as 200 suspected leftists.[4] Similar U.S.-supported activity has long been apparent in El Salvador, but only recently has documentation appeared in mainstream media, such as

---

* Excerpted from "Salvadoran Rightists: The Deadly Patriots," a series by *Albuquerque Journal* investigative reporter Craig Pyes, December 18–22, 1983, and reissued in pamphlet form. For further excerpts from this pamphlet, see Reading 19. Some of this material has been rearranged slightly.

[1.] The most popular presentation of this view, if not the most convincing, is in C. Wright Mills, *The Power Elite* (New York, 1959). For Marxian views, see W. Weslowski, "Ruling Class and Power Elite," and "Class Domination and the Power of Interest Groups," *Polish Sociological Bulletin*, Nos. 1–4 (1962–1965); Michael Parenti, *Democracy for the Few* (4th ed., New York, 1983).

[2.] The main exponent of pluralism is Yale University political scientist Robert Dahl, whose works include *Who Governs? Democracy and Power in an American City* (New Haven, 1961) and *Pluralist Democracy in the United States: Conflict and Consent* (Chicago, 1967).

[3.] We do not here consider whether in the past, political and social power in the United States depended upon the terrorization of oppressed groups, especially enslaved or tyrannized blacks. For a discussion of such issues, see Richard Hofstadter and Michael Wallace, eds., *American Violence: A Documentary History* (New York, 1970). For evidence of persistence of such practices in the contemporary United States, see Parenti, *Democracy for the Few,* chapters 8 and 9.

[4.] Dispatch of *New York Times* Central American correspondent James LeMoyne, February 14, 1986.

the Albuquerque Journal, *which late in 1983 published the account by Craig Pyes presented in this reading.*

An associate of the Center for Investigative Reporting, Pyes was, with journalist Laurie Becklund, co-recipient of the 1984–1985 Outstanding Media Coverage award from the Latin American Studies Association for their reportage on El Salvador's death squads.

In a parallel report issued about the same time, journalist Allan Nairn actually interviewed one of the U.S.-trained Salvadoran security officials, who fled his country and later settled near Minneapolis. This former official graphically described the techniques of torture learned from his North American mentors:

If [the suspected subversive is] . . . a Marxist or a revolutionary, it's not easy to make him talk, so you have to psychologically harm the prisoner. If the person is important —if he's, let's say, a journalist or a teacher or a labor or student leader, or if he's a person with some leadership or has something to offer—he isn't treated cruelly at the beginning. Well, of course, they may hit him at some time, but after that, when he's taken to one of the interrogation rooms, you start by talking to him as a friend, you try to convince him that you understand his idealism. . . .

When the actual physical torture begins, there are a lot of different methods: cutting off pieces of his skin, burning him with cigarettes. They teach you how to hit a person in the stomach, but in a sophisticated way so the person suffers a lot of pain but you don't see signs on the outside. Or sometimes you just beat his hands and beat him in the stomach, either with fists or with heavy sticks. Beat him, and beat him, and beat him.

After that, if he still doesn't talk, you take him to a toilet filled with excrement. You put on gloves and shove his head in the toilet for thirty seconds or so. You pull him out, then shove his head in again. You do this over and over.

Then you wash him and take him to the electric shock room. There's a special torture room in the Treasury Police; only the intelligence section can enter, no uniformed men are allowed. It's soundproof so they don't hear anything outside.

You learn how to give electric shocks, shocks to the brain, shocks to the stomach. There are some very sophisticated methods for this kind of torture. . . .

In general, you will kill the prisoners because there's an assumption they shouldn't live. If we pass them to the judge, they'll go free and we'll maybe have to pick them up again. If there's lots of pressure—like from Amnesty International or some foreign countries—then we might pass them on to a judge, but if there's no pressure, then they're dead. When it's over, you just throw him in the alleys with a sign saying Mano Blanco, *ESA (Secret Anticommunist Army), or* Maximiliano Hernández Brigade *[three names commonly used by Salvadoran Death Squads].*

You learn how to torture, how to cut the balls off a person when he's still alive. These are the things that happen in war.[5]

EL SALVADOR'S Nationalist Republican Alliance (ARENA) first made its appearance as an organized political party in the fall of 1981, behind the charismatic leadership of former army intelligence major Roberto D'Aubuis-

[5.] Rene Hurtado (pseudonym), quoted in Allan Nairn, "Behind the Death Squads," *The Progressive* (Madison, Wisc.), May 1984, 22.

son. . . . [Two years earlier] . . . a meeting took place in the baroque headquarters of Guatemala's ultra-right-wing National Liberation Movement (MLN) in downtown Guatemala City. Presiding was MLN leader Mario Sandoval Alarcon, a man whose name has become synonymous with right-wing terrorist violence in Central America. The meeting was the beginning of an extended program of aid and guidance from Guatemala's MLN to a group which would later become the Nationalist Republican Alliance in El Salvador.

Sandoval spoke in an electronic rasp caused by a cancer operation. He told his audience, a group of young Salvadoran businessmen worried by the leftist direction their country was taking, about the bloody history of the MLN and the sacrifice each of them would have to make to form a party like the MLN in El Salvador. Sandoval's own political organization has earned him the nickname "godfather" and the vice presidency of Guatemala. That organization is one of the largest and most disciplined in Central America.

Its origins go back to 1953, when the party was formed hastily as a mercenary army by the U.S. Central Intelligence Agency for the successful overthrow of Guatemalan reformist president Jacobo Arbenz Guzman the next year. During the 1980 Guatemalan presidential elections, the MLN advertised itself as "the party of organized violence."

Sandoval is an important figure in the rise of ARENA. He not only advised it politically, but loaned the Salvadorans advisers to train them in underground techniques. And Sandoval said he gave ARENA the MLN slogan: *"Dios, Patria y Libertad"* ("God, Fatherland and Liberty"), which the MLN received from the assassinated Dominican dictator Rafael Trujillo. . . . But the most important advice Sandoval said he gave his Salvadoran counterparts was to organize themselves politically.

The Guatemalan leader told the *Albuquerque Journal* that at first, when Roberto D'Aubuisson and the other Salvadorans came to see him in 1979, they were concerned only with getting arms and organizing their paramilitary underground. Sandoval said he tried to restrain them "from falling into the error of [becoming only] a terrorist organization. . . . If they kill you, you kill back," he said. But he warned that without a political organization they would lose within a year. To help them get started, Sandoval said, he raised money for D'Aubuisson's group, making "several trips to Miami to visit relatives." The sum was far less than $10 million, he said, and was earmarked for political purposes. The MLN also aided the Salvadoran rightists in smuggling weapons into El Salvador, according to a former highly placed Guatemalan official who asked not to be identified. . . .

D'Aubuisson first met Sandoval through a group of young Salvadoran rightists who had formed a group called the Salvadoran Nationalist Movement (MNS). One of its members, David Ernesto "Neto" Panama, who became a

D'Aubuisson aide, is Sandoval's nephew. Panama proudly describes his "uncle Mario" as "the biggest anti-communist leader in the world, now that Chiang Kai-shek [the former leader of Taiwan] is dead." When the MLN was established under Carlos Castillo Armas ("The Liberator")[6] in 1953, the group began as a paramilitary force and only later became a political party. In the mid-1960s, the MLN leadership integrated anti-communist civilians into the military's security apparatus to wage an anti-guerrilla campaign in eastern Guatemala.

In the cities, according to a well-informed Guatemalan politician, the MLN began a new organization called the *Mano Blanca,* or "White Hand," which began issuing death threats, followed by assassination teams. During the ensuing terror campaign, a program of mass political assassinations was directed against those who spoke out in favor of the poor. It was the first such terror campaign in Central America. During the two years of its duration, human-rights organizations estimate that between 3,000 and 8,000 Guatemalans were killed by rightist forces. When the Guatemalan guerrilla movement reappeared in the late 1970s, the Guatemalan death squads also returned, and thousands more were killed. Each time the death squads appeared in Guatemala, similarly named killing groups appeared in neighboring El Salvador. . . .

They believe in Jeffersonian Democracy and death squads. Their colors are red, white and blue. They are strident Salvadoran nationalists who have built the country's second-largest political party from a violent anti-communist paramilitary network. And in perfect English they learned in American schools, they defend the killing of thousands of civilians as necessary to preserve democracy and the free market. In short, they are fighting for what Americans cherish most with the methods Americans value least.

Uncontrolled killing of civilians is at the center of debate about growing U.S. involvement in El Salvador. Since 1979, and after nearly a billion dollars in U.S. aid, the commitment of U.S. advisers and training programs, 40,000 Salvadorans—the majority of them non-combatants—have been killed. Many died at the hands of leftist guerrillas and their sympathizers. But most were killed by forces allied with a government supported by the United States.

The so-called rightist death squads use terror as a weapon to forestall economic reform and prevent negotiations with leftist guerrillas to bring an end to the . . . civil war. [For further data on the death squads' activity in El Salvador, see Reading 19.—Eds.]

[6.] Carlos Castillo Armas was the head of the regime installed in Guatemala by the U.S. Central Intelligence Agency (CIA) after it engineered the ouster of the elected President, Jacobo Arbenz Guzman, in 1954. See Stephen Schlesinger and Stephen Kinzer, *Bitter Fruit: The Untold Story of the American Coup in Guatemala* (New York, 1982); Max Gordon, "A Case History of U.S. Subversion: Guatemala, 1954," in Jonathan Fried, et al., eds., *Guatemala in Rebellion: Unfinished History* (New York, 1983), chapter 2.—Eds.

8. *El Salvador's Divided Military**

BY SHIRLEY CHRISTIAN

El Salvador is a sobering and disillusioning place for anyone who believes that military and police forces are neutral agencies that evenhandedly defend the safety of all a country's citizens. The armed forces make ritual statements confirming such a benign role. For example, in an address at the Gerardo Barrios Military Academy in San Salvador, Defense Minister General Eugenio Vides Casanova proudly announced to the cadets in May 1985 that the Salvadoran military

> *is a monolithic organization that has eliminated internal antagonisms . . . [and is] trying to strengthen the country's unity, strictly for the community's welfare. . . . We have proven to the people [of El Salvador] that their Armed Forces is . . . a neutral and independent entity in the midst of complex and divisive circumstances that have been affecting our society.* [1]

Some months earlier, Vides Casanova's aide assured one of the editors of this book that whatever may have been the case in the past, the military has developed its professionalism to the point that it corrects its own mistakes internally by punishing soldiers who violate civilian laws and terrorize the population. [2]

In the essay that follows, Pulitzer Prize–winning journalist Shirley Christian shows a different side of the Salvadoran military—a long tradition of routine brutality and corruption that cannot be so easily swept aside with self-serving rhetorical declarations. Enjoying "contacts within the ranks of the Salvadoran military [which were] the envy of other reporters," [3] *she writes with inside knowledge about its splits and tensions.*

Having covered Central America for the Miami Herald, *Shirley Christian is now with the* Washington Bureau *of the* New York Times. *She is the author of* Nicaragua: Revolution in the Family *(New York: Simon & Schuster, 1985).*

ONE evening in March of 1980, a slightly built man wearing glasses and the three gold stars of a full colonel in the Salvadoran army went on television and told the nation that more than 200 of the largest private farms in the country were being expropriated, as part of the military's commitment to bring social and economic justice to the downtrodden. The next morning, army troops led by officers waving the new decree moved onto the farms to begin setting up

* From *The Atlantic Monthly* vol. 251, (Boston), June 1983.

[1] Vides Casanova's speech, as broadcast by Radio San Salvador, in Foreign Broadcast Information Service, *Daily Reports,* May 17, 1985.

[2] Marvin E. Gettleman, interview with Colonel Carlos Reynaldo López Nuila, San Salvador, January 10, 1985.

[3] Raymond Bonner, *Weakness and Deceit: U.S. Policy and El Salvador* (New York: Times Books, 1984), 53.

cooperatives run by peasants. During the coming weeks, in a temporary operations center at the High Command headquarters, an army major kept track
of completed takeovers by placing pins on a large wall map showing most of
the farms in the country. Because of the tense atmosphere caused by the
brewing guerrilla war and bitter opposition from well-armed landowners, it
was thought that only the Army enjoyed the power and security to set the
agrarian reform in motion, a job that otherwise would have been given to a
civilian agency.

One night a few months later, uniformed men pulled up to one of the newly
created farm cooperatives in an armored vehicle, awakened a dozen or so men
—including cooperative members and government specialists assisting them—
and shot them to death. Two agronomists died while they were trying to show
the troops their government identification cards.

Most of the outside world has come to look on the Salvadoran military as
a murderous, repressive, monolithic institution—the problem, if you will. But
there is also the other side of the Salvadoran military—the one that is looking
for solutions to the country's social, economic, and political problems, and that
is willing to break with the past to find them. It is a military that cannot be
characterized only with a set of good-bad, black-white images.

When I try to think of episodes or circumstances that capture the essence
of the Salvadoran army, it is neither the reforms nor the killings that come to
mind. Rather, it is the night . . . [in 1980] when a captain in his mid-thirties
sat before me, a bandage on one shoulder visible through his freshly ironed
yellow *guayabera* shirt. It was not a guerrilla-war wound that the bandage
covered but a wound from the army's own internal warfare. Someone had shot
the captain as he drove down the highway from Santa Ana, a provincial
capital. He thought it was one of the supporters of Roberto D'Aubuisson, a
vehement anti-Communist major who had been invited to leave the Army a
few months earlier, because he had refused to turn over to the new military-
civilian junta his files on leftist subversion and political prisoners.[4]

D'Aubuisson and about a dozen of his army and civilian friends were being
detained for allegedly plotting a *coup d'état* on behalf of rich men who had
lost land to the agrarian reform. Troops loyal to Colonel Adolfo Majano, one
of the two military officers in the ruling junta, had swooped down on an
isolated farmhouse the night before and captured the alleged plotters. The
wounded captain was in an agitated state. Majano, who was his colonel, might
be in danger; there had been threats from members of the D'Aubuisson camp.
The whole officer corps, about 700 men at the time, was in confusion as it began
several days of debate on the crisis.

It was tempting to characterize the debate—as the captain did—in terms
of Majano, a committed reformer, being under assault from a group of offi-

---

4. On D'Aubuisson's files and their uses, see Reading 19, below.—Eds.

cers serving the interests of big money. But it was just as much, or more, a dispute over the undefined rules under which the officers of the Salvadoran army hold themselves together as the ruling elite. Majano had ordered the arrests without consulting Colonel Jaime Abdul Gutiérrez, the other army officer in the governing junta. Gutiérrez was angry. He too supported reforms, and was not fond of D'Aubuisson, but he thought the way to deal with the problem would be quietly to ship those involved abroad, instead of arresting them and running the unacceptable risk of army officers killing other army officers. The issue of what D'Aubuisson and his friends had, or had not, been plotting became entangled with what Gutiérrez thought of as Majano's questionable methodology.

Gutiérrez appointed a military judge to rule on the charges against D'Aubuisson. In a fence-straddling decision worthy of Salvadoran military tradition, Gutiérrez selected as judge a major who was strongly identified with the so-called Majanista, or reform, sector of the Army but who also had graduated from the military academy in the same class as D'Aubuisson. Gutiérrez hoped that a man with allegiances in both directions might somehow decide the case on its merits. To Gutiérrez that meant a decision avoiding a permanent rupture in the military institution.

Within the week, D'Aubuisson went free and fled to Guatemala, and his alleged co-conspirators were dispatched in various directions. Majano lost a subsequent vote of confidence to Gutiérrez but remained in the junta until he was thrown out of the government, though not the Army, at the end of 1980. My captain subsequently did the unbelievable and took to the hills with the guerrillas. D'Aubuisson returned to relative glory last year, by founding a political party and getting himself elected president of the Constituent Assembly. Gutiérrez saw the government through to those elections, then stepped out of the picture and watched in dismay as some civilian politicians tried to undo the social programs he had helped put in motion.

THE APPEAL OF AN ARMY CAREER

Where it begins for most of these men is at the Captain-General Gerardo Barrios Military School, a place of waxed tile floors, fresh paint, tropical flower beds, and polite cadets. The teachers talk of rewards that come with loyal service to the nation, and the cadets learn that the welfare of the Army and the welfare of the fatherland are indistinguishable. Most of the cadets come from lower-middle-class families who struggle to put their sons through high school in the hope that they will pass the entrance examinations for the military school, which provides four years of free education and living expenses. Becoming an officer is the most certain way to rise socially for an intelligent, earnest young man lacking family means. It will never put him on the same social level as those whose ancestors built the great coffee estates, but it offers the imprimatur of respectability in a country where that is denied to all but a few. It has traditionally led, at the very least, to influence; to moderate and sometimes great wealth; and to cabinet ministries and maybe the presidency.

Many enter the academy, few finish. Most officers now deciding the future of the country graduated in classes of twelve to twenty men in the late 1950s and the first half of the 1960s. They emerged from the academy with strong alliances and a sense of shared past and future; most received advanced training in the United States, Panama, Taiwan, Argentina, and Chile, and at the Army's own school of high command. By law, a professional military career lasts thirty years, beginning the day a young man enters the academy, which means that most officers retire before they are fifty. Though their paths may cross only occasionally in the years during which they move to seniority and power, no one forgets his classmates. Together they constitute what Salvadorans call a *tanda*. We might call it a caste, each graduating class a subcaste of the larger caste. If a member deviates too much from a line that nobody can define, he gets a stint abroad for re-education, drumming on a desk in a cubbyhole at a Salvadoran embassy in some country that hardly knows El Salvador exists. Seldom is a member of the caste turned out permanently.

The military in El Salvador is divided into two groups of armed bodies: those traditionally concerned with defense of the national territory and those concerned with keeping internal order. The first group includes the 22,400-man Army plus the Navy and the Air Force, each of which has only a few hundred men. The second group includes the National Guard, with 3,300 men; the National Police, with 3,500 men; and the Treasury Police, with 1,700 men.

The creation of the internal-security forces is generally linked by historians to the conversion of El Salvador's agricultural economy, in the second half of the last century, to coffee-growing and private ownership of land by *criollos,* Spaniards born in the New World. Such farms needed labor, so the emerging military forces were used to persuade Indians, who had previously farmed in an informal communal system, to work on the farms. When the National Guard was created, it was for the express purpose of carrying out a new law against vagabondism aimed at any Indians who did not want to work for the *criollos.* The Guardsmen also protected private property against thieves or squatters. The Treasury Police was created after the turn of the century to combat trafficking in all kinds of contraband, on which the central treasury was being denied its tax revenue. Specifically, however, it was understood that the Treasury Police agents were to prevent Indians from getting drunk on *chicha,* the local version of corn liquor, and being unable to work. Treasury agents chased the *chicheros* who produced and sold the liquor to the Indians.

Of the three branches of the internal-security forces, only the National Police, which is assigned to handle police functions in the twenty largest urban areas, has dealt with anything remotely connected with protection of human life. Protection of the economic system was always the primary function of the security apparatus. By tradition, the toughest, meanest men in villages and rural townships were selected for the National Guard and Treasury Police, which offered lifetime careers that were attractive to men who had done their army draft duty and needed work. Because of the large size of many estates, groups of Guardsmen or Treasury Police were often based on the farms and worked virtually at the direction of the owner or his manager. No one ever told these men to use finesse in carrying out their assignments. The prevailing philosophy of the security forces was found in a phrase thought to have been brought to the New World by instructors from the Spanish Civil Guard and repeated often in the Salvadoran National Guard: "Authority that does not abuse loses its prestige."

In addition, the National Guard, too shorthanded to cover the entire country, organized canton patrols under the command of sergeants or retired sergeants and staffed by men who are not formally a part of the National Guard but are given uniforms and guns. As the war has developed, an additional paramilitary organization, called Civil Defense, has organized patrols in rural battle areas, with only loose connections with the nearest army base. The quality of the manpower, and the attitudes toward individual rights among these two groups, are, at best, on a par with those of the National Guard and the Treasury Police.

The Army developed as a garrison force, and until the war began, more than three years ago, its strength was held to only about a third of its present size. The young conscript soldiers, recruited among the peasants and urban poor for twelve to eighteen months of service, sat in barracks in the fourteen departmental capitals waiting for war with a foreign power, such as the hundred-hour war with Honduras, in 1969, while the academy-educated officers devoted themselves to building the only political party that mattered at the time.

To a large extent, the officers have been the only element connecting these various defense and security forces, and officers have traditionally come from that tight little network of graduates from the Army's military academy. In recent years, there has been some promotion from within the security forces, but the control and leadership of each force has remained with Army officers.

1932: THE MARTÍ UPRISING

Newspaper stories often say that El Salvador has been ruled by the Army for half a century. In fact, since Central America became independent from Spain, in 1821, El Salvador has almost always been governed by men whose right to power is based on guns. But historians usually treat 1932 as the watershed year in Salvadoran history. That was the year of a peasant uprising led by Farabundo Martí, one of the first Communists in Central America and the man whose memory the present guerrilla movement invokes in calling itself the

Martí National Liberation Front. A military dictator named General Maximiliano Hernández Martínez emerged to quell the uprising by killing a number of people, mostly peasants, put variously at between 7,000 and 30,000. He won for himself the designation of El Salvador's first modern military ruler. Before 1932, the rulers were men who commanded local armies or were combinations of landowners and warlords. After the bloodbath came a period of modernization. Highways were built, a communications system established, and a national currency created for the first time.

Even counting only from 1932, El Salvador has experienced the longest-running and most institutionalized military rule in Latin America. This rule has been centered in the military, in contrast to the personal dictatorships common in many other Latin American countries, where one man—a Somoza, a Trujillo, a Stroessner—ruled or rules through the military. In El Salvador during the past fifty years, no one individual has ever been allowed to place himself above the military, with the exception, to a certain extent, of General Hernández Martínez, who put the system in motion.

In the late 1940s, the Army organized a formal political party through which it governed the country, though other parties were not prohibited. At the beginning of the 1960s, the party was reorganized and named the National Conciliation Party, but the system of relying on senior army officers for leadership and for presidential candidates remained the same. The officers called elections every five years and established a national assembly. If the National Conciliation Party did not win the elections, the military stuffed the ballot boxes.

The National Conciliation Party and its predecessor were not ideological parties; they existed for the purpose of attaining and holding power behind a façade of legitimacy. An officer had to support the party. It was not something he learned in the academy but something he learned as he went along in his career. If he did not, he passed his days in dead-end hardship posts. The presidential candidate was always a military officer, though civilians were occasionally in the running for the nomination.

In 1966, General José Alberto Medrano, the head of the state intelligence agency (inspired, he says, by John F. Kennedy and the Alliance for Progress), founded a vast rural network called the Nationalist Democratic Organization, known by its Spanish acronym, ORDEN, to promote democratic virtues and to combat Communism. It served as the grass-roots structure for the party: white-collar civilians, particularly business and professional men, were also encouraged to support the party.

CORRUPTION IN THE ARMY

The birth of institutionalized army rule in the 1930s came about in tacit agreement with the landed rich, usually referred to as the coffee oligarchy. It was not a hand-in-glove arrangement, in which the rich pulled the military strings, but an unwritten pact to use and abuse each other for mutual benefit. One coffee grower told me that the arrangement guaranteed an "accommodating" attitude by the military toward those with economic power. Another member of his class explained that the "productive sector" agreed to finance the government—i.e., pay taxes and close its eyes to the fact that army officers steal a substantial amount—in return for being left in peace to make money. The rich financed the electoral campaigns and were allowed to name their own kind to the ministries dealing with the economy and foreign affairs. They looked down upon their military partners, who, in turn, felt great social resentment toward those who bankrolled, them.

Corruption is still extensive. Officers are routinely bought off or blackmailed by civilians seeking military influence. Some officers receive payoffs from men doing business in their territory; each provincial commander has the opportunity, for example, to make a profit on the monthly food budget for the 1,000 or so troops under his command. In some cases, it is difficult to draw the line between corruption and the granting of favors, such as the offering of bank directorships and jobs in private business after retirement from the military.

Some officers accept only what is dangled in front of them; others aggressively seek payoffs. In 1976, the chief of staff of the Army was convicted in U.S. federal court in New York and sentenced to prison for his part in a scheme to sell $2.5 million worth of submachine guns to American gangsters—guns he was intending to buy in the United States by submitting to the State Department a false certificate saying that the weapons would be shipped to his own army.

Corruption is so much a part of anything related to the Salvadoran military that any time an officer changes his position on any question, Salvadorans automatically assume that someone has bought him. Over the past four years, I have heard so many whispered charges and countercharges of corruption from officers and civilians that I conclude that the alleged corruption adds up to an impossible amount. Even the rare officer who joins the left or so much as proposes talking to the insurgents is likely to encounter the allegation that the guerrillas have offered him money. One theory of why U.S. military assistance is not more successful as a pressure device for ending human rights abuses is that it offers little prospect of individual rake-offs, because very little of it actually comes into El Salvador as money. Most comes as equipment and supplies or in the form of training Salvadoran soldiers in the United States and Panama.

MILITARY CHANGES FROM WITHIN

Despite the electoral framework created by the military and its pact with the rich, there have been periodic eruptions from within the military caused by various things: the desire for reform; individual officers' overstepping acceptable bounds of corruption; pressures from younger officers eager for their turn at the top; and external events. Each such eruption, however, has had some lasting effect, because each new group of officers has justified the assumption of power with promises to create a fair society and hold free elections, and has taken at least some steps toward keeping them. Two tumultuous periods of coups and government reorganizations, one in the mid-1940s and another at the beginning of the 1960s, resulted in substantial improvements, relatively speaking, in social and labor laws and the freedom to organize opposition political parties. This freedom led, in turn, to the birth and growth in the 1960s of the Christian Democratic Party, now the strongest single party in the country, though it lacks an outright majority. Some smaller opposition parties to the left of the Christian Democrats also developed, including a legal front organization for the Communist Party. Throughout the 1970s, the Communists participated in elections as part of the opposition coalition, but a split in their party spawned three of the present guerrilla groups, and the party itself opted to become a guerrilla force at the end of 1979.

It was obvious that this gradual opening up of the society would lead to a victory by the opposition, given free elections. When that came close to happening in 1972, the year the coalition led by José Napoleón Duarte got a plurality and possibly an outright majority of the popular vote, the Army went through another eruption. It announced false election results, giving the victory to its own candidate. A month later, several officers, dissatisfied with the fraud, attempted a rebellion. Perhaps because this rebellion raised the ultimate question—whether the military would actually give up power—the rest of the Army put it down with a hundred or more deaths and no significant change in the power structure. Duarte was arrested, beaten, and sent into exile, though he had played no role in organizing the rebellion. Today, many officers, as well as foreign analysts, believe that the failure to allow Duarte his victory contributed to the growth of guerrilla groups and social problems.

In May of 1979, a small group of officers began to meet. They saw a burgeoning leftist movement that not only was raising tens of millions of dollars by kidnapping wealthy Salvadorans or foreign businessmen but could put 200,000 demonstrators in the streets at one time. They looked at Nicaragua, where the Somoza dynasty was in its death throes, and saw that the United States was doing nothing to rescue the Nicaraguan National Guard, a military institution that had been, until recently, as strongly entrenched as that in El Salvador. Finally, they considered the occupant of the presidential palace, General Carlos Humberto Romero, who was isolated from many senior officers, deaf to the pleas of moderate civilians that he take drastic measures to correct national problems, and out of favor with the Carter administration because of the growing number of bodies turning up in trash cans and along the roads. The officers concluded that circumstances were such that the Marxist-Leninist guerrilla groups and their supporting organizations could carry out a successful insurrection by the end of the year. They decided to act before then.

THE 1979 COUP

On the morning of October 15, the three senior men in the small group of officers—Colonel Gutiérrez, Lieutenant Colonel René Guerra y Guerra, and Major Alvaro Salazar Brenes—took command of San Carlos, the headquarters of the First Brigade in the capital. Junior officers working with them demanded the surrender of barracks commanders around the country. Gutiérrez telephoned President Romero to request that he leave the country.

Another shaking of the military tree was under way, and everyone involved thought that this one would turn out to be more momentous than any in the past. Salazar Brenes had said during the planning sessions that it would have to be the last military coup in El Salvador for at least twenty years. The political planning that went into it was even more careful than the logistical planning. A proclamation was written containing a heavy dose of theory about the redistribution of wealth—primarily through an agrarian reform—a vague promise to call elections, and a commitment to work to repair the divisions in Salvadoran society, presumably meaning an attempt to patch things up with insurgents. In a country desperately short of skill in political analysis and organization, the three officers represented a remarkably large amount of what skill there was. Gutiérrez, an engineer, had respected administrative and managerial talents. Salazar Brenes had earned a degree in political science at the Central American University after finishing military school, an unusual education for a military officer. Guerra y Guerra, more highly born than most military officers, consulted closely with a relative among the Jesuit priests, who dominate the teaching and administration of the university.

After much jockeying in the final days before the coup, Colonel Gutiérrez and Colonel Adolfo Majano were selected to represent the military in the new ruling junta, which was also to include three civilians. Guerra y Guerra wanted to be a member of the junta, but Gutiérrez insisted that only full colonels should serve, so Guerra y Guerra and the younger officers working with him asked Majano, then deputy director of the military academy, to represent them. He played no role in organizing the coup and apparently hesitated at the last moment, not arriving at the San Carlos barracks until late on the day of the coup.

Majano was then forty-one and Gutiérrez was forty-three; both were part of the small elite that full colonels constitute in a country where few make general. Like the U.S. Senate, the colonels form an exclusive club of people with great influence and status. After the coup, nearly sixty senior officers, including all the generals and the majority of the colonels, were retired or sent abroad. Only about a dozen full colonels were allowed to remain, all of them handpicked by Gutiérrez, though the number was allowed to rise with promotions made in the months after the coup.

A CONTINUING MILITARY SHAKEDOWN

The 1979 coup was not the beginning and end of change in the military. The years since have brought an ongoing shakedown involving both power and ideas. The Salvadoran military has washed its linen in public as no other Latin American military institution has, providing a rare look inside a situation that would be reported with rumor and supposition in other countries. In part, this public display came about because the coup was followed by the assertion of a form of internal military democracy by the entire officer corps; for a while, everybody claimed the right to an opinion and a vote about every government policy. Gutiérrez thought that this was no way to fight a war, and set out to reassert the traditional top-to-bottom command structure. Eventually, some twenty-five commanders, all colonels or lieutenant colonels, assumed the power to make most military decisions, but the lingering effects of the democratization period have made it necessary for commanders to take into account the opinions of lower-ranking officers if they want their barracks to function. There was military unity when the coup was carried out in 1979, but within a few months it began to break down over various issues, and the consensus continues to be in debate today. Among the issues being debated are commitment or non-commitment to the promised reforms; past associations; corruption; relations with, and manipulations by, civilian groups; personal ambition; and, on occasion, conduct of the war.

Guerra y Guerra and many young officers, for example, viewed Gutiérrez as corrupt, because of his past position as head of the state communications corporation, a traditional source of rakeoffs. The left regularly dropped the suggestion that Gutiérrez worked for the CIA. Guerra y Guerra was distrusted by Gutiérrez and his friends, who saw him as too personally ambitious and for that reason damaging to the agreed-upon goals. Gutiérrez, a somewhat retiring person, thought that Majano hogged the limelight too much for a man who had done nothing to bring off the coup. Majano, known to friends and detractors alike for honesty, intelligence, and naïveté, thought that as the elected representative of a group of younger officers he had the responsibility to improve the miserable human rights record of the armed forces. Robert E. White, the American ambassador, encouraged him in this role.

In all the allegations of coup attempts and purges during 1980, it was never clear who was trying to do what to whom. Some officers accused Majano of flirting with the guerrillas, whose political front groups were tempting him to make a grab for total power with statements to the effect that they knew him to be "recuperable, not bloodthirsty." At the same time, some officers, particularly those friendly to the ousted Major D'Aubuisson, were viewed as being in the pay of the extreme right.

When the many versions of civilian government that have shared power with the military since the 1979 coup are added to this equation, the machinations and interests involved in any policy decision are multiplied. The first junta, made up of the two colonels and three civilians and backed by a cabinet that ranged from businessmen to Communists, lasted through ten weeks of tears, shouting, and mutual accusations before the inevitable self-destruction. Most of the civilians in the junta and the cabinet wanted Majano to assert the power of the younger officers to remove three senior officers the civilians perceived to be blocking progress: Gutiérrez, Defense Minister José Guillermo García, and Carlos Eugenio Vides Casanova, the director of the National Guard. Those three colonels, on the other hand, claimed that the civilians were being manipulated by the extreme left. Majano was apparently swayed against attempting a takeover by the fear that he might be destroying the military.

When the first junta broke apart, the Christian Democrats joined the military in forming a government, and while they had more collective staying power than the first set of civilians, they were shaken by the unsolved killings of various party activists and the flight of others to exile and affiliation with the insurgents. Though close to Majano in social ideas, the Christian Democrats found him a difficult loner in day-to-day affairs, and decided that Gutiérrez was more realistic and effective.

At the end of 1980, Gutiérrez and Defense Minister García made a written pact with the Christian Democrats that led to restructuring the government in the form that lasted until the elections in March 1982 for the Assembly, which began writing a new constitution. The catalyst for the 1980 restructuring, aside from the power struggles involving Majano, was the murder of four American missionaries by a National Guard patrol. The idea was to give a respected civilian, Duarte, more power by making him president of the junta (there had been none since the coup), and to establish firmer authority lines in the Army and security forces. In the process, García, Gutiérrez, and Vides Casanova became generals. A month later, however, the Reagan administration came into office almost simultaneously with the first big guerrilla offensive. The question of how to fight the insurgency on the battlefield quickly became more important than abuse of authority.

A TRADITION OF VIOLENCE

El Salvador's convulsions of the past four years[5] have drawn attention to the terrible violence that has existed seemingly forever but that has increased as part of the reaction and counterreaction to the insurgency. Somewhere along the line, the general principle that in wars people try to kill their enemies has been replaced in El Salvador with the notion that one kills whoever is easiest to kill. Usually, that has meant any young man between eighteen and twenty-four, families of government troops and of guerrillas, politicians who think it

[5.] For more recent discussions of violence and death-squad activity in El Salvador, see chapters 7 and 8.—Eds.

might be a good idea for the sides to negotiate, and nuns and other social activists who become involved with the intention of helping the poor.

The killings and abuses fall into several categories. One is crimes committed by so-called death squads or by individuals in them, which usually single out individual people or families, often those known nationally or in small towns for commitment to a particular cause, revolutionary or otherwise. It is accepted, among military officers and others, that the death squads are commanded by a few middle- or lower-level officers, who, in the pay of civilian groups, recruit gunmen, particularly enlisted men from the National Guard or Treasury Police, to carry out political assassinations. This theory is largely based on supposition, but there are some factual kernels that support it. Papers taken from the briefcase of a captain arrested with D'Aubuisson during the alleged farmhouse plotting three years ago revealed a list of last names of military officers suspected by other officers of receiving payoffs to run death squads.

Distinct from the death-squad killings are mass killings in rural battle zones. The circumstances of these killings are clouded by great confusion and lack of information, such as whether the victims were families of guerrillas and whether they were killed intentionally by government troops, caught in crossfire, or eliminated in a no-holds-barred cleanup sweep. Sometimes what the guerrillas describe as the site of a military massacre the Army will describe as a burial ground for guerrilla combat losses. A third category of killings is related to feuds in small towns and rural areas which are only nominally, if at all, related to any of the issues in the war. In the absence of legal and police authority, those who have guns—which seems to be almost everyone—resolve things in their own way.

Some analysts like to fix responsibility for this violence squarely at the top of the military structure, particularly on General García in his long reign as defense minister, beginning the day after the 1979 coup and ending with his resignation in April 1983, and a few other men in key positions, such as the heads of the National Guard and the Treasury Police. But the structure of the Salvadoran military is so diffuse that there is no such thing as a clear order. By tradition, the defense minister presides rather than directs. He is dependent on the willingness of the fourteen departmental commanders and of the heads of the three security forces to obey him. Even the link from the heads of the security forces to their troops is imprecise, because the security-force detachments in the fourteen departments are responsible first to the provincial army commander. When officers are inclined to clean up the units under their command, the old ways are often so imbedded as to prevent it. The two officers assigned to take over the National Guard and the National Police after the 1979 coup, General Vides Casanova and Colonel Carlos Reynaldo López Nuila, sought unsuccessfully in 1980 to be relieved of their posts, because they feared that it was impossible to get internal control of the organizations they were supposed to command. Further removed from the center of power and the command structure is the network of canton and civil-defense patrols in rural zones. These patrols, unpaid or badly paid, appear to take the brunt of guerrilla firepower and, in turn, to bear a large part of the responsibility in mass killings.

There have been efforts to deal with these problems, with mixed degrees of enthusiasm and success. The National Police, the National Guard, and the Treasury Police have dismissed several hundred men during the past three years as part of a campaign to weed out those who abuse their authority and to replace them with younger men who might carry out their assignments in a more humane way. Since the time when he wanted to throw up his hands in defeat in his effort to control the National Police, Colonel López Nuila, a lawyer who previously served on the army legal staff, has made some advances in teaching the police how to investigate crimes, particularly kidnappings, and in developing a code of conduct that includes keeping arrest records. Nevertheless, it is still routine for the police to beat up anyone they arrest. The Army High Command has held occasional meetings, which are well publicized, with the leaders of the canton and civil-defense patrols, to plead for better behavior.

A key element in the problems of violence, to which military leaders point as proof that they cannot bear the full responsibility, is the absence of a functioning judicial system. Many people concerned with achieving human rights progress in El Salvador, Americans as well as Salvadorans, believe that until the example of legal punishment is demonstrated, those who commit violent acts, whether they wear uniforms or not, will never change their ways. Some army officers speak bitterly of arresting people and turning them over to the civilian courts for investigation and prosecution, only to find them soon freed on technicalities. Salvadoran judges are known for being easy to buy off and easy to frighten. Bombs, threats, and terrorist attacks are the established methods used by people on all political sides to influence judges. A colonel told me about a large cocaine bust in which he played a significant role several years ago: the defendants, two Peruvian women arrested in a San Salvador hotel, went free after a large amount of money came into the country and, according to the colonel, was generously distributed among key people in the judicial system.

Finally, there is the matter of what José Napoleón Duarte calls the "culture of violence" that prevails in El Salvador.[6] Most Salvadorans are as convinced that extreme violence is part of their national character as they are convinced that corruption is endemic to the military and those who surround it. Government in El Salvador has traditionally been based on the authority of terror, implied even when not exerted. Rumor, cruelty, and ignorance are also at play

[6.] See Duarte's graphic representation of his doctrine of violence in Editors' Introduction to chapter 4.—Eds.

in many killings among the rural population, which is largely illiterate. Some argue that the issue of military abuse will be solved only as the entire society resolves its violence problem by a combination of education and legal punishment for the guilty.

THE COMPLEX TRUTH

"Each one has his own truth," a colonel commanding a post in eastern El Salvador once told me as he discussed the Army's degree of commitment or non-commitment to social change. Anyone trying to take an objective view will indeed find many truths about the Salvadoran military institution. A few truths are commendable, some are only barely palatable, and some are despicable. Some are simply facts that will not go away. Among them: the Salvadoran military has a lot of innocent blood on its hands, and admits it only reluctantly. It also has an ample historical sense of how its hands got bloody. It has reached a degree of consensus about the need to change the country's social and political attitudes, and to make the military put a high value on human life. But there are sectors in the armed forces not in agreement, men who believe that it is still possible to use the threat of a Communist takeover to justify oppression. There is also disagreement, even among the majority, about how to reach the national goals and how much internal change the military can absorb in time of war. Finally, as Salvadoran military history has shown, conflicts over ideas and policies often get deflected by personal ambition and greed. The error lies in believing only one of these truths about the Salvadoran military, whichever it may be, and ignoring the others. In the end, the military wants to survive, and its leadership wants to do what is necessary to ensure that.

Despite its own soul-searching of the past few years, the Salvadoran military, in large measure, looks to the United States to define what is necessary. The messages it gets are unclear at best, and often contradictory. Trying to interpret the demands coming from the many centers of power and influence in the United States—the White House, the National Security Council, the State Department, the Pentagon, Congress, the press, opinion polls, pressure groups, and demonstrators—leads some officers to conclude that it is enough merely to talk a reformist line, and others to see the disaster ahead if the military does not take the lead in effecting actual reforms. Without a clearer message from the United States, the officers may be unable to agree on what to do next. This is a military that is at war as much with itself as with the guerrillas.

9. The Roman Catholic Church in El Salvador: The Early Years*

BY THE STAFF OF CARIN/CENTRAL AMERICA RESEARCH INSTITUTE

Traditionally, and despite the occasional dissenting voice of an exceptional churchman, Latin America has seen what Alan Riding has called the alliance of Cross and Sword. The dominant Roman Catholic church not only has supported the unjust and oppressive colonial and postcolonial societies in the region, but through its own land holdings (vast until the expropriations in the mid-nineteenth century), was itself part of the system of injustice.[1] Hidden away in Christian doctrine, however, were seeds of radicalism that could flower under appropriate historical circumstances. The emergence of "liberation theology" in El Salvador and other places in Latin America shows that by the 1970s the time had come for a challenge to the alliance of Cross and Sword within the church. This development is treated in chapter 3. Here, we offer discussion of the social forces out of which liberation theology emerged in El Salvador.

THE CHURCH IN THE COLONIAL ERA

THE papacy actively promoted colonization and Christianization of the New World by the Spanish monarchy, in a series of mutual agreements designed to counter the Catholic Church's decline in Europe.

In 1493, Pope Alexander VI granted the Spanish Crown dominion over all of the Americas except Brazil. Subsequent agreements ceded the Crown the right to the tithes of the Church in the New World and the right of universal patronage—including the right to nominate bishops and archbishops for the colonies. In return, the Crown agreed to fund the establishment of the faith in the New World. Additionally, in 1478 Pope Sixtus IV granted the Crown complete control over the Inquisition, which was extended to the New World in 1570. This allowed the Spanish authorities to persecute and eliminate both religious and political dissent. Challenges to both official doctrine and royal authority were attacked as heretical rejections of the divine order of the empire.

Thus the Church and Crown collaborated closely in the strengthening of Spanish dominion in Latin America. As part of the subjugation of the indigenous population, all native culture and religion—including temples, shrines,

---

* Excerpted from "The Catholic Church in El Salvador," *El Salvador Bulletin* (later renamed *Central America Bulletin*), Berkeley, Cal., II, No. 2 (December 1982).

[1.] Alan Riding, "The Cross and the Sword in Latin America," *The New York Review of Books,* May 28, 1981.

religious books and images—were destroyed and replaced with [those] of the *conquistadores.* To this end, priests learned the native languages and counseled the Indians to accept the new order and religion. The first priest sent to El Salvador, for example, was sent in 1528 to help insure the docility of the Indians.

Dissenting Voices

A minority within the Church protested the barbarous exploitation of the Latin American Indians and asked for the absolution of their irreligion due to their "state of innocence." In 1551–52, Friar Bartolomé de las Casas urged the Crown to curb the forced exploitation of Indians in the mines and in the *encomienda* system of the great colonial estates, through which the Indians were placed under the control of the *conquistadores,* some as a serf-like and others, dispossessed of their lands, as a slave-like labor force. Many missionary clergy—in touch with the Indian population on a daily basis—argued that they be allowed to preserve their traditional lifestyle of communal agriculture.

Partially due to these efforts and partially as an attempt to save the rapidly dwindling Indian population from extinction at the hands of the *encomenderos* (which would have jeopardized the long-term tributes to the Crown), the Crown interceded on behalf of the Indians, limiting their exploitation and exempting them from the Inquisition. According to King Phillip II, more than ⅓ of the Indian population had been killed by 1581.

Establishment of Hierarchy

While initially the missionary clergy had been given relative independence in their work, as the colonial system was consolidated, a traditional ecclesiastical hierarchy was established in the New World. In the General Capitancy of Guatemala, which included most of Central America, the Bishopric of León de Nicaragua was established in 1531, Comayagua and Guatemala in 1534, and Chiapas in 1538.

Throughout the early 16th century, the ecclesiastical hierarchy struggled to wrest economic and religious control over the *cofradias* from the missionary clergy. The *cofradia*—a medieval Spanish socio-religious organization promoted by the Catholic Church—was strongest in Central America in the rural areas. Although in appearance its primary function was religious, it also served as a political administration of the indigenous population and an economic source of revenues for the local religious and political powers.

The basis of the *cofradia* was the communal land tenure practiced by the indigenous population in El Salvador. While most of the major agricultural product during the colonial era—indigo—was produced on a few large estates, some 40–50% of less important land remained in the collective hands of the local community, regulated and taxed by the Crown.

When in the mid-18th century Charles III awarded official control over the *cofradias* to the ecclesiastical clergy, the *cofradias* themselves rejected this. This struggle led to a slow reduction in the role of clergy in the *cofradias,* to the perfunctory performance of mass and other ceremonies.

By 1821 the Archbishopric of Guatemala had 20 vicars and 161 parish priests, serving 424 villages, settlements in 85 valleys, and 23 newly organized Indian communities. It had under its control 1,720 *cofradias.* Contemporary descriptions pointed out the uneven wealth of parishes, the unsystematic pastoral attention, the exploitation of the Indians, and in general the lack of clergy necessary to carry out all the duties of the Church in the region.

INDEPENDENCE

Towards the end of the 17th century, liberal ideas promoting the emancipation of the colonies penetrated the Catholic Church in the New World through clergy of creole background.[2] In El Salvador, the liberal priest Father José Matías Delgado led an abortive revolt against Spanish rule in 1811. The ecclesiastical hierarchy, however—closely tied to the Crown—actively opposed the Central American independence movements, using excommunication and other measures against progressive clergy.

In 1821, Central America achieved independence from Spain. El Salvador had constituted itself as a nation by 1840. The struggle between the conservatives, who supported the old political and religious order, and the liberals, who sought to restructure the economy and Church/State relations, lasted most of the 19th century.

Salvadoran liberals called for land reform to replace the communal lands with freely alienable private property, to meet the demands of El Salvador's integration into the world economy. The liberal program called for sovereignty of State over Church, including religious tolerance, civil marriage, and secular education. Most important, they sought to end Church control of land held in *mortmain* by restricting Church holdings to land upon which its buildings were located.

Once in power, the liberals moved to break up the traditional land structure to facilitate the production of export crops, specifically coffee, which by 1874–75 had become the principal export product. This process led to an enormous increase in the landless rural and urban working classes.

The Church in El Salvador had held relatively little property; its source of power was not so much economic as from the institutions it controlled. The ecclesiastical hierarchy supported the conservatives as long as they remained politically viable, warning that insurrection was a mortal sin and that State order was divinely ordained. With the liberal triumph, however, the institutional Church joined the new State in the break-up of the communal lands,

2. In its Latin American sense Creole (from *criollo*) means someone of Spanish or other European ancestry born in Latin America.—Eds.

moving to assert control over the *cofradias*. Archbishop Pérez Aguilar ordered parish priests to seize control over the *cofradia* funds. When many *cofradias* resisted, he ordered priests to rely on the military for support.

The peasants fiercely resisted seizure of their lands. In many areas there was open insurrection, and when that failed they often burned the fields they were forced to leave. The rural police was formed in 1889 to enforce the liberals' program.

Decline of Church Influence

Although the Church's collaboration with the State tipped the balance in its favor in the struggle for control of the *cofradias,* it ultimately did not enable the Church to take control of them; rather, it destroyed them. Attempts by the Church to incorporate the dispossessed *cofradias* or to recreate their structure failed. The few which remained in existence continued to resist the liberal reforms. In 1932, for example, the Izalco *cofradias* led by Feliciano Ama played a key role in the insurrection against the dictator Martínez.

Thus the presence of the Church in rural areas became sporadic, while with the rise of the liberals its general political power and economic control declined. Growing new institutions—government bureaucracies, workers' and artisans' organizations, political parties and economic groups—diminished the Church's political influence in the new order.

Attempts at the beginning of this century by modernizing economic sectors to diversify agriculture and to establish some manufacturing were cut off by the effects of the 1929 world economic crisis. This entrenched the coffee-producing oligarchy in power. Before the 1929 crisis, El Salvador was governed by coffee producers as presidents; afterwards—specifically after the 1932 peasant uprising and massacre—by the Armed Forces.

The Church as a whole collaborated with the powerful oligarchy and their governments. In the countryside, landowners invited priests and even bishops to celebrate mass in the private churches on their estates. In the cities, political figures bolstered their image with the support of local priests and Church hierarchy.

Throughout his 13-year reign, General Martínez continued to favor the coffee oligarchy at the expense of the country's industrial growth (for example, prohibiting the establishment of factories of over $8,000 capital). After World War II, supported by United States aid and rising commodity prices, attempts at modernization recommenced. Labor organizing grew, despite anti-labor laws and political repression.

The 1960's marked the regional integration of El Salvador into the Central American Common Market, favoring the new industrial economic sectors. In spite of the relatively rapid industrial and economic growth, the social and economic conditions of some sectors of the population—especially rural—did not improve and in fact deteriorated. Of 450,000 agricultural workers in 1961, only 290,000 owned small plots of land. In 1965 there were 54,000 landless families; in 1971, 72,000. As industry grew an average of 9% annually, industrial employment increased from 9% in 1950 to 13% in 1961. While minimum daily expenses for a Salvadoran family were estimated at 7.08 colones in 1961, the average industrial salary was 3.48 colones. In 1964 the average rural wage was only 1.61 colones.

Rural pauperization, urban migration, unemployment and poverty began to create a pressing problem for the regimes in power, which met attempts at labor organizing with repression. The growing misery and poverty were also to impact significantly upon the Catholic Church in the next decade.

[For further discussion of the religious movements in El Salvador, see Reading 11 and chapter 3 generally.—Eds.]

10. The Ideology of Salvadoran Christian Democracy*

BY STEPHEN WEBRE

Christianity, which was forced upon the indigenous populations of Latin America by the Spanish Conquistadores in the sixteenth century, has been hard put to escape its early role as the oppressors' religion. In the 1960s, Christian Democracy surfaced in the region as a serious alternative to the traditional religious viewpoint, which upheld the prerogatives of the Conquistadores' successors, the oligarchs and militarists, whose religious apologists preached popular passivity in the face of injustice.[1]

Except among diehard conservatives, reformist Christian Democracy was not only an improvement over religious backing for the status quo, but also a palatable alternative to left-wing revolution, especially after Fidel Castro's victory over the Batista dictatorship in Cuba in 1959. As Stephen Webre clearly demonstrates, for El Salvador Christian Democracy was the political ideology of a section of the middle class who found an eloquent spokesman in the U.S.-educated engineer José Napoleón Duarte. Duarte wanted to contest the political power monopolized by the oligarchy and the military, but he opposed the sweeping redistribution of wealth called for by socialist parties on the left. The right-wing opposition to Duarte did not make fine distinctions between reformists and revolutionaries; they considered the Christian Democrats "watermelon men"—"green[2] on the outside, red on the inside."

---

* From *José Napoleón Duarte and the Christian Democratic Party in Salvadoran Politics, 1960–1972* (Baton Rouge, La.: Louisiana State University Press, 1979).

[1.] The origins of Latin American and Central American Christian Democracy, including its possible links to similarly named, U.S.-funded parties in western Europe, badly needs not only country-by-country analysis, but also regional and global perspective.

[2.] In the electoral contests, the color of the Partido Demócrata Cristiano (PDC) is green.

The problems of a moderate Christian Democrat in a society as highly polarized as El Salvador's are analyzed further in chapter 4. In the excerpt below, Webre skillfully sets forth the background and hemispheric context of Duarte's quest for a middle way in El Salvador.

THE period of democratic experimentation in El Salvador in the 1960s coincided with a time of apparent electoral stability in many Latin American countries and thus served to confirm the beliefs of those who argued that the process of political development was linear and cumulative and would inevitably lead to a golden era of civil supremacy and parliamentary democracy. Somehow the collapse in 1964 of the boisterous Brazilian democracy went unappreciated amidst the general optimism. Few people would have guessed that the authoritarianism of the Brazilian colonels and not such enthusiastically welcomed democratic regimes as that of Rómulo Betancourt in Venezuela would come to characterize Latin America in the 1970s or that even such countries of long democratic tradition as Chile and Uruguay would ultimately produce repressive regimes.

What non-Communist progressives sought in Latin America in the years immediately following the Cuban revolution was a safe reformist alternative to the threat of a proliferation of Castroist revolutions in the area. The most substantial tradition for such a movement was that provided by the Peruvian APRA and such other "social democratic" parties as Acción Democrática in Venezuela and Liberación Nacional in Costa Rica. Although these movements enjoyed impeccable democratic credentials forged in the struggle against dictatorship that passed for revolutionary activity in most of Latin America before the triumph of Fidel Castro, they had over the years grown staid and conservative. Another possible model, although one peculiar to a single country, was the Mexican PRI.

A third alternative, which must have seemed to come virtually from nowhere in the late 1950s and early 1960s, was Christian Democracy. The expansion of this movement was remarkable. By 1964, the year of the first Christian Democratic victories in El Salvador, there were similar parties in sixteen of the twenty Latin American republics. Only Honduras, Paraguay, Haiti, and Cuba lacked them. For the most part, Christian Democracy in Latin America was a relatively recent phenomenon. Although the oldest parties, those of Uruguay and Chile, were of much earlier origin, most of the parties were founded in the period following World War II. Their leaders were inspired by the role European Christian Democratic parties had played in the postwar recovery of West Germany, Italy, and France.

The early 1960s were important years for Christian Democracy in all of Latin America. In 1963, the Peruvian Christian Democrats joined the government in coalition with Fernando Belaúnde Terry's Acción Popular and, by the end of the year, elected one of their own leaders mayor of Lima. In Venezuela, Rafael Caldera's Social Christian COPEI placed second in the 1963 presidential race and was the only party that actually gained in voter support over the previous elections. By far the most successful of all the Latin American Christian Democratic parties in 1964, however, was the Chilean PDC. In the municipal elections in 1963 the Christian Democrats had suddenly replaced the Radicals as Chile's leading political party. Then in 1964 Eduardo Frei Montalva's triumph in the presidential race made Chile the first Latin American republic to come under a modern Christian Democratic administration.

Many observers hailed Frei's victory as the coming of a new era in Latin America—an era in which social injustice would fall beneath the onslaught of humane and Christian government operating in an open atmosphere of democracy and liberty. To reformers, progressives, even revolutionaries who found communism distasteful, Christian Democracy seemed to offer an excellent alternative. Frei's defeat of a Communist-backed coalition led by Salvador Allende Gossens offered encouragement to those who feared that all of Latin America was in imminent danger of Communist takeover. The Communists themselves recognized the potential significance of this setback. Although Radio Havana attributed the Frei victory to fraud, intimidation, and bribery, Cuban Prime Minister Fidel Castro candidly admitted that "sometimes our opponents surpass us in ability."

By the end of the decade, it would become abundantly clear that Christian Democracy was no more a panacea or a wave of the future than had been the APRA movement or even the guerrilla socialism practiced by Castro in Cuba. In particular, observers tended to overlook the importance of the fact that Frei owed his victory to a coalition with Chile's intransigent right. Still, in 1964 when Frei's triumph was fresh, all was euphoria and optimism.

Latin American Christian Democrats state with pride that theirs is an ideological movement, a claim significant in a region where political parties have seldom been more than vehicles for personal ambition, with little goal other than the conquest and enjoyment of high political office. From the beginning, the leaders of the Salvadoran PDC emphasized this major difference between their party and the crowd of ephemeral, personalist parties that continued to characterize Salvadoran politics. Their party, they declared upon announcing its formation, would be "permanent [and] purely ideological in character, . . . something new in our country."

The most important single source of inspiration for the Christian Democratic movement has been the social doctrine of the Roman Catholic church, especially as set forth in Pope Leo XIII's encyclical *Rerum Novarum* (1891). Leo attacked both Marxist socialism and classical liberalism. He admitted the similarity between many socialist tenets and the teachings of the Gospel, but he condemned the notions of economic materialism and determinism as denials of the spiritual nature of man. He defended private property as a natural right but cautioned that it must be held and used in a socially just manner. He upheld the rights of labor against capitalist exploitation and called for state intervention on behalf of workers. He urged trade unionization, collective bargaining, experiments in agricultural cooperatives, cooperation among the classes (whose natural enmity he denied), and the preservation and strengthening of such traditional social institutions as church and family. In short, his was a call for Christians to work together to build a better society based upon traditional spiritual values and founded in the teachings of the Catholic church. Forty years later, Pope Pius XI echoed Leo's ideas in his *Quadraggesimo Anno* (1931), a condemnation of laissez-faire liberalism and defense of proletarian organization. More recently, two encyclicals of Pope John XXIII, *Mater et Magistra* and *Pacem in Terris,* have provided further reinforcement for the Social Christian position as has the important *Populorum Progessio* (1967) of Paul VI.

The Christian Democratic party of El Salvador emerged from a series of meetings dedicated to the study of the writings of these men and others. The men who participated in these discussions were mostly lawyers who had studied political theory at the National University. They were also Catholics attracted by the spiritual foundation of Christian Democracy. Roberto Lara Velado, Abraham Rodríguez, and such younger men as the student leaders Héctor Dada Hirezi, José Ovidio Hernández, and Carlos Herrera Rebollo, were all familiar with the works of Maritain, Caldera, and Frei. On the other hand, some were not so well read. Party leader Napoleón Duarte, an engineer by training and profession, freely admits the deficiency of his own ideological preparation. In the early days of the movement, he devoted his time and talent almost exclusively to the mechanical aspects of party organization, leaving theory to the lawyers and humanists.

Not surprisingly, the Catholic background of Christian Democracy at times caused the movement to be identified in the public mind with the church itself. In Latin America, where passivism and obscurantism rather than progressivism traditionally characterized the social attitude of the ecclesiastical establishment, this was potentially a source of great misunderstanding and embarrassment. The radical and Marxist Left often criticized the Christian Democrats for their supposed "clericalism." The truth was, however, that, despite the religious inspiration and symbolism evident in the movement, there were no formal and very few informal ties between it and the church. In fact, in most cases neither the parties nor the church was willing to accept or encourage any such cooperation. Christian Democracy is not a religion. It is a social and political movement concerned with worldly rather than heavenly kingdoms. The founders of the Salvadoran party made their position as clear as possible when they declared that the PDC "categorically denies that it is in any way directed by the Catholic Church or any other religious body, believing that politics and religion should not be mixed."

While the Left has attacked the Christian Democrats for their "clericalism," the Catholic Right has generally disowned them for their progressivism. There are some issues upon which the PDC and conservative churchmen and laity have found agreement, such as support for religious education and opposition to birth control, but there are many others on which they have remained antagonists.

In addition to the accusation of clericalism, another charge frequently leveled at the Christian Democrats was that they were an international party. They denied this, but Christian Democracy was in fact an international movement and the individual parties always stressed their ties with one another. Since 1947 there has been a hemispherewide confederation of Social Christian parties, the Christian Democratic Organization of America (Organización Demócrata Cristiana de América, ODCA), which, while it cannot compel adherence to its polities, does exercise a great deal of influence over its member organizations.

In the eyes of nationalists both right and left, the international character of the Christian Democratic movement was only slightly more suspect than its emphasis upon a foreign policy of international cooperation. The Salvadoran PDC was as concerned with national autonomy and rights as any nationalist group, but—with the notable exception of its wholehearted support of the government's position in the 1969 war with Honduras—it generally translated this concern into a call for cooperation, regional integration, and international social justice, instead of an irrational isolationism. Of particular interest to El Salvador's Christian Democrats was the strengthening of the Latin position in the Organization of American States, the defense of the rights of smaller countries in the United Nations and of producer nations in world markets, and the economic integration of Central America.

The PDC, in fact, favored an international order from which imperialism and colonialism of all types were absent. To critics who charged that Christian Democrats took their orders from Rome, Caracas, or Santiago de Chile, Roberto Lara Velado replied not only that this was not true but also that, even if it were, these were hardly sinister imperial powers on a level with Washington, Moscow, or Peking, from whom the official party and the Marxists derived their inspiration. Christian Democracy, Lara Velado explained, differed from the two major alternatives in that it was not an imperial ideology. According to him, liberalism and communism both required the subordination of smaller states to larger ones in order to function properly. Thus, while the liberal and Communist systems achieved their highest expression in the world's three great imperial states—the United States, Russia, and China—Christian Democracy was more suited to the small national or territorial state that wished only to safeguard its own rights and autonomy.

The Salvadoran PDC repeatedly condemned colonialism and was as critical of the Soviet version as of the North American, citing Cuba as a victim of both forms. The party's first national convention in San Salvador in 1961 condemned the Cuban revolution as a betrayal of the Cuban people's struggle for liberation and warned of the threat it posed of Soviet domination in the Caribbean. Equally conscious of a threat from the North, the Christian Democrat minority in the Salvadoran Legislative Assembly successfully urged the passage in 1965 of a resolution condemning the United States military intervention in the Dominican Republic. On the issue of economic penetration, Lara Velado opposed the establishment of a local branch of the First National City Bank of New York, as "another spearhead of foreign imperialism," and Abraham Rodríguez, in his 1967 presidential campaign, condemned the Rivera government's policy of floating large foreign loans for public works projects, then using the money to buy foreign materials and hire imported workers and technicians. In 1969, José Napoleón Duarte, then serving as mayor of San Salvador, shocked a gathering of Central American municipal officials in Vera Cruz, Mexico, by condemning United States policy in Latin America as designed to "maintain the Iberoamerican countries in a condition of direct dependence upon the international political decisions most beneficial to the United States, both at the hemispheric and world levels. Thus [the North Americans] preach to us of democracy while everywhere they support dictatorships."

Continentwide, Christian Democrats resist location within the simplistic typology of Right-versus-Left. A Nicaraguan Social Christian leader has made perhaps the most precise statement of this problem:

> If by left we understand the struggle for social justice, the great battle for the social and economic redemption of the people, the incorporation of workers and peasants into the mainstream of culture and civilization, then undoubtedly we are leftist. If, however, by left is understood historical materialism, communist totalitarianism, and the suppression of liberty, then in no way are we leftists. If by right is understood the conservation of the spiritual values of civilization, the historical legacy of humanity, and the dignity and liberty of man, then there can be no doubt that we are rightists. But if by right we understand the conservation of an economic order based on the exploitation of man by man, on social injustice, we energetically refuse the name of rightists.

Adhering to Catholic teaching, Christian Democrats rejected the belief in the ultimate perfectability of man and the determinism therefore inherent in laissez-faire liberalism and Marxist socialism. But the movement itself drew fire from critics for the "determinism" supposedly implicit in its own belief in the inevitability of revolution in Latin America. Christian Democrats believed that the inequities in Latin American society must eventually lead to violence if they were not corrected. Since they did not believe that most of these inequities could be remedied short of drastic structural change, they called in reality for a "revolution" of their own, a peaceful, Christian revolution to prevent a violent, materialist one.

The word "revolution" often appeared in the polemics of the Salvadoran party. A revolution, the party declared in 1966, was unavoidable. But, spokesmen hastened to add, the Christian Democratic revolution would not be violent or destructive of national institutions. Rather it would be a scientifically and technically planned process designed to effect, within the limits of liberty and national reality, a peaceful and rapid change in political, economic, and social structures. In his political memoirs, Napoleón Duarte rejects the Marxian notion that the clash of thesis and antithesis must necessarily lead to a constructive synthesis. It is just as likely to lead to the reinforcement of the thesis or to an orgy of wasteful violence. Change is necessary, Duarte is in effect saying, but it cannot be undertaken lightly or without careful preparation. He likens the revolution contemplated by the Christian Democrats to a controlled chain reaction produced in a nuclear reactor.

The Christian Democratic call for "revolution in liberty" aroused suspicion among observers of all political persuasions. One Uruguayan leftist saw it as an attempt on the part of the Catholic bourgeoisie to "short-circuit" the aspirations of the workers by bringing about minor social change, preserving capitalism, and restoring the temporal authority of the church. In El Salvador, a right-wing clerical polemicist who often faulted the Salvadoran PDC for the thoughts and actions of its Chilean counterpart accused the Christian Democrats of adopting Marxist theory and giving the concept of revolution priority over that of liberty. The notion of the inevitability of such a revolution he condemned as Hegelian and, therefore, presumably determinist, Marxist, and heretical. Finally, he charged that Christian Democrats prefaced democracy with the word "Christian" for the same reason Communists used "people's" —to deceive the masses.

The Christian Democrats had quite definite ideas about the kind of world they hoped to build as a result of their "revolution." The new regime would above all be one of democracy and social justice. From the beginning the Salvadoran party declared these popular aspirations to be its overriding goals. The PDC used the word democracy in the classic political sense—open elections, respect for the dignity of the individual, the guarantee of human and constitutional rights, and an end to persecution and imposition. By social justice the Christian Democrats meant the just payment of labor, the economic and cultural redemption of the peasantry, and a more equitable distribution of property and the fruits of production. Party leaders here placed the greatest stress on the right of the individual Salvadoran to gain a decent living from his work. Above and beyond any moral basis for this position, both Duarte and Lara Velado argued that a more just diffusion of Salvadoran wealth would be beneficial to the nation as a whole, as the increased number of consumers would serve as a stimulus to industrial growth and the widened propertied class would contribute to political stability.

The minimum acceptable standard of living in El Salvador, as defined by party leaders at a round table discussion in 1962, would be one in which every citizen would be guaranteed: (1) a nutritious and filling diet; (2) sanitary, comfortable housing; (3) adequate shoes and clothing; (4) access to medicine and health care; (5) the basic skills of literacy and sufficient vocational preparation to contribute in a productive fashion to the economy; (6) protection in his or her old age.

The key to social justice, according to the PDC, was structural reform designed to remove the obstacles the old order posed to the economic development of the country. It first set forth its plans to accomplish this on a national level in the presidential campaign of 1966–1967. In their platform of that year, the Christian Democrats declared their primary goal to be full employment at dignified wage levels. Since El Salvador had a large corps of unemployed or underemployed citizens, the necessity of a high rate of economic growth was obvious—especially since the rapid increase in population meant that more than 30,000 new workers joined the labor force each year. As more than 60 percent of the existing labor force was already competing for a limited amount of work in the agricultural sector, the PDC hoped to incorporate the increment into nonagricultural pursuits by fostering industrial development and national productivity in general. How this prodigious feat was to be accomplished never was clear, but party leaders constantly invoked the sacred precepts of economic planning and state direction as the answer to the nation's ills.

While they called for industrialization, the Christian Democrats placed virtually equal emphasis upon increasing productivity in the agricultural sphere. They urged a program to increase crop yields, but warned against the ruthless exploitation of the nation's soil resources without attention to the problem of conservation—a particularly important consideration in a country as small as El Salvador. The agricultural problem had a troublesome social aspect as well. Something must be done to insure a decent living for the vast numbers of landless or nearly landless peasants who lived by selling their labor to the large operators. The demand for itinerant farm workers was seasonal. The PDC estimated in 1967 that the average laboring *campesino* worked only 120 days out of the year and guessed the productive income lost each year due to this situation to be more than 80 million colones. The government could employ some of these workers on housing and transportation infrastructure projects, the party declared, but the only lasting solution would be some sort of alteration of the prevailing pattern of land use and ownership.

The Christian Democrats' moderate proposals received little criticism from the left in El Salvador, largely because the government was a more prominent target. Certain facets of the PDC program, however, scandalized traditional liberals on the right who chose to regard the party's approach to the problems of urban and rural labor as an attack upon private property. Very early, party leaders made it clear that they did not consider labor to be a commodity subject to the caprice of the law of supply and demand. When the editorial staff of *El Diario de Hoy* uncritically attacked this position as Marxism, Roberto Lara

Velado replied that workers were as much investors as were stockholders and, as such, deserved a share of the company's profits as well as a guarantee of a decent living. He went on to distinguish the Christian Democratic position, based upon the human dignity of the individual worker, from the alternative positions of liberalism and communism. Whereas in a liberal system the means of production remained in the hands of private capital and in a Communist system in the hands of the state, Lara Velado argued, in an ideal Christian Democratic community production would be a free and dignified collaboration between capital and labor. The concept of free collaboration of capital and labor along with the related concept of "communitarian" ownership of the means of production were popular themes in abstract discussions, but party ideologues rarely approached the question of practical implementation.

Although conservatives, usually arguing weakly from the Chilean experience, charged that Christian Democrats favored the destruction of private property as an institution, the position of the Salvadoran PDC on this issue was essentially conservative. In an early declaration the party maintained its belief that property was a natural right justified in that it constituted a fair reward for work and provided for the satisfaction of the individual's present and future material needs. The Christian Democrats, however, also believed that social justice required property-holding to be broadly diffused throughout society. To effect this, they urged just compensation for labor and easily accessible credit to encourage savings and consumption on the part of wage-earners. They also demanded state protection for small proprietors in agriculture, industry, and commerce. The stated economic and social aim of the PDC was the growth of a large, comfortable middle class. Such a class, it believed, would provide the backbone for a stable economy and a durable democracy. As party leaders declared on many occasions, the solution of El Salvador's social problems did not lie in pulling down the oligarchy, but in elevating the oppressed.

Of special concern to Christian Democrats in general and of the Salvadoran party in particular was the position in society of the family and, closely related to this, the position of women. The PDC saw the family as the basic unit of society and repeatedly expressed a determination to strengthen it. According to the party, the family was the primary nucleus of socialization, education, moral formation, and economic activity, and a strong family could provide the vanguard in every struggle from that against hunger to that against juvenile delinquency.

A major obstacle to the achievement of family strength and stability in El Salvador has been the large number (about 50 percent) of households formed from "free unions" instead of legal marriages. This has particular implications for the position of women in society. In the lower classes where the entire family must function as a productive unit in order to stay ahead of starvation, the needs of the family have forced the Salvadoran woman to serve as breadwinner as well as mother. Working-class men, repeatedly bested in the uphill struggle to maintain a hovel full of hungry children, often leave home in search of work, or simply out of frustration. Many never return, abandoning their families entirely. In the city of San Salvador, the vast majority of the market vendors are women, many of whom must provide for families without any assistance from men. In recognition of this situation, the PDC called early for legislation to protect the economic rights of wives and mothers and to require fathers and husbands to meet their domestic responsibilities. Only with her economic interests thus protected, the party declared in its Mother's Day message for 1961, could the Salvadoran woman be free "to accomplish her grand mission as queen of the home and educator of her children."

PDC concern for women's rights and interests was not completely altruistic, of course. Since 1945, women have become increasingly important as voters and political leaders in Latin America. Politicians, Christian Democrats not the least among them, have been quick to recognize this. Women have been particularly receptive to the message of Christian Democracy because of its religious inspiration and because of its emphasis upon social stability and family security.

From a broad examination of party pronouncements on various issues it soon becomes apparent that, although the rhetoric of the PDC may at times have been radical or even revolutionary, the ends and means it actually proposed in El Salvador were generally moderate and at times socially conservative. The PDC's interest in political reform and espousal of traditional Western democratic values are reminiscent of the program of the moderate rightist "Old Guard" PAR which it displaced in 1964 as the dominant opposition party. The movement's scriptural inspiration and its emphasis upon Christian morality appealed particularly to traditionalist sentiment in society as did its claim to be an ideology compatible with El Salvador's Hispanic heritage. The PDC's call for regional (that is, Hispanic) solidarity to be accompanied by the rejection of "alien" ideologies, such as communism and liberalism, represented an attachment to the fundamentals of Salvadoran culture and society. Similarly conservative was the party's desire to maintain an ordered society along established lines through the strengthening of traditional social institutions, such as the family and the church.

The economic programs of the Christian Democratic party may appear at first examination to have been more radical than its social goals. But one should remember that the economic changes the party proposed were designed specifically to achieve the restoration of its vision of an ideal social order. Party theorists were thoroughly committed to the concept of private property which they did not believe to be mutually exclusive with social justice. While they did recognize the need for more broadly distributed property-holding (and, therefore, a large middle class) in order to achieve social justice and political stability, they spoke more of diffusion than of redistribution. The goal was to create new wealth through industrial growth and increased productivity in general and to insure its fair distribution in society, rather than to divide up existing property. In the one area of Salvadoran economic life where this course was clearly impossible, that of land ownership, Christian Democrats agreed, however reluctantly, to the necessity of expropriation and redistribution. But, even here, the PDC opposed precipitous action. The process of redistribution must be keyed to the development of markets, roads, and technical education, in order to guarantee that the peasants would be able to exploit their new holdings in the most efficient manner. Above all, the Christian Democrats insisted that the expropriated landowners be compensated for their lost property.

Salvadoran Christian Democracy was in many ways an ideology well suited to the middle-class lawyers and other professionals who founded and led the party. While it adopted a moral orientation toward the question of social justice, it did not question the concept of class advantage itself. It retained private property as the foundation of economic life and assumed individual inequities in its distribution, condemning such inequities only when they were so gross as to threaten social order and development. It sought the support and cooperation of disadvantaged members of society in order to promote changes that it believed would contribute to the orderly expansion of a propertied middle class, and saw the growth of such a class as the best guarantee of political democracy and a tranquil social order. To manage social tensions from below, the PDC urged the organization of the masses into associations (syndicates, cooperatives, neighborhood organizations) similar to those interest and professional guilds (*gremios*) the elites had always employed to articulate and defend their class positions. The party also advocated measures designed to ease access to the middle class from below and welfarist programs designed to ameliorate the lot of those who inevitably would remain at the bottom. The Christian Democrats hoped through education not only to promote social stability but to inculcate the masses with middle-class values. Thus the PDC stressed wholesomeness and respectability in family life and campaigned against nonmarital unions, irresponsible fathers, alcoholism, and other such socially dissolutive practices as gambling and prostitution.

In spite of the protestations and denials of Christian Democratic leaders, not only in El Salvador but all over Latin America, it is hard to avoid the judgment of one North American scholar that Christian Democratic social theory is "essentially traditional, Catholic corporatism." Christian Democracy is not forward-looking; it is backward-looking: back past the dehumanizing rise of liberalism and nationalism, past the centralizing age of political absolutism, past the secularizing world of the Renaissance, back to the medieval ideal of unity and order, to a world where all Christendom was theoretically a community and where the moral laws that guided man's spiritual and personal life supposedly guided his political and economic activities as well. The applicability of this charming vision to modern industrial society is, of course, highly questionable.

Prescribing against the possibility of social violence from below was a simple matter when compared to the necessity to manage elite attitudes. The PDC's vision of an ideal society, while moderate, required significant concessions on the part of an established oligarchy that had developed an elaborate moral vision of its own to justify the existing order. While the goal of a revolution accomplished solely through Christian suasion and moral education is an attractive one to those who abhor bloodshed, one must be skeptical about its chances for success in any society, much less one such as El Salvador's where the privileged have routinely demonstrated their willingness to employ any means whatsoever to preserve intact their advantages by stifling all but the most innocuous attempts at change. One must particularly doubt the wisdom of advocating the diffusion of power and decision-making responsibility in a region where a major difficulty for governments (whatever their form) has always been that they have generally not been powerful enough to enforce compliance with policies other than those most favorable to established interests.

CHAPTER III

The Church and Liberation Theology

Editors' Introduction

Every religious viewpoint has to grapple with the problem of theodicy, the reconciliation of divine justice with the palpable reality of evil and suffering on earth. Most often this is accomplished by assuring people that God's infinite wisdom and mercy will eventually prevail, even if life looks grim in the present and injustice and exploitation run rampant. The problem of theodicy is raised in José María Argueda's moving novel of contemporary Latin America, *Todas las Sangres* (*All the Blood,* Buenos Aires, 1964), which includes among its characters a priest who tries to assure his parishioners that they must bear misfortunes because God is everywhere—with all people and all classes. But a peasant, a humble tiller of the soil, questions the priest closely on what appears like a rationale for humanmade injustice. "Was God in the heart of those who broke the body of the innocent teacher Bellido?" the peasant inquires. "Is God in the bodies of the engineers who are killing [the river] 'La Esmeralda'? In the official who took the cornfields away from their owners . . . ?"

Questions such as these have been increasingly raised within the Roman Catholic church in Latin America during the years since Pope John XXIII's Second Vatican Council in 1962. Many within the church have persisted in the traditional mold—focusing on salvation and evangelism strictly defined so as to exclude, either implicitly or explicitly, any call to social action or any challenge to the established order. Some within the hierarchy have counseled submission to authority instead of activism and given their blessing to unjust governments and structures. But increasingly, brave parish priests, and even an occasional bishop or archbishop, have stepped forward to speak out against injustice and oppression. Aligning themselves with the oppressed groups, these progressive churchmen risk the displeasure of the privileged elites, who often send gunmen to "liquidate" radical priests. Such martyrdom came to the outspoken Archbishop Oscar Arnulfo Romero, head of the Roman Catholic church in El Salvador until his assassination in the early spring of 1980. Romero might prove to be no less a threat to the Salvadoran oligarchs in death than in life.

In addition to animating the Latin American clergy and attracting missionaries from such places as the United States to assist in the struggles for social justice, the outburst of radical religious commitment has also taken the form of a new doctrinal outlook, the so-called liberation theology. The tenets of this theology stress the church's primary mission to minister to the poor and downtrodden rather than to serve the wealthy and powerful. Priests and lay "Delegates of the Word" in El Salvador and elsewhere have fanned out into the countryside as well as the urban centers, bringing the message that the people's poverty is not willed by God but is the result of historical patterns of oppression that cannot be overcome without action toward peace and justice.

During Pope John Paul II's 1983 visit to El Salvador and the rest of Central America, he voiced concerns about the direction and even the legitimacy of some liberation theology currents. The Pope urged priests and lay leaders to be "faithful transmitters" of church doctrine, responsive to the authority of their superiors. This attitude has caused concern among advocates of liberation theology; the papal approach to the issue is decidedly mixed. On the one hand, the Pope has reaffirmed the Vatican II emphasis on popular evangelization and the need for the church to stand with the poor in their struggles against unjust structures. The Pope has, however, warned against the use of Marxist analysis as a tool for understanding social and structural injustice, and against church alliances with Marxist groups. Such involvements, in the Vatican's view, constitute a flawed compromise with an ideology that at its heart denies transcendental aspects basic to the church and would subvert the church's role as an autonomous institution separate from partisan politics and guided by a hierarchy already in place. The Pope has, at once, affirmed a large part of that which we call liberation theology while seeking to define more narrowly the dos and don'ts for the church within that current.

The Salvadoran church, despite disagreements among its bishops over the nature of the political dynamic and the government, has consistently spoken out for a genuine land reform, a redistribution of power and income, and a negotiated settlement to the civil war. It has steadfastly supported freedom of association for all Salvadorans and played an important part in monitoring and publicizing violations of basic human rights. The church is currently mediating the dispute between the government and the opposition in order to "humanize" the conflict and, eventually, bring about a negotiated settlement.

Through its social-service agencies, the Salvadoran church has reached out to help all Salvadorans, regardless of political persuasion, to secure adequate food, shelter, health care, and, most importantly, human dignity. It is perhaps this sort of concrete work, more than this or that theological hypothesis, that has made the Salvadoran church an important factor in El Salvador's complex equation and its uncertain future.

11. The Rebirth of Christian Militancy in El Salvador*

By the staff of CARIN/Central America Research Institute

The upsurge of Christian radicalism, symbolized in El Salvador by the ministry, the teaching, and ultimately the martyrdom of Archbishop Oscar Arnulfo Romero, constitutes a challenge to the U.S. government's doctrine that popular unrest in Central America is the product of outside agitators—Nicaraguan, Cuban, Soviet. As veteran New York Times journalist Alan Riding put it, it is "an amazing tribute" to the abilities of these outsiders to "orchestrate from afar the revolutions that are erupting from the very bowels of Central America. In reality, these movements are being stirred by more powerful forces—the human instincts of hunger and faith. But U.S. policy toward Latin America has no room for such subtleties."[1]

Continuing the discussion of the Roman Catholic church in El Salvador from Reading 9, we present here discussion of the high degree of social activism carried out throughout the religious institutions of Salvadoran society.

... [THE] transformation of the church began in El Salvador in the 1960s with the establishment of community development programs, among them health education and savings and production cooperatives. During the 1970s it continued with the rapid growth of Christian Base Communities, organized on the local level by priests, who eventually trained leaders chosen by the groups.

---

* Excerpted from "El Salvador's Catholic Church," *Central American Bulletin* (Berkeley, California), 3 (March 1984; footnotes deleted).

[1.] Alan Riding, "The Cross and the Sword in Latin America," *The New York Review of Books*, May 28, 1981.

These leaders were known as Delegates of the Word and catechists. Pastoral work included the discussion of Biblical passages, which were reflected upon in relation to the daily lives of the community members and implemented in some form of social action. The Salvadoran government came to characterize this activity, and the organizing associated with it, as threatening and subversive.

El Salvador's then-Archbishop Luis Chávez y González and his auxiliary Arturo Rivera y Damas both actively supported the development and work of the base communities, and the right of the people to organize for improved social conditions, especially agrarian reform. When Chávez y González retired in 1977, Rivera y Damas was passed over as his successor; many believe this was because his support for reforms put him in too confrontational a position with the government.

Instead, the chosen archbishop was Oscar Arnulfo Romero, who had acquired a reputation as a conservative. However, Romero's views were deeply affected by developments during the late 1970s, including an increasingly high level of repression against the church. During Romero's term and subsequent transformation as archbishop, his closest ally in times of confrontation with the government over attacks against the civilian population and the church was Rivera y Damas.

The base communities and the priests and nuns committed to the promotion of the doctrine of Vatican II and Medellín became an increasingly important sector within the church—commonly called the 'popular church.' The government often associated the popular church with budding organizations working to improve social conditions—sometimes accurately and other times inaccurately. These organizations—known as popular organizations within El Salvador—later consolidated in the opposition FDR/FMLN (Democratic Revolutionary Front/Farabundo Martí Front for National Liberation).

In 1978 Romero and Rivera y Damas issued a pastoral letter "The Church and the Popular Organizations." In it they stated that the popular organizations were the only means open to Salvadorans for participation in the political affairs of their country. They also called for a dialogue between the popular organizations and the church.

The highest body of the Catholic Church in El Salvador is the Episcopal Conference (CEDES), composed of the bishops of the five dioceses in El Salvador: San Vicente, Santa Ana, San Miguel, Santiago de María and San Salvador (the archdiocese). Occasionally other bishops also participate. One of CEDES' principal tasks is to issue church policy statements reflecting the thinking of hierarchy on important issues facing their constituents.

Romero's strong stance on human rights and popular organizing caused tremendous tension within CEDES. Many bishops and priests were actively supporting the government. After Romero and Rivera y Damas issued their letter in 1978, the other bishops issued a statement prohibiting priests and lay workers from involvement with popular organizations. During his three year term, Romero came under increasing attack from the other bishops, especially San Vicente's Bishop Pedro Arnoldo Aparicio and San Miguel's Bishop José Eduardo Alvárez.

After Romero's assassination in March, the Vatican did not appoint a new archbishop immediately. Instead, it appointed Rivera y Damas as Apostolic Administrator of the Church.

THE POPULAR CHURCH

The popular church and its relationship with popular organizations has continued to be a source of tension and division in the church. The organization that coordinates and directs the pastoral work of the popular church—the National Coordination of the Popular Church (CONIP)—was formed in 1980, after Romero's assassination. The majority of parishes in which CONIP is present are located in the zones of control—areas of the country from which government forces have been driven by the FMLN and replaced by a local civilian administration. (See *El Salvador Bulletin,* July 1983, for details on the zones of control.) Many villages that had a strong base community movement in the 1970s are now in these zones, and CONIP has a strong presence in them.

Since its formation, CONIP has been condemned by CEDES as a whole and by bishops Aparicio and Alvárez individually. When asked about the popular church in March 1983, Archbishop Rivera y Damas referred to the 1979 bishops' conference in Puebla, Mexico, saying that it had been defined and sanctioned then as a "church that has grown from the people. . . . Nevertheless, in those areas where it has grown and developed, it has become a little too ideological and this has created some problems of division." Rivera y Damas, however, has not condemned the popular church outright. In 1982, when Bishop Aparicio accused priests working with Christians in zones of control of collaborating with guerrillas, Rivera y Damas responded by stating that pastoral work should be conducted wherever it is needed and asked for.

CONIP responded to Aparicio's accusation by saying that in the course of its pastoral work, it has suffered persecution, including imprisonment, torture and assassination, but it chose to be "where the people are creating their history." It added that in two-thirds of Aparicio's diocese, San Vicente, CONIP was the only church presence carrying out pastoral work.

Because zones of control have been slowly expanding and consolidating since 1981, and are relatively free from government forces, the work of CONIP has not been subjected to government persecution, as members of the popular church were during the 1970s. Therefore, the popular church acquires a stronger presence in El Salvador over time.

CONIP does not define itself "as a parallel church. It is not a church that grew out of the people in opposition to the church of hierarchy." It declares itself open "a) to the poor, because within our community we discover our mission and we regain our spirit in making an authentic church; b) to the hierarchy of the church and the ecclesiastical bodies, in order to receive from them their interpellations and to, as a community, construct the true church, the 'church of the poor'; [and] c) to the popular organizations, to accompany them in their construction of a more human, rational and fraternal society."

Tracey Schear visited Christian base communities in Chalatenango in late 1983, and describes their work. "Priests perform mass, while Delegates of the Word carry out the pastoral work including Bible study groups. . . . Services are held outdoors in some villages because church buildings have been destroyed in the bombing raids or counterinsurgency operations." According to Schear, the Bible is a primary tool in literacy programs as it is one of the few books available in the zones of control.

Church work in the zones involves both pastoral work and social obligations, as it did in the early Christian base communities. However, conditions of work for popular church members are very difficult in zones of control. A young catechist describes his work: "Work was more difficult every day because there was so much to do and I did not have time for everything. So I was asked to dedicate myself full time to pastoral work and to stop baking bread. On Sundays, presacramental meetings for baptisms and marriages were held. Monday through Saturday it was a matter of passing through the villages to evaluate tasks, to lift people's spirits and to plan the work together. We also had three-day courses with persons responsible for other parishes."

TENSIONS IN THE HIERARCHY

Despite Rivera y Damas' repeated calls for unity within the church, divisions are still evident. Some of these pertain to the existence of the popular church, as described in the previous section. Others pertain to the nature of church's role in the war.

CEDES' position on dialogue between the government and opposition forces provides an example of the latter. In November 1982, CEDES issued a call for dialogue. In January 1983, Aparicio, then-vice-president of CEDES, told the American Chamber of Commerce in San Salvador that he was opposed to dialogue because "it would be between criminals and the state."

Although Aparicio retired in June 1983, several other bishops remain who continue to work closely with the government. Alvárez is closely associated with the military; Marco René Revelo, bishop of Santa Ana, is a member of the government Peace Commission; and former Secretary of CEDES Freddy Delgado is a member of the government Amnesty Commission and Human Rights Commission.

Two new bishops were installed during the past year. Former Auxiliary Bishop Oscar Barahona replaced Aparicio as bishop of San Vicente, and former vicar general Rodrigo Orlando Cabrera became bishop of Santiago de María. The leadership in CEDES also changed in routine elections on March 22, 1984—Alvárez was replaced by Revelo as the president of CEDES. These changes, while they may help to lessen the polarization within CEDES somewhat, do not appear to resolve the basic division in the church, nor depart radically from past policy trends. Central American University publication *Carta a las Iglesias* reported in March 1983 that CEDES still remained divided between those who followed Vatican II and Medellín and those who did not.

POPE STRESSES UNITY, RECONCILIATION

In March 1983, Pope John Paul II visited Central America. Before and during his trip, the Pope stressed two objectives: to emphasize the need for reconciliation as a means for bringing to an end violence in the region, and to emphasize the need for unity within the church.

In El Salvador, expectations for his visit were displayed in a variety of ways. Rivera y Damas announced that the visit "is viewed as a source of hope for the Salvadoran people, because it will unite us and invite us to a reconciliation." Christians in the zones of control held meetings in which they formulated suggestions and requests for the Pope and sent them to him in letters. They asked that the Salvadoran Catholic Church receive him, and not the government; that the Pope be given a bouquet of flowers in memory of the martyrs of the violence; that he visit refugees, the prisons, the slums and Romero's tomb; that he issue a call for dialogue; and that he name and condemn those responsible for violence against civilians.

Cartas a las Iglesias wrote that the government and political party leaders remained silent on the subject of the Pope's visit for fear that he might repeat his August 1982 call for dialogue toward a political solution to the war. It also said that these political leaders hoped that the Pope would take a strong anti-Marxist stand during his visit.

The Pope was received by the church hierarchy and the Salvadoran government. On March 6, 1983 Provisional President Alvaro Magaña announced in his reception speech that presidential elections would be held before the end of the year.

The points most stressed by the Pope during his one-day stay in El Salvador had all been made before, and reflected the objectives of his trip. He called for dialogue among opposing factions in the war, for reconciliation and peace. He called for a "sincere dialogue" from which "no one must be excluded." John Paul responded to Magaña's announcement of elections with the comment that "the means announced and all the other adequate means could contribute to . . . peaceful progress." As the *National Catholic Reporter* noted, " 'means' have been 'announced' by the opposition, as well as by the government. . . . And the opposition's plan . . . includes a call of dialogue."

The Pope also called for unity within the church. "The strength of the church lies in unity," which is a "responsibility of all members of the church."

This message contained a warning to the popular church and to priests aligned with popular organizations to obey their bishops, and to stay out of partisan politics. The Pope told the priests to be "faithful transmitters" of church doctrine and admonished them not to let ideology or temporal considerations enter into their teachings. They were not "social leaders, political leaders or functionaries of temporal power."

Just prior to his visit, the Pope announced the appointment of Rivera y Damas as archbishop of San Salvador. According to Roberto Cuellar, director of Socorro Jurídico, a church-related human rights organization, Rivera y Damas' appointment was a show of "strong church support for the continued appeals for a peaceful solution to the conflict in El Salvador."

While Central American University publication *Estudios Centroamericanos* said that after his visit "the moral and religious authority of the Pope [was] still enormous," the popular church was disappointed with his visit. Father Rutilio Sánchez said that the Pope "did not address our problems. We feel the Pope spoke as if he were in a different country: he never mentioned our war, our political prisoners, the hunger we are suffering, the repression. He spoke as if El Salvador were at peace. We felt very disappointed."

ARCHBISHOP PUSHES DIALOGUE

Throughout 1983, Rivera y Damas has continued to call for dialogue toward a political solution to the war in El Salvador. This call was supported by the Pope, who sent a message in January 1983 called "Dialogue for Peace, an Urgent Need of Our Time." In response to this, the San Salvador Archdiocese Commission for Justice and Peace organized a day of prayer for peace on January 6, 1983 at which Rivera y Damas again urged the government and the FDR/FMLN to begin negotiations.

When he was apostolic administrator, Rivera y Damas defined the church's role in El Salvador as a non-partisan intermediary between the government and the opposition forces and as an active promoter of a non-military resolution to the conflict. He has offered the services of the Church as a mediator and has also supported various political initiatives toward the realization of dialogue. *Cartas a las Iglesias* reported that the church was involved in the process of bringing the various sectors together, but that the work was being done in secret.

Rivera y Damas has also expressed support for the efforts of the Contadora group—Panama, Mexico, Colombia and Venezuela—to bring about a political solution in Central America.

During the fall 1983 preparations for the March 1984 elections in El Salvador, Rivera y Damas reaffirmed the need for dialogue between the Salvadoran government and the opposition forces. He explained that such dialogue "would serve to avoid what happened in the March 1982 elections which resulted in a government that instead of favoring internal reforms has set them back." In February 1984 CEDES issued a pastoral letter once again calling for dialogue. And one week before the March 25 elections, Rivera y Damas said that conditions for free elections did not exist. "The elections are supposed to be free and democratic, but the spirit of the event is violent."

PRELATES DENOUNCE HUMAN RIGHTS VIOLATIONS

The archbishop's office continued to monitor and report on the human rights situation during 1983, supplying one of the most consistent and authoritative sources of informaton on the political violence. Auxiliary Bishop Gregorio Rosa Chávez announced at the end of 1983 that 6096 people died of political violence in El Salvador that year. He said "it is almost a rare thing to die a natural death in this country. It is almost a miracle."

In their Sunday homilies, Rivera y Damas and occasionally Rosa Chávez cite the level of violence of that week and the prevailing practices in human rights violations, and warn against increased U.S. military involvement in El Salvador. They are careful to balance these citations with denunciations of both government and FMLN actions. However the emphasis is usually on the more severe and violent army and death squad activity.

Rivera y Damas also notes trends in the human rights situation. In January 1983, he said he didn't understand how military service could be said to be obligatory when only the poor were enlisted. In May, he denounced the indiscriminate use of mortar fire against civilians. And, as death squad activity increased in the summer and fall of 1983, Rivera y Damas and Rosa Chávez condemned their activities. In one such denunciation in July, Rosa Chávez said that even though death squad members belong to government security forces, they remain anonymous. He called on the government not to give false information about disappearances and murders.

Rivera y Damas and Rosa Chávez have continued to make statements on political affairs that affect the human rights situation in El Salvador. In July, Rosa Chávez expressed the church's concern with the deployment of the U.S. flotilla off the Central American coast. This "is not a rational or peaceful solution," he said. In August, as the constitution was being written, Rosa Chávez asked the Constituent Assembly not to vote by party or political block, but according to their conscience. He warned that if they continued with the same partisan attitude, they would give El Salvador a constitution devoid of any substance. During September 1983, Rivera y Damas addressed the U.S. presence in the region by saying "the Central American people do not want to suffer the economic, political or military dependence on another country any longer, nor to become the piñata of the superpowers."

When the Kissinger Commission report was issued in January 1984, Rosa Chávez commented on behalf of the church that "we again insist that fomenting the prolongation of the conflict means condemning to death more Salvadorans and . . . increased suffering."

REPRESSION OF THE CHURCH

The Catholic Church continues to be the target of human rights violations in El Salvador. Since 1981, 17 priests, nuns and religious have been killed. In 1983, a number of incidents point out the continuing tension.

On April 6, 1983, two members of the christian community in San Ramón were abducted, tortured and shot by the National Police. Later that month, the National Police also abducted two members of the Salvadoran Lutheran Church, the Rev. Medardo Gómez and Dr. Angel Ibarra.

As death squads became more active in the summer and fall of 1983, attacks against the church increased. During September, the Jesuit residence in San Salvador was bombed. According to Socorro Jurídico, four members of the social secretariat of the archdiocese were kidnapped for ten days and then remitted to Mariona Prison. That same day, it was revealed that Rivera y Damas had received a death threat.

In October, the Anti-Communist Brigade killed four people and left them in a parking lot. In a communiqué left with the bodies, the brigade accused one of them of being the "contact for the Archbishop, Mons. Rivera y Damas, as intermediary to . . . the contact with the Mexican Embassy" who had supposedly helped coordinate church efforts to bring about negotiations.

By November, both Rivera y Damas and Rosa Chávez had received death threats from the right-wing death squad Maximiliano Hernández Martínez Brigade, warning them not to continue their denunciations of human rights violations. In October Rosa Chávez' 74-year-old father was abducted by members of the armed forces, detained and then released. Despite these threats, Rivera y Damas and Rosa Chávez continued to report on the violence and comment on the political situation.

Since becoming apostolic administrator, Rivera y Damas has had to contend with a church divided and clearly polarized between those whose work supports the government and those whose work supports the opposition. The church continues to be divided. Many priests work in the zones of control; others, including most of the bishops, participate in government-sponsored programs which ultimately are part of the counterinsurgency campaign.

Rivera y Damas has called for unity within the church, and has been careful not to condemn too strongly either sector, while at the same time not embracing either. This has been backed up by the Pope, who gave his support for Rivera y Damas' job in leading the church of El Salvador, by warning the popular church not to become too far removed from the hierarchy and calling for a negotiated settlement to the war.

Cartas a las Iglesias summed up Rivera y Damas' term as archbishop in March 1983 as following the legacy of his two predecessors "Mons. Rivera y Damas has reclaimed the right of the people to organize; has insisted on the necessity of including the left in finding an authentic solution to the military conflict; [and] has denounced the injustices and atrocities of both side in the conflict, without fear of being accused of partiality when the bulk of the denunciations directly accuse the armed forces and security bodies. At the same time, on repeated occasions, he has sought the humanization of the conflict and has proposed dialogue and negotiations as the most rational and christian resolution; on the other hand, Mons. Rivera y Damas has tried to keep alive the spirit of Mons. Romero."

12. Oscar Romero: Archbishop of the Poor*

By Patrick Lacefield

These excerpts are from an interview with Archbishop Oscar Arnulfo Romero in August 1979—two months before the coup that overthrew the military dictatorship of General Carlos Humberto Romero and ushered in the first junta. Interviewed near the chapel where he would be gunned down while celebrating mass on March 24, 1980, the Archbishop expressed hope that peaceful channels for social change in El Salvador were still real possibilities.

Under Romero's successor, Archbishop Arturo Rivera y Damas, the Salvadoran church honors the slain prelate as a martyr and has taken up his work for justice and peace. Rivera y Damas has spoken out against violence and the violations of human rights by both the government and the rebels. While decrying U.S. military aid and the escalating air war in the countryside in disputed areas, the church is sponsoring the dialogue between the government and the rebels in hope of reaching a negotiated settlement and putting an end to the civil war.

Patrick Lacefield: The principles of liberation, of liberation theology that emerged from Medellín and Puebla, have drawn a sort of battleline between the church and the government in many countries. How does the church in El Salvador apply these principles to the objective realities it encounters?

Monsignor Romero: This is a Latin American problem. There are two trends in the Latin American church. One is the conservative school which we tried to push a little in Medellín and Puebla and, of course, the other is the progressive. There are two trends in the church here also, but I do not particularly

* From *Fellowship* magazine, November 1979.

like to call these trends conservative and progressive because this implies a division within the church.

I do not wish to say that there is a division but rather that there is pluralism. The progressive trend promotes the liberation themes of Medellín and Puebla. The former Archbishop, Monsignor Chávez, initiated the application of the principles of the Second Vatican Council and Medellín. When I was appointed Archbishop three years ago, I only continued with the trend already initiated.

The circumstances in these last three years have been very hard and therefore our program has been more visible. There is much persecution of the church because the church is standing against repression and injustice, in accordance with the principles of Medellín and Puebla. The archdiocese of El Salvador becomes more and more aware every day that this is the correct and true interpretation. What happened at Puebla ratified the authenticity of these liberation principles. We can concentrate on these words emerging from Puebla: preferential treatment for the poor. It can be made concrete.

Q. Can you speak of the recent persecution of the church? I know that there was a priest, Padre Palaiso, killed in June.

A. These are the facts. There was the assassination of Padre Palaiso, and the expulsion of Padre Astor Luis, a Salvadoran whom the government will not allow to return from Colombia. When we attempt to investigate, to find the reasons for this, we are only told: "superior orders." There is also a Belgian priest, a Father Juan D'Planck, whom the government will not allow into the country. He visits Belgian priests working in Latin America.

The government has continued a campaign of misinformation about church activities, our communities and priests. There is support for campaigns denouncing me through the media, with radio programs and paid advertisements in the newspapers. I might also mention our inability to use the communications media because they are all under the control of the capitalists and the government, the oligarchy. The only exceptions are the archdiocese radio station [which broadcasts the Archbishop's Sunday homilies throughout the country] and our weekly paper *Orientación.*

There has been government interference with the frequency of the radio station. A recent declaration of the Human Rights Commission of the Organization of American States clearly says that there has been systematic persecution of the church in El Salvador.

Q. For many people, particularly in the countryside, the church is the only means of opposition communication, especially now since *La Crónica* is gone [the only opposition daily, whose offices were destroyed by the right-wing terror group, the White Warriors Union, in late June]. Is this not true?

A. It is not the "opposition" really, because the church is not a political party. Rather it is the Gospel's voice, denouncing injustice and oppression. With the return of Dr. Morales Ehrlich [the Christian Democratic vice-presidential candidate in the 1977 elections] from exile, he is becoming a voice of the opposition in the political field and this is hopeful. There is also a new press service, API—Independent Press Agency—that will take up much of the news that *La Crónica* printed.

Q. Are you optimistic or pessimistic about progress toward democracy and human rights in El Salvador? How will such progress come about—by elections, government reforms, or armed rebellion?

A. I am optimistic from the point of view of Christian hope. This is the hope I try to communicate to the people, because I am certain there is a God who is close to our problems and He will not let us down. But in addition to this, from a human point of view, I believe there are peaceful solutions. I believe in the ability of our people if only they are given an opportunity to participate. Here is where the difficulty lies. As long as there is repression and any discordant voice, any left voice against the government—whether a political party or a popular group—is repressed, there will be a problem. Elections alone are not the answer. If elections are a *part* of the process of freedom for the people, then I do believe in them. Because of this, it is imperative that these repressive actions by the government be stopped.

Q. And what of "The Dialogue" by General Carlos Humberto Romero following the massacre of demonstrators in May that the government and some opposition elements sit down to discuss national affairs?

A. There is no credibility for "The Dialogue." It is a forum, not a dialogue. A dialogue implies the presence of, and a toleration for, dissenting voices. In order for these voices to be heard, it is necessary to have a climate where repression is not feared. It is absurd that a national dialogue is called during a state of siege [a mild form of martial law], and that during this state of siege more acts of violence have been committed by the extreme right, and also—in revenge—by the extreme left. There is no appropriate climate for a dialogue at present.

Q. What were your feelings in May when government troops massacred peaceful demonstrators on the steps of your church, the Metropolitan Cathedral? What were your thoughts and what did you feel in your heart?

A. I expressed as always the rejection of such a crime, such violence. But as a Christian I am moved to call for conversion, for sinners to repent. I expressed my solidarity with the families of those killed and my solidarity with the just claims of the people. I pointed out the causes of these outrages, particularly social injustice and the lack of participation by Salvadorans in the goods of the society and the political process. As long as these profound conflicts exist, violence will continue and I regret that new crimes will be committed.

Q. In many Latin American countries, most notably and recently Nicaragua, Christians—even priests—have taken up arms in the struggle for liberation. Do you feel this runs counter to the Gospel tradition of love for all of mankind, the imperative for reconciliation and the belief in the inherent worth of all human beings?

A. Regrettably, it is an historical fact that many freedoms have to be won by bloodshed. Christian ethics admits of violence for a just cause. There are even constitutions that admit the right of the people to rebel; the church also admits this right. When there is a tyrannical situation, insufferable to the people, and it has not been possible to change the system by pacific means, then violence is justified on the condition that the evil of the rebellion does not become worse than the evil of the status quo.

In principle, Christians prefer peace. I believe that the power of nonviolence is much stronger than violence because it carries the power of love and the conviction that we are all brothers. This fraternal inspiration resolves unjust situations much better. The principles of the church are predicated on the conversion of mankind. However, as Pope Paul VI said, the Christian knows how to struggle and how to fight, but prefers peace. We too prefer peace but preach the legitimacy of the just war.

Q. You have been nominated for the Nobel Peace Prize by 132 members of the British Parliament and sixteen U.S. Congressmen. The church in El Salvador may be in the most difficult situation in the world and I know that you have received numerous death threats. What sustains you in your work, your commitment and your dedication?

A. Regarding the Nobel Peace Prize, I am deeply grateful for the nomination and have expressed my gratitude to the British Parliament, to the U.S. Congressmen, and all those who have indicated solidarity with this nomination. The nomination signifies to me very great moral and international support for our struggle. I am almost certain I will not receive the prize because there are so many political and diplomatic concerns that are not within my grasp. But the nomination itself is prize enough for me. I would accept it not for myself, but as an award to the cause of human rights.

What sustains me in the struggle is my love for my God, my desire to be faithful to the Gospels, and my love for the Salvadoran people—particularly the poor. I could not say whether the church in El Salvador is experiencing the most difficult times in the world today but churches all over the world—particularly in the United States—have given us beautiful testimonies of their solidarity.

Q. Can you talk very briefly about your background before you became archbishop?

A. I was born in a small town in the department of San Miguel [in eastern El Salvador] into a lower middle-class family. My father was the telegraph operator in town. I attended seminary in San Miguel, San Salvador and Rome and spent most of my life as a parish priest in San Miguel. I suppose I could have been called a conservative. However, I followed the principles of the Second Vatican Council with considerable interest. I noticed the changes that the Vatican was asking of us.

Later I came to San Salvador and served as secretary of the Bishops' Conference and in those years lived a very private life, anonymous you might say.

Then I was appointed auxiliary bishop in the town of Santiago de María where I became very close to the problems of the campesinos, and then the bloody repression began. This was 1975.

Then, in 1977, I was appointed archbishop. The circumstances were difficult. Priests were being exiled and, a month after I assumed office, Padre Rutilio Grande was assassinated. This gave me the impetus to put into practice the principles of Vatican II and Medellín which call for solidarity with the suffering masses and the poor and encourage priests to live independent of the powers that be. My predecessor had initiated this work and I continued on with it.

It was precisely those young priests involved in experiments of "conscientization" with the peasants and urban shantytown dwellers who feared that I was a conservative and would put an end to the process. However, circumstances made me very understanding of the plight of the church, and we have worked very well together.

Q. Is there any message that you would like me to take back to the Christian community in the United States?

A. I have expressed my appreciation to the U.S. religious community before and welcome this opportunity to reiterate that appreciation. I have received many expressions of solidarity from bishops, priests, religious communities and individual Christians, not only in the Catholic community but from all denominations. To all of them: I thank you for this fraternal feeling.

Some have been so kind as to say that we are an example of faithful followers of the Gospels. I would beg that they pray for this to be true because this praise is most encouraging. We will try to live up to their opinions of us.

13. Avoiding Bloodshed: A Letter to President Jimmy Carter*

BY ARCHBISHOP OSCAR A. ROMERO

In February 1980, less than two months after the resignation of the civilians from the first junta, Archbishop Oscar A. Romero sent a letter to President Jimmy Carter urging him not to supply military aid to the Salvadoran government. On March 14, U.S. Secretary of State Cyrus Vance replied, "We understand your concerns about the dangers of providing military aid assistance, given the unfortunate role which some elements of the security forces occasionally have played in the past" (emphasis added). Nevertheless,

* From *El Salvador Bulletin* (December 1980).

the aid was granted to the government. On March 24, 1980, Archbishop Romero was assassinated while saying mass. What follows are excerpts from the Archbishop's letter to President Carter.

February 1980

To President Carter:

It disturbs me deeply that the U.S. government is leaning toward an arms race in sending military equipment and advisers "to train three Salvadoran battalions." . . . Your government, instead of favoring greater peace and justice in El Salvador, will undoubtedly aggravate the repression and injustice against the organized people who have been struggling because of their fundamental respect for human rights.

If it is true that this past November, "A group of six Americans were in El Salvador supplying $200,000 worth of gas masks and protective jackets and giving training in their use," you yourself must know that starting at that time, the security forces—with greater personal protection and efficacy —have used even greater violence with death-dealing weapons in repressing the people.

Because I am a Salvadoran and Archbishop of the Archdiocese of San Salvador, I am responsible to watch over the condition of the faith and justice in my country. I ask that, if you truly want to defend human rights, you:

—Prohibit military aid to the Salvadoran government;

—Guarantee that your government will not intervene, directly or indirectly, with military, economic or diplomatic pressure in determining the destiny of the Salvadoran people.

In these moments our country is living through a grave economic and political crisis. It is beyond doubt that the people are rising to the times, each day becoming increasingly conscious and more organized, and beginning to summon the ability to direct, to take charge of the future of El Salvador. No power other than the people is capable of overcoming the crisis.

I hope that your religious sentiments and your sensitivity for the defense of human rights will move you to accept my plea avoiding, with such acceptance, any greater bloodshed in this suffering country.

—Monsignor Oscar A. Romero

14. The Option for Life: Challenge to the Church in El Salvador*

BY JON SOBRINO

Jon Sobrino is El Salvador's leading proponent of liberation theology. These excerpts from an article in the Salvadoran journal Estudios Centroamericanos *point out the opportunities, roadblocks and challenges facing the church as it carries on the work begun by the late Archbishop Oscar Romero.*

THE church in El Salvador is well-known. Its option for the poor and, above all, the consequences of that option—conflict, persecution, martyrdom, as well as its pastoral, liturgical, and doctrinal creativity—has attracted powerful attention. This true church of the poor achieved its maximum expression in the time of Monsignor Romero but has continued in its work with less brilliance since that time. Undoubtedly all of the church is not alike, but there is a part of the church that has maintained its faith in the Gospel, in Medellín, and in Puebla and that acts as a yeast within the ecclesiastical body.

Everything we shall say is a continuation of the following: The world of poverty is a world of death. For that reason, the option for the poor is an option against death and for life.

Many things can be said about the Salvadoran reality. There is an enormous idealism and generosity, a creativity and strength in the midst of the struggle and the suffering, the decision of all the people to survive. This is very novel in comparison with the resignation and fatalism of previous periods. This is a product of the hope of a people and generates hope for the future because it shows that El Salvador is not only a country torn and impoverished but also a people with great values and great capacities for winning the peace and constructing a just society.

El Salvador is and has been for a long time in the same condition as the whole of Latin America. The most striking factor is "the misery that marginalizes large groups of people," a product of "structural injustice" that truly constitutes "institutional violence" (Medellín). That misery is reflected in all economic indicators and expresses itself in infant mortality, starvation wages, 60 percent illiteracy in the countryside, inhuman crowding in the slums, chronic unemployment among *campesinos,* etc. It is now possible neither to accumulate statistical data nor to record the tragedy that is reflected in the faces of Salvadorans. As was said at Puebla, such poverty is "the most humil-

* Excerpted from *ECA/Estudios Centroamericanos,* May–June 1984. Translated by the editors.

iating and devastating scourge." Poverty is not a natural or inevitable fact "but a product of economic, social, and political situations and structures" (Puebla) that objectively produce great poverty and an ever-widening social division, leaving "the rich ever more rich at the expense of the poor becoming ever poorer." That poverty "cries out to heaven" (Medellín) and is "contrary to the plan of the Creator" (Puebla). It is a sin, absolutely in opposition to God, and cannot be condoned or tempered. It is not a lesser evil but rather a greater evil.

In El Salvador, as in Latin America and other countries of the Third World, poverty has a primary relationship with death. Poverty does not mean simply a scarcity of some goods accessible in societies of abundance. Poverty overwhelms the human being with the weight of existence, leaving him or her unable to control his or her own life on even the most elementary level. Poverty is indeed close to death, and the poor are destined to die before their time. This is why poverty is a cry for life, a cry for survival.

As Father Rutilio Grande said, the God that "gave us a material world . . . for all of us without frontiers" wants "a shared table for all humanity at which every man has his place and his position," and God today sees that his creation is threatened and destroyed. It is not pure metaphor to argue theologically that the creation of God has not arrived in El Salvador because life is not the predominant reality in a society of poor people. Nor is it metaphorical to state that there exists in Salvadoran society a serious sin because the socioeconomic system—the first idol, Monsignor Romero called it—is organized to produce a slow death for the poor.

In four years there are already close to 50,000 murdered by the repression, most at the hands of government forces and the death squads. That is without counting those who have died in combat on both sides. In 1983 alone, the Tutela Legal[1] of the archdiocese has denounced a total of 5,142 political murders by the right (1,259 at the hands of the death squads and paramilitary groups, 3,780 by the army, 27 by the security forces, and 76 by the national guard) and 67 political murders attributed to the guerrillas. To this it is necessary to add 6,000 disappeared persons, of whom only 549 have been given up for dead. To this are added the tortures, the faces flayed and disfigured with acid, the mutilations, the trunks without heads—sometimes in such great numbers that it is difficult to match the head and the trunk. It is not metaphorical to speak of a people crucified.

It is important to remember that those murdered are poor and die for being poor. The first is an empirical fact as much for the victims of the repression as for those who die in combat on one side or another because the poor are those who fight with the guerrillas and with the army. Those recruited do not include the sons of the oligarchy or the middle class but only the poor. The second is true because the ultimate reason for the repression—and now for the

[1] See Reading 32.—Eds.

war—is to eliminate the poor who are, by their mere anguished existence, a threat to the established system. Both the repression and the war seek to eliminate those who have organized themselves to combat the system and to terrorize those who are not organized. Those who are murdered who are not sociologically poor are murdered by the system for defending the poor.

This reveals that against the God of life and justice actively work the gods of death, who give death in order to defend and maintain themselves. It matters little what they are called. In El Salvador, Monsignor Romero spoke of the idol of "the doctrine of national security." What is important is that the idol of the rich is untouchable and that whoever touches it succumbs to the hands of the idol of security. As Monsignor Romero graphically put it: "I denounce, above all, the dictatorship of the rich. This is the greatest evil in El Salvador: the rich and private property as an untouchable dictatorship. Woe be to he who touches that high-tension wire. He burns himself."

In El Salvador the misery of poverty dominates, as does the agony of crucifixion; here, death rules. Faced with this situation, the church must choose life. This must be done insofar as a *Salvadoran* church is concerned, because without that option the church would not be responding to El Salvador and would be neither credible nor relevant. And it must be done insofar as a *Christian* church is concerned because as such it has a mission to announce and initiate the kingdom of God on earth, and this cannot arrive until the reign of death is ended and the reign of life begins.

The existing situation is different from that in the time of Monsignor Romero. It is different, above all, because it has worsened. The evils he denounced persist, and to them has been added the great evil of the war, which has outstripped all previous evils. There persist, for the most part, the challenges to which Monsignor Romero responded, and it continues to be necessary to respond to them in his spirit. A new situation exacts a new test for that spirit: the work, above all, for peace.

The programmatic response of the church to the challenges of the situation has been clearly expressed by Monsignor Rivera. On a doctrinal level, he stated it clearly upon assuming the position of Archbishop on April 8, 1983:

> In El Salvador we will . . . consider as our priority the problem of war and peace —to put an end to the war through pacific means, through a dialogue as requested by the church. . . . Among other things we ought to require of all parties a humanization of the conflict in order to lessen the shameful pain of the widows, the orphans, the homeless, the plundered, the prisoners, the wounded, etc. . . .
>
> Remembering that the promotion of justice is an integral part of evangelization, we will put emphasis on meeting human needs so that those in the most need can be makers of their own destiny, will be heard, and will be more than they are now.

In its daily work, the church is giving great priority to the dialogue and a negotiated settlement to the conflict. This Monsignor Rivera does in his homilies—proclaiming the need, explaining the reasons, and preferring it to any other solution, whether war or elections.

The church is trying to humanize the conflict, assisting thousands of refugees, especially those fleeing government repression, and programmatically defending their rights. The church has helped those persons and political prisoners who had to leave the country and has offered on several occasions to receive prisoners freed by the FMLN. The church is also working to speak the truth about the country, analyzing the true causes of the conflict and denouncing the repression in sermons and in reports from the Tutela Legal. The Church works for reconciliation, rejecting a Manichaean view of the conflict and insisting, in the words of Pope John Paul II, that it is a war "between brothers that take up arms."

The church has many serious problems in responding to the challenge. Some come from the outside, and others come from within the church. After years of repression and seven years of outright persecution, the church has been decimated and seriously weakened so far as human resources are concerned. Many priests and pastoral agents have been assassinated, have been expelled, or have abandoned the country under threat of death. A good part of the church has been terrorized, which has diminished on the whole its nearness to the poor, its promise to them, and the clarity of its criticisms of the repression. The weariness that accompanies the length of the conflict has made many Christians cease to be interested as Christians in the situation of the country. This disinterest has made comprehension and practice of the faith more individualistic and interior in a way that one finds in faith a refuge from personal problems but no motivation for the building of the Kingdom. For all these reasons the church has lost vigor as a body of service for the option of the poor and has seen its social influence diminish. All this is understandable given the climate of fear and the reigning weariness, but that does not keep it from being a serious problem for a church that desires to be effective in responding to the country's problems.

In order to defend life, Monsignor Romero analyzed the strengths of the forces undermining life. He then denounced them in proportion to their contribution to death. He unmasked the idols of absolute private property and national security and ordered soldiers not to obey the orders to kill. But he also analyzed and promoted the causes of life. He defended and inspired the organization of the poor, that they might become effective agents for structural change and masters of their own destiny. And today Monsignor Romero would denounce not only the war but also "the mystique of violence" that seeks a solution for the country through purely military force.

15. *Protestant Challenge in El Salvador**

By Marlise Simons

Although the phrase the Church *in El Salvador used to refer exclusively to the Catholic church, progress made by Protestant sects during the 1980s has begun to challenge that definition. Protestant churches, lavishly financed by their adherents in the United States and taking advantage of the chronic shortage of Catholic clergy, are making significant inroads in this heavily Catholic nation. This has prompted a response by the institutional Catholic church and the rise of a vibrant charismatic current within the Catholic grass roots. It is also a development with political ramifications, as the following reading demonstrates. Marlise Simons is a widely published writer on Latin American affairs for* the New York Times.

SAN SALVADOR—Only a decade ago revivalist preachers were viewed with hostility in deeply Roman Catholic El Salvador, at times even treated as alien sorcerers—stoned, tied up in village squares and run out of town.

But from its almost-clandestine beginnings, the Protestant evangelical movement has now won influence and respectability, with senior military officers, businessmen, teachers and students among its followers. Revivalist preachers now far outnumber the Catholic clergy and say they have converted one of every five adults from Catholicism.

The movement has also become closely identified with the battle against the country's Marxist-led guerrillas. While its leaders in the past invoked purely spiritual reasons for their mission, now some say openly that their "crusade" is part of the fight against Soviet encroachment in Latin America.

The dramatic growth of the sects here and elsewhere in Latin America is a result of an intense multimillion-dollar evangelical campaign by American-based churches and religious agencies. Their impact and anti-Communist focus appear especially strong in war-torn El Salvador. Preachers often refer to the leftist insurgents in theological terms, calling them "sinners," "forces of darkness" and "allies of Satan."

Because most of the sects here still receive considerable financing and guidance from their North American headquarters, their activities have further tightened the links between the United States and this small nation, which already depends overwhelmingly on American military and economic aid. American money has helped set up new temples, schools, clinics and radio stations.

Moreover, the movement's growth has widened the arena in which political

* From Marlise Simons "El Salvador Is Fertile Ground for Protestant Sects," *New York Times,* January 20, 1986.

conflicts are fought out under religious banners. The age-old mix of religion and politics in this region had centered largely on Catholic factions and disputing leftist, liberal and conservative views.

Now, like the new Catholic theologians on the left, the revivalist newcomers of the right use the Gospel as a vehicle to promote their political views.

Although several branches of Protestantism have been growing steadily here since the 1930's, ambitious plans by fundamentalists to intensify their work in Central America are relatively new. According to missionaries, several large denominations decided to step up their activities within the past 10 years.

"The Catholic left and the Marxists were looking like the only people with a new message, the people with the appeal and the vitality," said an evangelical development expert here. "Many of us knew that was wrong, that had to change."

BAPTISMS UP SHARPLY

Since then, missionaries supported by North American recruiting techniques and funds have helped establish new churches, training centers, bookstores and the region's first evangelical university, which opened in San Salvador in 1981.

According to Campus Crusade for Christ, an interdenominational agency, the number of Protestants baptized in El Salvador, which has a population of 4.6 million, jumped from 70,000 in 1975 to 250,000 in 1985. It says the movement has more than half a million followers and 2,465 large and small places of worship.

On recent visits to Sunday services in poor and well-to-do parts of San Salvador, church halls were full, despite rain squalls. At the Gamaliel Taberna-cle, a new Baptist church set among well-appointed homes, the proceedings were unusually orderly for a culture that normally thrives on improvisation. Attendants in dark blue uniforms firmly directed worshipers where to sit or move. Outside, a church bookstall offered translations of American authors giving testimony or advice on self-improvement or how to make money.

There is no single theology or mission strategy in a movement as fractured as this, which involves large denominations and many small, independent offshoots. Evangelical leaders in the past have been circumspect about discussing their financing or organization with outsiders. But apparently emboldened by the broad conservative mood in the United States and their growing acceptance here, leaders have become more willing to talk about their strategy.

RELIGIOUS AND IDEOLOGICAL

The California-based Campus Crusade for Christ, an agency specializing in recruiting and training, channels converts to churches of the Pentecostal movement, which makes up three-fourths of the Protestants here. Its leaders say they regard their mission as both religious and ideological.

"Our main objective is to influence the university," said Manuel Martínez, an executive at the Campus Crusade for Christ. "All mass movements and revolutions begin there. The conflict we have in El Salvador today began in the universities."

But in 1980, one of El Salvador's more turbulent years, Campus Crusade mounted a nationwide drive called "The Spiritual Battle for El Salvador." As a pivot, it used an American-made film called "Jesus," which according to the drive's organizers, has been shown in more than 100 towns and villages to 250,000 people.

Adonai Leiva, the national director for Campus Crusade, said that after a film show or a street rally people who "react most positively to our message" are visited by "Christian brothers or Campus Crusade coordinators."

"In our methods and strategy we emphasize the personal contact," Mr. Leiva said. "We usually follow a person through visits and contacts for three months, like a soccer player follows the ball. Then, if the person still resists, we incorporate him into a cell, a small group that often meets for prayer and discussion. Of course not everyone lets you go all the way."

"WE WERE CALLED BY GOD"

Mr. Leiva conceded that the agency's tactics were not dissimilar to those used by its opponents on the left.

"The Marxists infiltrate the universities," he said. "So do we. Marxism is the first thing humanities students hear. It's planned that way. Therefore we try and get to them first. So we start work in high schools and prep schools."

The Marxists, Mr. Leiva continued, "also use the most effective methods, the personal approach, the small groups."

"They learned that from the Bible," he said. "But we were called by God."

Increasingly, preachers appear in remote refugee camps and villages where the short-handed Catholic clergy do not reach. In 1985, in a move apparently initiated by Washington, the local office of the United States Agency for International Development signed its first cooperation agreement here with a Protestant group to distribute food to refugees.

There are also signs that the Protestants are receiving encouragement from the armed forces. "We now preach in the barracks and the jails," said Edgardo Montano, a preacher with the Assemblies of God. "Before, only the priests could go there."

In Chalatenango Province recently, soldiers first helped out on a Protestant housing project, then the zone commander himself attended the inauguration. Asked whether this might identify the project with the army and leave it a target of the guerrillas operating nearby, the project director, the Rev. Edward Ward, said: "The army has had a murderous image for so long. It also deserves some good publicity."

CHAPTER IV

Salvadoran Politics at the Top: Duarte and the Right-Wing Opposition

Editors' Introduction

José Napoleón Duarte's admirers among the U.S. press corps in the Camino Real Hotel in San Salvador (where most of the newspapers and press agencies have offices) generally characterize him as a man who has made a "Faustian bargain" with history.[1] As a member of several of the post-1979 juntas and as President of the Republic since 1984, Duarte has been in office during the bloodiest period in recent Salvadoran history, when as many as 15,000 to 20,000 noncombatant civilians may have been massacred by the death squads and armed forces. He has had difficulty justifying his decision to stay in office under these circumstances, especially since members of his own Christian Democratic Party (PDC) defected when it became clear to them and to many people that PDC participation in the government did little to stop *government* terror, much of it directed against Christian Democrats themselves. Explaining these anomalies to a group of visiting U.S. academics early in 1985, Duarte said that the "normal increment of violent criminality" in a country like El Salvador with its traditional "culture of violence" would amount to about 300 to 500 apolitical, noncombat deaths each month.[2] The

---

[1] Marvin E. Gettleman, interview with U.S. correspondents, San Salvador, January 9, 1985.

[2] In the fall of 1984, Duarte gave journalists Marc Cooper and Greg Goldin the somewhat higher figure of 400 to 500 deaths per month. See their interview with Duarte, *Playboy* (November 1984).

periods in which the killings substantially rise over the "normal" level are accounted for by the simultaneously and, to Duarte, morally equivalent violent efforts of the guerrilla left and the oligarchic right. He obligingly sketched a graphic representation of his theory, which is reproduced here.

One main problem with positing any such equivalency between left and right, as the material presented in later chapters of this book indicates and as many observers[3] have noted, is the awesome numerical preponderance of death squad-initiated and government-caused killings over violence perpetrated by the left. Not only the quantity, but also the quality of violence in contemporary El Salvador, so graphically revealed in Craig Pyes's prize-winning *Albuquerque Journal* reportage (Reading 19), suggests that the most brutal deeds by far are committed by the right-wing forces associated with the National Republican Alliance (ARENA).

But Duarte's theory of the normal increment of Salvadoran violence, however shaky its basis in fact, makes perfect sense as an expression of his own "Faustian" pact with what he conceives of as intractable political reality in El Salvador, which includes a powerful right wing convinced that Duarte and everything he stands for are evil. His current position also represents part of the ideological heritage of Christian Democracy in El Salvador, which drew on traditional Roman Catholic teachings on social questions.[4] But there were social and historical reasons for the emergence of Christian Democracy in Latin America in the 1960s, when it appeared to be a palatable alternative to the option of left-wing revolution introduced to the region by Fidel Castro's 1959 revolution in Cuba.[5]

Despite these moderate aims, conservative groups in the Salvadoran oligarchy and military see Christian Democracy as a barely disguised form of subversive Marxism. What appears at first glance to be surprising is the support given to Duarte by the conservative Reagan administration, since the PDC's welfare-state reformism is precisely what the Reaganites claim to be battling against in the United States. But several factors help explain official Washington's backing of the PDC, backing that includes significant amounts

---

[3.] Tom Buckley, *Violent Neighbors: El Salvador, Central America and the United States* (New York, 1984), chapter 5 and p. 147; in Raymond Bonner, *Weakness and Deceit: U.S. Policy and El Salvador* (New York, 1984), 63, this knowledgeable journalist concludes that 90 percent of the civilian deaths in El Salvador since 1979 are the result of murders by the official armed forces!

[4.] See Reading 10.

[5.] Christian Democratic parties also appeared in western Europe at the end of World War II, with the covert (and sometimes not-so-covert) support of the United States, which was anxious to counter the growth of local Communist parties, enjoying considerable popular favor earned by their prominence in the anti-Nazi resistance struggles. See Gabriel Kolko, *The Politics of War: The World and United States Foreign Policy, 1943–1945* (New York, 1968), 436–39; Gabriel Kolko and Joyce Kolko, *The Limits of Power: The World and United States Foreign Policy, 1945–1954* (New York, 1972), chapter 6, especially pp. 147–51 (on the situation in Italy).

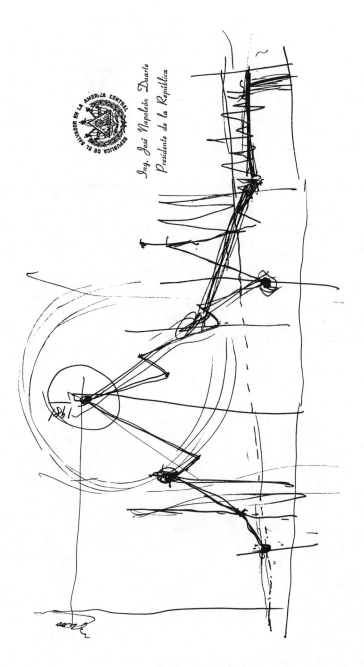

The curve of violence in El Salvador, as diagrammed by President Duarte, showing violence reaching its peak in 1981 and gradually tapering off in succeeding years.

of covert financial aid.[6] First, the price that Duarte had to pay for this backing, part of his "Faustian Pact," is the virtual abandonment of the Christian Democratic domestic-reform program, except as a rhetorical banner. This is one of the elements that make up what the author of Reading 21 calls "Duarte's Fix." A second factor explaining U.S. support for the PDC is that the alternative, backing the right-wing opposition, is less acceptable. Because of its terrorist activity and the unsavory reputation of some of its leaders—most notably, Roberto D'Aubuisson—this would be objectionable to all but a fringe of President Reagan's constituency.[7] But perhaps most important in understanding U.S. support for a Duarte is the long-term strategic design of U.S. foreign policy in the cold-war era, transcending political parties and administrations, to seek a "third force" in areas of the underdeveloped world experiencing economic dislocations and related political unrest stemming from long histories of repressive government. Conditions that spawn such unrest also invariably lead to the rise of Marxist-led armed insurgencies. The "third force" strategy is to back groups that will counter these leftist insurgents while avoiding the drawbacks of aiding right-wing repressive forces that further stimulate revolutionary opposition.

In El Salvador, this translates nicely into a policy of support for the Christian Democrats of José Napoleón Duarte, who with the endorsement of both Ronald Reagan and (perhaps reluctantly) the Salvadoran military, and barring assassination or other unforeseen developments, seems assured of retaining what power he has for at least the next few years.

16. At Home with José Napoleón Duarte*

By Tom Buckley

When he was interviewed by journalist Tom Buckley in 1981, José Napoleón Duarte had just become a member of the third military-civilian junta in the kaleidoscopic sequence of Salvadoran politics that followed the overthrow of General Carlos Humberto Romero in 1979. At that time, the Christian Democratic vision of social justice through such measures as land reform animated his conversation. A half decade later, backed by the Salvadoran armed forces and the Reagan administration, and now President of El Salvador, Duarte has narrowed his options. Even though the level of terror is currently diminished, his inability in the past to discipline the death squads, and to prevent the

[6.] On this, see Bonner, *Weakness and Deceit,* 170–71, 221–28, 241–42, and Buckley, *Violent Neighbors,* 303–15.

[7.] See Jeane Kirkpatrick's defense of authoritarian regimes in Reading 2.

* From chapter 6 of Tom Buckley, *Violent Neighbors: El Salvador, Central America and the United States* (New York: Times Books, 1984).

massacres of thousands of leftists, peasant organizers, and trade unionists, still haunts him. Land reform, once the keystone of PDC policy, has been virtually abandoned.[1] *Despite his 1984 electoral victory, his support from the U.S. embassy, his dramatic proposal at the United Nations for an end to the civil war in his country (see Reading 55), Duarte still has serious problems. The oligarchs snipe from the right, and the insurgents maintain their opposition on the left, going so far as to kidnap his daughter in late 1985 (see Reading 41). Duarte's hold on power may be only marginally better than it was when he had drinks with Tom Buckley in Escalón.*

Buckley, who reported for the New York Times *from Vietnam in the 1960s and 1970s, believes that there is little hope for El Salvador or the other countries of Central America and the Caribbean while the White House is occupied by someone like Ronald Reagan, who ignores the need for dramatic changes in the economic and political systems of the region.*

THE International Press Club was established at the Camino Real Hotel in San Salvador in March, 1981, while I was staying there. To mark the occasion, the management of the hotel provided free drinks. It was an act of generosity so entirely without precedent in the hotel's history that the clock in the lobby stopped.

The party had been in progress for an hour or so when Duarte arrived unexpectedly. He was in an ebullient mood. The guerrillas were licking their wounds, the populace had shown its loyalty to the government, and the weapons and advisers needed to suppress the rebellion were arriving on every plane. For 40 minutes Duarte responded, forcefully but amiably, to questions. When he had finished and was sipping a scotch, I introduced myself, told him that I was writing a long article about El Salvador for *The New Yorker,* and asked for an appointment.

"How about now?" he said. "Come on home with me."

I asked if I might invite two colleagues, and he agreed. We left the hotel shortly after 9:00 P.M. in a convoy of three armored sedans and station wagons, escorted by four motorcycle police. The curfew had just fallen, and the moon-bathed streets were empty and silent. Good citizens sat behind locked doors and drawn curtains, watching dubbed American sitcoms or Mexican soap operas on television. In their shacks, the poor lay down on their mats in the darkness and prayed that they would live to see the light of the morning.

Duarte lived on a treelined street in Escalón. The house was concealed behind a 15-foot brick wall topped with barbed wire. It was illuminated by floodlights and guarded by soldiers. Duarte led us inside, introduced us to his wife, one of his daughters, and a couple of grandchildren, and then escorted us onto the patio. It was a pleasant and roomy dwelling, but only a humble shelter compared with the mansions of the oligarchs in the vicinity.

[1.] Duarte admitted this to one of the editors of this volume in an interview at the presidential palace, San Salvador, January 1985.

Little had been written about Duarte, at that time, and not much since. I asked him to start at the beginning of his life and go on from there.

"The beginning is that I was born in San Salvador in November, 1925," he said, sipping a scotch and Coke that his military aide had poured for him. "I was the second son. My father came from a little town in Chalatenango. He was apprenticed to a tailor and took tickets in a movie theatre at night. My mother was—how do you say it?—a *modiste,* a dressmaker. She was from Santa Ana in the western part of the country. They had come to San Salvador to make a better life for themselves. They met, and they got married. By the time I was born, my father had opened his own custom tailoring shop. It was right across the street from the Casino Salvadoreño, the best men's club in the city. Many of the members were his clients. They knew his suits were just as well made as any that they could have bought in London or New York.

"In 1928, my father was elected president of the San Salvador Society of Artisans," he went on. "It wasn't a union, but an association of craftsmen. The society was mainly social and philanthropic, but conditions were very bad in 1932, and the members decided to back Arturo Araújo in the presidential election that year. When Hernández Martínez took over, he arrested all of Araújo's leading supporters, including my father. They were in jail for weeks, hundreds of them. Every day the guards would lead out a group of prisoners and tell them they were going to be shot, but they would shoot only one or two and send the others back to their cells. After a couple of weeks of that, my father and the others who hadn't been shot were freed. He tried to reopen his tailor shop, but Hernández Martínez sent two policemen to stand at the door. Everyone was afraid to go in. My father lost his clientele. He had to start from zero again.

"What he did was, he and my mother began to make candies at a little stove in the kitchen," Duarte continued. "Hard candies, toffee, things like that. The wrappers had little sayings or mottoes on them. No one had done that before, and they sold very well. He was able to increase his capital little by little. He bought candy-making machinery and hired people to work for him."

The parents did well enough to send their three sons, Rolando, who is a year and half older than José Napoleón, and Alejandro, to the Liceo Salvadoreño, which was run by the Brothers of the Holy Cross and was second in prestige in the city to the Jesuit school.

"I was a senior in 1944, when the people finally decided they wanted to get rid of Hernández Martínez," Duarte said. "Everyone went on strike, and we said we were going on strike, too. Our teachers warned us that if we did, we would be punished, but we went ahead anyhow. We marched in the demonstrations, and nothing happened to us. My father, though, stayed at home. He said he had had enough of politics.

"Our parents were very ambitious for us," Duarte continued. "My father always said, 'I want you to be big men, to excel.' He knew that if you wanted to be someone in our world, in El Salvador, you had to learn English and study abroad. He wanted us to learn something about American institutions and American business. The head of the *liceo* said he thought we could get scholarships at Notre Dame. Rolando went there in 1943. The next year so did I.

"I'll say this for Notre Dame—it taught me to have guts. Rolando and I didn't speak a word of English when we got there, so we had to study twice as hard. At the same time, I worked in the laundry. Later on I served in the cafeteria, and then I washed dishes. I got up at five A.M. and went to bed at midnight. I even tried out for the freshman football team. I had played soccer and basketball at the *liceo,* but not American football. One reason I wanted to go to Notre Dame was that the football team used to be in the newsreels we would see here. Anyhow, I went on the field, and they threw the ball to me. I caught it and ran about 20 meters, and then—boom!—I got hit by some great big guy."

He smacked his fist into his palm to illustrate his obliteration under one of the 220-pound tackles from the Pennsylvania coal region whom the Fighting Irish used to recruit.

"Boom!" he repeated, and laughed. "That was the end of my football."

At that, Duarte has the build of a football player or a brewery worker. He is about five feet 10 inches and 190 pounds, broad-shouldered and barrel-chested. He has acquired a bit of a belly, which may be why he wears a *guayabera,* a fancy short-sleeved shirt that is worn outside the trousers. His head is massive and set on a thick neck. His brown eyes are deep-set under upward-slanting eyebrows. He has a splendidly arched nose and a granitic chin with the hint of a cleft. His cheekbones are broad and high. The injuries that he suffered in 1972 have been corrected by plastic surgery. Duarte's hair is still thick and jet black, and his skin has the faintest coppery burnish. Almost every Salvadoran has at least a trace of Indian blood, and while, overall, Duarte's appearance is very Spanish, these details suggest that he probably does, too. His English is lightly accented and idiomatic, although he sometimes has to grope for *le mot juste.*

I mentioned that I had heard somewhere that his father had financed his entry into the candy business with a big prize in the national lottery.

"Not exactly," he replied. "He was already in the candy business and doing very well when he won the lottery. It was in 1944, the year I went away to Notre Dame. He won 40,000 colones [about $16,000]. He gave the ticket to his closest friend, José María Durán, and said, 'Here, go and collect the money for me. This is my new house.' Don José was also a poor boy from the country. He started as a carpenter and became a very successful contractor. He was also my father-in-law—he is dead now. When I got back from Notre Dame with my degree in civil engineering, I married his daughter Inés and went into business with him. His family lived next to us all the while I was growing up.

I am two years older than she is, so I can honestly say I have known her all my life."

If the sons or cousins of the oligarchy had been engineers and contractors, Durán-Duarte, as the firm was called, would have been building chicken coops, but they weren't, so the firm had a chance to get major contracts, and it prospered. Among its projects, Duarte said, were the Central Bank, a five-story Art Deco structure; the Bloom Hospital, one of the few privately endowed charitable institutions in the country; and the unfinished cathedral.

Duarte was a joiner and a booster, and it was his community activities, which are by no means as frequently undertaken in Latin America as they are in the United States, that eventually led him into politics.

"I was in the Boy Scouts, and I am still a member of the international training committee," he said. "When I went in the Boy Scouts, I took an oath, and it made a great impression on me. I've always been interested since that time in service. I used to be active in the Red Cross and the Anti-Tuberculosis Society and even the volunteer firemen. I traveled all over Central America founding chapters of the Twenty-Thirty Club. It's like the Kiwanis and the Rotary, dedicated to service, but for men between 20 and 30.

"It was because I have always been a man of concepts and principles that I decided to enter politics. One day in 1960, I was invited by a friend of mine to attend a meeting of a group that discussed the social doctrines of the church that you could find in the encyclicals like Leo XIII's *Rerum Novarum*. I began comparing what was being said with what I believed and with what I saw around me. In this country, which then had a population of 3,000,000, fewer than 100,000 people had any privileges at all. There were fewer than 2,000 teachers in the entire country. From that time I decided to form a political force to look for a solution to the country's problems."

That force turned out to be the Christian Democratic party. Its model was the reformist capitalist parties of that name in Western Europe.

"You must realize that until then there were no political solutions, no real political parties in El Salvador, only coups d'état," Duarte said. "The Christian Democrats represented an electoral solution. All the political intellectuals said we were crazy, but we decided to take part in the elections of 1962 against the whole machinery of government. They got 450,000 votes, we got 37,000 . . . something like that. We didn't give up. We kept working and in 1964 tried again. We won 37 mayors' offices, including San Salvador, which I won by 500 votes.

"I did things for the people. I went to the electric company, which was then owned by Canadians. I told them I wanted streetlights, which we had in only a few parts of the city, for everyone. I showed them how we could pay for them from the taxes I was collecting. They said no. So I went to a friend of mine and asked him to build a factory to make the poles and fixtures. When the electric company saw what I was doing, it changed its mind. When the lights went into service, people went out in the streets to dance. It was like a fiesta. They danced all night. The lights completely changed the attitude of the people. After that, every city and all the little towns in the country were demanding streetlights, too.

"I wanted to build a central market building," he continued. "We had never had one. When the national government found out what I was going to do, they took it away from me and did it themselves, to try to get the credit for it. It was the same with the Communitarian Action organization. I went to the poor people. I listened to them. I tried to help. When the government saw how successful it was, they made it a part of the presidential office and stopped doing anything."

This program of decentralization of authority, the creation of neighborhood organizations able to carry out self-help projects, is the heart of the doctrine of communitarianism, which was evolved by a Chilean philosopher, Jaime Castillo. Duarte has published a book by that title. Another of its exponents is Luis Herrera Campíns, the president of Venezuela. In the United States, the town meeting and neighborly cooperation date back to the Pilgrim Fathers, but communitarianism was a revolutionary doctrine in Latin America, where bossism is far more pervasive, corrupt, and violent than it has ever been in the United States, and is based on family and personal loyalties. Since colonial days, it has been customary for a local political leader, or *cacique,* to agree to become the godfather of scores, perhaps hundreds, of children. Godfatherhood establishes a patron-client relationship that often continues for generations.

"The question is 'What is a community?' " Duarte went on, in explaining communitarianism. "A family is a community, but a town is just a vicinity unless the inhabitants are connected to each other in some way. If you provide the connections so that the people can join together in dealing with social problems, you have created a community. The idea is for them to do as much as they can and leave to the municipality only the services, such as garbage collection, and capital investments, like public markets or streetlighting, that they cannot do efficiently or because they are too expensive.

"I went over the books, and I found out that the Regalado Dueñas family, the richest family in the country, hadn't paid their garbage or water taxes in 30 years," Duarte said. "There were a lot of families like that. I went around and collected from them—sometimes I did it myself—and used the money for community action. When I presented them with the bills, they got very angry at me. They said, 'Mr. Duarte is going to suffer because he is *touching* us.'

"When I was running for my second term, Tomás Regalado [Ernesto's father] invited me to his house. I had never been there before. No one I knew had. Three or four of the richest men in the city were there. They gave me a big drink, and we talked for a while. Then Don Tomás asked me to come upstairs with him. He said he wanted to show me a painting, but what he wanted to do was to talk to me about how I could serve them—the oligarchs.

How much did I want to resign and take a job with them? Whatever I needed they would give me. They would ask only one thing: that I drop out of politics. I said, 'Thank you for the offer, but no. . . .' I left the house and I never went back."

Speaking of the 1972 election, Duarte, between sips of another scotch, said, "We knew that the official party [the PCN] would try to cheat us, and they did, but they made a miscalculation. They had brought in polling experts, just like you have in the United States. The experts said that we would get about 200,000 votes, so they figured their cheating on that basis. They thought 300,000 would give them a great victory. But we got 324,000, and they had to stop counting the vote and go back to all the little towns and villages where they were in complete control. They still had only 316,000, so they just took 9,000 away from us and gave it to themselves. When my people found out what happened, they gathered in the streets. One word from me, and they would have burned down the city, but I told them, 'I believe in democracy. I don't believe in turmoil or violent solutions. You must be patient.' "

Duarte obviously didn't enjoy talking about Mejía's attempted coup. A shadow fell across his lively brown eyes. He was uncharacteristically evasive and, at some points, inexact in describing his role. The reason might have been that he now agreed that he should have acted more decisively.

"The police violated diplomatic privilege to arrest me," Duarte said. "They dragged me out of the house of a Venezuelan diplomat and took me to the central police headquarters with my hands handcuffed behind my back. I was blindfolded, and my mouth was covered with adhesive tape. They left me in the car for a while, and then they came back, one by one, no one saying a word, and began to beat me. They used their fists, blackjacks, brass knuckles, a pistol butt. I could feel the shape of whatever they were beating me with. They beat me unconscious in complete silence. Then they dragged me, still blindfolded, to a cell. When I came to, they began questioning me. They wanted to know how we got the money for the campaign. Was it supplied by the Communists? Because they had spent millions, they thought we had spent millions. I thought in the end they would kill me, but they threw me in a plane and flew me to Guatemala."

It was only after he got to Caracas that he was reunited with his wife and their younger children. He had plastic surgery for his facial injuries, and aside from a suggestion of bruises on his cheekbones and scars that are lost in the lines of his face, he bears no obvious marks of the beating. Most of the last joint of the three inner fingers of his left hand are missing. There is a persistent rumor that they were clipped off while he was in custody, although as a technique of torture it seemed far too subtle for the Salvadoran police. Duarte assured us that he had lost them as the result of an accident at a construction site in the Venezuelan hinterland.

"In 1974, I was notified that I could return to El Salvador," he said. "When

I arrived at the airport here, hundreds, maybe thousands of my friends were there to meet me. I returned to Caracas to help the family pack. Then I got another message from our embassy—I could not return after all. Why did they change their mind? Because they thought that by then I would be forgotten, but when they saw what happened at the airport, they knew I had not been.

"In the election of 1977, we decided to try a new formula to show the military we weren't against them," he said. "So we nominated Claramount for president and Morales Ehrlich for vice-president. Once again we knew the other side would try to rob us. This time I was not so naïve. If the United States government would say something, it might make a difference. I flew to Washington and met with Senator Kennedy and Vice-President Mondale. Neither one could give me much time. With Mondale it was 'Hello,' and then a photographer appeared."

Duarte's voice became distant and ironic, and he mimed the pushing together of the two men, the synthetic smiles, the handshake, and the sudden glare of the strobe light.

"After that, 'Good-bye.' I have the photograph still. I tried to arrange a meeting with the staff assistants of members of Congress. I am told they are very influential. The Republicans wouldn't talk to us at all. But we expected 20 or 30 Democrats at the meeting. We had . . . three! A lunch for newspaper people . . . five! We were trying to be heard; but nobody would listen, and the fraud this time was complete."

Duarte returned to Washington to protest the theft. He received a hearing before the House Foreign Affairs Committee, but for all the good it did him or the Christian Democrats he might just as well have spoken to the walls of his hotel room. In his testimony, Duarte pointed out the obvious—that nonintervention amounted to an endorsement of a corrupt and repressive government. "The United States, at this moment," he went on to say, "has an historic duty . . . [to] support those basic principles which form the basis of the so-called American way of life."

The first time that an American official got in touch with him, Duarte said, was in August or September, 1979, which was, not coincidentally, a month or two after the triumph of the Sandinistas in Nicaragua and at a time when the Romero government in El Salvador was already shaky. He had a visit in Caracas, he said, from Viron P. Vaky, then the Assistant Secretary of State for Inter-American Affairs. Duarte said that Vaky discussed the likelihood of Romero's overthrow. (Vaky later told me he had no idea that anything in the way of a coup was being planned.) Duarte said he made clear his opposition, as a matter of principle, to coups d'état, and advanced a program of his own.

"I said I had a formula so that Romero would accept a dialogue and that the Christian Democrats would wait until the elections for the National Assembly in 1980. All parties would then enter the government, and we would prepare for a presidential election in 1982."

Duarte said that his plan was scuttled by the leftists, who were the dominant civilian element in the first junta, and by the church, particularly the Jesuits who were Archbishop Romero's most trusted advisers. Their objective, Duarte said, was to head off the possibility of compromise with the center, as exemplified by his segment of the Christian Democrats, and the moderate right. He charged that the first junta resigned after only three months in office to precipitate a crisis.

"I found documents explaining why they had done so," Duarte said, without describing them further. "They wanted to end pluralism, to break up all the democratic possibilities, and, by letting the military rule, which is what they thought would happen, to create a civilian-military confrontation. We [the Christian Democrats] didn't want that, so we accepted the challenge of trying to govern. Mr. Ungo has lost his mind. He's lost his democratic concepts. He will accept no alternatives. He refused an invitation from the Christian Democrats to remain in the government. The left has lost the people, but the war will have to go on until the people isolate both the far left and the far right."

Duarte rejected the opinion expressed by Ungo and other officials of the Democratic Revolutionary Front, many of whom were old friends of his, that his long exile had put him hopelessly out of touch with developments in El Salvador and that he preferred to ignore the fact that the Christian Democrats had split down the middle. In their view, vanity, which Duarte, like most men in public life, has an adequate supply of, had reacted with disappointment to produce a corrosive compound that had eaten away at his judgment.

"I'm carrying out political change; but I'm doing it intelligently, and it can't be done overnight," he said. "The army, as an institution, is willing to accept political solutions, but the others, the National Guard and the National Police, have been trained for 50 years to do it the other way, and it will take time to change them."

Duarte said that he could already see a decline in the support that the *campesinos* were willing to give to the guerrillas. "The difference was the land reform," he said. "I spoke for it as long ago as when President Kennedy announced the Alliance for Progress. The political concept is simple—to take away the power of the *hacienda* owners and give it to the *campesinos.* Both the extreme right and the left tried to stop the land reform, but they failed, and if you look at the places where the guerrillas are strong now, the regions along the Honduran border, you will see that these are also the places where there were few *haciendas* to expropriate."

He finished a drink and stopped his aide from pouring him another. "There is no such thing as inevitability or historical determinism," he said, emphasizing his words by bringing down his fist and then stopping when he recalled the top of the table was made of glass. "You can change the laws of history by having the right people in the right place doing the right thing. I think I was selected by my people to be president in 1972. Now I have a second chance. The situation is very different. I have more enemies, and much of the world is against me, but I think we will succeed."

17. Promoting Democratization and Economic Vitalization*

By José Napoleón Duarte

Delivering the Salvadoran version of a state-of-the-union address in June of 1985, President Duarte touched on several major domestic as well as international and diplomatic issues. The speech was delivered in Salvadoran National Assembly, with key legislators, magistrates, foreign dignitaries, and representatives of the armed forces in the audience. In chapter 10 we will present his views on the important issue of "dialogue" between the Salvadoran government and the rebels. Here, we offer Duarte's appraisal of the nonmilitary aspects of the country's plight, even though in candid moments he could admit that "the war [that] accounts for 800 million colones[1] of our [yearly] budget . . . has become more important than the garbage department, public employees . . . drilling wells, providing [food] subsidies, and all the rest."[2]

As is usual in addresses of these kinds, whether delivered in San Salvador, Washington, Beijing, or Moscow, the speaker usually accentuates the positive achievements and hopeful prospects; the intractable difficulties (especially when they are in great measure due to the activities of members of the very audience before him) are usually slurred over.

Yet these difficulties are enormous, and they have resulted in drastic austerity measures, including devaluation of the currency and sharply increased gasoline prices. Announcing this austerity program early in 1986, Duarte sweetened matters by pledging to subsidize such basic consumer goods as corn, beans, cooking oil, rice, milk, and salt and raising the minimum wages for farmworkers. Permitting these economic concessions was a doubling of prices for Salvadoran coffee, due to crop failures elsewhere in Latin America, which will bring in the equivalent of several million unexpected dollars in the next two years. When such windfall benefits are removed, the prospects for the Salvadoran economy are bleak.

---

* Address to the National Assembly, June 1, 1985, Spanish text in *ECA/Estudios Centroamericanos,* 34 (May–June 1985), translated by the editors.

[1] Before recent measures an artificially low rate of 2.5 colones to the dollar was set to subsidize important petroleum and agricultural imports. The rate used in ordinary transactions was 4.85 colones to the dollar. In early 1986, the Duarte administration set a single rate of 5 colones. See James LeMoyne's dispatch from San Salvador in the *New York Times,* January 23, 1986.

[2] Duarte's remarks to provincial governors and mayors, as broadcast on San Salvador Radio, February 3, 1986, in Foreign Broadcast Information Service, *Daily Reports,* February 5, 1986.

UPON completing the first year of my tenure as constitutional president of the republic and general commander of the armed forces, I want to address you regarding the country's general situation. . . . [M]y message [describes] . . . the situation we are experiencing and the efforts we make so that El Salvador can succeed and we can decide our own fate. These efforts are contained in five major objectives, which I will discuss.

[We omit here the first two parts of Duarte's speech, covering "humanization of the conflict" in his country and the processes of "dialogue" and "pacification." His views on these subjects are spelled out elsewhere in this volume. —Eds.]

Third, democratization. When I assumed the presidency of the republic, I said that my government would promote the democratic process by encouraging the participation of democratic organizations in the new pluralist system established in the constitution of the republic. This has been possible thanks to the people's decisive support and to the strengthening of the institutions, particularly the armed forces, which has not only served to demonstrate an extraordinary moral and technical conduct in the struggle against subversion, but has also become the bulwark of the democratic system and a decisive factor in supporting the legally established government in the search for peace and a general solution to the country's problems.

This is what the people have hoped for and what they have expected from the armed forces. Today it has come true.

My commitment to democracy is based on a lifelong struggle on behalf of democracy and an absolute rejection of violence as a means to reach power. My ideal of democracy is not a static or cut-and-dried concept. It is dynamic, realistic, and participative with a profound humane dimension. To take advantage of democracy to manipulate men for economic, political, or ideological exploitation is to distort the real meaning of democracy. Therefore, I am pleased to see our country slowly but firmly moving toward an authentic democracy. In a recent letter to the Assembly, even the terrorists admitted the legitimacy and representativeness of the legislative branch as the result of the electoral processes and the people's will, and not as an imposition through the use of arms and violence. The international recognition of the progress we have made in this respect, which was obtained as a result of my trips to Europe, the United States, and Latin America, is the recognition of our institutional legitimacy obtained through the people's massive participation in the four elections we have held. In this manner, we have complied with the democratization of a government that governs.

Fourth, participation. Democracy is based on the people's participation in the government's decisions. That is why after I aspired to be President of the Salvadorans and was elected by the people, I agreed to sign a social pact with everyone based on making the participation of all sectors effective so that together we can work to achieve peace, full democracy, and social justice. The social pact is not a pact of interests. It is a bundle of will to attain social goals so that we can all forge ahead in harmony. This social pact implies the understanding and participation of all sectors in a permanent dialogue that will make possible the prevention of a social conflict so that together we can promote a feeling of solidarity for the good of our country.

Once again I urge all sectors to work conscientiously together on behalf of the country's dearest interests. However, we are all aware of the trade-union strikes that are taking place. Under the pretext of making labor demands, these strikes have an indisputable political background.

I have always believed in democratic trade unionism because it is a well-deserved gain by the workers. The trade unions are the channels of participation in the process and in the material and spiritual development of the peoples. What is unacceptable is for those channels to be used to manipulate people's needs. When the trade unions are infiltrated and used to promote war and destabilization, they lose their social function and the people's confidence. This is the sad, unjust objective planned by the FMLN/FDR, which we discovered in documents seized in Morazán from rebels who had surrendered and also found on the person of terrorist Nidia Díaz. . . .[3]

I must mention that many of the evils we are fighting today have been the result of the lack of social discipline in previous years. It is necessary that we realize that obeying the law is indispensable to having social harmony. We all know that we have a war economy, a large fiscal deficit, and a currency shortage; that half of our budget goes for national defense; that terrorism has greatly damaged our economic structure; that there is high unemployment; that there are almost no private or state investments; that as a result of the conflict the private sector has reduced job opportunities; and that we are facing a critical situation, and in order to overcome it we must make great efforts and sacrifices.

Under these circumstances, to demand outrageous wage increases and benefits that do not conform to reality is really unreasonable and shows a lack of patriotism. For this reason, I appeal to all Salvadoran workers to understand the country's difficult situation and make an effort not to help aggravate the crisis. The terrorists have publicly unveiled their intentions by appealing to workers to strike and cause disorder. However, I have faith and confidence that the workers will not heed or follow radical trade-union leaders because the workers understand that destabilization only weakens the democratic process, impedes the consolidation of the reform, and makes the struggle for the masses and the creation of jobs impossible, thus failing to meet the needs of thousands of jobless workers. Through participation we are trying to create a political

[3.] María Concepción de Valladares, whose *nom de guerre* was Nidia Díaz, was a high-ranking commander in the Revolutionary Party of Central American Workers (PRTC), one of the groups in the FMLN. Four months later she was exchanged for Duarte's daughter, Inés Guadalupe Duarte, whom the rebels had kidnapped in September. See Reading 41.—Eds.

space without clashes or confrontations. We act judiciously yet firmly because this is a true government.

Fifth, economic reactivation. I have established a process to stabilize our economy by facing the problems that affect most of our people. Our plans include the creation of new jobs for the thousands of jobless and to keep those who have jobs in them. I want to mention some of our efforts toward economic reactivation. As part of our economic reactivation program, on 14 May I announced specific ordinances that will benefit the national coffee-growing industry and all small, medium, and large coffee growers. This measure is necessary today more than ever to improve financing for coffee growing in order to preserve and strengthen one of our country's most important production structures. Thanks to the 600 million colones granted to us above former years' financing, this industry will employ more than 300,000 workers.

In addition, we have issued similar ordinances to help cotton growers, who also have suffered the impact of the crisis. Regarding sugar cane, it not only stabilized, but cultivation acreage increased. We have also issued specific instructions regarding basic grains. We have set up credit lines for more than 500 million colones. In addition, mechanisms have been expedited so that growers of basic grains have easy access to bank credits. It is important to point out that the grain growers have a sure credit and market. For this reason, we have speeded up the operation of the institute for the regulation of supplies and ordered the Agricultural and Livestock Development Bank, the Federation of Credit Institutions, and the Mortgage Bank, as well as the rest of the banking system, to cooperate in this marketing effort.

Regarding livestock, at the beginning of this month and during the inauguration of the Central American livestock exposition I said that this field deserves special attention. Cattlemen can rely on this government's cooperation. We have proudly confirmed the improved quality of this country's cattle breeds.

Agrarian reform requires consolidation. We have succeeded in breaking the legal stagnation of this sector, and 31 other estates have been returned to their former owners. These estates are worth approximately 38 million colones. In addition Salvadoran Institute of Agrarian Transformation [ISTA] has delivered 28 other farms to as many cooperatives. As part of the government's economic policy, it is worthwhile to stress that necessary measures have been taken to ensure the public expense's austerity and rationalization without increasing the 1984 general budget. By sacrificing other operational and investment expenses, the salaries of more than 149,000 public workers were increased by more than 130 colones monthly in July, thus benefiting their families.

As you can see, we have been concerned over state workers. Therefore, we made an effort and raised their salaries. We want to make our contribution so that social justice can be attained in this country. Public workers life insurance coverage was increased by 50 percent from 10,000 to 15,000 colones. In December, retirement and pension benefits for the central government's civil and military workers were increased proportionately. Some pensions for less than 100 colones were increased to 525 colones. A minimum of 150 colones per month was established for all retirement payments. This corrected the cases of many retired people who received 8 colones per month for many years because this adjustment had not been made for more than 50 years.

The tax policy centered its efforts on identifying new taxpayers. Tax registers were improved. The fiscal program was broadened. Taxpayers received assistance in the payment of their back taxes and procedures used by the tax administration were speeded up. The public credit policy was aimed at containing rapid indebtedness and achieving a rational utilization of domestic and foreign financing sources to contract for the strictly indispensable obligations to foster public investment and economic reactivation. The government, aware that the population's true income continues to be affected by inflation related phenomena, has speeded up the stabilization and price mechanisms. For this reason and becasue of a late charge regarding prices of some medicines, I have ordered the economy minister to open a public hearing to discuss this and make the necessary decisions.

The industrial sector, which is considered one of the strongest pillars in the economic reactivation policy, has received fiscal benefits to foster productive activities. The national industry has been protected and the consumption of our products has been urged and fostered. The organization, fostering, and development of the economy's nonformal sector has received priority treatment. Technical, financial, and managerial assistance has been given to this sector, as well as commercialization assistance, thus stressing its potential. We have taken into consideration that this sector is the one that provides the largest number of jobs in our country because this is a true government that thinks about the majority.

Salvadoran people, friends, the country's problems are many and difficult. Through the humanization of the armed conflict, we strive for our nation's pacification, the democratization of our society, the people's participation in the nation's activities at all levels, and the reactivation of the national economy. We do this because this is a true government. Therefore, this is a suitable opportunity to ask all sectors of the country to join forces and participate in this process to strengthen the five political aspects that I have outlined because we can forge ahead only in unity. Salvadoran people: I would like to invite all of you to feel that if the crisis that lashes at us is special, then the characteristics of our effort and willingness for work will also be special.

At this time, as El Salvador is living through one of its history's most dramatic chapters, I ask God, with all the force of my Christian conviction, to help me and give me the necessary moral strength to be firm and to always keep aloft the flag of faith and hope to keep asking for all Salvadorans' common unity and effort. I ask for help to be able to lead our homeland to a higher well-being, justice, democracy, freedom, and peace. If we have faith and are willing to struggle and work together, victory will be ours. Salvadoran people, government, Legislative Assembly, Supreme Court of Justice officials, members of the diplomatic corps, ministers of state, armed-forces members, Salvadoran people, thank you very much.

18. ARENA: The Salvadoran Right's Conception of Nationalism and Justice*

BY MAJOR ROBERTO D'AUBUISSON

The word fascism *is a term not to be thrown about lightly in the manner of careless soapbox orators; yet the ARENA party in El Salvador seemed, at least until its mid-1985 housecleaning, to be a reasonable facsimile of a Central American fascist organization. ARENA is the Spanish acronym for National Republican Alliance. In the classic European fascist parties, extreme nationalism and militarism were main ideological principles.* [1] *Roberto D'Aubuisson and other ARENA spokespeople stress the role of their party as upholder of Salvadoran nationalism and the honor of the military and are widely believed to be closely associated with the death squads and with the assassination of Archbishop Oscar Romero.* [2]

But if ARENA represents fascism in El Salvador, it is in a form different from the great power fascism of Nazi Germany. Although D'Aubuisson sometimes claims to be defending all the Americas against the Communist onslaught, [3] *there is also clearly a realistic acceptance of El Salvador's small-nation status, the country's power clearly circumscribed by tiny territorial extent, relatively small population, and weak economy. It may be that in the comparative analysis of fascism, a category must be reserved for small-power fascism. But this should not obscure the danger if even such a diminutive country as El Salvador becomes the trigger of a far larger conflict, particularly if great powers like the United States act on the belief that their national security requires outside support for the suppression of rebel challenges.*

* Statement presented to El Salvador's General Electoral Council meeting at the Salvadoran Center for Legal Studies, January 24, 1984, in U.S. Central Intelligence Agency, Foreign Broadcast Information Service, *Daily Reports—Central America,* February 22, 1984, 4–6. Text slightly rearranged and condensed.

1. On European fascism and Nazism, see Ernst Nolte, *Three Faces of Fascism,* trans. Leila Vennewitz (New York: Holt, Rinehart, and Winston, 1966); and John Weiss, *The Fascist Tradition* (New York: Harper & Row, 1967).
2. See Tom Buckley, *Violent Neighbors: El Salvador, Central America and the United States* (New York: Times Books, 1984), 5, 29; Raymond Bonner, *Weakness and Deceit: U.S. Policy and El Salvador* (New York: Times Books, 1984), 178, 204, 249, 309, 333, for judicious reviews of the available evidence.
3. D'Aubuisson, quoted in Buckley, *Violent Neighbors,* 11.

In this selection, ARENA's aims and ideology in the 1984 electoral campaign are set forth in a revealing and obviously spontaneous declaration by D'Aubuisson: intense nationalism, devout piety toward private enterprise, passionate hatred of the left, barely veiled justifications of terror and violence as legitimate means of political action, and several notions bordering on the bizarre. Surprisingly from a Salvadoran politican backed by such conservative North American figures as Senator Jesse Helms of North Carolina, [4] there is more than an undercurrent of hostility to the United States, some of whose policy suggestions are seen from the ARENA perspective as akin to Communism! ARENA lost the election to the candidate favored by the United States, José Napoleón Duarte, and his Christian Democratic Party, and subsequently disintegrated into squabbling factions. The pugnacious D'Aubuisson was replaced as ARENA chieftain by softspoken agro-export businessman, Alfredo Christiani, who evidently hopes to moderate the party's damaging reputation as a violent, possibly fascist organization. [5]

AS a nationalist, I want to offer in this most important forum the interpretation of what members of ARENA feel. Let us not delude ourselves regarding the situation that we are experiencing. The problem that is facing El Salvador is not [only] that this country is a target of international communism. We are guinea pigs. The two great world powers have come here to confront one another. The United States, the defender of our freedom, has come here to carry out alien experiments without even asking us if we wanted to be part of those experiments. They have come here to play with trilateralism. [6] They have come here to experiment with a number of other activities. They are supplying the weapons and the money for this confrontation, and unfortunately we Salvadorans are supplying the blood and the destruction of our people and of our fatherland. Based on this reality, we must respond to those two currents that are confronting each other here and that are playing and experimenting with us. . . .

On the topic of corruption, administrative corruption . . . must be fought. It is an evil that has developed gradually. There have been countries that have fallen into total chaos or are at the brink of failure because of corruption that has become almost institutionalized. However, the worst kind of corruption, in our view as National Republicans, is the nationalizations and state confiscations. [7] That is the worst germ of administrative corruption, because when there is nationalization, or state confiscation, corruption becomes routine.

Another kind of corruption that has become very widespread and harmful for our country is to allow intervention in the internal affairs of our people,

[4.] Buckley, *Violent Neighbors,* 103.

[5.] For recent changes in ARENA and in its leadership, see Infopress Centroamericana, *Central American Report* [Guatemala City], 12 (40; October 18, 1985), 318–19.

[6.] D'Aubuisson's reference here is to the multinational Trilateral Commission, consisting of representatives of industrialized nations. —Eds.

[7.] D'Aubuisson is apparently attacking here the agrarian-reform program in El Salvador.— Eds.

in our domestic affairs.[8] This kind of corruption, this surrendering, gentlemen, is the most harmful of all.

Corruption at the national level is highly dangerous because this corruption, together with the misinformation campaign of the great international Marxist plague, could place El Salvador in a very critical situation. It is corruption to allow this war to go on. Corruption is not having the courage to admit that we are in a state of war. We have been at war for four years already. Corruption is to allow it [to go on] by talking about things that are no longer comprehensible to us Nationalists, such as negotiating, holding dialogues, or forming a different government.[9]

It is corruption to allow this war for the financial benefit of those who supply us with weapons and those who are supplying the other side; those who are giving us loans, donations and a number of other things. They are making money, and that is also corruption.

As to justice, [it] . . . has been linked to respect for human rights. . . . I have heard how many deaths this war has caused, but I have not heard that those dead include some 2,000 young men of our Armed Forces. Where is the justice for those whose throats have been cut, as in the case of Colonel Baquerano in El Paraíso? Where was the clamor against the bombs that these terrorists placed in an unarmed civilian light plane that was carrying women and children? Where were the defenders of justice when the mother and daughters of a family in Aguilares were raped and the entire family killed? Only a young lady who was bathing in the river at that time was saved. Why did the guerrillas kill them? Because that lady was serving the troops that were on duty on Guazapa Hill. She would do their shopping in Aguilares, buy them cigarettes, candy, or take the newspapers to them.

Human rights and justice. This topic is also closely linked to violence. Who among us Salvadorans does not mourn a relative, or a comrade in arms, lost in this violence? I, for one, carry in my heart the memory of a great number of good Salvadorans, good servicemen, who have died violently, and not in combat.

Speaking of violence, gentlemen, the fundamental platform of our party is to attain peace, but we want to be very clear about this because we are not trying to deceive anyone. We believe that we will attain peace when El Salvador and our people obtain a victory. It is not true that we will continue negotiations to share with those gentlemen [the FMLN/FDR] a power to which they have no right. . . .

The topic of justice has been distorted. Gentlemen, there used to be four pillars here that were always the pedestal to keep out those doctrines that gradually infiltrated themselves, until those who espoused them ended up in

---

8. This is apparently a veiled reference to United States support for and financing of the electoral campaign of D'Aubuisson's political enemies, the Christian Democrats, in El Salvador. —Eds.

9. Thus, ARENA was opposed to most of the initiatives discussed in chapter 9.—Eds.

the mountains attacking us. One of those pillars was the productive sector, the men who knew how to work and give directions, from the man that tills the soil and the laborer up to the businessman. We are realists and I personally do not make distinctions between this kind and that when we speak about private enterprises. Everyone who produces and works honestly and freely is an entrepreneur.

For a government to fulfill a social function, it must have an income. The government's income comes from taxes. Who pays the taxes? Producers. That is why one of the principles that we most firmly believe is that productivity generates resources. . . .

The other pillars [of society] are the church, justice, the law and judges, and our Armed Forces.

Let us speak of justice that, being already undermined, has become a factor in the violence: the expropriations. Is it fair to expropriate violently? I think not, because if the government had felt secure and sure of popular support, it could have proceeded gradually in implementing its intention better to distribute the land. However, when a government feels unstable and follows foreign instructions it behaves in this way, and that does not constitute justice or compliance with the law. If you vote for . . . ARENA's position . . . it will be our obligation to correct those errors.

. . . Above all the things about which we have spoken to you so much, we say and will continue to say that El Salvador comes first, second and third. Thank you very much.

19. ARENA's Bid for Power*

By Craig Pyes

Although it is the fear of Communist revolution that excites the most heated U.S. rhetoric about El Salvador (as shown in chapter 1 of this book), it is the terror engendered by the death squads of the right that has created some of the most serious embarrassments for a succession of Washington administrations. As this reading (a continuation of Reading 7) by Albuquerque Journal *correspondent Craig Pyes makes clear, these death squads bear a distinctive "Made in U.S.A." label. Thus, Washington policy has vacillated between supporting movements like ARENA and occasionally excoriating such ARENA figures as Colonel Roberto D'Aubuisson for his links to the death-squad apparatus.*[1]

* Rearranged slightly and excerpted from "Salvadoran Rightists: The Deadly Patriots," a series by *Albuquerque Journal* investigative reporter Craig Pyes, which appeared December 18–22, 1983, and was reissued in pamphlet form. For another excerpt from this pamphlet, see Reading 7.

[1.] On this vacillation, see Walter LaFeber, *Inevitable Revolutions: The United States in Central America,* expanded edition (New York: W. W. Norton, 1984), 311. Early in 1986, after Congress ended a decade-old ban on U.S. police-training programs, the Reagan administration began

Beneath these policy shifts, and underlying the Reagan administration's support for the Christian Democratic government of José Napoleón Duarte, may have been sober reflections on the long-run futility of the kind of counterterror described here. As leading academic expert on Communist insurgency Chalmers Johnson pointed out during the Vietnam war, "Anti-guerrilla terrorism will more than likely spread the mass mobilization upon which guerrilla movements thrive."[2] But neither has the U.S. government pressured the Salvadorans to dismantle the terror apparatus that D'Aubuisson and his friends so carefully created; this apparatus stands in place ready to be reactivated when the Salvadoran oligarchy no longer perceives that "regular" counterinsurgency is effective and when popular political organizations again challenge the oligarchic-military establishment of that country. From current reports, they will not have long to wait.

A group of diehard veterans of French colonial Algeria helped right-wing leader Roberto D'Aubuisson map a secret plan for a campaign of terror aimed at seizing control of El Salvador's government.

The plan was drafted in Guatemala in April and May of 1980, D'Aubuisson said, when he met with former members of the French Secret Army Organization (OAS) who had been contacted by "Salvadoran millionaires."

D'Aubuisson said he and his French consultants laid out a political and operational strategy of counterterror adopted from techniques OAS developed in its struggle against Algerian nationalists in the late 1950s. The OAS veterans also had served as advisers to the ultra-right-wing National Liberation Movement (MLN) in its bloody anti-guerrilla campaigns in the 1960s.

After the October 1979 coup in El Salvador by a group of reform-minded young military officers, D'Aubuisson and other Salvadoran rightists moved to Guatemala and began working closely with the MLN in regional "anti-communist" paramilitary operations, including attacks on officials of El Salvador's U.S.-backed government.

D'Aubuisson's plan outlines organizational and operational guidelines for assassinations, kidnappings and military assault teams, to be coupled with a political organization engaged in international diplomacy and public relations.

D'Aubuisson called it "a good plan," based in part on "how we have been operating from October 1979 to May 1980." The Salvadoran leader never said how much of the plan had become operational, acknowledging only that "later the initial idea that we had seized on in that document became more con-

training all of El Salvador's police forces, "most of which," noted correspondent James LeMoyne, "have an unsavory record." Units of the treasury police and the national guard, he added, "were once considered by American diplomats to be little more than standing death squads." *New York Times,* February 25, 1986.

2. Chalmers A. Johnson, "Guerrilla Conflict," *World Politics* (July 1962), quoted in Michael McClintock, *The American Connection: State Terror and Popular Resistance in El Salvador* (London: ZED Books, 1985), 41. McClintock's chapter 4 is an insightful exploration of the limits of counterterrorism.

solidated." He added that it contained the organizational diagram that re-sulted in the Nationalist Republican Alliance (ARENA).

The document was seized from D'Aubuisson's attaché case during his May 7, 1980, arrest at a farmhouse northwest of San Salvador by forces loyal to Army Chief of Staff Col. Adolfo Arnoldo Majano, one of the army officers D'Aubuisson was working to overthrow.[3] The plan—a copy of which has been obtained by the *Albuquerque Journal*—was among a number of compromising documents seized at the time.

The others included a datebook containing the names and addresses of right-wing businessmen and military officers and records of payments to ac-tive-duty army officers, for weapons, notations of meetings, vehicles, prosti-tutes and safe houses.

"I believe this is a whole terrorist plan—it was a miracle to have captured this," said Majano. "Everything that was planned in this has come to be in these past years . . . the kidnappings, the dragging people out of their homes at night. It's all here."

Though the datebook was shared with authorities in the United States, U.S. officials claim they were never given a copy of the D'Aubuisson plan. . . .

The paramilitary organizational structure described in the document resem-bles a political death-squad network that U.S. officials today say is linked to D'Aubuisson's ARENA and high-ranking military officers strategically placed in intelligence sections of the Salvadoran security forces and army commands.

Some of these officers were among those arrested with D'Aubuisson at the farm, but all were released quickly "for insufficient evidence" by a military commission.

A few day. after D'Aubuisson's arrest, seven of El Salvador's most notori-ous death squads issued a proclamation announcing their unification under the banner of the "Secret Anti-Communist Army" (ESA)—one of the death squads operating in El Salvador today. The proclamation called for joining the extreme right's political groups with the military death squads, as outlined in the plan.

After his release, D'Aubuisson sent an explanatory letter to a member of the high command, asking permission to put the anti-guerrilla plan into effect. The *Journal* was allowed to see a copy of the May 25, 1980, letter, which is in the private files of a close D'Aubuisson associate. The letter concluded with an appeal to the Armed Forces Command for help and protection to "develop an anti-communist campaign in the country that is quite similar to that carried out in Guatemala, [a campaign that] would not signify any embarrassment for you because we don't plan to leave any tracks in that campaign."

[3.] On the aborted "Majanista" movement in the Salvadoran military, see Readings 6 and 8; and also McClintock, *The American Connection*, I: 272–75 and Raymond Bonner, *Weakness and Deceit: U.S. Policy and El Salvador* (New York: Times Books, 1984), chapter 10.—Eds.

D'Aubuisson publicly has denied any involvement with Salvadoran death squads.

The plan is the most significant documentary evidence so far to link the Salvadoran nationalist and his supporters to the planning of paramilitary terrorist groups.

It illustrates how terrorist actions could be carried out by tightly controlled but seemingly independent death squads which display no visible ties to either the military or political organizations. . . .

At the time the plan was drawn, Salvadoran rightists believed Marxist infiltrators in the Christian Democratic civilian-military junta were preventing the government's security forces from vigorously pursuing the battle against subversion.

Some of D'Aubuisson's OAS advisers came from Paris, others from South America, said a Salvadoran close to the operation. They were very "tight-lipped, more professional, more serious," he said, than other foreign advisers they had contacted.

He said the French had been promised funds to establish a commando school in Guatemala, including "weapons, and bullets, and arms and uniforms, and all those implements that are used to train people to be commandos," but the funds were not delivered.

D'Aubuisson said that, before meeting with the French, he received assurances from friends in Argentina and France that "they were honorable, motivated, trustworthy and that they had a lot of experience in these things."

"I laid it out to them how we had been working from October 1979 to May 1980," D'Aubuisson said, "how FAN [the Broad Nationalist Front, a right-wing civilian coalition he headed] was organized, what we had managed to achieve in these few months and what kind of economic help we had, with what infrastructure—that was my idea with respect to making political war.

"Then they told me that all we had done was good, that we were knowledgeable about our cause, but they recommended that I be more specific. Then they explained to me about the guerrilla war in Algeria," he added.

D'Aubuisson said the French advised the Salvadorans to form an organization which would operate independently of the government. "What we had to do was not to wait for the politicians to give the orders," D'Aubuisson explained.

At the top, according to the plan, would be a political directorate and a general staff made up of representatives of the military and right-wing civilians. The general staff was divided into four departments and a chief of combat operations: One department was charged with collecting funds through its agents and accounting for the expenditures. The description matches the date-book seized during D'Aubuisson's 1980 arrest.

Another department had responsibility for "psychological action," which was defined as maintaining liaison with international support groups in

Europe, South America and the United States, and distributing analysis and propaganda to local and international media. The press, the plan advises, "will be manipulated intelligently," suggesting "getting close to journalists, paying them, exploiting their professional ambitions. . . ."

The department of "Mass Organization" would be a civilian group to oversee food supplies, provide hideouts, distribute leaflets and obtain identity papers for the rightists. The civilian groups also would serve as an intelligence net, turning in the names of "subversives" to the brain of the organization: the Department of Searches and Information (DBI).

DBI's functions were to collect and analyze data and to direct the combat networks. The plan calls it "the point of the spear" in the anti-guerrilla war. Only the highest officers of the organization were to be allowed direct personal contact with DBI.

The director of combat would operate out of DBI. He would be the top of an organizational pyramid delivering orders to cells through post office box safe-drops down through its levels of command to individual combat cells of three soldiers each.

The DBI also would direct its urban combat units in assassinations, ambushes, military-type assaults, kidnappings, fund collection and sabotage. For the countryside, the document prescribes guerrillas in heavily armed small groups to disrupt the "red gangs" in their own territory, while trying to win over peasant families "in their tiny little towns" with gifts of money and food. The actions of the urban and rural guerrillas would have to increase gradually, the plan says, until the organization's support in the armed forces was sufficient to seize power.

During the Algerian war, French soldiers who joined the OAS operated in secret terrorist cells against the Algerian nationalist movement, even as the French government was working to reach a political accord for Algerian independence. The politicians, the OAS believed, had betrayed France in surrendering Algeria to the nationalists, and it vowed to kill de Gaulle and bring down his government. But, after more than half a dozen failed attempts at killing the French president, the OAS was broken up by French intelligence agents. Members of the secret terrorist organization dispersed, some to South America to become military advisers in the international anti-communist movement.

In the mid-1960s, at least one of the officers who worked with D'Aubuisson was in Guatemala to coach the MLN. The MLN carried out a counterinsurgency campaign similar to that later waged in El Salvador, using techniques that became the model for the Salvadorans. . . .

ARENA insiders describe a theory of counterinsurgency (anti-guerrilla) warfare which parallels the development of the party. The theory explains El Salvador's epidemic of death-squad killings as the implementation of a philosophy of selective and mass assassinations carried out in an organized manner.

D'Aubuisson is perhaps only the most public figure in ARENA, a political movement that contains others more powerful than he. The party organization spans all of El Salvador's 14 departments (provinces). It is divided into sectors that correspond roughly to the traditional divisions of Salvadoran society, such as youth, peasants and farmers.

But the party also embraces local military officers, security-force operations and a broad vigilante network of civil defense units suspected of being used to eliminate the party's political opposition.

Current U.S. intelligence indicates that ARENA may be connected to a single countrywide death-squad network, consisting primarily of three loosely knit regional organizations which in total do not exceed 50 persons.

In San Salvador the names of the operating groups are the Secret Anti-Communist Army, the Maximiliano Hernández Martínez Anti-Communist Brigade and the Comando Metropolitano, whose commander is known only as Comandante Leopoldo.

In the eastern part of the country, the death squad is known as the Gremio Anti-Comunista Salvadoreña. In western El Salvador, it is called the *escuadrón de la muerte* (literally translated, "the death squad"), which operates under the trademark "EM." . . .

The plan, explained one D'Aubuisson aide, was to establish a three-tiered organization containing a "political or propaganda level . . . to encourage and protect the military level; . . . a financial system where we would always have money to attack; and a military level—what the United States called right-wing death squads—people who go out and kidnap and kill the communists the way they were doing it to the rightists."

"We divided into a Salvadoran group and a Miami group," said the D'Aubuisson aide. "The Miami group was finances."

In the Miami group were members of El Salvador's oligarchy. They felt dangerously exposed after the 1979 coup broke its hold on the military and upset the old power structure. . . .

Those who put up the money at first, and who later became key financial backers of ARENA, which emerged later, were primarily planters with agribusiness and banking interests and who live in condominiums in Miami.

The identities of most of them are as well known in El Salvador as the names Rockefeller and Getty are in the United States. They include: Guillermo "Billy" Sol, Orlando De Sola, and relatives of Guatemalan rightist leader Mario Sandoval Alarcón.

Within the Salvadoran exile community in Miami, *Journal* sources said, there was talk in 1979 about hiring military men and foreign advisers to re-establish "a security network" that would operate its own death squads. Names of participants weren't revealed, but rumors put the fund-raising goal for this endeavor as high as $10 million.

The general plan was confirmed by former Salvadoran president and Christian Democratic Party leader José Napoleón Duarte.

"The people in Miami started to get military people," Duarte said. "I know at least three of the men they called. They were looking for people to create a structure outside the army, to do the things the army could not do." They wanted to find someone to put together a "military and guerrilla force, the same as the left had. . . . They were concerned about the intelligence work in particular."

"Terrorism cannot be fought with conventional methods," asserted Guillermo "Billy" Sol, a financier and right-wing activist and one of D'Aubuisson's earliest backers. The only answer, he said, is "destroy it." And to accomplish its destruction, "you need excellent intelligence. D'Aubuisson is excellent on that. He's U.S.-trained."

In fact, the intense, chain-smoking intelligence officer had spent most of his 20 years of military service tracking down enemies of the state. . . . In 1978, fresh from special training courses in Taiwan, D'Aubuisson composed a 64-page intelligence report for the National Guard which became *the* text on the relationships between social reformers and Marxist guerrillas for the various Salvadoran governmental intelligence services. D'Aubuisson was assigned to the elite of those services, the Salvadoran National Security Agency, ANSESAL.

ANSESAL was formed of the heads of the military services and internal security forces and answered directly to the president. From its offices in the Presidential Palace, it functioned as the brain of a vast state security apparatus that reached into every town and neighborhood in the country. By conservative estimate, at least one Salvadoran out of every 50 was an informant for the agency.

In addition to gathering intelligence, ANSESAL was used to carry out death-squad activities before the coup, according to Salvadoran and U.S. officials. After the coup, ANSESAL was ordered disbanded. Rebuilding that intelligence system, and using its data base for identifying the enemy, became a central goal of D'Aubuisson's nationalist movement. . . .

Rightist insiders involved with the paramilitary underground said that D'Aubuisson remained in contact with about 100 mostly low- and mid-level officers from the security forces, working closely with 15 to 20.

These sources pointed out the National Guard and Treasury Police, particularly their intelligence units, as the rightists' two main bases of support in 1980, which they called "a big paramilitary year." Both agencies have been accused by U.S. officials of conducting mass assassination campaigns.

The biggest target was the Christian Democrat Party (PDC), whose right wing maintained power with U.S. support after the civilians of the first junta resigned at the end of 1979. The PDC remained in power until the elections of March 1982.

ARENA party leaders told the *Albuquerque Journal* that they recognized the need for the moderate facade of Christian Democratic President Duarte during the junta period, in order to get military support from Washington.

But to the extreme right-wing network being assembled by D'Aubuisson, the rank-and-file Christian Democrats also were the foe. According to PDC spokesmen, more than 260 of the party's leaders, including 35 Christian Democratic mayors, have been murdered in the past three years. Many of these killings have been traced to former members of ORDEN. This group of rag-tag, machete-wielding peasants and conservative farmers formed the base of the government's disbanded ANSESAL internal espionage network.

But D'Aubuisson said he recruited and paid about eight of ORDEN's 14 departmental officials to maintain ORDEN's structure down to the local level, and rechristened the organization the "Democratic Nationalist Front."

The ORDEN network was formed in the mid-1960s by D'Aubuisson's mentor, former National Guard chief (now retired) Gen. José Alberto "Chele" Medrano, who was identified by U.S. officials as both a CIA liaison and head of the Salvadoran "White Hand" death squads in the 1960s.[4]

Medrano fashioned ORDEN to support his own political aspirations, building the organization around paramilitary power and political control. ORDEN recruited vast numbers of civilian agent-volunteers, put a chief in every town and a political leader in every area, who reported to the National Guard.

By the late 1970s, the governmental spy network was estimated to employ more than 80,000 "ears" and 6,000 paramilitary troops. A report by the Organization of American States recommended in 1978 that the government abolish the vigilante group for its participation in killings, torture, voter fraud and political intimidation.

Much of that network now has been absorbed into ARENA. Retired Col. Mario Rosales y Rosales, one of ORDEN's original organizers, controlled the organization and "all military for ARENA," said a high party official. The official, who asked not to be named, said Rosales put an ORDEN man in each province to run the party.

At the beginning, D'Aubuisson said, ORDEN was the foundation of the mass movement he was about to build.

*   *   *

[4.] Perhaps insufficiently emphasized in Pyes's otherwise penetrating exercise in investigative journalism is the North American origins of the Salvadoran death squads. Carrying out similar research at the same time, another U.S. journalist, Allan Nairn, found "a pattern of sustained U.S. participation in building and managing the Salvadoran security apparatus that relies on Death Squad assassination as its principal means of enforcement." Nairn's evidence includes not only Medrano's CIA connections, but data on the role of both the CIA and the U.S. armed forces in creating and organizing both ORDEN and ANSESAL, advising and arming both groups, including "instruction in methods of physical and psychological torture." Nairn, "Behind the Death Squads," *The Progressive* (Madison, Wisconsin), May 1984.—Eds.

To counter leftist support groups, D'Aubuisson said he began to put together an umbrella "civic organization" to support the armed forces politically and to extend military intelligence capabilities. Called the Broad National Front (FAN), its membership was made up of private enterprise associations, such as the coffee growers, cattle ranchers and young executives, plus the Women's Front and a youth organization called the Salvadoran Nationalist Movement (MNS). Each of these elements was later fused into the ARENA party.

MNS was one of the most idealistic segments of the burgeoning right-wing nationalist movement. Its young members were mostly American-educated aspiring businessmen who were the sons of upper-middle-class Salvadorans. They had sworn a "blood oath" dedicating their souls to the battle against communism. They were also one of the first groups to join D'Aubuisson. . . .

[Ricardo Paredes, one of the founding members of MNS and later ARENA vice minister of education,] described the civilian organizations as "counterparts to the army, giving it information [about persons ranging] from the peasants to very high-up people" to help destroy the urban guerrillas. . . . "It is not a civil war, an open war, a legal war," Paredes explained. "We don't want to fight a fair war. We have to go and beat their pants off."

Because the ultimate leadership of the communist organizations is always hidden, the intelligence services must be turned into "services of combat" to uncover the "the secret brain" and destroy it, D'Aubuisson explained. "If you destroy the [civilian] organization, the guerrillas will starve up in the mountains," Paredes said. . . .

Before the [1979] coup, almost 200 people a year were being killed, allegedly by government security forces. El Salvador was known in the international community as one of the world's worst violators of human rights. After the coup, the rate of killing rose steadily to 800 a month.

Both U.S. and Salvadoran officials attribute most of the increased post-coup violence to "independent anti-communist death squads" financed by the oligarchy and directed by the right-wing paramilitary underground. The Salvadoran military leadership said that D'Aubuisson was running these paramilitary operations from Guatemala. . . .

D'Aubuisson said that, after he left the army, his activities were directed toward building a network, both within and outside the armed forces, which he said had been compromised by pro-Marxist elements supporting the coup. Initially, he said, he met with former intelligence operatives and right-wing political leaders to salvage the intelligence system of the pre-coup regime.

MNS members said the organization did not participate in paramilitary activities but, for safety's sake, "decided to copy the enemy's strategy, operating with [other] secret groups in a combination of cell and chain." A number of these cells formed civilian defense groups which patrolled the upper-class neighborhoods, linked by CB radios and initiating actions under cover of their defense units.

The system was helped into place by Carranza, who explained the network with obvious pride. He said he personally organized Civil Defense Committee No. 1, which had about 20 people, mostly doctors, lawyers and businessmen, who patrolled in "sophisticated groups with radio systems hooked up to the National Police" and the armed forces. These groups, said D'Aubuisson, were integrated into FAN and formed "levels of defense more or less in leadership with me."

Beneath FAN was an underground network of civilian-military death squads. According to information contained in the organization's private files, members of its "clandestine arm" at one point considered calling themselves "The Army of National Salvation."

The name was never generally used in public, but one former Salvadoran junta member said that "The Army of National Salvation" was known to some of "the highest people in government," who thought it may have been the high command of the right controlling all the other paramilitary groups.

A few months before the March 1982 elections, the metamorphosis of FAN into ARENA was completed. ARENA burst into the open as a new Salvadoran political party. Its motto was "The Party of National Salvation."

20. Demonstration Elections in El Salvador*

By Frank Brodhead

Raymond Bonner witnessed the 1982 elections in El Salvador as a New York Times *correspondent and was observer of the intense involvement of a variety of U.S.-government agencies in the electoral contest. Not only was the Agency for International Development (AID) able to divert funds from human-rights and planning efforts while the CIA covertly channeled funds to Duarte and the Christian Democrats, but the American Institute for Free Labor Development (AIFLD), a nominally nongovernmental branch of the U.S. AFL-CIO, also threw itself into these elections.* [1]

But even deeper than these specific instances of U.S. involvement was the sense in which these and later elections were staged for a North American audience that needed a public spectacle of legitimate governmental activity, lest segments of the U.S. public, already uneasy about their country's increasing entanglement in what appeared to be another

---

* From *Resist Newsletter* (Somerville, Mass.), No. 164 (March 1984).

[1.] Raymond Bonner, *Weakness and Deceit: U.S. Policy and El Salvador* (New York: Times Books, 1984), chapter 15.

Vietnam, become actively anti-interventionist. Pioneering in this interpretation of the Salvadoran voting as a series of "demonstration elections" were Edward Herman and Frank Brodhead, whose book Demonstration Elections *was published by South End Press in Boston in 1982. In this essay, Brodhead summarizes the argument of that book and extends it to the eve of the 1984 presidential elections, in which José Napoleón Duarte, Washington's man in El Salvador, was the victor.*

ON March 25, 1984, more than a million Salvadorans will go to the polls. They will be casting their ballots in El Salvador's presidential election. Although the election will be interpreted as a vote for peace, it will be used by the Reagan administration to justify the continued U.S. military buildup in Central America. The Salvadoran election is not an exercise in democracy, but its opposite: a means to deny Salvadoran self-determination and to justify U.S. intervention.

For most Salvadorans the election ritual is meaningless and participation is compulsory. Voting is a means of keeping alive for another day. The election will affect Salvadorans chiefly by its impact on U.S. policy. It is for us, the citizens of the United States, that this election drama is conceived, written, staged, and interpreted. It is for us that the fine words of "democracy" and "self-determination" are scripted. It is for us—not the Salvadorans—that this election is called "free."

Our role in this election is not simply passive. As in much experimental theater, we as audience also have a role to play in the drama. If we find the election drama sufficiently convincing, our role may be expanded to support the dispatch of U.S. troops to Central America. Instead of a bit part, we may be offered the same leading role we had in Vietnam. But if we denounce the drama as a fraud, as not genuine, as insulting and laughable, the Reagan administration may be blocked from escalating U.S. military aid to its Salvadoran clients at a militarily critical stage in the war.

DEMONSTRATION ELECTIONS

The Salvadoran election of March 1984 may be best described as a "demonstration election." That is, it is an election whose secondary purpose is to select political leaders or even to ratify the political leaders chosen by the Reagan administration. The purpose of the demonstration election, rather, is to convince the citizens of the United States that their client government is freely chosen. While many colonial powers (including the Soviet Union) have sponsored fraudulent elections in client states, the demonstration election has become particularly important for U.S. intervention strategy. It is one of the major vehicles through which the United States legitimizes the expenditure of billions of dollars and thousands of lives in the slaughter of more thousands of lives in the defense of U.S. "interests."

It is significant that such an exercise, a demonstration election, has become necessary in managing U.S. interests in the Third World. For it was not always so. The United States intervened in Central America prior to the Second World War with no thought given to "electing" a Somoza in Nicaragua or a Ubico in Guatemala. The United States required no such justification when it appointed Diem the president of the imaginary country of "South Vietnam." Indeed, the United States has frequently exercised its influence in Third World countries to *prevent* a free election, as it did in Vietnam in 1956 and in El Salvador in 1961 and 1972. The U.S. support for free elections is *selective,* tending to support free elections which ratify a candidate of our choice while opposing free elections in which the outcome is problematic.

The rise of the demonstration election is distinctly a product of the growing anti-imperialist revolt in the post–World War II period. More specifically, the United States gave little thought to using elections to legitimize its counter-revolutionary work in the Philippines or Greece in the 1940s, in Iran in 1953, or in Guatemala in 1954. But the prolonged U.S. involvement in Indochina undermined automatic domestic support for the imperial enterprise. By 1966 the Johnson administration found it expedient to ratify its rescue of antidemocratic forces in the Dominican Republic by staging an election; and in the following year it staged another election to consolidate Thieu and Ky as the leaders of Vietnam, thereby legitimizing further U.S. intervention as a response to the request of a "freely elected government." In both elections the Johnson administration was at pains to present the election-day events and the mechanics of the election as on the democratic up-and-up. Election observers were provided to supervise the fairness of the balloting.

The elections in the Dominican Republic and South Vietnam set the pattern for future demonstration elections. In both these and later elections a critical role in their legitimizing and demonstration function was played by the mass media. Because the purpose of the election is to influence U.S. citizens, the election managers in the State Department, Pentagon, and CIA must rely on the privately owned U.S. mass media to shape the appropriate audience response to the election drama. There is clearly room for error here, as contradictory facts can (and often do) slip through. Yet on the whole the media fulfill their role by consistently accepting the *premises* of election drama, putting certain questions on the agenda and keeping others off the agenda. For example, the media can be counted on to play along with the "Will the guerrillas disrupt the election?" theme, and to accept the equation of a high voter turnout with political enthusiasm for the choices offered in the election. Most of the important questions, however, are kept off the agenda, or at least off the front pages. For example, completely lost in the media's fixation with political personalities and "Who will win?" are questions like:

1. Is there genuine freedom of speech? Could a candidate campaign for real land reform and the withdrawal of U.S. forces without being assassinated by government security forces or "death squads"?

2. Is there a free press? Could it support a candidate who was for real land reform and a withdrawal of U.S. forces? Would its reporters "disappear," would its editors be arrested, would its presses be bombed?

3. Can popular organizations grow and survive if they are independent and/or critical of the government? Are there trade unions, peasant associations, professional and artistic groupings? Are their officers assassinated or their militants routinely tortured by state officials? Ironically, this test—the existence of voluntary or "intermediate" organizations of citizens standing between state power and an atomized populace—is one stressed by liberal democratic theorists in criticizing the lack of democracy in totalitarian states. Yet the free press in the United States seldom raises these questions when considering the context of a U.S.-sponsored election in a Third World country.

4. Is there a limit on what kind of political parties can contest the election? Can candidates campaign safely? Can a party be established without turning over thousands of names to the secret police? Will the party that gets the most votes actually hold office? Will all the major political forces in the country be allowed to be represented on the ballot?

5. And, is the level of state-sponsored terror sufficiently low that people acting in a political manner might reasonably hope to survive? How much of a climate of fear is compatible with making a free choice in the voting booth? Can a free choice be made in an atmosphere dominated by the army and associated death squads?

These and other questions affecting the fundamental qualities of political life are never on the agenda when the U.S. media are discussing a U.S.-sponsored election in "our" sphere of influence.

A simple litmus test of media bias is to imagine a similar election within the Soviet sphere. In such cases the U.S. media has shown an astonishing ability to cut through rhetoric about "democracy" and to perceive the real meaning of an election ritual. In the Polish election of 1947, for example, the U.S. media accurately criticized the election as a farce. They ridiculed the idea that a high turnout meant political enthusiasm for the communist regime, and correctly analyzed it as an indication of coercion and fraud. They reported the restrictions on the opposition party's candidates, their difficulties in campaigning and getting on the ballot, their exclusion from the government-controlled press and radio, and the censorship placed on opposition party newspapers. During the Polish election of 1947 the U.S. media did not feature long lines of apparently happy voters eager to do their duty, as they did during the elections in the Dominican Republic, Vietnam, or El Salvador.

In short, it may be taken as a rule of thumb that the U.S. media will focus on the mechanics of the election and election day events when assessing a U.S.-sponsored election, while shifting its focus to the more fundamental (and allegedly undemocratic) parameters of political power when the election is in an enemy sphere of influence. Thus the *New York Times* passed on, without comment, Secretary of State George Shultz's criticism of Nicaragua's forth-coming election: "An election just as an election doesn't really mean any-thing," he said. "The important thing is that if there is to be an electoral process, it be observed not only at the moment when people vote, but in all the preliminary aspects that make an election really mean something" (Feb. 6, 1984). The U.S. media has placed off the agenda the "preliminary aspects" of U.S.-sponsored elections, i.e. precisely those qualities "that make an election really mean something."

EL SALVADOR

The election held in El Salvador in March 1982 was a classic demonstration election. The political climate in the United States was sceptical and increas-ingly critical of our Central American policy. Despite one of the most conserv-ative Congresses in many years, public opinion in the United States had forced somewhat cumbersome restrictions on the amount of U.S. aid sent to El Salvador. The March demonstration election was instrumental in stemming this tide of scepticism and criticism. It gave the Reagan administration some badly needed breathing room, letting it regroup its right wing, fire conciliators like Undersecretary of State Thomas Enders and Ambassador to El Salvador Deane Hinton, and increase the U.S. military presence in Central America without taking a beating from the Democrats and doubting Republicans in Congress. In thinking about the March 1984 Salvadoran election, therefore, it is useful to analyze how the last election achieved its demonstration pur-poses.

By March 1982 two years of state terror had cleared the ground for a free election in El Salvador. The country had been under a legal state of siege since March 1980. Freedoms of movement, residence, thought, and assembly had been suspended. All Salvadoran newspapers that were critical of the govern-ment had been closed. Among the 30,000 civilian victims of the security forces and death squads were priests and church officials, human rights workers and labor leaders, at least twenty leaders of the Christian Democratic Party, and more than 1,000 students. The media did not dwell on these longer term factors in the election. Instead they stressed the long lines of enthusiastic voters defying threats of guerrilla disruption to cast their vote. They did not reflect too much on the fact that the long lines were produced by allocating only a few polling places for each city (e.g. 13 in San Salvador), by making voting legally obligatory, and by identifying those who voted by marking their iden-tity cards. Neither the media nor the official U.S. observer team criticized the use of transparent plastic ballot boxes and transparent paper ballots. Although Salvadoran election officials and the U.S. Embassy predicted between 500,000 and 800,000 Salvadorans would vote, a turnout of more than 1,500,000 did not arouse scepticism. Two studies done by the Central American University in

El Salvador claiming that it was physically impossible for so many people to vote within the allotted time were quickly buried by the U.S. media. Nor did they spend much time puzzling over how a "massive vote for peace" could have resulted in the victory of those forces most determined to pursue the war against the guerrillas.

The cooperation of the U.S. media enabled the Reagan administration to pull off the demonstration election and to temporarily halt the rapid loss of popular confidence in its Central American policy. The promise of elections during the March 1982 certification hearings in Congress, and the results of the elections during similar hearings in July, allowed the Reagan administration to claim that it was supporting self-determination in El Salvador. At a minimum, the election undercut those liberal Democrats who claimed that the guerrillas had broad support and should therefore be included in negotiations. The election helped retain the support of Christian Democratic parties in Europe and Latin America for the alleged U.S. efforts to restore the mythical "center" in Salvadoran politics. It kept the congressional military aid pipeline open a little wider and a little longer. And, perhaps most important, it facilitated the Reagan administration's contrived "search for peace," whereby the scope of possible negotiations between the political forces in El Salvador was reduced to including the guerrillas within the next round of the electoral process. As the media and the U.S. Congress had largely accepted the legitimacy of this electoral process, the guerrillas were placed in the position of losing credibility if they refused to play the electoral game, or being defeated in an election drama controlled by the security forces and the Pentagon if they chose to participate.

MARCH 1984

Like its predecessor, the March 1984 Salvadoran election is a demonstration election. It is intended to pacify the home audience and to provide a suitable climate in which Congress can consider the recommendations of the Kissinger Commission for increased military aid. Whatever the additional consequences of the election for Salvadorans, its main effects will be in the United States. U.S. officials have been working on this election for a year or more. Special Envoy Richard Stone's first assignment was to (unsuccessfully) attempt to move the elections up to last fall. Members of the State Department and the last official U.S. observer team have been in El Salvador making arrangements for the election. The United States has put up $6 to $8 million for the election computers alone. The depth of the U.S. role in the election is indicated by a *New York Times* report last May:

> The Central Intelligence Agency plans to support the election by intensifying its collection of intelligence information about the guerrillas' military plans and opera-

tions so as to help the Salvadoran military block anticipated efforts to disrupt the voting. . . . Because the State Department and the Salvadoran Government lack expertise in conducting elections . . . a lot of the work will be turned over the private contractors. . . . A concern in El Salvador or the United States would likely handle an extensive print and television advertising campaign to promote the major voter registration drive that the Salvadoran Government hopes to conduct.

These efforts are being made for our benefit and not in the interests of Salvadoran democracy. They should be seen for what they are: the props, script, and stage lighting of a shoddy farce.

21. Duarte's Fix*

BY SAM DILLON

From the very start of José Napoleón Duarte's political career as a founder of the Christian Democratic Party and as its popular mayor of San Salvador, he has had his ups and his downs. By early 1987, the question is being asked once again: How long can Duarte hold on as Salvadoran head of state? Is he stronger than before or weaker? What of his foes in the military, on the Salvadoran right, among the guerrillas? What is the attitude of the Reagan administration toward his policies?

Since Sam Dillon's article detailing Duarte's prospects following his election as President over Roberto D'Aubuisson, the Salvadoran President has faced new challenges. The kidnapping of his daughter, Inés, by FMLN commandos in mid-1985 paralyzed his government for weeks until a swap involving kidnapped mayors, political prisoners, and wounded combatants could be arranged (see Reading 41). The exchange weakened Duarte's standing, as both the Salvadoran right (vocally) and the Reagan administration (sotto voce) opposed the trade. In addition, Duarte just barely convinced the Salvadoran military command, bitter over exchanging FMLN leaders they'd captured. The kidnapping effectively scotched any immediate resumption of the church-sponsored dialogue between the government and the rebels. With the current rebel emphasis on attacks against the infrastructure of the nation, the economy has taken a turn for the worst. In the slight political apertura that has resulted, the civilian left in the capital has made a tentative reappearance and workers in the unions that are part and parcel of Duarte's Christian Democratic base have turned their rising expectations and frustrations into militant strikes.

Still, this is not the whole story. Duarte was able to bring the military along on the exchange—however grudgingly—and that is no small feat given the traditional imbalance of power between civilians and the military in El Salvador. Duarte has utilized his 33-to-27 majority in the National Assembly to bolster the government propaganda apparatus to the benefit of his own personal standing and that of the Christian Democratic party. The Salvadoran right is in disarray, stymied by Duarte's working relationship with

* From *The New Republic* (Washington, D.C.), June 17, 1985.

their erstwhile solid ally, the military. The right is reduced to shrill, ineffective, and hypocritical flailing against corruption in the government and against a recent economic package that includes higher taxes against the coffee growers and restrictions on luxury imports that go to the oligarchy. Despite El Salvador's astronomical foreign debt and though there is no sign of any end to the war, the United States seems content to continue a level of aid adequate to prop up the tottering economy and fuel the Salvadoran armed forces.

Duarte, for all his pluses and minuses, is a survivor, and any attempt at predicting his future would seem a chancy undertaking at best.

Sam Dillon has written about Central America for the Miami Herald.

IN recent weeks El Salvador's president, José Napoleón Duarte, has triumphed as never before. In local elections on March 31, his Christian Democratic Party handily beat a coalition of rightist parties, seizing control of the country's legislative assembly, most of the country's 262 town governments, and every other major organ of civilian government except the judiciary. Meanwhile, the guerrillas have blundered their way into political and military reverses unprecedented in the five-year insurgency. Attacking unarmed peasants in La Paz province, razing municipal halls in nearly three dozen villages, executing two town mayors, and kidnapping several others, the insurgents have handed the government a series of unequivocal propaganda victories.

Duarte's fortunes have surged so suddenly, in fact, that they have obscured the continuing limits to his powers as El Salvador's first freely elected civilian president in three generations. The civil war is now five years old, and—Duarte's peacemaking intentions notwithstanding—could last ten. Despite the guerrillas' setbacks (one U.S. military officer estimated that the number of combatants had recently plunged by a third), they still hold the country's battered infrastructure at ransom. And they have begun to take advantage of the *apertura* his government represents by making inroads among unionists, students, and peasants. Meanwhile, the economy would collapse without U.S. aid; and although Duarte's victory has left the far right vanquished and confused, the U.S. Embassy and the military still hold significant power. They can prevent him from negotiating with the guerrillas too generously, pushing his populist economic policies too firmly, or prosecuting political assassins in the military too righteously.

Hours after his March election victory, Duarte announced that he would renew his peace efforts, calling them decisive to the Christian Democratic sweep. In the weeks since, however, he has set no date for the next encounter with the guerrillas, and the future of the dialogue remains in question. The successful first encounter between the guerrillas and the government at La Palma on October 15 was followed by a second ugly, stalemated meeting at the Ayagualo Seminary in late November. Duarte's top aide, Julio Rey Prendes, says the government will not risk another such embarrassment. Hint-ing at secret dealings, Rey Prendes says—as Duarte did at the White House on May 16—that before any new public dialogue the government will search for common ground with rebel leaders on limited issues in private talks.

The peace talks, of course, are about war, a bloody showdown over which the army is confident as never before. The high command is at once flush with new U.S. arms (its fleet of helicopter gunships has more than doubled since Duarte took office) and gleeful over the political ineptitude of the guerrillas' recent return to terror-style tactics. Defense minister General Eugenio Vides Casanova told me that although the army supports Duarte's dialogue efforts, the military he leads hopes to force the guerrillas to make major concessions. "If we act with more military force every day, the subversives will adjust their ideas to reality," Vides said. For their part, the rebels have recently reaffirmed their own faith in a long-term war of attrition, a war increasingly fought by roving terror squads planting Claymore mines and hurling grenades. With the major actors still committed to war, the prospects for negotiated progress appear limited to pacts over "humanization of the war"—the prisoner exchanges and other tactical agreements that only regulate the war's continuation.

Further complicating the prospects for a negotiated settlement are new fears. Christian Democrats have recently acknowledged with candor the immediate threat that political accommodation with the rebels could pose. "Six months after we sign a peace treaty, and these leftists start wandering around the country organizing legally, all the agrarian reform cooperatives would turn communist," said one of Duarte's aides. Miguel Parada, rector of the battered National University, where leftists have renewed organizing recently, made the same point about school-age youth. Parada said he believes that the left still enjoys wide organizing opportunities on the country's campuses and among unemployed youths.

In the labor movement as well, signs of leftward moves indicate that rebel agitators may find the ground more fertile than at any time since the rebels abandoned large-scale organizing in 1980 to wage the guerrilla war. The political picture inside El Salvador's unions has been especially complicated for the Duarte government by U.S. attempts to recast the labor movement around a new center-right federation. Since 1980, the AFL-CIO's American Institute of Free Labor Development has funded the Popular Democratic Unity, UPD, a political federation of peasant and trade unions. The UPD's leaders are street-smart peasant and trade union organizers—men who wear sandals but carry briefcases—and represent the only organized center-left force remaining in the country. The AFL-CIO's support has attempted to keep them centrist, and under control.

Three months after Duarte's 1984 presidential victory, UPD leaders publicly criticized Duarte for failing to prosecute army officers accused of political murders and, the unionists charged, for stalling on opening a dialogue with the guerrillas. To the AFL-CIO's Institute, that criticism proved the UPD had become too radical. Institute organizers, who because of their funding relationship with the U.S. government wear U.S. Embassy badges, initiated a transparent drive to break the UPD by creating a rival federation. UPD leaders say the drive so far has involved two elections rigged to oust key UPD leaders, bribe attempts to induce UPD leaders to cooperate with the Institute's newly created rival, and cutoffs of U.S. aid when they have refused.

The effort appears to have run aground, and the Institute's discredited director was recently transferred out of the country. Jack Heberle, the Institute's Washington-based spokesman, says that it never intended to weaken support for Duarte, only to tilt labor's influence back to the center. The opposite appears to have occurred. The UPD leaders, embittered by the interference, appear more militant than ever. At a recent summit in Sonsonate province, the assembled labor chieftains listed their post-election priorities: peace talks, freedom for political prisoners, and even a renewed "struggle for national sovereignty" by the Duarte government—a thinly disguised call for a reduction in U.S. involvement in El Salvador.

Beyond dialogue, UPD leaders are most insistent now in demanding that Duarte move to prosecute political murderers. Hundreds of the federation's own militants have been assassinated. In one celebrated case in February 1983, army troops intervened in a land dispute on Las Hojas, an Indian cooperative, slaughtering 74 peasants.

Perhaps Duarte's most troubling dilemma is how to maintain army loyalty while prosecuting guilty officers. His general tactic, according to Christian Democratic Party lawyer Humberto Posanda, will be to reform the judicial system rather than to push for punishment of past crimes. One of Duarte's first flourishes as president in 1984 was to secure $900,000 in U.S. funds for an investigative commission to probe celebrated political murders. But the assembly, then under rightist control, put a halt to that notion. The 12 supreme court justices and the attorney general—all rightists—blocked other attempts to punish political murder.

As one of its first measures, the new Christian Democratic Assembly emphasized its determination for judicial reform by replacing the rightist attorney general. The establishment of the investigative commission will come next, party leaders say. But Posanda maintains that the supreme court will remain untouched unless it commits impeachable offenses. Duarte's political fortunes will depend at least partly on the degree to which his supporters will accept mere judicial reform instead of retribution.

Before the March voting, U.S. officials worried that a Duarte sweep could provoke rightist violence. But the death squads have remained quiet, and the post-vote calm is a sign of progress in Washington's five-year effort to tame the semi-feudal Salvadoran right and modernize Salvadoran capitalism. Gradually the rich have accepted the Reagan administration's deal: play by constitutional rules, and the United States will provide the dollars and the guns to ensure that business prospers and the insurgency fades. Symbolically, Roberto D'Aubuisson—the dark prince of the feudal right—was the biggest loser; many believe his career as the oligarchy's standard bearer is finished. El Salvador's shattered right will have three years before new elections to lick their wounds and, perhaps, realign around new leaders. In the meantime, however, it has been deprived of formal power.

Christian Democrats say that in the vacuum they expect the Reagan administration to emerge as the strongest advocate of private sector interests. On economic issues, Reagan administration officials find more in common with the right's free enterprise prescriptions than with Duarte's *cooperativismo*. During Duarte's first ten months, U.S. officials brought constant pressure on him to build bridges to his business enemies, while bolstering the flow of U.S. aid to private sector organizations.

A month after Duarte took office in 1984, U.S. officials withheld dispersal of some $75 million in aid, demanding that he take measures to benefit the country's cotton, shrimp, sugar, and coffee exporters. Duarte complained, then complied. Last December U.S. officials withheld another $93 million, demanding changes in government import regulations. Recently the Reagan administration has increased its flow of aid to the private sector. Over the next three years, the administration will channel nearly seven million dollars to several private sector groups who have been among Duarte's sharpest critics. The funds will help businessmen develop strategies for negotiating more forcefully with the Duarte government over policy.

These parallel efforts—to weaken Duarte's grass-roots allies on the one hand, and to bolster his longtime business foes on the other—will dominate the Christian Democrats' second year in office. How successfully Duarte resists the pressures to veer right will determine the degree to which he keeps his promises of peace, reform, and justice in El Salvador.

Original members of the junta that assumed power in El Salvador in October, 1979 (from left): Mario Andino, Col. Jaime Abdul Gutierrez, Guillermo Manuel Ungo, Col. Adol Arnoldo Majano, and Ramon Mayorga. (World Wide Photos)

The late Archbishop Oscar Romero. (Patrick Lacefield © 1981)

José Napoleon Duarté, President of El Salvador. (Jane Halpern © 1985)

Members of the U. S.-trained Atlacatl Battalion, El Salvador's elite counter-insurgency force, at the Playa de Suchitoto in June, 1981. (Anne Nelson © 1981)

Combat veterans of the Farabundo Martí Liberation Movement in a government-controlled zone in January, 1985. (Edward Antopol © 1985)

Literacy class conducted in Salvadoran refugee settlement at La Virtud, Honduras in May, 1981. (Anne Nelson © 1981)

Young woman fighting with the guerrilleros, carrying an Israeli-made Uzi submachine gun and playing with a villager's child in October, 1980. (Anne Nelson © 1980)

Salvadoran Defense Minister, General Eugenio Vides-Casanova (center) at Salvadoran Army Headquarters in January 1985. To his right is intelligence officer Lieutenant Col. Ricardo Aristides Cienfuegos. (Edward Antopol © 1985)

Preparing for an anti-intervention rally in Oakland, California, in 1984. (Glen Korengold)

Children among the eight hundred refugees at the seminary of San Salvador in June, 1981. (Anne Nelson © 1981)

Bodies of the North American churchwomen slain in El Salvador at the end of 1980 in December, 1980. (Edward Hoagland © 1980)

The restaurant in San Salvador's Zona Rosa where the U.S. Marines were killed. This photo was taken the day after the killings in June, 1985. (Gilbert Schrank © 1985)

*Roberto D'Aubuisson,
founder and former head
of the right-wing party,
ARENA.* (Anne Nelson
© 1983)

*Arturo Rivera y Damas,
Roman Catholic
Archbishop of San
Salvador.* (Anne Nelson
© 1983)

CHAPTER V

The Salvadoran Rebels

Editors' Introduction

It is impossible to determine precisely the degree of popular support held by guerrilla movements in countries like El Salvador, lacking a peaceful democratic and electoral context. It is clear, however, that the Reagan administration's longstanding claim that the guerrillas are little more than a small band of Marxist terrorists, externally armed, advised, and organized, "interested only in obtaining power through brute force,"[1] is not to be taken seriously. Too many journalists, church groups, and congressional delegations, in visits to guerrilla and refugee camps, have found otherwise. In fact, the tactic employed by the Salvadoran military, with American support, of separating the guerrilla fish from the friendly peasant ocean—in recent years by aerial bombardments—is evidence that belies the propaganda. It is generally agreed that the guerrillas exercise considerable control in large portions of El Salvador, especially in the north along the Honduran boundary and in the southeast.

Moreover, the Democratic Revolutionary Front (FDR), a coalition of, among others, labor unions, professional associations, peasant organizations, and church groups, has in its leadership a large number of Christian Democrats, Social Democrats, and other non-Marxists, many of whom were until recently officials of the junta, including FDR president, Guillermo Ungo.

But legitimate questions can be raised about the degree of power held by FDR moderates. Will they, when and if victory comes, be shunted off by

---

[1] John A. Bushnell, Acting Assistant Secretary for Inter-American Affairs, before the Subcommittee for Inter-American Affairs of the House Foreign Affairs Committee, March 5, 1981, reprinted in the *Department of State Bulletin,* April 1981, 41.

radical Marxists in the Farabundo Martí National Liberation Front (FMLN)? The latter, after all, have the moral credentials—they did the fighting and the dying. More important, they will have the guns and *de facto* military control.

Even the case of a successful revolution in neighboring Nicaragua offers little in the way of what to expect in El Salvador. Nicaragua was less an example of a peasant war than that of a popular, multiclass uprising against an entrenched dictator.[2] Factory owners joined with their workers in the general strike linked to the final offensive against Anastasio Somoza in June 1979.[3] Also the extreme left in Nicaragua was never as influential as its counterpart in El Salvador. Last, the "final disposition" of the Nicaraguan revolution is yet to be determined.

We are led to the conclusion that no one can offer advance assurance that the revolution in El Salvador will not end up a left-wing dictatorship. Bloody civil wars often do in countries lacking democratic traditions, examples being China, Vietnam, and Cuba. On the other hand, Spain, Greece, and the Philippines show that when the right triumphs, years of authoritarian rule and coup-ridden regimes are the result.

But matters could be different in Central America if the United States gives the FDR and, in Nicaragua, the Sandinista government a degree of breathing room. Revolutionaries in both countries are undoubtedly aware that twenty years of revolutionary rule in Cuba have amply demonstrated the enormous difficulties that arise when a western-oriented economy in Latin America is totally severed from the United States. It is in the clear interest of whatever coalition comes to power in El Salvador—even the most left wing—to maintain economic relations with the United States. But will the United States be willing to maintain economic relations with a revolutionary El Salvador?

U.S. magnanimity has thus far been nowhere visible in postwar Vietnam. Nor has Washington ever suggested détente should include Cuba. Rap-

---

[2.] In this respect, Nicaragua can be compared to Cuba, where a multiclass struggle took place against Fulgencio Batista. One key difference between the two revolutions is the role played by the church. In Cuba, the peasants were less influenced by the church, which was tied to the middle and upper classes and soon became part of the counterrevolution. By contrast, the Nicaraguan church supported the revolution; even to the point of condoning armed struggle. Many of its priests and nuns have been mainstays of the revolution and part of its leadership, although the hierarchy has been increasingly opposed to the Sandinista government, perhaps fearful of the latter's commitment to a genuine social transformation, certainly hostile to the close relation it has established with Cuba and the Soviet bloc.

If Cuba ended up being a Communist state and a steadfast ally of the Soviet Union, it remains an intriguing historical question whether it had to turn out that way. Had there been no embargo, no Bay of Pigs invasion, no unremitting U.S. hostility the first years of the revolution, could Cuba have been more of a neutralist Communist regime, like Yugoslavia, even one more tolerant of dissent? Unfortunately, it appears that U.S.-Nicaragua relations are repeating the Cuban past.

[3.] See NACLA *Report on the Americas,* "Central America: No Road Back," 15, No. 3 (May–June 1981), 11.

proachement with China exists primarily because the latter promises to be
a useful card against the Soviet Union. The example of Chile, where the CIA
played a covert role in overthrowing the Allende government, even indicates
an unwillingness on the part of the United States to accept duly elected
governments that try to build socialism peacefully and democratically.

To a great extent, therefore, the ability of the Salvadoran revolutionaries
to carry out their commitment to structural change democratically and
without terror depends on the willingness of the United States to permit a
"socialist" state to exist in Central America.

In the introduction to this section in our first edition, written in 1981, we
pointed out that if "the United States escalates and prolongs the civil war by
an extravagant military commitment to the junta, the power and influence
of Marxist guerrillas in the FMLN will be strengthened at the expense of
moderate civilians in the Democratic Revolutionary Front." Recent reports
that guerrillas in the the Farabundo Martí National Liberation Front are
attempting to build a revolutionary party independent of the FDR (see
Reading 27)—surely a mark of the dispensability and weakness of the moderates—tend to confirm our previous formulation.

22. The Salvadoran Left*

BY ROBERT S. LEIKEN

*For years, the Salvadoran guerrillas have employed the slogan "The people united will
never be defeated." But unity has been an elusive ideal. The Salvadoran left squabbled
even as it fought the common enemy. This should occasion little surprise, for the left
everywhere, not just in El Salvador, is rarely unified. What causes disunity in El Salvador
is perceptively analyzed by Robert S. Leiken in the reading that follows.*

*Leiken is a senior associate at the Carnegie Endowment for International Peace. He
is coeditor, with Barry Rubin, of* The Central American Crisis Reader *(New York,
1986).*

GENEALOGY

THE FMLN has two main sources: radicalized religious activists, and the
Salvadoran Communist Party. Vatican II and the 1968 Conference of Latin
American bishops in Medellín, Colombia, had an especially powerful impact
on the Salvadoran clergy. "Christian base communities," small Bible-study

* From *Central America: Anatomy of Conflict,* edited by Robert S. Leiken (New York: Pergamon Press, 1984). Footnotes deleted.

The Salvadoran Opposition (FMLN-FDR)

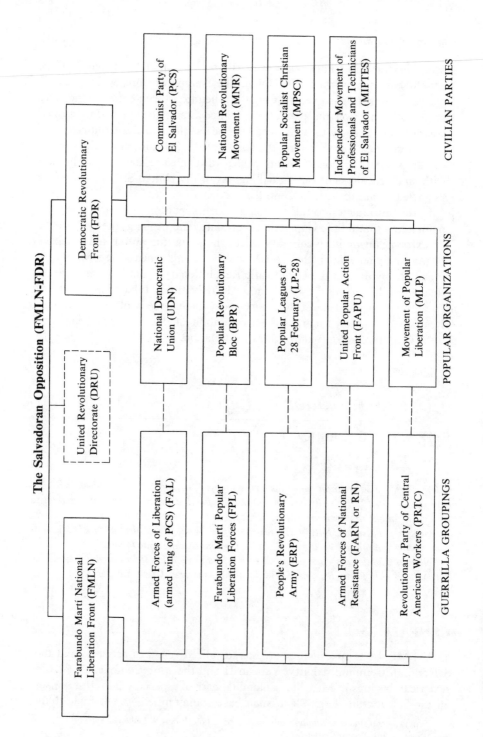

groups disseminating liberation theology's message of Christ's "preferential option for the poor," were formed in many parishes which later were to serve as rear-guard zones for the guerrillas.[1] The guerrilla-led mass "popular organizations" formed in reaction to the electoral frauds of the early 1970s drew many of their activists and leaders from these Christian communities.

The same was true for the "political-military fronts" that split off from the Salvadoran Communist Party. In 1970, Salvador Cayetano Carpio, a former seminarian and the secretary-general of the party, resigned and took underground the first cell of the Popular Forces of Liberation (FPL). They quickly recruited radicalized members of the Christian base communities and persecuted union activists. Shortly thereafter an amalgam of ex-party members, young Christian Democratic Party dissidents, religious activists, and student revolutionaries known as *El Grupo* ("The Group") publicly announced the formation of the People's Revolutionary Army (ERP). Two more organizations, the Armed Forces of National Resistance (FARN or RN), and the Revolutionary Party of Central American Workers (PRTC), were later to split from this grouping. The fifth guerrilla organization, the Armed Forces of Liberation (FAL), was formed by the Communist Party between 1977 and 1979. Thus, in varying degrees, all of the guerrilla organizations are products of the prolonged and turbulent struggle within the Salvadoran Communist Party.

The first apple of party discord, dating back to the Cuban Revolution, was the question of armed struggle. During the 1960s there developed in the PCS currents that favored the Cuban and Chinese criticisms of the Soviet line of "peaceful transition to socialism" which had repudiated armed struggle. Sympathizers of the Cubans gravitated to the FPL; of the Chinese to the ERP. The Soviet invasion of Czechoslovakia and enunciation of the Brezhnev Doctrine —each in turn endorsed by Fidel Castro and repudiated by the Chinese— sharpened the divisions in the party as well as among its dissidents. By the early 1970s the FPL, like the Cubans, was lining up with Moscow on international questions. The revolutionary groups engaged in ferocious polemics in their newspapers, in the National University, and in the "popular organizations" then beginning to form.

The first of the popular organizations was the United Popular Action Front (FAPU), a broad coalition of peasant, trade union, teacher, and student organizations, professors, radicalized clergy, and members of the Communist Party, the FPL, and the ERP. By then the ERP itself was beginning to subdivide into a "military" and a "political" wing. The latter, which eventually would become the National Resistance (RN), was responsible for work inside the FAPU. The differences within the FAPU between what was to become the RN and the FPL were to reemerge years later, after the formation of the FMLN,

---

[1.] See chapter 3, especially Reading 14.—Eds.

on the key question of political and military strategy for the revolutionary war.

In 1974–75 the two FAPU factions diverged on the role of reform versus revolution, the working class versus the peasantry, popular insurrection versus "protracted war," and on the matter of alliances with the middle class. The ERP-RN conceived the revolution as unfolding in stages leading to mass insurrection. Actions should correspond to "the historical moment," especially the level of awareness and organization of the masses. The struggle for reforms was necessary to consolidate the mass organizations, to create a political space in El Salvador, and for the masses to learn "from their own bitter experience" the futility of reformism. The same flexibility applied in choosing allies. All "democratic sectors" should be fused in a broad "anti-fascist united front." This would include not only those directly "represented," the workers and the peasants (with emphasis on the labor unions), but also ample sectors of the middle class and "democratic army officers."

The FPL considered the peasantry the key element in a worker-peasant alliance for a "protracted people's war." The FPL rejected the "anti-fascist united front" because it "liquidated class contradictions." The reform struggle and alliances with the middle class and military reformers would lead to co-optation. The mass organizations should provide the recruits for protracted war. Partly because of the large number of radicalized Christian militants, the FPL leadership inculcated a messianic spirit of self-sacrifice—in Cayetano Carpio's words, "a mystique . . . so that the members . . . are disposed to sacrifice their life . . . in any moment." The RN, by comparison, was a body of irresolute "politicians," disposed to compromise with the enemy.

As a result of these differences and the bitter rivalries among member organizations, the FAPU split, and, in July 1975, the FPL formed its own popular organization, the Revolutionary Popular Bloc (BPR). But even as this split was developing, the ERP itself was splitting. In 1975 its "Military Staff" tried and executed the group's leading intellectual, Roque Dalton, charged as a "Soviet-Cuban and CIA double agent." Dalton's supporters, members of the political faction of the ERP, subsequently left the group to form the RN.

By 1978 each of the three main guerrilla groups headed a "popular organization." The FPL-led BPR was the largest, with nine affiliated organizations and a membership of sixty thousand. Its main base was among the agricultural workers and peasants demanding wage hikes, reductions in land rents, and credits. The BPR frequently led peasant occupations of haciendas and uncultivated land. The RN-led FAPU (about half the size of the BPR) was strong among the urban trade unions of the National Federation of Salvadoran Workers (FENASTRAS). Belatedly, in February 1978, the ERP organized its own popular organization, the Popular Leagues of February 28 (LP-28). In late 1979 the PRTC founded the Popular Liberation Movement (MLP). By this time the Communist Party had formed a guerrilla wing, the Armed Forces of Liberation (FAL). Back in the 1960s the Party had gained control of the

National Democratic Union (UDN) and organized it as an electoral front. With the affiliation of trade unions and teacher organizations, it too gradually took on the character of a popular organization. By May 1980, all five popular organizations had united in the Revolutionary Coordinator of the Masses (CRM). At this time these mass organizations, capable of organizing truly massive street demonstrations in the capital, were the foundation of the guerrillas' power.

In 1975, FAPU demonstrators were gunned down in San Salvador. Thereafter mass demonstrations and meetings were accompanied by small contingents of discreetly armed militants. Government repression solidified the links between the popular organizations and the guerrilla groups. The former came to constitute recruiting ground for the latter. Demonstrations grew steadily in size and, in January 1980, four popular organizations announced a demonstration to celebrate their unification. Most prominent among the demands advanced by the organizers of the demonstration were calls for land reform, the creation of a "new people's army to replace the old," a national health care system, and a campaign against illiteracy. Estimates of the size of this demonstration vary widely, but it certainly was the largest in Salvadoran history. It was fired upon by the Salvadoran security forces, leaving dozens dead and hundreds injured. This and the massacre that accompanied the funeral of Archbishop Oscar Romero in March ended the epoch of large street demonstrations in San Salvador. The center of activity of the revolutionary organizations shifted to their rear-guard bases in the mountains. In May 1980 they announced the formation of the Unified Revolutionary Directorate (DRU), the precursor of the FMLN.

The revolutionary organizations had reacted in different ways to the reformist military coup of October 1979. The Communist Party welcomed the coup and prepared to join the government. The ERP called for an insurrection and set up barricades in San Salvador's suburbs. Later, in an about-face, it agreed to "study" any offer of participation in the junta. The FPL called the ERP's insurrections "suicidal" but opposed the junta as a U.S. plot. Its BPR occupied the headquarters of the economic, planning, and labor ministries, taking three hundred hostages to exchange for political prisoners, wage increases, and price controls. The RN favored "dialogue" between the junta and the popular organizations.

The October junta was composed of reformist and traditional military officers as well as Christian Democrats, Social Democrats, and Communists who later were to join the guerrilla-led popular organizations in the FDR. The revolutionary organizations' attitudes toward the junta were consistent with past and future divergencies. The ERP leapt at the prospect of armed insurrection. The FPL was cautious militarily but intransigent politically. The RN perceived an opening toward an "anti-fascist front" and sought an understanding with the reformist middle class politicians and military officers. When the junta collapsed under the weight of its own internal contradictions, all sides could claim vindication. But Cynthia Arnson's assessment is more accurate:

> By failing to appreciate divisions within the military and between the civilian and military representatives of the junta, the left played into the hands of the coup's betrayers. The High Command and sectors of the Army security forces furthest to the right ordered a stepped up campaign of violence and repression on the premise of restoring "law and order." The junior officers acquiesced to their superiors. . . . The attitude of the left caused the younger officers to feel that they, too, were regarded as the enemy.

AT WAR

The legacies of the FMLN's prehistory were smoldering, and sometimes violent internal struggle and an organic linkage with significant mass organizations. The latter have provided not only a reserve of guerrilla fighters and sympathizers but also the bulk of the "militias" that now play a key role in the FMLN military structure. Along with 6,000–8,000 guerrillas, the FMLN claims to have up to a million sympathizers, including one hundred thousand militia members. The latter provide food, storage, a postal service, intelligence, and back-up support in military operations. Militia members "keep a gun and some ammunition in their hut or farm" and "follow a certain discipline." In the cities they are supplemented by block and neighborhood committees that stockpile arms, ammunition, food, water, and medicine and provide logistical support, erect barricades, and dig trenches during conflicts.

As the war has deepened, the guerrillas have consolidated their support system, but their reservoir of popular sympathy seems to have diminished significantly, especially in the capital. According to ERP commander Joaquín Villalobos, the guerrillas failed to earn sufficient popular support early in 1981, just when their military capacities appeared to have matured and they undertook the "final offensive." "What happened was that we lost the propitious moment." In fact, they have consistently overestimated the readiness of the masses to support their tactics and heed their calls for strikes and insurrections. The guerrillas' onslaught on the economy has destroyed factories, stores, buses, private cars, and public utilities, causing widespread disruption, unemployment and misery. In January 1982, trade union leaders sympathetic to the guerrillas' moderate program, if not their immoderate methods, told me that three years before, at the time of the great street demonstrations in San Salvador, "the guerrillas spoke for all people." Now they believed that no longer was the case. This alienation is one reason why an incipient "third force" has emerged in El Salvador from among the unions and other sectors. It supports neither the FMLN nor the government but peace talks between them.

However, the elections of March 1982 should not so much be interpreted as a repudiation of the guerrillas as of the war. When elections are carried out under conditions of civil war, such as those held in Algeria between 1948 and 1954, in South Vietnam in 1967 or Zimbabwe-Rhodesia in 1979, the results can be deceptive. In the case of El Salvador the elections reflected, among other things, the changing conditions of the war. As is customary in Third World revolutionary wars, the locus of guerrilla power had shifted to the countryside. The government controlled most of the major cities (though they remain subject to guerrilla incursions), the guerrillas much of the eastern and northern countryside. The election turnout was heavy in the government-controlled cities and quite light in areas dominated by guerrillas.

Since the failed "final offensive" of early 1981, the guerrillas have carried out several offensives, each larger, better coordinated, and more damaging than the last. Guerrilla assessments of the war tend to correspond to the divergent approaches of the major groups.

The ERP has been inclined to triumphalism. After the FMLN's successful January 1983 offensive, leading ERP *comandantes* were predicting the Salvadoran army's collapse by the end of the year. The ERP is also by far the FMLN's most effective military force. This summer it inaugurated a full-size brigade, the Rafael Arce Zablah, capable of undertaking a variety of strategic missions. It was apparently trained in the ERP's "zone of control" in northern Morazán province, where the ERP runs two "military academies." These are directed by former Salvadoran army captains. In early September the Arce brigade initiated the latest, and spectacularly successful, guerrilla offensive by taking and holding for the better part of one day, the country's third largest city, San Miguel.

The other two major groups have been more restrained in their analyses. The RN and the FPL stress that although the government's new "National Pacification Plan" failed as soon as the guerrillas pushed against it, the army still retains "relative control over the strategic economic zones" and "abundant tactical resources." Above all "the masses are not insurrectionary." Nonetheless they stress that the nature of the war is changing from one of isolated guerrilla attacks to a "war of movement" utilizing ever larger guerrilla contingents able to move freely and openly through greater areas of the countryside.

The guerrillas assert that their military successes have increased their numbers, leading in turn to grander exploits. The widening of their "zones of control" in 1982–83 enables them to incorporate more peasants into their ranks. The expansion of the areas of conflict, from which the guerrillas withdraw upon arrival of the army, allows them to create clandestine networks. This, in turn, facilitates travel from areas of conflict into controlled zones where recruits can undergo military training. With each temporary occupation of a village—they claim seventy were taken in their offensive of fall 1983—the guerrillas are able to propagandize and to establish an underground organization.

TAKING SIDES

The RN and ERP have shown the greatest independence in developing their international views and in their international dealings. Among RN intellectuals and political leaders genuine non-alignment has been a basic ideological tenet. Among many lower-level RN cadre, however, strong sympathies for Cuba prevail. The ERP is fiercely nationalistic, impatient with ideology, and suspicious of "socialist" solidarity. Both the ERP and the RN have been quite critical of the Cuban presence and influence in Managua. ERP leaders have said that they would not want to see "so many Cuban doctors, teachers, and advisers in El Salvador." A leading RN official considers Nicaragua's press censorship a grave error. "If they didn't like *La Prensa,* they should have created a better newspaper." He was critical too, of the Cuban role in Sandinista economic planning and thought that together they were leading the country toward economic disaster. But the Sandinistas' greatest error has been their sectarianism, "not incorporating the masses into the revolutionary process."

Historically, the FPL has been the group closest to Cuba and Nicaragua. It is especially intimate with the Protracted People's War (GPP) faction of the Sandinistas, which has proved to be the most proficient at infighting in Managua. Cuban officials consider the FPL to have "the most developed Marxist-Leninist analysis of Salvadoran reality." But the FPL's former leader Cayetano Carpio's intransigent opposition to a political settlement has led to frequent tensions with Havana. With respect to the Soviet Union, the FPL has had two orientations over the years. The old leadership from the Salvadoran Communist Party retained few criticisms of Moscow once the USSR had abandoned its line of "peaceful transition." Characteristically they defended the invasion of Afghanistan and martial law in Poland. Younger leaders and militants with Christian activist origins, on the other hand, consider the Soviet Union corrupt and oppressive. Like others in the FMLN, they criticize Moscow not from an East-West perspective, but from a North-South perspective.

The Salvadoran Communist Party, with its Armed Forces of Liberation (FAL), remains firmly in the Soviet camp. It has gained some measure of influence within the PRTC, hitherto quite independent. Nonetheless, a PRTC congress in the spring of 1983 reaffirmed its independence.

The FPL is the largest of the FMLN groups in membership but not in armed guerrillas. As of early 1983 the ERP, with close to 40% of the guerrillas, was, by far, the biggest and most effective fighting force. The FPL is next largest with about 20%, followed by the FARN with 15%. The FAL and the PRTC each have less than 10% of the guerrillas, and the remainder is not permanently attached to any single group. A major argument against negotiations with the FDR-FMLN is that "the Marxist-Leninists have the guns." Yet among these "Marxist-Leninist" guerrillas, it is the organizations that stand at the greatest distance from the Soviet Union which control nearly two-thirds of the fighting force.

It is not certain that the FMLN will pursue real non-alignment. The Cubans have been assiduously courting the ERP, with whom they share a militarist orientation. The PRTC, as we have seen, is vulnerable to penetration by the Salvadoran Communist Party. Furthermore, as the war drags on and threatens to regionalize, the FMLN must perforce draw closer to its Nicaraguan and Cuban allies. On the other hand, the recent events within the FPL disclose this group as a rather unreliable wedge for Cuban-Soviet penetration.

NEGOTIATIONS AS STRATEGY

The most neuralgic point of difference within the FMLN has been the question of negotiations. As we have seen, all of the groups now comprising the FMLN —with the exception of the RN—refused to negotiate with the reformist October 1979 junta which included many of their current colleagues of the FDR. After the failure of the "final offensive" in February 1981, the political diplomatic commission of the FMLN-FDR approved an internal document which committed it for the first time to negotiations. Yet the document supported negotiations only as a "tactic," a "maneuver" for "gaining time and diplomatic initiative." These reservations were the price exacted by Cayetano Carpio's FPL hard-liners from the rising number of FMLN-FDR members who supported a political solution.

In the second half of 1981 the FPL became increasingly isolated on this issue as the other guerrilla groups and even the FPL's main outside backer, Cuba, endorsed "negotiations as a strategy."

Under Cayetano Carpio's leadership, the FPL had become an increasingly isolated, recalcitrant opponent both of negotiations and of the military and political unification of the FMLN. The other FMLN groupings bitterly complained of the FPL's refusal to coordinate military actions with the other groups. They regarded this as a major reason for the failure of the guerrillas' March 1982 election offensive.

Carpio's intransigent, fiercely independent attitude eventually created dissension in his own organization. Second-in-command Melida Anaya Montes (a.k.a. "Ana María") became the voice of the opposition. In October of 1982 Ana María supported the decision of the other FMLN groupings to present a concrete negotiating proposal to the government. Cayetano Carpio balked, but was forced to go along when the other groupings threatened to present the proposal without him.

Cayetano Carpio's line was finally and decisively overthrown at a meeting of the FPL's central command (Co-Cen) in January 1983. There, the FPL accepted negotiations as "an auxiliary but strategic factor in our struggle"; approved "unity of the FMLN" as a "strategic objective" and pledged to "eliminate from our vocabulary all objectives which offend the other organizations"; and accepted that alliances were now to include all "non-oligarchal" sectors. The document was approved overwhelmingly by the Central Command, signifying that Ana María was now the de facto leader of the organization.

Less than three months later, Ana María was repeatedly and grotesquely stabbed to death by Cayetano Carpio's closest comrades. According to an official communiqué of the FPL, Cayetano himself, resentful at his "political and moral defeat" in the Co-Cen meeting became "the principal initiator responsible for the assassination. . . ."

It has been rumored by unofficial FMLN sources and diplomats in Managua that Tomás Borge, a leader of the Sandinista's National Directorate and Minister of the Interior, went personally to Cayetano Carpio's house three days after Ana María's murder. Borge is reported to have told Carpio that he had to choose between suicide and public disclosure of his own and his comrades' involvement in Ana María's murder. Suicide would assure that the murder would remain an internal FPL affair.

Borge had originally denounced Ana María's assassination as a "CIA plot." Subsequently, both Managua and the FMLN quietly dropped that allegation, but there has been speculation of international involvement from another source. Historically, Borge's own GPP faction of the Sandinistas had been close to Cayetano and the FPL. This was especially true of National Directorate *comandante* Bayardo Arce of the GPP and his assistant Julio López. These two head the international section of the Sandinista Party and are charged with relations with fraternal organizations. According to Sandinista defector Miguel Bolanos Hunter, his former superior in the Interior Ministry accused Julio López of having failed to guarantee Ana María's security. Bolanos claims she was killed for "political reasons—she was just back from Cuba and wanted to have more dialogue between the guerrillas and the Salvadoran government." The GPP is reported to be the most intransigent of the Sandinista factions, though Borge himself, after a sharp turnabout this summer, now champions the Nicaraguan negotiation campaign.

The international reverberations of the deaths in Managua do not stop here. On May 25, U.S. Navy Lieutenant Commander Albert A. Schaufelberger, a military adviser in the American embassy, was killed in San Salvador. The FPL, and later the FMLN as a whole, took responsibility for the action, but the manner in which they did it raises questions. The FPL "communiqué" was delivered to a commercial Salvadoran radio station on stationery without the group's customary letterhead. Moreover, normally such communiqués are read over the guerrillas' own radio stations. The FMLN delayed in acknowledging responsibility for the action. Subsequent events were to suggest that this and other urban terrorist actions carried out during the same period were committed by a breakaway group of Cayetano Carpio's supporters within the FPL.

In August, the FPL held a "unity congress" dedicated to Ana María and reaffirming the hegemony of her line. But the unity was short-lived. Three months later, Cayetano Carpio's closest followers had split from the FPL, repudiating its new leadership. In early December a new faction, the Revolutionary Workers' Movement/Salvador Cayetano Carpio (MOR), claimed responsibility for several bombings in San Salvador. The split and the terrorism confirmed earlier speculation that there had been a dissident terrorist faction inside the FPL since April. Within days of the MOR declaration, the FPL issued a communiqué denouncing Cayetano Carpio and the "backward, sectarian and anti-unity position of MOR."

Certainly for the FPL, violence has been "the midwife of history." The main result of their fratricidal struggle has been the consolidation of positions favoring negotiations and unity with the other FMLN groups. According to FMLN and FDR sources the FPL now cooperates militarily and politically with the other groups. The spectacular military successes of the guerrillas in the latter part of 1983 appeared to corroborate this claim. Politically, the guerrillas now appear firmly united around the FMLN-FDR October 1982 proposal for unconditional negotiations.

What has led these guerrilla organizations down the path from no dialogue with the reformist October junta—which included their current associates in the civilian wing of the FDR—to unconditional negotiations with the present right-of-center government? In the light of the guerrillas' steady military progress, weakness cannot be the explanation. The guerrillas do acknowledge war-weariness, but they give more stress to the toll on the civilian population. The importance of the FMLN's links with the popular organizations has never been properly understood in Washington. The popular desire for peace is one reason the majority of organizations in the FMLN have rejected the strategy of protracted war.

The FMLN holds that a military victory over the Salvadoran armed forces is possible, but recognizes that a government produced by a military victory would have serious internal and external problems. Among the external problems would be the hostile attitude of the United States. The reconstruction and development of the war-devastated economy would become insuperably difficult should the U.S. seek to embargo the Salvadoran economy—one far more industrially developed and hence more dependent on foreign imports than that of Cuba or Nicaragua.

These factors help explain why the FMLN-FDR has progressively softened its negotiating position even as it has gained ground militarily. The FMLN has now agreed to the preservation of the "institutionality of the army" in a negotiated settlement. They are also prepared to participate in elections, and to guarantee a non-aligned foreign policy, and a mixed economy.

These concessions could form part of a framework for negotiations that could safeguard legitimate U.S. security interests. In this framework the security forces would be cleansed, professionalized, and placed under the effective jurisdiction of the Interior Department, where they could be integrated with FMLN forces into a territorial militia. The Salvadoran army's officer corps would be preserved, and only individual officers guilty of major abuses and convicted after proper investigation and due process would be retired with compensation. The same would be true for members on both sides of the territorial militia.

When the Sandinistas came to power in Nicaragua, the failure of previous mediation efforts led to their enjoyment of a vital monopoly of military and political resources. This has been a major factor in the country's evolution toward a monolithic political apparatus and alignment with the Soviet bloc. Should there be negotiations in El Salvador, a multiplicity of political actors, each with military and political resources, will contend for power. Among them will be the moderate pro-government political parties; the civilian parties in the FDR; the different FMLN groupings with their conflicting agendas; military reformers and more conservative military officers; the church; and the trade unions. Negotiations will not end the struggle but they will shift it to different terrain—the political and economic. On this terrain the Cuban-Soviet bloc is at its weakest.

As we have seen, conflict in the FPL does not seem to prefigure fissures within the FMLN. It is unlikely that the FMLN will split *before* a political settlement is achieved in El Salvador. However, there is danger that if the sectarian past reasserts itself, internal conflict could develop after a political settlement. It is also unlikely that the "democratic elements" of the FMLN-FDR would split off from the guerrilla organizations before the end of the war. Both the Carter and Reagan administrations have endeavored to lure the FDR away from the FMLN via elections. This has little chance of succeeding as long as its civilian adherents believe that a rupture of their alliance with the FMLN would deliver them into the hands of the armed oligarchy. After the October 1982 disappearance from San Salvador of several leaders of the FDR just as the latter was proposing negotiations, such fears seemed warranted.

Furthermore, the drawing of hard and fast distinctions between the "democratic" and the "violent" members of the opposition is not always useful. This is not only because the "democrats" support the armed struggle but also because the integration of the FMLN and the FDR's civilian organization is horizontal as well as vertical. The FPL has gained a certain measure of influence in the Social Democratic MNR of Guillermo Ungo. Ruben Zamora of the Popular Social Christian Movement—split off from the Christian Democratic Party—is highly respected and trusted by the ERP and the RN. The immanent line of demarcation within the FMLN-FDR is not so much between democracy and revolution but between non-alignment and Soviet alignment.

SOCIALISM AND SOVIETISM

In Central America, as in the rest of the Third World, revolutionary groups display a variety of attitudes toward the Soviet bloc. But in the American "backyard" the left is more inclined to Soviet alignment than in other parts of the Third World. Many, but certainly not all, Central American dissidents have come to regard world events as a contest between "reactionary forces" led by "Yankee imperialism"—of which they have had firsthand experience —and "progressive forces" led, or at least assisted, by the Soviet Union—of which they have had none. A history of U.S. opposition to legitimate change in Central America, revolutionary or otherwise, has been the main propagator of this view. Currently the principal justification for resumption of such policies has been the assumption that revolutionary movements eventually must link themselves to Soviet expansionism. Yet the diversity and even collision of views among the Salvadoran revolutionary groups in particular, and Central American groups in general, should force us to examine this assumption.

El Salvador is only the most graphic example of the division between non-alignment and Soviet alignment within the Central American left. Many of the *Terceristas* in Nicaragua envisioned a non-aligned course for the revolution in which the country would stand equidistant from the two superpowers. Between 1979 and 1983 a line similar to the old FPL line in El Salvador—that of the GPP tendency—seemed to have prevailed in Managua. There is reason to hope that the old *Tercerista* positions may reassert themselves in Managua.

In Guatemala and Costa Rica similar divisions exist among leftist groups. The Guatemalan Revolutionary Organization of the People in Arms (ORPA) and the Rebel Armed Forces (FAR) replicate some of the RN and ERP agnosticism toward Moscow. The People's Guerrilla Army (EGP) is closer to the Salvadoran pro-Cuban FPL while the Guatemalan Workers' Party (PGT) is directly backed by Moscow. In the summer of 1982, the Costa Rican electoral front, *Pueblo Unido* (People United), split twice over the issues of broad alliances and the Soviet Union. Eric Ardon, the leader of the Revolutionary Movement of the People (MRP) declared that a major reason for separating from the *Vanguardia Popular,* the pro-Soviet party, was that "they are permanently aligned with the Soviet Union." This same Eric Ardon was accused of Sovietism after he interrupted President Reagan during his visit to Costa Rica in December 1982.

Over the past decade, U.S. political leaders and policymakers have learned to distinguish leftism, even some varieties of Marxism-Leninism, from Sovietism. In other parts of the Third World non-Soviet and pro-Soviet insurgent groups have parted company after the winning of power. This has been the case in Angola, Zimbabwe, Egypt, China, and Indochina, among others. Recently, a virulently anti-Soviet guerrilla group emerged in Peru. In a number of Asian and African countries, revolutionary regimes have spurned alignment with the

Soviet Union. Marxist-Leninist China, with one quarter of the world's population, remains a bulwark against Soviet hegemonism. Marxist-Leninist Yugoslavia receives U.S. aid.

Nonetheless, we have been reluctant to apply these distinctions in the U.S. "backyard." These distinctions will have to be made if the U.S. is to live peaceably with its southern neighbors. By ignoring them and by its wholesale opposition to the entire Central American left, U.S. policy pushes the non-aligned left into the arms of those who are pro-Soviet. U.S. national security would indeed be threatened by Soviet-aligned regimes in the Caribbean Basin, but not necessarily by independent leftist regimes—even if they do speak the language of Marxism and seek to practice socialism. This discrimination will be fundamental to developing future U.S. policies for the region.

23. The Guerrilla Army*

By Radio Liberation and an FMLN Commander

The Farabundo Martí National Liberation Front (FMLN) seems to be modeled on the guerrilla armies of China, Cuba, and Vietnam. Part of their success can be attributed to an ability to induce large numbers of the enemies' armies to defect. The statements that follow make clear that the FMLN is making a similar effort. Successful guerrilla armies do more than fight. By concerning themselves with the health, education, and social needs of the peasants, guerrillas win their sympathy and support.

A. RADIO LIBERATION (JANUARY 17, 1981)

THE fighting people are building a new army. In our fatherland there is suffering but there are also heroic sacrifices that are building a new society, erected on the ruins of the old oppressive structures. It is a fact that the fascist army is collapsing at the same time that the people's army is growing.

The people's army is completely different from the gorilla [*sic*][1] army. Besides its growth, in our army's ranks there is friendship and brotherhood. There are no arbitrary and cruel chiefs in it. All its members see each other as brothers without distinctions in seniority, social position or ranks. What unites us is the resolute decision to fight and our eyes are always set on the great objective of achieving a bright future of peace and freedom for our fatherland.

* Radio Liberation, January 17, 1981, from Foreign Broadcast Information Service, *Daily Reports,* January 19, 1981, and from *Barricada,* Managua, June 1, 1981, Foreign Broadcast Information Service, *Daily Reports,* June 5, 1981.

[1.] For the meaning of *gorilla*, see p. xix.—Eds.

In his message to his comrades in arms who are still in the despicable army of the fascists, Lt. Col. Ricardo Bruno Navarrete has described the joy he felt at the warm reception he received when he joined our army. Lt. Emilio Mena Sandoval and Lt. Marcelo Cruz, along with the compañero commanders of the FMLN [Farabundo Martí National Liberation Front], have been at the head of the battles of our forces in Santa Ana where they are getting ready for new offensives. They remain in the frontline despite the fact that the liar junta has tried to misinform the people by saying that they are in Guatemala. The troops, which joined the Farabundo Martí National Liberation Front along with the lieutenants, continue alongside our brother fighters in the common struggle.

Another thing that distinguishes the new army from the fascist army is the high morale of its fighters which has led them to acts of great heroism. Our army is not an army of mercenaries because it is an army with ideals of justice and freedom. The FMLN fighters struggle and face death with heroism for the noble and just cause of the people. It is led by our political-military leadership, forged in the daily struggle, filled with privations and sacrifices which has armed it with a courage of steel, revolutionary conscience and a spirit of sacrifice, characteristics that the fascist officers of the gorilla army do not have and will never have because they are a handful of corrupt and murderous traitors.

In the new army of the liberated fatherland there is room for the troops and officers of the enemy's army who join the ranks of the people. The democratic revolutionary government will create a new type of army made up of the popular revolutionary army and the honest and patriotic individuals in the ranks of the troops and officers of the current army. The incorporation of officers Mena Sandoval, Cruz and Navarrete has already made a reality the proposal contained in the platform of the Democratic Revolutionary Government.

Long live the Democratic Revolutionary Government! Long live the new popular revolutionary army! Long live the incorporation of the honest officers, noncommissioned officers and soldiers in the ranks of the FMLN!

B. FMLN COMMANDER RIGOBERTO HERNÁNDEZ (JUNE 1, 1981)

The concerns and needs of the community are constant. Children, women, old people and fighters need food. People must learn to read and write, and they require medical attention and an armed defense. It is here that the FMLN power comes into play. The FMLN plans the mechanisms for the planting of staples, mainly corn and beans. Coordination is established with the few revolutionary doctors stationed in the military area so that they can attend to the people's health. Coordination mechanisms are established with the militias and they distribute the tasks of building defenses against air and artillery attacks, construction of communications trenches and so forth.

The organization also guarantees the safety and maintenance of the troops who are constantly fighting inside and outside the region.

In order to promote production, fighters have a schedule in which each unit participates in planting and cultivating staple grains. This is coordinated by the FMLN directorate.

They teach reading and writing. A literacy campaign is being promoted by teachers and clergywomen at the battlefront. Every morning and afternoon children and adults attend makeshift classrooms or sit under trees where they are taught to read and write in a manner adapted to the specific conditions in which Salvadoran workers live. When the junta's army attacks, pencils and notebooks are immediately exchanged for rifles, shotguns, antipersonnel bombs or any other manufactured or homemade weapon.

The FMLN power in rural areas, scattered throughout the country, is the structural base for a new people's power on Salvadoran territory, a power parallel to the one supported by the armed forces of the junta to keep power in the hands of a local oligarchy which, allied to the United States, has maintained this system over 50 years. It is slowly but surely crumbling.

24. Platform of the Revolutionary Democratic Government*

On February 27, 1980, the coordinating committee of the Salvadoran revolutionary organizations (CRM) made public its programmatic platform excerpted below. Calling for such economic measures as nationalized banking, foreign trade, and electricity distribution and a deepening agrarian reform, along with such social measures as low-cost housing, a national health system and a literacy campaign—all within a framework designed to benefit small and medium-sized private businesses, owners of real estate, and landowners—the writers of the platform see the revolution they espouse as "popular, democratic and anti-oligarchic" and the only path to "true and effective national independence."

A few months later, a Revolutionary Manifesto of May 1980 (see the U.S. Department of State release, June 17, 1980) was issued by the Unified Revolutionary Directorate (DRU). The formation of DRU was a significant step toward the unity a successful guerrilla struggle requires. The various guerrilla groups still remained separate entities but now had "a single leadership, a single military command and single command unit." (Later, in October, they were to merge into the Farabundo Martí National Liberation Front.) This manifesto—more inspirational in tone—echoed the programmatic platform

---

* From *Barricada*, March 4–5, 1980, published in Managua. The translation is by Intercontinental Press.

without its detail. The Reagan State Department characterized this manifesto as follows: "In May 1980, the leftist opposition to the government formed the Unified Revolutionary Directorate (DRU), which in its manifesto is dedicated to the establishment of a Marxist, totalitarian government in El Salvador" (U.S. Department of State Bulletin, *March 1981, 10).*

At a later stage in the civil war, the FMLN issued a detailed proposal for a provisional government (Reading 25).

THE economic and social structures of our country—which have served to guarantee the disproportionate enrichment of an oligarchic minority and the exploitation of our people by Yankee imperialism—are in deep and insoluble crisis.

The economic and political crisis of the dominant classes on the one hand, and on the other the forward impulse of the decisive political force in our country, the people's movement, have given rise to a revolutionary process and to conditions in which the people can assume power.

The revolutionary transformation of our society—submitted up to now to injustice, betrayal, and pillage—is today a near and possible reality.

It will be the revolution that will gain true political independence for our country, giving the Salvadoran people the right to freely determine their destiny and attain true economic independence.

This revolution is therefore popular, democratic, and antioligarchic, and seeks to conquer true and effective national independence.

The decisive task of the revolution on which completion of all its objectives depends is the conquest of power and the installation of a *revolutionary democratic government,* which at the head of the people will launch the construction of a new society.

Task and Objectives of the Revolution . . . :

To overthrow the reactionary military dictatorship of the oligarchy and Yankee imperialism . . . and to establish a *revolutionary democratic government,* founded on the unity of the revolutionary and democratic forces in the People's Army and the Salvadoran people.

To put an end to the . . . power of the great lords of land and capital.

To liquidate . . . the . . . dependence of our country on Yankee imperialism.

To assure democratic rights and freedoms for the entire people—particularly for the working masses.

The Democratic Revolutionary Government—Its Composition and Platform of Social, Structural and Political Changes. The revolutionary democratic government will be made up of representatives of the revolutionary and people's movement, as well as of the democratic parties, organizations, sectors, and individuals who are willing to participate in the carrying out of this programmatic platform.

Immediate Political Measures: A halt to all forms of repression against the people and release of all political prisoners. . . .

Disarming and permanent dissolution of the repressive bodies— ANSESAL, ORDEN, National Guard, National Police, Treasury Police, and Customs Police, along with their respective "Special Sections"; of the Gotera "Counterinsurgency School" and the so-called Armed Forces Engineering Training Center in Zacatecoluca; of the cantonal and suburban military patrols; of the oligarchy's private paramilitary bands; and of all other kinds of real or nominal organizations dedicated to criminal action or slander against the people and their organizations. The current misnamed security bodies will be replaced by a civilian police force.

Dissolution of the existing state powers (executive, legislative, and judicial); abrogation of the Political Constitution and of all decrees that have modified or added to it.

The *revolutionary democratic government* will decree a constitutional law and will organize the state and its activities with the aim of guaranteeing the rights and freedoms of the people. . . . The *revolutionary democratic government* will adhere to the United Nations' "Universal Declaration of Human Rights."

The *revolutionary democratic government* will carry out an intense effort of liberating education, of cultural exposition and organization among the broadest masses, in order to promote their conscious incorporation into the development, strengthening and defense of the revolutionary process.

The People's Army will be strengthened and developed. . . .

The new army will be the true armed wing of the people. . . .

The revolutionary democratic government will establish diplomatic and trade relations with other countries without discrimination on the basis of differing social systems, on the basis of equal rights, coexistence, and respect for self-determination. . . . Close fraternal relations with Nicaragua will especially be sought, as the expression of the community of ideals and interests between our revolution and the Sandinista revolution.

Our country will become a member of the Movement of Nonaligned Countries and will develop a steadfast policy toward the defense of world peace and in favor of détente.

Structural Changes . . . :

Nationalize the entire banking and financial system; . . . Nationalize foreign trade; Nationalize the system of electricity distribution, along with the enterprises for its production that are in private hands; Nationalize the refining of petroleum.

Carry out the expropriation, in accord with the national interest, of the monopolistic enterprises in industry, trade, and services.

Carry out a deep-going agrarian reform, which will put the land that is now in the hands of the big landlords at the disposal of the broad masses who work it. . . .

The agrarian reform will not affect small and medium landholders, who will receive stimuli and support for continual improvements in production on their plots.

Carry out an urban reform to benefit the great majority, without affecting small and medium owners of real estate.

Thoroughly transform the tax system, so that tax payments no longer fall upon the workers. . . .

Establish effective mechanisms for credit, economic aid, and technical assistance for small and medium-sized private businesses. . . .

Establish a system for effective planning of the national economy. . . .

Social measures . . . :

Create sufficient sources of jobs so as to eliminate unemployment in the briefest possible time.

Bring into effect a just wage policy, based on:

Regulation of wages, taking into account the cost of living.

An energetic policy of control and reduction of the prices charged for basic goods and services.

A substantial increase in social services for the popular masses (social security, education, recreation, health care, etc.).

Put into action a massive plan for construction of low cost housing.

Create a Unified National Health System. . . .

Carry out a literacy campaign that will put an end to the social defect of illiteracy in the shortest possible time.

25. Proposal for a Provisional Government*

BY FDR/FMLN

The following, a platform for an incoming provisional government, was issued in early 1984, when the prospects for taking power seemed good.

However, with the application of massive air power, in combination with the emergence, however tentative, of a political center personified by José Napoleón Duarte, the revolution has been sidetracked. Even guerrilla leaders now speak of a long war of attrition. Nonetheless, what the FDR/FMLN considered to be worthy of inclusion in such a document is of historic interest, revealing its conception of power, government, and society (or possibly its conception of what programs it thinks will further the revolutionary process).

* Excerpted from English-language press release of the FDR/FMLN, January 31, 1984.

THE proposal to form the provisional government of broad participation is the result of the development of the democratic and revolutionary forces of the Salvadoran people in the military and political arena.

The basic objectives of the provisional government of broad participation:

1. To rescue national independence and sovereignty.
2. To dismantle the repressive apparatus and to lay the grounds for a true democracy in which human rights and political freedom are fully respected and where broad popular participation to achieve a definite peace becomes a reality.
3. To respond to the most immediate and pressing needs of the popular majorities and to adopt basic economic and social measures to change these structures.
4. To establish the practical conditions needed to solve the current state of war.
5. To prepare for and hold general elections.

Representatives of the labor movement, peasants, teachers, workers, professional associations, universities, political parties, the private sector, representatives of the FMLN-FDR, and of an already-restructured national army will compose the provisional government of broad participation.

The government institutions will be an expression of the representatives of all the above-mentioned sectors. The oligarchy, individuals and sectors that are against the objectives of the provisional government or that advocate the maintaining of the dictatorship will be excluded.

Immediate measures:

1. To repeal the political constitution of 1983, and to substitute it with a constitutional statute that will guide the action of the provisional government of broad participation.
2. To repeal the state of siege and all the decrees promulgated since 1980, that coerce social and individual freedoms.
3. Freedom for all political prisoners and disappeared, as well as the suspension of all sentences dictated based upon repressive and emergency decrees.
4. Full guarantees to exercise collective and individual rights of agricultural and state workers to organize themselves. Trade unions will be compensated for damages against their property, caused by the repression since 1979. The popular power organizations that have emerged in several areas of the country during the war will be legitimized.
5. The dissolution of the security forces, death squads and their political arm, the A.R.E.N.A. party. A new civilian police force will be created under the Ministry of the Interior.

6. Withdrawal of U.S. advisers, a halt to U.S. military aid, as well as that coming from other countries, and the halt of all arms shipments.

7. Restructuring of the governmental armed forces, and once it is achieved, the incorporation of its representatives in the structures of the provisional government of broad participation.

8. Investigation and bringing to trial of the military and civilians responsible for the genocide, political crimes, torture, disappearances and illegal abrogations of individual freedoms. The deaths of FMLN combatants and army soldiers and officers in military combat do not constitute a crime.

9. The Supreme Court of Justice will conduct the immediate investigation and trial for crimes against human rights. At the same time, it will undertake a restructuring and reorganization of the judicial system. The nongovernmental human rights organizations that defended the people during the dictatorship will be asked to help in these tasks.

10. The return of the exiled and refugees, and the implementation of an emergency program to absorb and assist in the most urgent needs of the refugees, the displaced, those disabled due to the war, the idling elements of the armed forces and of the families or individuals in abandonment because of the war on either side. The provisional government of broad participation will ask the collaboration of international agencies and nongovernmental organizations in these tasks.

11. Execution of an emergency program for the reconstruction of the economic, educational and health-care infrastructure damaged or destroyed by the war.

12. A moratorium on all debts of small and medium entrepreneurs. A lenient financial program will be implemented for these sectors, in the industrial and agricultural sectors, thus stimulating the economic recovery.

13. Price control of the basic products of popular consumption, thus improving the real value of wages. Reorganization and control of the commercialization and distribution system of the basic popular consumption products.

14. Reorganization of the external debt, based on reorganizing the financial commitments contracted by the previous governments.

15. Reestablishment of the autonomy of the National University of El Salvador, assigning the necessary resources for its functioning and reorganization. The installations of the university campus will be immediately handed over to its legitimate authorities.

16. Undertaking a massive literacy campaign and a democratic program of adult training in the areas of health, education, agricultural production and community organization.

17. The development of a massive employment plan through the promotion of private and governmental investment in labor-intensive sectors of the economy. An emergency program will be implemented for the acquisition

of raw materials, as supplies, necessary for the economic recovery. Adequate channels and profit margins for the producers will be guaranteed.

18. Promotion and development of a program of popular organization through the broadening and consolidation of the municipalities, communal and local organizations. Participation of these structures in the planning, execution and evaluation of the projects that benefit the community.

19. Development of a massive communication program, implementing the creation of massive popular communication means of local interest.

20. To establish an electoral institution, which, by agreement of the parties, prepares the holding of general and free elections. Reliable electoral registers will also be created.

Economic and social reforms

1. To lay the grounds for the full achievement of agrarian reform, insuring the free participation of the rural workers in its execution. To develop programs of cooperative organizations with small individual owners.

2. To lay the grounds for the full achievement of the nationalization of the country's banking and financial system, with the purpose of making the financial structure and the credit system serve the interests of the national majority.

3. To lay the grounds for the full achievement of foreign trade reform, including the control of exports of the main products: coffee, cotton, sugar cane, fishing industry and meat. To include control over the import of raw materials, supplies, spare parts and technology necessary for the national production.

4. To lay the ground for the adequate solution of the housing conditions of the low income sectors, as well as for the progressive expansion of the social security services, and to reorient foreign investment so it can effectively contribute to the fullfilment of the social needs.

Foreign Policy

The provisional government of broad participation will develop its foreign policy based on the following criteria:

1. The provisional government of broad participation will promote an international relations policy oriented at preserving peace, against the arms race and nuclear proliferation. It will defend the principles of peaceful coexistence, self-determination and non-intervention as follows:

   Will join the Movement of Non-Aligned Countries and consequently will reinforce the struggle against colonialism, neocolonialism, Zionism, race discrimination and apartheid.

   Diplomatic relations with other countries will be established independently of their social regime, and based on national interests.

Will comply with the obligations contracted in the international organizations, and will seek the active participation in international forums for the discussion and solution of the problems stemming from the economic relations among the nations.

Will reaffirm Bolivar's convictions and consequently will make efforts in the promotion of, and participation in the regional forums which strengthen the positions of the Latin American countries regarding the political, diplomatic, economic, financial and social regional problems.

2. In its relations with the United States:

   2.1. Proposes the signing of agreements that will guarantee the national security of both countries as follows:

   The provisional government of broad participation commits itself not to allow the installation of foreign military bases and/or missiles in its territory, and on its part, the Government of the United States should commit itself not to undertake, promote or encourage aggressive or destabilizing activities against the Provisional Government of Broad Participation, and the government that is created from said process.

   The Salvadoran Government will not allow its national territory to be used to destabilize the governments of neighboring countries, nor will it allow the transit of arms and foreign troops in its territory.

   Will promote the signing of agreements of non-aggression and non-intervention in the internal affairs of the countries of the area.

   2.2. The relations of the Government of El Salvador and the United States and Central America will be reoriented on the basis of the unconditional respect for the right to self-determination, independence and national sovereignty, as well as mutual cooperation and independence as follows:

   It will make efforts towards achieving the Morazanic ideal of the Central American unity, and that our region be free of foreign military forces. It will not participate in military alliances. Consequently, it will withdraw from C.O.N.D.E.C.A.

   It will actively participate in the promotion and development of regional organizations that will guarantee political solutions to the international conflicts, and will sign agreements that promote economic, social and political integration.

—General Command of the FMLN
Executive Committee of the FDR

26. *"Dual Power" in the Guerrilla "Zones of Control"**

BY JAMES LEMOYNE

During the period of the Vietnam war few western journalists had any first-hand experience with the areas held by the rebels of the National Liberation Front for South Vietnam, the group commonly called the Vietcong. One noteworthy exception was the Australian reporter Wilfred Burchett, who had a quarter century of experience in the region before he revisited the area in 1963–64. Burchett's glowing report, Vietnam: Inside Story of a Guerrilla War *(New York: International Publishers, 1965), was contemptuously dismissed as the apologetics of a Communist sympathizer. What was valid and accurate in his reporting (and it turned out that a good deal was) was precisely what was missing in the mainstream western press—insight into the revolutionary society the NLF was building in its zones and the rebels' determination to achieve victory.*

This account of life and politics in the rebel-held territories of El Salvador, written by New York Times *bureau chief in Central America James LeMoyne, on the basis of actual forays into the regions controlled by FMLN forces, is consistent with the observations of such previous observers as Raymond Bonner.*[1] *They indicate the considerable extent to which these regions exhibit "dual power," a situation in which the insurgents begin exercising sovereignty even before the power of the previous regime is extinguished. One rebel spokesman described the new political institutions in these areas, the PPLs (Poder Popular Locales) as "a common phenomenon in the history of humankind." Declared FMLN spokesman David Nachon:*

No society goes from one type of organization to another without living through a period of dual power. It has been present in all revolutions in different forms. It may be a territorial duality, where the established government controls a certain area and the revolutionary forces control others, but where no new political power structures evolve. [Or] it may be a political dualism, where . . . the PPLs function clandestinely alongside the established government. . . . During this time the state apparatus becomes like a vacuum, like an empty building [which the people seize]. . . . In other words, in a large portion of the country a seed of the new society exists, developing an alternate government in which all the people participate.[2]

No wonder the Salvadoran armed forces see these zones of control as their prime targets.[3] *For if the rebels can claim genuinely popular dual power, then the counterclaim that the revolutionaries are subversives, undermining rather than creating political insti-*

* James LeMoyne, "How Rebels Rule in Their Corner of El Salvador," *New York Times,* December 26, 1985.

[1] Raymond Bonner, *Weakness and Deceit: U.S. Policy and El Salvador* (New York: Times Books, 1984), 108–34.

[2] David Nachon, n.d., in FMLN press release.

[3] See *New York Times* dispatch, February 16, 1986, describing intense army efforts to destroy the rebel base on the Guazapa volcano, just outside the capital city of San Salvador.

tutions, foreign directed rather than indigenous, will be revealed as a falsehood that may serve the interests of the oligarchy, the military, and their Miami and Washington allies but does not accurately reflect the situation in El Salvador.

LOS ALBERTOS, El Salvador—With his small blue backpack, white cowboy hat and hip-high son tagging along behind him, Evaristo López makes an unlikely looking senior political official.

But for the peasants in this and other neighboring villages who support leftist rebels trying to overthrow the Salvadoran Government, Mr. López serves as a kind of combination governor, commune organizer and trade union activist.

To be precise, he is the president of the subregional junta of the "popular power" government set up by the guerrillas and their followers in this area in Chalatenango Province 70 miles northeast of San Salvador.

The rebel administration is part of a network of guerrilla services and institutions in the area. Rebel officials say it is the most developed administration they have in the country.

FEW AREAS OF REBEL CONTROL

The region is one of the dwindling areas where the rebels of the Marxist Farabundo Martí National Liberation Front are dominant. It is unlike most of the country in being drastically depopulated by war. The small groups of peasants who have stayed on in villages like this one are committed to the rebels' war against the Government and actively support it.

Army operations and flagging public support appear to have limited the rebels' ability to expand their influence elsewhere in the country. But their political practices here offer an indication of how they might govern in the unlikely event that they ever defeat the Government army.

Two reporters had a rare opportunity to visit the zone for a week recently in the company of guerrilla escorts. They walked 40 miles through the rebel-dominated region and spent time with hundreds of rebel supporters in 11 villages.

The political structure the rebels have organized in these hill towns is based on the demands of subsistence agriculture and practical Marxism at the local level. The rebels are concerned principally with ordering village life collectively, maintaining political support and supplying guerrilla military units.

3,000 TO 4,000 REMAIN

Since the rebels drove permanent army garrisons out of the region four years ago and do not recognize the Government of President José Napoleón Duarte as legitimate, the rebel administration is the only political authority known to the 3,000 to 4,000 people who remain here.

Villages have armed militias that keep 24-hour guard against army incursions. There are also small repair shops, a few stores, three hospitals, rebel military training schools, weapons factories and a rebel radio station that broadcasts four times a day, according to rebel officials and their supporters.

There is even a guerrilla mailman who totes a pouch on one shoulder and an aged M-1 carbine on the other. As he ambles down the mountain paths, peasants and rebel officials give him scribbled notes to deliver in villages further down the trail.

The "popular power" government is organized in ascending tiers from the village to regional level, according to Mr. López and others. At the top is the central committee and military command of the rebel Popular Liberation Forces, the Marxist group that has deeply embedded itself in the region for more than a decade.

"DIRECTION" FOR "THE MASSES"

The central committee appears to be made up chiefly of former Marxist trade union activists and student leaders who organized a rebel army in this isolated zone. The top leaders are known as "the direction" to peasant supporters, who call themselves "the masses."

The central committee sets the policies that village leaders carry out after discussions in village meetings, according to Mr. López and other village officials.

Asked how he applied his Marxist beliefs to the business of government, a member of the central committee who gave his name only as Elias said: "Our job is to go cultivating certain values in people in satisfaction of needs. People cooperate in a social way and try to eliminate egotism."

The rebels have shown less beneficence to the elected mayors in the towns surrounding this area of guerrilla control. They kidnapped nine mayors in September, forcing them to resign. The rebels accused the mayors of trying to limit guerrilla activities.

STRONG COMMITMENT SHOWN

The political commitment called for in the system the rebels have created goes far beyond that seen in the capital of San Salvador. Much of daily life here is devoted to public activities, and political discussion is constant in twice-monthly village meetings, according to several villagers.

For those willing to accept the basic assumptions and hardship of life in these small politicized communities, the form of government that has developed appears to offer some attractions. There seems to be a much higher degree of participation in village life than in most Salvadoran peasant communities, and the political structure appears well suited to helping villagers survive the war.

The highest authority is the subregional junta that Mr. López heads. He said that it was formed in 1983 and that its representatives were still learning how to be administrators.

The junta consists of a president and delegates specializing in health, education, militias, the economy and public works and judicial matters, Mr. López and other officials said.

All representatives are elected by secret balloting in villages, they added, a method that could not be confirmed by a reporter. They now serve one-year terms, but that may be extended to 18 months in the next election, Mr. López said.

One of the chief concerns of the local rebel authorities is the use of land and the production of the crops on which the region and rebel combat units depend.

The subregional junta has a university-trained accountant, whose job is to travel the region with calculator and account books, estimating the size of the harvest and the needs of farmers in the new season.

The accountant, who gave his name only as Eric, said the rebels depended on financial aid from rebel sympathizers in the United States and Europe to buy fertilizer and seeds each year to distribute to villages for planting.

Village "popular power" committees decide how much land will be cultivated collectively and how much will be devoted to growing beans, corn and sorghum to feed rebel military units, Eric and Mr. López said.

Peasant families then decide how much land they want to cultivate for themselves.

If the Government army burns a family's food supplies or cuts down their crops, as appears to happen two or three times a year, the village donates food to see them through, Eric said.

One task of village leaders seems to be to serve as therapists for residents suffering the psychological and physical trauma of the civil war, which has taken hundreds of lives and destroyed many homes in this region.

PERSONAL VISITS MADE

When a family has suffered especially harshly, local officials go to speak with them, as do political organizers who work for the central committee, according to Amado Vallés, head of the "popular power" committee in the village of Portillo del Norte.

"One tries to explain it for the people to understand," Mr. Vallés said, adding that the Government troops "do this to demoralize us and have us abandon the zone."

Such contact is an indication of why the Popular Liberation Forces has survived repeated army attacks. More than other rebel forces, it has devoted itself to maintaining close ties with its peasant followers as much as to military preparations.

Despite such attention to local administration, however, the region's population has fallen drastically during the years of war, and many hamlets and farming valleys are now almost deserted.

"When this started, we never believed it was going to last so many years," said Paco Dubon, a rebel follower in the once-thriving, now nearly silent town of Arcatao.

RADIO FARABUNDO MARTÍ

The day starts early at a guerrilla radio station hidden in the mountains of Chalatenango Province.

By 5 A.M. a dozen rebel newscasters, soundmen and reporters are up and about. After 15 minutes of calisthenics, they stand to attention and sing the "International." The early morning session ends with a series of chanted political slogans.

"If Nicaragua won, El Salvador will win!" the radio team shouts into the morning air. "Revolution or death!"

They call their station Radio Farabundo Martí after a Communist Party leader executed by the army in 1932. They switch locations at least once a month to avoid discovery by the army, they say.

TWO TREES FOR ANTENNA

During a visit by two reporters who were brought to the site blindfolded on horseback, the radio was situated in a small clearing. Two trees draped with wire served as an antenna, and a small wooden table held a sound mixer, microphones and tape recorders ready to transmit the evening broadcast.

"This is Radio Farabundo Martí, the rebel signal," a female announcer named Erandi shouted into a microphone.

"Soldiers, don't keep defending the interests of the rich," she continued. "Leave the rich to defend themselves. The slogan is: Develop the war of all the people."

The radio is only one of a number of services and facilities the guerrillas have organized in this mountainous zone visited recently by a reporter with guerrilla escorts.

MEDICAL CARE

Four doctors move through the area, working at three carefully concealed hospitals, according to one who gave his name only as Francisco.

He said he had worked with rebel forces for four years. He has learned how to carry out an amputation by flashlight, as well as use a broken door with tree branches for legs as an operating table.

Because the army regularly destroys rebel medical facilities, all operating equipment and medicine are kept in backpacks, ready to be carried away on the run. A small rebel clinic visited by a reporter was well hidden in a narrow, heavily forested canyon.

Two patients lay on stretchers, a small wood stove served to boil water to sterilize instruments, and nurses were on hand to aid in surgery. Dr. Francisco, who is 35 years old, said the most common ailments are parasites, malaria and malnourishment among children,

He has chosen to work with the rebels, he said, because he feels politics is inseparable from his practice as a doctor.

"We are not going to cure hunger and disease with medicine," he said. "We have to fight to change this system or else our profession will be the useless giving of pills."

MILITARY SCHOOL VISITED

The rebels consider this region to be their strategic rearguard, and they have tucked military facilities into its many abrupt valleys. A reporter's request to visit a bomb factory was not granted. But a military training school provided a look at the sort of preparations underway in the region.

The school was visited on the condition that its precise location not be revealed. It is administered by a 28-year-old rebel named Alex, who said he had five years of combat experience.

An abandoned farmhouse served as a classroom. It contained an American-made M-60 machine gun, and its walls were posted with rebel propaganda. There was also a series of carefully drawn diagrams detailing how to build a variety of the bombs and mines that Salvadoran officials say now account for more than 40 percent of army casualties.

About 20 rebel students were taking the 18-day course in explosives and weapons. One was a European who said he had raised funds for the guerrillas abroad.

A CLENCHED FIST

The instruction includes political discussions, and the classroom wall was dominated by a red banner and a poster of a clenched fist, sharply outlined in black ink. Each finger of the fist held a separate slogan.

The image appeared to represent the Farabundo Martí National Liberation Front, which is composed of five rebel factions.

Rutilio, a 15-year-old student, already appeared comfortable with his M-16 automatic rifle.

"We are being taught how to strike the enemy," he said.

27. FMLN: Toward a Single Party*

BY COMMANDER LEO CABRAL

In El Salvador, as Reading 22, by Robert Leiken, makes clear, the left is riven by sectarian rivalries and historic enmities. Some semblance of political unity was achieved in April 1980 with the formation of the Democratic Revolutionary Front (FDR). The various guerrilla groups also attained a degree of military coordination with the formation of the Unified Revolution Directorate (DRU) a month later, reformulated later that year as the Farabundo Martí National Liberation Front (FMLN).

The full degree of unity guerrillas believe necessary to win a long war of attrition, however, has apparently not been achieved. For this reason, in the fall of 1985 they announced that they were attempting to consolidate into a "single revolutionary party."[1] Since each of the five factions that make up the rebel front is Marxist-Leninist, it is not unreasonable to assume the single party they are seeking to create will also be Marxist-Leninist. (Past ideological orientations suggest this amalgam will not necessarily be pro-Moscow unless the war or postwar situation forces a dependency.)

Several important questions can be raised about this tendency toward Marxism-Leninism in the Salvadoran left. One involves the historic differences among the five groups making up the FMLN, and whether such FDR moderates as Ruben Zamora or Guillermo Ungo will have much of a political role in the new structures that are envisioned.

QUESTIONER: We have asked Commander Leo Cabral, second secretary of the FMLN's National Resistance, to comment on the importance for our revolutionary process of the line traced by our general commander—that we should advance toward the consolidation of a single revolutionary party and a single people's army.

Cabral: First, in order to answer this question we must refer to a situation we have experienced throughout these years in unifying the FMLM's strategic and tactical lines of action. Specifically, we have implemented a process of coordination and cooperation among all our forces, using our human and material resources, in order to channel our military, popular, and international lines in one direction. In this sense, we have confirmed in practice that we are more capable of defeating the enemy's plans. We can say with absolute certainty that the FMLN's line is being implemented by the single commands we have created in some of the combat zones in our country, with the single

---

* Broadcast over Radio Venceremos, September 9, 1985. From Foreign Broadcast Information Service, *Daily Reports—Central America,* September 12, 1985.

[1.] At the same time the FMLN announced their intention to form "a single people's army" as well. On this military issue, see Editors' introduction to chapter 6.

political-military directorates. This, in turn, is a step forward in creating a single party and a single revolutionary army.

In addition to and parallel with this process of building the single political-military directorates, we have also found ourselves submerged in an accelerated process of sharing our experiences; it is precisely this that has enabled us to become familiar with the particular functions of each of the organizations during all these years. We have not only learned about how they have solved their internal problems in organizing the party and army, but also the concrete ways in which they have faced the enemy's operations, both in rural fronts and in the cities.

In addition to seeking the unification of the strategic and tactical lines, in the political field we are currently striving to achieve our ideological unification. In this respect, all the organizations are working toward drafting a single political platform; in other words, a platform for a single party. The internal debates within each organization will lead to the creation of a single, revolutionary party. However, this is a process, and as I said, we are currently exchanging experiences. Regarding ideological unification, we must stress the importance of the efforts we have begun to unify our training; in other words, preparations in the ideological, political, and military fields. These will be specific steps that will enable us to maintain closer and more direct relations in order to know each other better, so that the strategic line traced by the FMLN General Command can be assimilated and implemented in a unified manner.

In sum, these are our views regarding the immediate perspectives of the line traced by our General Command, which calls for the unification of the five organizations into a single party and a single revolutionary army struggling for power.

CHAPTER VI

The Civil War

Editors' Introduction

Helicopters and screaming jets descend over a jungle village. Bombs explode, carving craters, leveling ancient forests. Villages crumple as families crying out in terror scramble to reach bombshelters. Children caught in billowing walls of fire run screaming down dirt roads, the clothing burned from their bodies. In less than an hour a village has been destroyed, 100 civilians have been killed, more than 4,000 are homeless.

This is not Vietnam. This is El Salvador.[1]

Rethinking the significance of the Vietnam War and its relationship to events in Central America is—should be—a central intellectual and political task of our time for thoughtful citizens. Elsewhere in this volume, historian George C. Herring, reexamining the connections between the Indochina struggle and the one in El Salvador (Reading 52), makes a good analytic start. But there are aspects of both conflicts that need further clarification, and one of them is the question of what constitutes a civil war.

The U.S. Civil War of the mid-nineteenth century was a clear example of an internal conflict, relatively uncomplicated by outside intervention.[2] Viet-

[1] Gar Smith, "The Invisible War," *Not Man Apart,* July–August 1985.

[2] The main external factor during the American Civil War was diplomacy with Great Britain. The breakaway southern Confederacy sought to enlist British support for its own efforts to smash the U.S. government's coastal blockade. The Union side strove to keep Britain from diplomatically recognizing the Confederacy, and to prevent construction of Confederate blockade runners in British shipyards. For a succinct summary, see Norman A. Graebner, "Northern Diplomacy and European Neutrality," in *Why the North Won the Civil War,* ed. David Donald (New York, 1962), [chapter 3].

nam and El Salvador are far more complex in that the struggles there became enmeshed in wider conflicts of global dimensions, with undeniable outside interventions in both cases. In the case of Vietnam, the major outside intervention came from the United States, which poured hundreds of billions of dollars into Indochina, sent more than two million troops, and subjected the area to a bombardment that probably exceeded the total firepower expended in all previous wars in the history of humankind.[3] There was some attempt to equate this massive U.S. involvement with the presumably comparable North Vietnamese interference in the struggle waged in the southern part of that country, but such efforts to create interpretive symmetry cannot stand up to serious analysis.[4] For one thing, the almost self-contradictory proposition that Vietnamese can be portrayed as outsiders in their own country is frequently overlooked by those who wish to view the Indochina war in a light favorable to the United States.[5]

But a more plausible case can be made for seeing Vietnam not as a civil war at all. At least after the Communist-led Vietminh defeated the French in 1954, no other local independent force in Vietnam was capable of sustaining itself without outside influence. By this view, the Americans did not intervene in a civil war in Vietnam, but rather created and maintained a series of client regimes in Saigon that, aside from Washington's backing, had little support.[6]

In the sense of having more of the trappings of a genuine internal conflict, the situation in El Salvador more nearly approaches the model of a civil war. Naturally, Washington and the U.S.-backed government in El Salvador deny this, refusing to credit the rebels with any popular constituency and charging that the insurgents are nothing but outside agents of the world Communist conspiracy. These assertions must be understood in part as ideological pronouncements, weapons in the conflict itself. They must also be evaluated in light of the realities of the struggle inside El Salvador, where the Marxist

[3.] The most convenient and reliable summary of the costs of the Indochina War are to be found in the special double issue of *Indochina Newsletter* (Box 129, Dorchester Mass. 02122), No. 18 (November–December 1982). See also Marvin E. Gettleman, Jane Franklin, Marilyn Young, and H. Bruce Franklin, eds., *Vietnam and America: A Documented History* (New York, 1985), especially Reading 64.

[4.] Even so perceptive a student of Indochina as George C. Herring (Reading 52) attempts to picture the northern Vietnamese as "outsiders" in the conflict.

[5.] This is a point of view adopted by a group of Vietnam War "revisionists," of whom Guenther Lewy, author of *Vietnam in America* (New York, 1978), commands the most authority. In his view, indigenous factors virtually fade away as Vietnam is seen mainly as an arena for clashing great-power interests, in which the validity of U.S. aims is an unquestioned article of faith.

[6.] A forceful statement of this interpretation is to be found in "The Lessons of the Vietnam War—an Interview with Noam Chomsky," *Indochina Newsletter*, No. 18 (November–December 1982), and in Chomsky, "The Best-Selling of Vietnam," *Boston Review* (February 1984). See also George C. Herring, *America's Longest War: The United States and Vietnam, 1950-1975* (2d ed., New York, 1986), especially chapters 1 and 2; Gettleman, Franklin, Young, Franklin, *America and Vietnam*, parts III and IV.

groups united under the banner of the Farabundo Martí National Liberation Front (FMLN) may or may not have ideological affinities with different Communist states.

Seen historically, the civil struggle in El Salvador has ebbed and intensified as grievances accumulate, popular mobilization threatens oligarchic power, and the oligarchy and its military allies (sometimes including outside support) repress suspected rebels, resist reform, and consolidate their own power. The *Matanza* of 1932, the crushing of the peasant uprising, clearly marked one phase of the struggle. Another began with the overthrow of the regime of General Humberto Romero in 1979 and the increase in rebel activity that followed.[7] Overestimating its strength, the FMLN launched what its propaganda called a "final offensive" early in 1981 but failed to topple the ruling junta, which was aided by military support from the United States.[8] But the insurgency stubbornly refused to fade away, since the basic conditions that gave rise to it—political repression and absence of meaningful social and economic reform—have not changed substantially.

Now, at mid-decade, El Salvador may be in a period of a new intensification of struggle, in which the rebels and their supporters face a relentless air war. The guerrillas seem no longer able to engage the military in large-unit combat. The territory under FMLN control is now subject to savage reprisals, as the Salvadoran military and their U.S. advisers seek to separate the guerrillas forcibly from the populace that gives them backing. This is strikingly reminiscent of the American resort to air power to weaken the link that the Vietnamese insurgents had forged with the peasantry in the countryside. Since early 1984, civilians in the countryside have been subject to "indiscriminate attacks in conflict zones where the guerrillas are believed to enjoy significant support," as reported Americas Watch, a human-rights group based in Washington.[9] In addition, the Salvadoran military is intensifying efforts to organize the civilian population within zones sealed off from the guerrillas. In order to "win the hearts and minds" of the people, to borrow a phrase much in use by the United States in Vietnam, "psychological operations" have been mounted to persuade civilians to collaborate with the army —for example, videos are shown to suspected guerrilla supporters and followed by discussions of FMLN sabotage.

The guerrillas have responded to the air war and related counterinsurgency programs with a strategic shift of their own to a war of attrition in which small-scale guerrilla units engage in such operations as economic sabotage or

[7.] See Readings 5 and 6.

[8.] On the guerrilla strategies and defeats of the early 1980s, see Tom Buckley, *Violent Neighbors: El Salvador, Central America and the United States* (New York, 1984), chapters 7, 18; Raymond Bonner, *Weakness and Deceit: U.S. Policy and El Salvador* (New York, 1984), chapter 6; Robert Armstrong and Janet Shenk, *El Salvador: The Face of Revolution* (Boston, 1982), 183–87.

[9.] "Preliminary Report on the Human Rights Situation in El Salvador During the Last Six Months of 1984," Americas Watch, 30 January 1985, as cited in *Central America Bulletin,* June 1985, 4.

political assassinations. As FMLN commander Joaquín Villalobos stated the new policy, the struggle would be carried to the affluent neighborhoods of the capital city, and U.S. personnel would be included among the targets. Thus, in June 1985, a group of FMLN commandos attacked off-duty U.S. Marines in the posh *Zona Rosa* of San Salvador, killing four of them and a number of bystanders. (See Reading 38.) In its new strategy, the rebel command has by no means ceded control of the countryside to their opponents. In the spring of 1985, they were able to conduct an elaborate international press conference in a remote village in the rebel-dominated province of Morazán, without apparent fear of the Salvadoran military.[10]

Does this switch in strategy indicate that the tide has turned against the guerrillas, and that the optimistic picture given out by U.S. Embassy briefing officers and Salvadoran military officials[11] is a correct assessment? The answer must be a mixed one: The intensified air war (in which the guerrillas, of course, lack anything faintly resembling air power themselves) has clearly hurt the rebels; yet many options remain. The rebels may be able to retain a measure of initiative by combining small-scale hit-and-run tactics in the countryside with operations in the cities—highly visible demonstrations, strikes, and disruptions of public facilities. Above all, the guerrillas seem to be girding themselves for the long haul, convinced that time is on their side in any war of attrition. "We are in no hurry," remarked commander Villalobos. "We can resist as long as necessary."[12]

28. *Stalemate in El Salvador**

BY ANNE NELSON

When in the fall of 1984 leftist guerrillas met with Salvadoran President José Napoleón Duarte in the mountain village of La Palma, hopes were raised that peace might be on the agenda after years of civil war (see chapter 10). A year later, reporter James LeMoyne recorded his strong impression "that exhaustion is gaining hold in a country that has

[10.] James LeMoyne, "Salvador Rebel Vows to Spread War," *New York Times,* July 7, 1985.

[11.] Marvin E. Gettleman, interviews with Vittorio Brod, political counselor, James Steele, U.S. military adviser, and Ambassador Thomas Pickering, U.S. Embassy, San Salvador, January 8, 1985; interviews with General Carlos Eugenio Vides Casanova and General Adolfo Blandón, Salvadoran military headquarters, San Salvador, January 8, 1985.

[12.] *Los Angeles Times,* March 28, 1985, as cited in *Central America Bulletin,* June 1985, 5. The long view was also expressed by an FMLN activist in commenting on the guerrilla forces' decision, during the summer of 1985, to merge into one army: "It may take a year, maybe five years, maybe even 10 years, to integrate the armies.... This is a process." See Clifford Krauss, "Salvador Rebels Unite; Woes Remain," *Wall Street Journal,* August 19, 1985.

* From *Christianity and Crisis,* July 22, 1985.

joined Northern Ireland and Lebanon as a land in which violence is normal." As an elderly Catholic priest who works with refugees put it, "What one sees most of all is the suffering of the common people. They don't see an exit. There isn't an exit."[1]

Just as the announcement of the Salvadoran Army that it had killed Joaquín Villalobos, senior military commander of the Salvadoran rebel movement, was later shown by Mr. Villalobos himself to have been "premature," so too the optimistic claim in the spring of 1985 that the improved training of the Salvadoran military had the guerrillas on the ropes has been discredited by events. The guerrillas, for example, still had the capability to kill more than forty Salvadoran soldiers in a single attack in October 1985.

The stages of this endless, brutal war and its rules of engagement are traced by journalist Anne Nelson, who has reported on Central America and the Caribbean since 1978 for a variety of media, including Life, *the* Los Angeles Times, *the* Nation, *and the British Broadcasting Corporation. Her book on Puerto Rico,* An Island Tragedy, *was published by Ticknor & Fields in 1986.*

IN 1985, for the first time in several years, the military stalemate between the Salvadoran government and the guerrillas has started to give way, in favor of the government. Yet the "Requiems for the Revolution" that are starting to appear in some publications are premature. The Reagan administration and its ally, President José Napoleón Duarte, have based their strategy and their claims to victory on the idea of defeating the guerrillas on the battlefield while racing to create a political "center." But so far, nothing in their game plan has affected the country's old grievances of monopolized land ownership, low wages, and repression of civil liberties. These have gone largely unchanged since 1979, and indeed, since 1950. What has changed, and remains in a constant state of fluidity, is what military analysts call the "rules of engagement."

When Hercules wrestled Proteus, he was confounded to find that his opponent changed into a different creature with every round of the match. That is how Duarte must feel facing the Salvadoran left. For as soon as his army can credibly claim an upper hand militarily, he is faced with an event like the march in San Salvador on July 5, [1985]. More than 20,000 peasants turned out to demand land reform measures that coincided with the guerrillas' platform, and which were clearly impossible for Duarte to deliver while maintaining his current working alliance with the military and the right. Only a few weeks earlier, his administration was caught up in the travails of a bitter strike by STISS, the Social Security workers' union, which was active in one of the leftist "mass organizations" in the late 1970s. The strike made headlines in the U.S. only when members of government security forces mistakenly shot and killed other security force members raiding a hospital that had been occupied by the strikers. And only days earlier members of a small guerrilla group killed four U.S. Marine embassy guards, among others, at a chic cafe in San Salvador.

[1] James LeMoyne, "A Year After Talks, Salvadoran Peace Recedes," *New York Times,* October 14, 1985.

The march and the strike would have been impossible only a few years ago, when the military routinely opened fire on demonstrations and imprisoned or "disappeared" inconvenient union leaders. And the targeted killing of Americans lay outside the unwritten "rules of engagement" the FMLN guerrilla front has followed. Over the course of a long stalemate, the Salvadoran government changed the rules of chess and called it victory; the guerrillas are changing from one chessboard to another to show there has been no defeat. The strategic questions tend to get lost in the tactical discussions, but they still loom over the situation as a whole: Are there significantly greater numbers of people who feel their grievances can be addressed by peaceful means? Are their allegiances changing from one side to another? A look at the evolving patterns of the war suggests not.

FISH IN THE SEA

To understand the military course of the war, one must look first at the part social forces have played throughout. For the guerrillas, popular support is the single element essential for their survival, as they face an enemy receiving ever greater amounts of assistance from the United States. The unions, peasants, and radical Christians have been the underpinnings for their efforts. But the left also learned that to use these groups as instruments of political expression within the law was also to invite their repression, or destruction. For the past five years leftist forces in El Salvador have alternated between striving for a military victory and periodically testing the waters of Duarte's new democracy.

The course of the civil war in El Salvador to date can be broken down into four stages, and each can be defined by a characteristic relationship between the guerrillas and their civilian supporters on the one hand and the response of the government and the military on the other. The years from 1970 to 1979 were a period of gestation, in which left and center-left political forces experimented with elections (1972 and 1977) only to have them usurped by the military. These forces gradually polarized between those who chose to play by the traditional political rules and those who threw in their lot with the guerrilla groups. The guerrilla insurgency had started out in 1970 with a split from the Communist party, and built support from a base of Christian, union, and peasant organizations, also feeling frustration with the lack of means to change the status quo. . . .

The second stage, from late 1979 to January 1981, began when a clique of young military officers carried out a coup against the government of General Carlos Romero, largely to prevent a revolutionary victory along the lines of the Sandinista triumph in Managua the previous July. The second stage was marked by the brief and ambivalent period of grace granted by the left and center-left to the new government (ambivalent because many on the left felt that a full military victory was within reach), by a drastic increase in anarchy and death squad activity in the capital, and by the beginning of large-scale army search-and-destroy missions in the countryside. The guerrilla organizations grew rapidly, and in January 1981 made an ill-fated attempt to seize power in the "final offensive." Their defeat was due less to the government's popular support or the army's military capabilities, than to the guerrillas' lack of consolidated popular support and the fact that most of their supporters were not armed and incorporated into their military structure. The 1981 offensive, however, had the effect of drawing the attention of the United States to El Salvador as potentially the most dangerous trouble spot in the hemisphere. It earned a priority status in Washington through its violence that neither its poverty nor its coups had ever achieved.

The third stage was brief but interesting. From 1981 to 1982 the guerrilla forces enjoyed an unprecedented prestige. The Reagan administration met the January offensive with a blast of its own propaganda whose virulence weakened its own credibility. When then-Secretary of State Alexander Haig released a "White Paper" on Soviet, Cuban, and Nicaraguan arms shipments to El Salvador, a number of publications ended up devoting as much space to debunking its hyperbole and criticizing its methodological shortcuts as to reporting its findings. International relations also flourished for the Salvadoran left over this period. A strong new Socialist government in France and a not-yet-collapsed Mexican economy were responsible for the French-Mexican peace initiative, which dealt with the Salvadoran guerrillas as a legitimate army in a civil war instead of a band of terrorists (and brought down the wrath of the Reagan administration upon the offending French and Mexicans). Meanwhile, support for the Sandinistas continued to run very high in the Socialist International and democratic Latin America, and the extent to which the Sandinista revolution seemed to have chances for long-standing success reflected well on the aspirations of the Salvadoran revolutionaries.

Following their military setback of January 1981, the guerrillas regrouped and developed a strategy that depended on the use of "liberated zones." These were areas in the northern third of the country (and also its poorest area) where civilian support for the guerrillas ran high. The guerrillas made use of the civilian population to supply a much-needed logistical base. After all, the guerrillas could easily keep up their stock of guns and boots, routinely stripping them from army soldiers and comrades alike who had fallen in battle. But it was harder for the guerrillas to supply themselves with food, living quarters, and other necessities on a regular basis. In large stretches of the northern provinces of Morazán, Chalatenango, and Cabañas, and major pockets in the central regions of Guazapa, San Vicente, and Usulután, entire communities participated in the guerrilla war effort. Farmers grew crops for the guerrillas, their wives cooked meals, their children served as scouts and messengers, and often their older sons and daughters fought alongside them (occasionally against their will). The "liberated zones" had another advantage for the guerrillas; they were living proof of active civilian support. As the Sandinistas demonstrated, a military force does not give a civilian population access to arms unless it trusts the population not to turn the arms against the military.

A CLEANED-UP CAPITAL

The guerrillas were badly in need of such proof. The government forces had devoted their strength to securing the economically vital south, especially the capital. The kinds of strikes, marches, and acts of civil disobedience that the left and center-left had depended upon during the 1970s were now impossible. Security forces and death squads had "disappeared" church, peasant, and labor leaders who pressed publicly for radical social change. The aim was to decapitate *("descabezar")* the leftist movements by depriving them of leadership.

In the short term, it worked. The capital looked "clean" to the new embassy personnel and press corps (both communities tend to be entirely replaced with abnormal frequency, the usual generational span being about two years). The Americans would come to El Salvador, work the capital and the army-controlled highways, and see little sign that the guerrillas even existed as a political force, a perception reflected and mutually reinforced in the round of briefings, cables, and press reports. Surviving leaders who had been active within the political (as opposed to the military) sphere went into exile or joined the military forces in the mountains (where they felt enriched by the experience but sometimes useless and out-of-place). Overall, then, international support for the political goals of the FDR/FMLN and, to a large degree, its own internal morale depended on the sense of well-developed communities within the liberated zones, where something that verged on a network of provisional local governments was taking shape, complete with judiciary and constabulatory services and facilities for religious and educational activities.

The Reagan administration was well aware of the guerrillas' gains in international diplomatic terms and support in the countryside, and their losses in the cities. The fourth stage of the war, which began gradually with the Constituent Assembly elections of March 1982, was designed to eliminate the guerrillas' strengths and intensify their weaknesses. At the same time, the administration looked at the most highly publicized complaints against the Salvadoran army and government and set about rehabilitating their images. The first part of the strategy was to give El Salvador a democratically elected government, without weakening the military power of the army or the economic power of the elite, both of which were seen as crucial to the country's stability. The elections were held in three tiers: Constituent Assembly in 1982, presidential in 1984, and Legislative Assembly in 1985. Christian Democrat leader José Napoleón Duarte was the key figure in the elections, using his rapidly-fading past reputation as a reformer to win a broad-based support, but soft-pedaling his former concerns for human rights and land reform to avoid angering the military on the one hand and the oligarchs on the other.

The next step of the Reagan administration's plan was to reshape the Salvadoran military. This was a vital and difficult task; defense analysts had long taken a dim view of the prospects of U.S. troops fighting in El Salvador, and diplomats and military advisers alike looked back to Vietnam and decided the problem was not "Vietnamizing" the war soon enough.

In El Salvador, "Salvadorizing" the war meant "Americanizing" the Salvadoran army. The only army methods of counterinsurgency were clumsy and ineffective. They entailed moving several thousand troops into a guerrilla-held area for a "sweep," which usually resulted in guerrillas escaping on foot to fight another day on their own terms. The high casualty figures largely represented civilian deaths; this brought international and press criticism on human rights grounds and created blood enemies among the victims' survivors. The Salvadoran army ran on a cult of cruelty; in 1981 a frustrated U.S. military adviser told me that he couldn't get it through the Salvadoran officers' heads that it was bad for morale when they routinely beat their troops.

The U.S. trained the Salvadoran officers' corps on an unprecedented scale. The 55 military trainers in residence in El Salvador worked on site, while hundreds of Salvadorans traveled north for training in the States. Slowly, field tactics began to change. Battalions were broken down into smaller units in the attempt to make them more mobile, helping them to adopt the most profitable conventions of guerrilla warfare, and incidentally reducing the officers' opportunities for plunder presented in the large-scale transport of troops and logistical support. "Human rights training" was stressed, largely for the sake of a pay-off in terms of public relations. If peasants knew they would not be massacred if they turned themselves in, the guerrillas could be deprived of important support in the countryside, and the guerrillas themselves might desert in increasing numbers.

Just as importantly, the U.S. led the Salvadorans to take the war off the ground and into the air, greatly updating and nearly doubling the capacity of the Salvadoran air force, training pilots in the use of A-37s loaded with 500- and 750-pound bombs, as well as in machine-gunning. U.S. military advisers boasted that their students were capable of distinguishing civilians from guerrillas from the air, and could conduct "surgical bombing." . . . Morale in the Salvadoran armed forces rose dramatically.

LIFTING THE LID

Appearances were not neglected. After a series of negative press reports on the extreme right and political killings, Vice President George Bush visited El Salvador to read the riot act to the death squads, whose activities instantly dropped to a fraction of their former levels. The Security Forces—the National Guard, National Police, and dreaded Treasury Police—were deemphasized, while the long-neglected Salvadoran Navy and Air Force were boosted to new importance. But putting an official damper on the death squads and extrajudicial killings also opened the door for public political activities that had not been possible since 1980. The National University was reopened. Opposition labor leaders nervously rented new offices and leftist clergy experimented with keeping regular hours.

Part of the government's new strategy was to deprive the guerrillas of their civilian support—not necessarily by killing them, but by deliberately creating a large new refugee population. More than 20 percent of El Salvador's population of five million has already been displaced by the war, and refugees are continuing to steam into camps across the country. The U.S. Agency for International Development (AID) has earmarked $120 million over the next three years for Salvadoran refugee programs that are often in competition, rather than collaboration, with ongoing Catholic and Protestant church efforts. Salvadoran Catholic spokesmen have accused the United States and AID of "politicizing" the refugee situation for military means.

Now, more than ever, the civil war in El Salvador is defined as a battle for "hearts and minds." U.S. military advisers express confidence that within the year, their counterinsurgency methods will reduce the guerrillas to "just a bunch of bandits in the hills." Yet embassy officials freely admit that they have no magic solutions to what they call "El Salvador's unviable economy," which is based on the production of export crops that are worth less and less on the world market. The stillborn land reform is not being displayed as a showcase for reporters any more, and the presence of 20,000 peasant protesters on the street further undermines its public relations value. The U.S. response to El Salvador's inequitable distribution of wealth has been to apply a dose of Reaganomics to the country's economy. Wages have been frozen since 1980 in the attempt to promote exports, and workers are still waiting for the "trickle down."

And Duarte has attempted to monopolize the meaning of democracy. When he holds elections, that is democracy. When peasants march and unions strike, he declares that "[t]hey are using the political characteristics of democracy to destabilize democracy. If they want to use the public space, they can do it, but they want to function within an antidemocratic space. That is the phenomenon I cannot permit" (*New York Times,* June 16, 1985).

It cannot be denied that the policies of the Reagan administration and the Duarte government have created certain political structures that are new to Salvadoran society, and that could be democratic in their function. But, as Duarte's quote demonstrates, those structures have been created on the condition that they can be monopolized by forces that exclude the left. For Duarte, "democracy" is a static and rigid convention that exists to shut "the communists" out, not an organic system of government that adjusts to the social forces within it.

So long as the Reagan administration and the Duarte government define all opposition as "communists" and "bandits," they undermine what little chance for long-term stability the Salvadoran government may have. The war in El Salvador is far from over, and until the social base of the government is truly broadened, the chess board will continue to be littered with fallen knights and pawns.

29. The Escalation of the Air War: A Congressional View*

BY REPRESENTATIVE JIM LEACH, REPRESENTATIVE GEORGE MILLER, AND, SENATOR MARK O. HATFIELD

The air war being waged by the Salvadoran military against villages suspected of being sympathetic to the guerrillas is hauntingly evocative of Vietnam. Just as it did in Southeast Asia, terror from the air has created vast numbers of refugees in El Salvador. During a recent eight-month period, more than 100,000 were driven from their homes—the equivalent in the United States of more than four million—many forcibly rounded up and removed by the Salvadoran army.

A 1985 New York Times *article by correspondent James LeMoyne supports the conclusion that in 1983 and 1984 the Air Force engaged in "indiscriminate attacks" on "defenseless civilians." Not being in a position to be an eyewitness, LeMoyne finds it difficult to evaluate the effectiveness of the stricter rules of aerial engagement issued by President José Napoleón Duarte in September 1984.[1]*

But whether discriminate or indiscriminate, depopulation of the countryside is a reality. Some have suggested that this is not a side effect but the very purpose of the bombardment: Guerrilla fish cannot swim in an empty sea.

The congressional authors of this report do not approve of the use to which American aid has been put, and elsewhere they suggest that the air war not be funded and that the United States seek a political, not a military, solution in El Salvador (see Reading 51).

*In a personal inspection, later in the year, of a number of small villages near the Honduran border, LeMoyne concluded that in depopulated areas inhabited almost exclusively by guerrillas and their civilian supporters, "the armed forces appear to bend the rules governing bombing of towns and destruction of property" (*New York Times, *December 20, 1985).*

* Selection from "U.S. Aid to El Salvador: An Evaluation of the Past, a Proposal for the Future—A Report to the Arms Control and Foreign Policy Caucus" from Representative Jim Leach (R-IA), Representative George Miller (D-CA), and Senator Mark O. Hatfield (R-OR), February 1985. (Most footnotes deleted.)

[1] James LeMoyne, *New York Times,* July 18, 1985.

Further evidence of indiscriminacy is a statement in January 1985 by Colonel Sigifredo Ochoa, a top Salvadoran commander, that he has established in Chalatenango free-fire zones. In addition, the Salvadoran armed forces press office admits to using bombing operations to "soften up" contested areas. See Congressional Record, *March 6, 1985, E 787.*

THIS Section [of the Report to the Congressional Arms Control and Foreign Policy Caucus] analyzes in more details the "Direct War-Related Aid" category, and by doing so describes the overall U.S. strategy reflected by that aid. In describing the uses of the aid, it reveals a step-by-step escalation of a strategy for a military victory, and shows that our original attempt to expand and upgrade the Salvadoran Army has broadened and deepened, resulting in a counterinsurgency strategy, reminiscent of Vietnam, of aerial bombardment and air mobile assault, which has heightened casualties among the civilian population. This Section also shows that a once fairly simple strategy of getting the Army out of the barracks to fight in small mobile units has become a vastly more sophisticated and technological one, requiring increased U.S. involvement in providing both funds and equipment, and consequently involving U.S. personnel more directly in combat-related activities.

STEP ONE: EXPANDING THE ARMY

Since the U.S. initiated its war-related aid program in FY81 [fiscal year 1981], the size of the Salvadoran Army and security forces has grown from a combined strength of 12,000 in 1980 to 42,000 in 1984. This nearly four-fold expansion has been accomplished through the massive training, arming and equipping of Salvadoran soldiers, using U.S. funds. Of the roughly 30,000 members of the Army, 19,000 have been trained with U.S. military aid. Another 7,000 have been trained with U.S. funds but are no longer active in the Army. Among the units trained were 6 "Immediate Reaction" battalions (850–1000 men each), 8 mid-sized battalions (600 men each) and 11 "Hunter" battalions (350 men each).

In order to train this many soldiers without exceeding the limit of U.S. trainers in El Salvador, the U.S. military trained large numbers of Salvadorans at the Regional Military Training Center in Honduras (known by its Spanish acronym "CREMS"), beginning in 1983. Some 100 Green Berets from the U.S. Special Forces were stationed at CREMS, training primarily newly-formed Salvadoran units.

The expansion of the Army has meant a change in the number and role of U.S. advisers in El Salvador.

The Executive Branch's ongoing assurances to Congress that "at no time are there more than 55 U.S. trainers in El Salvador" are true only if one overlooks changes in how the 55 are counted. In 1981, nine members of the U.S. Military Group at the U.S. Embassy were counted as part of the 55; in 1984, the 11–16

Milgroup members were not counted as part of the total. Similarly excluded from the 55-man cap are 20–25 medical trainers sent in 1984, private U.S. contract personnel providing maintenance services on U.S.-supplied aircraft, and members of the Defense Attaché's office, whose staff has quadrupled from an average of six in 1981 to 26 in early 1984. Also not included are the several hundred members of a U.S. Intelligence Battalion based in Honduras who regularly fly missions over El Salvador to gather battlefield intelligence.

Changes in the numbers of U.S. advisers have been accompanied by a relaxation on the rules governing their deployment in El Salvador. As the expanded Armed Forces moved more frequently into the countryside, U.S. personnel increased their direct supporting role. In 1981, U.S. military personnel were restricted to secure areas near San Salvador (with the exception of a naval team based in La Unión); but by 1984, Operational Planning and Assistance Teams (OPATs) of 2–3 "trainers" had been stationed in each of El Salvador's six Army brigade headquarters throughout the country, assisting commanders in management and planning, and even moving with the headquarters during field operations.

Similarly, as recently as July 1983, three "trainers" were relieved from duty for traveling by helicopter over a combat zone; yet by October, 1984, the head of the U.S. Milgroup and several trainers flew into the heart of rebel territory during an air mobile assault, and remained at the command post overnight. Finally, U.S. personnel began to increase their aerial reconnaissance role: an Army intelligence battalion of several hundred members began to fly reconnaissance missions in OV-1 observation craft from Honduras over El Salvador; U.S. Air Force C-130s flew similar flights from Howard Air Base in Panama; and CIA flights, such as the one from Salvador's Ilopango Air Base which killed four Americans in the fall of 1984, also probably perform battlefield reconnaissance.

Throughout the 1981–1984 period of Army expansion and increasing U.S. involvement, the size of the rebel force also expanded—from roughly 2–3,000 in 1980 to 9–11,000 in late 1984. The rebels have continued to hit economic targets such as bridges and power lines, and for the most part have managed to avoid fixed battle with the Army—succeeding instead in melting away and regrouping for their next operation.

STEP TWO: THE "NATIONAL CAMPAIGN PLAN," OR PACIFICATION

In the summer of 1983, the Salvadoran Army initiated a program known as the National Campaign—a model pacification backed by the U.S. Milgroup and patterned after a component of U.S. strategy from the Vietnam War. The National Campaign was devised to implement a new, aggressive style of counterinsurgency: instead of fighting a "9 to 5 war," the Army would saturate the countryside with constant day and night patrols. Instead of sending thousands of troops into battle against guerrilla forces, only to withdraw when the operation was over, the Army would clear and hold a rebel-held area; enhanced security would then permit peasants to return to their homes, plant crops and revive the economy. Security would be maintained by organizing civilians into "civil defense patrols" loyal to the government. "Civic action" and public works projects would also be instituted in an attempt to gain public support. The National Campaign was given its trial run in San Vicente province, under the name "Operation Well-Being," and was judged so crucial to overall policy that U.S. military strategists declared that "we will win or lose on this operation."

The small units and "civic action" crews moved into San Vicente in June of 1983, but rebel forces evacuated the area, again resisting combat on the Army's terms. A number of civic action projects were initiated, but by the end of the year, Operation Well-Being was faltering. Rebel forces returned to San Vicente in August, inflicting substantial casualties on Army troops and hurting morale. A rebel offensive in other provinces in September drew off most of the crack troops stationed in San Vicente, leaving behind second-tier forces which "reverted to the same kind of behavior that the Americans say had cost them the initiative in the past, digging in rather than advancing by small night patrols and often giving up weapons in the face of unexpectedly fierce guerrilla attacks." U.S.-financed civic action projects, including the reopening of schools and roads, continued to go forward in a number of areas, but largely at the sufferance of rebel commanders also trying to win the loyalty of the peasants. By December of 1984, only three of the 33 municipalities in El Salvador asked to form civil defense units had complied with the order.

U.S. Ambassador Thomas Pickering assessed Operation Well-Being in December, 1983, in these words: "The Army has not shown the capacity to deal with the counteroffensive and the area of the plan. We had said that was a clear test."

The floundering program in San Vicente led to another shift in Salvadoran war-fighting tactics. Salvadoran commanders turned away from the small units proposed by U.S. strategists, and reverted to more conventional "sweep" operations through rebel zones involving large numbers of government troops. At the same time, the aerial bombing of rebel-contested zones surged. The stepped-up air war appeared to have two complementary objectives: to disrupt the rebels' ability to mass for attack, and to drive civilians out of areas in the countryside that the rebels controlled or contested, thereby denying the rebels a base of logistical support.

STEP THREE: THE AIR WAR

(A) Aerial Bombardment

An intensification of aerial bombardment of rural areas in the five northeastern provinces where the rebels were most active began in late 1983, as the National

Campaign of pacification was winding down. According to Pentagon figures, average flying hours for UH-1H helicopters and A-37 strike aircraft—the core of El Salvador's air attack capability—increased by over 220 hours per month between July, 1983 and February, 1984. UH-1H flight hours increased 60 percent (from 364 to 582 per month), and A-37 flight hours increased 68 percent (from 31 to 52). Britain's *Jane's Defence Weekly* also reported an increase in A-37 air strikes, citing U.S. military sources for a figure of 227 air strikes in all of 1983 (an average of 19 each month), versus 74 air strikes in the month of June, 1984, alone. Air attacks from UH-1Hs were especially heavy during the election period of March–May, 1984, when helicopters were flying at three to four times their previous frequency. The stated aim was to enhance security for the elections.

U.S. officials categorically deny that U.S. personnel have in any way advised or encouraged the Salvadoran Air Force to bomb rebel zones to disrupt life there and drive out civilians. But while there is no direct evidence that U.S. advisers encouraged the strategy, there is little doubt that U.S. aid provided the ways and means to carry it out.

Through U.S. military aid, El Salvador received seven A-37s since 1982 (three more are on their way in 1985), and (in 1982) $1.2 million worth of 500 and 750 pound iron bombs. Beginning in 1982, the U.S. also provided the "nose rods" to convert the iron bombs (which normally explode when they hit the ground) to anti-personnel fragmentation devices that explode in the air. U.S. intelligence may also have helped to pinpoint bombing targets: the step-up in bombing raids by the Salvadoran Air Force coincided with published reports that U.S. pilots were flying reconnaissance missions out of bases in Honduras and Panama.

The Executive Branch denies that there is any "indiscriminate" bombing, and asserts the A-37 pilots have developed "near surgical precision" in their bomb deliveries. These assertions have been challenged by a growing body of evidence from U.S. journalists, both Salvadoran and U.S. independent monitors of the war, and President Duarte himself—who last September actually issued new regulations to the Air Force to minimize damage to civilians and encourage respect for human rights. The core of the problem appears to lie in the Salvadoran officers' failure to distinguish between civilians and guerrillas in zones of conflict; this failure is reflected in the remarks of a Salvadoran officer who, explaining an incident where 42 peasants died, said "there are no people living in those hamlets—only terrorists." But perhaps the most direct evidence of the effect of the bombing is its contribution to the swelling population of displaced persons: displaced persons registered by the Red Cross in zones of conflict increased from 80,000 to 105,000 between January and July of 1984; and displaced persons in government-controlled areas rose from 262,000 to 342,000 from November 1983 to May 1984. In less than eight months, over 100,000 civilians were driven from their homes.

While the increase in aerial bombardment appears to have hurt the rebels in certain ways—such as making it riskier for them to mass for attack—the view that the strategy could actually be counterproductive was reflected in a classified report to the Pentagon by a team headed by retired Major General John Singlaub. "Dropping 500-pound bombs on insurgents is not the way to go," said Gen. Singlaub. "There is a need for very discriminate firepower."

(B) Air Mobile Assault

With the rebels somewhat dislocated by the effects of aerial bombardment, an expansion and escalation of the air war has taken place, known as air mobile assault.

Air mobile assault is designed to keep the rebels on the run through unexpected helicopter assaults in rebel zones, and eventually to wear them down to a small number of rural "bandits" who pose no substantial military threat. The air-mobile concept was initiated in 1984 (although U.S. strategists hoped to implement it as early as 1981), with the approval by Congress of vastly increased military assistance (although Congress' knowledge of its strategic implications was less than complete).

FY84 and FY85 military assistance totaling $328 million has allowed the Salvadoran Armed Forces to almost triple the number of helicopters in its inventory from 19 in January of 1984 to 46 by the end of the year. The increase in the number of helicopters is intended to support the "air cavalry" technique used widely in Vietnam, in which government troops make surprise raids into guerrilla areas or rapidly reinforce troops under attack. As *The New York Times* described it:

> To catch the guerrillas, the army is developing long-range reconnaissance patrols of 10 to 20 men. The patrols are trained to enter guerrilla areas to gather intelligence and carry out ambushes at night. With a fleet of 40 to 50 helicopters, the army is expected to be able to send small patrols to make contact with the guerrillas and immediately reinforce them by air with a 500- to 800-man battalion.

As part of the air assault capability, the U.S. has begun providing AC-47 gunships, equipped with three pilot-controlled .50-caliber machine guns. The guns, which can deliver up to 1500 rounds per minute, represent a significant increase in the firepower of the Salvadoran Army.

It is unclear whether this air mobile assault technique can actually overcome the rebels. It may enhance the mobility of the Army to the point that the rebels are permanently on the run. On the other hand, the Army may rely on the increased technology too much, and revert to its traditional behavior of stressing firepower from a safe distance rather than aggressive small-unit tactics. In addition, helicopter operations are riddled with problems. First, they are vulnerable to ground fire—last winter, 28 soldiers died when two helicopters collided while trying to avoid rebel ground fire—and could become more vulnerable if the rebels acquire the SAM-7 hand-held missiles they are rumored to be seeking.[2] Second, it is far from clear that the expanded helicopter fleet can be successfully operated and maintained: helicopter maintenance is a "logistical nightmare": last July, for example, roughly half were grounded at one time. Third, the complexity of the maintenance might require U.S. military or contract personnel to oversee. Fourth, there is a shortage of trained Salvadoran pilots and copilots to operate them. And finally, they are likely to increase human rights abuses, as Salvadoran troops continue to fail to discriminate between civilians and guerrillas in rebel-contested zones—as proven by recent instances.[3]

The three separate strategies which have been pursued since 1981 to achieve a military victory over the Salvadoran guerrillas have each failed to achieve their desired result. In spite of increased U.S. financial aid and increased U.S. involvement of personnel, conditions within El Salvador continue to deteriorate. The number of displaced people grows daily. The number of civilian casualties increases, and threatens to worsen under increased aerial assaults. And finally, official estimates of the number of rebels have climbed steadily, from 2,000 (1981), to 4–6,000 (1983), to 9–11,000 (1984), and now, in the most recent interview at the end of 1984, "10, 12, 13, 14,000."

30. Living under El Salvador's Air War*

BY MARY JO MCCONAHAY

According to Chris Hedges, former Salvadoran correspondent for the Christian Science Monitor, *the bombing of guerrilla strongholds in Cuscatlán, Chalatenango, and Morazán provinces by A-37s now occurs three times a day. Moreover, according to Vicki Kemper (*Sojourner, *April 1985), bombing is more sophisticated: Bombs are designed to explode a yard or two above the ground, thereby extending the range of shrapnel, leading to more injuries, death, and property destruction.*

[2.] On May 22, 1985, in Managua, Nicaragua, Guillermo Ungo, a leading member of the FDR, was quoted as saying, "For the time being, we do not plan to acquire SAM-7 missiles, but I don't know if they will be necessary in the future." Foreign Broadcast Information Service, *Daily Reports–Central America,* May 24, 1985.—Eds.

[3.] In one particularly chilling incident in August 1984, helicopter-borne troops encircled and opened fire on hundreds of unarmed peasants and a small number of armed rebels in Chalatenango province. Salvadoran Archbishop Arturo Rivera y Damas condemned the incident, in which he said 50 people had died, and called for an investigation. According to Catholic Relief Services, almost 1,000 refugees fled El Salvador for Honduras in the two months following this incident. Interview of CRS official by staff of Rep. George Miller (D-CA), January 10, 1985; "Salvador Prelate Asks Study of Grisly Reports," *New York Times,* September 17, 1984.

* From *Pacific News Service,* February 26 and 28, 1985.

Mary Jo McConahay, an editor of Pacific News Service, *describes, in two reports, what life is like in guerrilla-controlled territory. (A third report, not included here, describes the efforts—thus far successful—to keep a candy factory in operation, the product being a morale builder for the guerrillas.)*

AIR attacks and hunger are shrinking the civilian population of this mountain zone. The people here are guerrilla supporters—"masas"—and this has long been a stronghold of the rebel Farabundo Martí National Liberation Front [FMLN].

FMLN officials and civilian "popular power" authorities say they have been "sending out" the old, the very sick and some families with many children to refugee camps and other locations in government-controlled zones for the last several months. The exodus, they say, is partly also in response to increased government operations on the ground. And some of the "masas," rebel officials admit, have left "without permission."

The several thousand peasant "masas" who remain are subject to bombing and gunfire from the air when there is no apparent combat situation. During five days near here in February, two North American reporters were forced to take cover from air attacks on three occasions.

Peasants are also finding it increasingly difficult to feed themselves. On walks through the area each lasting several hours, reporters observed fruit groves, a corn field and other pieces of land which appeared to have been recently burned. In several cases residents claimed that government troops had set fire to their fields deliberately. In some cases, they said, fires started after bombs fell.

Residents of three hamlets reported that soldiers destroyed stores of corn amounting to several hundred pounds. Corn is a staple of the rural diet.

"If they did not destroy the fields, we would have sufficient food to feed ourselves," said Francisco Valle, 44, the civilian official responsible for agricultural production in the La Cruz hamlet near here.

Peasants here work both for themselves and for the guerrillas. They spend three days on their own fields, and three days without pay on communal fields whose products are given to guerrilla units, and to community members such as teachers or medics. Now, Valle said, so many fields have been burned that all stores are being shared with those who lost crops, shrinking everyone's share of food.

("This is a war of attrition, and food—or an attempt at starvation—has become a weapon too," said a religious worker in San Salvador whose duties include interviewing peasants displaced from conflict zones such as this one.)

The International Committee of the Red Cross has tried to deliver emergency food to two towns in this zone. But the regional Salvadoran army commander has forbidden this on the grounds that the food would go to the guerrillas, according to an informed source.

Merchants of Tejutepeque, a town of 8000 about four hours walk from here, have complained to military authorities of a similar incident as they were bringing in stock. In early February they were stopped by National Police at a road block 17 kilometers from Tejutepeque. There they were forced to give up all but a minimum of goods and accused of supplying guerrillas.

These charges seem to be borne out by San Salvador Archbishop Arturo Rivera y Damas who announced in his Feb. 17 Sunday homily that military authorities in the neighboring zone of Chalatenango were impeding the delivery by Caritas of emergency food supplies to "the civilian population who urgently need them." Caritas is the charity organization of the El Salvadoran Bishops Conference.

Armed Forces spokesmen denied the archbishop's claim, and said that "it interests the Armed Forces more than anyone that help should reach countrymen who suffer the torments of this war, imposed by international communism."

Given the difficulties of continuing to live in a zone under fire, what is surprising is that peasants stay at all. According to census figures provided by local "popular power" authorities, the number of "masas" is down by a third to a half in the last year to 18 months.

Those who remain may not be easily convinced to abandon the mountains. A majority of the dozens interviewed said they would die first before leaving.

"Our strength comes from the faith we have in changing the system we used to live under," said Freddy, 23, secretary of the civilian directorate in a hamlet called San Antonio. His work includes going house to house to solicit food for families which run out of supplies or find them destroyed.

"We have a school, a store and food production, and we're not peons any longer on someone else's land," Freddy said. "We've built that structure. You can't buy that."

"We are sending people out because we are hoarding up, preparing for a worse time yet," said another young civilian, the governor of the easternmost of three "subzones" which make up the FMLN's Central Front.

Some who have been encouraged to leave, however, refuse to go.

"My parents say they don't want to leave their children and grandchildren here," said Tonio Vanegas, 33, of La Criba, the local civilian security officer.

After the last army operation, he said, his mother Carmen, 70, lost her left arm when she exploded a mine planted on a path from her house to a water trough.

Other residents said there had been several explosions of mines or grenades left by the army over the last few months involving nylon trip lines. These were camouflaged, they claim, wrapped in corn husk leaves or tamale leaves and left on the ground. It was not possible to verify the reports independently.

Day by day, what seems to grind the nerves is the air war. One morning reporters woke to the sound of an exploding mine or mortar, which residents agreed was "far away." Yet within 20 minutes all had scattered, alarmed at the sound of aircraft heading for their hamlet, and hid as rockets, bombs and machine gun fire covered the area for about half an hour.

The next morning at another hamlet, an 02 spotter plane, flew low over houses, then—as children ran into shelters dug a few feet away—returned to fire rockets. There had been no sounds of combat before or after the attack.

The peasants here say what they fear most are the ground operations by the Salvadoran army and U.S.-trained elite battalions. These bring up to thousands of government troops into the area for days, even weeks, at a time. Such moves used to come once every month or two, they say, but recently they occur about every two weeks.

At those times, peasants flee to mountain caves or other hiding places with as much food as they can carry, and wait for the operation to end.

* * * *

By the time the first jet appeared, screaming over the top of the mountain from the north, peasants here were already running for cover in every direction.

"Juga!" yelled a 60-year-old named Joaquín, as he dived behind a wall of stones, using the local word for a U.S.-made "ground assault" jet. At the same moment, the first bomb exploded close enough to shake the ground under the some 150 inhabitants of this hamlet, their faces pressed into the quaking dirt.

Only about 50 miles northeast of the modern, bustling capital of San Salvador, a small nation-within-a-nation of pro-rebel civilians is trying to conduct its own separate system of education, health care and farm production—all in dangerous accommodation with the air war.

Classes are held in a bombed-out house a few feet away from two of the thousands of "tatus" that pepper these hills, caves where children can run to shelter during an air attack. During a five-day visit to the area, reporters saw farmers going into the fields on only three days—on the other two there was bombing, and peasants stayed close to home to be ready for quick evacuation.

To watch the peasants slapping additional layers of earth on their shelters in hope of protection against the army's new Hughes 500 helicopter "mini-guns," which spray some 6,000 bullets a minute, or to see them rush to snatch drying clothes from tree branches at the sound of approaching aircraft—which can pick out the colors that signal human habitation from thousands of feet —is to see that this fight has something of David and Goliath about it. Yet, after some two and a half years of escalating air war, peasants seem to have found a way to live with the giant.

The artifacts of daily life certainly indicate there is a war going on.

—The handle of a home-made knife turns out to be a finely-crafted, large caliber machine gun shell.

—Small children play house in a sturdy wood box dropped during a recent operation, its markings, in English, announcing 40 mm shells from Tennessee.

—"Safe-conduct passes"—3 by 6 inch mimeographed sheets inviting guerrillas and their supporters to give up, signed by Army Chief of Staff Col. Adolfo Blandón, and dropped by the hundreds from aircraft during one of the new psychological operations efforts—are used as bathroom tissue.

Even within the terror that is a sudden air attack, certain apparently well-practiced routines are set in motion.

On the morning the jets came, villagers first lay low where they were as bombs and rockets hit nearby for about 10 minutes, all miraculously missing people, small houses and camouflaged shelters. When the planes flew toward a distant, isolated road—where an explosion had been heard—residents grabbed a few necessities and ran down a grassy mountain slope to the safety of a natural grotto, well-hidden from the air.

In the grotto, one could make a quick sketch of the community.

Marisol, 38, a local officer of the women's organization associated with the Farabundo Martí National Liberation Front, the FMLN, was caught at the grotto with her water jug and stayed, hugging the moist stone walls in fear.

There is Raul, the serious 24-year-old governor of the "subzone," running by with a plastic bag stuffed with notebooks—full of hand-printed records, census and production figures—which he will hide further down the trail in a "tatu."

Moments later, he is followed by a breathless Roberto Aguilar, a teacher who had come here two weeks before from another FMLN area to reorganize the tiny school and start an adult literacy class. He carried a package of workbooks under each arm.

Last came Jesús, the small, soft-spoken medic, a brown day-pack containing the town's entire dispensary in one hand, a guitar in the other.

At the grotto, 19-year-old Maribel, eight months pregnant, held fast to the metal corn grinder she had quickly dismantled. Others smoked furiously, but Maribel politely refused a cigarette, saying it was bad for her health.

At first glance, peasants seem no less terrified than a visitor who is experiencing the explosions and confusion of aircraft on all sides for the first time. (The bombings are now killing more people than the death squads, according to the Archdiocesan Legal Aid Office in San Salvador.)

In fact, however, those who stay in these mountains have learned to live with the air war in a certain way. They often call the planes and helicopters "animales," and seem to have developed almost a sixth sense for their distinctive sounds, capabilities—and limitations.

For instance, no one runs at the first pass of an 02 spotter plane. If it loops or changes course, however, residents scatter for protection from the rockets which inevitably follow.

They know the schedules of commercial airliners, and rarely confuse them with an oncoming jet attack. And even children can recount certain rules, as Amilcar, 14, did at the grotto: "For helicopters with machine guns, keep the house between you and the 'animal,' but for A-37s, get away from the house."

Peasants say one thing they dread is being caught alone and unaware by an aircraft, and not "freezing" fast enough. They claim government aircraft will attack "anything that moves" in a guerrilla-controlled zone. Government officials have denied there are "free fire zones."

Two reporters attempting to leave the FMLN-controlled zone on their own experienced an incident that would seem to corroborate the peasants' claim. Walking on an open stretch of the little-used road between the towns of Cinquera and Tejutepeque, well inside the guerrilla zone, reporter Peter Katel of the Albuquerque (NM) Journal and I took cover at the sound of approaching aircraft.

There had been no sounds or signs of combat, and we had seen no one else on or alongside the road. We remained pinned down by rocket and machine gun fire from two airplanes for about 10 minutes.

When the planes departed, we walked as quickly as the heat and terrain allowed, still hearing no sounds of combat—and encountering no one else on the road until we reached the outskirts of the government-controlled zone, one and a half hours later.

31. The Invisible War on the Environment*

BY GAR SMITH

Not only does the air war exact a frightful human toll, but—as one might expect to learn in a publication of the Friends of the Earth—its ecological effects are devastating as well. Gar Smith, formerly with Friends of the Earth, is a freelance writer in Berkeley.

"NATURAL resources are a specific target of military action," writes Mexican researcher María del Carmen Rojas Canales. "Bombs, napalm, white phosphorus," she states in her report "Ecological Effects of the War in El Salvador," are used "against both civilian populations and vegetation."

El Salvador, which has lost much of its rich and diversified forests to agriculture and cattle ranching, now faces a new threat from the air and ground war. Native plant species like the chicozapote, sincuyo, and cabeza de muerto are on the path to extinction; rubber trees and willows are threatened.

El Salvador lies at the same latitude as Vietnam, and, like Vietnam, has a hot, humid climate favoring mangrove swamps and tropical forests.

* From *Not Man Apart* (the newsmagazine of Friends of the Earth), 15, No. 6 (July–August 1985).

Unlike Vietnam, El Salvador has served for millenia as a land bridge and a "zone of fauna filtration" retarding the migration of mammals from North America to South America. Native wildlife now falling under the pressures of troop movements and bombardment includes forest-dwelling sloths, tiger cats, howling monkeys, iguanas, and deer.

In addition, El Salvador is part of the great Central American refuge that serves as a wintering home for millions of migrating North American songbirds—tanangers, warblers, kingbirds, and vireos. More than 150 species of North American birds are dependent on a rainforest refuge, which has lost 75 percent of its cover in the last three decades. Some environmentalists have warned that development pressures could eradicate the remaining rainforests before the end of the century. Already scientists have noticed fewer songbirds returning in the spring migrations.

HOW THE WAR IS KILLING THE LAND

"One of the departments most affected is that of Cuscatlan, both because of the type of arms used and the intensity of the attacks," reports Rojas Canales. Cuscatlán is largely semi-evergreen rainforest with croplands devoted to corn, beans, sugar cane, zapote, mamey, mango, nispero, nance, and maranon. "The types of attacks are bombing with napalm and white phosphorus, 200-pound bombs, burning of cane plantations and destruction of coffee crops."

"It can be inferred," Rojas Canales observes, "that many of the fruit trees were damaged by bomb fragments, making way for diseases caused by bacteria and fungi, principally." Presumably similar damage has been done in the natural forest areas. The effect of incendiary weapons would tend to "diminish plant cover and lead to soil erosion, which would be accelerated due to the heavy rainfall of the area." Beyond the problem of erosion "the entire ecological balance is damaged by extinguishing the primary producers that serve as food and refuge for many other organisms such as rodents, many birds, and other creatures which, if not of commercial interest, do contribute to the maintenance of the balance of the ecosystem."

War-caused fires in the pine-oak forests "provoke changes in the composition and the structure of the ecological communities. Many forests of this type die, because they cannot reproduce and perpetuate." The forests then decline into secondary "scrub forests" or grasslands. This leads to aggravated erosion, "the drying up of natural springs, water pollution, floods, filling up of reservoirs and dust storms."

"If the war continues and intensifies the use of conventional as well as chemical weapons," Rojas Canales concludes, "the deterioration could reach a point that would impede the recuperation of ecosystems even in the medium term; there would be zones that, as in the case of Vietnam, would be unusable for more than 50 years."

242 EL SALVADOR: CENTRAL AMERICA IN THE NEW COLD WAR

BOMBS, BULLETS, AND BATS

In March of 1985, Gus Newport, the mayor of Berkeley, California, attempted to visit Berkeley's sister city of San Antonio Los Ranchos in Chalatenango Province. The city had been nearly destroyed by a bombing raid in the fall of 1983, shortly after Berkeley announced its sister-city affiliation. Newport and his colleague, Diane Green of an organization called New El Salvador Today, never reached their goal. In the middle of their cross-country hike their party came under a government air attack.

Newport and Green huddled in a dark bunker with a dozen terrified children as the rockets pounded the village they had taken shelter in. One rocket destroyed a nearby home killing the family of 11 cowering inside.

"The army is destroying fields and homes. They have destroyed anything that is for living," Newport told a press conference upon his return. Fighting back tears, Newport confided his fears that he "might never see again" many of the friends he had made during his visit to Chalatenango.

Diane Green brought back vivid memories of the environmental havoc that's raging over the countryside. "We observed lots of land that had been burned by mortars. They can start fires which can burn for days," Green recalled. "The army drops incendiary rockets, gasoline rockets. We saw lots of land—acres and acres—that had been charred."

Green repeated the charge that the Salvadoran Army routinely destroys crops. "When the Salvadoran Army invades," she stated, "they always burn the crops and destroy the waterpipes in the villages. They cut down the fruit trees, kill the cows, destroy all the tools they find. Fishing boats are sunk." Both Newport and Green reported seeing many people (many of them children) suffering from malnutrition as well as machinegun wounds. There is no dairy protein for the children where the army has killed the cattle and milk cows.

"This is what counterinsurgency is all about," says Christina Courtright. "The government has tried very hard to destroy the means of subsistence of the people in the countryside. They have intentionally destroyed crops and homes. Dead bodies are thrown into wells to poison the water supplies."

"Ecological imbalances are occurring all over," Courtright continues. "One of the most macabre involves bats." In Central America it is a common sight to see blood trickling down the necks of cattle every morning. It is part of the natural ecology. The war has changed that, Courtright says. "Vampire bats are now attacking humans for the first time because the army has killed off the cows."

"The bats first lick the victims' necks in the night," Courtright explains. "Their tongues have a mild anesthetic so the victim doesn't feel the bite. But the bite also injects an anticoagulant. This is fine for the bat, but it's not good for the victim if the victim happens to be a small child. Small children can die from loss of blood in the night. And they have."

In her pioneering report on ecology and war in El Salvador, María del Carmen Rojas Canales and her scientific colleagues render a sobering verdict:

"The menace to the natural resources of El Salvador constitutes a situation that should be taken into consideration by the international ecology, conservation, and peace movements. We call upon them to announce their support for a stop to the war, a negotiated political solution, and a halt to the destruction of the ecosystem of El Salvador."

CHAPTER VII

Special Aspects of the Civil War: Terror and Human Rights

Editors' Introduction

One of the functions of political leadership is to translate the complex reality of the passing scene into *issues* about which policies can be developed. In doing this, political leaders bracket and frame parts of reality, in line with their ideology and political interest.[1] U.S. policies in Central America provide an interesting example of this. The Jimmy Carter presidency highlighted the issues of "human rights," whereas the administration of Carter's successor has attempted to relegate human rights to the background and has given primacy instead to the issue of left-wing international terrorism.[2] But reality cannot be so readily molded even by powerful political leaders, and Ronald Reagan has expressed concern about human rights violations by established governments in Asia, Africa, the Caribbean, and even Central America, some of them "friendly" to the United States.[3] But the Reagan administration has not abandoned its overall perspective—that in what is usually called the

[1] The serious interpretive issues involved in the function of political leaders in the modern era are provocatively discussed by C. Wright Mills in *Power, Politics and People*, ed., Irving Louis Horowitz (New York: Oxford University Press, 1963), part II, and in his *The Sociological Imagination* (New York: Oxford University Press, 1959); and by Erving Goffman in *Frame Analysis: An Essay on the Organization of Experience* (New York: Harper & Row, 1974).

[2] See, for example, "Remarks on Central America and El Salvador to the National Association of Manufacturers," March 10, 1983, in *Public Papers of the Presidents: Ronald Reagan*, 2 vols., 1983 (Washington, D.C.: U.S. Government Printing Office, 1984), 1; 372–77, etc.

[3] Interview with Walter Cronkite, CBS News, March 3, 1981, *Public Papers*, 1981 (Washington, D.C.: U.S. Government Printing Office, 1982), 196, etc.

Third World, leftist terrorism, rather than inhumane and authoritarian dictatorships, is the main problem.

But problems of defining just what is included in the definition of terrorism are formidable. Recent violent events—car bombings of U.S. military emplacements in Beirut, the highjacking of airplanes and cruise ships with North Americans aboard, the gunning down of U.S. Marines in the Zona Rosa of San Salvador—have offered President Reagan opportunities to lash out verbally at terrorism. But terrorism cannot be convincingly reduced to violence directed at U.S. citizens or those "friendly" folk the President labels the "good guys."

There is the question of when, even in the midst of war, military actions taken are forms of terrorism. For example, were the World War II bombings of civilian centers like London or Dresden legitimate exercises of military force or were they acts of terrorism? What about the unleashing of atomic bombs on Hiroshima and Nagasaki in 1945? In El Salvador too, as the previous chapter indicates, the government is waging a devastating air war —using U.S. aircraft and ammunition paid for by U.S. taxpayers—killing many civilians (as well as guerrillas) and producing hundreds of thousands of refugees. Is this not terrorism too, a form of state terrorism?

On their side, the Salvadoran guerrillas, like insurgents in many other places fighting against established governments, lack the sophisticated military equipment of their opponents. The FMLN can deploy no AC-47 gunships, HUEY helicopters, or jet bombers. They are, like their Spanish predecessors in the peninsular wars of the early nineteenth century,[4] forced to fight an "irregular war" and do their killing on more of a face-to-face basis. Are we to call them terrorists simply because they lack an air force?[5]

No government is ideologically pacifist. Washington approves of guerrilla "terror" when it is employed by Afghan insurgents against Soviet and Soviet-supported troops. The U.S. government has also financially aided, armed, and directed the counterrevolutionary *contras* striving to overthrow the Sandinista government of Nicaragua. Reliable observers have shown that these U.S.-backed *contras* regularly kill, rape, and maim Nicaraguans they encounter, including civilians, and destroy property, crops, and institutions on their murderous forays.[6] How to distinguish "legitimate" terrorism from "bad" terrorism has to be one of the most troubling moral dilemmas for concerned citizens in these violent times. We do not claim to solve any of these problems here, but we aim merely at providing reliable documentation of the terror that has wracked El Salvador for most of the past decade. Although the use

[4.] For discussion of the first "guerrillas" to be so designated, see page xvii.

[5.] Even former CIA agents, like Harry Rositzke, accord wars of national liberation a status different from random hijackings, kidnappings, and assassinations that serve no discernible political purpose. See his remarks quoted in the *New York Times*, July 20, 1981.

[6.] Christopher Dickey, *With the Contras: A Reporter in the Wilds of Nicaragua* (New York: Simon & Schuster, 1985).

of terror is of course an integral part of the raging civil war in that country, we assign a separate chapter of our book to it because it is so endemic and because it presents such agonizing moral issues.

By all responsible accounts, most of the terror in El Salvador has been carried out by right-wing death squads, which, financed by the oligarchies and by the United States (see Reading 7), ran rampant, kidnapping, torturing, mutilating, killing tens of thousands—mostly labor leaders, peasant organizers or students suspected of that most subjective of offenses, subversion. Particularly horrendous episodes from this stream of terrorism often surface in the U.S. mass media: the assassination of Archbishop Romero or the slayings of North American churchwomen (Readings 11 and 34). More rarely does the news get out about a mass killing, such as the Sumpul River massacre (Reading 37).

Although right-wing terror, and its far less numerically significant left-wing response, have become a way of life in El Salvador, the tempo does vary. Reaching a kind of peak in the early 1980s death-squad activity has diminished, especially as the main urban popular organizations were decimated. But it can never be repeated too often that the structure of the Salvadoran terror apparatus remains intact. Though terror has been curtailed for the present by the influence of the Reagan administration and by prudent people in the government and military, its resumption is a realistic possibility. The guerrillas have added daring acts of ambush and killing to their array of tactics, and the reactivation of popular militancy in the cities brings the likelihood of yet another cycle of terror in the ravaged country. No people would be more happy than the editors of this book to be proved wrong about this grim prediction.

32. *Recording the Terror: El Salvador's Tutela Legal**

BY THE STAFF OF TUTELA LEGAL

In the conflict-ridden society of contemporary El Salvador, even the statistics on the terror are contested. The U.S. Embassy frequently attacks the Roman Catholic church agency Tutela Legal ("Legal Trust"), which collects and publishes the grim lists and charts of deaths and disappearances. Former U.S. Ambassador Thomas Pickering claimed that Tutela Legal's data are suspect and slanted in favor of the guerrillas.[1] The

* Excerpted from Oficina de Tutela Legal del Arzobispado, Comisión Arquidiocesana de Justicia y Paz, San Salvador, Informe No. 30 (October 1984).

[1.] Marvin E. Gettleman, interview with Thomas Pickering, U.S. Embassy, San Salvador, January 8, 1985.

director of Tutela Legal, former philosophy professor María Julia Hernández, was all too familiar with these charges, and although she admitted that one of its statistical reports (in early 1983) was in error, she pointed out that the U.S. Embassy figures are drawn from newspaper accounts and from government officials. All of El Salvador's newspapers (except, of course, clandestine sheets put out by the FMLN), especially the main San Salvador daily, Diario de Hoy, are right-wing publications under the control of the oligarchy.[2] Casualty reports emanating from such sources, Hernández pointed out, have a built-in bias against all data that might show government, armed-forces, and death-squad brutality. Tutela Legal makes on-the-spot investigations where possible and draws the rest of its data from eye-witnesses to the brutal events it records and chronicles.[3]

OFFICE OF THE TUTELA LEGAL OF THE ARCHBISHOPRIC
THE ARCHDIOCESE COMMISSION ON JUSTICE AND PEACE
SAN SALVADOR, EL SALVADOR, C.A.
Report No. 30, October 1984
Deposition No. 4

In San Salvador, in the Office of Tutela Legal of the Archbishopric of San Salvador, at 10:15 on the 16th of October 1984 testifies Mrs. _____, 60 years old, in domestic work, a widow, from Sensuntepeque, who cannot identify herself with her identity card because she misplaced it, who swears to tell the truth, and only the truth about the events that she describes as follows: On the 10th of October of this year at 11 in the morning planes of the Air Force came to bomb the area of El Chile canton close to where I lived. I had to run out to hide because besides their bombing, soldiers came and everyone there fled to the hills in the direction of the river Lempa. They stayed there until 5 in the afternoon on that day; then on the 11th of the same month and year, they bombed again and came on the ground and because of this, fearing they would kill us, we fled from there and didn't go back because whenever they come they destroy the place and kill people, and also all of these months they have come to bomb at different times. In June I witnessed the bombings of the 16th and the 12th; in the one of the 16th a woman named Ingacia died; she was about 60 years old; a bomb fell where she was, for it was nighttime and she was getting ready to go to sleep when they came and the bomb fell. Also they wounded a little fellow named Victor, about 13 years old, and a man named Uvaldo, 30 years old, a day laborer; both of them came from San Juan Buena Vista. From then on, in July, August, and September, they came to bomb as well, but thank God we hid ourselves well and they didn't get us; but now on the 10th of October we got more frightened and we left there for good because we couldn't return to risk their killing us. Last year in one of these bombings they killed my two sons who were at home after they came back

[2.] Marvin E. Gettleman, interview with President José Napoleón Duarte, Presidential Palace, San Salvador, January 10, 1985.

[3.] Marvin E. Gettleman, interview with María Julia Hernández, offices of the Archbishop of San Salvador, January 9, 1985.

from work when the bomb fell, and I was not there at that moment because I was out bringing water. Everything I have to declare is the truth and only the truth and having had this read to me I leave my fingerprints because I can't sign my name.

[Prints of the Witness]

Deposition No. 9

In San Salvador, in the office of Tutela Legal of the Archbishopric of San Salvador, at five minutes past ten o'clock, on the 31st of October 1984, a young woman, 14 years of age, single, a domestic worker who was originally from the Cerros de San Pedro Canton, in the jurisdiction of San Vicente, who was not identified by *cédula* [identity card] because she was a minor and not having a birth certificate, for it had been taken from her during the events that will be related, and WHO PROMISED TO TELL THE TRUTH ABOUT THE DEEDS THAT WILL BE DETAILED:

About 15 days ago in October of this year, a combat force of soldiers of the [Salvadoran] armed forces appeared, I don't remember exactly when, but it was approximately the 18th of October, but on that day they arrived at about 1 in the afternoon, those that were coming over land, and also they arrived to bomb at about 7 in the morning and in A-37 airplanes. The bombardment lasted an hour and a half, and later helicopters also arrived, a total of five and two small planes, those which they call A-7, and then that day plenty of people died as a consequence of the invasion by elements of the army, who came and began to kill the poor people of the civilian population and among them I found out about six. They killed six persons, of them one was an old woman of approximately 60 years of age, on whom a bomb had fallen and severed her hands and foot and left her with a great many of *esquirlas* [shrapnel fragments] in her body. Also, another man died, about 50 years of age. They took him and cut off his head after interrogating him. With this man were two children, one age six and the other eight, and the children, upon seeing what had been done to their father, began to cry, and the older one, the eight-year-old, was shot in the head, and there he was left stretched out with his father and the soldiers took away the other boy, but he kept crying as the soldiers led him away on the road, they cut off his head with a machete. I found out about this because the other people who were fleeing, and saw it and told me. I also realized that two other young children died, one only 3 days old, and the other six months. A big bomb fell on them and they died. There were also two wounded people, I don't know their names but I know that shrapnel hit one on the hand and the other on the legs.

That day, I was with my family in my house, and when we were advised that the soldiers were coming near we left, fleeing for the mountains to hide ourselves because if we didn't they would have killed all of us. Also on March 2 of this year, there was another invasion in the same place, while I was getting olive seeds to make soap. I was accompanied by two other people, MARTINA ALVARADA, approximately 65 years old, and who was my aunt, and was helping me chop the olive seeds; also a man called ELIO, whose last name I don't remember but who was about 35 years old. He was nearby cutting firewood when around 4 o'clock in the afternoon an A-37 plane passed and it dropped a bomb which killed Mr. Elio and tore off a leg. He died rapidly because shrapnel struck him all over his body, and my aunt MARTINA's hand was blown off and she was all bruised. She survived 12 days but because of the injuries she could not eat and she too died. Shrapnel hit me in the leg, getting me on my leg, right on the knee, and cut my veins, and destroyed the knee. Then gangrene set in, and after about 4 days they amputated my right leg.

Also five years ago some National Guardsmen in uniform came to take three relatives into custody: my father MERCEDES PALACIOS, 52 years old, my mother's brother, my uncle PEDRO JUAN ALVARADO, 48 years old, along with my brother, MARIO PALACIOS. The soldiers used ropes from the oxen tied nearby and with these same ropes bound them, beat them and took them away, and since then we have not known their whereabouts. That was the 29th day of May of 1979.

Around August of 1980 my other brother DANIEL PALACIOS, who was 20 years old, that day he came to visit us and some men from ORDEN[4] were waiting in the road; already they were waiting in the road for him, and then they shot him several times, and also struck him with machetes, and left his body thrown on the road. Lately, the Army came constantly to make war, and then they came all the time to bomb every week.

Due to so much suffering, I came here [to San Salvador] because there one can't live anymore, [the Army] ruined our crops, they burned them, and also they burned the few good clothes we had and they destroyed our house in a way that leaves us nothing. Thus, having nothing we came to San Salvador in search of help.

That is all I have to declare to you and it is all the truth and nothing but the truth and in good faith I leave my fingerprints because I do not know how to sign.

FINGERPRINTS OF THE DECLARER

OFFICE OF TUTELA LEGAL
Victims of Political Violence
Report No. 30, October 1984
Note: Deaths Attributed to Death Squads During the Month of October, 1984.

[4.] On the right-wing paramilitary National Democratic Organization (ORDEN), see Readings 7 and 19. —Eds.

1. REYNALDO ECHEVERRÍA: 37, *Licenciado* and Professor of Letters at Universidad Centroamericana José Simeón Cañas (UCA), killed on October 3, 1984, as he arrived at his house in Colonía Metrópolis in the department of San Salvador. A gray-colored vehicle with tinted windows followed the aforementioned *Licenciado,* his wife, and daughter. A person armed with a G-3 gun got out of the above vehicle and fired several times at the said *Licenciado* and subsequently fled down the street in the opposite direction.

2. UNKNOWN (2): found dead on October 2, 1984, on the Panamerican Highway, in the territory of El Congo en Coatepeque, with gunshot wounds, with their hands and thumbs tied behind their backs, and without identity papers.

4. LUIS DAGOBERTO RODRÍGUEZ: 48, employed, killed by an unidentified paramilitary Squad when he was taken from his house on October 8, 1984, by armed men in civilian dress, in Colonía Santa María in San Marcos, and found the same day in Reparto Bosques del Río in the district of Soyapango.

5. FRANCISCO ANTONIO REYES: 24, mechanic, found dead on October 29, 1984, on the coffee farm of the El Molino plantation on the outskirts of Santa Ana near San Salvador in the vicinity of the cemetery; found nude with visible marks of blows and signs of strangulation, with 2 leather straps around his neck, and without personal identification papers; it is believed he died elsewhere and had his body left in the place described above, killed by an unidentified paramilitary squad.

Total: 5 victims

OFFICE OF TUTELA LEGAL

Persons Taken into Custody Who Subsequently Disappeared on Dates Prior [to October] (Information Received During the Month of October [1984])

Peasants

1. AYALA MARTÍNEZ, ARCADIO, 21 years old, single, day laborer, and a resident of the department of San Vicente, was taken into custody March 8, 1984, at 8 A.M., in a place known as Las Vegas in the department of San Vicente, when the mentioned youth was on his way to go fishing on the banks of the Lempa River; a group of soldiers duly uniformed accosted him and after identifying him proceeded to take him into custody, taking him to a destination unknown to this day.
(declaration received 18-Oct '84)

Workers

2. DERAS MARTELLI, MILTON ALFONSO, 22 years old, single, worker and resident of the Department of San Salvador, was taken into custody on September 28, 1984, at 8:30 P.M. when two heavily armed men in civilian

clothes appeared at his house and upon identifying him proceeded to take him into custody and led him into a small truck, telling his family that they were taking him for investigation. He was driven to a destination unknown to this day.
(declaration received 18 Oct. '84)

3. MARINO COTO, ROGELIO, 25 years old, married, who worked as a driver and was a resident of Zacatecoluca in the Department of La Paz, was taken into custody on September 21, 1981, at 9 A.M. on the litoral highway by the Blanco River in the Department of La Paz, on which he was riding on a bicycle. He was intercepted by a group of duly uniformed soldiers who were at the site, who after identifying him proceeded to take him into custody along with a friend who was riding with the young man ROGELIO, and about whom nothing is known, and drove them to a destination unknown to this day.
(declaration received 4 Oct. '84)

Employees

4. LANDAVERDE RAMÍREZ, HUGO WALTER, 22 years old, single, employed resident of the Department of San Salvador, was taken into custody October 11, 1982, at 4 P.M. in the Finca Suchinango en Apopa, where he was working in the coffee harvest, when elements of the National Guard and the National Police appeared in uniform, and after identifying all the young people at the place, proceeded to take the youth HUGO into custody, together with a friend named DOMINGO LÓPEZ, of whom no more is known. They were carried off in a white pick-up vehicle, driven by the aforementioned elements [of the uniformed forces] to a destination unknown to this day.
(declaration received 30-Oct. 1984)

Teachers

5. MACHADO, BALBINO, 38 years of age, single, a schoolteacher in San Miguel, and a fifth year law student at the National University of San Miguel, and resident of the same Department. He was taken into custody January 3, 1984, at 9 A.M. at a café in the center of San Salvador, when heavily armed elements in civilian dress appeared and after identifying him proceeded to take him into custody along with a friend named CATARINO, of whom no more is known, taking them to a destination unknown to this day.
(declaration received 29-Oct. 1984)

OFFICE OF TUTELA LEGAL
Victims of Political Violence
Deaths Caused by Guerrilla Units
Report No. 30, October, 1984

1. AGAPITO DE JESÚS BARAHONA: 20, unmarried, worked as a driver, resident of Cantón La Lucha, killed while transporting National Guardsmen in a private pickup, ambushed by guerrilla units on the highway leading from Zacatecoluca to San Vicente, at the 75km. mark, in the district of Tecoluca, October 7 of this year.

2. LAZARO DE JESÚS CRUZ: 17, unmarried, worked as a conductor [fare collector], resident of Cantón La Lucha, death occurred when he was transporting National Guardsmen in the pick-up he was conductor for; ambushed on the highway leading from Zacatecoluca to San Vicente at the 75km. mark in the Tecoluca district on October 7 of this year.

3. UNKNOWN: death occurred on October 23 when a group of guerrillas penetrated the town of Santiago de María; they came to the house of the farmer Atilio Soriano where the main gate was dynamited; the victim was asleep in the garage of the house in an intoxicated condition and died as a result of the explosion.

4. PEDRO VÁSQUEZ ROSAS, 78, died on October 31 of this year as he walked by the side of the highway that leads from Nueva San Salvador to Santa Ana in the Palo Negro Cantón district of Santa Ana. At the moment he passed by, a bomb intended for ambushing a National Police patrol exploded, killing the aforementioned gentleman.

5. DANIEL PINZÓN LUCERO, 6, died on October 31 of this year as a result of the explosion of a bomb that guerrilla units had intended in an ambush for a National Police patrol; the boy was walking by the side of the highway that leads from Nueva San Salvador to Santa Ana in the vicinity of Palo Negro Cantón district of Santa Ana.

6. RAUL MELÉNDEZ AQUINO, 62, supervisor and security guard at the U.S. Embassy, killed on the first block west, behind the Maternity Hospital, by three members of the FPL[5] riding in a vehicle; moments after the action, they took responsibility; it took place on October 26 of this year.

GENERAL ACCOUNTING

Total Victims of Political Violence During October 1984

Victims of killings imputed to death squads and the armed forces during October	29
Victims of military actions	72
Deaths imputed to the guerrillas	6
Total victims of political violence	107

[5] Fuerzas Populares de Liberación—Popular Liberation Forces, the armed wing of the BPR, Bloque Popular Revolucionaria (Popular Revolutionary Bloc)—Eds.

33. The Death of a Salvadoran Church Worker*

BY TERRY TROIA

The author of this moving tribute to one of the anonymous victims of the death squads is Terry Troia, a doctoral candidate at Union Theological Seminary in New York City. She spent six months in 1984 traveling throughout Central America and has spoken at universities and churches in the United States since her return.

I was seeking the pastor of a poor Catholic parish located somewhere on the outskirts of San Salvador. It had been a laborious search. Nobody in El Salvador, not even the most faithful of churchgoers, will tell you the name of their pastor. Not that they don't know. It is just that handing over a name to a stranger is treason in El Salvador.

But I did nail down the right pastor after a week of asking. And after he pulled his pick-up truck into the rectory, which was really a garage, we had some time to talk. We would never know last names. That was an unspoken rule. We agreed to a Tuesday morning meeting to discuss the work of the church in El Salvador. He promised to have church workers with him. I promised not to ask their names.

We had set our Tuesday appointment for 8 A.M., but when I arrived at the rectory, the assistant pastor was there alone, reading the book of Isaiah and chain-smoking non-filtered cigarettes. His first words were an offer of breakfast. His eyes were weary and his face drawn. "Something terrible happened here last night," he began. "They killed one of our people—a catechist of the children. The cadaver is in the street. Father's gone to find someone to take the body away."

He didn't know where the body was. "I'm new here [in El Salvador]," he continued. "It isn't a good idea for me to go to the cadaver. I have got to say Mass for the Mothers of the Disappeared at 10 A.M. And now this. . . ." His voice trailed off. He ran his fingers down his face. Then he lit another cigarette.

There was no need for him to explain further. The Committee of the Mothers of the Disappeared—a group started by Archbishop Oscar Romero—was considered subversive by the Salvadoran military. I knew that first hand. The week before I had been picked up by the National Police for carrying subversive material—documents of the Mother's Committee—in my pack.

I decided to search out the body myself. At the first street corner, I met a young boy selling newspapers. I asked him where the body was. He ignored

* From *Sojourners*, March 1985.

me. I asked again, this time adding that I was a friend of the pastor. Without looking at me, he finally whispered, "Straight ahead."

I followed a dirt road. Houses lined one side, an empty lot with garbage on the other side. In the middle of the street, people were gathered around a station wagon.

She was there in the midst of them, lying in the back of the car. Her face was calm and relaxed. Her features were like those of the indigenous people, with soft, mocha-colored skin and thick black hair pulled back, much like my own hair. She had bled from a bullet wound above the right eye, and the blood had trickled down the side of her face. Her cotton pants had been torn from the knee down. Whether she had been macheted or machine-gunned in the knee was difficult to tell: I couldn't find the knee in the midst of this sea of blood. The crowd backed away quietly as, between my own heart beats, I took photos of the body. Then the station wagon drove her away.

Who was this young woman of 15 years? Was she a David who tried to slay Goliath and was met with machine-gun fire? Was she Judith trying to enter the enemy camp under cover of darkness, caught in her act? Yet this was not the ground of the enemy. This street was her barrio.

Back at the rectory, with the testimony of unnamed witnesses and church workers, a story begins to unfold. She taught communion class to the parish children. Last night the lights went out at 6 P.M. in this barrio. A squad of 12 members of the Civil Defense, a division of the Armed Forces, was patrolling the streets. At 7:30 P.M., a barrage of machine-gun fire was heard. A witness recounted that then the squad of soldiers turned the corner from the street where her body lay. There the body remained, unclaimed for 13 hours. No one touches the body of someone slain by the military in El Salvador.

And her name. No one would say her name. But in the rectory hung a memorial of those church workers slain by the military. Some of the names are familiar to us—Oscar Romero, Ita Ford, Maura Clarke, Dorothy Kazel, Jean Donovan. But many names were unfamiliar. And somehow I felt that this unspoken name had already taken its place among them.

That afternoon only one of the newspapers reported the death: "Idalia ——— appeared dead of bullets that were fired last night at 7:30 P.M. in Barrio ———, when there were no lights. The death of the youth, it is said, was reported to the parochial church, anonymously."

Idalia never had a funeral. She was buried in secret, far away from her family and church. This is the fate of those murdered by the military: marked in death, as she was in life.

Neither President Reagan, nor the members of Congress who voted to continue this madness, will ever meet her. But I met Idalia in the back of a station wagon. And I know the truth that her death tells. A broken candle in the night, she was. And what in God's name are we?

34. A Tragic Nuns' Tale*

BY THE SPECIAL PRESIDENTIAL MISSION TO EL SALVADOR

In early December 1981, the world was shocked to learn of the brutal slaying in El Salvador of three American nuns and an American lay churchworker. Coming only days after the assassination of the six civilian leaders of the Democratic Revolutionary Front, this outrage prompted the Carter administration to respond by suspending military aid on December 5. A special U.S. mission was then sent to El Salvador. Its members were William D. Rogers, former Under Secretary of State for Economic Affairs and Assistant Secretary of State under President Ford, and Assistant Secretary of State William G. Bowdler (accompanied by Luigi R. Einaudi of the Department of State's Bureau of Inter-American Affairs). Their report is reprinted below.

Whatever history's final verdict on America's role in El Salvador, it will not likely pay tribute to the sensitivity of those Ronald Reagan appointed (or sought to appoint) to high office. Consider, for instance, the statement made two weeks after the killings by Jeane Kirkpatrick, then ambassador-designate: "No. I don't think the government [of El Salvador] was responsible [for the murders]. The nuns were not just nuns. The nuns . . . were political activists on behalf of the frente[1] . . . and somebody who is using violence to oppose the frente killed these nuns. The death squads are not agents of the Salvadoran government."

Then there is the flippant reference of Ernest Lefever, Reagan's sorry choice for human rights commissioner—later denied the appointment by the Senate—to "nuns hiding guns beneath their habits." Finally, there was the outrageous comment of Secretary of State Alexander Haig, who, months after the murders, suggested against all evidence "that perhaps the vehicle that the nuns were riding in may have tried to run a roadblock. . . ." Haig made light of the barbarous incident, noting under questioning at the Senate Foreign Relations Committee that he has never met "pistol-packing nuns," having previously suggested on no basis whatsoever, "There may have been an exchange of fire."

SISTER Ita Ford was an American citizen and a member of the Maryknoll order. She had been requested by the Apostolic Administrator of San Salvador to go to the refugee settlement in Chalatenango in July, 1980. She worked under the supervision of Father Efraín López distributing food, clothing and medicine to the poor and the dispossessed and lived in a modest parish house. Sister Maura Clarke joined Sister Ita in Chalatenango in August of 1980.

Chalatenango is an area particularly marked by competing violence between the left and right. During the latter part of November, it is reported that a sign appeared over the door of the Chalatenango parish house stating that all who

---

* From U.S. Department of State press release, December 12, 1980. The editors have added a brief Epilogue.

[1]. There was no evidence at the time that this was true, and none has been unearthed since. See Ana Carrigan, *Salvador Witness: The Life and Calling of Jean Donovan* (New York, 1984).

lived there were Communists and anyone who entered would be killed. Neither Sister Ita, Sister Maura nor local clergy gave the sign any special attention.

All the Maryknolls of the Central American region meet in assembly every year. Sister Ita Ford and Sister Maura Clarke, together with Sister Madeline Dorsey and Sister Teresa Alexander, two other Maryknoll sisters who work in the Diocese of Santa Ana (and whom we interviewed), left El Salvador by plane on November 26 to go to the annual meeting, held in Managua, Nicaragua.

The four Maryknolls could not obtain reservations on the same plane back to El Salvador. Accordingly, Sisters Madeline and Teresa returned on a TACA flight arriving at the El Salvador International Airport at about 4:30 P.M., Tuesday, December 2. There they were met by two other American citizens, Ursuline Sister Dorothy Kazel and Jean Donovan, a lay volunteer, both of whom were engaged in similar parish work in the city of La Libertad. Sister Dorothy and Jean Donovan drove Sister Madeline and Sister Teresa to La Libertad, then returned to meet Sisters Ita and Maura at the airport. Sisters Madeline and Teresa understood the four intended to sleep at the parish house in La Libertad, and that Sisters Ita and Maura planned to drive to Chalatenango the following day.

Sister Ita and Sister Maura arrived at the El Salvador International Airport from Managua on a COPA flight at approximately 6:30 P.M. the evening of December 2. Sister Dorothy Kazel and Jean Donovan arrived in their white 1978 Toyota van at approximately the same time to pick them up.

The airport was filled with foreigners arriving to attend the funeral the next day of the leaders of the leftist Democratic Revolutionary Front (FDR) kidnapped and murdered on November 27. The level of tension was high throughout El Salvador. Security forces patrolled the airport and its access roads.

The four Americans met and, while waiting for their baggage, chatted with a group of Canadian churchmen. The Canadians left the airport first, at approximately 7:00 P.M.

We have not identified anyone who saw the four American churchwomen alive after the Canadian group left them at the airport baggage pickup station. [Father Schindler of the La Libertad parish, after informing the U.S. consul that the women were missing, spent the next day searching for them.] At about 8:00 P.M. that night, he found their Toyota van on a road about ten miles northwest of the airport, in the direction of the City of San Salvador. The license plates had been removed and the van was burned so badly it had to be identified by the engine number.

[On the following day, the U.S. Ambassador, Robert White, was informed that the Vicar of the Diocese of San Vicente] had been told that the bodies of the "American nuns" were buried near Santiago Nonualco, a remote village some 15 miles northeast of the airport, and about 20 miles from where the van had been found northwest of the airport.

The Ambassador and the Consul drove there immediately; the trip into what is a rugged and mountainous part of the country took some time. After several inquiries, a local villager directed them to the grave, which he called that of the "American women," beside a back road some way out of Santiago Nonualco. When they arrived at the site, at about 1:30 in the afternoon, Father Paul Schindler was already there. He too had received word from the parish priest. Reporters from San Salvador and foreign media representatives began to arrive. Some villagers started to open the grave. No authorities were present when they began. About 3:00 P.M., the secretary of the Justice of the Peace, who performs the functions of a county coroner, arrived from Santiago Nonualco. He gave permission for the bodies, already uncovered, to be removed from the grave. Shortly thereafter the Justice of the Peace, Juan Santos Ceron, appeared.

All four women had been shot in the head. The face of one had been destroyed. The underwear of three was found separately. Bloody bandanas were also found in the grave.

According to the accounts given the Ambassador and others on December 4, one victim had been found nude below the waist; out of respect, a villager had replaced her jeans before burial. The villagers took the bodies to be those of "blond foreigners" and subsequently informed church authorities.

[After being notified by the commander of the local militia of the dead women, the] Justice of the Peace and his secretary had then cooperated in the burial, following procedures they said had become standard at the direction of the security forces. They told the Ambassador that two or three such informal burials of unidentified bodies occurred every week.

According to the brief report on the cause of death prepared at the direction of the Justice of the Peace before the informal burial, one of the victims had been shot through the back of the head with a weapon that left exit wounds that destroyed her face; the other three had entry wounds, one in the temple, the others in the back of the head, but apparently no exit wounds. Those present at the disinterment, however, had the impression that the wounds were more extensive, that several had been caused by high-caliber bullets, and that the bodies were also bruised.

EDITORS' EPILOGUE

From the beginning, the Salvadoran government was engaged in a cover-up. Unfortunately, as Ana Carrigan makes clear in her biography of one of the deceased, Jean Donovan, the State Department, fearful, perhaps, that this sordid affair would endanger its military solution to the civil war in El Salvador, felt it necessary to cover up the cover-up.[2]

As Bill Ford, brother of Ita Ford, one of the deceased nuns, remarked:

[2.] Ana Carrigan, *Salvador Witness.* See especially, "Chronicle of a Cover-up," 263–317, on which much of this epilogue is based.

The realization that the State Department was not interested in pursuing the case was something that dawned on us gradually. As I went through my personal crash course about what was happening in El Salvador, it became clear to me that the death of the women was just an inconvenience to American policy. The American government, both under the Carter and the Reagan administrations, has a fixed policy in Salvador, and that policy will not bend to reason, or eyewitness, or anything else.

Initially, it's a terrible personal tragedy, but gradually there intrudes upon the sense of personal tragedy the surrounding facts, and it was like a growing, horrible realization: we were supporting a government; that government had killed my sister; and my government didn't care.[3]

By voting 54–42, in September, 1981, to require the president to certify semiannually that progress was being made in the area of human rights— specific mention being made of the investigation of the four murdered nuns— the Senate forced the administration to go through legalistic contortions in order to be able to deliver the requisite aid to its client government.

Eventually, U.S. pressure did result in the conviction on May 24, 1984, of five low level National Guardsmen, the first successful prosecution since 1979 of anyone in the Salvadoran military for the tens of thousands of murders they were responsible for. Within twenty-four hours, the State Department, announcing with apparent relief that justice was done, released millions of dollars to Minister of Defense General Carlos Eugenio Vides Casanova, who at the time of the killings was commander of the National Guard.

Nonetheless, in spite of the desire of the Reagan administration to call the case closed, the matter cannot be laid to rest. There remains a widespread belief that the five convicted guardsmen had been ordered by higher-ups to do the murders. Two months earlier, in March 1984, Walter Cronkite had interviewed on CBS Evening News a former high official in the Salvadoran military (who at the time assumed a disguise). The informant stated point-blank that the order to kill the nuns was given by Colonel Edgardo Casanova, cousin of Vides Casanova, and that not only the latter, but also President Duarte, must have known of the cover-up.

Two months later, Ana Carrigan interviewed the same man (who has since gone public), Roberto Eulalio Santibáñez, who went over in detail what happened the night of the murders. She finally asked him, "Why did Colindres Alemán [the sergeant in charge of the group that did the actual killings] bother to contact Lieutenant Colonel Casanova for instructions? Why, in light of the intelligence that he had, and the urging he received from his colleagues in Chalatenango and La Libertad, did he not act on his own initiative?" He looked at me as though I were slightly demented. "But they were Americans," he said. "No sergeant would take such an action against four Americans without checking first with his superior officer."[4]

[3.] Ibid., 267.
[4.] Ibid., 315–16.

35. *Communiqué from a "Death Squad"**

By the Maximiliano Hernández Martínez Squad

Proudly claiming credit for the November 27, 1980, abduction and assassination of six civilian leaders of the Democratic Revolutionary Front (FDR), the Maximiliano Hernández Martínez Squad takes as its name that of the general responsible for the massacre of some 30,000 peasants in 1932.

The six included Enrique Alvárez Córdoba, president of the FDR, and Juan Chacón, secretary general of the People's Revolutionary Bloc. The "death squad" abducted the FDR leaders from a press conference being held in an archbishopric legal assistance office in a San Salvador seminary. The Democratic Revolutionary Front and the archbishopric legal assistance office attributed the murders to the government's security forces, but the governing junta denied any complicity and officially denounced the slayings.

*While the bodies lay within the metropolitan cathedral of San Salvador, a powerful bomb exploded at its main door and set the church on fire. A church bombing should occasion little surprise when groups like the Maximiliano Hernández Martínez Squad have publicly warned that "priests who favor the Marxist terrorist bands" will be killed "if they continue with their sermons which are poisoning the minds of Salvadoran youths" (*La Prensa Gráfica, *November 28, 1980, reprinted in the Foreign Broadcast Information Service,* Daily Reports, *December 1, 1980).*

Not long after Reagan became President, this death squad, also called Maximiliano Hernández Martínez Anti-Communist Brigade, broadened its "enemies list" to include thieves, muggers, miscreants and swindlers." In Santa Ana, the brigade took credit for murdering ten circus workers, including two clowns, it claimed were drug trafficking. [1]

THE "Maximiliano Hernández Martínez Squad," which claimed credit for the abduction and assassination [of the six leaders of the Revolutionary Democratic Front], has issued a message in which it "calls on the national conscience not to be intimidated by false prophets who say nothing when communists destroy businesses, burn coffee sheds, kill peasants, and cruelly assassinate military personnel, security agents and soldiers, but react profusely when communists are executed."

The "squad" notes that the leaders of the Catholic Church "said nothing when South African Ambassador Dunn was killed, when progressive industrialists were kidnapped or when peasants were massacred in San Pedro Perulapan and San Esteban Catarina, where the communists had imposed their will

---

* From *El Diario de Hoy,* San Salvador, December 1, 1980, reprinted by the Foreign Broadcast Information Service, *Daily Reports,* December 3, 1980.

[1.] See Raymond Bonner, *Weakness and Deceit: U.S. Policy and El Salvador* (New York, 1984), 330.

by force. In those cases, there was no clamor for respect for human rights, nor was there any [cry of] injustice. In those cases, no defenders were forthcoming for those humble sons of the people. Now that six criminals, who led the mobs, have been executed by the people, however, the church leaders come out in defense of human rights. That is hypocrisy," the communiqué states.

Lastly, the "squad" urges the church hierarchy, U.S. diplomats and military leaders not to allow themselves to be deceived and instead urges them to react in the proper manner to this event which is nothing special since it is an action which is being taken to demand justice in the face of ineffective laws.

36. The Execution of Hammer, Pearlman, and Viera: No Justice in Sight*

BY SENATOR EDWARD KENNEDY

In 1984, Senator Edward Kennedy (D-MA) sought by an amendment to a funding bill to cut off military aid to El Salvador "unless that government has initiated a prosecution of those involved in the murder of two American Labor advisers in 1981." (A Salvadoran, José Rodolfo Viera, was also murdered.)

The deceased, Michael Hammer and Mark Pearlman, were employees of the American Institute for Free Labor Development (AIFLD), a nonprofit organization funded by the U.S. government Agency for International Development. AIFLD was originally founded in 1962 with the goal, in part, of combating the "threat of Castroite infiltration . . . within [labor movements in] Latin America."[1]

Supported and partially financed by the AFL-CIO—George Meany was its first president—AIFLD is often accused of being a CIA front.[2] In El Salvador, the institute attempted to build an anti-Communist base by promoting agrarian reform. The unpopularity of this program among extreme conservatives and the oligarchs undoubtedly explains the coldblooded murder of the AIFLD employees.

Though Kennedy's amendment did not pass, in June 1985 the investigation was reactivated and on February 14, 1986, two enlistees in the National Guard were convicted of the murders. Even though the two gunmen gave detailed accounts implicating two army officers, Lieutenant Rodolfo Isidro López Sibrian and Captain Eduardo Avila, and a right-wing businessman, Hans Christ, in planning, ordering, and overseeing the killings, the latter are not being prosecuted. A spokesman for AIFLD, Jack Heberle, aptly

* From the *Congressional Record*, 30, No. 42, April 3, 1984, S3669–70.

[1.] Tom Barry, et al., *Dollars and Dictators* (New York: Grove Press, 1983), 105.

[2.] The controversial Philip Agee, a former CIA operative, has described AIFLD as a "CIA-controlled [organization] . . . used as a front for covering trade-union organizing activity." Ibid., 106.

sums up the situation: "The convictions are unfortunately further evidence that Salvadoran Army officers are immune from prosecution for even the most heinous crimes."[3]

OVER 3 years ago, on January 3, 1981, Michael P. Hammer and Mark David Pearlman joined a Salvadoran friend for dinner at the Sheraton Hotel in San Salvador. Mr. Hammer and Mr. Pearlman were employees of the American Institute for Free Labor Development of the AFL-CIO, and they were in El Salvador as advisers to El Salvador's land reform program. They were with José Rodolfo Viera, a campesino labor leader and the head of the Land Reform Institute for the Government of El Salvador. Mr. Viera had been the target of three prior attempts on his life.

As they sat together at their table drinking coffee, two gunmen came into the room with a machinegun. They walked over to their table and shot them dead. It was a brutal, premeditated, politically motivated act of cold-blooded murder.

Michael Hammer was 42 years old, Mark Pearlman was 36, and José Viera was 43.

What do we know about that crime today?

Because of an investigation conducted by the American Institute for Free Labor Development we know that, on that same evening, there was another dinner party being held at that same hotel. That dinner party included a part-owner of the hotel, Ricardo Sol Meza. He is a Salvadoran businessman. Accompanying Mr. Sol Meza were three members of the Salvadoran Armed Forces. There was Maj. Mario Denis Moran, a military classmate of Roberto D'Aubuisson. Major Moran was at that time head of the intelligence section of the Salvadoran National Guard. There was Lt. Isidro López Sibrian. He worked in the intelligence section of the national guard. And there was Capt. Eduardo Alfonso Avila, an associate of Mr. D'Aubuisson and the nephew of one of the founders of the Arena Party. In addition, there was Mr. Sol Meza's brother-in-law. Hans Christ, a large landowner and a wealthy Salvadoran businessman.

According to the AIFLD investigation, Mr. Christ spotted the two American labor advisers and the Salvadoran labor leader as they entered the dining room of the hotel. Approximately one-half hour later, Captain Avila and Lieutenant López Sibrian walked to the front of the hotel where two bodyguards were waiting. According to the AIFLD investigation, López Sibrian and Eduardo Avila gave the two national guardsmen—who were serving as their bodyguards that night—a machinegun and ordered them to go into the hotel to kill the two Americans and the Salvadoran. Mr. Christ then led the two guardsmen through the hotel and pointed out the three targets. Hammer, Pearlman and Viera were then executed.

[3.] *New York Times,* February 15, 1986.

What has happened since then?

Today, more than 3 years after those men were murdered, despite confessions and admissions and solid evidence, no one has been tried.

In April 1981, the Salvadoran Government arrested Ricardo Sol Meza and requested the extradition of Hans Christ, who had fled to Miami. In the fall of 1981, a Salvadoran judge suspended all action in the case on the grounds that there was insufficient evidence to implicate Christ and Sol Meza in the murders. That decision was upheld by a Salvadoran court of appeals in April 1982, and Sol Meza was released. An appeal of that decision is still pending before the supreme court.

As for Major Moran, he has seen service over the last 2 years in various Salvadoran embassies in South America, and he was recently brought back to El Salvador by Vides Casanova, the Defense Minister, to take charge of a command in the army.

The two national guardsmen who actually pulled the triggers are in detention. One of those two guardsmen was Major Moran's second in command in the intelligence section of the national guard. In September 1982, they confessed and, in their confession, they implicated Lieutenant López Sibrian and Captain Avila.

After the national guardsmen confessed, they were remanded to a civilian court along with Lieutenant López Sibrian. But in December 1982, the case against López Sibrian was dismissed. The trial of the guardsmen cannot begin until appeals involving their codefendants have been resolved.

In April 1983, an appellate court upheld the dismissal of charges against López Sibrian, and the case was presented to the supreme court for review. In November 1983, the supreme court denied the appeal. The case against López Sibrian is over; it will not proceed unless new evidence is introduced within 1 year after the supreme court's decision.

On December 19, 1983, 3½ months ago, as a result of direct intervention by Vice President Bush, it was announced that Captain Avila had finally been arrested by Salvadoran authorities. He was not charged with the murders of the three labor leaders but only with a minor military infraction—leaving his post without permission. And then on March 22, 1984—a mere 10 days ago —Captain Avila was suddenly released.

A spokesman for the U.S. Embassy in El Salvador has stated:

We are convinced from early interviews in which polygraphic examinations were used that Captain Avila knows a great deal about the murders. We continue to expect the Government of El Salvador to meet its obligation to obtain that testimony.

Captain Avila is reported to have appeared in court last Saturday. It has been reported he has now denied under oath that he had anything to do with these murders. This testimony is in direct conflict with earlier statements which acknowledged his involvement in the matter.

Captain Avila's uncle is a justice of the supreme court—Dr. Ricardo Avila Morera. He is also a founder of the Arena Party.

What is the significance of all this? An editorial that appeared in this morning's Washington Post answers that question. The Post wrote:

> It's simple to understand the calculus at work here. The armed forces—which shield, if they do not actually harbor, the killers in the two American cases and in Salvadoran cases beyond counting—tend to protect their own. The national tradition and the practice of intimidation and bribery put them effectively beyond civilian political or judicial control . . . stonewalling and token concessions on the part of the Salvadorans have ensured that none of those who killed the Americans has been brought to justice. None.

After the American labor advisers had been murdered in January 1981, the U.S. Embassy public affairs officer at the time stated:

> One day Mark Pearlman is giving us a briefing on agrarian reform, and the next day he's killed by those mad-dog types who are supposed to be on our side. They killed our own people, our friends, our own damned people, and what can we do about it?

Mr. President, there is something we can do about it. And we must do it today.

We have said the United States is for human rights in El Salvador. We have said that death squads must be eliminated in El Salvador. We have called for justice in El Salvador. Today we must make our deeds match our words. Today, if we pass this amendment, the actions of the U.S. Senate will speak louder than any words we could possibly say. Today if we pass this amendment, our message will be conveyed—not only in words—but also in deeds.

In the name of justice, in the name of those murdered Americans whose only sin was to work for social progress for the people of El Salvador, in the name of the people of the United States, let us tell the Government of El Salvador that these killers must be called to account. Better late than never.

37. Massacres in El Salvador

When in 1982 the Christian Phalangists massacred hundreds of Palestinians in the West Beirut refugee camps of Sabra and Shatila, there was an outcry the world over. Israel was blamed—its military, after all, was in control and had apparently winked its approval.

In El Salvador, there have also been massacres—many of them—and some even more bloody than the one in Lebanon.[1] By and large, though, the world has remained silent.

[1.] Massacres have occurred other than those documented below. For example, the *New York Times* recorded one that took place in late 1981 in the village of Mozote in Morazán province.

But the Salvadoran army is not altogether an independent entity; it is equipped and trained by the U.S. government. If Israel could be legitimately censured for massacres others committed in Israeli-occupied Lebanon, the United States may someday have to admit that its hands are equally stained with the blood of Salvadoran civilians.

New York Times *Bureau Chief in Brazil at the time, journalist Warren Hoge, wrote in 1981 that "reports of deliberate killings of noncombatants during El Salvador's civil war" are difficult to confirm. "Many times no one has been left to tell what happened."*[2] *Tragically, it can be reliably reported that a mass killing took place at the Lempa River on the Honduras border on March 17, 1981. Eyewitnesses include the Rev. Earl Gallagher, a Brooklyn-born Capuchin priest working in Honduras, and Yvonne Dilling, a refugee worker from Fort Wayne. With low-flying Salvadoran helicopter pilots firing down on refugees trying to cross the Lempa into Honduras, and with a Salvadoran gunship and Salvadoran soldiers raining down rockets, automatic-weapons fire, and grenades, children clung to Father Gallagher's beard as he swam them to safety while Ms. Dilling tied infants to herself with her bra straps to carry them over the river. More than 200 are believed to be dead or missing.*

Father Gallagher had also visited the site of an earlier and even larger massacre on the Sumpul River—also on the Honduras border—the day after it took place. "There were so many vultures picking at the bodies," he recalled, "that it looked like a black carpet." Included below [A] is a brief account of the earlier massacre in which perhaps 600 died. The event has been compared to the My Lai atrocity in Vietnam.[3]

Also included below [B] are excerpts from a letter to Congressman Joe Moakley (D-MA) from Holly Burkhalter, Washington representative of Americas Watch, a respected human-rights organization, documenting two civilian massacres that took place during the summer of 1984. In the dreadfully violent climate that exists in El Salvador, both sides are not only engaged in armed confrontations, but are also fighting a continuous war of propaganda. Whenever large numbers of civilians are slaughtered, there are claims and counterclaims. Nonetheless, it is generally agreed that until 1985 most, if not all, massacres initially blamed on guerrillas were later found to have been the work of the regular Salvadoran army.

The Salvadoran military appeared to possess an exclusive franchise for producing massacres. But there is no dispute that on April 8, 1985, one of the guerrilla groups— the Popular Liberation Forces (FPL)—entered the town of Santa Cruz La Loma and proceeded to murder nineteen citizens, including unarmed civilians.[4] *According to blood-*

More than 900 persons were killed by government soldiers of the Atlacatl Battalion, according to the count of the Human Rights Commission of El Salvador, an organization that works closely with the Catholic church. See Raymond Bonner, "Major Massacre Is Reported in Salvadoran Village," *New York Times,* January 27, 1982. Another massacre that has received widespread attention is the one that took place at Las Hojas on February 23, 1983. It is believed that 74 villagers were killed in a massacre that had little, if anything, to do with the guerrilla war. It was simply one of the "procedures" used by the Salvadoran landowning class for resolving a dispute! See *New York Times,* February 25, 1985.

2. *New York Times,* June 8, 1981.

3. In 1968, an American military company, headed by Lieutenant William Calley, entered the Vietnamese village of My Lai and without provocation gunned down 347 civilians, most of them women and children, some infants.

4. Pacific New Service, April 10, 1985, "Response to New U.S. Program—Massacre Marks

stained mimeographed sheets strewn over the bodies, guerrillas were "carrying out justice" against those who had cooperated with the army. Apparently, this was an attempt to undermine the government's counterinsurgency effort, which had recently created civil defense units in forty-seven towns, including Santa Cruz La Loma. Whether this was an incident marking the beginning of a new stage in which guerrillas regularly attack those "sea lanes" in which they can no longer swim freely, or simply an isolated attack, remains to be seen. If the former, it is bound to lose for the guerrillas much of the political capital they had earned in opposing a military perceived to slaughter peasants like animals.

A. The Sumpul River Massacre*

BY A PRESBYTERY OF HONDURAS

THE most evident example of harassment and cruelty happened last May 14. The day before, several trucks and vehicles of the Honduran Army arrived filled with soldiers. Without stopping, they went 14 kilometers further down, to near the Sumpul River, the border between Honduras and El Salvador, near the Honduran towns of Santa Lucia and San José. The megaphones directed to Salvadoran territory shouted out the prohibition against crossing the border.

On the opposite side, at around 7 A.M., in the Salvadoran village La Arada and its surrounding area, the massacre began. A minimum of two helicopters, the Salvadoran National Guard, soldiers and the paramilitary organization ORDEN opened fire on the defenseless people. Women tortured before the finishing shot, infants thrown into the air for target practice, were some of the scenes of the criminal slaughter. The Salvadorans who crossed the river were returned by the Honduran soldiers to the area of the massacre. In mid-afternoon the genocide ended, leaving a minimum number of 600 corpses.

Days before, according to the Honduran press, in the city of Ocotepeque, bordering Guatemala and El Salvador, there was a secret meeting of high military commanders of the three countries. The news was officially denied shortly afterwards.

A minimum of 600 unburied bodies were the prey of dogs and vultures for several days. Others were lost in the waters of the river. A Honduran fisherman found five small bodies of children in his fishtrap. The Sumpul River was contaminated from the village of Santa Lucia.

Shift in Guerrilla Tactics in Salvadoran Countryside" (reported by Mary Jo McConahay from San Salvador).

* From testimony entered into the *Congressional Record,* September 24, 1980, by Senator Edward Kennedy, S13375–S13379.

B. *Massacres in Cabañas and Chalatenango Departments**

By Holly Burkhalter

TWO particularly well-documented massacres of civilians took place during the last half of 1984. In July, the Army massacred at least 68 civilian noncombatants at Los Llanitos in Cabañas Department. Church officials and western journalists visited the site of the massacre days after the incident, viewed the bodies, took testimony from survivors and family members still present in the area and compiled a list of victims. Roughly half of the 68 dead were children under 14 years of age. *The New York Times, Christian Science Monitor* and *Boston Globe* all carried detailed accounts of the incident. The *Boston Globe* of Sept. 9, 1984 reported the following:

"Villagers of Los Llanitos, a hamlet of 183 residents, said government troops combed the areas for guerrillas three times earlier this year. But in the July campaign, villagers said, the soldiers for the first time avoided open roads. Instead they scaled rocks and cut through bush and brambles to take to the hills above the hamlets before village lookouts spotted them. When word finally went out at dusk on July 18 that the 'enemy' was ready, nearly 1,000 peasants from seven hamlets grabbed their children and set out on a frantic march, stumbling in the darkness down ravines and over promontories, the villagers said. They hoped to reach the caves and gullies where they had hid safely during past army incursions.

"On the morning of July 19 the soldiers came down after them, according to the villagers. With sticks, troops beat in the roofs of empty houses and one elementary school. 'We weren't there,' said Tula Escobar, 'so the houses had to pay.'

"Napoleon Gómez, 35, said he was crowded in the bushes on one side of a ravine with 36 villagers when soldiers fired on them with a machine gun from the other side. Gómez said a woman named Gloria Vides, 24, and her two children, one aged 2 and the other 6 months, froze with fear and were left behind as others pressed up on the hill. Minutes later, Gómez and other witnesses heard a soldier call out to his commander. 'Do I leave her or kill her?' 'Light the fire,' Gómez quoted the officer as shouting. 'Then we heard rifles rattling' Gómez said. Gómez said he found the three bodies when he returned to his home July 22nd.

"Gómez' sister Teresa, 28, fell behind because of a bad hip. Witnesses said they saw her being captured by troops. She did not reappear. Villagers believe

* From *Congressional Record,* March 6, 1985, E787.

that she and six other persons were beaten to death and their bodies pushed into a public school latrine. They said they found clothing tatters and parts of human limbs there.

"Villagers said that later in the afternoon of July 19, soldiers burned 22 bodies, including 9 children, in a wooded clearing. From his hiding place, farmer Aquidio Rosa, 28, saw three bonfires. Reporters who visited the site saw a mound where guerrillas were said to have dug a mass grave. The area was littered with human bones, many burned, and nearby trees were sprayed with bullet holes."

A second massacre took place in August 1984 in Chalatenango Department where approximately 600 civilians (with several armed guerrilla escorts) attempted to flee the village of Las Vueltas and nearby hamlets when the Army began shelling homes with mortar fire. The Army opened fire on the fleeing civilians and at least 50 died in the attack.

38. Marines Killed in San Salvador: New Stage in the Salvadoran War

On the evening of June 19, 1985, a contingent of armed gunmen opened fire on patrons of an outdoor restaurant in a posh district of San Salvador known as the Zona Rosa. Thirteen were killed, including four Marine guards assigned to the U.S. Embassy and two American businessmen. In the course of expressing his outrage, President Reagan warned, "We also have our limits—and our limits have been reached." In the days that followed, the Reagan administration proposed a new aid package for El Salvador designed to counter urban terrorism, threatened retaliation against Nicaragua for its alleged support of the Salvadoran insurgents, and announced that the United States would pay up to $100,000 for information leading to the capture of those responsible for killing the six Americans.

Although Caspar Weinberger was to announce in July that the Salvadoran Army had captured or killed those responsible for the slayings, the Defense Department later "clarified" his statement to mean that there was a successful attack on the Central American Revolutionary Workers Party, a guerrilla group that had taken responsibility for the assault. Late in the summer, President Duarte was to announce the arrest of three guerrillas suspected of participating in the attack, though the guerrilla organization denied that those captured had anything to do with the action.

For its part, Nicaragua denied involvement. "Nicaragua has neither practiced nor supported terrorism nor has it been involved in any terroristic act," stated Sandinista leader Daniel Ortega, replying to the diplomatic note delivered to Managua by the United States. Nicaraguans, he said, were "victims of United States terrorism," alluding to the American-supported contras who are attempting to overthrow the Sandinista government.

If much sympathy for the guerrilla cause has been based on the widespread belief that up to now most of the violence in El Salvador has come from the right—from the death squads and the various military organizations—an interesting question is whether an increase in urban terrorism will squander the political capital of the guerrillas, not only with their allies abroad, but also with their supporters at home. One person whose voice counts is Archbishop Rivera y Damas. It is of note that on this opportunity to deliver an unqualified condemnation of the left, he instead tempered his criticism of leftist terrorism with equally strong criticism of terrorism from the right.[1] What follows is a statement by President Duarte and a reply from rebel radio Venceremos.

A. Sincere Condolences*

BY JOSÉ NAPOLEÓN DUARTE

Two days after the slayings, seeing off the bodies of the U.S. Marines at Ilopango Airport in San Salvador, President José Napoleón Duarte offered his condolences to the American people.

TO the American people, on behalf of the Salvadoran people, to the U.S. Government; to President Reagan; and to the relatives of these heroes, these marines, who are returning to their homeland today covered with the honor of the U.S. flag, to all of them; to the U.S. Marine Corps; to the U.S. diplomatic corps in El Salvador:

On behalf of the homeland and by the powers that the people have granted to me, I express my sincere condolences.

It is for us, the Salvadorans, a moment of sadness to deliver the bodies of these four honorable men. We are delivering them surrounded by representatives of our Armed Forces because as brothers we feel the pain of the loss of these four men who had come to our fatherland to serve. This is a moment of great sadness for me because an act of barbarism, a savage act, an act that surpasses all dimensions of human respect was perpetrated in our homeland.

There are people in the world who have lost their minds. The doctrine of terrorism has been created. The religion of death has been created. They have no regard for life. They attack without any risk. They place bombs in public places in order to kill people and arrive, carrying machine guns, at places to kill unarmed and innocent people.

In El Salvador, we have gone through great crises in these past few years,

[1.] See Foreign Broadcast Information Service, *Daily Reports,* June 25, 1985.

* From Foreign Broadcast Information Service, *Daily Reports–Central America*, June 24, 1985, 4–5.

but amid all this death, we have never witnessed an act as savage as this one. This is not a coincidence because just a few days ago FMLN-FDR representatives sent me an ultimatum. They threatened me. They said that they were going to kill all my family, my relatives, Armed Forces officers, and everyone they could. A threat of this kind only indicates that these murderers have lost their minds.

The Salvadorans of good faith, the Salvadorans who want peace, the Salvadorans who believe that our fatherland has a better destiny, of justice and freedom, are sad and hurt to see that this savage attack was carried out. We think that efforts must be increased to continue progressing in our task of giving security to all those who are in our fatherland and to all Salvadorans. For this reason, we are going to do everything we can to investigate this massacre, this savage attack. We are going to do everything we can, and we are going to ask for the necessary help to investigate this case. There are already witnesses, as you saw on television, who can give a verbal description of those who savagely carried out this massacre at a city restaurant.

I pray to God that our homeland will not go through this experience again. I pray to God that the souls of these four marines and of the other people killed innocently will be received by God in heaven. I pray to God that hatred won't take root in the hearts of Salvadorans because that is what terrorists want. They want to unleash vengeance and retaliation. However, the fatherland and the Salvadorans want to find the path of peace. For this reason, when these four men appear before God they will tell him that they gave their lives for this homeland where they died.

I repeat my condolences to the U.S. people, and President Reagan, whom I will call in a few moments to express my sympathy. My condolences also go to the U.S. diplomatic corps, the U.S. Marines, and to the relatives of each one of these men who are the glory of the U.S. people. May God bless them!

B. *"Crocodile Tears"**

BY RADIO VENCEREMOS

In 1981, Radio Venceremos ("We Will Win") made its inaugural broadcast from a peasant hut in the village of Guacamaya. Radio Venceremos currently broadcasts four times a day, reporting on battles and airing drama, satire (directed against Ronald Reagan, the U.S. ambassador and his wife, and José Napoleón Duarte), and music and in general broadcasting propaganda and "subversion." (It once gave directions on how to make a Molotov cocktail.)

* From Foreign Broadcast Information Service, *Daily Reports–Central America,* June 24, 1985.

Even though destruction of Radio Venceremos is a high-priority goal of the Salvadoran government, the station has never been taken. Efforts to jam its operations are largely ineffectual. An estimated 60 percent of the population tunes in. (In the United States it can be heard Monday through Saturday at 7:15 A.M. and 1:30, 7:00, and 9:30 P.M. on 6.560 and 6.850 megaHertz. [2]

Hours after President Duarte's memorial speech (the previous reading), Radio Venceremos made the following commentary.

THE following is our commentary on José Napoleón Duarte's speech during the funeral farewell ceremony for the U.S. soldiers at the Ilopango Military Airport.

The crocodile tears shed by Duarte, his hysterical lament at Ilopango Airport when he bid farewell to the bodies of several U.S. soldiers who came to make war on us, are understandable. Duarte has many reasons to cry for those invaders. They made him president. They breast-feed him and support him. During the sickening lament before his masters Duarte tried to justify his Armed Forces' lack of capacity to protect the military advisers, U.S. soldiers, and CIA agents who were together when they met the justice of a people who repudiate them.

Duarte's speech was a blunder; it was confusing and full of lies. The invaders are not innocent unarmed people as Duarte said; they are war technicians, experts at killing and torturing. They are the creators of the clandestine jails; the ones who plan the shelling of the civilian population; they are the North Americans who plan terror against the peasant population. A CIA official or U.S. soldier in our country is never unarmed as Captain Schauffelberger was never unarmed.

Duarte's cynicism reached an untolerable level when he asserted that these people come to our homeland to defend democracy. Amidst his defeat, Duarte wiped his tears with one hand while extending the other like a beggar, asking for mere Yankee aid, which has proved so useless in facing the FMLN.

The usual melodramatic note could not miss in his funeral speech; it is characteristic of a madman, of Duarte's megalomania. He asserted ridiculously that the FMLN had sent him an ultimatum threatening his life. If U.S. Army members and CIA agents died in El Salvador it was because they came to attack our people. No one had summoned them; they died as a result of the interventionist policy carried out by President Reagan, whose intervention grows day by day. Reagan will have to assume full responsibility for his deeds. These will not be the last invaders to be sent off by Duarte under similar funeral circumstances. The U.S. people must stop Reagan's policy, or a new Vietnam awaits thousands of U.S. youths, irresponsibly sent by Reagan to die.

The Salvadoran people's duty is to defend our homeland and our rights.

[2] Information on Radio Venceremos from Gerry L. Dexter, "The Guerrillas Take to the Airwaves," *The Progressive,* June 1985.

Duarte, who is only Reagan's puppet, has every right to cry before his master and try to justify his inability to protect them, even with the $2 billion given to him for the war. However, we cannot accept Duarte's words in Ilopango because he said that the armed invaders' execution is a terrible act, the likes of which had never been seen in the country.

We cannot accept this, because Duarte's words mock the blood shed by 50,000 Salvadorans murdered by his Armed Forces, the raped women, and the workers dismembered by death squads. Duarte's words insult the blood shed by Msgr. [Oscar Arnulfo] Romero, whose murderers share power with Duarte.

Duarte is mocking the thousands of people he massacred in December 1981 in Morazán Department. Neither Msgr. Romero, the woman killed during the attack against the Social Security Hospital, the two ANDA workers assassinated by the Arce Battalion, nor 50,000 Salvadorans murdered by Duarte have merited a minute of silence at the Legislative Assembly or official ceremonies to declare them martyrs of the homeland. The silence for them has been the silence of the murderers and those who bless the criminal Army's weapons, provided by the Yankees, because Duarte also thinks that the genocidal invaders are the heroes. . . .

This time Duarte's heroes, who are the heroes of traitors and oppressors, have left this afternoon in coffins, fully defeated. Meanwhile, the people, the Salvadoran people, remain firm, united, and ready to win!

39. Abuses by Salvadoran Guerrillas*

BY ARYEH NEIER

As the guerrilla armies responded to the intensified air war with their own escalation, including kidnappings and assassinations, they have increasingly been criticized by human-rights activists. One prominent critic is Aryeh Neier, vice chair of Americas Watch, whose comment is reprinted below.

Such criticisms are likely to mount. Guerrilla radio announced in October 1985 that they now consider the Reagan administration and American military personnel their main enemies. As New York Times *correspondent James LeMoyne points out, this decision—to shoot Americans—"appears to be carefully thought out." If previously they had gone out of their way to avoid this kind of provocation, they now appear less timid. They said:*

The Government of Ronald Reagan must realize once and for all that we are not afraid of the intervention of its troops and that it cannot pretend to make war on

* From *New York Times*, July 26, 1985, 27.

our people without suffering and paying the consequences. We are decided to van-
quish North American intervention in our homeland.[1]

FOR several years, human rights groups concerned with El Salvador have
focused the great bulk of their attention on abuses by Government forces.
Though these forces continue to be responsible for most of the civilian suffering, a recent deterioration in the practices of the guerrillas makes it essential
that we speak out more forcefully now to denounce their abuses against
noncombatants.

Compared to such guerrilla groups as Sendero Luminoso (the Shining Path)
in Peru, waging a savage war in the Andean highlands, and to the "contras"
in Nicaragua, who are systematically violating the laws of war, the Salvadoran
guerrillas had a relatively good reputation. This rested principally on their
treatment of prisoners of war. Over the past six years, they have released
thousands of captured soldiers unharmed, either through the International
Committee of the Red Cross or through local civilian officials. Whether carried
out for humanitarian reasons or propaganda purposes, this policy contrasted
sharply with the practices of the Salvadoran armed forces, which have been
suspected of summarily executing most prisoners they captured in combat.

This is not to say that the guerrillas committed no human rights abuses in
past years. On three different occasions in mid-1983, they executed a number
of captured soldiers. They have also been responsible for several assassinations
and have shot at vehicles that crashed through their roadblocks, wantonly
killing and injuring civilian passengers.

For several months in 1981, the guerrillas practiced forced recruitment in
areas they controlled. Though not prohibited by the laws of war, this caused
grief to many civilians, leading at least 1,500 to flee their homes and join the
enormous population of displaced persons—most of it created by the armed
forces' attacks on civilians in guerrilla-controlled areas. Criticism of forced
recruitment in the press and among human rights groups seemed to have an
effect, however: in September 1984, the guerrillas abandoned the practice.

It is in the last eight months that the practices of the guerrillas have become
especially disturbing. There has been an increase in assassinations, often of
right-wing political leaders. The main guerrilla organization denies any connection with the group known as the Clara Elizabeta Ramírez Front, which
has claimed "credit" for the killings. But the guerrillas have not denounced
the assassinations, explaining that to do so "would deepen contradictions"
between the forces on the left.

Other recent guerrilla abuses include an episode in April at Santa Cruz
Loma, a village near the capital, in which the guerrillas executed unarmed
members of the local civil defense and also killed a number of civilians. Shortly

[1.] James LeMoyne, *New York Times,* October 12, 1985, 3.

thereafter, the guerrillas began kidnapping mayors in several regions, claiming that the Government was trying to use these mayors to exercise civil authority in areas that the guerrillas consider under their control. In practice, the mayors are being held as hostages, apparently so that they can be exchanged for captured guerrilla commanders.

Most dramatically, on June 19, the guerrillas attacked an outdoor restaurant in San Salvador, killing four United States Marines and nine civilians. The guerrillas claim that the Marines were a legitimate target because they were members of the armed forces of a party to the conflict. This is insupportable, however, because the Marines' sole-duty was to guard the United States Embassy, and they took no part in hostilities. Moreover, even if the Marines could have been considered a legitimate military target, the circumstances made it almost inevitable that there would be a heavy civilian death toll.

In denouncing the attack on the Marines and the civilians killed with them, Archbishop Arturo Rivera y Damas of San Salvador said it would be hypocritical not to also condemn the continuing use of terror tactics by the Government's armed forces. The reverse is also true: Critics of the Government must not hesitate to condemn the mounting abuses against noncombatants by the Salvadoran guerrillas.

40. Why We Kidnap Mayors*

BY THE FMLN

During the spring of 1985, Salvadoran officials claimed that guerrillas "killed 2 newly elected mayors, kidnapped 8 others and burned 32 mayors' offices."[1] According to New York Times *correspondent James LeMoyne, one of those killed was Edgar Mauricio Valenzuela, a liberal member of Duarte's Christian Democratic Party. He had previously been temporarily kidnapped and warned not to assume office as mayor of San Jorge, a town sixty miles east of San Salvador. Not heeding this advice, he was seized two days later and killed with a single shot to the head. A senior official of the FDR, the political front of the guerrillas, told LeMoyne he had opposed these attacks but could not convince the People's Revolutionary Army (ERP) to refrain from them. Below is a statement from the ERP about why they are attempting "to attack and dismantle" local administrations.*

Later in the year, a total of twenty-three kidnapped mayors were exchanged, along with Duarte's daughter, for rebel prisoners (see Reading 41).

* From Radio Venceremos, May 11, 1985, in the Foreign Broadcast Information Service, *Daily Reports–Central America,* May 16, 1985.
[1] James LeMoyne, *New York Times,* May 12, 1985.

THE ERP reports:

1. Yesterday, a guerrilla unit of our army captured the mayor of Gualo-cocti, Morazán Department, who is a member of the Christian Democratic Party [PDC]. This mayor can be added to the ones we have already captured in the eastern region and whom we are holding captive.

2. Since the beginning of the war we have pursued a line opposed to local administrations across the country because they are a fundamental component of the counterinsurgency plans financed and sponsored by the United States through the AID [Agency for International Development]. This enemy policy has now taken on greater importance with the expansion of U.S. intervention. Among other things, local administrations are the bases on which the PDC plans to create fascist organizations, information networks, and the already known and repudiated Civil Defense.

Therefore, in addition to representing the central government in our area, local administrations are a fundamental belligerent component of the enemy's political and military plan. For this reason, our forces have decided to attack and dismantle local administrations more actively than ever. It is not acceptable for the government to seek to continue exercising power where it definitely no longer has control and where there is a duality of power between the FMLN and the Armed Forces. Therefore, it is inadmissible for the government to seek to establish mayors' offices and authorities in those areas. A total of 50 out of 86 municipalities in the eastern region now have dual power structures.

3. Before the elections we clearly and directly issued warnings in all areas that we would not accept mayors or political parties in zones under our control or disputed zones, and that we would take measures before, during, and after the elections. Some persons who were forced to become candidates resigned and withdrew from their parties.

4. We do not consider the PDC, Duarte, and the other leaders to be innocent or to represent a third force in this conflict. Mr. Duarte and the rest of the PDC members are fully aware that they have committed themselves to an antipopular, repressive, and surrender-oriented plan in cooperation with the Army. Therefore, they also are active and belligerent parties in this war and are directly responsible for repression, crimes, and the disappearance of people in these past few years. We will deal with them in accordance with their actions.

5. The mayors we have captured have been classified as prisoners of war involved in counterinsurgency plans against our forces and our people.

6. Commander Janet Samour and Compañera Maximina Reyes Villa Toro were captured in San Miguel by the National Guard on 30 December. The two women had been captured, but the Armed Forces Press Committee denied it. In this way the Duarte government and the Armed Forces high command demonstrated a total disregard for our compañeras' prisoner of war status.

The two compañeras have been subjected to cruel tortures by the National Guard. Nothing has been heard of them because they refused to cooperate with the enemy. Our public and private efforts to determine their whereabouts have produced only vague and misleading answers, with which the Armed Forces have tried to win time or make us forget about the matter. The Salvadoran church has not cooperated much with our efforts either.

7. Our organization has fully respected the rights of prisoners of war and has facilitated their release, both publicly and privately. We have captured more than 1,000 soldiers, dozens of officers, the well-known criminal Captain Medina Garay, and former Defense Minister Colonel Castillo. We also currently have in our hands three CIA agents, two Hondurans and one Colombian. The rights of all of them have been respected. This is our forces' substantial contribution to the humanization of the conflict.

8. A unilateral attitude in the process of humanizing the conflict is unacceptable. For this reason the nonresolution of the case of Compañeras Samour and Reyes hampers and jeopardizes any possibility of reaching agreements to humanize the conflict.

9. As the result of all we have presented so far, we assert that the situation of all mayors captured by our forces will only be settled if the Duarte government resolves the case of Commander Samour and Compañera Reyes.

10. Considering the fact that the church, through Msgrs Rosa Chávez and Rivera y Damas, has made efforts to obtain the release of the mayors we hold as prisoners, we hereby assert that we are willing to accept their mediation provided they are allowed to visit and observe the situation of our compañeras.

11. We want to make clear that what we propose is fundamental respect for the right of our compañeras to live and be tried in court. We reiterate that the violation of this right cannot be tolerated at this stage of the war because we have constantly treated the enemy prisoners of war fairly.

12. Duarte's government, the PDC, and the high command should bear in mind that there will continue to be prisoners of war of all kinds and on both sides in this war. Leaving this case unresolved could bring serious consequences and will aggravate the war.

13. Finally, we hold Duarte, the PDC, and the Armed Forces high command responsible for our compañeras' lives and situation. Let Duarte, the PDC, and the high command be assured that we will not let this criminal action go unpunished. With an unbreakable determination to fight for the Salvadoran revolution until we win or die, revolution or death, we will win.

[Signed] ERP General Command, Morazán, 10 May 1985

41. The Kidnapping of President Duarte's Daughter*

From Central American Broadcast Sources

Months later, the repercussions of the fall 1985 guerrilla kidnapping of 35-year-old Inés Guadalupe Duarte Durán were still apparent in El Salvador. According to New York Times correspondent James LeMoyne, both "she and her family have been . . . deeply scarred by the experience."[1] *Although the kidnapping drew criticism from European and Latin American governments, and even from some members of the Salvadoran FDR,*[2] *it seemed to be a net gain for the rebel movement as a whole, which won freedom for more than a score of its leaders held in prison and passage out of the country for more than 100 wounded insurgents. What's more, it threw President Duarte off balance, politically as well as psychologically. Rebels released photos and tape recordings that indicated certain sympathy for the rebel cause on the part of Señora Duarte Durán, reinforcing conservative suspicions that the President's Christian Democratic movement is just a bunch of Communist supporters. Aside from driving a wedge between Duarte and his backers in the army and oligarchy, the rebels' kidnapping operation, their ability to hide Duarte Durán and her companion in their zones of control, and their managing of the complicated negotiations for the exchange of prisoners indicated a high degree of international diplomatic and logistical sophistication.*

We present the story here as it unfolded in the press in the weeks of the kidnapping, showing the complex event from several viewpoints.

A. FIRST DISPATCH, SAN SALVADOR RADIO, SEPTEMBER 10, 1985

The daughter of President José Napoleón Duarte, Inés Guadalupe Duarte Durán, 35, communications student at the New San Salvador University, UNSA . . . in this city, was kidnapped at approximately 1515 this afternoon by three unidentified men who were waiting for her to arrive at the UNSA.

Mrs Duarte Durán was driving her Toyota . . . when a beige Toyota intercepted her. Two men got out, forcibly seized her, and, although Mrs. Duarte Durán struggled with them, they managed to drag her into the Toyota, while other persons fired at her bodyguards. One of her bodyguards was killed instantly, and the other two were badly injured. The injured bodyguards were taken to a hospital.

---

* From Foreign Broadcast Information Service, *Daily Reports–Central America*, September 11–November 7, 1985.

[1] James LeMoyne, "Kidnapping Still Taking a Toll on Duarte," *New York Times*, February 16, 1986.

[2] See the remarks of Guillermo Ungo in section F of this reading.

Since a military blockade has surrounded the university and nearby blocks, and since the authorities are not allowing us to gather information, it was impossible to learn the names of the slain bodyguard or the two injured bodyguards.

Mrs Duarte Durán is in charge of Radio Libertad, Radio Cadena Libertad. It was reported that she was head of Radio Libertad's news and that she studied communications science at the UNSA. . . .

B. PRESIDENT DUARTE'S REACTION, PANAMA CITY RADIO, ACAN, SEPTEMBER 11, 1986

ACAN has learned from unofficial sources that Salvadoran President José Napoleón Duarte was told about the kidnapping of his daughter Inés 3 hours after it occurred and that he suffered "a slight heart attack" upon hearing the news.

C. A DAY LATER, RADIO MANAGUA, SEPTEMBER 12, 1985

After more than 24 hours since the kidnapping of Mrs Inés Guadalupe Duarte, President José Napoleón Duarte's daughter, none of the armed groups in El Salvador has claimed credit for the kidnapping, while government spokesmen announced that a 23-year-old woman accompanying the president's daughter —Ana Cecilia Villeda—was also kidnapped.

President Duarte has received solidarity and support from all traditional political sectors of El Salvador, as well as many messages of support from political leaders throughout the world, headed by President Reagan, who condemned the kidnapping in a letter he sent a few hours ago to the Salvadoran president.

One of the leaders of the FDR, Ruben Zamora, said in the past few hours: Up to the moment we have absolutely no reports on the kidnapping.

D. PLEA TO KIDNAPPERS, AGENCE FRANCE PRESSE DISPATCH FROM SAN SALVADOR, SEPTEMBER 12, 1985

Rodolfo Castillo Claramount, foreign minister and vice president of El Salvador, has issued a dramatic plea to the kidnappers of President José Napoleón Duarte's daughter, to respect her physical and moral integrity. Likewise, he urged them to give some information concerning the health of 35-year-old Inés Guadalupe Duarte, who was kidnapped by heavily armed men on Tuesday.

During a statement to AFP, the foreign minister stated categorically that "there are no new developments" because no communication has been received, so "we continue in this cruel uncertainty." Castillo said he hopes that

Inés Guadalupe "is not being mistreated . . . so that her physical and psychological integrity does not suffer in the least, and that she may soon return home."

E. MILITARY SEARCH, SAN SALVADOR RADIO, SEPTEMBER 13, 1985

This morning combined Armed Forces units carried out an operation in which they discovered and searched 12 residences that probably were being used by guerrillas in San Salvador. These combined units were searching for the eldest daughter of President José Napoleón Duarte, who was kidnapped 2 days ago, according to an official Army spokesman.

Colonel Carlos Armando Aviles, chief of the Armed Forces Press Committee [Coprefa], said that the search of some of the houses was based on intelligence reports and information secured with regard to the kidnapping.

F. FDR LEADER DEPLORES KIDNAPPING, PANAMA CITY RADIO, ACAN, OCTOBER 3, 1985

During an interview with ACAN in this capital, Guillermo Ungo today accused "certain politicians" who have tried to link him with Inés Guadalupe Duarte's kidnapping on 10 September of "vulgar opportunism."

Ungo was responding to a statement by Ricardo Arias Calderón, top leader of the Panamanian Christian Democratic Party, who charged the civilian leaders of the guerrillas with being "accessories in the terror tactics" or "figureheads with no political decision-making power."

On the kidnapping of Señora Duarte Durán, Ungo said: "We deplore it; we hope and expect that her life, her physical integrity, will be spared; however, we cannot stop at this case but must regret the situation of dozens of thousands of fathers and mothers who have lost dozens of thousands of children and many hundreds of other people who are experiencing the sorrow of having missing children.

"The FDR [which is headed by Ungo] is not the political arm of the guerrillas, and the FMLN is not the military arm either," Ungo stressed.

"It is an alliance; they are two bodies that share a political line," he added.

"It would be as if we tried to link Duarte's administration and the Salvadoran Christian Democratic Party [PDC] with the murder of over 60,000 Christians and several thousand missing people, although Duarte is the Armed Forces commander in chief, while I am not," Ungo added.

G. THE REBELS DEFEND THEIR ACTION, CLANDESTINE RADIO FARABUNDO MARTÍ, SEPTEMBER 15, 1985

The Pedro Pablo Castillo Front [a unit of the FMLN] assure[s] the People of El Salvador that the struggle of the people will break all locks, all rocks, will open all the dungeons, and we will once again join in an embrace of freedom and independence.

This morning, the traitor José Napoleón Duarte cried when he spoke from Liberated Plaza to address the fatherland which he is selling out to a foreign power, the imperialist power. With tears, the butcher Duarte tried to exploit the sentiments of the people. Duarte apparently thinks that our people have forgotten the repression he has unleashed in our fatherland. Duarte travels constantly to the United States as the puppet of imperialism. Duarte has remained silent on the massacre of refugees . . . and continues to cover up the murder of Msgr Romero.

When Duarte speaks about the Salvadoran family he is thinking of the 14 oligarchic families. He is responsible for the situation of the refugees, for the situation of the families that have been forced to flee their homes, for all the persons who have been imprisoned and are missing.

We wish to refresh Mr. Duarte's memory. What happens to our political prisoners? From the moment they are captured they are tortured, they are kidnapped, they disappear. Men and women are cruelly tortured. and their belongings are stolen from their relatives. Duarte, who this morning spoke of liberty, is chiefly responsible for the persons who are missing, who are in prison, who are tortured.

Mr Duarte: Where are our sons? Where are our daughters? Our children, Mr Duarte, where are they? Where are our brothers, Mr Duarte? Why are so many Salvadorans disappearing? Is it moral to torture? Is it moral to murder many fellow countrymen in the dungeons of the repressive forces? Is it perhaps, Mr Duarte, that the Salvadoran people do not have human rights?

H. A DEAL TAKES SHAPE: DUARTE IN CONTACT WITH THE FMLN, REUTERS, BUENOS AIRES, SEPTEMBER 15, 1985

A top-level source told REUTERS that the first contact between the kidnappers and the government was established late on Friday, but the communication was cut when a helicopter motor was heard in the background.

The government has said there is reason to believe that the FMLN was responsible for the kidnapping, but the rebel stations which normally claim responsibility for these actions have remained silent. One of Duarte's advisers told REUTERS that the government hoped the abductors would not make some kind of public statement, but try to establish private contact to reach an agreement. There were some unconfirmed reports that the kidnappers had demanded the release of important leaders who had been arrested by Duarte's government in exchange for Duarte's daughter.

According to the officials, the government has in detention at least five important guerrilla leaders, including Nidia Díaz, second in command in the Revolutionary Party of Central American Workers (PRTC), and Americo Mauro Araujo, one of the top-level leaders of the Communist Party of El Salvador. An important military official said that if the abductors insist on the release of all the captured rebel leaders, then "Inés will die, because we will never release all of them."

Nevertheless, one of Duarte's advisers said that the government was prepared to negotiate the release of the president's daughter in exchange for Nidia Díaz. Duarte has appointed a commission, comprised of a close adviser, one of the president's sons, and the defense minister, to prepare answers to all possible demands from the kidnappers.

Last year, when the guerrilla forces kidnapped Eduardo Vides, brother of Defense Minister Carlos Eugenio Vides Casanova, secret negotiations between his kidnappers and the Army—with the church acting as mediator—led to his release. Weeks later an important guerrilla leader was released from the Salvadoran prison of La Esperanza.

I. THE ROLE OF THE CHURCH, SAN SALVADOR TV, SEPTEMBER 15, 1985

[In a homily delivered at the Sistine Cathedral in San Salvador, Archbishop Arturo Rivera y Damas said:] We must bear in mind the sacrifices of all our forefathers and all the Salvadorans who have struggled and suffered to attain our people's welfare, because we cannot continue to consider independence as a gift derived from something which has already been accomplished. In addition to becoming passive, and resigned to our fate, we would be celebrating the beginning of a process without really becoming aware that we must continue with our efforts. This process and our people's efforts must be aimed at achieving total liberation, and the church wants to contribute to the achievement of this goal. We understand that total liberation is comprised of all the various aspects and dimensions in which man is involved: political freedom, trying to build a just society; economic freedom, seeking to build an equitable society; human freedom, creating a new, free man who chooses his own destiny; and freedom from sin, because we are trying to eradicate injustice among men and their society, opening our hearts to a communion with God and all men.

This is the integral, total liberation we want as people and nations, and it has brought us much suffering. Something new is being created with much suffering and many deaths; the church is here and wants to contribute with its faith. This faith urges us to love all men, even our enemies; this love discards the friend-enemy concept and does not conceive of peace as an absence of war; it does not conceive of peace as an imposed peace, the peace of cemeteries, but as a permanent achievement, the fruit of love and a gift from God.

In this concern, frequent calls will be issued to our national awareness to stop so much violence and seek the roads to a dialogue in order to humanize the conflict. I shall leave the detailed report on this week's events for next Sunday; however, I must point out the most recent case, which has shaken our nation and the world, concerning the kidnapping of the president's eldest daughter, Inés Guadalupe Duarte Durán, and her fellow student, Ana Cecilia Villeda Sosa. As soon as we learned of this sad event, we raised our pleas to God, asking him that such a difficult test have a quick and comforting outcome.

However, our prayers also included all the other brothers who are prisoners for political reasons or because they are victims of a kidnapping—either for economic or political reasons. While the legal assistance office works for the political prisoners, how could we not pray for the 13 mayors and other officials who are being held prisoner by the guerrilla groups; or for businessman José Luis Zablah and many others who—perhaps due to their humble origin—have not deserved a newspaper headline? In addition to prayer and work, the church's moral support will join many voices being raised without hesitation to condemn all kidnappings because these are terrorist actions, regardless of the reasons behind each of them.

Above all, we wish to assert our concern for the lack of sensibility which might prevail among us concerning these abominable actions, until we come to the point where daily violence is viewed as a spectacle or a statistic and not as what it really is: disdain for human dignity. We also wish to point out that if this kidnapping has political connotations, it could accentuate the deterioration of the dialogue, which needs not only a good dose of good will but also respect for persons who have nothing to do with the country's problems—particularly women.

We must be positive and overcome the temptation to treat people as mere objects, as pawns which one can discard at will during a chess game, if we want to embark on the road toward peace. Inés Guadalupe's kidnapping eloquently highlights what must not be done. God willing, this will be the last time we have to deplore such actions. Otherwise, this celebration at the cathedral should encourage all to renew our inner selves, love our brothers, and continue building a much more human way of living. May the Holy Virgin, identified with her people's suffering, be the one to accompany us during our pilgrimage for faith, hope, and the search for a better world. Amen.

J. THE ARMY SUPPORTS DUARTE, RADIO SAN SALVADOR, SEPTEMBER 26, 1985

"The Salvadoran Army will support any decision adopted by President José Napoleón Duarte with regard to the kidnapping of his daughter, Inés Guadalupe Duarte, and her friend, Ana Cecilia Villeda," Culture and Communications Minister Julio Adolfo Rey Prendes said yesterday afternoon.

He made this clarification in view of rumors and reports circulating about disagreement in the military ranks about the demands of the kidnappers of the president's daughter. The minister did not give details of the demands, but he clarified that these rumors are false. He also said that other rumors indicating that a deadline had been set for an exchange of prisoners are false.

K. NEGOTIATIONS, PANAMA CITY RADIO, ACAN, OCTOBER 5, 1985

This afternoon Salvadoran President José Napoleón Duarte communicated with the kidnappers of his daughter, Inés Guadalupe, and informed them that he is ready to release 22 jailed guerrillas. Communication between the president and the kidnappers was established through a shortwave radio monitored by several newsmen. During the communication Duarte said that three of the rebels whose release is being demanded in exchange for his daughter's release have already been set free. . . .

After providing the names of the rebels the government is willing to surrender, President Duarte asked the kidnappers about his daughter's health and that of Ana Cecilia. The radio communication was cut at this point, although Duarte insisted on asking several times about Inés Guadalupe Duarte's health.

L. SEÑORA DUARTE DURÁN IN CAPTIVITY: INTERVIEW WITH THE FMLN, OCTOBER 24, 1985 (BROADCAST BY RADIO VENCEREMOS, NOVEMBER 7, 1985)

The first question to Mrs. Duarte was: Could you briefly describe the conditions under which you were held while in the territories controlled by the FMLN?

Mrs. Inés Guadalupe Duarte answered: About this, I could say that in spite of the difficulties, their treatment was very humanitarian and very respectful. Within the limitations they had they tried to cover everything for us: food, clothing, and we had a doctor permanently with us. For any problem we had, we consulted him, and he immediately gave us some medicine. We had a girl accompanying us throughout the entire captivity. I would like to say very nice things about her. She was very kind to us. She was always attentive to us. She would take us in the morning to take a bath, and I could say that the (?others) who took care of us, such as those from security, were also very respectful boys. Well, within this same attention that there was during the 45 days of my captivity, I could say that I must be very grateful for the treatment they gave us as it was really very respectful, and with great humane quality.

The question [next] was whether Mrs Inés Guadalupe ever had any contact with the civilian population in the territories controlled by the FMLN. To that question, Mrs Duarte Durán answered in the following manner: Well, it is true. There were no bombings in the area where we actually were [apparently in the vicinity of the Guazapa Volcano.—Eds.]. However, between 17 and 19 October there were two bombings that were really very close to where we were. More or less, about 15 or 20 minutes. I can truly tell you this was horrible. I felt the bombs crashing nearby. To see the [word indistinct], to see the small plane, the one they call La Carreta, see how it drops the grenades, I can tell you, I was very afraid. It is a very sorrowful impression and very anguishing when one is not psychologically prepared for that. I think of the fear of the civilian population when they see those planes flying.

Our compañero interviewing Mrs Duarte Durán asked her if she was ever in contact with the civilian population. Mrs Duarte Durán answered as follows: I asked to see the civilian population. They thought I was a reporter. I could not explain to them. They told me about their experiences. They told me everything they think, and I really understood them because I had just experienced the bombing.

M. SEÑORA DUARTE DURÁN FREED, AGENCE FRANCE PRESSE DISPATCH FROM SAN SALVADOR, OCTOBER 24, 1985

Inés Guadalupe Duarte, the daughter of the Salvadoran president, and her companion Ana Cecilia Villeda were freed this morning at 1000 in Fantasma Municipality, Tenancingo Department, 42 km east of this capital, Communications Minister Adolfo Rey Prendes reported.

Rey Prendes made this statement today at the General Staff headquarters where a news conference was called to await the released women, who were in the hands of the guerrillas for 44 days.

Reliable sources said that 22 political prisoners and 96 war-maimed guerrillas, who were exchanged for the 2 women and 33 municipal officials, will leave for Panama today at 1400. Rey Prendes said that the entire operation is the result of a major coordinated action by the International Red Cross Committee, the diplomatic corps, the government, and the church which stationed priests throughout the country to receive the mayors and the war prisoners.

N. REUNITED WITH HER FAMILY; PRESIDENT DUARTE'S PRESS CONFERENCE, SAN SALVADOR RADIO, OCTOBER 25, 1985

I will begin by saying that Inés Guadalupe is fine. At this time, she will not make statements, so I ask you not to ask her to make statements. She is tired and apparently she was made to walk for 3 consecutive days. She is suffering from nervous tension, and I am sure that you will understand that this is normal after being held hostage for more than 40 days. However, she is fine. She is very happy at home with her father and mother, and with her children. She is resting at home at present with her three children.

We know that these persons now being released [in exchange for Señora Duarte Durán] will pick up a rifle again and continue to possibly do harm to the nation. That is unfortunately something we cannot ignore. Neither can we ignore that the entire conflict is wearing on not the government, but the Salvadoran people. Then, my work should be to help the Salvadoran people come out of this conflict and gain peace, and to seek its humanization through the effort of democratization by all in order to find the political space required so that all sectors, from the extreme right to the extreme left, may abandon violence in favor of peace and participation, in which this government is interested. Thus, all things considered, this will be positive for the country.

O. THE AFTERMATH: SEÑORA DUARTE DURÁN WAS FORCED TO MAKE STATEMENTS, PANAMA CITY RADIO, ACAN, DISPATCH FROM SAN SALVADOR, NOVEMBER 7, 1985

A ranking [government] official said today that the Salvadoran president's daughter, Inés Guadalupe, was forced by the guerrillas to make statements for a rebel station moments before her release.

Culture and Communications Minister Julio Adolfo Rey Prendes said at a press conference that Inés Guadalupe Duarte, who was held for 44 days, "was forced to make statements under the threat that if she did not do so she would not be released."

P. THE AFTERMATH: "STOCKHOLM SYNDROME," AGENCE FRANCE PRESSE DISPATCH FROM PARIS, NOVEMBER 4, 1985

Inés Guadalupe Duarte, kidnapped by Salvadoran guerrillas for 44 days, is not presently "in a condition to make objective statements" about her experience as a hostage, President José Napoleón Duarte said here today.

Duarte presented Inés Guadalupe during a news conference held at a downtown Paris hotel but asked newsmen not to ask his daughter questions because of the emotional state she is in, mentioning the phenomenon known as the "Stockholm Syndrome." Duarte mentioned the so-called "Stockholm Syndrome," which was referred to in the case of the U.S. passengers kidnapped in the TWA plane who were placed in quarantine in Frankfurt after their release. (This syndrome, which was reportedly studied in the Swedish capital, is characterized by a disturbance in the conscience of those who have been kidnapped and which leads them to sympathize with their kidnappers.)

Inés Guadalupe Duarte, with a shy smile on her face, posed by her father's side for a while and then retreated without making any statements.

Q. THE AFTERMATH: FREEDOM OF SPEECH, RADIO FARABUNDO MARTÍ, NOVEMBER 4, 1985

Duarte has violated freedom of expression even in his own home.

After Inés Guadalupe Duarte Durán was released, her father, the president of the Republic, has not allowed her to say one word to the news media, which has tried to get a statement from her. . . .

A few minutes before she was released, Inés Guadalupe told Radio Farabundo Martí that she had been treated with great respect and great human decency by the FMLN, and that she was impressed by the brotherly attitude and solidarity among the members of the FMLN. She also spoke against the Air Force's raids on the civilian population and she also admitted that she had changed her opinion of the members of the FMLN, who are struggling for an ideal and have very high morale. . . .

[T]he people have already answered their own question after listening to Napoleón Duarte's statements to U.S. news media during his recent trip to the United States. According to Duarte, his daughter was brainwashed to turn her against him and for this reason she is seeing a psychologist. In other words, Duarte is not allowing his daughter to make statements to the news media, because she would make statements in favor of the FMLN.

[Early the next year, rebel Radio Farabundo Martí reported that it was no longer observing the part of the agreement negotiated in October by which the FMLN would no longer kidnap relatives of government and military officials, in exchange for the government's agreement not to capture suspected leftists without giving their families notice. According to a *New York Times* dispatch of February 23, 1986, by correspondent James LeMoyne, the latter practice of "disappearing" such suspects has diminished but not ceased. The guerrillas called for "immediate liberation of all the disappeared" and declared themselves "no longer . . . obliged to to continue complying with the agreements made in . . . October 1985." Radio Farabundo Martí, February 22, 1986.—Eds.]

Chapter VIII

"Agrarian Reform" and the Revival of Labor

Editors' Introduction

Not only in El Salvador, but throughout the nonindustrial world, land short-ages and rising population growth have provided the matrix for social strug-gle and demands for land reform.[1] The situation in El Salvador, the most densely populated area in Latin America, is particularly critical and is intri-cately involved with the political problems of that tiny country.

In El Salvador land has always meant power—either directly as in the case of the landowners themselves, or indirectly, through the military or civilian elites who have served the oligarchy so long and so well. Since the breakup of the communal Indian lands in the 1870s by the free-market liberal govern-ment of the day, El Salvador's land has been tied up in agricultural commodi-ties for export—first in indigo, later in coffee, cotton, and sugar cane. Efforts at redistributing the land and, hence, the power in El Salvador have been in vain, whether those efforts were the results of mass political movements or even modest proposals broached by the military.

The land-reform program initiated by the military–Christian Democratic junta in March of 1980 was, however, supposed to be different. Hailed by the United States and bankrolled largely by it, the measures were supposed to be proof positive of the reform credentials of the government and yet another reason for vigorous efforts to defeat the rebellion.

[1]. See Paul R. Ehrlich, Anne H. Ehrlich, and John P. Holdren, *Ecoscience: Population, Resources, Environment* (San Francisco, 1977), chapter 7; Emma Rothschild, "Food Politics," *Foreign Affairs* (January 1976).

From the beginning, though, land reform was sabotaged by its enemies. After one year, Leonel Gómez, former chief adviser to Rodolfo Viera, the assassinated head of ISTA, El Salvador's institute for land reform,[2] could (from the safety of U.S. shores) dismiss it as a failure that functioned mainly to bolster the reformist image of the oligarchic regime in El Salvador.[3]

By now, debate over its merits has ended; the reform is a dead issue. No longer attached as a condition for further U.S. aid, no longer followed closely by policymakers or the press, the land reform fell victim to the ascendancy of the Salvadoran right.

With their victory in the March 1982 Constituent Assembly elections, ARENA and the PCN (the National Conciliational Party) acted immediately to gut the reforms at the behest of the oligarchy. The military–Christian Democratic junta had already "postponed" indefinitely phase 2 of the reforms that would have cut deeply into the large coffee *fincas,* stating that such action would at the present time cripple "the productive sector."

Roy Prosterman's "Land-to-the-Tiller" program, designed to "breed capitalists like rabbits," faltered from the start, ill-conceived and underfunded but, most importantly, carried out with abysmal ignorance of the *modus operandi* of Salvadoran agriculture.[4]

As Irving Howe wrote in 1981, "Land reform would/could make a major difference only if it were accompanied by physical security for political dissidents and recalcitrant peasants were able to create their own free and autonomous institutions."[5] Even the smashing Christian Democratic victory in the Constituent Assembly elections of March 1985 seems unlikely to put the land-reform program back on track, despite continuing pressure from *campesino* and trade-union groups within the Christian Democratic base.

If in the rural areas *campesinos* have been unable to wrench reforms out of the oligarchy, their urban counterparts—the Marxist-oriented unions— seem to be displaying an unexpected vitality. Strikes and demonstrations have reappeared, especially in the government sector, and have put President Duarte on the spot. El Salvador's economy remains "ravaged and stagnant,"

[2.] See Reading 36.

[3.] See *Food Monitor,* July–August 1981; No. 22.

[4.] Roy Prosterman had previously attempted a similar program in Vietnam, with similar results. In an interview with one of the editors of this book in early 1985, President José Napoleón Duarte delivered himself of a bitter reminiscence of Roy Prosterman's role in the U.S.-sponsored land reform. Pointing out that the "Land-to-the-Tillers" phase of the agrarian reform could not possibly go into effect until at least $100 million was made available for credit to the new peasant-owners and for compensation for the previous owners, Duarte was reluctant at first to support the measure. Prosterman urged him to sign the law, promising him that the U.S. government would supply the needed funds. According to Duarte, he signed but Prosterman "disappeared and never came back." Nor was the $100 million forthcoming. (Marvin E. Gettleman, interview with President José Napoleón Duarte, Presidential Palace, San Salvador, January 10, 1985.)

[5.] Irving Howe, "Looking into El Salvador," *Dissent* (Summer 1981), 285–88.

with unemployment and underemployment over 50 percent.[6] But without a
transformation in the countryside, there is no way an impoverished agricultural country can find the wherewithal to pay urban workers the wages they
expect and simultaneously reduce mass unemployment. In the economic
sphere, Duarte and his American sponsors face a tough road ahead.

42. The Failure of Land Reform*

By Raymond Bonner

*Elsewhere in this book (see Reading 52) the question of the relationship between the
current struggle in El Salvador and the earlier Vietnam conflict is discussed. Land reform
is an issue on which the two countries may also be fruitfully compared, especially in light
of the interesting fact that the designer of the ill-fated land-reform program in El
Salvador, University of Washington professor Roy Prosterman, also served in a similar
role in Vietnam in the 1960s.[1]*

In the reading that follows, former New York Times *reporter Raymond Bonner, who
covered El Salvador in 1981, describes the role of the AFL-CIO agency, the American
Institute for Free Labor Development (the group Prosterman worked for), in the struggles
over land reform in El Salvador after the revolution of 1979. Bonner's journalism won
him a prize from the Latin American Studies Association. Previously he had been a
lawyer and had served with the U.S. Marines in Vietnam. No longer on the* New York
Times *staff, Bonner is currently completing a book on the Philippines.*

AIFLD, which was expelled from El Salvador in 1973 but returned after the
coup in 1979 . . . tried to subvert the land reform program that was being
considered by the first junta. AIFLD was opposed to taking land from all the
largest landowners, arguing instead that only one or two farms be expropriated
and converted to peasant cooperatives, "as pilot projects," said Leonel Gómez,
deputy director of the Salvadoran Institute for Agrarian Transformation
(ISTA) at the time. The AIFLD representatives also tried to persuade José
Rodolfo Viera not to take the job as head of ISTA, offering him a position with
AIFLD at $1,000 a month. But after consulting with Archbishop Romero,
Viera, a peasant with only three years of formal schooling, became the ISTA
director. At point AIFLD rented him a suite at the Sheraton, "for no

[6.] James LeMoyne, *New York Times,* October 20, 1985, Section 4, 2.
* From Raymond Bonner, *Weakness and Deceit: U.S. Policy and El Salvador* (New York:
Times Books, 1984), 191–203, 317–319.
[1.] For Prosterman's role in the Salvadoran land reform, see Peter Shiras's article in *Food
Monitor* (Washington, D.C.), No. 20 (January–February 1981), and Prosterman's reply, ibid., No.
22 (July–August 1981).

reason at all," said Gómez. "They were just trying to buy him. But they couldn't."

AIFLD did, however, effectively buy the largest Salvadoran peasant union, [Unión Comunal Salvadoreño], known by its Spanish initials as the UCS, and the Democratic Popular Unity (UPD), an umbrella organization for four labor groups. Peasant unions were banned from 1932 until the late 1960's, when the government set up the UCS with assistance from AIFLD. It was about that time that Michael Hammer first worked in El Salvador. When AIFLD became involved with the UCS again in 1980, it paid some 400 UCS members salaries of $160 a month—a hefty amount for a peasant—to work as promoters, going into the countryside to explain the law and seek new members. Each peasant paid 25 centavos (about 60 cents) a month to be a member of the UCS; the rest of the organization's annual budget of nearly $2 million came from AIFLD. The UCS has become little more than an alter ego for AIFLD and the U.S. policy.

During one crucial period when President Reagan had to certify that progress was being made in the land reform program in order to continue military aid to El Salvador, the UCS complained in a letter to Duarte that "the failure of the agrarian reform process is an immediate and imminent danger." Just three days after that negative letter had been made public, in a front-page story by Karen De Young in *The Washington Post,* AIFLD released another letter purportedly written by UCS leaders, this time praising the Duarte government's efforts in behalf of peasants. This letter was the basis of a front-page story in *The New York Times* under the headline SALVADOR PEASANTS PRAISE LAND POLICY.

The letter was dated January 25 and purportedly written in El Salvador. AIFLD made it public with a press release on January 28. But mail does not arrive from El Salvador in three days, and the name of one of the UCS leaders, Samuel Maldonado, who supposedly signed the letter, was misspelled. In fact, the letter was written by AIFLD in Washington.

AIFLD has used the UCS and its leaders on other occasions, flying them to Washington to testify before congressional committees skeptical about continuing aid to El Salvador. But AIFLD leaders have never allowed them to say publicly what they voice in private, such as their support for negotiations to end the war.

When it comes to Phase III of the Salvadoran land reform, the land-to-the-tiller law, there can be no doubt that it was a U.S. program, in spite of State's insistence that the United States provided only technical assistance. Phase III, also called 207—the number of the government decree enacting it—"had to be shoved down their throats," said a diplomat noting the nearly universal Salvadoran government, civilian and military, opposition to it. An internal AID [Agency for International Development] document described Phase III as having been "designed virtually in its entirety by Americans, and slipped into legislation without their [the Salvadoran government's] being consulted. The fact is known and resented."

The land-to-the-tiller law was Prosterman's idea. It was one of the changes in the program that he had pressured Gutiérrez to accept at their meeting in early March. Prosterman argues: "Douglas MacArthur pushed through the sweeping land reform in Japan after World War II, transforming the tenants into small family farmers, which effectively destroyed the communists as a political force, and helped set the stage for the economic miracle in that country. Chiang Kai-shek, with U.S. support, carried out an equally sweeping land reform in Taiwan after losing the mainland, with equally positive results, as did South Korea, just before the North invaded in 1950 (which is a key reason why there was never any 'behind the lines' problems in that conflict)." These land reform programs, Prosterman insisted, are a "strikingly better model for other Latin American countries" than what had been tried in Chile and Peru.

"The Salvadorans used to get amused at Prosterman sometimes," recalled [former U.S. Ambassador, Robert E.] White. "His frequent allusions to Taiwan, Japan, Vietnam. That's not Central America. He didn't know anything about Latin America." But Prosterman knew how to stop a leftist revolution —or thought he did. To a hostile audience of Salvadoran businessmen he argued that the land-to-the-tiller law would "breed capitalists like rabbits" and that there was no one more conservative than a landowner. And even though White said he didn't think Prosterman knew much about Latin America, he, too, was enthusiastic about land to the tiller. "It was going to build a middle class, a group of people who had a stake in society," he said.

But there was opposition to the law, even among Salvadorans and American officials who recognized the need for Phases I and II. They pointed out that a considerable number of Phase III parcels—all plots smaller than seventeen acres were affected by the law, but most of them were only two or three acres —were owned not by wealthy individuals but by schoolteachers, shopkeepers, widows, and others who had managed to save enough money over the years to buy a plot of land, which uninterested in farming themselves, they rented. Phase III, because it was hastily drafted to thwart the leftists' appeal, did not take into account any hardship cases.

There were also serious economic and agricultural deficiencies in the program. In a comprehensive report on the Salvadoran land reform program, Oxfam America, the Boston-based humanitarian and development organization, noted that the law altered the peasant practice of crop rotation. Under the renting system, a peasant moved to a new plot every couple of years, allowing the soil of his former field to lie fallow and regenerate. But when a peasant owns a tiny plot, he is forced to plant every available inch every year in order to feed his family. The soil is quickly depleted. From an agricultural and economic perspective, it would have been wiser to combine the small plots into cooperatives owned by several peasant families. Economies of scale would have operated, and while the farmers had grown enough corn or beans in one area to feed everyone, another section could have been left fallow.

Gómez and Viera, the ISTA officers, were also opposed to the land-to-the-tiller program—not because of the concept but for the practical reason that the government did not have the resources to implement it while it was also trying to carry out Phases I and II. Prosterman countered that land to the tiller was self-executing, that a peasant need only present proof that he had been working the parcel as a tenant for the prescribed period and title would automatically be issued to him.

In later months and years American diplomats and AID officials realized that the opponents had been right on many counts. The land to the tiller's "bequests upon the landless will be largely at the expense of small investors and those whose lives were improved by the chance of inheritance," Hallman, the embassy political officer, wrote in his January 1981 Dissent Channel cable. "This is not a political net plus." An AID report noted: "If campesinos were to cultivate a single plot with poor soil on a steep slope for three years in succession, it would be converted to a sterile desert." And the law was hardly self-executing. "It is abundantly clear that Decree 207 is not, by any stretch of the imagination, 'self-executing,' " said another AID report. When 207 was enacted, the government said some 150,000 rural families would be beneficiaries; three and a half years later, as of November 1983, only 4,767 definitive titles, and 53,401 provisional ones, had been issued.

But in the spring of 1980 the Americans didn't think they had time to examine all these concerns. Land reform was hastily enacted because something had to be done to counter the growing strength of the left. "It was rushed through more for its political impact than its social impact," White said. "The left fears land reform," Prosterman assured the Salvadoran businessmen. "It deprives them of their most valuable weapon in implementing revolution because they can no longer appeal to the landless." He even went so far as to declare that "the leftist onslaught will be effectively eliminated by the end of 1980."

Of all the myths generated by the land reform, this is one of the most pervasive: that it took the banner from the left. It was a "logical conclusion," said one diplomat, but "no one ever offered us any proof—and the press never questioned it."

The land reform probably did take some of the wind out of the revolutionary sails, but not nearly to the extent that American and Salvadoran officials proclaim. For one thing, the program just didn't benefit that many people. "The overall numbers of people benefited [under Phase I] are relatively small," noted a Confidential State Department memorandum written two years after the program had begun. Only about 30,000 peasant families have become cooperative members under Phase I, the one phase most fully implemented.

Even if all three phases were completed, there would still be 1.8 million Salvadoran peasants without land. More important, giving a peasant title to a plot of land won't bring the schools, water, electricity, and health care that have more meaning for the daily lives of peasant parents and their children than a piece of paper that bestows certain legal rights. It is also debatable whether peasants will be better off as the owners of the cooperatives than they were when they were working for an absentee landlord. "Many of the people working on the [Phase I] cooperatives may not be really aware of much change," noted a Confidential State Department memorandum in March 1982. "Some of them are even being managed by the same people who were formerly the agents of the large land-owners, so the net impact is lessened."

A significant reason that the real benefits of the land reform program did not match the rhetoric was that Phase II was never implemented. The Carter administration was ambivalent about Phase II—Pastor, at the NSC, thought it was a mistake—and the Reagan administration was unequivocally opposed. But the Salvadoran peasants desperately wanted it. Maldonado, the head of the UCS, said in an interview in mid-1982 that U.S. aid should be conditional on the implementation of Phase II, an opinion that AIFLD did not have him make publicly in any letters or congressional appearances.

If the purpose of the land reform is to effect a meaningful distribution of the wealth, as opposed to being primarily a political tactic to stop the revolution, then Phase II is essential. Many wealthy landowners avoided losing their lands under Phase I by subdividing them among family members into farms that were within the Phase II size—247 to 1,235 acres. Moreover, under a fully implemented Phase I, there would be some 325 cooperatives, affecting only 15 percent of the nation's farmland and benefiting 34,658 families, or 7.2 percent of the total farm families. Phase II, on the other hand, would have affected some 1,700 farms, covering 18.5 percent of the farmland and 50,000, or 10.5 percent, of rural families. From the perspective of redistribution of the wealth, only 13 percent of the nation's coffee is cultivated on Phase I properties, at least 30 percent on Phase II-size farms.

The Salvadoran land reform was designed to prevent a revolution. This is in contrast with the land reform in Nicaragua, which was designed to implement one. It is beyond the scope of this book to examine the Nicaraguan reform in any detail, but Lawrence Simon of Oxfam America, who has studied both countries' land reform efforts, described the Nicaraguan project as "more democratic and sweeping." It is more democratic in that the Salvadoran program was "imposed from abroad or above"—as Archbishop Romero said —while Nicaragua's was designed with considerable input from the peasants, who at one point marched on Managua to demand, successfully, that the Sandinista government expropriate and distribute more lands. But though the Nicaraguan program is more sweeping—affecting a greater percentage of farmland and rural families—it is also less radical in some respects than El

Salvador's. While the Sandinistas took some lands for political reasons—from people who had fled the country and from those who joined the counterrevolutionary forces—productivity, not size, was the principal criterion used by the Sandinistas in deciding which farms to expropriate. One 44,000-acre privately held sugarcane plantation, for example, was not touched by Nicaraguans.

There is another, and perhaps more significant, reason why the Salvadoran land reform didn't silence the revolutionary surge or generate more converts to the government: The repression continued unabated.

"On July 18 [1980], in a surprise move at night, the Army surrounded the Hacienda, which is called San Lorenzo, obliging its members that were on watch to lie face downward, then with their hands against the wall accusing them of being Communists, and tying up cooperative member Pedro Antonio Mijango. They took him away and the next day he was found dead near the road to Santiago de María."

Thus did the members of the Santa Catalina Agricultural Production Cooperative Association describe their plight in a plea to Archbishop Rivera y Damas. After this raid, they wrote, "all the cooperative members were terrified and did not go to town that night. Eight days later when they went to work they found the storehouse and part of the roof burned, with all the fertilizers completely destroyed, all the irrigation equipment, furnishings, agricultural containers, etc." The army returned again one month later, in August. "The Army put all the cooperative members and other workers face downward in the cultivated areas on top of ants' nests, tied up several of them." This time two members of the cooperative were seized by the soldiers, "taken to the edge of the Hacienda and publicly assassinated in a ravine." After that "no one came to work, much less to do guard work, and we lost in crops 80 manzanas [about 136 acres] of corn, 60 [102 acres] of millet, 2 [3.4 acres] of tomatoes, 1 [1.7 acre] of chile, the small projects of onions, peppers, jicama fruit and 8 manzanas [13.6 acres] of coffee, and things of lesser value such as wire, wood, tools, etc." The peasants concluded their letter to the archbishop: "We hope you will forgive us for having to add one more problem to your many concerns but after having reflected on who we might turn to, we decided that you were the most appropriate."

Another of the myths fostered by U.S. officials is that the land reform demonstrates that the Salvadoran military is no longer in service to the country's oligarchy, that after the coup it was transformed "from an institution dedicated to the status quo to one that spearheads land reform," as the head of State's Latin American bureau, Thomas Enders, proclaimed in 1982. In a similar vein, when the Subcommittee on Foreign Operations of the House Appropriations Committee was considering the Carter administration's request for $5.7 million in "nonlethal" aid in early 1980, the State Department's John Bushnell argued that the aid would be a "symbol" to those military officers who are "committed to reform." Moreover, he assured the congressmen, the military aid was needed so that the armed forces could "provide security to these farmers who have received land. To do that they need transport and communications equipment so they can respond when there is an incident and provide security in the countryside."

But about the only evidence that the military was supporting the reforms came on the day they were announced, when army units surrounded the banks and occupied many of the Phase I properties to prevent any interference with the expropriations. What happened after that, U.S. policymakers didn't bother to tell Congress and the American public. Salvadoran officers used the American trucks and communications equipment not to spearhead reform but to thwart it by continuing to repress the peasants, as they always had.

"How can this present process succeed if the peasants are repressed on a daily basis merely for organizing themselves?" Christian Democrat Héctor Dada asked rhetorically in his resignation letter submitted when he left the junta a few days before the land program was announced. "How can this process hope to reach fruition when the organizations representing thousands of peasants have not even been consulted while, to the contrary, the daily and growing repression against those organizations renders impossible any dialogue with them? How can this process serve democracy if, far from the democratic framework in which the Party envisioned it taking place, it is carried out under a state of siege?"

The state of siege was declared on the day the reforms were announced. It was to be in effect for thirty days. Ritually, every thirty days, except for one very brief period in early 1982, it has been extended for another thirty days.

"In reality, from the first moment that the implementation of the agrarian reform began, what we saw was a sharp increase in official violence against the very peasants who were the supposed 'beneficiaries' of the process," the deputy agricultural minister, Jorge Villacorta, wrote in his resignation letter, submitted a few weeks after the reforms had been announced.

It was reform with repression.

It was barely light when the soldiers pushed through the creaky gate into El Peñón, a farm near the Pacific. A few days earlier the peasants had elected the leaders of their cooperative. The soldiers had a list of the names. From the lines of peasants going into the fields for the day's work, they pulled out eight, took them down a dusty road, past the oxen lugging carts, lined them up against a dirt bank, and executed them.

At San Francisco Guajoyo, the largest original UCS cooperative, the assassins arrived at about three-thirty in the morning, while the 160 families were sleeping. They were dressed in military uniforms; a small armored personnel carrier was brought along in case things got out of hand. The men went from door to door, rounding up peasants whose names were on a list. ISTA employees showed their identification. To no avail. Fourteen peasants were shot, as the other members of the cooperative were forced to watch. Junta members Morales Ehrlich and Colonel Gutiérrez told AID officials that the perpetrators of the massacre were guerrillas who had dressed in army uniforms and stolen the small tank. But one person had survived. When Leonel Gómez, the ISTA deputy director, and an AID official found him in the Santa Ana hospital, they spirited him away, knowing that survivors are often hunted down and killed in their hospital beds. He was laid on a mattress in the back of a pickup truck, with the AID man holding his plasma bottle. The survivor provided the details: The killings had been carried out by the National Guard. Concerned AID officials visited Guajoyo after the incident. A few days later, according to a classified "Memorandum to File," the Guard returned and killed more peasants.

El Peñón, San Francisco Guajoyo, Santa Catalina weren't random or isolated incidents. They were part of a pattern. According to an AIFLD memorandum, 184 peasants, government employees, and others associated with the land reform were "killed violently" during the eight months after the reforms had been enacted. Gómez, who tracked the repression for ISTA, testified before the House Subcommittee on Inter-American Affairs that between March and December 1980, 240 leaders of cooperatives were killed. AIFLD and Gómez blamed the government for most of the killings.

The land reforms "have been attacked very strongly, from both the Right, so-called, and the Left, so-called," Jeane Kirkpatrick declared soon after becoming Reagan's ambassador to the United Nations. In one quick stroke she had absolved the government from any responsibility and accused the left. She was wrong, on both counts. But she was not alone in that assessment.

The obverse of the myth that the Salvadoran armed forces respected the land reform was that the left attacked it. Bushnell, when he was arguing for the $5.7 million in military aid, told the congressional subcommittee that the guerrillas were attacking the cooperatives because "it is clear to them that if this government reform program succeeds, they will be very badly set back." He added that the guerrillas were moving onto cooperatives and evicting peasants who had been given the land by the government. The belief that the left was attacking the reforms was reinforced by most reporters, including this one, who heard that line used repeatedly by U.S. officials, in El Salvador and Washington, and who did not have access to classified government reports that showed the contrary. The author of one Confidential embassy memorandum, for example, reported being told by the manager of cotton lands that were expropriated under Phase I that "twenty tractors were burned during the expropriation, not by the guerrillas but by the Christian Democrats."

There was never "a concentrated plan of attack on the land reform from the left," an AIFLD official said in an interview as late as mid-1983. Internal government documents support what he said, presenting a far different picture of the attacks on the land reform from that presented publicly by Kirkpatrick, Bushnell, Enders, and other officials.

"While innocent campesinos are being hit from both sides of the political spectrum, there is a good deal of evidence that much of the violence is being carried out by Government Security Forces," according to an AID evaluation of the land reform prepared in August 1980. AIFLD's director in El Salvador, Richard V. Oulahan, in a memorandum dated November 12, 1980, wrote that of the 184 land reform-related killings, "[m]ilitary forces, police, para-military forces and a right-wing terrorist group with links into the Treasury Police" were allegedly responsible for 133 deaths. The other 51 persons were killed by "unknown sources," he noted, "probably a collection of those military and para-military groups already mentioned, plus leftist guerrillas and common bandits." Then he added, "Very few, if any, of these deaths have or will be investigated and the authors brought to trial, especially where police and military were involved. Government has not been willing to stop actions by the right-wing 'Death Squad.' "

In another memorandum Oulahan summarized the reactions of the military to the land-to-the-tiller law. In the province of Cabañas, he reported, a local commander, "in collusion with the Guardia Nacional, is responsible for the death of two promoters and almost had a UCS lawyer assassinated for investigating the same." In San Miguel, Oulahan informed Washington, the army major in charge ordered his subordinates not to allow UCS promoters to talk with peasants about the land-to-the-tiller law and the benefits of joining the UCS. In several provinces, Oulahan noted, UCS promoters were being harassed by the canton patrols, the rural civil defense forces. "In all cases the Canton Patrols and ORDEN are the same." (This was one year after the coup, which American officials continued to insist had resulted in the abolition of ORDEN.)

Similarly, in his congressional appearance Gómez testified that of the 240 peasants killed, 80 percent "died at hands of the Army and security forces." Two had been killed by guerrillas, he said. The killers of the others were unknown. He also provided the subcommittee with the names and circumstances surrounding the deaths of the UCS and ISTA employees, individuals, Gómez said, who "had been paid with U.S. money." There was Edith Matamoros, a member of the San Jacintena cooperative, pulled from his home and "cruelly killed" by soldiers from the Third Infantry Brigade in San Miguel. There was Juan Francisco Velásquez, a UCS promoter, pulled from a bus by soldiers near Comalapa and later assassinated. There was Mario Ramírez, the UCS departmental secretary, who was captured in Ahuachapán, forced into a vehicle, and later found dead. And so on. There were 92 government or UCS workers on the list. Telling the subcommittee that 47 had been killed by the army and 13 by the security forces, Gómez noted, "This is very significant because there is a widespread myth in the United States that the security forces, National Guard, National Police, and Treasury Police, with connections to the local oligarchy, commit most of the human rights violations. The Army, made up of conscripts, it is claimed, is cleaner and able to resist the pressures of the local landlords. The truth," Gómez declared, "is different."

The [National] Assembly's [1983] actions against the land reform created serious problems for the Reagan administration. In order to continue military aid to El Salvador, the administration had to certify every six months that the Salvadoran government was making "continued progress" in implementing the land redistribution program. After the suspension of the land-to-the-tiller law, the Salvadoran government launched a highly visible campaign designed to demonstrate that it was still committed to the land reform. Army units reinstated some evicted peasants, and in ceremonies around the country attended by high-ranking civilian and military officials, titles were delivered to peasants. During one elaborate affair in the ornate second-floor chamber of the Presidential Palace, President Magaña, flanked by a military honor guard of white-gloved soldiers holding rifles mounted with silver-plated bayonets, candidly acknowledged that the delivery of the titles was designed primarily for foreign consumption, to demonstrate "to the entire world" that El Salvador's land program was "going forward." The ceremony was held on the very day that President Reagan sent his certification to Congress. "Pure theater," said a senior Salvadoran official who was present. He was right. "After certification" there was "a lack of interest in completing the [land reform] program," Deputy Agricultural Minister Jorge A. Peña Solano told *New York Times* reporter Bernard Weinraub three months later. "Before certification we wanted to give an impression to the American people and Government how fast we were giving titles. Now certification is over." A few months earlier Peña Solano had told me, "If I were in their [the Reagan administration's] socks, I would stop aid, if what I believe is they [the Salvadorans] should go on with the reforms."

The Salvadoran land reform program never fully recovered from the assaults in the spring of 1982, failing even to meet the minimal goals set by the Reagan administration. The number of potential beneficiaries under the land-to-the-tiller program, according to the Salvadoran government, was between 125,000 and 150,000. In June 1982 the State Department in a Confidential cable to the embassy in El Salvador established certain goals that would be necessary in order to justify certification. Among them was the issuance of 12,000 definitive titles to land-to-the-tiller beneficiaries by the end of 1982. When the administration issued its certification in January 1983, the number of definitive titles issued was only 408. At the end of June 1983 the number had risen to 2,453. Yet the Reagan administration again certified that progress was being made on the land reform. And Senator Percy, along with other members of Congress who loudly protested the actions against the land reform, routinely voted for more aid.

More titles had not been issued primarily because of guerrilla attacks,

Enders told the Senate Foreign Relations Committee in August 1982. Senator Dodd questioned this, saying that he had been told by the peasants "that in fact the left really did not bother the land reform that much because it was too sacrosanct an issue to really disrupt it and thereby run the risk of incurring even further opposition in the countryside." Roy Prosterman, who was also appearing before the committee, said that "there is actually very little substance, very little support, for Secretary Enders' suggestion." He explained that the guerrillas were not willing "to interfere physically with the actual land reform process, because they know if they do that they will gain the enmity of vast numbers of campesinos who are beneficiaries of that process."

Nevertheless, a few months later, at the time of the January 1983 certification, the administration again insisted that "guerrilla attacks" on agrarian reform promoters and workers in the Salvadoran National Financial Institute for Agricultural Lands (FINATA) were interfering with the titling process. But the independent consulting firm hired by AID to evaluate the land reform reported: "FINATA staff told us that the guerrillas have seldom attacked them, and at times when FINATA promoters have been stopped by guerrilla roadblocks, they have been released with good wishes."

The administration also distorted the problem of evictions. In its July 1983 certification it reported that 3,656 evicted peasants had been reinstated. That may well have been accurate. But the administration failed to advise Congress on the number of peasants who had been evicted and not reinstated—nearly 10,000, according to the Salvadoran peasant organization—and also failed to report that many peasants reinstated one day were evicted the next.*

The Salvadoran Assembly delivered its final blow to the land redistribution effort in December 1983, passing a constitutional provision that cut in half the amount of land available for distribution. As originally drafted, El Salvador's land program placed a limit of 360 acres on the size of farms that could be privately owned. The constitutional provision, adopted by a coalition of ARENA and other rightist parties, permits individual ownership of up to 600 acres. "I congratulate it [the rightist coalition] for succeeding in definitely ending agrarian reform," said Julio Rey Prendes, a leader of the Christian Democrats, whose deputies voted against the provision.

But peasants who lost only a future right to become landowners or were merely evicted from their lands were in some respects fortunate, as the army continued gruesome attacks on cooperatives. A unit of some 150 soldiers, for example, raided La Florida, a cooperative sixty-five miles west of the capital that was financially supported by the Episcopal Church in the United States

* Although Salvadoran peasants continued to suffer from the dismantling of the land reform program begun by the Assembly in 1982, progress was made on behalf of the former owners, reflecting the priorities of the Reagan administration and the Salvadoran government. Prior to the elections in March 1982, no landlord of parcels claimed by peasants under the land-to-the-tiller law had received any compensation. By July 1983, $6,022,412 had been paid to 271 former owners.

and the Anglican Church of Canada. The soldiers seized seven members of the cooperative, hauled them away, tortured and killed them. One man had his nipples cut out. The testicles were slashed off another; the ears off a third. Brains spilled out of one man's head. All had their heads partially or completely severed. None had any bullet wounds. "This is the most horrendous thing I have ever seen in my entire ministry," said the Reverend Luis Serrano, the priest for the 220-member congregation at the cooperative, as he wept. The assassinations left behind widows and 24 orphans. No one was prosecuted.

43. *Economic Recovery in El Salvador?**

From *Proceso*

In addition to the civil war now raging in El Salvador, that tiny Central American country is also experiencing a chronic economic crisis that seriously threatens the government of José Napoleón Duarte. In the past half decade, the U.S. government has channeled nearly $2 billion in economic and military aid to "protect democracy and strengthen free enterprise."[1] But despite this massive assistance, the Salvadoran economy has, by every available measure, gone downhill. Its gross national product has fallen to 77 percent of its 1978 levels; per-capita income has dropped to 73 percent; unemployment is close to 40 percent, with another 25 to 30 percent of the work force underemployed. Although a few rural cooperatives have benefited from the land-reform program (see Reading 42), the majority of the Salvadoran campesinos are either landless or, if they do have land, are without access to sufficient credit to make a go of farming. And despite (or, as the Salvadoran conservatives would say, because of) the nationalization of banks and foreign trade, the economy continues to stagnate, as this analysis by a respected academic research institute in El Salvador suggests.

Since the publication of the Proceso *analysis in late 1984, the situation has changed in several respects: Inflation has soared, with prices rising by a third during the six months prior to March 1986. Rising expectations on the part of Salvadoran workers have prompted waves of strikes and demands for wage increases, as well as calls for resumption of the stalled "dialogue" process (see Readings 55–57). Amid right-wing charges that President Duarte's "communitarian" economic outlook is barely disguised communism (see Reading 10), and the left attacks on the funneling of resources into military operations and to private sector support, Duarte announced in February 1986 a new economic "package" designed to ease this crisis. It includes increased taxes on coffee growers (who are enjoying sudden prosperity because of the recent devastation of the Brazilian coffee*

* From "Recuperación," in *Proceso: Informativo Semanal del Centro Universitario de documentación e información* (University of Central America, San Salvador), 5, No. 164 (November 5, 1984). Translated by the Editors.

[1.] *Public Papers of the Presidents of the United States: Ronald Reagan,* 1981 (Washington D.C.: U.S. Government Printing Office, 1982), 191–193.

crop), prohibition of importation of certain classes of luxury goods, new standard curren-
cy-exchange rates, and increased prices for transportation and other basic services. With
Duarte's solid majority in the National Assembly, passage of this program is virtually
assured. The larger question is whether this, or any other economic prescription, can boost
productivity, spur development, and increase prosperity for the Salvadoran people without
a resolution of the civil war.

WHILE official [Salvadoran] economic data speak of economic recovery, and
a projected 2% growth rate in 1984, despite a zero growth rate in the previous
year, and while the government presents an attractive picture of the country's
steady advance toward democratization, one element remains constant in its
progressive increase: the impoverishment of the masses of the people.

A recent inquiry into prices of basic consumer items available in the stores
and markets of San Salvador carried out by the Department of Agricultural
Economics reveals that the costs for basic foods are much higher than those
established by the Institute for the Regulation of Supplies, as much as 66.7%
higher in the case of red beans. For pasteurized milk, which during 1983 was
priced at 1.70 colones per liter, a new price of 2.20 colones has been authorized,
the second such increase in the course of 1984.

While debates in the National Assembly have reached no decision on
whether to raise the price of gasoline "for private uses," the users of mass
transit have criticized increases in urban bus fares from 30 to 40 centavos.
Notwithstanding the official insistence that any rise in gasoline prices will not
affect raw materials for basic production, any increase in petroleum prices will
have wide direct and indirect effects on basic consumer products. Already, it
is precisely in the production of these things where the unregulated and
"informal" structures prevail.

The progressive deterioration of the purchasing power of the Salvadoran
people, aggravated by the delay in payment of public-sector salaries, contrasts
sharply with the government's policy of providing positive stimulus to the
private sector. It also helps explain the rising tide of labor unrest that is
becoming apparent. Close to 15,000 public employees affected by arrears in
salary payments have been insistently pressing claims to obtain what is due
them. For example, the workers in the Coffee Ministry are in the second week
of a strike (which affects coffee production in its period of greatest activity).

At this point is is appropriate to ask ourselves anew what effect U.S. economic aid has on the Salvadoran economy. This aid, the most given to any
country in this hemisphere, has mainly been earmarked to stimulate the private sector. Its overall effect has probably been to retard the falling of production and to generate expectations of prompt economic recovery. But this influx
of funds does not seem to bring much benefit to the people most lacking in
necessities and with the least purchasing power. On the other hand, U.S.
economic aid swells the Salvadoran government's rising foreign debt. Official

figures indicate that the total public debt has increased in the 1979 to 1983 period to 3,455.8 million colones from 853.2 million. In the same period, the foreign debt has risen from 65.1 million colones to 1,555.3 million, while U.S. economic aid, including donations, amounts to approximately $600 million in the period, with the official exchange rate set at 2.5 colones to the dollar.

Total U.S. aid [including military aid] for the same five-year period is $984 million. Despite this influx of money, El Salvador has not been able to overcome its chronic *hard* currency shortage. According to the Monetary Committee: "The situation involving the availability of *hard* currency is very critical. At this date [October 1984] imports totalling $169 million already authorized, or about to be authorized, cannot be delivered because of this currency shortage."

Given this data, one would have to ask if the expected 1984 economic growth rate of 2% is an illusory one in the light of the 43.2 increase in the public debt over the last five years, the alarming rates of unemployment and underemployment, and an internal market reduced with each passing day. It is also appropriate to inquire about the possibilities of recovery through an explicit policy of support for the private sector involving transferring the main economic burden onto the backs of the poorest groups in the population. If this is recovery, then for whom?

44. Radical Unions Revive in El Salvador*

BY CLIFFORD KRAUSS

In the new phase of the civil war that is unfolding in El Salvador, the U.S. media have tended to focus on the military tactics of the guerrilla organizations. The rebels freely admit that they intend to engage in small-unit attacks, including ambush and sabotage, and predict there will be a long war of attrition.

Less publicized in this country is the resurgence of mass political activity, including public demonstrations, work stoppages, and strikes. Workers, who have lost as much as 50 percent of their earning power during the five-year civil war, have once again taken to the streets, utilizing the space Duarte's political success has created. Some 20,000 marched on May Day of 1985. That same month, more than 20,000 teachers were on strike, as were thousands of social-security and water-works employees.

Perhaps the most dramatic event in this period on the labor front was the June 2 invasion by 500 national police of San Salvador hospitals, which had been occupied by striking personnel for almost a month. The assault led to the death of a pregnant patient as well as four police accidently killed in the confusion by their own forces. Troops then

* From *The Wall Street Journal*, September 24, 1985.

arrested the leaders of the striking union. A protest march two days later drew some 7,000 participants, organized by an umbrella group of independent left-leaning unions.

Duarte's electoral victories helped make this kind of activity possible, but after the spate of June strikes and demonstrations, he called the labor protests "a maneuver by the armed left" and "subversive,"[1] an ominous charge in a land in which more than 5,000 trade unionists have been assassinated.[2] The truth of this somewhat vague charge is open to question: It is known that the rebels have increased their ties to leftist unions, but it is not believed that they have taken them over.

After the U.S. Marines were killed in the Zona Rosa attack (see Reading 38), Duarte's government stepped up its attacks on the union movement. Radio programs "explained the supposed links between union activity and the FMLN military strategy."[3] Government intimidation, however, may backfire. There is evidence of greater unity within the labor movement—sympathy work stoppages and increased financial support of other unions on strike, among other measures.[4]

What the foregoing makes clear is that the struggles of labor have become one of the critical factors in El Salvador's future. The reading below is an overview of the labor situation by Clifford Krauss, staff reporter for the Wall Street Journal.

. . . IN the countryside, the war is going badly for the revolutionaries. But here in the capital, on a recent Saturday morning, there is evidence that a different phase of their struggle is gaining speed.

A mass of 6,000 workers winds through the streets, in a march sponsored by a coalition of radical unions. The workers jeer the government and wave banners promising, "From strike to strike we will triumph." Poor people slip out of their shacks to peek at the protest. Some bystanders smile and even wave. Union activists board city buses to politely ask passengers to contribute a few centavos. Many do.

Only three years ago, such a march would have been unthinkable. At that time, during the height of the civil war, the radical labor movement had been chased underground by the military and the political Right. More than 5,000 of its members and a full generation of its leaders had been killed, many by shadowy death squads, between 1978 and 1982.

But times are changing. The government is winning the war with U.S. assistance, and the Left is digging in for the long haul. The economy is in a mess, and real wages are declining. President José Napoleón Duarte is trying to open up the country's political system. Death squad activity has tailed off.

Given the opportunity to protest without suffering high casualties, the radical labor movement is back at the barricades, striking and protesting in a way unseen since the 1970s.

[1] *Latin American Regional Reports,* Mexico and Central America, June 7, 1985, and *Latin American Weekly Report,* June 14, 1985.

[2] FENESTRAS, Washington DC, office listings of Human Rights violations against labor, as cited in *Central America Bulletin,* January 1986.

[3] *Central America Bulletin,* January 1986.

[4] Ibid.

So far this year, Marxist-oriented unions, which represent about half this country's 100,000 urban unionized workers, have led major protests at several key government agencies, plus in the textile, sugar and transportation industries. If the current level of activity continues, there will be about 200 strikes and work actions this year, double last year's total; nearly all involve radical groups. Some 20,000 workers marched in the streets of San Salvador for May Day this year, twice the number of 1984.

"We're invigorating the masses to develop the class struggle," says Carlos Zometa, 28 years old, a leader of the National Syndicalist Federation of Salvadoran Workers, a leading radical group. Like other leftist labor organizations, his isn't formally connected to the guerrillas, but it shares many of their goals, including the overthrow of the government and the eventual installation of a socialist regime.

Miguel Angel Parada, rector of the National University and a Marxist, says the strikes mean the nation is "entering a new phase of great agitation and mobilization." He adds: "Lenin said that even when a revolution suffers setbacks and people tire, the revolution can come back when the social contradictions are right."

The government sees it similarly. "It's the first stage of the new urban war," says Col. Rinaldo Golcher, director of the powerful Treasury Police. "It's also the first test to prove whether or not this democratic government will respond with the repressive methods of the past." Col. Golcher thinks the leftist unions want "to provoke us and cry repression." (At least eight labor leaders have been killed or have disappeared this year.)

President Duarte is responding firmly—partly to reassure the powerful political Right, which distrusts his moderate politics. When the left-wing Social Security Workers Union occupied 25 hospitals, seeking $50-a-month raises for its 6,000 members, he sent in the military to clear out the strikers. When state water workers went on strike in support of the social security workers, for the second water strike this year, the government fired top union leaders and activists.

"We're not trying to break the unions," says Atilio Vieytez, leader of Mr. Duarte's Christian Democratic party in the National Assembly. "But we're not going to give them a break either."

Marxist labor unions are as typically Central American as marimba music; they have challenged democracies and military dictatorships alike since the 1920s, when the Russian and Mexican revolutions were viewed by many workers as glorious labor victories. The banana workers union is a traditional center for leftist organizing in Costa Rica, a country that otherwise is strongly anticommunist. In Honduras, radical unions are the vanguard of the small opposition to the U.S. military presence there.

"In Honduras, El Salvador and Guatemala, radical unions have legitimized radical politics and organized protest," says Phil Shepherd, a professor at

Florida International University. "Radical unions have brought workers into the system and made organized workers power contenders."

El Salvador's radical labor movement seems to live nine lives. It was nearly wiped out by a ferocious government response to a failed 1932 peasant rebellion, but it made a comeback in the late 1950s under the guidance of the Communist Party. In the 1970s, with the communists on the wane, the radical unionists split with them and began joining peasant and student groups in "popular organizations" that eventually established ties to guerrilla groups.

The popular organizations disappeared in the last crackdown; but some union leaders joined the guerrillas, and a few now serve as guerrilla comandantes. Most of the radical unions are loosely aligned with the Moscow-controlled World Federation of Trade Unions.

Col. Carlos Reynaldo López Nuila, vice defense minister for public security, calls the renewed union activism "the most delicate problem we face today."

45. *Labor Woes for Duarte**

BY CHRIS NORTON

Chris Norton was the El Salvador correspondent for In These Times, *an independent socialist newspaper published in Chicago. In early 1985 he filed a report on the situation in El Salvador in which he stated that unemployment is officially calculated at 36 percent. When combined with those underemployed, the total is more than 60 percent. Actual levels, he wrote, are probably higher.*

By any standard, these are appalling statistics. President Duarte, he wrote, was "in a Catch 22—he can't have an economic reactivation until he ends the war, which eats up 50 percent of the budget. Yet until he improves economic conditions for broad sectors of the population, he can't remove the war's causes." [1] *This report, written four months later, makes clear that for Duarte, the situation has deteriorated.*

A WAVE of public sector strikes is revealing a critical weakness of President Napoleón Duarte's regime—the disintegration of his social base as he delivers austerity to the working class while making concessions to the private sector and the military.

The striking unions are not leftist, demonstrating the widespread frustration with the Duarte government's failure to improve the economy. As *In These Times* went to press, the Ministries of Agriculture, Public Works and Tourism were all paralyzed. A strike by San Salvador municipal workers has cut off the

* From *In These Times,* November 27–December 10, 1985.
[1.] *In These Times,* July 10–23, 1985.

city's meat supply and is stopping burials in the city cemetery, which has not been struck since 1947. "Some of these municipal unions are among the most passive and conservative, but they're angry now," said a Salvadoran journalist. "They're not scared of the government's threats."

Finance Ministry workers stopped work for 19 days, ending their strike November 8 after the government had been forced to concede a generalized wage hike to all public workers—a 130–150 *colones* raise equal to a $21 monthly raise on salaries averaging around $150 a month, according to the black-market rate of six *colones* to the dollar. The First of May Committee, which groups together leftists and centrist unions, gave the Finance Ministry workers important support with a widespread solidarity strike on September 28 affecting the Education Ministry, the telephone company, social security, the national lottery, the post office, the pension institute and various of the nationalized banks.

At first the government took a hard line, threatening to fine and fire striking workers, but quickly backed down and granted the pay hike and a Christmas bonus of almost $90. The government itself provoked strikes in two vital services—the post office and the government-run telephone company—by arresting the head of the postal workers union as a subversive and also arresting two sons of a telephone union leader in connection with the kidnapping of Col. Omar Avalos, the head of Civil Aeronautics. In addition to freeing their leader, the postal strikers also asked for the firing of postal officials they claimed were corrupt and who owed their positions to militancy in the Christian Democratic Party, as well as the nullification of the recently passed Decree 162 that allows the government to move public employees to different ministries. Decree 162 is a move by the Christian Democrats to consolidate their hold over the governmental bureaucracy, and will likely be used against non-PDC employees and union activists.

The postal strike ended November 12 after the government released the union leader and agreed to fire the corrupt officials. The telephone workers strike continued at press time, although the government presented a video of the two sons admitting to being members of the armed wing of the Communist Party, the Liberation Armed Forces (FAL), and participating in the colonel's kidnapping. Confessions are being extracted by security forces after days of sleep deprivation, beatings, threats and sometimes torture.

At the same time as the sons and a third young man were being presented on television, the FMLN formally took responsibility for the colonel's capture on Radio Venceremos, the guerrillas' short-wave radio. They accused him of bombing the civilian population as a combat pilot and of being an agent for the CIA, since he was allegedly recruited during Air Force training in the U.S. Avalos was the head of the Presidential Guard under Presidents Magaña and Duarte and is a close friend of Duarte. Still, he is considered by some to be a military hardliner.

The CIA-linked head of the Hacienda Police, Col. Rinaldo Golcher, recently arrested many supposed FAL members, apparently in retaliation for the Avalos kidnapping. Observers, however, see some of the arrests as ill-advised because of the strikes they provoked. Still, the arrests may restrict the harder line the military has forced the government to take in the aftermath of freeing the guerrillas for Duarte's daughter.

Héctor Bernabe Recinos, perhaps El Salvador's best known unionist, recently returned to El Salvador for the first time since his October 15, 1984, release after four years in prison. He attended the convention of the leftist union federation, FENASTRAS, of which he is secretary general. (Recinos headed the electrical workers union and was imprisoned after the union cut off electricity throughout the country in 1980. The government militarized the electrical plants and abolished the union.) After the convention, Recinos left the country. Yet many observers consider his brief return and the high-profile meeting as significant steps for left-wing unions—a testing of the political waters.

Yet aside from their one-day solidarity strike in support of the Finance Ministry, the left unions have been relatively quiet. However, a conference of agricultural and urban workers is in the planning stages and some see strikes by left unions and peasant associations on the horizon. Strikes by agricultural workers could help win higher salaries, especially if supported by guerrilla highway stoppages.

But so far, the current strikes "are more an indication of the errors of the Christian Democrats than inroads of the FMLN," said an academic analyst who requested anonymity. "Duarte started with the benefit of the doubt—internationally and nationally—but he had little leeway to make mistakes, and he's making them one after the other, especially with the working class."

"He's using the easy scapegoat of 'Marxist destabilization' to ignore the legitimate complaints of workers with fixed incomes," the analyst continued. (Public sector wages were frozen in December 1980 and since then there has been only one increase—forced in the spring of 1984 by a wave of public sector strikes.) "At the same time, he's handing it over with a heavy spoon to the private sector. The Christian Democrats are destabilizing themselves."

Despite the Duarte government's constant concessions, the private sector hasn't been won over completely. Conservative business groups such as the Chamber of Commerce and Industry are urging the government to take a hard line with the unions, saying the strikes are heading El Salvador toward "anarchy and chaos." ARENA front groups are criticizing Duarte's handling of his daughter's kidnapping and reprinting newspaper columns calling for his resignation.

The kidnapping's upshot, according to the analyst, is that "Duarte will be forced to abandon monopoly of the executive branch of government. He will have to make concessions to business and to the parties to his right."

"Duarte seems to be out of touch with the grassroots," said a diplomat who also requested anonymity. "You can cope with the guerrillas, but if you allow your power base to erode, you have nothing."

Duarte's union power base never was very strong, consisting mainly of union leaders who sold themselves either to the Christian Democrats or to the U.S. American Institute for Free Labor Development or both. Now, with a sharpening of the economic crisis and the left unions' resurgence, pressure on union leaders is mounting. But the rank and file are unlikely to follow them unless they adopt more militant positions.

Yet Duarte, instead of trying to rebuild his working-class base, seems more intent in playing the role of the good U.S. ally in the region, with his anti-Nicaraguan pronouncements and his denunciations of "terrorism." He asks unions to tighten their belts because of the country's current economic crisis and he warns them not to become allies of the "two extremes" who are trying to destabilize the government.

"But the crisis is caused by the war," said centrist union leader Miguel Angel Vasquez, head of the CTS, whose Ministries of Agriculture and Public Works are on strike. "Yet they [the government] prefer to buy more and more guns. Hunger is the greatest terrorist. It makes people violent."

CHAPTER IX

U.S. Policy and the Civil War in El Salvador: The Decision to Intervene

Editors' Introduction

In 1981, the civil war in El Salvador seemed ideal as a setting for reasserting U.S. muscle on behalf of a Third World anti-Communist regime imperiled by a mass-based, Marxist-Leninist guerrilla movement. El Salvador's location in our own geographic backyard and traditional zone of influence appeared to make a policy of military assistance—including U.S. military personnel as advisers—to the government in San Salvador as salable to the U.S. public and Congress as it was logistically simple. Geographically, as well as psychologically and politically, El Salvador was no distant Vietnam or Iran, two countries in which dictatorships friendly to the United States had been *allowed* to fall—or so the new Reagan administration argued. The setting in El Salvador more closely resembled the situation in Nicaragua, also in our backyard, before the victory of the Sandinista-led revolution in 1979. This time, the Reagan team would not permit, as the Carter administration had, another "loss" in Central America.[1]

[1.] See the editors' introduction to chapter 1. The foreign policy of the Reagan administration has been called "Reassertionism." See *U.S. Foreign Policy and the Third World: Agenda 1985–86,* edited by John W. Sewell, Richard E. Feinberg, and Valeriana Kallab (published as "U.S.-Third World Policy Perspectives No. 3" for the Overseas Development Council by Transaction Books, Rutgers, New Jersey, 1985). Another designation is the "Reagan Doctrine"—see the defense of it by the columnist credited with devising the term, Charles Krauthammer, "The Poverty of

A suitable political public relations campaign was mounted by Washington to justify a policy of military intervention, short of U.S. combat troops, to support the military-civilian junta in El Salvador. For those who considered Carter policies too soft and utopian in a world governed by the harsh laws of *Realpolitik* (Carter had placed human rights at the top of his foreign-policy priorities), President Reagan's new Ambassador to the United Nations, Jeane Kirkpatrick, had provided just the right kind of ideological tonic, the tough-minded arguments that purported to prove that supporting tyrannies of the right was preferable to the risk of totalitarianism on the left. For those needing less contorted exposition, Secretary of State Alexander Haig did his best to inflame fears of aggressive Soviet intentions in Central America. As U.S. military assistance and counterinsurgency specialists were readied for El Salvador, Washington marshaled dubious evidence of a Soviet-Cuban master plot in a celebrated White Paper, "Communist Interference in El Salvador."[2]

Half a decade later, Washington's backing of the military-civilian junta and its successor, the Duarte regime, has probably been the most important factor in denying victory to the insurgents. Yet Reagan's campaign to win U.S. domestic opinion over to unqualified support for his policies continues to provoke opposition—from the U.S. public, especially from a "solidarity" movement reminiscent of the anti–Vietnam War campaign; from Congress; from the media; from friendly Latin American nations, especially the "Contadora" group of Mexico, Panama, Venezuela, and Colombia; and even from within the western alliance.

In an eloquent plea for understanding Third World revolutions, President François Mitterrand of France told a joint session of Congress that the "roots [of revolution] lie deep in the legacy of the past. Thus, the peoples of Central America have a long history marked by military oppression, social inequality and the confiscation of economic resources and political power by a few. Today, each of them must be allowed to find its own path toward greater

Realism," *The New Republic,* February 17, 1986. A convenient, if seriously flawed, analysis of the Sandinista revolution is Shirley Christian's *Nicaragua: Revolution in the Family* (New York, 1985). For a critical review that faults Christian for making a prosecution case against the Sandinistas without sufficient attention to the "grim record" of the Somoza dynasty they overthrew, see Robert E. White in *Commonweal,* November 1, 1985. For a more favorable review, see Ronald Radosh in *Partisan Review,* 53, No. 1, 1986. Radosh accepts Christian's view of the Sandinistas' hidden agenda to establish a Marxist-Leninist regime but questions whether a policy of overthrowing or subverting the Sandinistas follows.

2. For Kirkpatrick, see Readings 2 to 4. For Haig, see various statements in the first edition of this volume (New York: Grove Press, 1981). For the White Paper and its critics, see Readings 46 and 47. To the penetrating critique of the White Paper by James Petras and others should be added the report by Craig Pyes suggesting that Roberto D'Aubuisson was responsible for channeling to the U.S. State Department certain documents that formed the basis for the questionable conclusion that "the insurgency in El Salvador [is] a textbook case of indirect armed aggression by communist powers. . . ." See the section "D'Aubuisson Says He Recruited Uncle Sam for a Civil War," in the *Albuquerque Journal,* December 18–23, 1983.

justice, greater democracy and greater independence and must be allowed to do so without interference or manipulation."[3]

That Ambassador Kirkpatrick and Secretary Haig are no longer at their posts is no proof that the Reagan administration has abandoned the policies associated with their names, although the kind of rhetoric the two championed has few echoes in Washington today. (There is always Secretary of Defense Caspar Weinberger. Late in 1984, in connection with administration arguments that international law permitted the use of force against Nicaragua, he was reduced to invoking the Monroe Doctrine, something that Washington has rightly avoided for decades for fear of offending the sovereignty of Latin American nations.[4]) Widespread domestic criticism of U.S. interventionism, especially by a Congress that controls military purse strings, has led to more subtle strategies than exaggerated invocations of the Red Menace (translate: Soviet expansion). One such attempt was the mustering of a bipartisan commission chaired by Henry Kissinger, National Security Adviser and Secretary of State in the Nixon and Ford administrations, to devise some policy recommendations of the sort that would silence the critics.

To no one's surprise, the Kissinger Commission came up with some bland proposals midway between outright U.S. military intervention and outright U.S. noninterference in the Salvadoran civil war. The administration continued along this path, and critical voices were not stilled (see Readings 48 and 49).

Of greater surprise is U.S. behavior in other parts of the Third World. The Reagan administration has undertaken policies it once castigated the Carter government for espousing—criticizing, even getting rid of, friendly dictators for human-rights and other abuses. Early in 1986, two long-standing tyrannies saw their foundations shaken by popular movements. In the Philippines, U.S. ally Ferdinand E. Marcos was finally persuaded by Washington to hold elections in which his opposition would be allowed to campaign. Fraud and violence directed by Marcos's supporters were so apparent and his electoral "victory" so specious that even Washington urged him to leave office when mass protests raised the specter of civil war. In Haiti, Washington did not even bother to press "demonstration elections" on the hated dictatorship of Jean-Claude Duvalier, "Baby Doc," the son and heir to the throne ("President for Life") established by his father, the notorious "Papa Doc," François Duvalier, three decades ago. At the very end Washington not only refrained from helping him stay in power, but provided (as it later did for Marcos) the jet transport that took him out of the country into exile.[5]

[3.] See *New York Times*, March 23, 1984. Mitterrand's comments were, as the *Times* put it, "a polite but strong note of demurral" to President Reagan's remark earlier that week that the problem in Central America was "a power play by Cuba and the Soviet Union, pure and simple."

[4.] *New York Times*, November 13, 1984.

[5.] The Reagan administration faces two similar quandaries—having to withhold support from friendly dictatorships, or at least chastise them, because of political repression amid popular

In Africa, the Reagan administration has pursued contradictory policies that baffle many observers. On the one hand, covert assistance is approved to harass the Marxist government of Angola, similar to the aid that goes to the *contras* fighting the Sandinista government of Nicaragua. On the other hand, the administration, with the enthusiastic support of U.S. corporations, established warm relations with the Marxist government of Samora Machel in Mozambique.[6]

Small wonder, then, that over these and other issues, many of President Reagan's champions on the right, advocates of uncompromising hostility to Marxist governments and movements everywhere, see in administration policies a betrayal of their cause. Incensed especially by the failure to render all-out support for efforts to crush the Sandinistas in Nicaragua and the guerrillas of the FMLN in El Salvador, many conservatives have called for the resignation of Secretary of State Shultz. Burton Yale Pines, of the conservative Heritage Foundation, summed up the problem ruefully: "Much of the neoconservative analysis . . . is that the foreign policy premises which drove the United States in the 70's were flawed, and yet Ronald Reagan seems to be conducting foreign policy on those flawed premises." Those premises, he added, include the "false assumption fully developed under Jimmy Carter" that U.S. options in reacting to crises are extremely limited. "We are not some giant tied down by the Lilliputians," Pines said.[7]

What all of this suggests is that perhaps the Reagan administration, like its predecessors, must often realize that the application of great power and the grand theory or dogma behind it is inevitably frustrated by variable, complex circumstances—whether those presented by the Soviet Union or by the unceasing restlessness of the Third World. If Pines had in mind movements and nations in the Third World when he referred to "Lilliputians," his conclusion was wrong: The giant *can* be tied down—the power of nationalism and the thirst for independence based on social and economic justice are a mighty force that can resist and challenge superior military strength, as both the U.S. and the Soviet Union have discovered in the recent past and as the European imperial powers learned earlier.[8]

opposition—in Chile and South Korea. The ironies of Reagan foreign policy in the Third World (does Reagan resemble a Jimmy Carter in wolf's clothing?) are pointed out by Jefferson Morley in "What Jimmy Knew," *The New Republic,* July 29, 1985.

[6.] "What's the political difference between Nicaragua and Mozambique?" asked the *Washington Post* archly. "Not much—except that we're propping up the regime in Mozambique." See Michael Isikoff, "Sometimes We Help Keep Marxists in Power," *Washington Post* national weekly edition, June 24, 1985. The almost politically surrealistic paradoxes of the situation in Angola, where Cuban troops protect U.S. oil interests against a former Maoist strongman, Jonas Savimbi, who is supported by the U.S. and South Africa, are summarized in "Upside Down in Angola," by Michael Massing, *The New Republic,* March 3, 1986.

[7.] For the campaign against Shultz, see *New York Times,* July 28, 1985. Pines's comments are in ibid., July 12, 1985.

[8.] The bloody and still unsuccessful attempt to pacify Afghanistan by the Soviet Union is the most prominent example from the side of the noncapitalist powers. Earlier, the U.S.S.R. saw its

Second, contrary to what Mr. Reagan's critics on the right assert, his administration does employ the big stick; U.S.-supported force *is* being applied in Central America and elsewhere, as noted in the introduction to chapter 1. The size of the stick is the real issue agitating the conservatives and neoconservatives. What seems to be shaping up in Reagan policies throughout the Third World is a consistent pattern of what Pentagon analysts call "low-intensity conflict," or L.I.C., a strategy of limited use of force against the left in the Third World—Cambodia, Afghanistan, Angola, and Central America are current examples.[9] In Central America, the policy operates in two different forms with a single anti-left objective—in Nicaragua force is directed against the Sandinista government through instruments dubbed by Washington "freedom fighters" (the *contras,* or counterrevolutionaries); in El Salvador force is directed toward preserving the Duarte government against the insurrectionary threat of the FMLN.

The L.I.C. strategy has dangers and opportunities. The dangers emanate from the ever-present possibility of escalation as the limited force continues to fail. In Nicaragua, the *contras* have yet to seize a single town and have only aroused the Nicaraguan people to close ranks with the Sandinistas despite the latter's economic failings and often heavyhanded attempts to stifle dissent. In El Salvador, limited force has propped up the Duarte regime, but the props are extremely fragile and continuously unsettled by a weakening economy, by the persistence of death-squad and other terror, and by the absence of substantive agrarian reform. Among the guerrillas, meanwhile, the resolution to wage a long war of attrition stiffens with the arrival of every U.S. helicopter gunship (see chapters 5 to 8).

Escalation of U.S. military efforts may delight Mr. Reagan's conservative critics. But it can only inaugurate war without end, a war, moreover, that could engulf the entire region and convert it into a zone of East-West conflict. Surely, this is the lesson of the history of our misguided involvement in Vietnam. Vietnam, too, it should be remembered, was once an arena of "low-intensity conflict" (see Reading 52).

But the opportunities suggested by the relatively small scale of U.S. military intervention in Central America are no less significant than the dangers. So long as the intervention remains limited, the way out through negotiation, compromise, and diplomacy remains clear.

influence in Egypt and Somalia summarily curtailed. A revision of Moscow's strategies is seen by Jerry Hough, who argues that "despite the Reagan administration's incessant alarms, Soviet intervention in the Third World has declined in recent years." "The Revolutionary Road Runs Out," *The Nation,* June 1, 1985. See his *The Struggle for the Third World: Soviet Debates and American Options* (Washington: The Brookings Institution, 1985).

[9.] See Michael T. Klare, "The New Strategic Doctrine," *The Nation,* December 28, 1985.

46. "Communist Interference in El Salvador": The U.S. State Department White Paper*

As early as 1681, according to the authoritative Oxford English Dictionary, *official governmental reports in Great Britain were known as "White Papers." Along with much other political nomenclature and practice, the preparation of such reports became part of the political tradition of the United States. During the period of the Vietnam War, the U.S. government issued two notable White Papers on that fateful Indochina conflict—* A Threat to the Peace: North Vietnam's Efforts to Conquer South Vietnam *(U.S. Department of State Publication 7308, December 1961); and* Aggression from the North: The Record of North Vietnam's Campaign to Conquer South Vietnam *(U.S. Department of State Publication 7839, February 1965). These White Papers share at least one important feature with this comparable State Department publication on El Salvador: the fervent, even obsessive attempt to link local insurgency with some nefarious outside conspiracy.*

SUMMARY. This special report presents definitive evidence of the clandestine military support given by the Soviet Union, Cuba, and their Communist allies to Marxist-Leninist guerrillas now fighting to overthrow the established government of El Salvador. The evidence, drawn from captured guerrilla documents and war matériel and corroborated by intelligence reports, underscores the central role played by Cuba and other Communist countries beginning in 1979 in the political unification, military direction, and arming of insurgent forces in El Salvador.

From the documents it is possible to reconstruct chronologically the key stages in the growth of the Communist involvement:

- The direct tutelary role played by Fidel Castro and the Cuban government in late 1979 and early 1980 in bringing the diverse Salvadoran guerrilla factions into a unified front.
- The assistance and advice given the guerrillas in planning their military operations.
- The series of contacts between Salvadoran Communist leaders and key officials of several Communist states that resulted in commitments to supply the insurgents with nearly 800 tons of the most modern weapons and equipment.
- The covert delivery to El Salvador of nearly 200 tons of those arms, mostly

* United States Department of State, Special Report No. 80 (February 23, 1981).

through Cuba and Nicaragua, in preparation for the guerrillas' failed "general offensive" of January 1981.

- The major Communist effort to "cover" their involvement by providing mostly arms of Western manufacture.

It is clear that over the past year the insurgency in El Salvador has been progressively transformed into another case of indirect armed aggression against a small Third World country by Communist powers acting through Cuba.

The United States considers it of great importance that the American people and the world community be aware of the gravity of the actions of Cuba, the Soviet Union, and other Communist states who are carrying out what is clearly shown to be a well-coordinated, covert effort to bring about the overthrow of El Salvador's established government and to impose in its place a Communist regime with no popular support.

I. A CASE OF COMMUNIST MILITARY INVOLVEMENT IN THE THIRD WORLD

The situation in El Salvador presents a strikingly familiar case of Soviet, Cuban, and other Communist military involvement in a politically troubled Third World country. By providing arms, training, and direction to a local insurgency and by supporting it with a global propaganda campaign, the Communists have intensified and widened the conflict, greatly increased the suffering of the Salvadoran people, and deceived much of the world about the true nature of the revolution. Their objective in El Salvador as elsewhere is to bring about—at little cost to themselves—the overthrow of the established government and the imposition of a Communist regime in defiance of the will of the Salvadoran people.

The Guerrillas: Their Tactics and Propaganda. El Salvador's extreme left, which includes the long-established Communist Party of El Salvador (PCES) and several armed groups of more recent origin, has become increasingly committed since 1976 to a military solution. A campaign of terrorism—bombings, assassinations, kidnappings, and seizures of embassies—has disrupted national life and claimed the lives of many innocent people.

During 1980, previously fragmented factions of the extreme left agreed to coordinate their actions in support of a joint military battle plan developed with Cuban assistance. As a precondition for large scale Cuban aid, Salvadoran guerrilla leaders, meeting in Havana in May, formed first the Unified Revolutionary Directorate (DRU) as their central executive arm for political and military planning and, in late 1980, the Farabundo Martí People's Liberation Front (FMLN), as the coordinating body of the guerrilla organizations. A front organization, the Revolutionary Democratic Front (FDR), was also created to disseminate propaganda abroad. For appearances' sake, three small non-Marxist-Leninist political parties were brought into the front, though they have no representation in the DRU.

The Salvadoran guerrillas, speaking through the FDR, have managed to deceive many about what is happening in El Salvador. They have been aided by Nicaragua and by the worldwide propaganda networks of Cuba, the Soviet Union, and other Communist countries.

The guerrillas' propaganda aims at legitimizing their violence and concealing the Communist aid that makes it possible. Other key aims are to discredit the Salvadoran government, to misrepresent U.S. policies and actions, and to foster the impression of overwhelming popular support for the revolutionary movement.

Examples of the more extreme claims of their propaganda apparatus—echoed by Cuban, Soviet, and Nicaraguan media—are:

- That the United States has military bases and several hundred troops in El Salvador (in fact, the United States has no bases and fewer than 50 military personnel there).
- That the government's security forces were responsible for most of the 10,000 killings that occurred in 1980 (in their own reports in 1980, the guerrillas themselves claimed the killings of nearly 6,000 persons including, noncombatant "informers" as well as government authorities and military).

In addition to media propaganda, Cuba and the Soviet Union promote the insurgent cause at international forums, with individual governments, and among foreign opinion leaders. Cuba has an efficient network for introducing and promoting representatives of the Salvadoran left all over the World. Havana and Moscow also bring indirect pressure on some governments to support the Salvadoran revolutionaries by mobilizing local Communist groups.

II. COMMUNIST MILITARY INTERVENTION: A CHRONOLOGY

Before September 1980 the diverse guerrilla groups in El Salvador were ill-coordinated and ill-equipped, armed with pistols and a varied assortment of hunting rifles and shotguns. At that time the insurgents acquired weapons predominantly through purchases on the international market and from dealers who participated in the supply of arms to the Sandinistas in Nicaragua.

By January 1981 when the guerrillas launched their "general offensive," they had acquired an impressive array of modern weapons and supporting equipment never before used in El Salvador by either the insurgents or the military. Belgian FAL rifles, German G-3 rifles, U.S. M-1, M-16, and AR-15 semiautomatic and automatic rifles, and the Israeli UZI submachinegun and Galil assault rifle have all been confirmed in the guerrilla inventory. In addition, they are known to possess .30 to .50 caliber machineguns, the U.S. M-60 machinegun, U.S. and Russian hand grenades, the U.S. M-79 and Chinese RPG grenade launchers, and the U.S. M-72 light antitank weapon and 81 mm mortars. Captured ammunition indicates the guerrillas probably possess 60mm and 82mm mortars and 57mm and 75mm recoilless rifles.

Recently acquired evidence has enabled us to reconstruct the central role played by Cuba, other Communist countries, and several radical states in the political unification and military direction of insurgent forces in El Salvador and in equipping them in less than 6 months with a panoply of modern weapons that enabled the guerrillas to launch a well-armed offensive.

This information, which we consider incontrovertible, has been acquired over the past year. Many key details, however, have fallen into place as the result of the guerrillas' own records. Two particularly important document caches were recovered from the Communist Party of El Salvador in November 1980 and from the Peoples' Revolutionary Army (ERP) in January 1981. This mass of captured documents included battle plans, letters, and reports of meetings and travels, some written in cryptic language and using code words.

When deciphered and verified against evidence from other intelligence sources, the documents bring to light the chain of events leading to the guerrillas' January 1981 offensive. What emerges is a highly disturbing pattern of parallel and coordinated action by a number of Communist and some radical countries bent on imposing a military solution.

The Cuban and Communist role in preparing for and helping to organize the abortive "general offensive" early this year is spelled out in the following chronology based on the contents of captured documents and other sources.

Initial Steps. The chronology of external support begins at the end of 1979. With salutations of "brotherly and revolutionary greetings" on December 16, 1979, members of the Communist Party of El Salvador (PCES), National Resistance (FARN), and Popular Liberation Forces (FPL) thank Fidel Castro in a letter for his help and "the help of your party comrades . . . by signing an agreement which establishes very solid bases upon which we begin building coordination and unity of our organizations." The letter, written in Havana, was signed by leaders of these three revolutionary organizations.

At the April 1980 meeting at the Hungarian Embassy in Mexico City, guerrilla leaders made certain "requests" (possibly for arms). Present at this meeting were representatives of the German Democratic Republic, Bulgaria, Poland, Vietnam, Hungary, Cuba, and the Soviet Union.

In notes taken during an April 28, 1980 meeting of the Salvadoran Communist Party, party leader Shafik Handal mentions the need to "speed up reorganization and put the party on a war footing." He added, "I'm in agreement with taking advantage of the possibilities of assistance from the socialist camp. I think that their attitude is magnificent. We are not yet taking advantage of it." In reference to a unification of the armed movement, he asserts that "the idea of involving everyone in the area has already been suggested to Fidel himself." Handal alludes to the concept of unification and notes, "Fidel thought well of the idea."

Guerrilla Contacts in Havana. From May 5 to June 8, 1980, Salvadoran guerrilla leaders report on meetings in Honduras, Guatemala, Costa Rica, and Nicaragua. They proceed to Havana and meet several times with Fidel Castro; the documents also note an interview with the German Democratic Republic (G.D.R.) Chairman Erich Honecker in Havana. During the Havana portion of their travels, the Salvadoran guerrilla leadership meets twice with the Cuban Directorate of Special Operations (DOE, the clandestine operations/special forces unit of the Cuban Ministry of Interior) to discuss guerrilla military plans. In addition, they meet with the Cuban "Chief of Communications."

During this period (late May 1980), the Popular Revolutionary Army (ERP) is admitted into the guerrilla coalition after negotiations in Havana. The coalition then assumes the name of the Unified Revolutionary Directorate (DRU) and meets with Fidel Castro on three occasions.

After the Havana meetings, Shafik Handal leaves Havana on May 30, 1980 for Moscow. The other Salvadoran guerrilla leaders in Havana leave for Managua. During the visit of early June, the DRU leaders meet with Nicaraguan revolutionary leaders (Sandinistas) and discuss: (1) a headquarters with "all measures of security"; (2) an "international field of operations, which they (Sandinistas) control"; and (3) the willingness of the Sandinistas to "contribute in material terms" and to adopt "the cause of El Salvador as its own." The meeting culminated with "dinner at Humberto's house" (presumably Sandinista leader Humberto Ortega).

Salvadoran Communist Party Leader's Travels in the East. From June 2 to July 22, 1980, Shafik Handal visits the U.S.S.R., Vietnam, the German Democratic Republic, Czechoslovakia, Bulgaria, Hungary, and Ethiopia to procure arms and seek support for the movement.

On June 2, 1980, Handal meets in Moscow with Mikhail Kudachkin, Deputy Chief of the Latin American Section of the Foreign Relations Department of the CPSU Central Committee. Kudachkin suggests that Handel travel to Vietnam to seek arms and offers to pay for Handal's trip.

Continuing his travels between June 9 and 15, Handal visits Vietnam where he is received by Le Duan, Secretary General of the Vietnamese Communist Party; Xuan Thuy, member of the Communist Party Central Committee Secretariat; and Vice Minister of National Defense Tran Van Quang. The Vietnamese, as a "first contribution," agree to provide 60 tons of arms. Handal adds that "the comrade requested air transport from the USSR."

From June 19 to June 24, 1980, Handal visits the German Democratic Republic (G.D.R.), where he is received by Hermann Axen, member of the

G.D.R. Politburo. Axen states that the G.D.R. has already sent 1.9 tons of supplies to Managua. On July 21, G.D.R. leader Honecker writes the G.D.R. Embassy in Moscow that additional supplies will be sent and that the German Democratic Republic will provide military training, particularly in clandestine operations. The G.D.R. telegram adds that although Berlin possesses no Western-manufactured weapons—which the Salvadoran guerrillas are seeking—efforts will be undertaken to find a "solution to this problem." (NOTE: The emphasis on Western arms reflects the desire to maintain plausible denial.)

From June 24–27, 1980, Handal visits Czechoslovakia, where he is received by Vasil Bilak, Second Secretary of the Czech Communist Party. Bilak says that some Czech arms circulating in the world market will be provided so that these arms will not be traced back to Czechoslovakia as the donor country. Transportation will be coordinated with the German Democratic Republic.

Handal proceeds to Bulgaria from June 27 to June 30, 1980. He is received by Dimitir Stanichev, member of the Central Committee Secretariat. The Bulgarians agree to supply German-origin weapons and other supplies, again in an apparent effort to conceal their sources.

In Hungary, from June 30 to July 3, 1980, Handal is received by Communist Party General Secretary Janos Kadar and "Guesel" (probably Central Committee Secretary for Foreign Affairs Andras Gyenes). The latter offers radios and other supplies and indicates Hungarian willingness to trade arms with Ethiopia or Angola in order to obtain Western-origin arms for the Salvadoran guerrillas. "Guesel" promises to resolve the trade with the Ethiopians and Angolans himself, "since we want to be a part of providing this aid." Additionally, Handal secures the promise of 10,000 uniforms to be made by the Hungarians according to Handal's specifications.

Handal then travels to Ethiopia, July 3 to July 6. He meets Chairman Mengistu and receives "a warm reception." Mengistu offers "several thousand weapons," including: 150 Thompson submachineguns with 300 cartridge clips, 1,500 M-1 rifles, 1,000 M-14 rifles, and ammunition for these weapons. In addition, the Ethiopians agree to supply all necessary spare parts for these arms.

Handal returns to Moscow on July 22, 1980 and is received again by Mikhail Kudachkin. The Soviet official asks if 30 Communist youth currently studying in the U.S.S.R. could take part in the war in El Salvador. Before leaving Moscow, Handal receives assurances that the Soviets agree in principle to transport the Vietnamese arms.[1]

[1.] Handal categorically rejected the State Department's charges of an arms agreement between him and Soviet-bloc countries, and countercharged that the White Paper "is a maneuver to justify the growing supply of U.S. arms and military personnel to the genocidal Christian Democratic military junta and prepare the ground for an eventual military aggression in Central America." See *New York Times,* February 27, 1981, for Handal's full statement. Another Salvadoran insurgent leader reported to a Latin American correspondent of the Paris newspaper *Le Monde:* "If

Further Contacts in Nicaragua. On July 13, representatives of the DRU arrive in Managua amidst preparations for the first anniversary celebration of Somoza's overthrow. The DRU leaders wait until July 23 to meet with "Comrade Bayardo" (presumably Bayardo Arce, member of the Sandinista Directorate). They complain that the Sandinistas appear to be restricting their access to visiting world dignitaries and demanding that all contacts be cleared through them. During the meeting. Arce promises ammunition to the guerrillas and arranges a meeting for them with the Sandinista "Military Commission." Arce indicates that, since the guerrillas will receive some arms manufactured by the Communist countries, the Sandinista Army (EPS) will consider absorbing some of these weapons and providing to the Salvadorans Western-manufactured arms held by the EPS in exchange. (In January 1981 the Popular Sandinista Army indeed switched from using U.S.-made weapons to those of Soviet and East European origin.)

The DRU representatives also meet with visiting Palestine Liberation Organization (PLO) leader Yasir Arafat in Managua on July 22, 1980. Arafat promises military equipment, including arms and aircraft. (A Salvadoran guerrilla leader met with FATAH leaders in Beirut in August and November, and the PLO has trained selected Salvadorans in the Near East and in Nicaragua.)

On July 27, the guerrilla General Staff delegation departs from Managua for Havana, where Cuban "specialists" add final touches to the military plans formulated during the May meetings in Havana.

Arms Deliveries Begin. In mid-August 1980, Shafik Handal's arms-shopping expedition begins to bear fruit. On August 15, 1980, Ethiopian arms depart for Cuba. Three weeks later the 60 tons of captured U.S. arms sent from Vietnam are scheduled to arrive in Cuba.

As a result of a Salvadoran delegation's trip to Iraq earlier in the year, the guerrillas receive a $500,000 logistics donation. The funds are distributed to the Sandinistas in Nicaragua and within El Salvador.

By mid-September, substantial quantities of the arms promised to Handal are well on the way to Cuba and Nicaragua. The guerrilla logistics coordinator in Nicaragua informs his Joint General Staff on September 26 that 130 tons of arms and other military material supplied by the Communist countries have arrived in Nicaragua for shipment to El Salvador. According to the captured documents, this represents one-sixth of the commitments to the guerrillas by the Communist countries. (NOTE: To get an idea of the magnitude of this commitment, the Vietnamese offer of only 60 tons included 2 million rifle and machinegun bullets, 14,500 mortar shells, 1,620 rifles, 210 machineguns, 48 mortars, 12 rocket launchers, and 192 pistols.)

we only had half the weapons the enemy attributes to us, we'd have no trouble overrunning several of its barracks and grabbing the matériel the Salvadoran army is receiving from the United States by plane and boat (via the Panama Canal)." Francis Pisani, "Where El Salvador's Guerrillas Get Arms," *Manchester Guardian Weekly* (March, 8, 1981). —Eds.

In September and October, the number of flights to Nicaragua from Cuba increased sharply. These flights had the capacity to transport several hundred tons of cargo.

At the end of September, despite appeals from the guerrillas, the Sandinistas suspend their weapons deliveries to El Salvador for 1 month, after the U.S. government lodges a protest to Nicaragua on the arms trafficking.

When the shipments resume in October, as much as 120 tons of weapons and matériel are still in Nicaragua and some 300–400 tons are in Cuba. Because of the difficulty of moving such large quantities overland, Nicaragua —with Cuban support—begins airlifting arms from Nicaragua into El Salvador. In November, about 2.5 tons of arms are delivered by air before accidents force a brief halt in the airlift.

In December, Salvadoran guerrillas, encouraged by Cuba, begin plans for a general offensive in early 1981. To provide the increased support necessary, the Sandinistas revive the airlift into El Salvador. Salvadoran insurgents protest that they cannot absorb the increased flow of arms, but guerrilla liaison members in Managua urge them to increase their efforts as several East European nations are providing unprecedented assistance.

A revolutionary radio station—*Radio Liberación*—operating in Nicaragua begins broadcasting to El Salvador on December 15, 1980. It exhorts the populace to mount a massive insurrection against the government. (References to the Sandinistas sharing the expenses of a revolutionary radio station appear in the captured documents.)

On January 24, 1981 a Cessna from Nicaragua crashes on takeoff in El Salvador after unloading passengers and possibly weapons. A second plane is strafed by the Salvadoran Air Force, and the pilot and numerous weapons are captured. The pilot admits to being an employee of the Nicaraguan national airline and concedes that the flight originated from Sandino International Airport in Managua. He further admits to flying two earlier arms deliveries.

Air supply is playing a key role, but infiltrations by land and sea also continue. Small launches operating out of several Nicaraguan Pacific ports traverse the Gulf of Fonseca at night, carrying arms, ammunition, and personnel. During the general offensive on January 13, several dozen well-armed guerrillas landed on El Salvador's southeastern coast on the Gulf of Fonseca, adjacent to Nicaragua.

Overland arms shipments also continue through Honduras from Nicaragua and Costa Rica. In late January, Honduras security forces uncover an arms infiltration operation run by Salvadorans working through Nicaragua and directed by Cubans. In this operation, a trailer truck is discovered carrying weapons and ammunition destined for Salvadoran guerrillas. Weapons include 100 U.S. M-16 rifles and 81mm mortar ammunition. These arms are a portion of the Vietnamese shipment: A trace of the M-16s reveals that several of them were shipped to U.S. units in Vietnam where they were captured or left behind.

Using this network, perhaps five truckloads of arms may have reached the Salvadoran guerrillas.

The availability of weapons and matériel significantly increases the military capabilities of the Salvadoran insurgents. While attacks raged throughout the country during the "general offensive" that began on January 10, it soon became clear that the DRU could not sustain the level of violence without suffering costly losses in personnel. By the end of January, DRU leaders apparently decided to avoid direct confrontation with government forces and reverted to sporadic guerrilla terrorist tactics that would reduce the possibility of suffering heavy casualties.

III. THE GOVERNMENT:
THE SEARCH FOR ORDER AND DEMOCRACY

Central America's smallest and most densely populated country is El Salvador. Since its independence in 1821, the country has experienced chronic political instability and repression, widespread poverty, and concentration of wealth and power in the hands of a few families. Although considerable economic progress took place in the 1960s, the political system remained in the hands of a traditional economic elite backed by the military. During the 1970s, both the legitimate grievances of the poor and landless and the growing aspirations of the expanding middle classes met increasingly with repression. El Salvador has long been a violent country with political, economic, and personal disputes often resulting in murders.

The Present Government. Aware of the need for change and alarmed by the prospect of Nicaragua-like chaos, progressive Salvadoran military officers and civilians overthrew the authoritarian regime of General Carlos Humberto Romero in October 1979 and ousted nearly 100 conservative senior officers.

After an initial period of instability, the new government stabilized around a coalition that includes military participants in the October 1979 coup, the Christian Democratic Party, and independent civilians. Since March 1980, this coalition has begun broad social changes: conversion of large estates into peasant cooperatives, distribution of land to tenant farmers, and nationalization of foreign trade and banking.

Four Marxist-Leninist guerrilla groups are using violence and terrorism against the Salvadoran government and its reforms. Three small non-Marxist-Leninist political parties—including a Social Democratic Party—work with guerrilla organizations and their political fronts through the Democratic Revolutionary Front (FDR), most of whose activities take place outside El Salvador.

The government of El Salvador—headed since last December by José Napoleón Duarte, the respected Christian Democrat denied office by the military in the Presidential elections of 1972—faces armed opposition from the extreme right as well as from the left. Exploiting their traditional ties to the security forces and the tendency of some members of the security forces to abuse their authority, some wealthy Salvadorans affected by the Duarte government's reforms have sponsored terrorist activities against supporters of the agrarian and banking reforms and against the government itself.

A symbiotic relationship has developed between the terrorism practiced by extremists of both left and right. Thousands have died without regard for class, creed, nationality, or politics. Brutal and still unexplained murders in December of four American churchwomen—and in January of two American trade unionists—added U.S. citizens to the toll of this tragic violence. The United States has made clear its interest in a complete investigation of these killings and the punishment of those responsible.

Despite bitter resistance from right and left, the Duarte government has stuck to its reform programs and has adopted emergency measures to ease the lot of the poor through public works, housing projects, and aid to marginal communities. On the political front, it has offered amnesty to its opponents, scheduled elections for a constituent assembly in 1982, and pledged to hand power over to a popularly elected government no later than mid-1983.

The government's pursuit of progress with order has been further hampered by the virtual breakdown of the law enforcement and judicial system and by the lack of an effective civil service.

The introduction of the reforms—some of which are now clearly irreversible —has reduced popular support for those who argue that change can only come about through violence. Few Salvadorans participate in antigovernment demonstrations. Repeated calls by the guerrillas for general strikes in mid- and late 1980 went unheeded. The Duarte government, moreover, has made clear its willingness to negotiate the terms of future political processes with democratic members of all opposition forces—most notably, by accepting the offer of El Salvador's Council of Bishops to mediate between the government and the Democratic Revolutionary Front.

In sum, the Duarte government is working hard and with some success to deal with the serious political, and economic problems that most concern the people of El Salvador.

U.S. Support. In its commitment to reform and democracy, the government of El Salvador has had the political support of the United States ever since the October 1979 revolution. Because we give primary emphasis to helping the people of El Salvador, most of our assistance has been economic. In 1980, the United States provided nearly $56 million in aid, aimed at easing the conditions that underlie unrest and extremism. The assistance has helped create jobs, feed the hungry, improve health and housing and education, and support the reforms that are opening and modernizing El Salvador's economy. The United States will continue to work with the Salvadoran government toward economic betterment, social justice, and peace.

Because the solution in El Salvador should be of the Salvadorans' own making and nonviolent, the United States has carefully limited its military support. In January, mounting evidence of Communist involvement compelled President Carter to authorize a resupply of weapons and ammunition to El Salvador—the first provision of lethal items since 1977.

IV. SOME CONCLUSIONS

The foregoing record leaves little doubt that the Salvadoran insurgency has become the object of a large-scale commitment by Communist states outside Latin America.

- The political direction, organization, and arming of the insurgency is coordinated and heavily influenced by Cuba—with active support of the Soviet Union, East Germany, Vietnam, and other Communist states.
- The massing and delivery of arms to the Salvadoran guerrillas by those states must be judged against the fact that from 1977 until January 1981 the United States provided no weapons or ammunition to the Salvadoran armed forces.
- A major effort has been made to provide "cover" of this operation by supplying arms of Western manufacture and by supporting a front organization known as the Democratic Revolutionary Front to seek non-Communist political support through propaganda.
- Although some non-Communist states have also provided material support, the organization and delivery of this assistance, like the overwhelming mass of arms, are in the hands of Communist-controlled networks.

In short, over the past year, the insurgency in El Salvador has been progressively transformed into a textbook case of indirect armed aggression by Communist powers through Cuba.

47. Blots on the White Paper: The Reinvention of the "Red Menace"*

BY JAMES PETRAS

During the Vietnam War, responsible journalists such as I. F. Stone refused to take government pronouncements at face value. Stone in particular subjected the 1965 Vietnam White Paper, Aggression from the North, *to withering analysis in* I. F. Stone's

* The Nation (New York; March 28, 1981), 353, 367–372, by permission.

Weekly *(March 8, 1965), reprinted in Marvin E. Gettleman, ed.,* Vietnam *(1965, 1970). In a similar spirit, Latin American expert James Petras subjects the 1981 El Salvador White Paper to close scrutiny in this reading. Professor of Sociology at the State University of New York, Binghamton, Petras is the author of several books on Latin American society and politics and was a member of the international People's Tribunal on El Salvador that met in Mexico City in February 1981.*

THE State Department's white paper entitled *Communist Interference in El Salvador*[1] purports to provide evidence demonstrating:

(1) "the central role played by Cuba and other Communist countries . . . in the political unification, military direction and arming of insurgent forces in El Salvador";

(2) that "the insurgency in El Salvador has been progressively transformed into another case of indirect armed aggression against a small Third World country by Communist powers acting through Cuba"; and

(3) that "Cuba, the Soviet Union and other Communist states . . . are carrying out what is clearly shown to be a well-coordinated, covert effort to bring about the overthrow of El Salvador's established government and to impose in its place a Communist regime with no popular support."

The white paper fails to provide a convincing case for any of those propositions. On the contrary, its evidence is flimsy, circumstantial or nonexistent; the reasoning and logic is slipshod and internally inconsistent; it assumes what needs to be proven; and, finally, what facts are presented refute the very case the State Department is attempting to demonstrate. The document, in a word, has the aura of a political frame-up in which inconvenient facts are overlooked and innuendoes and unwarranted inferences are made at crucial points in the argument. In demonstrating this, I will follow the format of the white paper, discussing the sections in order, under their original titles, and making cross-references to material in other sections where it is warranted; for example, when the authors contradict themselves.

I. A CASE OF COMMUNIST MILITARY INVOLVEMENT IN THE THIRD WORLD

The first technique that is employed in the white paper is to conflate what is happening in El Salvador with other alleged examples of Soviet and Cuban military involvement. The political opposition is reduced to a group of extreme leftist guerrillas manipulated by Cuba and in turn manipulating "small, non-Marxist-Leninist parties" in order to deceive public opinion. Opposition activity is labeled terrorist. Journalists who describe the U.S.-backed regime's behavior as terrorist are labeled as witting or unwitting dupes of an orchestrated Communist propaganda effort.

[1] See Reading 46. —Eds.

What is most striking about this description of the opposition to the junta government is the complete absence of even a minimal account of the numerous social, political and civic movements that have developed in El Salvador over the past decade, which represent a wide range of political views and social strata. This collective omission on the part of the State Department is necessary if one is bent upon labeling the opposition as Soviet-Cuban manipulated and if one wishes to reduce the conflict to an East-West military confrontation.

The fact of the matter is that over the last decade an enormously rich variety of social organizations have emerged in El Salvador, embracing the great majority of professional and technical workers, peasants, labor and business people. Their membership is in the hundreds of thousands and they are an integral part of the main political opposition group, the Revolutionary Democratic Front (F.D.R.). Almost all union members, peasant associations, university and professional people are members or supporters of social and civic organizations that are sympathetic to the front. The white paper clearly falsifies the political and social realities by excluding an account of the social forces involved with the opposition. Moreover, the origins of the opposition are clearly rooted in the social realities of the country—a point which the document admits in Section III in a politically vague and unspecified fashion when it notes that: "during the 1970's, both the legitimate grievances of the poor and landless and the growing aspirations of the expanding middle classes met increasingly with repression."

What the paper fails to acknowledge is that these "legitimate grievances" and "growing aspirations" found expression and were embodied in the mass organizations which are the essential components of the opposition groups that make up the F.D.R. The guerrilla movement is part and parcel of a larger political and social movement that has been and is repressed. Its activities stem from social realities of Salvadoran history, which the paper concedes is one of "repression, widespread poverty and concentration of wealth and power in the hands of a few families." Because it is intent on demonstrating that the problem is Soviet-Cuban intervention, the paper fails to examine the crucial relationship between the repressive nature of the state, social inequalities and the growth of opposition and guerrilla movements.

The "Non-Marxist" Opposition. The striking feature of the Salvadoran revolution is the broad array of political forces that have united to oppose this regime—Christian Democrats, Social Democrats and Liberal Democrats, as well as independent Marxist groups and pro-Moscow coalitions. What is particularly unique in the Salvadoran case is the substantial leadership and its popular base of support that has developed among Christian communities. In all areas of social and political organization, a plurality of political tendencies are represented—among peasants, workers, professionals and so on. The attempt by the white paper to reduce the opposition to a handful of Marxist guerrillas manipulating the "non-Marxists" is a crude oversimplification and gross distortion of reality. What is remarkable in the document is the systematic exclusion of any mention of the mass-based Christian opposition, the twenty-eight Christian priests, nuns and community leaders murdered by the regime for their opposition activities. A discussion of these facts would complicate the State Department's job of selling intervention to the U.S. public.

In describing the emergence of the guerrilla forces, the document downgrades accounts of repressive political conditions under the junta. Yet detailed descriptions are available from the Organization of American States, the United Nations and, most comprehensively, from the Legal Aid Commission of the office of the Archbishop of El Salvador, which has compiled a lengthy dossier of the regime's systematic violence against all legal public organizations opposed to it in any way. Churches, trade unions, independent newspapers and peasant co-ops have been assaulted and bombed, leaving almost 9,000 dead between January 1980 and January 1981. The precondition for the growth of guerrilla activity was the closing of political channels by the U.S.-backed regime—not Soviet intervention.

Shortly after the first junta was established in October 1979, and before the rightist military took over, the guerrillas and political opposition groups offered a cease-fire. The rightists in the armed forces responded by escalating the number of assassinations, which touched off renewed hostilities. The decision to seek a military-political solution was forced upon the opposition by the military regime when it murdered Archbishop Oscar Romero on March 24, 1980, and then the six leaders of the F.D.R. meeting in San Salvador on November 27, 1980. The subsequent purge of the moderate Christian Democrats and reformist military officers from the first government junta is further proof that political options had been taken away. The white paper overlooks this context of regime violence in order to invent a Cuban-inspired conspiracy and to impute the violence of the regime to its victims. The killings by the military regimes increased from 147 in 1978 to 580 between January and October of 1979 and to 8,952 between January 1980 and January 1981. This increasing reign of terror clearly was instrumental in lowering the rate of popular participation in public activity and swelling the numbers of clandestine groups. Oblivious to this reality, the white paper describes the increase in guerrilla activity as a willful act of the "extreme left."

In its attempt to cast doubt on the opposition's legitimacy, the paper omits any mention of centrist defections from the U.S.-backed junta to join the leadership of the Revolutionary Democratic Front. The shift of a significant body of centrist opinion to the opposition is described disparagingly in the following fashion: "For appearances' sake, three small non-Marxist-Leninist political parties were brought into the front, though they have no representation in the D.R.U. [Unified Revolutionary Directorate]." These former Christian and Social Democratic allies of the U.S.-backed coalition had been described by U.S. officials a few weeks earlier as major political forces representing significant reform-minded sectors of Salvadoran public opinion. The fact that the pro-Moscow Communist Party of El Salvador is a marginal political force in the opposition coalition is never discussed by the white paper, nor is the fact that three of the four major leftist groups are critical of the Soviet Union.

Moreover, the paper's charge that Fidel Castro was responsible for unifying the left overlooks the fact that the unity of the leftist forces was under way prior to December 1979 as a result of increasing repression by the regime and pressure from the rank and file of all the groups. The F.D.R. was formed in El Salvador, not in Cuba, and was supported and promoted by European social-democratic forces. It was certainly not a product of the alleged machinations of Castro. As the participants stated at the time, the needs of the popular struggle, the limited options open to all opposition groups and the example set by the success of the Nicaraguan revolution were the main impulsions to unity.

Conspiratorial Hypothesis. The effort by the white paper to discredit the F.D.R. by describing it as a "front" disseminating propaganda for the guerrillas systematically ignores the popular support that these groups draw away from the junta, the internal political debates within the front and between the front and the guerrillas and the influence they have had in shaping the program in a reformist direction. The white paper's conspiratorial view requires that its authors overlook the importance of these moderates and their internal and external influence. The paper says nothing about the widespread international support for the front and the isolation of the junta. Indeed, it expands its conspiratorial hypothesis to find Cuban and Soviet-sponsored deception behind the front's success.

The numerous and detailed accounts of repression by the regime compiled by the Archbishop's Legal Aid Commission which have swayed world public opinion are not mentioned; nor are Amnesty International's publicized accounts of widespread systematic torture. In place of careful consideration of these documents, the white paper labels the 10,000 deaths attributed to the junta (13,000 by the time the paper appeared) an "extreme claim" of the guerrilla propaganda apparatus, which is parroted by the Cuban, Soviet and Nicaraguan media. Actually, the principal source of data collected on the regime's repression is non-Communist, Catholic and respected by most non-U.S. government sources. In summary, through omissions and distortions, through labeling and simplification, the white paper early on fabricates a case against a broad-based popular revolutionary movement in order to prove "Communist military involvement."

II. COMMUNIST MILITARY INTERVENTION: A CHRONOLOGY

This section is the longest and most convoluted. It is also the section that is supposedly based on secret documents purporting to demonstrate Soviet-Cuban intervention and direction in El Salvador. We have no way of authenticating the documents nor the particular quotations which are cited.[2] Nevertheless, even in the terms in which the documents are presented, there is serious doubt that they make the case the white paper claims, despite the self-serving assertions by the authors that the evidence is "incontrovertible."

In the first section, the white paper describes the revolutionaries prior to September of 1980 as "diverse guerrilla groups . . . ill-coordinated and ill-equipped, armed with pistols and a varied assortment of hunting rifles and shotguns." In effect, the document affirms that up to a few months ago, the guerrilla movement consisted of local forces employing their own resources and forging their own programs with no outside support, let alone control. The subsequent aid then is directed toward a leadership and organization that has been shaped by organizational and political experiences rooted in many years of independent activity. It is highly unlikely that such groups would suddenly submit themselves to foreign tutelage or be subject to foreign manipulation. The initial document which purports to "demonstrate" Cuban involvement is a letter of salutation from the guerrillas to Castro thanking him for help. There is no mention of arms, political direction or military coordination; rather, the emphasis is on the need for Salvadoran groups to build and coordinate their activities among themselves. The next reference is to a meeting of guerrillas at the Hungarian Embassy in Mexico City at which the word "requests" was apparently mentioned. Without any rhyme or reason, the white paper extracts the word and appends a parenthesis: "(possibly for arms)." To this gratuitous appended parenthesis is added a list of the Eastern European ambassadors present, presumably to suggest a neo-Comintern conclave.

Alleged Soviet Help. Inadvertently, however, a document cited by the white paper does demonstrate the *absence* of pro-Soviet forces within the actual

---

[2.] For a skeptical analysis of these documents and the white-paper arguments they purport to substantiate, see Robert G. Kaiser's article in the *Washington Post,* June 9, 1981. The white paper, writes Kaiser, "contains factual errors, misleading statements and unresolved ambiguities that raise questions about the administration's interpretation of participation by communist countries in the Salvadoran civil war." Similar skepticism was expressed by *Wall Street Journal* staff reporter Jonathan Kwitny in his article "Tarnished Report?" June 8, 1981. The article was based on a three-hour interview with the principal author of the white paper, 37-year-old Jon D. Glassman, a U.S. Foreign Service officer with a Ph.D. in Soviet studies. Glassman conceded that parts of the report were "misleading" and "overembellished" and that it included a number of "mistakes" and examples of "guessing." He also acknowledged misattribution of a number of key documents upholding the white paper's main thesis of outside military support for the Salvadoran guerrillas. "We completely screwed it up," Glassman admitted to Kwitny. Apparently skeptical himself of some of the documentation, Glassman submitted the material to the U.S. Central Intelligence Agency with the question " 'Did you fabricate any of the documents, or is there any indication they were fabricated by anyone else?' And the answer was no to both." Glassman still held that the white paper was, according to a later State Department briefing, "an accurate and honest description of the development of communist support for the Salvadoran insurgency" and that the very shortcomings of the documents on which it was based testify somehow to its truthfulness. —Eds.

guerrilla struggle. It quotes Shafik Handal, secretary general of the Salvadoran Communist Party, as mentioning the need to "speed up reorganization and put the party on a war footing." As late as April 28, 1980, the Salvadoran Communist Party is not yet prepared to engage in the ongoing guerrilla struggle. Then the white paper quotes Handal as saying, "I'm in agreement with taking advantage of the possibilities of assistance from the socialist camp. . . . We are not yet taking advantage of it." From this we can deduce incontrovertibly that, the socialist camp was not involved at all up to then in El Salvador; that any assistance was a "possibility"; and that the overriding concern of the Salvadoran Communist Party was how to use the "socialist camp." This is hardly the attitude of a docile tool of Moscow conspirators.

Finally, regarding unification of the left, Handal mentions that "the idea for involving everyone in the area has already been suggested to Fidel himself. . . . Fidel thought well of the idea." In other words, the idea of unifying the left did not even initiate with Castro; it came from the Salvadorans and Castro merely granted his approval.

What the white paper fails to mention in all its accounts of guerrilla and leftist meetings with the Communists are the frequent contacts among all the opposition groups—including centrist Social Democrats and Christian Democrats—and their political counterparts in other countries, from Stockholm to Mexico City, from Washington, D.C., to Bonn. Requests for aid and support were laid before U.S. State Department officials and European Social Democrats. Outside the United States these ideas have, at least in part, met with favorable responses. Europeans favor a "Zimbabwe solution" in El Salvador —unifying the opposition and working for a center-left regime. The white paper's attempt to attribute this idea to secret Communist cabals is willful ignorance. The paper's selective discussion of meetings between guerrillas and Communists and its omission of meetings by other opposition forces in the European and Latin American left is a tactic more appropriate to a lawyer's brief.

Handal is also supposed to have visited Nicaragua to hold discussions about setting up an office there from which to disseminate propaganda and make political contacts. Such overtures from dissidents in one country to officials in another are commonplace the world over. In this case, the possibility was merely *discussed*—which would seem to be within the bounds of propriety for officials of a sovereign government.

Handal's Travels. The heavy stuff is still to come. The next itinerary for the peripatetic Handal is listed as "travels in the East." During his stop in Moscow, supposedly in search of arms, Handal, we are told, met with a Soviet official. This official merely suggested that Handal travel to Vietnam and offered to pay for his trip. (The white paper's sources apparently could not determine if it was one way or round trip.)

The white paper goes on to claim that in Vietnam Handal gained concrete support—sixty tons of arms. The East Germans told him they would put out a search for available arms, as did the Czechs, Bulgarians, Hungarians and Ethiopians. Lieutenant Colonel Mengistu, chairman of Ethiopia's Provisional Military Administrative Council, we are told, promised "several thousand weapons." The white paper adds that the Russians asked if they could send thirty student volunteers to take part in the "war," and agreed to ship the Vietnamese arms. Eventually, even the Palestine Liberation Organization and Nicaragua pledged arms. According to the white paper, a total of 780 tons of arms were to be transported to Nicaragua via Cuba, and then to El Salvador. By September 26, there were supposedly 130 tons of arms cached in Nicaragua. The paper claims that "in September and October the number of flights to Nicaragua from Cuba increased sharply. These flights had the capacity to transport several hundred tons of cargo."

Yet we learn that at the end of September the Sandinistas "suspend their weapons deliveries to El Salvador for one month. . . . When the shipments resume in October, as much as 120 tons of weapons and matériel are still in Nicaragua and some 300–400 tons are in Cuba." There are curious discrepancies in this account. For example, we are told that there were 130 tons of arms in Nicaragua by September 26. We are also informed that shipments to El Salvador were "suspended" for one month at the end of September but the flights from Cuba continued through October. Yet when the shipments resumed in October "as much as 120 tons of weapons and matériel are still in Nicaragua. . . ." Since no weapons were going to El Salvador and presumably loaded planes were continuing to arrive from Cuba, it seems odd, to say the least, that at the end of the one month's suspension, Nicaragua had a net loss of ten tons of arms in its stores for shipment. Apparently, the white paper's several authors didn't bother to coordinate their stories.

Swamped with Arms. After reporting that only about 2.5 tons were shipped in November, the white paper authors step up the pace dramatically. In December, we are told, there was such a deluge of arms that the Salvadoran insurgents complained that they could not absorb them. Yet earlier in the white paper we were told how poorly armed the 4,000 to 5,000 guerrillas were in September 1980 ("ill-coordinated and ill-equipped, armed with pistols and a varied assortment of hunting rifles and shotguns"). Is it conceivable that within a few weeks in December the guerrillas were inundated with arms? What is more, the flood mysteriously turned into a drought, because in the March 1 *New York Times* the guerrilla leaders are said to be complaining that they do not have an adequate supply of arms, a shortage that hindered their January offensive.

During this period of supposedly massively flowing arms, no specific figures are ever given, nor is there any detailed explanation of how so many (undisclosed) arms flowed into El Salvador. There are only references to a Cessna that crashed, and it is *speculated* that it had arms ("unloaded passengers and possibly weapons"). A second plane strays into government hands, and "numerous weapons are captured." We are told of shipments in motor launches and overland, but there is no evidence that any of these were captured, even though the roads and seaways are easily policed and at least some large shipments should have been intercepted. But the security forces' total bag is one trailer truck carrying 100 U.S. rifles and some mortars. The Honduras-El Salvador border is heavily patrolled, and needless to say the roads that would be passable by trucks loaded with arms are closely watched. The paucity of evidence suggests that the arms flow is minimal; thus, the claims of massive outside intervention are unsubstantiated. The failure of the guerrilla offensive in January was in part the result of inadequate armaments coupled with massive infusions of U.S. arms to the regime's forces. Even junta spokesman José Napoleón Duarte and former U.S. Ambassador Robert White (who originally promoted the story of a massive weapons influx) would question the need for further U.S. arms.

The white paper's evidence of outside Communist arms shipments supports only a small fraction of its claims. Such shipments as there were did not approach the flow of weapons, advisers, napalm, helicopter gunships and the like to the military-civilian dictatorship from the United States.

III. THE GOVERNMENT: THE SEARCH FOR ORDER AND DEMOCRACY

The massive propaganda efforts to focus attention on outside Communist intervention is a way of diverting attention from the repressive regime that the United States is supporting. The Reagan administration's tactic is to win backing for the junta not because of what it stands for (few democratic governments would support a government whose army has killed 13,000 civilians) but to "draw the line" against "outside intervention."

In its opening section the white paper claims that El Salvador experienced "considerable economic progress" during the 1960s, "although . . . the political system remained in the hands of a traditional economic elite backed by the military." The facts are that between 1961 and 1975 the proportion of landless laborers rose from 11 percent to 40 percent; the level of unemployment climbed from 10 percent in 1960 to 25 percent in 1979. Whatever economic progress took place did not benefit the workers and the peasants. Rather, the growth of El Salvador's gross national product was intimately tied to its repressive system. Prosperity for some was matched by the repression of the many. The white paper notes that the "legitimate grievances of the poor and landless and the growing aspirations of the expanding middle classes met increasingly with repression." The paper does not go on to identify the organizations and leaders which come to express these "legitimate grievances" and middle-class "aspirations" because they are not found in the current junta but among the opposition. Moreover, these aspirations and grievances are not answered by the military measures and repressive forms of rulership undertaken by the current regime. The document's systematic evasion of the sources of violence and the U.S. Government's responsibility is revealed in its attempt to blame it on everyone: "El Salvador has long been a violent country."

In fact, El Salvador has not been a violent country—its U.S.-backed oligarchical-military regimes have been violent, killing 30,000 people in 1932 and running the country with an iron fist ever since. Between 1946 and 1979, the United States has provided Salvadoran military dictatorships with more than $17 million in military assistance and trained 2,000 military officers while providing the ruling oligarchy with $157.7 million in economic aid.

The "Progressive" Coalition. The white paper describes the governing coalition that took over after the coup in October 1979 as being made up of progressive civilian and military officers. Yet the great majority of these progressives defected to the F.D.R. or were killed by the rightist faction which is now in control. The "three small non-Marxist-Leninist political parties" that the white paper earlier dismisses as window-dressing in the F.D.R. leadership are later portrayed as significant progressives when they were in the first coalition. The white paper's inconsistency is apparent in the way it attempts to reclaim the progressive character of the original junta while discrediting the genuine progressives who resigned from it in protest or were pushed out. The systematic purge of the progressives by the rightist faction within the junta between October 1979 and March 1980 is described in the same vacuous, euphemistic language that is used throughout the white paper when the authors wish to cover their tracks: "After an initial period of instability, the new government stabilized around a coalition that includes military participants in the October 1979 coup, the Christian Democratic Party and independent civilians." The white paper leaves out the purge of the Majano reformists, and the bulk of the Christian Democrats who are now in opposition, along with the university faculty and students. It does not say that ultra-right forces deeply involved in repressive actions are all that remain of the original junta that took power in October 1979.

The white paper claims that "since March 1980, this coalition has begun broad social changes." Actually, the number of peasants killed and co-ops that fell under military occupation rose sharply: peasants killed increased from 126 per month in February, to 203 in March, to 423 in July, totaling 3,272 for the glorious year of agrarian reform! The paper then repeats the falsehood that the opposition to this "reform" consists of Marxist-Leninist guerrilla terrorists and the three significant non-Marxist-Leninist political parties operating outside of the country. Once again, the authors omit mention of the absence of any political rights in El Salvador, and the state of war that the junta has declared against all opposition.

Extremist Symbiosis. The white paper then proceeds to argue that the government "faces armed opposition from the extreme right as well as from the left. . . . A symbiotic relationship has developed between the terrorism practiced by extremists of both left and right." This notion has been systematically refuted by the Archbishop's Legal Aid Commission report on repression, which adduces evidence showing that in 1980, 66 percent of the assassinations were committed by government security forces, and 14 percent were committed by right-wing death squads. Moreover, voluminous testimony, documents and photographs have emerged to substantiate the frequent and close collaboration between the death squads and the regime's security forces. The "symbiosis" causing most of the violence is between the regime and the death squads, not the right and left.

In this regard it is important to note that not one right-wing death squad assassin has ever been apprehended, let alone prosecuted, despite the public nature of most of the killings. This in itself should dispel any notion that the regime is innocent in the activity of the death squads. The Legal Aid Commission study further demonstrates that the bulk of victims were poor peasants, students and wage workers—the groups in whose names the purported reforms were carried out. In fact the reforms were mere facades for the militarization of the country. The escalation of regime terror against the peasants is the surest indication of this.

The white paper voices concern about the murder and rape of the U.S. nuns, but it fails to mention the fact that the nuns were opposed to U.S. policy, and were murdered by the junta along with more than a score of other church people working for the poor. While the white paper claims to be interested in a complete investigation of these killings, former Ambassador White stated emphatically that Washington has not made any effort to pressure the junta and has effectively collaborated with the regime in covering up the murders —rewarding its perpetrators with additional arms and economic aid.

In one of its more cynical statements, the paper notes that "few Salvadorans participate in anti-government demonstrations"—implying that they support the government. The scores of dead protesters, including mutilated and decapitated corpses that appeared in the wake of every protest march, have no doubt had a dampening effect on demonstrations. But to equate a terrorized population with one that approves the government is a grotesque distortion which only indicates how out of touch this administration is with the political reality in El Salvador and the rest of the Third World. There is not only an absence of all forms of political protest in El Salvador, there is an absence of all forms of political expression; the dictatorship is total. The support for the front and the guerrillas has not diminished—it has gone underground. The white paper's claim that U.S. aid "has helped create jobs and feed the hungry" is belied by the accounts of church sources. U.S. economic aid has contributed to massive military corruption; military aid hardens the resolve of the military dictators and increases the rate of killing. U.S. economic aid does not keep up with the massive flight of private capital estimated at more than $1.5 billion during the past year. The collapse of the Salvadoran economy and the massive exodus of refugees from repression in rural areas hardly testifies to the "success" of what the paper describes as the "Duarte government." The latter is a figment of the State Department's imagination, for real power continues to be vested within the military. . . .

Conclusion. The white paper is a thin tissue of falsifications, distortions, omissions and simplifications directed toward covering up increased U.S. support for a murderous regime. It has sought to transform a war between the regime and its people into an East-West struggle and to deny the internal socioeconomic and political roots of the struggle. The purpose of these distortions is to mobilize U.S. public opinion behind the new administration's policies not only in El Salvador but throughout the Third World. The hypocrisy suffusing the white paper is vice's tribute to virtue, for it tacitly recognizes that if the truth were presented, the American people would balk at supporting a regime that is rewarded for killing its noblest sons and daughters who seek social justice in El Salvador.

48. The White House Searches for a Consensus: The Kissinger Report*

BY HENRY KISSINGER, ET AL.

The Report of the President's National Bipartisan Commission on Central America, which quickly became known as the Kissinger Report from the name of the commission's chair, Henry A. Kissinger, Secretary of State in the Nixon and Ford administrations, was the effort of a group created by presidential order in 1983. The commission was charged with studying "the nature of United States interests in the Central American region and the threats now posed to those interests" and with providing advice on formulating "a long-term United States policy that will best respond to the challenges of social, economic, and democratic development in the region, and to internal and external threats to its security and stability" (Executive Order 12433 of July 19, 1983). In the words of one observer, the Reagan administration "hoped the Kissinger commission would decrease congressional criticism and provide a bipartisan framework for future strategy along essentially the same lines it had been pursuing"—that is, seeking the destruction of the

* Excerpts from *Report of the National Bipartisan Commission on Central America,* January 1984, U.S. Government Printing Office, Washington, D.C. An appendix to the report, including staff documents, papers by consultants, and selected testimony (often critical of the assumptions on which the commission was to base its conclusions), is also available (U.S. Government Printing Office, March 1984). The report was also published in 1984 by Macmillan Publishing Company, New York.

Sandinista regime in Nicaragua and the defeat of the guerrillas in El Salvador. See Barry Rubin, "Reagan Administration Policymaking and Central America," in Robert S. Leiken, ed., Central America: Anatomy of Conflict (New York: Pergamon, 1984).

WHAT WE LEARNED

- First, the tortured history of Central America is such that neither the military nor the political nor the economic nor the social aspects of the crisis can be considered independently of the others. Unless rapid progress can be made on the political, economic and social fronts, peace on the military front will be elusive and would be fragile. But unless the externally supported insurgencies are checked and the violence curbed, progress on those other fronts will be elusive and would be fragile.

- Second, the roots of the crisis are both indigenous and foreign. Discontents are real, and for much of the population conditions of life are miserable; just as Nicaragua was ripe for revolution, so the conditions that invite revolution are present elsewhere in the region as well. But these conditions have been exploited by hostile outside forces—specifically, by Cuba, backed by the Soviet Union and now operating through Nicaragua—which will turn any revolution they capture into a totalitarian state, threatening the region and robbing the people of their hopes for liberty.

- Third, indigenous reform, even indigenous revolution, is not a security threat to the United States. But the intrusion of aggressive outside powers exploiting local grievances to expand their own political influence and military control is a serious threat to the United States, and to the entire hemisphere.

- Fourth, we have a humanitarian interest in alleviating misery and helping the people of Central America meet their social and economic needs, and together with the other nations of the hemisphere we have a national interest in strengthening democratic institutions wherever in the hemisphere they are weak.

- Fifth, Central America needs help, both material and moral, governmental and nongovernmental. Both the commands of conscience and calculations of our own national interest require that we give that help.

- Sixth, ultimately, a solution of Central America's problems will depend on the Central Americans themselves. They need our help, but our help alone will not be enough. Internal reforms, outside assistance, bootstrap efforts, changed economic policies—all are necessary, and all must be coordinated. And other nations with the capacity to do so not only in this hemisphere, but in Europe and Asia, should join in the effort.

- Seventh, the crisis will not wait. There is no time to lose. . . .

U.S. INTERESTS IN THE CRISIS

When strategic interests conflict with moral interests, the clash presents one of the classic challenges to confront societies and statesman. But in Central America today, our strategic and moral interests coincide. We shall deal later in the report with the specifics of those interests. But in broad terms they must include:

- To preserve the moral authority of the United States. To be perceived by others as a nation that does what is right *because* it is right is one of this country's principal assets.
- To improve the living conditions of the people of Central America. They are neighbors. Their human need is tinder waiting to be ignited. And if it is, the conflagration could threaten the entire hemisphere.
- To advance the cause of democracy, broadly defined, within the hemisphere.
- To strengthen the hemispheric system by strengthening what is now, in both economic and social terms, one of its weakest links.
- To promote peaceful change in Central America while resisting the violation of democracy by force and terrorism.
- To prevent hostile forces from seizing and expanding control in a strategically vital area of the Western Hemisphere.
- To bar the Soviet Union from consolidating either directly or through Cuba a hostile foothold on the American continents in order to advance its strategic purposes.

In short, the crisis in Central America is of large and acute concern to the United States because Central America is our near neighbor and a strategic crossroads of global significance; because Cuba and the Soviet Union are investing heavily in efforts to expand their footholds there, so as to carry out designs for the hemisphere distinctly hostile to U.S. interests; and because the people of Central America are sorely beset and urgently need our help. . . .

As Nicaragua is already doing, additional Marxist-Leninist regimes in Central America could be expected to expand their armed forces, bring in large numbers of Cuban and other Soviet bloc advisers, develop sophisticated agencies of internal repression and external subversion, and sharpen polarizations, both within individual countries and regionally. This would almost surely produce refugees, perhaps millions of them, many of whom would seek entry into the United States. Even setting aside the broader strategic considerations, the United States cannot isolate itself from the regional turmoil. The crisis is on our doorstep.

Beyond the issue of U.S. security interests in the Central American-Caribbean region, our credibility worldwide is engaged. The triumph of hostile forces in what the Soviets call the "strategic rear" of the United States would be read as a sign of U.S. impotence.

Thus, even in terms of the direct national security interests of the United States, this country has large stakes in the present conflict in Central America. They include preventing:

- A series of developments which might require us to devote large resources to defend the southern approaches to the United States, thus reducing our capacity to defend our interests elsewhere.
- A potentially serious threat to our shipping lanes through the Caribbean.
- A proliferation of Marxist-Leninist states that would increase violence, dislocation, and political repression in the region.
- The erosion of our power to influence events worldwide that would flow from the perception that we were unable to influence vital events close to home.

THE PROBLEMS OF GUERRILLA WAR

Despite these high stakes, the debate over Central America has been polarized in the United States. One reason may be the seeming paradox in which important security questions are raised by small conflicts in an area which we have customarily neglected.

On the one hand, the territories involved are not large, and neither is the number of soldiers, policemen, and insurgents active in each country. The current amounts of U.S. military assistance are also not significant by global standards. In the last fiscal year, for example, U.S. military aid to all countries in Central America combined amounted to $121.3 million, or 3 percent of U.S. military assistance worldwide.

On the other hand, there is the extreme intricacy of the struggles. They proceed concurrently in the realms of internal politics, regional diplomacy, and the global East-West competition, including worldwide propaganda; they comprise both guerrilla and terrorist phenomena as well as more conventional confrontations among armed forces; and they are governed by very complicated interactions between violence in all its forms and the political, social, and economic circumstances of each country.

Thus what is being tested is not so much the ability of the United States to provide large resources but rather the realism of our political attitudes, the harmony of Congressional and Administration priorities, and the adaptability of the military and civil departments of the Executive. What is more, Central American realities often clash with our historical experience and with the disparity between our resources and those of the threatened countries.

The fundamental dilemma is as follows: both the national interests of the United States and a genuine concern for the longterm welfare of Central America create powerful incentives to provide all necessary assistance to defeat totalitarian guerrillas. At the same time one of the principal objectives of the guerrilla forces is to destroy the morale and efficiency of the government's administration and programs.

We thus labor under an immediate handicap. Unlike the Soviet Union in Afghanistan, the U.S. cannot—and should not—impose its own administration, even for such laudable objectives as implementing political, social and economic reforms; it cannot place its own experts in each village and town to gather political intelligence; and it cannot supervise the conduct of each soldier and policeman in all dealings with the population. For all these goals, the U.S. Government must rely on the abilities and good faith of the government under attack.

But that government—already fragile because of history and structure and conflicting attitudes—is being systematically weakened further by the conditions of guerrilla warfare in which it must function.

Much attention has been paid—correctly—to the shortcomings of the El Salvador government. But it is important—and only fair—to recall the many demands that have been made upon it and the progress that has been made in many fields. It carried out impressive elections in 1982, despite severe intimidations by the guerrillas, and will conduct another one this March. It has been going forward with an extensive land reform program. It allows debate, freedom of assembly, opposition and other aspects of democracy, however imperfect. Albeit belatedly and due to U.S. pressure, it is beginning to address the problem of right-wing violence. It has made offers to the insurgents to resolve the conflict through the political process. All of this has been done in the midst of a bitter war. It is a record that compares very favorably with El Salvador's past and with that of its neighbor, Nicaragua.

There is, of course, a darker side as well in El Salvador. The United States obviously cannot accept, let alone support, the brutal methods practiced by certain reactionary forces in Central America. Some of these actions are related to counter-insurgency. Their common denominator is the systematic use of mass reprisals and selective killing and torture to dissuade the civil population from participating in the insurgency or from providing any help for the insurgents. Historically, such reprisals, along with the static guard of key installations and the occasional ambush of betrayed insurgent bands, have often proved capable of preserving colonial rule and unpopular governments for a very long time, even centuries. Other violence has in fact nothing to do with insurgency at all. It is designed to terrorize opponents, fight democracy, protect entrenched interests, and restore reactionary regimes.

Whatever their aims, these methods are totally repugnant to the values of the United States. Much more enlightened counter-insurgency models were pursued in, for example, Venezuela and Colombia in the 1960's when military action was combined with positive economic and political measures. The methods of counter-insurgency developed over the last generation by the armed forces of the United States are consistent with such models. They depend upon gaining the confidence and support of the people and specifically exclude the use of violence against innocent civilians.

Yet these methods are expensive. In addition to continued action on the economic and social fronts, they require two forms of military action, to be carried out by two distinct types of forces. First, local popular militias must be formed throughout the country (with whatever minimal training is feasible and with only the simplest weapons) to prevent the insurgents from using terror to extract obedience. These must include members trained as paramedics to deliver basic health care, which evokes strong local support for these forces. Since this localized protective militia cannot be expected to resist any sustained guerrilla attack, U.S. counter-insurgency methods also require the availability of well-trained and well-equipped regular forces in adequate numbers. These methods assume that the regular units will be provided with efficient communications and suitable transport, notably helicopters, to enable them to provide prompt help for village militias under attack, and to allow them to pursue guerrilla bands on the move.

The present level of U.S. military assistance to El Salvador is far too low to enable the armed forces of El Salvador to use these modern methods of counter-insurgency effectively. At the same time, the tendency in some quarters of the Salvadoran military towards brutality magnifies Congressional and Executive pressures for further cuts in aid. A vicious cycle results in which violence and denial of human rights spawn reductions in aid, and reductions in aid make more difficult the pursuit of an enlightened counter-insurgency effort.

The combination of the tactical guidance given by U.S. advisers and levels of aid inadequate to support that advice creates a potentially disastrous disparity between U.S. military tactics and Salvadoran military resources. U.S. tactical doctrine abjures static defense and teaches constant patrolling. But this requires the provision of expensive equipment such as helicopters. In their absence, the Salvadoran military abandon their static defenses for intensive foot patrolling, only to find the strategic objective they had been guarding destroyed in their absence.

In the Commission's view it is imperative to settle on a level of aid related to the operational requirements of a humane anti-guerrilla strategy and to stick with it for the requisite period of time.

Another obstacle to the effective pursuit of anti-guerrilla strategy is a provision of current U.S. law under which no assistance can be provided to law enforcement agencies. This dates back to a previous period when it was believed that such aid was sometimes helping groups guilty of serious human rights abuses. The purpose of the legislation was to prevent the United States and its personnel from being associated with unacceptable practices. That concern is valid, but, however laudable its intentions, the blanket legal prohibition against the provision of training and aid to police organizations has the paradoxical effect, in certain cases, of inhibiting our efforts to improve human rights performance. For example, while it is now understood in the Salvadoran armed forces that human rights violations endanger the flow of U.S. assistance, in the police organizations there is no training to professionalize and humanize operations. And in Costa Rica, where the police alone provide that country's security, we are prevented from helping that democracy defend itself in even the most rudimentary fashion.

We therefore suggest that Congress examine this question thoroughly and consider whether Section 660 of the Foreign Assistance Act should be amended so as to permit—under carefully defined conditions—the allocation of funds to the training and support of law enforcement agencies in Central America.

A final problem is philosophical. Our historic tendency as a nation is to think about diplomacy and military operations as antithetical. The fact is that the principles outlined here will enhance the prospects of a political solution whose characteristics are outlined in the next chapter. Experience suggests that a lasting political solution will become possible only when the insurgents are convinced that they cannot win through force, and are therefore willing to settle for the next best option: taking advantage of opportunities for democratic competition and participation.

In this regard, a military stalemate will not enhance but rather would inhibit the prospects for a political solution, since it would confirm that the government cannot prevail. This is itself a chief goal of an insurgency that aims to undermine a government's legitimacy. In a guerrilla war, a stalemate is not the same as a balance of power. Moreover, while an insurgency can sustain itself over time if it has access to sanctuaries and external sources of support, there is nothing to suggest that a government, especially a weak one, can endure the cumulative toll of protracted conflict. A successful counter-insurgency effort is not a substitute for negotiations. But such an effort—the more rapid the better—is a necessary condition for a political solution.

THE SITUATION IN EL SALVADOR

The war is at a stalemate—a condition that in the long term favors the guerrillas. They have relatively little popular support in El Salvador, but they can probably continue the war as long as they receive the sort of external support they are now getting.

The guerrilla front (the Farabundo Martí National Liberation Front—FMLN) has established a unified military command with headquarters near Managua. The dominant element of the five guerrilla groups making up the FMLN is now the People's Revolutionary Army (ERP), which is active in eastern El Salvador. ERP strategy is one of systematic attacks on the economic infrastructure, in order to precipitate an economic and political collapse, and military actions designed for political and psychological effect. The ERP leaders are keenly interested in the impact of guerrilla actions on international public opinion, especially in the U.S., where they hope to discourage further support for El Salvador's Government.

The number of guerrillas has remained basically unchanged for the last two years: there are an estimated 6,000 front-line guerrillas and a slightly larger number organized in militia and support units. But these latter forces have been increasingly well armed and involved in operations with the front-line forces. The insurgents can now put perhaps as many as 12,000 trained and armed fighters in the field. Currently the Salvadoran armed forces, including defense and public security forces, have about 37,500 men. That gives the government less than a 4-to-1 advantage over the insurgents. A ratio of 10 to 1 has generally been considered necessary for successful counter-insurgency, though this ratio varies by individual case and clearly depends upon the capability and mobility of the government forces. In any event, the guerrillas have been able to demonstrate an increasing ability to maneuver and to concentrate their forces, and to react to Salvadoran Army moves.

In 1983, as in the past, the war was characterized by a cyclical pattern, in which the initiative swung between government and guerrilla forces. The ebb and flow of field operations has enabled the guerrillas to strengthen their presence in the eastern departments over the past two years. In the absence of significant Salvadoran military forces, armed guerrillas operate at will throughout the countryside. They have established the rudiments of a civil administration and have enforced a tax regime in areas under their control. Increasingly, they are able to mass their forces and overwhelm isolated garrisons or ambush relief columns.

The severity of guerrilla attacks on the transportation and electrical network in the eastern departments has resulted in the effective isolation of much of that area. The nature and extent of guerrilla operations have led to speculation that the military objective of the guerrillas in the eastern departments might be the establishment of a "liberated" zone, as a prelude to the extension of the war into the central departments.

The situation is not uniformly favorable to the guerrillas. Their bases in San Vicente have been disrupted. They have lost their infrastructure in western El Salvador and have been unable to reconstitute their support network in the cities. But although the military situation continues to be essentially a stalemate, the guerrillas' campaign of economic disruption and sabotage has helped to devastate the Salvadoran economy. In large part due to the violence, the country's gross domestic product has declined 25 percent in real terms in the last four years. In eastern El Salvador, the economic decline has been even more precipitous.

In part, the Salvadoran military's difficulties in containing the guerrilla threat are related to manpower problems—their training, their retention, their equipment, and their development. About three quarters of the Salvadoran armed forces are deployed in static positions that protect fixed installations. This leaves insufficient maneuver forces to carry the war consistently to the guerrillas.

The Commission has heard testimony that as the end of the U.S. fiscal year approaches the Salvadoran armed forces husband ammunition and equipment until the scale of congressional appropriations for U.S. assistance becomes clearer. At present assistance levels there are critical shortages of basic equipment, including communications, medical equipment and airlift assets.

The Salvadoran armed forces have also suffered from inadequate command and control, coordination and leadership. A recent major reorganization of the military command structure is designed to achieve needed improvements in command and control and coordination, and to lead to a more aggressive prosecution of the war. But to end the stalemate will require much more in equipment and trained manpower. . . .

MILITARY ASSISTANCE

While important U.S. interests are engaged in El Salvador, and while we pay a high political price at home and abroad for assisting the armed forces there, the United States has not provided enough military aid to support the methods of counter-insurgency we have urged. At the same time, the United States cannot countenance the brutal alternative methods of counter-insurgency which wreak intolerable violence upon the civilian population. In our judgment, the current levels of military aid are not sufficient to preserve even the existing military stalemate over a period of time. Given the increasing damage —both physical and political—being inflicted on the economy and government of El Salvador by the guerrillas, who are maintaining their strength, a collapse is not inconceivable.

The Salvadoran Government's National Campaign Plan combines military operations with follow-up civic actions to restore agriculture and commerce. The plan is designed to provide secure areas within which the Salvadoran *campesino* can grow, harvest and market his crops, and where industry can again operate. The plan assumes that sufficient security can be established countrywide to reduce the insurgency at least to a low level within two years. But the government's forces must be significantly and quickly strengthened if the plan is to succeed. Their requirements include:

- Increased air and ground mobility, to enable the government forces to reach and assist static positions under attack and, eventually, to seek out and engage the guerrillas.
- Increased training to upgrade the forces tactically and to generalize further the use of modern, humane, counter-insurgency methods, including civic

action as such. This last includes not only road building and basic engineering projects, but especially the provision of basic health care by paramedics.

- Higher force levels, to enable the government forces both to protect important installations and to carry the war to the guerrillas; at present the choice is between allowing the destruction of vital infrastructures, or the indefinite prolongation of the war.
- Greater stocks of equipment and supplies to support a consistent war effort.
- Improved conditions for the troops in order to retain trained personnel, particularly by providing medical evacuation; at present, for the lack of evacuation helicopters, the fatality rate is very high.

There might be an argument for doing nothing to help the government of El Salvador. There might be an argument for doing a great deal more. There is, however, no logical argument for giving some aid but not enough. The worst possible policy for El Salvador is to provide just enough aid to keep the war going, but too little to wage it successfully.

As we have already made clear in this report, the Commission has concluded that present levels of U.S. military assistance are inadequate.

We are not in a position to judge the precise amounts and types of increased aid needed. We note that the U.S. Department of Defense estimates that it would take approximately $400 million in U.S. military assistance in 1984 and 1985 to break the military stalemate and allow the National Campaign Plan to be carried out. The Department believes that thereafter assistance levels could be brought down to considerably more modest levels.

The Commission recommends that the United States provide to El Salvador —subject to the conditions we specify later in this chapter—significantly increased levels of military aid as quickly as possible, so that the Salvadoran authorities can act on the assurance that needed aid will be forthcoming.

The training and improvement of the Salvadoran forces to the point where they can effectively wage counter-insurgency will take time. Indeed, given the complexity of the internal as well as external problems confronting El Salvador, the situation there will remain precarious, even with increased military assistance. Such assistance alone cannot assure the elements of national unity and of will that are necessary for success. But it is the Commission's judgment that without such aid the situation will surely deteriorate. . . .

OTHER MEASURES

To be effective, U.S. military assistance programs require greater continuity and predictability. As we have seen, local commanders are now uncertain whether an adequate supply of such critical support items as ammunition will be on hand. The result in El Salvador has all too often been a less than vigorous prosecution of the war. *The Commission believes the Administration and the Congress should work together to achieve greater predictability. That could be most effectively achieved through multi-year funding. . . .*

HUMAN RIGHTS

The question of the relationship between military aid and human rights abuses is both extremely difficult and extremely important. It involves the potential clash of two basic U.S. objectives. On the one hand, we seek to promote justice and find it repugnant to support forces that violate—or tolerate violation of —fundamental U.S. values. On the other hand, we are engaged in El Salvador and Central America because we are serving fundamental U.S. interests that transcend any particular government.

Our approach must therefore embrace, and pursue, both objectives simultaneously. Clearly, sustained public and international support rests heavily on our success in harmonizing our dual goals. Against this background, we have stressed the need to make American development assistance strictly conditional on rapid progress towards democratic pluralism and respect for human rights, as well as economic performance. Respect for human rights is also of great importance to improved security in Central America, as well as to the self-respect of the United States. We recognize, however, that how the problem is addressed in this regard is vital because Central America is crucial to our national security.

While the objectives of security and human rights are sometimes counterposed against each other, they are actually closely related. Without adequate military aid, Salvadoran forces would not be able to carry out the modern counter-insurgency tactics that would help keep civilian losses to a minimum. Were military aid to be cut off, it would open the way for the triumph of the guerrillas, an eventuality that no one concerned about the well-being of the Salvadoran people can accept with equanimity. Such a development would be unacceptable from the standpoint of both human rights and security.

The Commission believes that vigorous, concurrent policies on both the military and human rights fronts are needed to break out of the demoralizing cycle of deterioration on the one hand and abuses on the other. We believe policies of increased aid and increased pressure to safeguard human rights would improve both security and justice. A slackening on one front would undermine our objective on the other. El Salvador must succeed on both or it will not succeed on either.

The United States Government has a right to demand certain minimum standards of respect for human rights as a condition for providing military aid to any country.

* * *

With respect to El Salvador, military aid should, through legislation requiring periodic reports, be made contingent upon demonstrated progress toward free elections; freedom of association; the establishment of the rule of law and an effective judicial system; and the termination of the activities of the so-called death squads, as well as vigorous action against those guilty of crimes and the prosecution to the extent possible of past offenders. These conditions should be seriously enforced. . . .

As an additional measure, the United States should impose sanctions, including the denial of visas, deportation, and the investigation of financial dealings, against foreign nationals in the United States who are connected with death-squad activities in El Salvador or anywhere else. . . .

EL SALVADOR

Obviously, the future of Central America will depend in large part on what happens in El Salvador. That nation most immediately faces critical choices about the course of its internal politics; it is wracked more severely by internal strife and conflict than any of its neighbors; it most requires intelligence and subtlety in the day-to-day conduct of U.S. diplomacy.

The dilemma in El Salvador is clear. With all its shortcomings, the existing government has conducted free elections. But it is weak. The judiciary is ineffective. The military is divided in its concerns, and in the degree of its respect for human rights. Privileged Salvadorans want to preserve both their political and economic power.

We have described in other chapters the economic, social and security measures we believe are necessary to make progress in economic development.

In the political field two broad options have been presented: either elections, or what is commonly referred to as power-sharing.

The government of El Salvador has consistently stated that a solution to the conflict "must be essentially political and democratic." This means that a political solution must result from the free choice of the Salvadoran people expressed through elections. The political parties represented in the Constituent Assembly, from the center-left Christian Democrats to the right-wing ARENA party, have formally endorsed this view. The United States has supported this position.

The Salvadoran Peace Commission was established last year—again in consultation with the political parties—for the "purpose of promoting the incorporation of all social and political sectors in the democratic process." The Commission has offered to discuss with the guerrilla fronts, the FMLN/FDR, the conditions under which the left could take part in the elections scheduled for March 25, 1984. The issues of security guarantees, access to the media and freedom to campaign would be included in such discussions.

The insurgents have rejected this offer. They assert that their security could not be assured. In any event, they hope for a collapse of American support, and eventually for a military victory. They evidently want to maintain unity among the various guerrilla groups, which they perceive would be put at risk by rifts over tough political decisions. They may well judge that a contested election would reveal their low level of popular support. So they seem to have cast their lot with continued military struggle unless the government is prepared to abandon the scheduled elections and install a coalition government.

The insurgents most recently set forth their formal position in September of last year, following contacts with Ambassador Richard Stone and the Salvadoran Peace Commission. In a document entitled "The Situation of Human Rights in El Salvador in Light of the Geneva Convention" and under the heading "Prospects for a Political Solution," the Political-Diplomatic Commission of the FMLN/FDR stated: "the Salvadoran people need a negotiated settlement between the government and the FMLN/FDR—to bring about peace; they do not need elections." The document went on to detail the FMLN/FDR position calling for comprehensive negotiations on the following agenda:

a) Composition of a provisional government.
b) Restructuring the armed forces.
c) Structural reforms.
d) Salvadoran foreign policy.
e) Mechanisms for future elections.
f) The process to achieve a ceasefire.

This is more than a refusal to campaign under the currently insecure conditions in El Salvador. Evidently the insurgents do not view power-sharing as merely an interim measure needed in order to hold elections in which the left could participate with security. Rather, it is a means of scrapping the existing elected governmental structure and armed forces and creating a provisional civil and military authority in their place in which the rebel leadership would have a major role—and in which they would eventually gain a dominant position well before the electoral "mechanisms" were in place.

Therefore, the Commission has concluded that power-sharing as proposed by the insurgents is not a sensible or fair political solution for El Salvador. There is no historical precedent suggesting that such a procedure would reconcile contending parties which entertain such deeply held beliefs and political goals, and which have been killing each other for years. Indeed, precedent argues that it would be only a prelude to a take-over by the insurgent forces.

To install a mixed provisional government by fiat would scarcely be consistent with the notion that the popular will is the foundation of true government. It would tend to inflate the true strength of insurgent factions that have gained attention thus far through violence and their ability to disrupt the functioning of government. It would provide openings for them and their foreign supporters to forestall democratic politics. The likely final outcome of power-sharing would be the imposition on the people of El Salvador of a government unwilling to base its authority on the consent of the governed.

We believe that a true political solution in El Salvador can be reached only through free elections in which all significant groups have a right to participate. To be sure, elections do not solve a nation's problems. They can be the beginning, but cannot be the end, of political development. This is particularly true in El Salvador, which is threatened by a fragmentation of political life affecting most, if not all, of its institutions.

How elections are conducted will be crucial. Given prevailing conditions in El Salvador, all factions have legitimate concerns about their security. Neither supporters nor opponents of the regime can be expected to participate in elections so long as terrorists of the right or the left run free. No political efforts at reconciliation can succeed if the Government of El Salvador itself aids and abets violence against its own people. Unless it effectively curbs the actions of the death squads—unless it provides basic security for teachers, editors and writers, labor and religious leaders, and generally for the free and secure expression of opinion, the political process recommended here will break down. A secure environment must be established for all who wish to take part, whether leftists, centrists or rightists. The U.S. Government—to be credible —must insist that these conditions be met.

Thus the El Salvador Government must take all appropriate measures to make the March 25 elections as safe and open as possible. This should include the introduction of outside observers to help insure the security and fairness of the process.

The political process should not—indeed cannot—stop after the March elections. Following the elections, basic U.S. strategy for El Salvador should include firm support for the newly elected legitimate government. Along with providing military assistance, we should encourage it to pursue negotiations and reconciliation with all elements of Salvadoran society that are prepared to take part in an open and democratic political process, to promote rapid progress towards the protection of human rights, to strengthen civilian authority, and to undertake comprehensive reform of both political and military institutions. Such reform is essential to the creation of a stable, democratic government and for the reconciliation of disparate elements within Salvadoran society. U.S. economic assistance should be a key instrument in helping to secure these ends.

Even if the insurgents do not take part in the March elections, their participation in subsequent elections—at least participation by those prepared to accept the results of the balloting—should be encouraged. The Commission believes that a proposal along the following lines—which amplifies the government's approach—would constitute a genuinely fair chance for all to compete peacefully for political power in El Salvador. The basic principle would remain that of consulting the popular will, not imposing a government on the people through power-sharing. It would test the intentions of the insurgents.

We understand that El Salvador contemplates holding municipal and legislative assembly elections in 1985. The elements of the following approach could be applied to that process.

1. *The Salvadoran government would invite the FDR-FMLN to negotiate mutually acceptable procedures to establish a framework for future elections.* Although the details of the framework would have to be worked out by the parties to the talks themselves, the United States would energetically support their efforts and encourage other appropriate arrangements for elections in which all parties could participate as a first step toward a peaceful settlement of the conflict.

2. *As part of this framework a broadly representative Elections Commission would be established, including representatives of the FDR-FMLN.* The Salvadoran Government would thus be inviting participation by the political front of the guerrilla movement in the conduct of elections. The Commission would help ensure that all parties could compete openly and safely and that all citizens could receive political literature, attend meetings and rallies, discuss partisan issues freely, and cast their ballots without fear or intimidation. The insurgent opposition should have a significant voice and vote both in the Elections Commission and in developing security arrangements for the campaign and election. But this should not become a subterfuge for the sharing of power with regard to the responsibilities of government, which we have rejected in this report.

3. *Violence should be ended by all parties so that mutually satisfactory arrangements can be developed among the government, pro-government parties, the different opposition groups and insurgent groups for the period of campaigning and elections.* To that end, certain developments are needed. The Salvadoran security forces and guerrillas should cease hostilities against one another. Guerrilla terror against military, government, and economic targets should end. Civilian and military violence of the right should also end.

4. *A system of international observation should be established to enhance the faith and confidence of all parties in the probity and equity of arrangements for elections.* This might include senior advisers to the Elections Commission drawn from the OAS, Contadora nations or third countries agreed upon by all parties to the conflict.

In sum, the United States should make a maximum effort to help El Salvador to create a self-sustaining society dedicated to open participation in its political process, to social justice, and to economic freedom, growth and development. An El Salvador that works toward these goals deserves our continuing support. This should include adequate levels of economic and military aid, which in turn can produce pressure for a politically negotiated end to the fighting.

What happens in El Salvador will have important consequences in the other nations of Central America. If the shaky center collapses and the country eventually is dominated by undemocratic extremes, this will lead to increased pressures on El Salvador's neighbors. For Guatemala and Nicaragua, the experience of El Salvador could carry a clear message: the best means of earning the support of the United States, and of promoting political, social, and economic development, lies in adopting both the form and the substance of democracy. . . .

In the meantime, the United States has a dual task: to create those economic conditions in Central America that thwart the export of revolutions and to make clear the risks of expanded violence. Social reform, economic advance and political stability in Central America will discourage Cuban adventurism in the region. But we must also bring home to Havana a due appreciation of the consequences of its actions.

As for the Soviet Union, it has been pursuing a strategy of progressively greater involvement in the Western Hemisphere, particularly in reaching beyond Cuba to Central America and the Caribbean. It has employed gradualism, ambiguity, and proxies. For Moscow, this strategy has entailed few risks, either military or political; except in the case of Cuba, it has been inexpensive; and it has held the potential for significant gains. Soviet objectives, beginning with Cuba in the early 1960's, have been to end unchallenged U.S. preeminence within the hemisphere and possibly to see other "Cubas" established, to divert U.S. attention and resources from other parts of the world that are of greater importance to Moscow, to complicate our relations with our West European allies, and to burnish the Soviet Union's image as a revolutionary state.

Preserving U.S. interests in Central America and the Caribbean against the Soviet challenge will be a significant concern for years to come. We reject the proposition that the establishment of a Soviet military base in Central America is the sole, or even the major, threat to U.S. interests. Unless current Cuban-Nicaraguan designs are checked, long before Moscow feels ready for such a move the turmoil in Central America will have reached a point of crisis that could not be contained in Central American dimensions. In designing a basic policy toward the region, we must make the Soviet Union understand the limits of its activity, especially before its practice hardens into precedent. Moscow must be forestalled from making gains that would give it major advantages either within the region or in wider aspects of East-West relations.

Excluding Soviet involvement in Central America altogether—extending to trade, diplomatic relations, and the gaining of some influence in individual countries—is no doubt impossible. At the other extreme, clearly any Soviet involvement in the region that poses a strategic threat to the United States is unacceptable. The policy questions are, first, to decide at what point between these two extremes of Soviet involvement the balance point of U.S. interests lies; and second, to take those actions necessary to preserve those interests.

The United States cannot accept Soviet military engagement in Central America and the Caribbean beyond what we reluctantly tolerate in Cuba.

We will also need to define specific situations as precisely as possible and to make those definitions clear to Moscow. At the same time we must avoid the inference that Soviet actions we have not proscribed are thus acceptable to us. If we do challenge directly any particular Soviet military activity in the region, we must be prepared to prevail.

On the other hand, some Soviet involvement in Central America and the Caribbean is likely to fall into gray areas. Except where a Soviet position of dominance is either imposed or preserved through force of arms, Moscow depends for its opportunities on conditions both within the region and within individual countries. Where political, social and economic programs forestall violent revolution, Soviet ability to fish in troubled waters is severely limited. Where we can agree with countries in Latin America that Soviet actions pose a threat to hemispheric interests, we can share leadership in opposing those actions. Where countries of the region can agree on mutual security and the pooling of benefits, collective actions can reduce Soviet opportunities.

Against this backdrop, the Commission sees little promise in negotiating with the Soviet Union over Central America. The Soviets would almost certainly use negotiations to legitimize their presence in the region. They would welcome discussion about superpower spheres of influence, which would prompt Soviet assertions of primacy and the need for U.S. abstention on the Soviet periphery, in such places as Eastern Europe and Afghanistan. For the United States, however, such a concept of spheres of influence is unacceptable. Should the United States now accept that concept, the Soviet Union would reap substantial gains.

In sum, the United States cannot eliminate all Soviet political involvement and influence within Central America and the Caribbean. But we must curb Soviet military activity in the hemisphere. And we can reduce Soviet opportunities and increase the incentives for others to abstain from forging ties with Moscow that damage U.S. and regional interests.

49. Failings of the Kissinger Report*

By Arthur M. Schlesinger, Jr.

Historian Arthur M. Schlesinger, Jr., is Albert Schweitzer Professor in the Humanities at the City University of New York and author of, among other books, A Thousand Days *(1965), a history of the Kennedy administration, in which he served as an adviser.*

* *New York Times*, January 17, 1984.

THE Report of the National Bipartisan Commission on Central America is a serious document. It is literate, at times eloquent; it conveys much useful information; it is reasoned in analysis and humane in values; and it represents a valiant attempt to deal with intractable problems. It is also seriously deficient in its sense of political reality.

The Kissinger commission's thesis is that the exploitation of Central American unrest by the Soviet Union and Cuba threatens our security interests. The answer, the commission says, lies in offering pro-United States regimes military assistance to defeat externally supported insurgency and economic assistance to overcome the misery and depression that set off insurgency.

1. THE SOVIET THREAT.

Moscow unquestionably aims to benefit from Central American turmoil. But how? What goals are attainable? What risks is it prepared to run? What costs to pay? Instead of rigorous analysis, the commission rests its case for a dire Soviet threat on what Senator Daniel Patrick Moynihan correctly calls a "doctrinal position," dressed up with perfunctory military arguments.

The report broods about the danger to our Caribbean shipping lanes. But in what circumstances would Moscow try to "interdict" shipping? Only in the event of general war—and, with nuclear missiles flying, the sinking of oil tankers would be of small consequence, nor would Soviet military installations matter in Cuba or elsewhere. And Moscow knows it cannot establish nuclear missile bases in the Western Hemisphere in 1984 any more than it could in 1962. As for economic aid to pro-Marxist states, why, as the Latin Americans put it, would Moscow fatten a lamb in the jaws of a lion? For Moscow, Central America is a windfall, a target of opportunity, not of deep strategic purpose. The Kremlin will keep the revolutionary pot boiling, but it knows how vulnerable its investment will be.

The report also uses the domino argument: Guerrilla victory in El Salvador would spread Soviet influence through Central America. Actually, Communist success is quite as likely to galvanize anti-Communism and to move countries like Mexico to the right. In assessing the threat, Washington should listen to countries directly threatened, such as the Contadora group (Mexico, Panama, Venezuela, Colombia). It is too bad President Reagan did not assemble an *international* bipartisan commission, in which Latin American democrats might have joined in recommendations for multilateral action.

The commission's final argument it that failure in Central America will damage our worldwide "credibility." It may well be that the Administration's determination to inflate stakes and invest a civil war with global significance has made El Salvador a "test" of our "resolve." This does not, however, lead ineluctably to a military solution.

2. THE COMMISSION'S PROGRAM.

The commission acknowledges the difficulty of combining military victory with social reform. Its answer is the military-shield concept—the idea that, if we help provide a military shield, we can persuade the regime taken under protection to make the changes necessary to win popular support.

But regimes requiring military shields against their own people are under siege precisely because they don't give a damn about poverty and exploitation. The shield concept works when it helps governments already committed to agendas to democratic reform; but Romulo Betancourt (Venezuela) and Ramón Magsaysay (Philippines) were the exception, not the rule. Most of the time, the shield approach only nourishes the arrogance of the regime whose repression created the revolution. For, as soon as we insert the magic shield, we lose most of our leverage. The guarantee of military protection means that we renounce the ultimate sanction—the withdrawal of support. Once we declare our commitment to a regime's survival, it becomes increasingly hard to make a beleaguered oligarchy do things it sees, probably correctly, as fatal to its privilege and power. The military shield turns into a blank check.

The report invokes history against alternative policies, like power-sharing. But when have we ever been able to force a right-wing regime, confident of our continuing support, to take action contrary to its own ideology and interests? We tried it in China, in Vietnam. When we bind ourselves to a client regime, we become the client's prisoner.

The report fails to note how skilled native elites manipulate their patrons. We are being manipulated by oligarchies in El Salvador, Honduras and Guatemala and by ex-oligarchs in flight from Nicaragua, using the "credibility" line to ensnare us into saving their property and power.

The men who run El Salvador do not believe in the splendid reforms urged by the commission—in civil liberties, in trade unions, in land reform, in redistribution of income. Vice President Bush rightly said of the death squads: "These right wing fanatics are the best friends the Soviets, the Cubans, the Sandinista *comandantes* and Salvadoran guerrillas have." They are also the Salvadoran regime's best friends.

Does the commission really mean it when it conditions aid on "demonstrated progress" toward human rights? Does it expect Washington to end aid after the report's own vivid portrayal of guerrilla victory as a grave defeat for the United States? The Administration, once it deepens its military commitments, will certainly heed the footnote signed by the chairman and two other members and decline to "interpret conditionality in a manner that leads to a Marxist-Leninist victory."

The commission's program is bathed in political unreality. Democratic economic development depends on restoration of peace and on a domestic will to reform. But militarism entrenches in power the people most opposed to social change. Peace restored by giving military victory to a crowd whose survival depends on the elimination of the democratic alternative—and who torture and murder their own democrats—will simply reproduce all the conditions that drove peasants and the middle class to revolution.

3. THE UNITED STATES' ROLE

The commission's program requires our "purposeful" leadership. But the report's sanitized historical review does not adequately suggest the credentials, or lack thereof, we bring to resolution of Central American problems. Distrust runs deep, understandably: Why should any Central American believe we have democratic interests at heart? Even Franklin D. Roosevelt's Good Neighbor Policy co-existed cheerfully with Somoza ("our own S.O.B.")[1] and other Central American dictators.

While there should be due consultation, the report says, "the United States cannot use the Contadora process as a substitute for its own policies." True enough; yet nothing has got us into more trouble through the long years than the delusion that we understand the interests of other countries better than they understand their own interests. The Contadora nations know the terrain far better than we do, are more directly threatened and are equally determined to protect themselves. If they do not see the threat as apocalyptically as we do, who is to say that they are wrong and we are right? If they still see possibilities in diplomacy, why should we put our chips on military power?

4. AND THE ALTERNATIVE?

Victory for the revolutionaries would be an international setback for us. And it would not lead to Central American regimes of sweetness and light.

Still, if the military solution makes social change impossible, and if social change is impossible until peace is restored, what do we do? Negotiate. The commission insists that only the prospect of military defeat will bring the guerrillas to the table. "A successful counter-insurgency effort . . . is a necessary condition for a political solution." This may well be so, but it sends us down the military road again. The Contadora countries still work at negotiation. But if they fail, which seems all too possible, and if they refuse to endorse our military solution, do we go it alone and back our own S.O.B.'s? It is against the American grain to suppose there are problems we cannot lick with sufficient arms and money. Moreover, abstention would disturb those, like this writer, who feel an obligation to the many decent Central American democrats who share our values and deserve our support. One can only say that a military

---

[1] Schlesinger's reference is to a statement reportedly made by President Franklin D. Roosevelt about the Nicaraguan dictator Anastasio Somoza (in other versions, about the Dominican dictator Rafael Trujillo)—"He may be an S.O.B., but he's our own S.O.B."—Eds.

solution is problematic as a way of saving them, since it confirms their enemies in power. And the international repercussions for us would be less if we pursued a policy of accommodation to the inevitable, like the French withdrawal from Algeria, than if we tried to force our will and failed, or succeeded at protracted and grievous cost.

Civil war is a historical experience through which nations, including our own, achieve national identity. History takes its own time. Its ways are inscrutable and often tragic: People find their own paths to nationhood, and these paths often run with blood. Reflecting on the itch to save other lands from their own historical logic, a wise British Ambassador to Washington (Lord Harlech) said, "Every country has a right to its own Wars of the Roses."[2]

Obviously, it would be wonderful to have in Central America a set of devoted, tranquil, prosperous, pro–United States countries. Equally, it would be unacceptable to let Central America become a Soviet base. Actually, both extremes are beyond the power of either the United States or the Soviet Union to achieve. We cannot attain the first, and we can prevent the second. We may well face an anguished time in Central America (Costa Rica always excepted) for a while to come. I believe we can live with that. It is conceivably better than trying to beat the revolution by installing—and it would probably take G.I.'s to do it—a new generation of Somozas, who would only sow the seeds of later and fiercer revolutions.

50. Substantial Progress One Year after the Kissinger Report?*

By George P. Shultz

Former Secretary of State Alexander Haig attempted to scare the American public and Congress with melodramatic and hyperbolic rhetoric about the state of affairs in Central America. The region, he said, was on a Soviet "hit list," and he threatened to go "at the source," meaning Cuba, to resolve the "problem" of El Salvador, which he defined as "external intervention in the internal affairs of a sovereign nation in the hemisphere— nothing more, nothing less."

[2] The War of the Roses was a struggle for the throne of England, 1455–84, between the rival houses of York (the white rose insignia) and Lancaster (the red rose).—Eds.

* Excerpts from "Sustaining a Consistent Policy in Central America: One Year after the National Bipartisan Commission Report"—Report to the President from the Secretary of State, United States Department of State Special Report No. 124, April 1985. For a later report, "Implementing the National Bipartisan Commission Report," see the State Department's Special Report No. 148, July 1986. A recent official U.S. overview of "The Situation in El Salvador" is offered in Special Report No. 144, April 1986.

Haig's successor as Secretary of State, George P. Shultz, still accepted Haig's major premise of Cuban-Soviet (and Nicaraguan)[1] responsibility for the civil war in El Salvador, but his statements have been more temperate and he has sought congressional and public support by emphasizing purported gains in human rights, the economy, and political democracy in El Salvador. Moreover, he could pursue the administration strategy of denying military victory to the FMLN and refusing them a share in political power by referring to the recommendations of the Kissinger Report, which was instrumental in persuading Congress to make funds available to the Duarte regime in the summer and fall of 1984.

THE report submitted to the President on January 10, 1984, by the National Bipartisan Commission on Central America is at the core of U.S. policy in Central America. The Commission concluded that fundamental strategic and moral interests of the United States require a long-term national commitment to economic opportunity, human development, democracy, and security in Central America.

The Commission proposed a comprehensive approach—an active diplomacy in support of democracy, supported by economic aid to get at root causes of poverty and social unrest and by security assistance to protect peaceful development.

The Commission recommended an immediate supplemental appropriation of $400 million and an additional $8 billion in economic aid for the succeeding 5 years. The Administration's proposal was similar: a $400 million fiscal year (FY) 1984 supplemental, $5.9 billion in appropriated funds, and $2.0 billion in insurance and guarantees for FY 1985–89.

The Commission also recommended increased military assistance to permit the application of modern, humane counterinsurgency strategies which require greater mobility, more training, higher force levels, and more equipment. The Administration proposed a $259 million supplemental for FY 1984 and $256 million for FY 1985.

Bipartisan congressional majorities approved increases in both economic and military assistance close to what the Commission recommended and the President proposed for FY 1984–85.

---

[1] See the State Department's " 'Revolution Beyond Our Borders'—Sandinista Intervention in Central America," which concludes, "The Sandinistas can no longer deny that they have engaged and continue to engage in intervention by: Providing the arms, training areas, command and control facilities, and communications that transformed disorganized factions in El Salvador into a well-organized and -equipped guerrilla force of several thousand responsible for many thousands of civilian casualties and direct economic damages of over $1 billion. . . ." United States Department of State Special Report No. 132, September 1985.

CURRENT STRATEGY

Our increased economic assistance is being used to:

- Arrest declines in incomes, employment, and economic activity through major balance-of-payments assistance;
- Establish the basis for long-term economic growth through improvements in economic policy and the infrastructure needed to export;
- Assure the widest possible distribution of the benefits of growth through assistance aimed at improving health, education, and housing for the poorest groups; and
- Support democratic processes and institutions through assistance for the administration of justice, technical training, and the development of leadership skills.

At the same time, security cooperation has been put on a firmer professional footing. The improved performance of the armed forces of El Salvador and the increased readiness of those of Honduras are directly linked to increases in both the quantity and the steadiness of U.S. security assistance and military cooperation. . . .

NEXT STEPS

This year we again seek bipartisan support for the balanced and mutually reinforcing mix of political, economic, security, and diplomatic activities that the Commission concluded we should pursue simultaneously. For FY 1986, the Administration's economic assistance request totals $1,053 million; the military request is $261 million. Legislation that would authorize appropriations for non-military programs for FY 1986–89 would provide a critical assurance of U.S. commitment and an important tool for public and private planning in Central America. . . .

CENTRAL AMERICA ONE YEAR LATER

Almost as soon as the Commission issued its report, developments in Central America began to confirm the accuracy of its analysis and the soundness of its judgment. In early 1984, many in the United States, in Western Europe, and even in Latin America believed that El Salvador was caught in an endless war between the guerrillas of the left and death squads of the right. But the Commission saw a different future. It saw electoral democracy, reform, and political dialogue as realistic alternatives to the antidemocratic violence of the extreme left and right—provided El Salvador's democrats got the support they needed.

Today, El Salvador's problems are closer to resolution than a year ago. In 1984 there were two rounds of national elections leading to the presidential inauguration of Christian Democrat José Napoleón Duarte; the trial, conviction, and imprisonment of the murderers of four American churchwomen; changes in military and security personnel and in the procedures which govern their behavior; improved economic and military performance; a marked reduction in the number of political crimes; and President Duarte's initiation of a dialogue with the FMLN/FDR [Farabundo Martí National Liberation Front/Revolutionary Democratic Front] guerrillas. At the same time, the United States increased both economic and military assistance while West Germany, the United Kingdom, and Japan all resumed or increased aid during 1984. . . .

El Salvador

has improved incentives to exporters by permitting them to sell their earnings on the more favorable parallel exchange market. The government also has improved the management of foreign exchange and has taken a more active role in the promotion of nontraditional exports.

- A project supported by AID is being implemented by the Ministry of Foreign Trade to explore new market opportunities in the United States and other countries.
- An international trade fair was organized with AID support and technical assistance from the U.S. Foreign Commercial Service which attracted U.S. and other foreign investors to El Salvador. Several investment proposals resulted.
- A new business organization, "The Salvadoran Foundation for Economic and Social Development," is working with AID assistance to help small business owners, traders, and skilled crafts people develop and promote new export products.
- A new private finance company is being organized with AID assistance that will provide financial and technical support for productive enterprises. The new facility should add flexibility, initiative, and expertise to the commercial banking system. . . .

Employment Programs.

In El Salvador, AID contributed to 137,000 full-time jobs in 1984 as part of public works employment programs for the general population and displaced persons. Contributing to these employment levels were AID-financed imports of raw materials and intermediate goods.

Humanitarian Relief.

The U.S. Government also has expanded humanitarian relief efforts as recommended by the Commission. One-half million displaced Salvadorans have benefited through the Health and Jobs for Displaced Persons Project and through U.S. contributions to international and private organizations. In August 1984, AID authorized an additional $60 million for El Salvador which, over the next 3 years, will finance vital services such as health and sanitation services and increased food deliveries and relocation. . . .

Educational Opportunities.

The Commission also recommended support for programs designed to bring about substantial improvement in the availability and quality of educational opportunities. Thus, using a mix of FY 1984 supplemental and FY 1985 funds:

• In El Salvador, AID is beginning a $17.68 million program to improve the quality of primary education and make it more available to poor children. . . .

DEMOCRATIC PRACTICES

In El Salvador democratic political development was affirmed by presidential elections in March and May 1984 in which nearly 80% of the Salvadoran electorate turned out in the presence of hundreds of international observers to elect José Napoleón Duarte. Nine political parties representing a broad range of opinion campaigned in the March 1985 legislative and mayoral elections, which completed the constitutional renewal despite guerrilla attacks and harassment.

Political murder in El Salvador by "death squads" declined dramatically from the levels of previous years, particularly after President Duarte took office. Urban killings by guerrilla groups, however, have increased.

Due to the guerrilla threat, the state of siege restricts some constitutional rights. Nevertheless, the government has reinstated the right of assembly for political parties and peaceful organizations, including church and labor groups. Groups sympathetic to the guerrillas have freely run advertisements and held marches, demonstrations, and a human rights congress dominated by anti-government speeches. . . .

ADMINISTRATION OF JUSTICE

Implementing the recommendation of the Commission report, we have begun an intensive effort to help the Central Americans strengthen their judicial systems. Indeed, in his speech to the November 1984 General Assembly of the

Organization of American States (OAS), Secretary Shultz highlighted the importance of the administration of justice to the consolidation of democracy throughout the hemisphere.

In September 1984, the United States committed $9.23 million in FY 1984–85 ESF funds for a 3–5 year program in support of the Salvadoran Government's effort to strengthen the administration of justice. This program includes:

- Support for a revisory commission to identify the legislative, procedural, and administrative problems that prevent the judicial system from functioning effectively and to design and oversee the implementation of solutions to those problems;
- Support for a criminological institute, which is to include a permanent investigative capability and a modern forensic laboratory;
- Support for a judicial protection capacity (which began with U.S. funding to provide security for the trial of the murderers of the four U.S. church-women) to help shield participants in the judicial process from intimidation; and
- Assistance to the court system to improve general efficiency and responsiveness.

Under the program, an intensive, 6-week training of the initial group of investigator recruits was completed in Puerto Rico, and a full-time trainer-consultant in criminal investigation has been assigned to work with the unit and to assist the Government of El Salvador in planning the operation of the criminological institute.

The efforts of President Duarte, continuing those of President Magaña demonstrate the Salvadoran Government's commitment to improving the administration of justice. Despite the notable success evident in the May 1984 conviction of the killers of the U.S. churchwomen, President Duarte still faces an extremely difficult political task in brokering enduring reforms among the executive, legislative, and judicial branches. Strong, continued U.S. support will be necessary. . . .

SECURITY

The Commission encountered a sobering security situation in Central America. During the 1970s, the steady growth of Cuban military power, backed by the direct Soviet military presence in Cuba, was accompanied by reductions in U.S. military presence in the Caribbean Basin. Then, after the Sandinistas came to power in Nicaragua in 1979, the U.S.S.R. shifted from opposition to support of Cuban advocacy of armed struggle. The belief that revolutionary conditions prevailed throughout Central America, especially in El Salvador, was widespread. . . .

In 1984, El Salvador's elected government and increasingly professional armed forces made significant progress in dealing with the guerrilla war as a political as well as a military struggle. But the activities of Cuba and Nicaragua, with sizable Soviet cooperation and material support, continue to pose a serious threat to Central American governments and to U.S. interests in the region. Direct Soviet arms deliveries to Nicaragua and Nicaragua's continued support for the armed insurgency in El Salvador underline again the gravity of current security concerns and of the potential strategic risks at stake. . . .

Nicaragua serves as a conduit for money, arms, munitions, medical supplies, and communications and logistical support to the Salvadoran guerrillas. The Salvadoran guerrillas maintain training facilities and command and control centers in Nicaragua. However, there are indications that some Salvadoran guerrilla units are experiencing difficulties in receiving supplies. This disruption of supplies is due to several factors, including more effective intelligence and patrol operations by Salvadoran Government forces, more active Honduran patrols along the border and in refugee camps, and armed resistance activities within Nicaragua.

The Administration and Congress approved the Commission's recommendations to significantly increase military aid to El Salvador. This assistance is already making a positive difference in the military situation.

As recommended by the Commission, U.S. military aid has been administered with close and continual attention to human rights considerations. Under Public Law 98-332, the Executive now reports to Congress on El Salvador every 60 days. The four reports issued so far document steady improvements in respect for human rights by the Government and armed forces of El Salvador. The number of civilian deaths attributable to political violence has declined sharply. The Federal Bureau of Investigation is investigating individuals residing in the United States who may be directing, financing, or otherwise involved in "death squad" activities in El Salvador.

In its treatment of the guerrilla war in El Salvador, the Commission felt that it was imperative to settle on a level of aid related to the operational requirements of a humane counterinsurgency strategy and to sustain that aid over time. The Commission specifically recommended providing the Salvadorans with increased air and ground mobility: increased training; support for higher force levels; greater stocks of equipment; and better troop conditions, especially an improved capability to evacuate the wounded and to provide prompt medical attention.

These recommendations formed the basis for the Administration's request for increased assistance to El Salvador, which was included in two supplemental appropriation bills passed by Congress. In June 1984 the Congress passed an urgent supplemental including $61.8 million in military assistance. In the FY 1984 supplemental, the Congress appropriated an additional $70 million. Together with the FY 1984 Continuing Resolution, military assistance for El

Salvador in FY 1984 amounted to $197 million. Though short of the $243 million requested by the Administration, it was, nonetheless, a substantial increase over the $81 million appropriated for FY 1983. For FY 1985 Congress appropriated $128.25 million, $4 million short of the amount requested.

With U.S. support, including training as well as materiel, the Salvadoran Armed Forces have been able to maintain the battlefield initiative. They are now larger, better trained and led, and have improved mobility and communications. In addition, the military now has an aeromedical evacuation capability which, together with an expanded corps of trained medics, has improved morale and decreased the mortality rate among wounded Salvadoran troops. The arrival of two C-47 aircraft with mounted machine guns has provided the armed forces with the capacity to respond to units under attack by guerrilla forces. On January 7 and 8, 1985, a Salvadoran Army battalion withstood a guerrilla force twice its size because of the critical help of the armed C-47s. The Salvadoran military will occasionally suffer some battlefield setbacks, but it is undoubtedly a better military force now than a year ago.

As anticipated by the Commission, this improvement in the military situation for the Salvadoran Government contributed to the FMLN/FDR decision to accept President Duarte's October 1984 offer at the United Nations to meet with the insurgents. This historic step offers some hope for the eventual reincorporation of FMLN/FDR members into the greatly strengthened Salvadoran democratic process. The short-term results, however, have been disappointing. That the guerrillas have by no means abandoned the goal of complete power is evidenced in their intransigent November 30, 1984, demands for power-sharing, recognition of areas "under guerrilla control," the amalgamation of government and guerrilla forces, and the formation of a new government as preconditions for elections.

Still, the guerrillas are beginning to demonstrate a lack of resolution in the face of the Salvadoran military's increased effectiveness and professionalism. The increased ability of government troops also has strengthened President Duarte's hand in dealing with the armed forces as an institution. The more self-confident military knows that the peace dialogue can be limited to a constitutionally based discussion of the FMLN/FDR's participation in the democratic process.

The humane pursuit of the war has been a central theme for President Duarte and his government. At La Palma and again at Ayagualo, Salvadoran officials proposed an agreement to end all attacks on the economic infrastructure and populated areas. Although their proposals were rebuffed by the FMLN/FDR, President Duarte has enforced strict compliance with rules of engagement to minimize noncombatant casualties. The government's National Plan envisions the extension of increased government services and programs to the civilian population in conflictive areas. We strongly support efforts to monitor closely the rules of battlefield engagement and to increase assistance to the National Plan to help displaced persons. . . .

51. "Insufficient, Misleading and False Information" from the Administration*

By Representative Jim Leach, Representative George Miller, and Senator Mark O. Hatfield

One of the consequences of the Vietnam War was the demise of the traditional blank check Congress extended to the President and State Department in foreign policy matters, especially for military assistance, both overt and covert, to client regimes and counterrevolution in the Third World. Interventionist policies now face critical scrutiny from a Congress that is more sensitive to questions from the public about justifying huge expenditures in the name of national security or fighting communism.

Since the beginning of the Salvadoran civil war in 1980, the U.S. has provided $1.7 billion to the Central Bank, the armed forces, and the successive regimes battling the guerrillas in El Salvador. How is the money spent and in service to what goals?[1] How accurate are administration reports of "progress" against the guerrillas? Are there alternative political strategies to a military resolution of the conflict? Representative Jim Leach (R-IA), Representative George Miller (D-CA), and Senator Mark O. Hatfield (R-OR) prepared the following critical review.

THIS report is intended to provide Congress with an analysis that will focus debate over U.S. aid to El Salvador on the *purposes* and *effects* of that aid, rather than simply on the *amount* of aid to be provided, or on the *conditions* that the Government of El Salvador must meet to obtain it. In brief, this report should help Members of Congress become familiar with the content and strategy of U.S. funding for El Salvador—the "what" and "what for," in addition to the amount or the "how much." . . .

Unfortunately, as this section will document, the Administration has provided insufficient, misleading and in some cases false information to Congress. As a result, Congressional-Executive relations have become increasingly strained. Following are examples of the insufficient, misleading and false information which have provoked increasing Congressional skepticism of Administration representations.

---

* From "U.S. Aid to El Salvador: An Evaluation of the Past, a Proposal for the Future: A Report to the Arms Control and Foreign Policy Caucus," February 1985. The Arms Control and Foreign Policy Caucus was formerly known as Members of Congress for Peace through Law. The full text of this report appears in the *Congressional Record*, 131, No. 18, February 22, 1985. See another excerpt, Reading 29.

[1] For a revealing report on how corrupt members of the Salvadoran officers' corps siphon U.S. assistance dollars into their own pockets, making the civil war a profitable enterprise, see "Officers' Mafia in El Salvador," by Kenneth E. Sharpe, *The Nation*, October 19, 1985. Such officers are hardly receptive to negotiated, peaceful settlement of the war. Similar entrepreneurial practices developed among our clients in the Vietnam War, and the Chinese civil war.

EXAMPLES OF INSUFFICIENT INFORMATION

• Classified and unclassified Congressional Presentation documents for FY84 [Fiscal Year 1984—Eds.] Supplemental and FY85 aid to El Salvador, from both AID and DOD [the Agency for International Development and the Department of Defense—Eds.], were unusually meager in their descriptions of the content of proposed funding. AID requested all $120 million of FY84 Supplemental funds and $140 million of $290 million in FY85 funds under the single line item "New Activities," rather than providing the usual project titles and descriptions for its requests. No break-down of "New Activities" was made available to Congress until *after* House and Senate floor votes on both the authorization and appropriation.

DOD's request was even less informative than AID's, being three as compared to 18 pages long, in a request for $311 million. Neither specific *types* of equipment nor total *quantities* were listed. Formal attempts by Members of Congress to get more details resulted in the transmittal of data only on past, not proposed, aid. For both AID and DOD programs, Members of Congress knew how much funding was to be provided, but not what it was intended to buy.

• The Administration failed to inform all relevant committees of plans to build an air base in eastern El Salvador. The closest they came to disclosing these plans was to suggest that the existence of only one field in the country hampered helicopter efforts to cover the whole country. The Administration acknowledged that the air base was being built over a month *after* Congressional floor votes on the aid request, and, perhaps coincidentally, only after *Newsweek* had reported the construction plans.

• The Administration hid from virtually all Members of Congress, including those on specific Committees of jurisdiction, its intention to supply El Salvador with four AC-47 gunships. Although the AC-47s represented a major increase in the level of violence in the civil war (since they can deliver 18,000 rounds per minute and blanket the size of a football field,) they were not listed in the Administration's aid requests or included in briefings prior to floor votes in both houses.

Following press reports of U.S. intentions to supply the four gunships, Members of Congress protested that the issue had never been discussed during review of the aid requests. As a result, an agreement was reached to send only one AC-47, and that one a downgraded one which would be used on a trial basis under rules precluding its use in populated areas. Without information from the media, the original four gunships would have been delivered.

EXAMPLES OF MISLEADING INFORMATION

- In response to Congressional inquiries about corruption in the U.S. Cash Transfer program in El Salvador, AID repeatedly denied that corruption was a significant problem, and stated that "management actions" in the Salvadoran Central Bank had corrected whatever problem had existed. AID's position was contradicted by its own internal studies of the problem of corruption in the Salvadoran Central Bank. AID's Inspector General found that 20 percent of the transactions reviewed by the Central Bank in a spot-check for corruption were fraudulent, and a respected AID contractor, the Arthur Young accounting firm, concluded that corruption was "far beyond the control" of the Central Bank personnel charged with detecting it.

  AID also restricted information about corruption, by classifying the Arthur Young report, which also documented the existence of a massive "black market" for foreign exchange in El Salvador.

- The Administration has provided Congress with overly optimistic reports on the progress of the Salvadoran Armed Forces and the military situation in El Salvador. In a haunting reminder of Congressional-Executive relations during the Vietnam War, the Administration has at times appeared to take on the role of cheerleader rather than analyst in its military reports to Congress, as exemplified by the statement of the commander of U.S. forces in Central America, General Paul Gorman, that up to 90 percent of the Salvadoran countryside would be under Army control in two years. Other top Administration officials have claimed that the military stalemate in El Salvador has been broken, in favor of the Salvadoran Armed Forces.

  The situation on the ground does not appear to offer as optimistic an assessment: the ratio of active forces has remained roughly four to one (Army over rebel) since 1980; the ability of the rebels to cripple the economy with attacks on power lines, dams, roads and crops has not diminished; and the rebels continue to be able to mass, attack military targets at times and places of their choosing, and disperse safely—as proven by a recent battle at El Salto, where the rebels reportedly inflicted heavy damage on one of the Army's top battalions.

- The Administration is also providing Congress with overly optimistic reports about the Salvadoran economy, asserting that a "recovery" is underway there whose benefits will be "widely distributed throughout the society." In fact, domestic product has dropped between 25 and 35 percent since 1979; unemployment stands between 40 and 50 percent; 20 percent of the population has been driven to refugee camps or exile; massive capital flight of over $1 billion has cut public investment to half, and private investment to one-quarter, of previous levels; the tax system is non-functional in entire areas and taxes raise less than one-half of the Salvadoran budget; and rebel attacks on the economy that are responsible for many of these indicators show no signs of abating.

- Finally, the Executive Branch has apparently misled Congress about the very nature of U.S. strategy in El Salvador, by repeatedly asserting that the pursuit of economic and social reform was favored over the pursuit of a military victory over the rebels. And yet in spite of repeated claims that U.S. aid is "three to one" economic over military, the next section of this report will show that, under a more realistic evaluation, military aid is double that of our aid to reform and develop the economy. This reflects a military strategy devoted to prosecuting the civil war, and not one addressing the economic and social problems leading to the civil war.

EXAMPLES OF FALSE INFORMATION

- In seeking $93 million in FY84 Supplemental military aid for El Salvador, the Administration claimed that a dire "emergency" existed in the supplies available to the Salvadoran Army, when in fact, the Pentagon's own management data show that this claim was false.

  Administration officials stated that "without these funds, the El Salvadoran Armed Forces will either go back to the barracks or collapse." Secretary of State Shultz affirmed that the Salvadorans were "running out of supplies right now," and President Reagan claimed that Salvadoran soldiers were going into battle with "one clip" of ammunition for their rifles.

  In fact, there was no emergency: Pentagon management data obtained by Caucus Chairman Leach confirm statements by personnel in the field, including the Chief of Staff of the Salvadoran Armed Forces, that adequate supplies were available to continue a high rate of operations through the elections. According to this data, supplied by the Defense Security Assistance Agency (DSAA), there was $32 million of military aid available in the pipeline, much of which could have been diverted to arms and ammunition if necessary. In any event, the majority of the Supplemental aid was used not to resupply existing units in the field, but rather to continue expanding the Army by building new units.

  In the five months prior to the "emergency" request, DSAA records show that general military expansion was emphasized over emergency supply of fighting units in the field: in these months, 44 percent of military aid funds were spent on U.S. personnel for training and technical assistance, and only 30 percent on arms and ammunition—the reverse of the percentages spent on these categories in the previous three years.

  Not only was there no emergency in Salvadoran supplies, but the materiel requested was largely inappropriate for emergency use in any case. Some $26 million was to be used for training and equipping nine *new* battalions (none of which were scheduled for combat duty in the immediate future); another $29 million was allocated to expanding the helicopter fleet by 12, and purchasing new trucks and supporting equipment; and finally, $4 million was to upgrade the Salvadoran communications network. Over 60 percent of the original request, then, could not have been used to offset a shortfall in arms and ammunition, even if one had existed.

• The Administration has denied the existence of an intensified air war on non-military civilian targets in El Salvador, which seeks to drive civilians out of rebel zones. Extensive press reports, Salvadoran government actions and reports from independent monitors of the situation strongly contradict these claims. For instance:

—Although DOD stated that no bombing had taken place on Guazapa Volcano early in 1984, at least one newspaper *(Christian Science Monitor)* reported that the area "resembles a ghost town," with "every structure damaged by bombing."

—Similarly, although Assistant Secretary Motley[2] denies "indiscriminate" bombing and asserts that the Salvadoran pilots have developed "nearly surgical precision" in their bombing, independent human rights observers assert that the evidence is "overwhelming" that the army engages "regularly" in "indiscriminate attacks" on civilians.

—Finally, in contradiction of official claims that civilians are exempt from bombing, President Duarte has issued guidelines to the Air Force to reduce civilian casualties from air strikes.

• The Executive Branch has provided false information to Congress concerning the number of U.S. military personnel operating in El Salvador, about the roles they are performing, and about the duration of their presence there:

—Although in 1981 DSAA testified that the trainers "have gone there with the idea the jobs would be done in months or at most one year," they remain there four years later;

—Although the Administration agreed to and has widely publicized the 55-man cap on U.S. military personnel in the country, in fact total U.S. military personnel there on a given day is probably twice this number. This is because of DOD's new definitions of what falls under the 55-man cap: originally, the ceiling included all personnel except Embassy Guards and employees of the Defense Attaché's office. Now, however, the cap excludes not only guards and attachés, but also 11–16 members of the "Milgroup" which oversee the use of military aid and advise the Salvadoran High Command on strategy and tactics; 23 military trainers helping Salvadoran soldiers learn battlefield medical skills; an undisclosed number of advisers on "temporary duty" of one-two weeks at a time; and about a dozen civilian contract personnel from private U.S. contractors. Some 50 of these "excluded" personnel, on top of a rapid increase in the Defense Attaché's office

[2.] Former Assistant Secretary for Inter-American Affairs Langhorne A. Motley. The present holder of that office is Elliott Abrams.—Eds.

from 6 in '81 to 26 in '84, indicates that the 55-man cap is exceeded. If one includes personnel "in or over" El Salvador, yet additional personnel would have to be included, such as the U.S. pilots who regularly fly reconnaissance flights from Honduras and Panama.

—Although the Executive Branch since 1981 has maintained that U.S. personnel are not in areas which would expose them to hostilities (and thus also trigger the War Powers Act), in fact U.S. trainers have been stationed in six Salvadoran brigade headquarters throughout zones of conflict, and members of the U.S. Milgroup and trainers travel to the site of combat operations to assess the performance of the Salvadoran Army. Some have come under hostile fire.

- As recently as late 1984, the Administration pledged to Congress to deploy only one AC-47 gunship to El Salvador, until completion of an "interim" period in which the effect of the gunship's operations on human rights would be evaluated in consultation with Congress. The State Department has conceded that in fact a second gunship went into battle *on the same day* that the first was initially deployed (Jan. 8, 1985). The Administration claims that the Salvadoran Air Force armed the second AC-47 with the spare armament for the first one, without U.S. consent. However, the Administration has now affirmed its intent to retain *both* gunships in El Salvador during the evaluation period—in contradiction of the original agreement.

Congressional frustration with insufficient, misleading and false information has motivated this report. . . .

RECOMMENDATIONS: HOW U.S. AID COULD ENCOURAGE A NEGOTIATED SETTLEMENT

El Salvador has experienced a national trauma of major proportions over the past five years. Some 50,000 Salvadorans have been killed (roughly 40,000 of whom were non-combatants), the per-capita equivalent of 2,400,000 people being killed in the United States. The economy has virtually collapsed under the strain of the civil war, with Gross Domestic Product dropping between 25 and 35 percent, and unemployment standing between 30 and 40 percent. Only U.S. aid equivalent annually to 55 percent of the Salvadoran Government's budget and 15 percent of the Gross Domestic Product has kept the Government, the Armed Forces and the economy functioning.

Tragically, if U.S. aid is composed in the future as it is at present, the next five years will be as violent and unproductive for El Salvador as the past five years. Under current U.S. aid strategy, there is no light at the end of this tunnel.

U.S. aid strategy has favored a military solution to the civil war, focusing twice as much funding on direct war-related aid to the Armed Forces (30 percent) as on aid for reform and development which aims to change the conditions that led to the civil war (15 percent). The largest share of aid (44 percent) simply neutralizes the ever-increasing effects of the civil war; permitting the Government and Armed Forces to continue their search for a military solution.

Yet a military solution remains elusive. Rebel strength and activity have kept pace throughout the civil war with increases in the Armed Forces' size and operations. Although it is difficult to assess the long-term impact of the current air war on the military balance, rebel attacks on both military [and] economic targets are continuing now much as they did a year or two ago. The overall level of military violence, especially that which affects civilians, is increasing with the technological escalation of the air war.

We propose a major shift in U.S. policy in El Salvador, and a major shift in the composition of U.S. aid to implement it. Our policy must be maximum support for a cease-fire, followed by intense and serious negotiations for a swift settlement. U.S. policy must unequivocally reject a military solution in favor of a negotiated settlement, and then redirect U.S. aid to support this policy.

Our recommendations for implementation of this new policy are, in summary:

Reduce the level of violence by stopping funding for the air war;

Encourage reform and negotiations by redirecting the Cash Transfer to Reform and Development projects;

Limit U.S. combat support by returning to the numbers and roles of U.S. personnel assisting the Salvadoran military effort in 1981; and

Require that direct U.S. military action can be undertaken only with the prior consent of the Congress. . . .

52. Vietnam, El Salvador, and the Uses of History*

By George C. Herring

Critics and defenders of the Vietnam War share a troubled conscience. For the critics, U.S. intervention in Vietnam was a tragic misapplication of American military power on the basis of misguided information for ends that were never clear. For defenders, American defeat represented a failure of nerve, a capitulation to ill-informed, naïve, even un-American liberal and radical domestic critics, and a sellout of anti-Communists in

* From Kenneth M. Coleman and George C. Herring, eds., *The Central American Crisis: Sources of Conflict and the Failure of U.S. Policy* (Wilmington, Delaware: Scholarly Resources Inc., 1985). Most reference notes deleted. Additional explorations of the Vietnam–El Salvador analogy are in the original edition of the present volume (New York: Grove Press, 1981), 263–82.

Indochina and elsewhere. Both critics and defenders are determined, therefore, that there shall be "no more Vietnams."

U.S. intervention in El Salvador has not yet reached the scale of our involvement in Vietnam, but the trend has been pointed enough to alarm critics and encourage defenders. Both sides now invoke the Vietnam War to buttress their cases with what they see as its lessons. The Muse of History has become a partner in contemporary political debate, as the following reading shows. George C. Herring is professor of history and chair of the History Department at the University of Kentucky and is the author of Aid to Russia, 1941–1946: Strategy, Diplomacy and the Origins of the Cold War *(New York: Columbia University Press, 1973) and* America's Longest War: The United States and Vietnam, 1950–1975, *2d ed. (New York: Alfred A. Knopf, 1986).*

MORE than ten years ago, toward the end of the Vietnam War, the Harvard historian Ernest May examined a series of case studies from World War II through Vietnam. He concluded that, in responding to foreign policy crises, policymakers and the public were invariably guided by history, especially by their memory of the recent past. May went on to say that equally invariably they used history badly. Their historical knowledge was at best superficial. Their historical reasoning was "thoughtless and haphazard." Indeed, he specifically argued that such reasoning had been a major cause for American involvement in Vietnam.

Similar to the case studies May considers, from the time El Salvador became a major national issue it has been inextricably linked to Vietnam. It is instructive, therefore, to consider the ways in which Vietnam and El Salvador have been compared, to analyze the extent to which and the reasons why they are in fact analogous, and, proceeding from there, to discuss how history can be useful in dealing with the problems of today. In general, it should be noted that history is no better used now than in the instances May studied a decade ago, and this is true of those who oppose U.S. involvement as well as those who support it.

Looking first at how Vietnam and El Salvador have been joined in public discussion in recent years, no matter what one's point of view, analogies have been discovered, memories evoked, and lessons drawn. To start at the beginning, and at the top, there are indications that the Reagan administration, in undertaking its initial, firm commitment to El Salvador, thought that it could win a quick victory and in so doing erase the stigma of defeat in Vietnam and exorcise the so-called Vietnam syndrome, the perceived public reluctance in the wake of Vietnam to take on commitments in the Third World.

When the quick victory turned into an illusion and President Ronald Reagan's commitment aroused the popular apprehensions it was supposed to dispel, the president and his advisers immediately sought to distance themselves from Vietnam. Then Secretary of State Alexander M. Haig, Jr., went to great lengths to show that Vietnam and El Salvador were drastically different. The United States had clear-cut, indeed obvious, vital interests in El Salvador, he insisted, something which had not been the case in Vietnam (a statement that must have come as a shock to the generation of policymakers which had based an escalating commitment in Vietnam on precisely the opposite grounds). Since early 1981 President Reagan has repeatedly stated that there is "no comparison with Vietnam and there's not going to be anything of that kind [in El Salvador]." Reaganites like Ernest Lefever have echoed this refrain, arguing that the United States failed in Vietnam because it did not act decisively and at least implying that Reagan will not make that mistake in El Salvador. The more apt analogy, Lefever insisted, was Greece where, under the Truman Doctrine, the United States turned back an insurgency between 1947 and 1949. Other Reagan supporters insist that the Dominican Republic, where Lyndon Johnson successfully intervened in 1965, is more relevant.

American conservatives have supported the president's commitment in El Salvador, but, where Reagan has attempted to evade the Vietnam issue, his conservative brethren have pronounced numerous lessons from Vietnam that should guide policy in El Salvador. George Will harks back to Woodrow Wilson to find that the cause of American problems, in general, in Vietnam, El Salvador, and Third World countries is the effort to force feed democracy on nations that simply are not ready for it. The United States pressed elections on Vietnam, he warned, and Saigon "is now Ho Chi Minh City." Henry Kissinger has emphasized different lessons. Never an admirer of the American democratic system, he proclaimed, upon accepting chairmanship of the commission on Central America, that "it is imperative [in dealing with problems there] that we avoid the bitter debates that characterized the Vietnam period." Norman Podhoretz, editor of *Commentary,* adds yet another lesson; namely, that "fighting a war on the cheap is a sure formula for defeat." If in Central America U.S. military power is called for and we do not use it or use it halfheartedly, he notes, we will "reveal ourselves as a spent and impotent force." More recently, and along the same lines, the Kissinger Commission Report evoked memories of Vietnam when it warned of the dangers of a stalemate in El Salvador. In words almost identical to those Kissinger used in his famous 1969 *Foreign Affairs* article on Vietnam, the report stressed that "the insurgency is winning if it's not losing, and the government is losing if it's not winning."

On the other side of the political spectrum, liberal critics of Reagan's policies have gloomily forecast a replay of Vietnam in El Salvador. The Coalition for a New Foreign and Military Policy, responding to the president's "no comparison" statement, points to the long history of oppression in El Salvador and an unpopular regime backed by U.S. money and insists that the comparisons are all too obvious. To George Ball, Johnson's in-house critic on Vietnam, El Salvador's "music and words sound like plagiarization. I have the feeling that we've heard it all before but in another setting." Liberal journalist Tad Szulc warns that, if the United States persists in its present course in El Salvador, it will become bogged down "in an endless, Vietnam-style guerrilla war in the Salvadoran mountains and jungles," a "scenario for absolute disaster," he describes it.

Outside the formal debate, similarly, discussion of El Salvador invariably begins with, or comes back to, Vietnam. When Congress discusses El Salvador, one legislator concedes, Vietnam is a "ghostly presence; it's there in every committee room, at every meeting." Many of the top U.S. advisers in Central America, men like Ambassador John Negroponte and General Paul Gorman, are old Vietnam hands, and most of the U.S. military advisers served apprenticeships in Indochina. The programs being applied by American advisers often seem to be retreads of programs that worked in Vietnam or programs modified in the light of Vietnam failures.

The military brings to El Salvador an exceptional amount of Vietnam baggage. "All I want to do is win one war, that's all, just one," an adviser told a reporter, as though wars, like baseball, were tallied in win-loss columns. "It'll be like winning the world series for me." Another adviser expressed fear of a repetition of the final days of April 1975. "If the sense spreads that the U.S. will desert them," he said of the Salvadorans he is working with, "I don't know what they'll do. It's Vietnam all over again." Among senior U.S. military officers, Adam Smith has written, Vietnam is a "silent obsession. It lurks in nuances and ellipses, even when the discussion is about something else." They are unwilling to go through in Central America what they experienced in Vietnam. They are reluctant to see the army committed, as General Edward Meyer affirmed in the fall of 1983, unless the nation itself is committed. The presence of Vietnam in the military mind was clearly manifested in September 1983 in the famous Freudian slip of Marine Corps commandant General P. X. Kelley who, before a committee of Congress, inadvertently used the word Vietnam when he meant to say Lebanon.

If the polls mean anything, the American public, at least partly because of Vietnam, has little stomach for any such commitment. Polls taken in the spring and summer of 1983 revealed that a solid majority of Americans (75 percent) saw the likelihood that U.S. involvement in El Salvador would turn into another Vietnam, and a smaller majority (54 percent) opposed sending troops even if the government was about to be defeated by leftist forces.

Wherever one turns, then, discussion of El Salvador invariably refers back to Vietnam and discussion of Vietnam invariably moves forward to El Salvador. A political cartoon portrays President Reagan, waist deep in quicksand, rifle held above head, doggedly plunging forward, while a nervous Uncle Sam inches along cautiously behind. "Quit grousing!" Reagan orders Sam. "I'm telling you it's *not* Vietnam!" "It doesn't look like Munich either," a still wary Sam responds. In her book *The March of Folly*, even Barbara Tuchman, who once said that the purpose of history was "not to instruct but to tell a story," sets out to find "lessons" from Vietnam and wonders how the United States can continue in El Salvador the "imbecility" it practiced earlier in Southeast Asia. The discovery of lessons is not limited to Americans. A representative of the Salvadoran right wing, protesting American interference in his country's internal politics, exclaimed in frustration that El Salvador should "fight the war without the influence of foreign advisers who were defeated in similar conflicts and have nothing to teach the valiant Salvadoran soldiers."

Since the two situations are so often joined, it is not only appropriate but also essential to determine the ways in which they are in fact similar and the ways they differ. On the surface, at least, the similarities seem obvious and compelling. Both wars occur in small, tropical, underdeveloped countries. In each case insurgents are attempting to overthrow an established government. Each insurgency is composed of a coalition of leftist groups in which Communists play a leading role. Significant outside support comes from the major Communist power in the region and from the Soviet Union. The government in both cases comes from the right of the political spectrum, unrepresentative and unresponsive to the needs of many of its people, especially rural peasants, and it is therefore especially vulnerable to insurgency. It enjoys large-scale support from the United States. The wars themselves are remarkably similar in form. The insurgents rely on guerrilla tactics, ambushes, hit-and-run raids, and sabotage, from bases deep in the countryside. Government forces relying on U.S. aid and advice fight a 9-to-5 war, often indifferently and with indecisive results.

Historical analogies are never exact, however, and these superficial similarities obscure a world of important differences. To start with the obvious, Vietnam is in Southeast Asia, its political culture derived to a large extent from China. El Salvador, only about one-eighth the size of Vietnam, is in Central America and is of the Hispanic political tradition.[1] At this point, the level of intensity of the war remains lower than it was in Vietnam almost from the inception of the insurgency there. So far, and despite their survival and successes, the Salvadoran insurgents do not seem to be in the same league with the Viet Cong.

There are much more important differences in the origins of the insurgencies, their composition, and the nature and extent of their "outside" support. War originated in Vietnam in 1945 as a nationalist revolution against French colonialism, and the second phase—the American phase—was an extension of that struggle. In El Salvador the revolution began in response to a narrowly based and reactionary regime that was totally unresponsive to the needs of a

[1.] For extended commentary on the importance and role of political culture in the Vietnamese revolution, see John T. McAlister, Jr., and Paul Mus, *The Vietnamese and Their Revolution* (New York, 1970); Frances FitzGerald, *Fire in the Lake* (New York, 1972); and David Marr, *Vietnamese Tradition on Trial* (Berkeley, 1982). For comment on the role of political culture in Central American revolutions, see Richard Morse, "Toward a Theory of Spanish American Government," in Howard Wiarda, ed., *Politics and Social Change in Latin America* (Amherst, 1974); and Eldon Kenworthy, "Dilemmas of Participation in Latin America," *Democracy* 3 (Winter 1983): 72–83.

great majority of its own people. Both wars in time became to some degree internationalized, but there is a crucial difference in the nature and extent of outside support. In Vietnam the major source of outside support was from the North Vietnamese who were fanatically committed to liberating their southern brethren and driving out the foreigners. China and the Soviet Union provided important assistance, but the Vietnamese dimension was decisive to the outcome. External support in El Salvador comes from Nicaragua, Cuba, and the Soviet Union, none of which would appear to have the same level of commitment as North Vietnam did in the earlier war.

It is extremely difficult to compare the respective insurgencies. In each case the guerrilla forces are made up of a loose coalition of leftist groups led by hard-core Marxist-Leninists. But the National Liberation Front of Vietnam appears to have been much more tightly knit than the FMLN, a somewhat unwieldy and apparently divided coalition of five groups including pro-Soviet Communists, Cuban-trained Trotskyites, and Maoists. In Vietnam, moreover, there was nothing quite comparable to the moderate leftists, Christian Democrats, and Social Democrats who have joined the Salvadoran opposition.

Again, despite surface similarities, there are important differences between the two governments. As narrowly based as it was, the government of South Vietnam probably enjoyed broader support than the narrow oligarchy which dominates El Salvador, and there was nothing in Vietnam comparable to the right wing and its death squads in El Salvador. Indeed, at certain times the government of Nguyen Van Thieu would seem a paragon of civil liberties compared to El Salvador. In Vietnam the army more often than not was a tool of the government in power rather than a power in its own right, as appears to be the case in El Salvador. The role of the Catholic church is quite different. The church and its people represented the one secure base of support for the Diem and Thieu governments in South Vietnam. In El Salvador it is badly split. Like all historical events, then, Vietnam and El Salvador are fundamentally different. It is reasonably safe to assume that the revolutions and wars there will take different courses and that whatever government emerges in San Salvador will be different from that in Hanoi.

All things considered, the closest similarity may not be the wars in Vietnam and El Salvador themselves but the way in which the United States has responded to them. American policies clearly reflect the same Cold War mind-sets and world views. In each case U.S. policymakers defined what began and, despite outside Communist support, remained indigenous struggles primarily in terms of the larger Cold War conflict. American involvement in Vietnam was thus justified in terms of preventing the Chinese, who at various times were or were not held to be Soviet proxies, from extending Communist domination over Southeast Asia. In El Salvador, President Reagan has said that the United States must draw the line in Central America against Communist "aggression" instigated by the Cubans who act as Soviet proxies. In each situation the domino theory has been employed to justify commitments to countries whose intrinsic significance is not obvious. The fall of Vietnam, it was argued, would set off a chain reaction which might have repercussions as far away as Hawaii or the Middle East. In the same way, we are told, the fall of El Salvador after the "loss" of Nicaragua could cause the loss of Guatemala, Honduras, Costa Rica, and even Mexico. And that might not be the end. "We are the last domino," candidate Reagan warned ominously in 1980. In February 1965 and February 1981—the coincidence is eery—the United States issued White Papers, which might have been carbon copies, supporting these arguments. [See Readings 46 and 47—Eds.] In each case the United States has made the outcome a test of its credibility. In each case, at one time or the other, administrations declared their intention to do whatever was necessary to save their client states from communism, and presidents assured a worried nation that they saw no need for combat troops.

At least at the outset in both cases, bold rhetoric was usually matched by cautious action, the pattern of involvement one of gradual escalation. First came economic and military aid, then a steadily growing stream of advisers, and with Vietnam, advisers were followed by combat troops. To keep things in some kind of perspective, it is worth noting that the fifty-five-man military advisory team now in El Salvador is smaller than the sixty-five-man Military Assistance and Advisory Group sent to advise the French in Indochina in late 1950.

American relations with its client states in Saigon and San Salvador are also hauntingly similar. We beg, plead, threaten, or cajole, and the governments go on much as before, making occasional gestures to placate us but never exactly following our direction. Further, there is a marked similarity in the way the two armies respond to U.S. military advice.

The domestic debate in the United States is so similar that it cannot but evoke a sense of déjà vu. The official line emphasizes the importance of outside support for the insurgency; the opposition argues that it is indigenous. Critics stress that the government is reactionary and oppressive; the administration concedes it is not perfect but warns that the situation would be much worse if the Communists gain power. Washington contends that slow and steady progress is being made; its critics question such assertions. Most important, out of the domestic divisions in each case there emerges something of a standoff: the opposition prevents the government from doing what it thinks is necessary to win the war; it is not strong enough to force a withdrawal, however, and indeed most opponents are unwilling to shoulder responsibility for the loss of Vietnam or El Salvador. As a result, the United States year after year does just enough to perpetuate a bloody and destructive stalemate.[2]

2. For commentary on this point, see Leslie Gelb, *New York Times,* July 24, 1983. The dilemma was neatly summed up by Representative Stephen Solarz of New York in the spring 1984 debate on Central America. "The American people do not want any more Cubas in Central America," he said, "but neither do they want any more Vietnams." Some congressmen might reverse the order of concerns. Solarz's statement was reported by the Associated Press, May 11, 1984.

Despite these similarities, there would appear to be one major difference, the importance of which is not yet clear. In the case of El Salvador, Vietnam already has happened, and it is very difficult to see how, in the light of this, it will happen again. Because there was a Vietnam, the media are much more skeptical and critical than they were in the early stages of Vietnam, even though television, in particular, could still be much more critical than it is. Congress is much more cautious, and it has consistently challenged Reagan's modest steps far more than it did the larger steps taken by Presidents Dwight D. Eisenhower and John F. Kennedy. Opinion polls indicate that the public foreign policy permissiveness of the 1950s and 1960s has been replaced in the wake of Vietnam by caution and fear. As noted earlier, the army is extremely fearful of becoming engaged in another "no win" conflict like Vietnam, whereas in the 1960s, having passed out of the "never again" phase that immediately followed Korea, it was in a "can do" mood and ready to go to Vietnam. As a result, while American handling of El Salvador to date strikingly resembles earlier policy toward Vietnam, the fact that we have only recently gone through the trauma of Vietnam would appear to add a powerful restraining factor that did not operate in the years of escalation in Southeast Asia.

Given these similarities and differences, does the Vietnam analogy have value in dealing with the problems of Central America today? It is clear first, as Ernest May concluded of the period 1945–1965, that thus far history has been badly used. Each side in the current debate has been extremely sensitive to the Vietnam analogy, especially since Vietnam is so close and fresh in the popular mind. But the analogy has misled rather than guided, obscured rather than clarified. Conclusions on both sides have been based on superficial historical knowledge and faulty historical reasoning. Each side has blatantly abused history for partisan purposes; and each has demanded more than history can possibly deliver by asking it to forecast outcomes.

The Reagan administration stretches our credulity to the breaking point by asking us to believe that there is no comparison between El Salvador and Vietnam. The comparisons are all too obvious, and, more important, to say that El Salvador is not another Vietnam does not, as the president seems to wish, eliminate the need for further discussion. To reject the Vietnam analogy for analogy with Greece in the 1940s or the Dominican Republic in the 1960s, moreover, is the most blatant form of argument, by historical expediency, of selecting the example that has the desired outcome and using it.

The effort to apply lessons from Vietnam to El Salvador is equally misleading. It violates what David Hackett Fischer has called "the didactic fallacy," the attempt to extract specific lessons from history and apply them literally to contemporary problems without regard to the differences in time, space, and historical circumstances. The lesson that we failed in Vietnam because we did not use our power decisively, and therefore in future situations like El Salvador we must apply it quickly and without stint, breaks down at several points. We cannot be sure first that a different application of American military power in Vietnam would have produced better results; it might have provoked a nuclear war. The relevance of this lesson for the distinctly different situation in Central America is, in any event, open to question.

On the other hand, the opposition's ominous warning that El Salvador will be another Vietnam is as much an abuse of history as the administration's arguments and, indeed, as the so-called Munich analogy was for American involvement in Vietnam. It violates another of Fischer's fallacies, the "fallacy of the perfect analogy," the "erroneous inference from the fact that A and B are similar in some respects to the false conclusion that they are the same in all respects." Vietnam and El Salvador are different in important ways, and it is highly unlikely that the outcome will be the same, namely, an unsuccessful effort to prop up a non-Communist government which cost 58,000 American lives and $150 billion. As Fischer suggests, each historical situation is unique, and we cannot make superficial comparisons and draw facile conclusions that, because such and such occurred before, the same or the reverse will happen this time.

Does this concede the administration's point that, since Vietnam and El Salvador are really not alike, we have nothing to worry about? No, it does not. A new Vietnam in Central America is obviously a worst case scenario; there are many possible outcomes to the current crisis, short of another Vietnam War, that could damage U.S. interests in significant ways.

Does rejection of the Vietnam analogy deprive the opposition of its strongest argument? On the surface it would seem so since Vietnam has such an emotional ring with the American public. When looked at from another perspective, however, the analogy may be a dangerous and self-deceptive argument for the opposition to employ. By focusing on the issue of whether we can succeed at an acceptable cost, we ignore what may be the more important question of whether we should be intervening in the first place. More significant, perhaps, as long as the president can show that El Salvador is not another Vietnam, he can do almost as he pleases there, and that leaves him considerable room to maneuver.

Even more important, the Vietnam analogy inhibits discussion of El Salvador and Central America on their own merits and terms. Rather than indulging in the nondebate of whether El Salvador will become another Vietnam, we should be addressing the major issues in El Salvador itself. What is the nature of the struggle there? In what ways, if at all, does it threaten our vital interests? Can we morally justify intervention in support of the existing government? Can we tolerate doing nothing? What are the possible consequences of deeper involvement, including military intervention? All of these questions have been raised at one time or another, but we have never really confronted them in a systematic or sustained way.

Does this mean, then, that history has nothing to teach us, or, more specifically, that the Vietnam analogy is useless in dealing with our present dilemma in Central America? Obviously, this is not the case. History in general, and the history of American involvement in Vietnam in particular, have much to teach us, but we must use them with discretion and caution and not expect too much.

We could learn a lot that is of value from the study of the unique histories of El Salvador and other Central American nations, and from the study of our traditional relationships with these nations. Discussion of the current crisis in Central America thus far has been almost totally devoid of historical context, an alarming and perhaps dangerous omission given its importance. Such analysis would provide us with a much clearer picture of the origins and nature of the difficult and distinctive problems in each of the Central American nations. Understanding of our traditional role would make the United States more sensitive to the ways in which Central Americans view us. It might suggest a great deal about the extent of our influence there and the possible responses to programs we initiate.

Although history does not offer specific lessons, it can provide a desperately needed perspective on contemporary problems. From studying our involvement in Vietnam, for example, we can learn much about ourselves and how we deal with other peoples. The mind-set which got us into Vietnam is quite similar to that which the Reagan administration is operating from today and therefore is worthy of critical analysis. Many scholars believe that in dealing with the Vietnamese we consistently worked from a base of ignorance and cultural blindness. We should be sensitive to the same errors in our dealings with Central Americans today. Study of the interplay within the Moscow-Beijing-Hanoi triangle during the Vietnam War can shed light on, although obviously it will not foretell the direction of, the relations among the Communist nations in dealing with Central America.

When used cautiously and with due regard to its limitations, the Vietnam analogy may even provide guidance, if not outright lessons, that could be useful in handling specific problems in El Salvador. American relations with the Saigon government, for example, suggest, seemingly paradoxically, that the deeper our commitment the smaller our leverage in getting that government to take necessary actions for what we believe are necessary for its survival. Policymakers should at least be alert to this possibility as our involvement in El Salvador and other Central American countries becomes more and more complex.

Above all else the Vietnam experience suggests the centrality of local circumstances in international conflicts. From the outset, American policymakers defined the problem in Vietnam in the context of the Cold War. To a considerable degree, however, local forces explained the origins, the peculiar dynamics, and the outcome of the war. By wrongly attributing the conflict to external forces, the United States drastically misjudged its internal dynamics. By intervening in what was essentially a local struggle, it placed itself at the mercy of local forces, a weak client and a determined adversary. What might have remained a localized struggle was elevated into a major international conflict, with enormous and fateful consequences for Americans and especially for the Vietnamese. The circumstances in El Salvador and Central America are different, and the outcome will certainly not be the same. But the point should be clear: we ignore local forces at our own peril.

Without suggesting to us outcomes that are foreordained, the study of history might also teach us a healthy caution. "History does not teach lots of little lessons," historian Gordon Wood recently wrote; "it teaches only one big one: that nothing ever works out quite the way its managers expected or intended." In the final analysis, however, one of the most important functions of history, or the historian, may be to expose the falseness of historical analogy. As a wise Englishman, James Lord Bryce, once put it, "The chief practical use of history is to deliver us from plausible historical analogies." Let us study Vietnam and study it carefully and with an open mind. But let us be conscious that the purpose of our study is to gain perspective and understanding, not hard and fast lessons. With tongue planted firmly in cheek, the historian and Vietnam policymaker James Thomson once proposed that we learn one central lesson from Vietnam: never again "take on the job of trying to defeat a nationalist anti-colonial movement under indigenous Communist control in former French Indochina," a lesson of "less than universal relevance," he quickly and redundantly added. Thomson obviously overstated for effect, but again the point should be clear. Each historical situation is unique, and the use of analogy is at best misleading, at worst, dangerous.

Writing in 1970 about the misuse of historical analogy in dealing with Vietnam, Fischer suggested that the problem had to be "studied and solved in its own terms, if it is to be solved at all." Perhaps the best way to conclude this analysis of the use of the Vietnam analogy in the debate on El Salvador would be to paraphrase Fischer and change the point of reference. As valuable as an understanding of Vietnam may be to us, the problems of El Salvador and Central America can best be studied and solved in their own terms if they are to be solved at all.

53. The El Salvador Solidarity Movement in the United States*

By Barton Myers and Jean Weisman

Opposition to U.S. policies in El Salvador has been a consistent feature throughout the 1980s as Washington's involvement has deepened. Apart from critical voices in Congress

* Written expressly for this volume.

and sections of the media, a movement seeking a wide popular base of opposition has emerged recalling aspects of antiwar activity during the Vietnam era, [1] *protests that may have been an important factor behind Washington's decision to leave Indochina. Some participants in the current movement describe their efforts as an expression of solidarity with the Salvadoran people. Many are impelled to protest U.S. policies for moral or religious reasons; others protest out of anti-imperialist political convictions. Some in the movement are immigrants from Central America, often refugees from repression in their countries.*

Here, two activists survey some of the groups and activities involved in the movement. Barton Myers, associate professor of psychology at Brooklyn College, is a member of the New York City chapter of the Committee in Solidarity with the People of El Salvador (CISPES) and serves on the steering committee of the New York downstate region of the Pledge of Resistance (see Reading 54). Jean Weisman, of the City College Center for Worker Education in New York, is coordinator of the New York Educators Committee on Central America and a founding member of the District Council 37 (American Federation of State, County and Municipal Employees) Central America Committee.

IT can be as little as wearing a button or displaying a car bumper sticker that proclaims "El Salvador is Spanish for Vietnam" or "Stop U.S. Intervention in Central America." It may be the repetitious work of getting out a mailing or of handing out leaflets. It can take the form of a house party with a slide show, a talk, and a pitch to raise money. It can include cultural events with music, dance, or films. It may mean marching in a protest demonstration. And it sometimes involves a commitment to illegal activity such as nonviolently occupying congressional offices or supporting sanctuary for Central American refugees. All these activities and more, when they are integral to aiding the struggle of the Salvadoran people, fit under the rubric of working in the Salvador solidarity movement.

The movement embraces extensive contact between Salvadorans and North Americans, including U.S. missionaries who now return after years spent in El Salvador. In addition there are also many Salvadorans who have lived for long periods in the United States and others who have been driven from their country more recently and have sought refuge in the United States. They bring first-person accounts of death-squad torture and assassination, of army massacres, and of hunger and disease due to the exploitation of the great majority of the people. In addition, numerous delegations of North American trade unionists, students, educators, physicians, and others have visited El Salvador for briefer periods and have borne witness to the suffering imposed by U.S. policy. [2]

[1.] The most complete account to date of this movement is Nancy Zaroulis and Gerald Sullivan, *Who Spoke Up? American Protest against the War in Vietnam, 1963–1975* (Garden City, N.Y.: Doubleday and Co., 1984).—Eds.

[2.] Many of these delegations to El Salvador have published reports, such as the academic human-rights group FACHRES/CA (Faculty Committee for Human Rights in El Salvador/Central America), the National Labor Committee in Support of Democracy and Human Rights in

Many activists in the solidarity movement also participate in organizing for housing, health care, jobs, and education in the United States. They see discrimination and attacks against blacks, Latinos, Asians, and Native Americans in the United States as a reflection of the racist domestic and foreign policies of the Reagan administration and the system it represents. They protest the racism of the Reagan administration's view that the Salvadoran people could not possibly be organizing their own struggle for self-determination, that they must be controlled by the Nicaraguans, who are controlled by the Cubans, who are controlled by the Soviets. Unionists, concerned that their members are losing jobs, point out that multinational corporations are fleeing to Central America in search of cheap labor and higher profits. Students, struggling against financial-aid cutbacks, insist that funds need to be spent on education rather than for military intervention. Many of the demonstrations include a call for an end to apartheid in South Africa as well as an end to U.S. intervention in Central America. Activists demand that money should be used for decent housing, jobs, health care, and schools and not to kill people in Latin America, Asia, or Africa.

The result has been the growth of a diverse and vigorous movement composed of many organizations, of which the following play a leading role.

THE COMMITTEE IN SOLIDARITY WITH THE PEOPLE OF EL SALVADOR (CISPES)

CISPES was founded in October 1980 at conferences held in both Los Angeles and Washington, D.C. It is the largest Central American solidarity organization in the United States and one of the most important. CISPES supports the self-determination of the Salvadoran people and therefore has declared its solidarity with both the Democratic Revolutionary Front (FDR), the broad coalition of forces in opposition to the San Salvador government, and the Farabundo Martí National Liberation Front (FMLN), the armed opposition that is allied with the FDR. It opposes U.S. government intervention on the side of the repressive government in San Salvador.

Within the first year of its existence, CISPES organized a national demonstration of 100,000 people in Washington, D.C., to protest the El Salvador policy of the Reagan administration. Since that time CISPES has staged other national demonstrations as well as countless decentralized protests. The character of these actions has ranged from marches, rallies, and cultural events, to blockading federal government office buildings. The great diversity and wide geographical dispersion of these activities has been made possible by the fact that CISPES has more than 400 chapters and affiliates in the large cities and small towns of 48 states.

CISPES's national organization publishes a newspaper, *Alert!* which is one

El Salvador, Aesculapius International Medicine, etc. For a directory of such solidarity groups, see the appendix to this book.—Eds.

of the best sources of information available on Central America in general and on El Salvador in particular. CISPES chapters and affiliates have raised more than $500,000 for material aid for El Salvador (see below). Currently, CISPES has set a national goal of $130,000 for its campaign entitled Healing the Wounds of War; Health Care for the People of El Salvador. Some of the events that will raise money for this campaign include a door-to-door canvass in Brooklyn, New York, a crafts fair in Mobile, Alabama, and a bike-a-thon in Santa Cruz, California. CISPES has arranged innumerable forums, film presentations, and slide shows that have contributed to the education of the U.S. public. At this time, many of these community activities are focused on the national Stop the Bombing Organizing Project. In Chicago, Detroit, Kalamazoo, Michigan, Champaign-Urbana, Illinois, Washington, and other locations, this very promising grassroots organizing is being conducted in the districts of congresspersons whose votes waver on El Salvador policy and can, perhaps, be changed by citizen pressure campaigns.

CISPES has also sent individuals and delegations to El Salvador to investigate conditions among students, trade unionists, and prisoners in the areas controlled by the San Salvador government. On a few occasions, members of these delegations have managed to travel out of San Salvador into zones controlled by the FMLN. There they have met with the rural population and with leaders of the FMLN and have even come under attack by jet aircraft manufactured in the United States. CISPES has also contributed to education about El Salvador by helping to arrange speaking tours in the United States for Salvadoran trade unionists, refugees, members of the FDR, and others. In fact, wherever solidarity work of any kind is occurring, CISPES, alone or in cooperation with other groups, has often contributed to the success of the activity.

LABOR

Many of those who are deeply concerned about U.S. foreign policy in El Salvador are active members of trade unions. The violation of the basic rights of Salvadorans to organize unions, the bombing of all major union halls, and the murder of thousands of trade unionists by government-supported right-wing death squads deeply affected North American trade unionists. Fully aware that the AFL-CIO leadership had supported U.S. involvement in Vietnam, they began to mobilize within their unions for a strong position against U.S. intervention in El Salvador. In California in 1981, the International Longshoreman's and Warehouseman's Union announced that they would refuse to load any military equipment bound for El Salvador.

In April 1981, a group of labor leaders in New York, including Moe Foner of District 1199, the hospital workers' union, Ida Torres of RWDSU, the storeworkers' union, and Sol Stetin of ACTWU, the clothing workers' union, joined together to form the New York Labor Committee in Support of Democracy and Human Rights in El Salvador. The New York committee inspired the formation of the National Labor Committee in Support of Democracy and Human Rights in El Salvador. This committee was co-chaired by Douglas Fraser, President of the United Autoworkers Union, Jack Sheinkman, Secretary-Treasurer of the Amalgamated Clothing and Textile Workers Union, and William Winpisinger, President of the International Association of Machinists. In March 1982, both committees placed an ad in the *New York Times* that supported the right of self-determination for the Salvadoran people, opposed U.S. military aid to El Salvador, opposed the sending of North American men and women to support unpopular regimes, and stated that U.S. funds should be used for social services rather than for military intervention.

Rank-and-file activists and local leaders formed similar committees in Seattle, Portland, San Francisco, San Jose, Los Angeles, Chicago, Indianapolis, Boston, Philadelphia, Washington, and other cities throughout the country. Numerous official committees were formed within unions to organize their members in opposition to U.S. intervention in El Salvador. They succeeded in getting hundreds of resolutions passed at labor conventions, organizing labor contingents at demonstrations, publishing articles in union newspapers, and sponsoring tours of labor leaders from El Salvador and other countries in Central America. Several delegations of labor leaders from the United States went to El Salvador, where they met with trade-union activists whose friends and relatives had been murdered, whose union halls had been bombed, and who had themselves been injured and imprisoned. The National Labor Committee helped to organize an international campaign that succeeded in bringing about the release of ten leaders of STECEL, the electrical workers' union. These leaders had been imprisoned for four years after they organized a strike. In 1985 delegations of North Americans went to El Salvador to attend the conventions of ANDES, the teachers' union, and of FENESTRAS, a major labor federation.

It is this type of organizing which caused the first major debate in 40 years to take place at an AFL-CIO convention. While the majority of the leadership of the AFL-CIO continues to support U.S. foreign policy in Central America, the 24 presidents of the national unions that belong to the National Labor Committee (and who represent one-half of the organized workers in this country) have become increasingly vocal in opposition to that policy. At the AFL-CIO convention in Anaheim, California, in October 1985, they succeeded in getting a compromise resolution passed that opposed Reagan's emphasis on a military solution to the conflict in Central America. The resolution stated:

Thus the AFL-CIO reiterates its insistence that military aid to the government of El Salvador be conditioned on its demonstrable progress in guaranteeing trade union rights, implementing land reform, ending the attacks and killings by right-wing "death squads," reforming the judicial system, and bringing to justice the murderers of AIFLD [American Institute for Free Labor Development—Eds.] representatives Michael Hammer and Mark Pearlman and Salvadoran labor leader José Viera. . . . A negotiated settlement, rather than a military victory, holds the best hope for the social, economic and political justice that the people of Nicaragua and El Salvador deserve.[3]

Although many other parts of the resolution basically support U.S. foreign policies in Central America, the fact that the resolution was at all critical of Reagan's position was an important accomplishment. In the past the AFL-CIO, through its lobbying efforts, through the American Institute for Free Labor Development, and through Lane Kirkland's participation in the Kissinger Commission, has supported a military solution to the conflict in El Salvador.

The level of the disagreement in the AFL-CIO with Reagan's policy is demonstrated by the following excerpts from a speech given by Kenneth Blaylock, President of the American Federation of Government Employees, at the AFL-CIO convention. Blaylock had participated in a labor delegation to El Salvador organized by the National Labor Committee.

As we condition our support for military aid in El Salvador in this resolution, we fail to mention that the activities and the campaigns of terror by the death squads have been replaced by military action, planned, supported and connived by military advisors in El Salvador and our embassy in El Salvador.

As I sat in the military commander's office last February, he glibly told us that "We will have this little war wrapped up in six months, because we have adopted a policy and a strategy of sanitization."

Now for those of you who do not know what in military terms sanitization means, it means with foot soldiers, with artillery and with aircraft you completely run all of the people out of an area.

As I sat in a church late one night and listened to mothers who had come down from those areas tell about the atrocities being perpetuated against them and their families by this technique of military operation, it would literally bring tears to your eyes. . . .

Again our military action, again our government's policy and I think in our resolution we surely should mention our government's policy and the role they're playing. Now I don't know about the rest of you people here, but when I look at Iran, I look at Vietnam, I look at Nicaragua, I look at El Salvador, Guatemala, I would like for one time for my government to be on the side of the people, not on the side of the rich dictators living behind high walls. . . .

Now we saw the results in El Salvador. The union leaders, there, as you people noticed this morning, the leaders from that country are very young. There are no old leaders left. The old ones have been killed.[4]

[3.] For the Hammer, Pearlman, Viera murders, see Reading 36. —Eds.

[4.] Proceedings of the AFL-CIO Convention, Anaheim, California, October 29, 1985.

This speech in many ways summarized the work being done within the labor movement to oppose U.S. intervention. It reflects both the sense of moral outrage and the strong critique of an administration that supports the repression of workers.

THE RELIGIOUS COMMUNITY

Organizing in the religious community grew rapidly after the murder of four religious women—three nuns and a lay worker—by the Army in El Salvador and after the murder of Oscar Romero, the Archbishop of El Salvador. The Inter-Religious Task Force in El Salvador, which works out of the National Council of Churches, was formed in 1981 and now has 350 local committees throughout the country. With the regionalization of the war, the committee changed its name to the Inter-Religious Task Force in Central America. It includes the leaders of 20 religious denominations such as the Presbyterian church, the Roman Catholic church, the United Methodist church, the Unitarian Universalists, the American Friends Service Committee, the Episcopal church, and the Christian Church-Disciples of Christ. A second organization, the Religious Task Force on Central America, which is primarily Catholic, works closely with the Inter-Religious Task Force.

According to Darlene Cuccinello, the chair of the Inter-Religious Task Force, the primary purpose of these committees is to educate the American public about questions of morality in order to bring about a change in U.S. policy in Central America. Their work consists of activities such as educational programs within their religious communities, lobbying, prayer vigils, support for the Pledge of Resistance (see Reading 54), and support for the sanctuary movement. She stated:

> This is the first time the grass roots and leadership are saying the same thing on a foreign-policy issue. This is the first time that the bishops of major denominations have called for stopping U.S. military intervention. The solidarity groups can be written off as leftists by the public because they take a political stance. The church's position, which is not talking right or left, is harder to argue with. It is especially important because the administration is trying to use theological rhetoric to justify its position. The work in the religious community is the most important because it is the largest and the most credible opposition.

The Pledge of Resistance has emerged as a key solidarity organization whose central activity is organizing demonstrations to protest U.S. policy toward Central America. Its origins trace to activists in the religious community who formulated a pledge to offer nonviolent civil disobedience in response to any U.S. invasion of Nicaragua. This commitment was then formalized as the Pledge of Resistance by a wide array of religious, peace, and solidarity groups and published in the August 1984 issue of *Sojourners,* a religious magazine. Its publication contained an invitation to U.S. citizens to sign it and to commit themselves to this course of action. In October 1984 the pledge was broadened to include not only a U.S. invasion of Nicaragua but also a variety of other significant escalations by the United States or its surrogates in any of the Central American nations.

The response was immediate. In every region of the country, people began to sign the pledge in large numbers and to develop plans of action to implement it if that proved necessary. The words spoken by some of those at the first mass public signing of the pledge, in October 1984 in San Francisco, convey the depth of feeling and determination that it evokes:

> I'm a pastor and as a person of faith I'm called to live out what's called the good news, that is the good news of God's peace and justice. I feel that by signing this pledge of nonviolent resistance that's one small embodying of the good news.

> I'm a mother of a 17-year-old son who I don't want to see fight in Central America, and I take this pledge of disobedience in the name of the Salvadoran refugees who lead me to this decision with their struggles and their stories.

> I'm a veteran of two wars. I'm not sure about the morality of those wars, but I'm very sure of the immorality of this war that's going on now in Central America. I've signed the pledge of resistance, and I'm going to stand behind it.

> I've never been arrested before. I'm signing the pledge not just for the people of Central America, but also for the people here in this country. We've got to wake people up to what is being done in our name all over the world.[5]

By November 1985, more than 68,000 people had signed the pledge. Coming from both the religious and secular political communities, they represented the broad unity of the U.S. people in opposition to the Central America policy of their government.

The pledge has mounted demonstrations in locales not traditionally associated with militant protests. These protests have occurred in Bangor, Maine, Decatur, Georgia, Jackson, Mississippi, Little Rock, Arkansas, San Antonio, Texas, Eureka, California, and Juneau, Alaska, as well as in New York City, Boston, Chicago, and San Francisco. Quite commonly they have involved occupations of the offices of congresspersons who have voted for aid to the Nicaraguan *contras* or for the Salvadoran military's air war. For example, during the September 21–24, 1985, pledge actions against the air war in El Salvador, eleven people in Fresno, California, were arrested in their congressperson's office after they demanded hearings on the bombing and on upcoming aid requests for the region; in Minneapolis 150 people were arrested while sitting in at two congressional offices; and in Seattle a mock Salvadoran village was built in the plaza of the Federal Building and destroyed to the taped sounds of bombing and helicopters. To date, thousands of people activated by

---

[5] *¡Basta! No Mandate for War. A Pledge of Resistance Handbook* (San Francisco: Emergency Response Network, 1985).

the pledge have demonstrated and been arrested while protesting U.S. policy toward El Salvador and Nicaragua.

After more than a year of its existence, the pledge needs to reassess its rationale for action. It was originally organized in the aftermath of the U.S. invasion of Grenada as a network that could be activated by "telephone trees" to respond on an emergency basis to a U.S. invasion of Nicaragua. In many regions the networks were organized by congressional district, and the pledge was conceived as a vehicle to bring organized pressure on congresspersons to vote for withdrawal of invading U.S. troops. Its wide geographical dispersion, its organizational structure, and the deep moral commitment of its signers constitute real strengths. However, in the face of current U.S. policy to wage protracted "low-intensity conflict" in El Salvador and guerrilla warfare in Nicaragua, in both cases largely with surrogate troops, the pledge has encountered difficulties in keeping its forces in readiness and in understanding clearly what events demand using the networks for actions. Accordingly, discussions are underway at all levels of the pledge to adjust to the current situation.

MATERIAL-AID ORGANIZATIONS

A different kind of solidarity organization is that whose primary purpose is to raise money for nonmilitary material aid for El Salvador. Because the government in San Salvador is corrupt and profoundly antagonistic to the interests of the masses, these groups do not channel aid through that government. Rather, aid is distributed through opposition organizations such as the FMLN and the local popular governments (*Poderes Populares Locales,* or PPLs) in the zones controlled by the FMLN so that the aid will, in fact, reach and benefit the people.[6]

In addition to providing essential aid to Salvadorans, the campaigns to raise money for material aid have several striking effects on North Americans. First, these campaigns translate abstract U.S. geopolitical strategy into the concrete terms of hunger, illness, and illiteracy that are easily comprehended and deeply felt and that lead people to side with the victims of the U.S. government. Second, donating money for and working in these campaigns helps to overcome the feeling of frustration that sometimes accompanies educational events or demonstrations, the feeling that nothing tangible is being accomplished. Donors are able to make an actual contribution to the welfare of the Salvadoran people. Finally, by aiding the people and the organizations against whom the U.S. government is waging war, donors place themselves in direct confrontation with their own government.

Medical Aid for El Salvador was founded in 1981 and was one of the first organizations in the United States to provide material aid. Since that time it has

[6.] In addition to material-aid groups that channel assistance through the FMLN, many other organizations direct aid in other ways, mainly through religious networks. See the roster of organizations in the appendix.—Eds.

distributed more than $700,000 for medical supplies for victims of the war, most of it going to people in the zones of control of the FMLN. This money has been spent on projects as diverse as the purchase of neurosurgical kits, the training and equipping of *brigadistas* (highly trained medics with knapsacks full of medicines and medical instruments who travel in the FMLN zones of control to administer health care and teach preventive medicine), and the support of a medical clinic in Guazapa, El Salvador, that was formerly administered by Charlie Clements, a North American physician who spent a year there.

Medical Aid participated in a dramatic relief mission involving Nidia Díaz, a commander in the FMLN. When captured by the Salvadoran military in April 1985, she was shot in the back, arms, leg, and hand. Because of the refusal of the Salvadoran government to permit surgery on her hand, permanent paralysis of the hand was imminent. After being pressured for months by members of Congress and by human-rights groups, the Salvadoran government finally gave permission in August 1985 for Medical Aid to dispatch a surgical team to operate on Díaz. Accompanying this team as an observer was Mike Farrell, an actor who portrayed a surgeon in the TV comedy *M*A*S*H*. Because of the political controversy surrounding the operation, no local surgical aide would participate. Therefore, Farrell was pressed into service. He scrubbed up and assisted, and the operation on Díaz was successful.[7] (Life imitates art!)

A number of methods are used by Medical Aid to raise funds. It receives a great deal of money in response to direct-mail appeals. All over the country, solidarity organizations, religious and community groups, and individuals put on events to raise money for Medical Aid. These events have been extremely diverse. They have included door-to-door canvassing, benefit concerts, and walk-a-thons with money pledged by friends and acquaintances for each mile participants walked. Countless house meetings have been arranged at which there is a talk or video presentation and a pitch made for money for Medical Aid. In New York City, a $100-a-plate dinner hosted by Ed Asner, Harry Belafonte, Colleen Dewhurst, and others raised $17,000. In Lawrence, Kansas, there is a rice-and-beans dinner every Thursday night with the proceeds going to Medical Aid. In Boulder, Colorado, Ed Asner attended a cocktail party and then addressed a community gathering in a church; there was extensive media coverage in Boulder and Denver, and $6,000 was contributed.

New El Salvador Today (NEST) is another material-aid organization. Since its founding in late 1983, NEST has sent $157,000 to El Salvador. This money has been channeled to the PPLs to fund their projects for health clinics and disease control, community literacy campaigns, and food production. These projects contribute to combatting parasites and malaria, to providing paper and pencils for the literacy campaigns, to supporting poultry and fishing

---

[7.] In October 1985, along with twenty-five other political prisoners, Díaz was released in an exchange for Inés Guadalupe Duarte, the kidnapped daughter of the Salvadoran president. Díaz returned directly to her FMLN unit. See Reading 41. —Eds.

cooperatives, and to growing beans, corn, rice, sorghum, and vegetables, much of which is destroyed by government aerial bombings and ground invasions and which, therefore, must be grown in great quantities.

The following quotations, from NEST pamphlets, of peasants in the zones of control governed by the PPLs make clear the need for this aid:

> The Salvadoran Army attacked our village and destroyed everything. But as soon as we could we returned and rebuilt our homes and replanted our crops, thanks to help from people around the world.
>
> Our appeal to you is urgent at this writing because our situation has been greatly affected by waves of hundreds of people fleeing the Army operations. The operations have involved bombings and invading ground troops. More refugee camps have been set up, creating a situation of even worse poverty, fear, and tension among the civilian population. Within this context we present our requests for your support. Adequate nutrition is at the base of all else and especially among the children. Malnutrition is an affliction that affects us all. We must increase our food production at this time, regardless of how tremendous the difficulties resulting from war. We must confront this on a daily basis and provide for the basic necessities of life.

NEST raises money by essentially the same methods as Medical Aid. Additionally, Boston and Berkeley, California, have adopted sister cities in El Salvador, and groups in Evanston, Illinois, West Lafayette, Indiana, Olympia, Washington, and other places have adopted sister communities. In these cases, fundraising is accomplished specifically for those cities or communities in El Salvador and channeled through NEST.

THE SALVADORAN COMMUNITY

The presence of more than 600,000 Salvadoran refugees in the United States has had a profound impact on the development of the solidarity movement. The war has forced many Salvadorans to flee their country after their names were placed on death lists, their relatives and friends were murdered, or their villages were destroyed. When they come to this country, they face tremendous difficulties in finding housing, jobs, and health care.

Many of the Salvadorans have moved to cities such as Houston, Austin, San Francisco, Los Angeles, Chicago, Newark, New York, and Philadelphia. In each of these cities, committees of Salvadoran refugees, such as Casa El Salvador or Comité El Salvador, have been formed. They have encouraged the development of the movement for a peaceful, political settlement to the conflict in El Salvador. They have provided direct personal testimony of the repression in El Salvador to various groups of Americans. These committees have worked closely with the solidarity movement. They organized the First National Salvadoran Caravan for Peace and Justice in Central America, which carried their message to cities and towns all across the country. They have marched from New York to Washington and have held hunger strikes in numerous cities. They have also worked on material-aid campaigns to send medical, office, and school supplies to the popular movement in El Salvador.

Increasingly, the Salvadorans have been facing repression in this country. Many Salvadorans have been deported. In October 1985 in Houston, twenty-two people in seven families were interrogated by the FBI. Their homes were entered, their property destroyed, and their personal identification confiscated. The FBI was working with the Immigration and Naturalization Service, and two of those who were interrogated were detained, although later released. They were accused of having ties with and directly supporting the FMLN. The prosecution of members of the sanctuary movement provides further examples of this repression.

Artists, teachers, professors, and lawyers have formed groups to organize people in their professions and to offer their talents and expertise to the solidarity movement. Limitations of space do not permit a full description of their valuable activities or those of countless others who have made important contributions to the solidarity movement, but they have mounted art shows, developed curricular materials, published reports on abuses of human rights, placed ads in newspapers, defended Salvadorans and solidarity activists in the courts, and raised funds for the popular opposition in El Salvador.

CONCLUSIONS

This sketch of the solidarity movement with El Salvador gives an impression of its character. A number of different organizations and networks are in place. Their members and constituents are both those who have become experienced in previous political struggles (notably, against the U.S. war on Vietnam) and those whose political analysis and practice have been developed by the Central American situation.

During the early days of the Reagan administration, marked as it was by the crudely bellicose threats of Haig, Kirkpatrick, and Reagan against El Salvador and Nicaragua and by the invasion of Grenada, the solidarity movement was at its peak in its ability to attract activists and resources and to mobilize people for its activities. There is every reason to believe that this mass, militant mobilization was a factor in slowing Reagan's hand in pursuing military measures yet more extreme than the ones chosen in El Salvador. (Indeed, a key message of the *Pentagon Papers* was that despite Nixon's public-relations effort to the contrary, the antiwar movement in the Vietnam era made a significant contribution to the defeat of the U.S. government's war effort.)

Now, with the use in large part of surrogate troops, the decision to wage "low-intensity conflict" in Central America, the institution of "democratic" reforms in El Salvador and Guatemala as a cover for the continuing militarist policies, and a generally lower profile in Washington for Central American policy, there has been a decline in visible protest. In part, the current size of the solidarity movement is a measure of its success in previously slowing the U.S. juggernaut.

Nonetheless, the solidarity movement continues to make important contributions. Moreover, the organizations and networks remain in place and provide the infrastructure for a mobilization even more massive and more militant than previous ones, should the U.S. introduce troops in significant numbers or otherwise massively escalate the war.

The challenge for the solidarity movement is to discover a way to remain ready to counter such dramatic U.S. government moves in Central America while, at the same time, managing to mobilize North Americans to oppose the slow but steady intensification of U.S. intervention in El Salvador and other Central American nations. It is our hope that the solidarity movement will accomplish this task and contribute significantly to the liberation of our Central American brothers and sisters.

54. Opposing U.S. Policy: The Pledge of Resistance*

FROM THE SOLIDARITY MOVEMENT

During the period of opposition to the Vietnam War, one of the most important protest documents was the 1967 "Call to Resist Illegitimate Authority," which described U.S. involvement in the Indochina conflict as "unconstitutional and illegal."[1] This "call" was signed by several thousand opponents of the war, and the government prosecuted five of them—including the pediatrician Dr. Benjamin Spock—on the grounds that they "did unlawfully, willingly and knowingly conspire, confederate and agree together and with each other, and with diverse other persons . . . to commit offenses against the United States." These alleged offenses were to "aid and abet" resistance to the draft.[2] The subsequent trial was a major cause célèbre of the 1960s, and the decision against the defendants was reversed on appeal.[3]

This Pledge of Resistance is modeled in part on the earlier Call, but in an era when the drafting of young men into the armed forces is not in effect, the acts of resistance called for are different. In fact, the pledge has two forms, one including possibly illegal acts of nonviolent protest, the other limited only to "acts of legal protest."

* The Pledge of Resistance (n.d.), widely distributed at Central America demonstrations and other events.

[1.] The text of the 1967 document is reprinted in Marvin E. Gettleman, Jane and Bruce Franklin, and Marilyn Young, eds., *Vietnam and America: A Documented History* (New York: Grove Press, 1985), Reading 47.

[2.] Indictment of the "Boston Five" in U.S. District Court, January 5, 1968, in Jessica Mitford, *The Trial of Dr. Spock, the Reverend Willam Sloane Coffin, Jr., Michael Ferber, Mitchell Goodman, and Marcus Raskin* (New York: Alfred A. Knopf, 1969), Appendix 1.

[3.] Mitford, *The Trial of Dr. Spock* is a penetrating account of the Boston Five conspiracy action through conviction and later reversal.

CIVIL DISOBEDIENCE PLEDGE

If the United States invades, bombs, sends combat troops, or otherwise significantly escalates its intervention in Central America, I pledge to join with others to engage in acts of nonviolent civil disobedience as conscience leads me at Congressional field offices, the White House, or other pre-designated U.S. federal facilities, including federal buildings, military installations, offices of the Central Intelligence Agency, the State Department, and other appropriate places. I pledge to engage in nonviolent civil disobedience in order to prevent or halt the death and destruction which such U.S. military action causes the people of Central America.

Name (Print) _____ Date _____

Signature _____

Address _____

City _____ State _____ Zip _____

Tel. (office) _____ (home) _____ Cong. Dist. _____

Have you had nonviolence training? _____ or Rep. _____

LEGAL PROTEST PLEDGE

If the United States invades, bombs, sends combat troops, or otherwise significantly escalates its intervention in Central America, I pledge to join with others to engage in acts of legal protest as conscience leads me; including such actions as participating in demonstrations, vigils, leaflettings, and appeals to Congress and the White House. I also pledge to demonstrate my support for those who engage in acts of nonviolent civil disobedience in order to prevent or halt further death and destruction in Central America.

WHY NONVIOLENT RESISTANCE?

U.S. citizens have a long history of nonviolently resisting injustice and war. Nonviolent direct action was used effectively by the women's suffrage movement to gain women's voting rights, by the civil rights movement to end segregation in the South, and by the anti-war movement to help terminate the war in Indochina. As Martin Luther King Jr. said, "Nonviolence, when effectively organized, is an unstoppable force. When people are caught up in what is right and are willing to suffer for it, there is no way of stopping it short of victory."

LET US PLEDGE TO
STAND WITH THE PEOPLE
OF CENTRAL AMERICA

The sheer danger of expanding an already long and bloody war in Central America calls us to engage in strong, dramatic, nonviolent resistance. Such nonviolent resistance to government policy is a very serious step. But the seriousness of U.S. escalation in the region demands that we consider this form of active, nonviolent witness. In the event of an invasion, tens of thousands more will die in a tragic war. The lives of the people of Central America depend on our joining together—from every walk of life and every age group—to nonviolently oppose this growing disaster *before it worsens.*

CHAPTER X

Dialogue and the Prospects for Peace

Editors' Introduction

The term *dual power* was popularized in Petrograd in 1917 as a description of the political situation prevailing after the fall of tsarism. Two sets of authorities, a "provisional government," and a network of "soviets" (the Russian word for popular "councils"), emerged, each committed to different goals and each commanding allegiance from different sections of the population. Put another way, the same condition could be described as "dual powerlessness"—for a certain period, neither side had the political strength to assure its authority over the whole of the nation.[1]

Such situations existed long before the Russian Revolution and long after. They are inevitable wherever old orders have been broken or challenged and new ones are not yet in place or consolidated. Patterns of revolution, counter-revolution, and civil war—the last being the most extreme and violent manifestation of "dual power"—have been a part of national histories in the twentieth century in locales the world over.[2]

From this broad perspective, Central America in general and El Salvador

---

[1] For a classic account see Leon Trotsky *The History of the Russian Revolution,* 3 vols., translated by Max Eastman (New York: Simon and Schuster, 1936). See especially the historical and theoretical discussion in Vol. 1, chapter 11. For a recent treatment, see Alexander Rabino-vitch, *The Bolsheviks Come to Power: The Revolution of 1917 in Petrograd* (New York: W.W. Norton and Company, 1976).

[2] Eric Wolf analyzes six revolutionary transformations involving protracted civil wars in his *Peasant Wars of the Twentieth Century* (New York: Harper & Row, 1970).

in particular are no exceptions. In El Salvador, the end of the 1970s brought an erosion of the traditional contours of oligarchic/military rule, and the 1980s have led to a contest between two would-be successor regimes—the Duarte government, claiming sovereignty by virtue of "free elections," and the movement of popular resistance known as the FMLN. As of the end of 1986, a rough balance of forces exists between the two sides, warranting the description "dual power," a characterization favored by the FMLN.

Each side is convinced of its own strength and legitimacy. The Salvadoran military firmly believes that their new U.S.-supplied equipment and the professionalism the armed-forces leadership is trying to foster will result in a decisive victory over the rebels. For their part, the rebels are proud of their ability to cope with the intensified counterinsurgency. They have developed defensive techniques of their own, relying on mobility and dispersion in the face of deployment of such sophisticated military technology as a spotter plane using infrared sensors that even at night can locate, by body heat, concentrations of guerrilla forces.[3] Morale remains high among both camps, although the Duarte government is experiencing difficulty in retaining the support of an urban social base, particularly among labor groups.[4]

Can this conundrum of dual power be resolved without subjecting Salvadorans to the constant bloodletting that has already ravaged their tiny nation for nearly a decade? Can the civil war be settled peaceably through mutual accommodations and concessions in ways that ensure the political stability of the resulting new regime?

A survey of dual-power situations and civil wars in the twentieth century does not yield hopeful conclusions about such a possible outcome. Usually, nothing less than total and unconditional victory by one side over the other settles the conflict. Force has indeed been the midwife of history. Yet exceptions and novelties, as well as regularities, are characteristic of political dynamics. In recent times, the example of Zimbabwe (formerly Rhodesia) comes to mind. In the course of a long civil war, the white-settler colonial regime of Ian Smith at length accepted the inevitability of black-African rule and opted for a surrender of political authority to the Marxist movement of Robert Mugabe in return for a minority voice in government.

A simple imposition of the Zimbabwe model on El Salvador cannot hold. Is the FMLN an analogue to Mugabe's movement, and Duarte a facsimile of Ian Smith? Such analogies may be plausibly constructed in hypothesis, but

---

[3.] FACHRES delegation, interviews with Generals Carlos Eugenio Vides Casanova and Adolfo Blandón, San Salvador, January 10, 1985; FACHRES delegation, seventh visit to El Salvador, January 1986, briefing, New York City, March 2, 1986.

[4.] Robert C. McCartney, "Even Duarte's Supporters Are Down on Him These Days," *Washington Post,* national weekly edition, April 7, 1986. By early 1987, Duarte was facing serious trouble from the right. In January business executives and opposition parties organized a successful one-day business strike to protest increased taxes.

they are not reliable guides to conditions in El Salvador, where, for example, the racial dimension is absent. We don't know whether Duarte or representatives of the FMLN thought about Zimbabwe when they agreed to conduct their widely acclaimed dialogue at La Palma and Ayagualo late in 1984 (see Readings 55 and 56). Whatever crossed their thoughts, leaders on both sides recognized, however briefly, that, as Churchill once expressed it, talk, talk, talk is better than war, war, war.

The talks were inconclusive and bitter. Still, dialogue ought to be seen as a process, a lengthy one, and not as a single dramatic resolution. Echoes of dialogue continue to be heard long after the two sides parted at Ayagualo. Reading 57 in this section excerpts a call of November 1985 by rebel military leaders for renewed negotiations based on the FMLN's familiar "power-sharing" formula. In March 1986 Duarte proposed negotiations with the FMLN if the Sandinistas agreed to negotiate with the Nicaraguan rebels (the *"contras"*). In April 1986, meeting in Lima under the auspices of Peruvian President Alan García, representatives of the two social-democratic parties that are allied with the FMLN held talks with officials of the Salvadoran government.

The rebel call of November 1985 was ignored by the Duarte government, and Duarte's proposal to the FMLN and Managua was generally dismissed as a ploy suggested by Washington to pressure the Sandinistas and influence congressional voting on military assistance to the *contras*. As for the unpublicized talks in Lima, no agreements or follow-up materialized, but on June 1, 1986, in a speech marking the second anniversary of his presidency, Duarte called for a new round of talks with the guerrillas. The FMLN and the DRF promptly accepted the offer, and over the next three months, representatives of the rebels and the government, with the support of the church, traded proposals on the time, place, and agenda for the new talks. On August 23, after discussions in Mexico, a communiqué signed by Archbishop Rivera y Damas announced that both sides had agreed to hold the talks in the Salvadoran town of Sesori, 95 miles northeast of the capital, beginning September 19. Hopes for the renewed dialogue, however, were dashed amid mutual recriminations after the rebels demanded, and the government refused, the removal of army units recently brought into the Sesori region. Said Guillermo Ungo, head of the DRF, "This confirms my view that Duarte started this as a propaganda game with no room for maneuver." The same day Duarte accused the rebels of boycotting the talks "because they don't want to negotiate for peace. They want a dialogue of war."[5]

[5.] *New York Times*, September 16, 1986. "In September Duarte and the guerrillas agreed to hold peace talks in a small town in northern El Salvador. Colonel [Roberto Mauricio] Stabén, in violation of the arrangements Duarte had approved, moved his troops into the area around the town. The guerrilla leaders, not eager to be Stabén's next kidnapping victims, declined to show up." Jefferson Morley, "Prisoner of Success," *The New York Review of Books*, December 4, 1986.

In the Salvadoran deadlock, much depends on Washington. As chief economic supplier of the Duarte regime and provider of its military arsenal, Washington holds important keys to the Salvadoran civil war. From its inception, the Reagan administration has been fond of the crusading rhetoric of anti-Communism and counterrevolution. But overall, its policies have revealed large doses of pragmatism. Moreover, in Central America, Washington has in recent years directed its political obsessions at Nicaragua, not El Salvador. It is intriguing to speculate that in the long run the Reagan administration may yet be flexible on El Salvador. For the present, unfortunately, no major shift in Washington's strategy of refusing to recognize the legitimacy of the Salvadoran rebels—of denying, that is, the reality of dual power—is discernible. So long as Washington remains adamant on this, prospects remain remote for a genuine dialogue process that leads to a just peace.

55. An Offer of Peace*

By José Napoleón Duarte

In this address delivered at the United Nations the newly elected Salvadoran president announced his plan for a meeting, which in fact took place later that same month at the town of La Palma in Chalatenango province and was covered extensively by the press. Duarte explained later that it took him almost a half year to "get in position" to start the process of dialogue by inducing the death squads to reduce their murderous activity and by "getting a handle on world public opinion."[1] When the full story of the Salvadoran "dialogue" becomes known, however, it is likely that the role of the church and Archbishop Arturo Rivera y Damas, as well as the FMLN/FDR leadership, in initiating this process will be accorded a more prominent role than is now the case.[2]

What is of considerable interest in the portions of Duarte's U.N. talk reproduced here is his reversal of the conventional view that the guerrilla leaders of the FMLN are the radical, Marxist "extremists," whereas the civilian leaders of the FDR[3] are the reasonable moderates.[4] Duarte here argues that the FDR leaders in exile are the ideologically dogmatic radicals, whereas the rebels in the hills are pragmatic folk who can be convinced

---

* Excerpted from the translation of Duarte's address to the United Nations, New York, October 8, 1984, in 39th U.N. General Assembly, *Provisional Verbatim Record* (A/39/PV.24).

[1.] Marvin E. Gettleman, interview with José Napoleón Duarte, Presidential Palace, San Salvador, January 1985.

[2.] Marvin E. Gettleman, interview with a widely respected observer of the Salvadoran scene, who must remain anonymous, January 1985.

[3.] See Readings 22–27 for the components of the Salvadoran rebel movement.

[4.] This is the main thesis of Enrique Baloyra, *El Salvador in Transition* (Chapel Hill: University of North Carolina Press, 1982), among many other studies of the Salvadoran insurgency.

that they made a mistake in taking the insurrectionary path and should rejoin "the democratic political stuggle" in the war-ravaged country. Although Duarte's argument was obviously motivated by rhetorical considerations, it does suggest that the relationship between different segments of the insurrection may be more complicated than is usually conceded.

Commenting favorably on the U.N. speech was rebel leader Joaquín Villalobos, who, from his base in Morazán province, expressed satisfaction that Duarte had finally acknowledged "the strictly domestic roots of the war" and had thus negated all previous statements that "it was imported from abroad."[5] However, almost a year later, Duarte reverted to the formulation that outside agitators were responsible for the conflict. As he put it in his June 1985 address to the National Assembly: El Salvador's civil war was "imposed on us with the aid and sponsorship of the Soviet, Cuban and Nicaraguan Marxist governments."[6] It is not only rebel commanders who find Duarte's theory of the war incredible, but many independent observers as well. Of course, official Washington, with its vision of omnipresent agents of the unified Moscow-directed world conspiracy (see chapter 1), probably likes to have those it supports echo its own perceptions of reality. The relevant question may very well be: Is Villalobos as dependent on Moscow, Havana, or Managua as Duarte is on Washington?

I came before the United Nations General Assembly in October 1981 as President of the Revolutionary Junta of El Salvador to explain to the world the crisis which was facing my country and to explain to you the process of democratization which we proposed to accomplish and which we have indeed fulfilled, in holding the first free elections in El Salvador to elect the National Constituent Assembly, which brought back a state of law and received, without any reluctance whatsoever, from the Revolutionary Junta, the full powers of a democratic and a republican nation. That message was received with satisfaction by representatives at the United Nations, although scepticism led them to doubt the possibility of free elections proposed by a *de facto* Government which had committed itself to ensuring that its people would come in large numbers to vote, even under fire, to demonstrate its desire for democracy and its rejection of violence. . . .

I am very happy to state here before all the peoples of the world that El Salvador, despite having gone through one of the most difficult periods in its history, has given specific examples of what a people can do and obtain when it truly believes in democracy as the best possible way to solve the differences which are inherent in all organized societies.

For more than four years now El Salvador has suffered from the effects of a merciless war which has caused us bloodshed and impoverishment. More than 30,000 Salvadorans have been the innocent victims of a fratricidal con-

[5] Interview with Villalobos, broadcast by clandestine Radio Venceremos, October 13, 1984, in Foreign Broadcast Information Service, *Daily Reports,* October 18, 1984.

[6] Duarte's Address to the National Assembly, June 1, 1985, in *ECA/Estudios Centroamericanos,* 34 (May–June 1985), 430.

frontation. More than half a million persons have had to leave their homes and their property. Subversive forces have engaged in a campaign of terror and systematic destruction, and our people [are] tired of it. It must end.

One after another, the speakers who have preceded me at this rostrum have referred to peace in the strongest of terms.

Peace undoubtedly is the greatest yearning of all men, and its maintenance is the main function of the United Nations. I too come before the Assembly to speak of peace in the same strong terms.

But I shall not refer to the dangers confronting the world as the consequence of the unbridled arms race, nor to the threat of total destruction represented by the senseless accumulation of nuclear weapons although, of course, I share the concerns of all of you, as well as your frustration in the face of the seeming inability of the community of nations to fulfil not only the letter but also the spirit of the Charter of the United Nations.

I shall not speak of nuclear confrontation because others have done so here with great eloquence and profound knowledge of this problem.

May I therefore be permitted to depart from the usual procedure and, in greeting all the nations of the world, I should like to take this opportunity to describe and define the position of my Government in the face of the problems and the crisis which beset us, because in this manner I shall furthermore establish the principles of the foreign policy of my country, which is based on peace and harmony among all human beings.

I am convinced that to give this information is part of the responsibility which we have taken upon ourselves in the face of disinformation, stereotypes and commonplace statements. We must dispel uncertainties, clarify goals and purposes, state the course we intend to take and inform the world of the reality of life in El Salvador. . . .

El Salvador's conduct has always been based on its dedication to the principles and tenets which govern relations between States. We are convinced that adherence to those principles is an indispensable requirement for a more harmonious coexistence of international society. El Salvador thus fulfils its international commitments and regrets that some countries that speak half-truths and deliberately conceal their own violations appear before various bodies of this Organization not in order to settle differences but rather to use the Organization as a mere platform for propaganda, regardless of the cost and the degree to which they undermine this body, whose protection they claim to seek. El Salvador believes that the Contadora process is the only course open to us. In this context we support an honest regional dialogue so that we Central Americans may determine our destiny on the basis of a consensus. We Central Americans must not become the tools in a struggle of the interests and ideologies of foreign Powers and certainly not the mere instruments of those Powers, thus denying our own nationalism and characteristics and frustrating the aspirations of our peoples and their right to live in peace and freedom. . . .

The history of my country is similar to that of many of the underdeveloped countries in the world. If I describe it briefly, many representatives listening to me will find amazing similarities with the history of their own countries. It is the history of a common struggle, of anguish, of triumphs and of failures. It is a common history of ideals—it is our history.

El Salvador emerged from colonialism to become an independent State on 15 September 1821 as a member of the Federal Republic of Central America. The struggles between the conservatives and the liberals culminated at the end of the century in the absolute triumph of the latter. From that time on, a coffee oligarchy controlled the economic and political life of our country. The larger and better ranches, banking and trade in the principal export products were in their hands. Controlled elections led to a succession of Presidents of the Republic who were the representatives of that oligarchy until 1931. Then for the first time a progressive party came to power, but a few months later it was defeated. The world crisis, the fall in coffee prices and the losses suffered by our farmers led in 1932 to a popular uprising, which was put down by force. After that an alliance emerged between the armed forces and the oligarchy, which used it to keep political control and economic privileges. Following a dictatorship that lasted for 13 years, and after 1944, various military Governments, Government juntas and provisional Presidents came to power. In 1984 the first civilian Government in 50 years was elected by the free vote of the people. . . .

In October 1979, a group of officers and officials acting on behalf of the armed forces overthrew the ruling authoritarian Government and issued a proclamation pointing out the corruption of the system of government and promised to open the path to democracy, as well as to undertake a series of structural reforms and, in particular, to lay the bases for thorough agrarian reform.

The Revolutionary Junta that was set up that year included, along with the armed forces, the political parties and the social, economic and religious forces that still believed in a democratic solution and that had harshly criticized those who had taken up arms. The Communist Party, the National Revolutionary Movement—of social democratic orientation—and the Christian Democrats took part. The armed subversives stepped up their attacks against the new régime. Many thought that the triumph of the guerrillas was imminent, and in the face of that possibility the Communist Party and the Social Democratic Party left the Government and its democratic position and joined the armed struggle.

At the same time, the leaders of the mass movements also withdrew and joined the guerrillas. In other words, they all burned their bridges and opted for armed struggle and violence as the sole solution. I believe that this attitude was their first historical error: to abandon the democratic political struggle and the struggle of the masses and opt exclusively for armed struggle.

In accordance with the historical analysis carried out by the subversives, in applying their ideological position to reality they never thought that the Salvadorian armed forces would break their traditional alliance with the oligarchy and that, therefore, the economic and social reforms could ever be achieved. They thought that the establishment of pluralist democracy would continue to be a Utopian goal and out of the question.

The only political sector that did not lose faith was the Christian Democratic Party—my Party—and by means of an agreement with the armed forces it rebuilt the 1980 Government. Despite the negative forecasts of the extreme left, with the active participation of the armed forces the most profound agrarian reform in Latin America was carried out, the banking and finance system was reformed and foreign trade was nationalized. These reforms brought in hundreds of thousands of peasants as a major social and political force, henceforth organized in co-operatives and in owning the best and biggest ranches of the country.

Faced with the faulty analysis of the extreme left that structural changes were impossible, the subversive groups made a new and fatal mistake with the most serious consequences for their objectives: in acting in the same way as the extreme right they lent themselves to bringing about the failure of the reforms. Thousands of peasants were murdered, as were hundreds of Christian Democrats; crops were burnt, houses and machinery destroyed and the publicity campaigns of both extremes denigrated both nationally and internationally the reforms that had been initiated. Their only success, however, was to distance the people from extreme positions and to begin to strengthen the democratic revolution. . . .

Many of those who took up arms did so out of rebellion and frustration: they wanted agrarian reform, they fought for a banking system that would serve the majority and they wanted respect for the will of the people through free elections. These justifications were valid in 1979; today they have lost all validity.

At that time it could be argued that the objective and subjective conditions were in keeping with the historical dialectics of the class struggle and that, in response to rightist totalitarianism, the concept of revolutionary violence should gain validity and force.

The Marxist strategy of a prolonged people's war against imperialism and the oligarchies, the oppressors of a people deprived of justice and freedom, was based on that concept and thousands of young people joined a process that began with social confrontation and civil disobedience and went on to the use of arms in the various phases of the destruction of life and the destruction of services and firms, until it resulted in the greatest crisis in our country's history.

I am convinced that the historic path of mankind is not one of violence but of democratic revolution.

It is understandable that those compatriots who left El Salvador years ago cannot or refuse to understand that things have changed; however, I know that the great majority of Salvadorians, and even the guerrilla commanders and fighters roaming about in the mountains of our homeland, are aware of this new situation.

Unfortunately, the Revolutionary Democratic Front does not understand that we are experiencing a new reality, and therefore it is still trying to change things that no longer exist: a mediaeval agrarian structure, a financial structure at the service of the interests of a minority, an army at the service of a political system dominated by an economic élite. All those things no longer exist. In 1979 a profound process of change began, and it has been consolidated. Today we have a new agrarian structure which has placed our best lands at the service of the farmer. We have a new financial structure which supports and strengthens the new agrarian structure. We have a new trade structure for the products that we traditionally have exported, and this makes available to the country the hard currency thereby generated. We now have an armed force that works for the people. And we have a people that has demonstrated its unshakeable faith in democracy and has elected a Government by its own free will; we have a people that are working, suffering and dying to achieve peace and justice.

From this rostrum I ask those who advocate the ideology of armed subversion in El Salvador to change their strategies because of the new reality in my country. The El Salvador that they left in 1978 and 1979 is not the El Salvador that exists in 1984. Today our country is breathing the air of freedom. Political parties are respected and encouraged. The people freely choose their leaders. Abuses of authority and violations of human rights have been reduced to the very minimum, and those who commit them are prosecuted and punished. Banks are lending large sums to farmers, who are actively participating in the social and political struggles. There is a very different society in El Salvador today.

I wish at this point to address some observations to the nations that have committed themselves, in one way or another, to undermining my country, as well as to the guerrilla leaders—not those who are living comfortably in and giving orders from Managua or Havana, or to other nations that claim to be democratic but in fact export violence and murder, but to the leaders of the guerrillas who are in the mountains of my country, those who are suffering from the elements, unsheltered, those who are aware of the real position of the Salvadorian nation when they attack the people and who are waiting—in vain —to be welcomed as liberators when the truth is that their purpose is to oppress those people. I am addressing myself to the leaders who take their ideals for reality; to those who are mistaken about the people because they have a different view of truth; to the leaders who are now committing this historical error. The guerrilla leaders in the mountains are aware of this dilemma, but they are egged on by subversive leaders from abroad, who try to conceal this truth and distort this reality in order to justify their anti-historical position before the whole world.

The people of El Salvador now have no doubt that subversive violence has lost its mystique and its raison d'être. Terrorist violence has become an end in itself, which proves that its objective is no longer liberation, and certainly not democracy.

In El Salvador the terrorists have committed excesses but they have failed, because the people do not support them and because we have the political will to build a united, pluralistic and democratic society. By persisting in their anti-historical obstinacy, they have dedicated themselves to the oppression of the simple farmers who are the victims of their reign of terror; they are robbing and killing people; they are leaving citizens without any means of communication because they are blowing up bridges and railroads; they are destroying electrical power lines and water systems; they are setting fire to plantations producing coffee, cotton and food crops. That leaves the poorest element of our population without work or hope.

It is so easy to destroy. Services which are needed by the people and which took so many years to build up, the infrastructure that is part of our national heritage and that was established by the efforts and sacrifice of our people, can be destroyed in an instant by the criminal hand of the terrorist, who uses dynamite and is financed by nations that have in mind only world domination and are perhaps labouring under a misunderstanding of history.

This new reality is misunderstood by the members of the Revolutionary Democratic Front, because they live outside our country; it is being experienced today by all the Salvadorians who have not abandoned their homeland. But it has penetrated the guerrilla forces. We know this from the testimony of the guerrillas who have abandoned their weapons and violence and have set out on the path to peace. We know it because the guerrillas are not getting so many volunteers and are obliged to fill their ranks with young people. We know it because they are becoming weaker each day.

For all those reasons, I address the Salvadorian guerrillas and ask them to accept the new reality, to stop killing our brothers, to stop destroying bridges, to stop destroying the infrastructure of the nation, the public transport services, the plantations and the railroads. In a word, I ask them to stop killing and destroying and, together with all the rest of our people, to engage in the building of a new country, a free and democratic country in which peace will be the basis for our development.

I now wish to make an offer of peace.

Ever since I became President, by the freely expressed decision of the citizens of my country, I have been aware that my principal task is to work for the achievement of social harmony and internal peace in the Republic, which has been convulsed by a conflict with both internal and external causes. The time has come to put an end to that conflict. I am more convinced today than ever before that the existence of this conflict not only affects the life of my compatriots but is an element of friction that threatens the peace and security of other nations of the world, and particularly of our brother nations in Central America.

Hence, there could be no more appropriate time than this, when I am at this rostrum, to make before the peoples of the world an offer of peace, which would ensure for all Salvadorians—without any distinctions flowing from political or ideological position—social harmony and security. This offer is made within the framework of the Salvadorian Constitution, which has established the system of democracy and political pluralism, under which the most varied ideologies can coexist.

Of course, the acceptance of this proposal by all sectors—those that are in the opposition to my Government, within the constitutional system, as well as those that are fighting by violent methods—will require a change of mental attitude, under which hatred will be replaced by understanding and tolerance. For, after all, the peace which is manifested by outward signs is but the result of an individual and social state of mind which rejects aggression and all forms of violence and promotes dialogue and the democratic political struggle whose results are seen at the ballot box.

Quite naturally, it is hard to convince those who up to now have viewed weapons and violence as the only way to ensure their political space that there can be a climate in which they can express their own thoughts without thereby suffering reprisals from their adversaries.

But I have come here to affirm that as President of the Republic and Commander of the Armed Forces I am in a position to maintain those measures which, within our constitutional process, make it possible for them to abandon an attitude that runs counter to the history of the political evolution of the people of El Salvador. Furthermore, in due course I shall propose to our Legislative Assembly general amnesty for political crimes. We are exercising control over abuse of authority and eliminating all the methods of repression that have existed in our country in the past and have in part been at the root of a rebellion for which there is no longer a need.

This means that I am offering the safety and security of a political place within a pluralistic, constitutional, democratic system which Government is defending. As part of those efforts I invite the heads of the guerrilla movement now in our mountains, to come without weapons to the village of La Palma, in the Department of Chalatenango, at 10 A.M. on 15 October, the anniversary of the insurrection movement of 1979 and in the presence of the representatives of the Churches and the world press, to discuss with us the details and scope of this proposal for their incorporation into the democratic process and the establishment of an atmosphere of freedom for the next election. I am convinced that our people, tired of violence, will take this proposal as a sign of hope emanating from its lawful Government.

56. La Palma and Ayagualo: Brief Peaceful Encounters in a Long Civil War

The prospects for peace in El Salvador seem dimmer than ever, as both sides dig in for a protracted struggle and Washington shows no interest in pressing for a negotiated settlement that would diminish President Duarte's political control along the lines of power sharing with the FMLN.[1] At one point, however, late in 1984, the two warring parties met, with the blessings and in the presence of the Salvadoran church hierarchy, to initiate what many hoped would be the essential process of dialogue for ending the savage conflict. President Duarte met face to face with representatives of the FMLN/FDR at the town of La Palma, Chalatenango province, on October 15, 1984. In the village of Ayagualo, La Libertad province, on November 30, 1985, officials of the Duarte government met rebel leaders. These meetings raised expectations that were soon dashed as both sides, having presented their respective positions, returned to the battlefield.

The following reading and ensuing exchange analyze the significance of the meetings in the light of political realities in El Salvador—or in light of what each side perceives to be the realities. Were the meetings a forgettable interlude in the civil war, merely a platform for airing political positions? Or were they what may someday be seen as the start of a search for peaceful paths toward settlement?

Terry Lynn Karl teaches in the Department of Government, Harvard University. In April 1985, she visited El Salvador as part of a delegation to monitor the process of dialogue, sponsored by the Washington-based Commission on U.S.–Central American Relations. Edward S. Herman teaches at the Wharton School, University of Pennsylvania, and is author and co-author of several books on the United States and the Third World.

A. After La Palma: The Prospects for Democratization in El Salvador*

BY TERRY LYNN KARL

PRESIDENT José Napoleón Duarte's dramatic decision to hold peace talks with the FDR-FMLN in October 1984 ushered in a new phase of El Salvador's painful political transition. Duarte's La Palma initiative marks an important breakthrough in the stalemated civil war: by agreeing to meet with the FDR-FMLN (Democratic Revolutionary Front–Farabundo Martí National Libera-

[1.] For a sophisticated early argument for this kind of solution, see Piero Gleijeses, "The Case for Power-Sharing," *Foreign Affairs,* Summer 1983.

* From *World Policy Journal* (New York), 2 (Spring 1985).

tion Front), the Christian Democratic president has effectively granted formal recognition to another "representative political force" and an alternative center of power in the country. For the first time, the rebels and the government stand in a position of political parity—backed by separate armies. Although fighting resumed just after the La Palma meetings and negotiations are now in abeyance until after the March 1985 elections, the two sets of talks that the government and the FDR-FMLN held before Christmas have nonetheless created hopes for a political solution of the war and for peace at some point, however remote, in the future.

Is optimism warranted in this deeply torn nation? What accounts for President Duarte's sudden willingness to negotiate after several years of refusing to do so? What are the prospects for democratization in El Salvador—a country that over the past four years has suffered 50,000 deaths and the displacement of 27 percent of its population? How can U.S. policy facilitate this process? Even a superficial glance at Salvadoran history reveals the powerful obstacles to the construction of a fully competitive party system. Throughout its modern history, El Salvador has lacked a solid pluralist tradition. It has been ruled by an antidemocratic alliance between the oligarchy and the military: the agrarian private sector has relied on the armed forces to govern by suppressing peasant- or worker-based associations and autonomous partisan expression. Does Duarte's call for the FDR-FMLN to join a democratic process reflect any real change in this respect? If so, how should the United States respond to these developments?

Perhaps it is best to state some conclusions at the outset. There is little question that the La Palma initiative, regardless of its actual results, signals an important—if uncertain—increase in the opportunity for democratization in El Salvador. Although it is difficult to gauge the changes that have taken place between 1979 and 1985, the stalemate that has been established between the government and the FDR-FMLN, as well as that which has emerged between the Reagan administration and the U.S. Congress, have produced new incentives for compromise on the part of all Salvadoran political actors, particularly within the armed forces and the private sector. This stalemate in El Salvador results from domestic and international vetoes that rule out either a return to the old regime or a revolutionary triumph. These vetoes, by preventing an outright military victory by any side, might conceivably result in a democratic instauration by compromise. This does not mean that a democratization will necessarily occur—a forecast no political observer could make in the face of the tremendous uncertainties that exist in the region—but rather that an *opportunity* for democratization exists.

Within the context of this stalemate, the Christian Democratic Party (PDC) lies at the center of current democratization efforts—the place where domestic and international forces meet and where strategies and alliances are forged and discarded. Today its actions are critical in the determination of El Salvador's future. This has not always been the case. From 1980 to 1982, the PDC governed only nominally; after failing to win a sufficient majority in the 1982 elections, it was forced to the sidelines. Now, for the first time since the outbreak of the civil war, the party has been thrust to the forefront of Salvadoran politics. Its new position is largely the result of changing circumstances beyond Christian Democratic control rather than of a self-conscious democratic design. Nevertheless, since the 1984 elections, the PDC's capacity to influence events has grown: it has more leeway than ever before to try to negotiate a peace and to implement a deliberate democratic strategy. Yet because of the ideological discord in Christian Democratic thinking, the contradictory lessons of past practice, the *personalismo* of Napoleón Duarte, and the uncertainty of the political pressures that might be brought to bear upon the PDC, its course in 1985 is difficult to predict.

Ultimately, the contribution the PDC makes to the resolution of El Salvador's crisis depends on the U.S. government. Although the PDC has enhanced its own ability to exert domestic influence by making itself politically indispensable to the Reagan team, only the administration and the U.S. Congress, acting in the context of a stalemated war, hold the power to pressure the armed forces and the traditionally antidemocratic private sector into giving up past privileges and playing by democratic rules. If the United States strongly supports the move toward negotiations by maintaining certain incentives, like the cutting of military aid and the tying of economic funds to progress on peace and reform, then democracy will gradually appear to be the more advantageous—or the less disadvantageous—choice to those forces that have previously rejected democracy in El Salvador. Under these circumstances, other options such as authoritarian rule or revolution would become less attractive. The decision to sustain or increase pressures for democratization is a U.S. policy choice—one that so far has been opposed by the Reagan administration, even after the La Palma talks, and supported only erratically by Congress. Yet in the year ahead, strong pressures are needed to keep the spirit of La Palma alive and tilt the delicate balance away from a ruinous civil war toward a future political settlement in El Salvador—and perhaps in the rest of Central America.

THE CHRISTIAN DEMOCRATIC STRATEGY TO DEMOCRATIZE EL SALVADOR

Napoleón Duarte's sudden decision to meet with the FDR-FMLN on October 15, 1984, took the Reagan administration and most political observers by surprise. Although the press, with some validity, attributed this about-face to Duarte's impetuous character, the decision to negotiate had its roots in Christian Democratic ideology and practice as well as in specific partisan interests. Perhaps more than any other political force in El Salvador, the Christian

Democratic Party has understood that its own long-term survival ultimately depends upon the successful construction of an anti-authoritarian alliance that can forge a compromise on the procedures for democratization and the parameters of a future political regime. In any transition to democracy, this step is contingent on the ability of antagonistic domestic political actors to produce acceptable interim agreements or pacts about the new rules of the political game as well as mutual guarantees that these rules will be respected by all parties concerned, regardless of the outcome. These pacts are usually put together by parties that occupy the center of the political spectrum—the position the PDC has chosen for itself in El Salvador.[2]

There can be little real debate over the PDC's credentials for this bargaining role. Since its inception, the party has played a pact-making game—first with the left until 1972, then with the right after 1980, and now perhaps with the left again. The PDC has been the most important political organization to appear during the flurry of associational activity that took place in El Salvador over the past two or three decades. Formed in 1960 when International Christian Democracy was showing substantial gains throughout the continent—especially in Venezuela and Chile—the PDC rapidly demonstrated its ability to construct a durable organization, build a mass base in largely urban areas, and govern the city of San Salvador. Its successes resulted in part from the popularity of party leader Napoleón Duarte. By March 1972, the PDC was able to produce a national electoral victory in coalition with two other parties, now represented by the FDR-FMLN. This victory was subsequently snatched away through electoral fraud by the armed forces.[3]

Although the PDC's critics emphasize recent U.S. influence over the party to explain its political behavior, the PDC's current strategy for democratization owes far more to Christian Democratic ideology and its own participation in that international movement than it does to direct U.S. pressure. The PDC's guiding principles for democracy are based upon certain key Christian Democratic tenets: anticommunism; belief in the need to build consensus; a reformist conception of private property rights, which results in advocacy of land reform; the right of individual political expression primarily through the right to vote; and the rule of law. This vision has a strong conservative bias stem-

---

[2.] For a discussion of the importance of pacts in the transition to democracy, see Terry Karl, "Petroleum and Political Pacts: The Transition to Democracy in Venezuela," in Guillermo O'Donnell, Philippe Schmitter, and Laurence Whitehead, eds., *Transitions from Authoritarian Rule: Latin America* (Baltimore: Johns Hopkins University Press, 1985); Guillermo O'Donnell and Philippe Schmitter, *Political Life after Authoritarian Rule: Tentative Conclusions about Uncertain Transitions* (Baltimore: Johns Hopkins University Press, 1985); and Adam Przeworski, "Some Problems in the Study of the Transition to Democracy," forthcoming in the same four-volume series.

[3.] For a historical description of the party, see Stephen Webre, *José Napoleón Duarte and the Christian Democratic Party in Salvadoran Politics, 1960–1972* (Baton Rouge: Louisiana State University Press, 1979). [See Reading 10.—Eds.]

ming from Catholic precepts of ordained order and zealous opposition to the spread of atheistic thought, represented by communism; yet the emphasis upon socioeconomic change gives the movement a reformist cast. In many Christian Democratic parties, the ideological discord between these twin preoccupations of order and reform has often resulted in a confused political definition, strong internal factionalism, and party divisions.[4]

The PDC's strategy of democratization has been influenced by the party's two decades of political practice. During its formative years, the PDC was forced to grapple with the question of allying with the military. At that time, it rejected any type of collaboration, preferring to continue to build its own separate political base. In 1960 Duarte sealed his status as a major party figure by maintaining party unity during the strong debate over a possible alliance with the military. The party maintained its policy of noncooperation with the military until after the 1972 election, when the military denied the PDC its victory. Forced into exile in Venezuela, Duarte and other party leaders came to the conclusion that any future reform in El Salvador could only be achieved in alliance with the army, particularly the young officers. As early as 1973, they were discussing the possibility of an interim government that could unite civilians, including the PDC, and military progressives. By the October 1979 coup, much of the PDC leadership had set aside its reluctance to join with the military. In a highly controversial decision in 1980, the Christian Democratic Party, led by Duarte, joined the military government at the very moment when army-led repression was forcing other civilian parties into open, armed opposition.[5]

To a unique extent, the experiences of other Christian Democratic parties, particularly those of Chile and Venezuela, have affected the Salvadoran party's strategy and perceptions of reality. The Venezuelan example of regime transformation in the aftermath of 1958 has had a particularly strong impact. During his seven years of exile in Caracas, Duarte absorbed significant lessons through his close political relationship with the leaders of the Venezuelan Christian Democratic (COPEI) party. Because Venezuela's own democracy was an elite-negotiated enterprise, party officials there emphasized the importance of political pact-making with the army, the private sector, and other political parties as well as the need to relinquish certain reformist aspects of

---

[4.] For a discussion of Latin American Christian Democratic ideology, see Michael T. Fogarty, *Christian Democracy in Western Europe: 1820–1973* (London: Routledge and Kegan Paul, 1957); Edward Williams, *Latin American Christian Democratic Parties* (Knoxville: University of Tennessee Press, 1967); and Mario Solarzano Martínez, "El Papel de la Democracía Cristiana en la Actual Coyuntura Centroamericana" in Hugo Assman, ed., *El Juego de los Reformismos frente a la Revolución en Centroamérica* (San José, Costa Rica: Collección Centroamericana DEI, 1981).

[5.] This treatment of Christian Democratic democratization strategy is drawn from interviews conducted by the author in El Salvador, Mexico, and Venezuela. Discussions with Napoleón Duarte, Fidel Chavéz Mena (PDC), Hector Dada (former leader of the PDC), José Miguel Fritis (IVEPO), Rafael Caldera, and José Rodríguez Iturbe (CAREF, Venezuela) were particularly useful.

the original party program. Duarte, noted for his highly personalistic and messianic style, was particularly taken by the Venezuelan model and considered himself El Salvador's equivalent of Romulo Betancourt.[6]

The Venezuelan experience did provide an important instance of the voluntary withdrawal from power by an undefeated military. In exchange for an amnesty for past human rights violations and political crimes as well as substantial economic benefits, the Venezuelan Armed Forces had accepted a new self-definition as an "apolitical, obedient, and nondeliberative body." True, the military was already deeply divided over its own role in government and chose to withdraw from power in order to maintain its institutional integrity. Yet Betancourt's legendary artfulness was of critical importance: he courted the military, nurturing its leaders' allegiance to his own emerging regime. When a guerrilla war broke out after the establishment of democracy, Betancourt was able to translate his widespread popularity into broad national support for the military's effort to quash the uprising. Among Venezuelan politicians, this produced a strong belief in the possibility of "democratizing" a country's armed forces—a belief they willingly shared with their Salvadoran counterparts.

There were additional lessons for El Salvador in the Venezuelan agreement that established the "rules of the game" in the political realm. The Pact of Punto Fijo, signed prior to the holding of any elections, was a classic example of an interim agreement to create a formula for compromise. It guaranteed that all parties would respect the result of the elections, whatever they might be, and established a political truce between parties previously in dispute, particularly the Christian Democrats and the Social Democrats, while excluding the Communist Party. Although the pact did not commit the parties to explicit quotas of power-sharing, as did a similar pact in Colombia, it did recognize that the benefits of state power must be equitably distributed to guarantee the prolonged political truce necessary for the formation of a coalition government. Thus, regardless of who won the elections, each party was promised a share of the political and economic pie through access to state jobs and contracts, a partitioning of the ministries, and a complicated spoils system that would assure the political survival of all signatories. In 1982, the Salvadoran PDC would attempt a similar agreement through the Pact of Apaneca.[7]

The Venezuelan parties had also negotiated an economic pact with the

[6.] As Duarte remarked: "We believe that we can do what the Venezuelans did. . . . We are following the Venezuelan example and I am Romulo Betancourt." Interview with José Napoleón Duarte, San Salvador, October 1983. This description of the influence of the Venezuelan model of democratization was also drawn from interviews with COPEI members and officials from the Foreign Ministry and CARE in Caracas, Venezuela, November 1983.

[7.] On August 3, 1983, the PDC, ARENA, the PCN, and the PPS signed this agreement as a means of easing tensions and reaching some form of governability during the civil war. The pact pledged to lower the level of interparty disputes, established a timetable for a new constitution and the next elections, and set up a political commission to work out disagreements. See Tomás R. Campos, "El Pacto de Apaneca, Un Proyecto para la Transición," *ECA,* September 1982.

private sector that established the broad outlines of a development model—an important means for limiting uncertainty during the formative stages of a democracy. All political parties in Venezuela agreed to respect foreign and local private capital accumulation as well as to subsidize the private sector. This agreement thus ruled out the possibility of expropriation, but it did provide for a program of land reform based on compensation paid for by Venezuela's petroleum wealth. In return for their support of basic property rights, the parties won the elite's aquiescence to the expansion of the state, the right of workers to organize, and a policy of guaranteed benefits in health, education, social security, and wage rates. Given U.S. interests in Venezuelan oil, the economic pact was closely tied to an informal modus vivendi with the United States. In exchange for assurances that U.S. holdings would *not* be expropriated and that Venezuela would maintain a pro-U.S. foreign policy, the U.S. government refrained from intervening to support its previous ally, Perez Jiménez, and eventually promised its full backing to the new regime. PDC leaders hoped that a similar arrangement could be made in El Salvador, providing reassurance to both the Salvadoran agrarian elites and the U.S. administration.

To a lesser extent, the experiences of Chile, whose democratic political system was overthrown by the 1973 coup, also influenced the Salvadoran Christian Democratic Party. Unlike their Venezuelan counterparts, the Chileans in their advice to Duarte were skeptical about the possibility of democratizing a military like El Salvador's through simple persuasion; instead, they stressed the importance of the U.S. role in producing a military withdrawal from government. In addition, they were aware of the deep divisions likely to be caused by a substantive agrarian reform—particularly one lacking the petroleum revenues that had financed the Venezuelan program.

Chilean Christian Democrats were speaking from their own experiences of failure in Chile. They traced this failure to their inadvertent destruction of a pragmatic centrist party during the mid-1960s before the election of Salvador Allende, and warned the Salvadoran PDC against a similar mistake. In particular, these Chileans felt that their party had failed to continue the practice followed by its predecessor, the Radical Party, of occupying the political center by forming alliances with both the left and the right. On the one hand, the party had become sectarian, adopting a *partido único* majoritarian strategy that polarized politics, making it more difficult to formulate compromises. This factor, combined with party tactics emphasizing mobilization at the expense of client relationships, upset the normal rules of Chilean democracy by encouraging popular organization and real political competition in previously unincorporated rural areas. On the other hand, the party could see in retrospect—given the power the Communist Party had gained and the 1970 victory by the Popular Unity Coalition—that it had been unnecessarily intransigent toward those factions of the left that wanted to play by electoral rules, contributing to a destabilization through polarization, mobilization, and the breakdown of a center. "We have to avoid that here," argued José Miguel Fritis, a Chilean PDC member working in El Salvador, "by building a pragmatic center-right coalition in this country."[8] Once cemented, this alliance could later turn its attention to negotiations with the left.

This combination of Christian Democratic ideological predisposition and party experience in several countries produced clear if inconsistent guidelines for the democratization of El Salvador. First and foremost, the Salvadoran PDC believed that it should try to "turn enemies into partners" by forming an alliance with the military in order to convince it to leave power. This explains the PDC's 1980 decision to govern with the traditionally repressive military, to give unqualified support to the Salvadoran armed forces while attempting to conduct serious political work inside the government, and to renounce all active efforts to seek a political solution. In light of this strategy, it seems unlikely that the party would risk alienating the Salvadoran High Command in the future by entering into agreements that could strain the nascent PDC-military relationship.

Second, the party has been committed to occupying the center of the political spectrum, wherever that might be, through pragmatic policies, nonmobilizing actions, and alliances with both the left and the right. Because the PDC's association with the military prohibited political negotiations with the left, this strategy called for the formation of flexible and frequently changing alliances that were aimed at assuaging the fears of the private sector and the political right and that resulted in the gradual abandonment of PDC's centrist position. It might be expected that, in order to regain the center, the party would make some move toward the left to the extent permitted by the Salvadoran Armed Forces.

Third, the PDC has always believed in the importance of pursuing a careful program of agrarian and technocratic reforms to improve the efficiency of the market and the state while solidifying a social base for a conservative political democracy. Yet this goal collided with the desire to soothe antireformist agrarian interests and the effort to build a center-right coalition. In practice this meant that the party's position on the importance of and timetable for various reforms shifted constantly according to the political winds of the moment, a behavior that would be unlikely to change without a strong electoral majority. Ironically, the party's own constant vacillation has made the achievement of such a majority less and less likely; this, as we shall see, became an important impetus for the La Palma talks and foreshadowed the backpedalling that would occur as reaction to negotiations intensified.

[8] Interview with José Miguel Fritis, Chilean Christian Democrat working in IVEPO, San Salvador, October 1983. For an analysis of the destruction of the political center in Chile, see Arturo Valenzuela, *The Breakdown of Democratic Regimes: Chile* (Baltimore: Johns Hopkins University Press, 1978).

Finally, like all other forces in El Salvador, the PDC believed it should seek international support for its own program—an awkward task as the party twisted and turned through these other imperatives. On the one hand, potential democratic allies in Latin America and Europe had trouble with the PDC's decision to join a repressive military regime; on the other hand, the Reagan administration found it difficult to support a program of state-led reform, given its own militant bias in favor of free enterprise. As the PDC's fortunes dipped throughout 1982, its only firm ally until the 1984 elections remained its sister members of International Christian Democracy. Most international actors measured out their support for the Salvadoran PDC according to their own foreign policy positions regarding the desirability of a political settlement. This created additional long-term pressure for negotiations.

STALEMATE AND THE 1984 ELECTIONS

Given the obvious contradictions in these strategies, it is no wonder that the Christian Democratic Party can be credited with little actual success until 1984. Yet not even a coherent strategy could have brought democracy to this deeply divided country. Democratization has been blocked by the ongoing search for a military solution; breaking this deadlock required a widespread perception that the current situation would only bring continued losses to all sides. This perception crystallized in the 1984 elections.

Democracies are usually made "on the installment plan," as events unfold.[9] They result from concrete steps and sequential decisions, unintended consequences and pure luck, which, when taken in toto, increase the probability of a competitive or semicompetitive polity. In general, transitions to democracy have been a by-product of other goals and intentions on the part of reactionaries and revolutionaries. For antidemocratic actors, democracy is by definition a second-best option chosen only when no single other regime preference can prevail. A democratic compromise can emerge from and terminate a prolonged and inconclusive struggle that would otherwise bring significant losses to all political forces involved. Indeed, democracy's greatest attraction may well be this institutionalization of stalemate through the construction of a polity based upon uncertain outcomes yet offering the possibility of future change. Thus the clear perception of stalemate can be conducive to democracy's emergence—a situation that began to take shape only in 1983.

The period from 1980 to 1983 marked a clear failure of Christian Democratic strategy in El Salvador. The decisive pressure from the Carter administration, rather than any subtle "democratization" of the military, had convinced the armed forces to accept the PDC as a junior partner in the ruling junta in 1980 and to lend some support to land reform. The military's subse-

[9] See Dankwart Rustow's seminal article, "Transitions to Democracy," *Comparative Politics,* April 1970, 337–366, and those works listed in note 2.

quent agreement to the holding of elections was a concession to the United States, not to the military's hated Christian Democratic allies.[10] When these U.S.-sponsored elections took place in 1982, the Christian Democrats, tarnished internationally and domestically by their complicity with a repressive regime, were unable to win the electoral majority they needed to govern. They could not defeat the ultraright, represented by the National Republican Alliance (Arena). Indeed, only open U.S. intervention in the selection of the country's president kept ultrarightist Roberto D'Aubuisson out of the nation's highest office; he was replaced by a compromise candidate, Alvaro Magaña, who had not even participated in the elections. The right, furious at U.S. interference, retaliated by appointing D'Aubuisson President of the Constituent Assembly and promptly adopting legislation that effectively annulled much of the Christian Democratic land reform. By 1983, each pillar of Christian Democratic strategy—the alliance with the military, the occupation of the political center, the insistence upon reform, the desire for international linkages—was in serious trouble.

What changed this context in 1983 was the dawning realization of a political and military stalemate, a stalemate defined by several hard realities. The Reagan administration, pursuing a hard-line strategy in Latin America, remained committed to the defeat of any revolution on its watch—a fact that ruled out a military victory by the FDR-FMLN. At the same time, the U.S. Congress, which controls the strings on the purse that is the sole maintenance of the Salvadoran government and economy, refused to condone an alliance with the violent ultraright, represented by Arena, or military escalation in El Salvador, with its potential for involving U.S. troops. This ruled out both the total defeat of the opposition and the full restoration of the old regime. Finally, the FDR-FMLN demonstrated that it was too strong, both politically and militarily, to be defeated by the Salvadoran military alone. Since it could deny an economic recovery or peace until its political demands were met, the FDR-FMLN retained the power to prohibit a successful center-right alliance in El Salvador. In sum, El Salvador faced a series of international and domestic vetoes that effectively prevented either military authoritarianism or revolution.

By 1983, this system of vetoes began to translate into crisis for both El Salvador and U.S. foreign policy. Inside El Salvador, the temporary breathing space opened up by the 1982 elections and the subsequent formation of a government of "National Unity" had closed by January 1983. The FDR-

[10.] In mid-July, at the height of international disapproval of the Reagan policies toward Central America and pressure for a political solution in El Salvador, Assistant Secretary of Inter-American Affairs Thomas Enders called for "prompt, free and open elections" as "the best course for ending civil violence and keeping peace." The army, however, reacted strongly against the idea. It believed that elections could produce a PDC victory and "a one-party state" with the permanent retention of Duarte. Only U.S. insistence and the apparent spreading of CIA money in appropriate places won the army's reluctant agreement to hold elections. See Raymond Bonner, *Weakness and Deceit: U.S. Policy and El Salvador* (New York: Times Books, 1984), 290–293.

FMLN had launched a highly successful military operation in October 1982; this culminated in an intense campaign at the new year. In January alone, the FDR-FMLN initiated 181 military actions, demonstrating a capability of attacking over broad areas of the country, including San Salvador, that belied predictions of its early demise. In late 1983, it overran a major army base in Paraiso, drove hundreds of government troops from a crucial bridge at Cuscatlán, and demonstrated the weakness of a U.S.-sponsored "National Plan" that was to be the centerpiece of the army's strategy in the coming year.[11]

The FDR-FMLN offensive, coupled with increased U.S. pressure to hold down human rights violations, exacerbated existing divisions within the armed forces. Appalled by losses through death and desertion of up to 20 percent of enlisted personnel, and hindered by supply shortages caused by congressional unwillingness to fund the war adequately, the Army Command was torn between a hard-line and a reformist course. An expanding faction, led by Defense Minister García, began to support land reform in order to assure continued access to U.S. aid. The January 1984 rebellion of Lt. Col. Sigifredo Ochoa, supported by the rightist party, Arena, signaled the discontent of the country's ultraconservatives with García's leadership, continued talk of land reform, and human rights-related restrictions on U.S. aid. This revolt was terminated only by a delicate military compromise involving the transfer of Ochoa and the eventual removal of García. Although different factions of the army eventually agreed upon General Vides Casanova as the new commander, the fragility of the army's unity could no longer be discounted.

The governing political parties were also deeply divided over the prosecution of the war, the state of the economy, and the extent to which reforms should be permitted. In early 1983, the alliance between Arena and the National Reconciliation Party (PCN), two rightist parties that had dominated the Constituent Assembly since the 1982 elections, collapsed in a shambles, leaving the country virtually ungovernable and weakening the base of Arena and the ultraright. After considerable turmoil, the Christian Democrats stepped in and, drawing upon their pact-making experience, joined with the PCN to forge a fragile, one-vote working majority in the Assembly. But it is clear that the PCN's association with the Christian Democrats was a stopgap measure, intended to prolong a deadline for the land reform. Crisis erupted at midyear over the Constituent Assembly's adoption of the new constitution. Arena and the PCN reunited to block future land reform in the constitution, using death squad threats as part of their "legislative" tactics. In return, the PDC tried to defend its program of agrarian reform by resorting to the unusual tactic of mobilizing peasants to march into San Salvador. In the tense period that

---

[11.] This description of the military situation in El Salvador and divisions within the Salvadoran Armed Forces and the political parties was gathered during a visit in October 1983. For a more complete treatment, see Kenneth Sharpe and Martin Diskin, "Facing Facts in El Salvador: Reconciliation or War," *World Policy Journal*, Vol. 1, No. 3 (Spring 1984), 517–547.

followed, the Christian Democrats were forced to accept a constitution that blocked the PDC party program by raising barriers to changes in land tenure patterns.

The Reagan administration faced a similarly bleak situation in 1983. Heightened pressure for political negotiations instead of a military solution came from a variety of sources: the unexpected strength of the FMLN offensive, the deterioration of the Salvadoran military and government, the visit of the Pope to Central America, the formation of the Contadora Group, and the positions of European allies. In addition, U.S. public opinion was strongly opposed to increased military involvement in Central America. Harris Polls from 1982 and 1983 showed that 79 to 85 percent of the respondents were against the introduction of U.S. troops into El Salvador; this figure dipped to 54 percent after the invasion of Grenada, but stayed at that level only briefly. To show its displeasure with administration policy, Congress began to block additional U.S. funds to the Salvadoran army, cutting a $60-million aid request in half to protest the Salvadoran government's lack of progress in the investigations of the deaths of four churchworkers and other U.S. citizens.

In general, support for the Reagan plan of massive military and economic aid aimed at producing a military defeat of the opposition had waned badly —a trend the president was unable to reverse through his unusual address to a joint session of Congress in April. Even the May shakeup of the Central America team with the removal of Assistant Secretary of State for Latin America, Thomas O. Enders, the visit of President Magaña to Washington, the formation of the Kissinger Commission, and the roving ambassadorship of Richard Stone did little to stem rising criticism. By November 1983, Reagan was forced to veto a bill that renewed the human rights certification requirements on aid to El Salvador since his own avowals of Salvadoran progress in curbing repression had become a political embarrassment.

As early as March 1983, the Reagan administration was seeking new elections in El Salvador both to escape from its own policy dilemma and to alleviate the country's internal crisis—a tactic that had proved at least temporarily effective in 1982. The administration even urged the Salvadoran government to advance the presidential elections from March 1984 to some time in 1983 as a demonstration of its commitment to democracy. Although the elections could not be moved up because of technical problems,[12] the Reagan administration did make certain not to leave their outcome to chance. Fearful

12. The idea of advancing the elections was supposed to appear as a Salvadoran initiative, but it was inadvertently made public by Special Envoy Richard Stone. The center-right agreed to the new date because they believed this would bring increases in U.S. aid, but all parties later insisted that the initiative had come from El Salvador, not the United States. One Reagan official was less diplomatic, stating that "the timing of the elections is essentially a Salvadoran issue to decide, but our position consistently has been that we support the elections at the earliest possible time in order to sort of get this thing wrapped up." In the end, the elections could not be advanced because of technical problems. *Washington Post*, March 3, 1984.

that Roberto D'Aubuisson might win an electoral majority, which would permanently jeopardize congressional approval of U.S. aid, and realizing that the Christian Democrats offered the best public relations advantages, the Reagan team poured over $10 million into the elections, paying for electoral technology and administration and the air fares of international observers. It gave support funds to the Unión Popular Democrática (UPD), a confederation of unions allied with the AFL-CIO that backed the PDC, and cooperated with Venezuela's COPEI government and the Konrad Adenauer Foundation of West Germany to channel money through a Venezuelan-sponsored Christian Democratic public relations firm.[13]

The results were satisfactory for both the United States and the PDC. In the final runoff between Roberto D'Aubuisson and Napoleón Duarte, the Christian Democratic candidate won 53.6 percent of the valid votes. The party, which had only nominally governed from 1980 to 1982 and had remained on the political sidelines in 1983, was given another chance.

THE ROAD TO NEGOTIATIONS

The 1984 elections reshaped the political game in El Salvador to the advantage of the Christian Democratic Party, giving its program the international and domestic credibility it had lacked during the 1980–82 government. Duarte's first act as president was to bring in massive amounts of new funding. His success was resounding, indicating a broad range of international support. The Reagan administration, delighted that it finally had an elected ally to present to Congress, sent Duarte to the House and Senate committees that had previously slowed or blocked aid and arranged for him to address the Senate. The new president, an effective campaigner in Washington as well as in El Salvador, won $61.75 million in immediate supplemental military aid. Within just three months of his inauguration, Congress had appropriated a total of $132 million in military aid and $120 million in economic aid, a sharp increase from the past. In addition, the amount set for fiscal year 1985 brought the total aid figure secured by the Duarte government to almost half a billion—an amount second only to Israel's. After his Washington stint, Duarte traveled to Europe,

---

[13.] The firm named IVEPO, a Venezuelan-sponsored institute staffed largely by Chilean Christian Democrats, denied receiving funds from the United States. But employees of IVEPO privately credited Konrad Adenauer, the Venezuelan government, and the United States for its money. Their campaign advice, provided free to the PDC, and their financing launched Duarte's campaign and kept the electoral process functioning. Jorge Rochac, the chief planner of the Elections Council, said: "IVEPO just pays the bills. They haven't said no to anything I asked for. The beauty of it is, IVEPO can give help in ten minutes that would take ten years if I had to go through the government." When asked where the money originated, he replied, "Sometimes it is better not to know things in this country." The U.S. government also gave money to the PCN to help draw votes away from Arena. *Boston Globe,* May 4, 1984; *Time* Magazine, May 21, 1984. Interview in IVEPO, San Salvador, October 1983.

where he received $18 million from West Germany's Christian Democratic government followed by money and support from the leaders of Portugal, Belgium, and Britain.[14] Even France and Mexico, FDR-FMLN's strongest backers except for Soviet allies, softened their positions toward El Salvador's new government.

Using this international backing as leverage, Duarte moved quickly to clarify the new conditions that would prevail under his government: the foreign aid the country desperately required depended on curbing the extreme right inside both the armed forces and the political parties. Although in the past there had been numerous pressures on the military to clean its own house, Duarte's success in Washington brought home the message that to receive substantial increases in U.S. aid El Salvador had to maintain a government acceptable to the U.S. Congress. The Salvadoran Armed Forces responded positively to this message by restructuring the military command. Four leading rightist officers—including Treasury Police head Nicolas Caranza—known to be supporters of D'Aubuisson and linked to death squad activity, were transferred to posts outside El Salvador. In addition, the military agreed to dismantle the intelligence unit of the Treasury Police, the reputed center of death squad activity, and to separate the command of the regular army from the security forces—a maneuver that would bring the security forces under closer governmental control. These shifts replaced the hard-line leadership of the National Police and the Treasury Police with moderates and conservatives— a boon to the Christian Democrats and a reflection of Duarte's persistent lobbying of the military.

Arena also felt immediate pressure to lower its extremist profile. When threats of a plan to overthrow Duarte surfaced, the new president quickly turned to his U.S. allies. In the past, the Reagan administration had been reluctant to intervene against Arena, despite the advice of former Ambassadors Robert White and Deane Hinton. But now the administration took a new stance, dispatching General Vernon Walters—the traditional expert at dealing with recalcitrant militaries—to El Salvador to tell D'Aubuisson that a coup would not be tolerated. In June, the State Department accused D'Aubuisson of complicity in a plot to assassinate Thomas Pickering, U.S. Ambassador to El Salvador, and subsequently denied D'Aubuisson a visa to enter the United States. Reagan feared that the ultraright might upset the U.S. diplomatic victory represented by the 1984 elections and demonstrated that his government now had a stake in Duarte's success: Arena would have to play by the recently established party rules or risk the open wrath of the region's dominant

---

[14.] Before Duarte's first visit to Washington after winning the presidency, one senior official delightedly remarked: "We will run him all over Capitol Hill, putting members of Congress in the palpable position of voting against democracy if they vote against aid to El Salvador." *Boston Globe,* May 6, 1984. For a report on Duarte's international trip and subsequent aid statistics, see *Central American Bulletin,* July-August 1984, and *Latin America Weekly Report,* July 27, 1984.

power. Since U.S. displeasure centered on D'Aubuisson's notoriety, new divisions began to appear in Arena over D'Aubuisson's future role in the party. Some conservatives turned their support to other rightist parties, such as the PCN.

Thus Duarte's election marked an important shift in the balance of power among the United States, the Salvadoran Armed Forces, and the Christian Democrats. In a sense, the least powerful member of this alliance—the PDC —temporarily gained the upper hand. While this realignment did advance democratization by propelling party politics into a more central role and restricting state violence, the actual changes it introduced were still quite tentative. The private sector continued to block land reform in the Constituent Assembly and to oppose the attempts of workers and peasants to organize. Death squad activities slowed but did not stop: a trade union leader and a university professor were killed. The Duarte government knew it was walking a fine line. As rumors of a leadership purge based on political sympathies spread throughout the armed forces, one high commander publicly warned, "If it stops here, it is okay, but if it continues, it could become worrisome."[15]

Yet the new president could not stop at this point if he wanted to succeed in future elections. Despite his initial actions, Duarte faced intense pressure from his party and electoral base. Worker and peasant organizations grew increasingly angry at his constant efforts to placate landowners at their expense. Impatient for change and trusting that repression would slacken under the new government, these groups became active after the 1984 election. Strikes and labor disputes increased at an alarming rate and demanded solutions.[16] At the same time, trouble arose in the PDC's relations with the UPD, an umbrella organization of labor federations and peasant unions. In the 1984 elections, the Christian Democrats had given promises of accelerated land reform in exchange for the UPD's support. But the PDC found itself unable to keep this commitment. Although Christian Democratic leaders explained that the peasant unions would have to build support for the party in order to win a majority in the 1985 Assembly elections that could reintroduce the land reform program, the Secretary-General of the nation's largest peasant union publicly threatened to withdraw support from the PDC if it did not deliver on its promises.

Other factors weakened the PDC's hold on its electoral base. The 1984 elections had communicated an important message: the party's constituency, and the Salvadoran population in general, favored some form of political

[15.] *New York Times*, May 25, 1984.

[16.] In early 1984, strikes occurred in the Social Security Institute, the IRA, the Salvadoran Teachers Union, the textile industry, and various financial institutions. At least 37,000 workers took part in work stoppages at this time, resulting in a ten percent public sector wage increase. This was the first strike activity in El Salvador since the virulent repression against the labor movement began in 1980. See the *Central America Bulletin,* July–August 1984.

negotiations with the opposition to bring peace and economic recovery. Pre-election polls showed that 70 percent of all Salvadorans considered the war and the economy to be the country's principal problems; 51.4 percent favored dialogue as the best means of resolving the war—a surprisingly high percentage to be openly expressing agreement with what was the formal position of the FDR-FMLN. Only 10.3 percent advocated military annihilation of the armed opposition, while just 10 percent called for a military intervention by the United States.[17]

One does not have to look far for the underlying causes of these trends in public opinion. The rapid deterioration of the economy since 1979 had dramatically affected the living standard of most Salvadorans. The price index rose about 25 percent per year. Yet since 1980, wages had been frozen by government decree: between 1979 and 1983, real minimum wages declined by 65 percent and consumption levels by 50 percent. Almost 80 percent of the population was unemployed or underemployed.[18] The war and the uncontained human rights abuses had taken an additional toll on the country. By 1984, it was generally acknowledged that there had been over 50,000 deaths and over 1.3 million persons displaced in this country of only 5 million inhabitants. The popular base of the Christian Democratic Party was clamoring for some visible and significant change.

Thus the 1984 electoral victory created a painful dilemma for the governing party. On the one hand, it was restricted by its key allies—the United States and the Salvadoran military—who had been opposed to any form of negotiations with the FDR-FMLN. On the other hand, the Salvadoran people had given Duarte a mandate to negotiate. To the extent that voters had been free to choose—given the exclusion of the FDR-FMLN and the abstention or failure to vote by a third of the eligible electorate—they had voiced a preference for a program of reforms, an end to the war, the termination of human rights abuses, an opening toward the FDR-FMLN, and the defense of the right of association.[19] Throughout the campaign, Duarte had claimed that D'Aubuisson had produced nothing but economic chaos and death during his

[17.] These polls, obviously limited in their reliability because of the atmosphere of intimidation in which they were conducted, are one of the few indicators of public opinion in El Salvador. The statistics favoring negotiations are particularly surprising since in early 1984 it was difficult to express support for negotiations, an FDR-FMLN position, without risking reprisals from the ultraright. See Ignacio Martin-Baro and Victor Antonio Orellana, "La Necesidad de Votar: Actitudes del Pueblo Salvadoreño ante el Proceso Electoral de 1984," *Estudios Centroamericanos: Las Elecciones Presidenciales de 1984,* April-May, 1984, 255–256. This entire edition contains several excellent analyses of the 1984 elections.

[18.] See Segundo Montes, "Condicionamientos Socio-Politicos del Proceso Electoral," *Estudios Centroamericanos,* April-May, 1984 and *NACLA, Report on the Americas,* Vol. 18, No. 2 (March–April 1984).

[19.] Ricardo Chacon, "Las Campañas de los Partidos," in *Estudios Centroamericanos,* April–May 1984, 229–252.

21-month tenure as president of the Constituent Assembly. The alternative Duarte had offered—the linchpin of his campaign—was a "pacto social," a government that would reconcile and integrate all Salvadorans into an effective plan for peace. Now Duarte had to deliver on this promise or else be vulnerable to the same charges he had leveled at D'Aubuisson.

Compounding all these difficulties was the continued pressure of the FDR-FMLN. It engaged in a heavy sabotage campaign through June and July, repeatedly seized control of the nation's roads, and launched a spectacular attack on the Cerron Grande dam, demonstrating a military capability that surprised U.S. advisers. Despite a lull in combat as the FMLN adjusted to an escalated air war—and despite frequent pronouncements in the U.S. press about the new successes of the Salvadoran armed forces—the enormous influx of aid following Duarte's election did not appear to diminish the opposition's capacity to continue fighting and disrupting the economy. The FDR-FMLN made its position clear: there would be no peace or economic prosperity until the fundamental issues of the distribution of power and wealth were resolved. Referring to its midyear offensive, the opposition said, "The attack is to make the government aware that there is no military solution. It is urgent that they take our dialogue proposal seriously."[20]

The Christian Democratic leadership was aware that the grace period opened up by the presidential elections would soon expire: the Constituent Assembly elections scheduled for March 1985 would determine the fate of reform and of the PDC. If the party could not gain majority control of the legislature, it could not hope to implement a land reform. Its tenuous position was obvious. As PDC leader Eduardo Molina explained: "There is no military solution to our conflict now, unless it is a military victory by the guerrillas. . . . If we continue to attempt to resolve the conflict militarily, we will lose. Only a dialogue and eventual incorporation of democratic elements of the left into our ranks offer any exit for us now."[21]

President Duarte, pushed from all sides, saw only one way out. The guerrillas had an apparently limitless capacity to maintain the war, while the PDC position could only deteriorate if the party failed to show some results before the 1985 Assembly elections. A coup by the right or a victory by the left perpetually threatened to bring down the Christian Democrats or to provoke a U.S. military intervention—which from the viewpoint of the PDC's nationalist members would be a disaster. Yet continued backing from the United States, if it could be contained, was critical. Duarte understood that the two leading forces historically opposed to negotiations—the Salvadoran military and the Reagan administration—needed him in order to extract aid from a

[20.] *Central American Bulletin,* June–July 1984.

[21.] *Christian Science Monitor,* March 8, 1984. Similar views were also expressed by President Duarte in *Playboy,* October 1984, and by leading party officials in interviews held in San Salvador, October 1983.

skeptical U.S. Congress. Especially with U.S. elections around the corner, and with the Contadora process revitalized by Nicaragua's acceptance of a regional peace agreement, the Reagan administration could not oppose Duarte. After surprisingly little consultation with the United States, Duarte gambled on his own indispensability to U.S. and Salvadoran hard-liners: in a dramatic speech to the United Nations, he invited the FDR-FMLN to negotiate.

DEMOCRATIZATION, U.S. POLICY, AND THE FUTURE OF NEGOTIATIONS

There is no viable political democracy in El Salvador today, despite the semi-competitive elections that took place in 1982 and 1984. Democracy depends on the achievement of a compromise protected by law—a fundamental agreement over a set of secure rules that determine who wins and who loses, that guarantee the game can be played again in future, and that set the broad parameters of a model for economic development. Clearly, such an agreement has not been reached—and may never be reached—in this deeply divided country. Yet in 1985, the prospects for democracy, peace, and reform in El Salvador are greater than at any moment since the outbreak of civil war. The current political stalemate in the United States over policy toward Central America and the military stalemate that has prevailed in El Salvador since 1983 have created a different set of probable political outcomes and changed the perceptions of most important political actors.[22] The extent of these changes, however, remains to be seen.

What is new in El Salvador's political equation is the temporary increase in the PDC's autonomy, as marked by the La Palma talks. Whether Duarte can turn his dramatic initiative into a first step toward genuine democratization is an open question. Its answer depends on political forces inside El Salvador and the U.S. government. There are certain hopeful signs. The FDR-FMLN, having openly called for negotiations since 1981, responded promptly to Duarte's invitation. Although the FDR-FMLN may have believed in the possibility of an all-out military victory just after the Sandinista defeat of Somoza in nearby Nicaragua, those heady days have passed and for some time the FDR-FMLN has been ready to discuss a settlement. The La Palma initiative, besides moving the situation past "the stupid pride stage where one side wouldn't talk to the other," has led to the creation of a joint commission of the Salvadoran government and the FDR-FMLN to direct a continued process of dialogue. Subsequent negotiations, though stalled on fundamental issues, did produce a partial Christmas truce and some plans to "humanize" the

[22.] For a discussion of the sequential creation of new probabilistic outcomes in the process of democratization, see Giuseppe Di Palma, "Party Government and Democratic Reproducibility: The Dilemma of New Democracies," presented at the workshop "The Future of Party Government," European University Institute, Florence, Italy, June 1982.

conflict. The small size of the country and its elite has facilitated these talks. Members of the government and the FDR-FMLN leadership are often from the same background and have worked together in the past.[23]

The Salvadoran people's longing for peace is the primary force driving this negotiation process: both the government and the FDR-FMLN have been forced to produce signs of progress after their meetings in order to please their constituencies. Nationalism also encourages dialogue; by demanding Salvadoran solutions for Salvadoran problems, it provides common ground on which the country's warring factions can negotiate. The importance of the national mood should not be underestimated. The Salvadoran people have expressed their desire for peace in numerous ways and, if negotiations fail, they can be expected to withdraw their support from whichever side is responsible.

Unexpectedly, some factions of El Salvador's traditional oligarchic alliance have also given tentative backing to the Duarte initiative. Affected by international pressure and the strains of continued combat with the FDR-FMLN, the Armed Forces initially agreed to attend talks with the opposition, though it has insisted that all discussions be limited to the parameters established by the 1983 constitution. Some sectors of the military have begun to understand that the violent ultraright in its ranks is a hindrance, that some form of land reform must occur, and that its own survival depends on a U.S. Congress that favors negotiations.[24] Certain groups in the agrarian private sector have also given Duarte's initiative lukewarm approval—a departure from their attitude in the past, when they feared the Christian Democrats as much as or more than the FDR-FMLN. Suffering economic losses and aware that they are losing their historic grip on the military, some agrarian elites have increasingly resorted to conservative political parties rather than death squads to represent their interests and to control the rural poor—a strategy utilized with notable success in the 1982 and 1984 elections.[25] If a military solution is ruled out, the perceptions of democracy's past opponents should continue to move toward support for some form of historic compromise.

Yet the present barriers to democratization are great. The majority of the

[23] *New York Times,* October 16, 1984. This has led to poignant moments during the La Palma talks. The FDR-FMLN military commander, Fernán Cienfuegos, reportedly asked the Salvadoran Defense Minister, Gen. Eugenio Vides Casanova, who was part of the government delegation, to send regards to Mr. Cienfuegos's family since the general was a friend of his parents. In other unexpected encounters, representatives of the two sides often embraced, sent messages to each other's families, and traded social gossip. *New York Times,* November 19, 1984.

[24] The views of FMLN Commander Fernán Cienfuegos, expressed in an interview by Chris Hedges, are instructive here. He divides the military into ultrarightists, whose power is diminishing, apolitical technicians trained in the United States, and nationalists, who form the support basis for a political settlement. *Christian Science Monitor,* October 18, 1984.

[25] The conservative Salvadoran business association, ANEP, issued a statement saying that it "supports the talks so long as Duarte heeds their advice not to agree to any power sharing arrangements." *Christian Science Monitor,* October 15, 1984. Members of the right believe that they can gain control over the Assembly and also think that the FDR-FMLN can not win an election. *New York Times,* November 17, 1984.

military and the ultraright have not yet committed themselves to negotiations. Conservative army officers are reported to have privately criticized Duarte for his decision to open talks with the FDR-FMLN and have demanded that the president refuse to discuss military activities, the combining of the Salvadoran army with the guerrilla army, and any form of power-sharing—the basic issues facing the country. Ultrarightists such as Roberto D'Aubuisson have actively opposed negotiations and have argued for delaying the talks past the 1985 municipal and legislative elections since they believe they can win a majority.[26] This growing rightist pressure is credited with having forced Duarte to delay further talks until after the March elections.

The distance between Christian Democratic and FDR-FMLN visions of democracy represent another substantial obstacle to compromise. As we have seen, the Christian Democrats have emphasized elite pact-making generally with parties of the right, electoral mechanisms, client relationships, the importance of individual political rights over the right of workers and peasants to organize, and slow reform. The competing vision of the FDR, whose members span a political spectrum from dissident Christian Democrats to Marxists, is mass-based and stresses political organization and mobilization as tools to achieve rapid socioeconomic reform. Within the FDR-FMLN itself, there are different notions of a political regime, with some guerrilla factions contending that a Leninist party is a viable model for the future—a view not shared by the majority of the current leadership.

These distinct visions create substantively different interpretations both of the current situation in El Salvador and of the steps necessary to achieve a basic compromise. On the one hand, Duarte's government maintains that profound changes have actually taken place between 1979 and 1985: that human rights violations are slowly being brought under control, that the antidemocratic character of the armed forces has changed, that the power of the landowners has been broken, and that all political parties—including those of the opposition—can now participate freely in fair elections. Asserting that the conditions that brought about civil war no longer exist, Duarte offers a general amnesty to the FDR-FMLN if it will lay down its arms, a facilitated process of resettlement to those who wish to leave the country, and the right to participate freely in future elections based on the rules established by the 1983 Constitution. As Duarte explained after the La Palma talks:

> My responsibility as president of the Republic is the Constitution and . . . I cannot go beyond the Constitution. . . . Therefore, if this sector [the FDR-FMLN] which today does not believe in the constitution wanted to change the constitution, the constitution itself provides them with the instruments to do that. These instruments are to participate in the elections, elect deputies, carry their propositions to the assembly, and win the adoption of their propositions.[27]

[26.] *New York Times,* January 23, 1985.

[27.] Transcript of President Duarte's press conference, held October 16, 1984, in San Salvador following the La Palma meeting.

In Duarte's view, democracy already exists in El Salvador, and the basic rules by which it was established cannot be abridged.

The FDR-FMLN offers a radically different interpretation. While agreeing with Duarte that certain changes have occurred in El Salvador, it maintains that the military and the death squads continue their systematic violations of human rights, that land reform has been blocked, and that as long as the country's repressive forces remain intact, the safety of opposition leaders and supporters could not be guaranteed during an election. Rejecting a settlement based on the 1983 constitution, which was designed without their participation under the leadership of Roberto D'Aubuisson, FDR-FMLN leaders offer a three-stage plan, to be implemented over an extended period. In the first phase, the government would present a concrete formula to guarantee security, end human rights violations, stop weapons imports, and send U.S. advisers out of the country. In exchange, the FDR-FMLN would agree to an arms freeze and to the termination of economic sabotage. During the second phase, there would be a formal cease-fire, with territorial concessions to both rebel and government forces. The final phase would include a broad national dialogue, the formation of a new government, a new constitution, and the reorganization of the armed forces. Only at this point would national elections be held.[28]

As long as the FDR-FMLN cannot be eliminated—an act that would require the involvement of U.S. troops—the pressure to implement a negotiated settlement lies most heavily on the Christian Democratic government. In the long run, continuing the war would favor the FDR-FMLN—a fact recognized by all contending forces. The Salvadoran rebels do not have to win the war; they simply need to remain strong enough to prevent the successful consolidation of any regime that might intend to exclude them. "The heart of this is the war," as one FDR-FMLN delegate remarked at La Palma, "and we are not losing the war."[29] Indeed, attempts by the Duarte government to eliminate the opposition by military means end up weakening the Christian Democrats more than they do the rebels. Bombings by the Salvadoran Air Force and army sweeps into contested territory are currently the overwhelming cause of civilian deaths; the PDC government is held to account for these strikes, which are unlikely to increase its popularity among those Salvadorans who are affected. Moreover, La Palma has opened a political space that now can not easily be closed, despite the intensification of the war on other fronts. If the Christian Democratic government claims that democracy and the rule of law now prevail in El Salvador, it can no longer rely on open repression, as it has in the past, and still maintain its credibility. Instead, it must address the burgeoning demands for reform and peace from labor, peasant organizations, and Christian base communities or risk an electoral setback.

[28.] See FDR-FMLN Political-Diplomatic Commission, La Palma: A Hope for Peace, November 1984.

[29.] *New York Times,* December 6, 1984.

The burden of forging a workable compromise rests largely on the Duarte administration, but can the Christian Democratic Party play this central statecraft role? Thus far the signals are mixed. There is little question that any agreement between the government and the FDR-FMLN must first establish definite safeguards on the rights of association and political expression, since there can be no successful settlement until the lives of all political leaders, and their followers, are guaranteed. At a minimum, this will require the complete dismantling of the structures of terror that have prohibited political participation in the past.[30] But it is not likely that the Duarte government could successfully insist upon this dismantling. During its period in power from 1980 to 1982, the PDC showed a knack for acting as surrogate for the military and the United States—behavior not conducive to a centrist role. It listened to Venezuelan party cohorts who have urged accommodation with the armed forces. Furthermore, the party's backpedalling from future talks after La Palma is an important indication of the power the army and the right still hold over the Christian Democrats.

The opportunity to face down these opponents, however, does exist. The PDC has demonstrated an ability to work with some sectors of the military. Most important, through a combination of statecraft and luck, the party has succeeded in casting itself as an indispensable ally to the United States, thus transforming its past surrogate role into a less asymmetrical situation of mutual need—as evidenced by Duarte's independent La Palma initiative. If Duarte and the Christian Democrats have the political courage and foresight to link their fate to negotiations, they may also prove themselves capable of using the United States as a sturdy, if reluctant, shield to protect the negotiation process. There are strong partisan reasons to adopt this strategy. If the PDC should succeed in presiding over a successful peace agreement, this historic accomplishment would cement the party's electoral standing for years to come; popular opposition to the war is so great that a Christian Democratic Party credited with ending it would undoubtedly triumph over the parties of the right and the FDR-FMLN in open political competition, a fact recognized by all sides.

[30.] Despite claims to the contrary, the government still is unable to guarantee the safety of political opponents of the regime, a fact dramatically highlighted during the recent release of Salvador's longest held political prisoners. As a gesture of national reconciliation, the Duarte government freed 10 trade unionists—all members of STECEL, the hydroelectrical workers union, who were jailed after they took part in a nationwide general strike protesting government repression in 1980. The union leaders and their families were sent directly from prison to the airport and were quietly flown to the Netherlands. "We are not leaving our country by choice," stated Héctor Recinos, the union's top leader whose wife and daughter were "disappeared" during his confinement in jail, "but because the death squads force us to do so. Giving us our freedom is easier for Mr. Duarte than punishing those responsible for so many deaths." Janet Shenk, "La Palma: A Report on the Negotiations," *NACLA, Report on the Americas,* Vol. 18, No. 6 (November–December 1984).

In the end, though, the ability to tilt forces and events toward a political solution in El Salvador lies beyond the control of the PDC. Despite Duarte's insistence upon a national solution for national problems, it is the United States that frames the structure of incentives that either encourage or discourage democratization. For this reason, the Reagan administration's escalation of the war just after the La Palma talks has seriously undermined the tentative and fragile move toward negotiations. Supporting the assumption of Salvadoran military officers that "there are times when you have to make war to achieve peace," the administration provided the Salvadoran Air Force with new gunships specially designed for attacking FDR-FMLN strongholds and, for the first time, allowed U.S. military advisers to participate openly in the direction of military operations whose explicit purpose was to sabotage the talks.[31] Reagan officials have downplayed the significance of a dialogue, requested new increases in military aid, and reiterated their claim that the Salvadoran military could defeat the FDR-FMLN by 1986, despite indications to the contrary.

These steps, combined with a series of rhetorical, inadequate U.S. responses to disturbing actions by the Salvadoran ultraright, indicate intentions on the part of the Reagan administration to seek a military victory—a posture that can only threaten current efforts toward compromise.[32] The Reagan administration's logic is, of course, to force the FDR-FMLN to accept Duarte's terms for negotiation. But the effect is precisely the opposite. U.S.-sponsored militarization merely increases the incentives for sections of the antidemocratic right and left to seek a "winning" solution while decreasing the probability of democratization through political compromise. In the end, ironically, the administration is undercutting the Christian Democratic Party, leaving its only "acceptable" political ally to pay the political price of ongoing civil war.

The La Palma initiative has forced stark choices on U.S. policymakers: to support dialogue and a negotiated settlement or to face the eventual prospect of sending U.S. combat troops to El Salvador to attempt to eliminate the

[31.] Lt. Col. Domingo Monterrosa, a U.S.-trained field commander, used this logic, reminiscent of Viet Nam, the day before he was killed directing an operation in Morazán province. According to Monterrosa, the purpose of the operation, planned in conjunction with U.S. advisers, was to surprise FDR-FMLN commanders in the midst of talks among themselves about the La Palma meeting. *Washington Post,* October 19, 1984.

[32.] A week before the La Palma talks, Undersecretary of Defense Fred Iklé announced that the Salvadoran military had broken a long stalemate with guerrilla forces and could "neutralize" the insurgents by the end of 1984. *New York Times,* October 7, 1984. General Paul Gorman, the commander of U.S. military forces in Latin America, has maintained that the Salvadoran military could have 80 to 90 percent of the country under control within two years if Congress approved sufficient military aid. These comments, taken in the context of mild responses to new activity by the ultraright—the mobilization of Col. Ochoa in La Palma the day before the first talks, death squad threats against President Duarte and members of the private sector for favoring negotiations, and the acquittal of a known rightist officer widely believed to have murdered two U.S. officials—keep alive the hope of a military solution in El Salvador.

FDR-FMLN. As long as domestic and international opposition to a U.S. war in Central America translates into a congressional majority that prohibits a military solution, democracy is still on the Salvadoran agenda. Thus if Congress takes a more positive stance in 1985 by cutting military aid and tying increases in economic support funds to progress in negotiations, human rights, and socioeconomic reform, it can maintain the stalemate that keeps the possibility of a democratic outcome alive.[33] In the past, Congress has successfully, albeit sporadically, demonstrated to the Salvadoran military and the ultraright that it will not support forces that systematically violate human rights in order to block political and economic reform—a stance that helped create the current opportunity for democratization. Despite El Salvador's requests for increased military and economic aid, 1985 is the year for Congress to redouble its efforts to restrict U.S. assistance until progress in peace can be clearly demonstrated. The importance of an active congressional veto of a military solution cannot be underestimated: without congressional pressure the impetus for negotiations and therefore the opportunity for democracy will disappear.

If, despite the Reagan administration's posture, Congress succeeds in curbing reactionary forces in El Salvador, an important precedent in U.S. foreign policy toward Latin America will have been set. Such precedents worry policymakers, who often do not welcome this kind of innovation. But contrary to their fears, negotiations that limit the power of antidemocratic forces will not pave the way for a take-over by an extremist faction of the FDR-FMLN. The essence of negotiation is the recognition of stalemate and the need for *all* sides to accept a "second-best" solution. Once this recognition becomes widespread, any faction that chooses not to play the democratic game will be isolated from domestic and international support. Those groups that refuse to compromise and continue to fight for the restoration of the past or for the implementation of a Leninist model will be effectively marginalized.

Negotiations do imply, however, that the U.S. government might have to accept a "second-best" solution as well. Indeed, if negotiations are successful, the United States could be faced with a democratic compromise in El Salvador that is significantly more broad in scope, participatory in means, and indigenous in content than previous Latin American democracies. This new democracy, forged through a compromise between warring parties, could play an important role in mitigating regional tensions. While this outcome is optimistic, given the traditional forces against change in Central America and the militarist cast of Reagan policy toward the region, the alternative is a civil and regional war without resolution that is strongly opposed by the Salvadoran population. Efforts by the Reagan administration to maintain the war at a low level in order to avoid a difficult political solution will result at minimum in

[33.] If U.S. economic aid were carefully targeted to pay for a land reform, the rightist opposition to democracy would be likely to significantly decrease.

continuing battles with Congress and at maximum in a U.S. military invasion strongly opposed by the majority of Americans. Faced with these choices, an independent—if uncertain—democracy in El Salvador might not look so bad.

B. La Palma: A Public Relations Stratagem by Duarte?*

BY EDWARD S. HERMAN

ALTHOUGH I found Terry Lynn Karl's "After La Palma" (Spring 1985) informative and scholarly, the article's emphases and interpretations suggest a promise of democratization in El Salvador that, though carefully qualified, is in my opinion overly optimistic.

To a great extent, I believe Karl's excessively sanguine prognosis results from her misreading of Salvadoran President José Napoleón Duarte. While she correctly points out that Duarte has allowed himself to serve as a surrogate for the Salvadoran military and the United States, Karl places Duarte's actions in the context of a Christian Democratic model of behavior in which this subordination is calculated, designed to capture eventual control through patient alliance-building. But one can construct an alternative model, based on Duarte's actual performance and numerous statements, that explains his behavior on the basis of opportunism, power hunger, intense anticommunism, and considerable self-deception. In this alternative model, Duarte is an opportunistic, albeit half-knowing, agent of his principals and their policy of seeking military victory.

Duarte's aggressive hostility toward the U.S. press—which he views as heavily infiltrated by communists—for its concern over civilian murders, and his unswerving determination to force the "subversives" to surrender, seem deeply rooted in his psyche and value system. According to Duarte, the hundreds of civilians murdered by the armed forces at the Sumpul River in May 1980 were "communist" guerrillas. In March 1984, Duarte peddled a similar line, accusing the human rights office of the Roman Catholic Church —Tutela Legal—of "permanently working under the direction of [those] trying to help the subversive groups." This behavior fits my alternative model very well. So does Duarte's important role in the escalated air war and his service to the Reagan administration in eliciting more military and economic aid. Karl stresses that these policies have made Duarte indispensable to both the Salvadoran army and the Reagan administration. But the other side of the

* From *World Policy Journal*, 2, Summer 1985.

coin is that in the process Duarte has committed himself to the escalated military effort sought by his two strong partners. He has, for example, consistently defended the new pacification program and air war.

The initiation of the La Palma talks between the government and the rebels was surely a response by Duarte to the demands of his civilian constituency; but there is no reason to believe that he ever thought that these talks would go anywhere. In his *Playboy* interview, cited by Karl, Duarte admits that the rebels could not safely lay down their arms now. This is why he puts first priority on achieving "security"! Karl fails to explore the possibility that La Palma was a public relations gesture—a stratagem designed by Duarte to placate his supporters—initiated with neither the hope nor the intent of serious consequences. In fact, Duarte did not make one realistic proposal at the La Palma talks; the ultraright Arena party has even sarcastically commended him for "seeming to be *arenos*" in refusing to advance beyond an agenda for rebel surrender.

Karl acknowledges the central importance of U.S. policy decisions in shaping any democratization process in El Salvador. Nevertheless, she arrives at her cautiously optimistic assessment by arguing that there is a stalemate between Congress and the Reagan administration that precludes a military victory for either side in El Salvador. Thus, in her view, even the Reagan team may be amenable to some kind of settlement short of victory, given that victory itself is unattainable. But Karl underrates the Reagan administration's ideological and political commitment, and she does not give adequate weight to the fact that the administration, not Congress, has the initiative: if it cannot win, the administration will almost surely keep trying. Furthermore, given the administration's success, with Duarte's help, in obtaining an increase in annual U.S. appropriations to the Salvadoran struggle—to perhaps a half-billion dollars—and given the further possibility of open or surreptitious escalation of weaponry, training, surveillance, and the mobilization of surrogate aid, it is not clear that the Salvadoran resistance cannot be worn down over a three-year period. These lines of thought and action will surely dominate the Reagan approach, rendering exceedingly remote Karl's scenario of stalemate leading to pressures for accommodation and democratization.

Karl provides an interesting analysis of the complex forces operating within El Salvador: with her view of Duarte and the impact of a Congress-Reagan stalemate, Karl sees these indigenous forces as capable of producing a peaceful settlement. But based on the alternative reading of Duarte and U.S. policies that I have outlined above, the indigenous peace constituency is doomed to frustration under Duarte-army-U.S. conjoint rule. From this perspective, Duarte is legitimizing the search for a military solution and is an important agent in the process of military escalation. Meanwhile, his actual contribution to a peaceful settlement is *negative,* regardless of the theoretical Christian Democratic component of his thought processes. I stand by my and Walden

Bello's earlier statement in this journal (Summer 1984) that the paradoxical effect of the election of Duarte, "who has loosened congressional purse-strings and expedited the flow of bullets, may well be a higher rate of civilian deaths than would have prevailed with a less generously funded D'Aubuisson." In order of probability, I would rate possible future scenarios in El Salvador during the second Reagan term as follows: (1) continued military stalemate, with no advance toward democratization; (2) the imposition of peace by a successful capital-intensive war of attrition, reducing the rebels to marginal guerrilla operations, also with no advance toward democratization; (3) a collapse of the Salvadoran army and a possible rebel victory, which would in all likelihood lead to a U.S. invasion. Genuine democratization by some kind of accommodation process during the Reagan term seems too unlikely to warrant listing.

C. A Negotiated Settlement Is Still a Viable Option: Reply to Edward S. Herman*

BY TERRY LYNN KARL

IN my article, "After La Palma," I attempted to establish a range of possible outcomes, including genuine political compromise, rather than a hierarchy of probabilities. This approach was based on the assumption that El Salvador's regime transition, like that of other countries, will undoubtedly be characterized by uncertain and unpredictable changes. Yet Edward Herman's proposed ordering of the likelihood of future scenarios, if risky, is also provocative. I would argue that there are presently two viable options in El Salvador: the continuation of a stalemated civil war or progress toward negotiated peace and democratic rule. These two options run on parallel, yet mutually contradictory, tracks. The marginalization of the FDR-FMLN (Democratic Revolutionary Front–Farabundo Martí National Liberation Front) by the U.S.-backed Salvadoran army or that army's defeat followed by a U.S. invasion—scenarios that Herman ranks above accommodation—are not, in my opinion, feasible now.

The short-term marginalization of the FDR-FMLN is unlikely for two reasons. First, although the Salvadoran army has been successful in forcing the FDR-FMLN to break down into smaller units and return to a classic guerrilla strategy, it has not won a single important military victory against the opposi-

* From World Policy Journal, 2, Summer 1985.

tion. Instead, the FDR-FMLN continues to maintain its capacity to strike throughout the country, attack civil defense units, and engage in economic sabotage. Second, the FDR-FMLN appears to retain its popular base among labor and the peasantry. This permits the FDR-FMLN to shift the confrontation from a rural territorial war to a reactivated urban political movement. Given the similarity of its objectives to those of a part of the Christian Democratic Party (PDC), the FDR-FMLN can often rely upon tacit cooperation from the PDC, which, according to some observers, owes up to 30 percent of its March 1985 electoral majority to the left. President Duarte may choose to meet the new level of social protest with a sophisticated form of the ferocious repression of 1980–81, but in the process he would risk losing his own domestic support as well as his access to desperately-needed international aid. As long as the FDR-FMLN does not isolate itself through abuses to civilians, the Duarte administration could have the most to fear from marginalization of the opposition over time.

The imminent collapse of the Salvadoran Armed Forces also is unlikely. In the past year, the Reagan administration has increased its military commitment to El Salvador through support for aerial bombardments of the countryside, daily reconnaissance flights, the introduction of an expanded helicopter fleet and AC-47 gunships, and the direct involvement of U.S. personnel in combat-related activity. The Salvadoran army has grown from 12,000 to 50,000 personnel and is better equipped and trained than in the past. The FDR-FMLN, aware that direct U.S. intervention could ignite an uncontrollable regional conflagration, has modified its 1980 call for a total military victory. In 1983–84, it pulled back from a highly successful military offensive in order to prevent a sudden defeat of the Salvadoran army and the subsequent entry of U.S. troops. A rare interview with FMLN commander Joaquín Villalobos, a hard-liner who had reputedly opposed dialogue with the government, reflects the FMLN's understanding of these realities. Villalobos avoided the language of total victory and instead chose to describe his army as a "veto force." He also proposed a cease-fire in exchange for an end to U.S. military aid and gave his full endorsement to political negotiations.

I agree with Herman that the most probable scenario in El Salvador today is a continuation of a stalemated war of attrition. This situation is primarily the result of last year's enormous increase in U.S. aid, which has rekindled the flagging confidence of the military and the private sector. Even though these groups lost much of their electoral clout with the defeat of the rightist coalition (which included Arena and the National Reconciliation Party, the traditional army party) in the 1985 Assembly elections, the military's access to high levels of U.S. aid has allowed the army to increase its direct pressure on the Duarte government. The High Command has set extremely narrow parameters within which the president can negotiate after the La Palma meetings. Not only has it ruled out a formal cease-fire, it also currently opposes the formal or informal implementation of agreements with the FDR-FMLN. President Duarte either acquiesces to or is helpless in the face of these pressures. "This is not our army," a Christian Democratic cabinet member admitted to me in a recent interview.

This resurgence of the Salvadoran Armed Forces has fostered another round of militarism. Although, as Herman points out, U.S.-imposed elections previously provided a political cover for military buildups, the fact that there are no elections scheduled in the immediate period ahead now accentuates the quest for a military solution. Despite their antidemocratic nature, demonstration elections had the unintended consequence of temporarily widening the space of permissible political activity in El Salvador. The knowledge of impending elections also forced the leadership of the Christian Democratic Party to take initiatives, like the La Palma talks, that reflect the positions of the majority of the party base. This political-electoral cycle has been replaced by a predominant military logic. "We have two years of U.S. aid and three years until we have to deal with another election in our country or yours. We have time to hit the guerrillas," a representative of ANEP, the leading business association, explained to me recently. The FDR-FMLN response is predictable: "We are prepared to fight to the ultimate consequence . . . [a U.S. invasion]."

Yet a negotiated establishment of some type of political democracy remains a viable future option. Compromise for a "second-best" solution is both a rational and humane choice in the face of a war without winners—a war that has already killed or displaced from their homes a full 33 percent of the Salvadoran population. If key Salvadoran elites do not make this choice—perhaps because they benefit in some way from the current stalemate or from the "soap bubble" economy that has resulted from the influx of $1.7 billion—several other factors in addition to those mentioned in my article could promote a negotiated settlement:

First, the process of dialogue has its own dynamic motion and independent life—regardless of the initial intentions of the negotiators. Despite the maximalist stance of the government in La Palma and the FDR-FMLN in Ayagualo, peace talks already have begun to produce an emerging consensus on some significant issues. Both sides now seek permanent and private means of communication until their next public meeting. Both claim to be interested in "partial accords," which would bring a halt to the opposition's economic sabotage in exchange for the army's respect for human rights and democratic political activity in certain zones. The PDC and the FDR-FMLN can also probably agree to mutually protect cooperatives in the reformed sectors of agriculture. Most important, the election of the new Christian Democratic majority in the National Assembly has created an opportunity to change the 1983 Arena-imposed constitution, the chief stumbling block in talks thus far. "Peace is more important than the constitution," Archbishop Rivera y Damas, the national symbol for a political solution, has stated. Although the army does not appear to share this view and has already undercut previously established accords, it cannot take an open stance against dialogue without jeopardizing President Duarte's international position.

Second, the Salvadoran army's growing dependence on the U.S. military support has an Achilles' heel: it will be extremely difficult for the United States to guarantee the enormous aid required to maintain the current stalemate over a period of, say, five years in light of approaching congressional battles over the U.S. budget and the consistent unpopularity of the administration's policy in Central America. When the present infatuation with President Duarte wears thin, as infatuations tend to do, Congress could put a serious hitch in the Reagan administration's unquestionable commitment to "draw the line" in El Salvador—just as the House of Representatives has done with policy toward Nicaragua. While I, like Herman, doubt that the Reagan team is amenable to a settlement short of victory, it is important to point out that the administration does not always get its way, regardless of its intentions.

Third, President Duarte is aware that he cannot stake his future solely on the United States. The Reagan administration, opposed to the state-interventionist bias of Salvadoran Christian Democracy, has sought to undercut the party in a number of ways since 1981; the U.S. Embassy's opposition to a Christian Democratic victory in the 1985 Assembly elections and the current efforts by the Agency for International Development to divide the Unión Popular Democrática, Duarte's main labor and peasant federation, are merely two recent examples. This perpetual tension with the Reagan administration, when combined with the unreliability of aid, the strength of the FDR-FMLN, and the domestic popularity of dialogue, may encourage Duarte—a Christian Democrat par excellence—to seek a national accommodation.

One final point: Herman's discounting of a negotiated settlement for democratization as "too unlikely to warrant listing" underscores our main difference over El Salvador's future options. His claim is based on President Duarte's "opportunism, power hunger, [and] intense anticommunism." While this description may well be accurate, these characteristics are, nonetheless, compatible with Christian Democratic ideology and do not constitute an "alternative model." Moreover, they fit a number of politicians who have played a key role in "pacted" regime transitions. Such compromised democracies are not necessarily made by nice guys.

57. "Blood Has Not Been Shed in Vain": Resolving the Crisis of Dual Power*

BY THE FMLN GENERAL COMMAND

In the year after the meetings at La Palma and Ayagualo, a political-military deadlock prevailed in El Salvador, a condition the rebels like to describe as "dual power" (see editors' introduction to this chapter). In the course of that year, the Duarte government intensified counterinsurgency operations, relying particularly on wider use of air power, while the rebels tooled up for a war of attrition, emphasizing hit-and-run combat operations in the countryside along with sabotage at all levels of the economy. (See chapters 6 and 7, on the civil war.)

No substantial initiatives for resuming peaceful negotiations came from the Duarte government during this period; evidently it was convinced that only further military pressure would force the rebels to accede to the proposals Duarte presented at La Palma. Late in 1985, however, the FMLN issued a new call for reopening the dialogue process, based on its claim for a legitimate share of power, given the military-political realities.

In the document below, the FMLN repeats prior positions but also includes what some observers viewed as two novelties: (1) The rebels acknowledge receiving outside military support, though in no way comparable to what the Duarte regime gets from the United States, and offer to end it in return for a similar concession by the government (point 13); (2) The rebels propose calling off their sabotage campaign in exchange for the government's "Armed Forces relinquishing" their "strategic weapons," that is, the air war (point 11).

Regarding them as novelties or not, Duarte—and Washington behind him—refused to take the proposals seriously. The war goes on.[1]

OUR country has already endured 5 years of war which might continue as a result of the growing level of political, military, and economic intervention by the U.S. Government, which has also been the greatest obstacle for the development of dialogue and which permanently plots to close the possibilities for national understanding.

From the first month of the war, the FMLN and the Revolutionary Democratic Front [FDR] presented several initiatives for a dialogue, one right after the other. At the Ayagualo meeting 1 year ago, we submitted a proposal for

---

* "[Radio] Farabundo Martí on FMLN Document on Dialogues," November 19, 1985, from Foreign Broadcast Information Service, El Salvador, November 22, 1985. For a fuller FMLN statement, see Foreign Broadcast Information Service, *Daily Report–Central America*, November 20, 1985.

[1.] See the Editors' Introduction to this chapter for the aborted dialogue scheduled for September 1986.

an overall political solution. Our initiatives have been systematically blocked. The U.S. Administration, the Salvadoran Government and Army, as well as the local oligarchy, have based their hopes on defeating us militarily, with the support of U.S. power.

However, the facts of war say something else. In spite of the growing and strong U.S. intervention, we have been extending ourselves throughout the national territory and developing our forces in quantity and quality. In 1981, we fought in only five departments of the country. In 1985, we are fighting in 12 of the 14 departments. However, Reagan continues relying on the military solution while Duarte and the high command, blinded by their ambitions for political and economic power, meekly obey the orders from the imperialists and sell national sovereignty.

While it talks about sovereignty, the oligarchy profits from the war, continues taking capital out of the country, and also thinks we will be defeated in the military field which will ensure that they maintain their privileges.

The 5 years of war have shown the capabilities of the FMLN to defeat, one by one, the various phases of U.S. intervention. The escalation of intervention is currently one of the greatest ones within the counterinsurgency experiences of U.S. imperialism. However, the euphoria of the alleged military successes of the Army over the FMLN dissipates and brings out in the open that we are also defeating the current phase of escalation.

Where is, then, the so-much announced military victory of the Army over our forces? The most optimistic estimates speak of several years. But such expectations have become very inexact. Reagan and his spokesmen have admitted it when they have said on various occasions that, without their military support, the Salvadoran regime would have already been defeated, and they do not rule out that it might be necessary to send their troops to El Salvador.

The situation our country is enduring can have only but two immediate possibilities: first, prolonging the war with a high probability of intervention by foreign troops, including U.S. troops; second, a political solution to the conflict that will attack the economic, political, and social causes that led to the conflict and that will lead to peace with independence, justice, and liberty. Only Reagan—who does not care about the destruction of the country if with that he manages to submit the country to his geopolitical dictates—and the irresponsible ones who place their personal interests above those of the nation can choose prolonging the war.

Prolonging the war entails a cost that will burden the workers and means: (A) a growing and greater capitulation of our national sovereignty to the U.S. Government: (B) a continuation of the loss of human lives of people displaced by war, prisons, torture, unemployment, hunger, and poverty for our people; (C) greater destruction of the already scarce material resources of the country; (D) the bankruptcy of small, medium, and large enterprises; and (E) the possibility that U.S. troops will stain our soil.

The FDR and the FMLN, convinced that we must strive to prevent a greater level of imperialist aggression and rescue our national independence—before it costs more human lives and destruction of the country—will continue promoting a political solution, through dialogue and negotiations. The basis of our constant search for a political solution cannot be found in concluding that all possibilities for a military victory will be closed if an option is imposed on us.

Let it not be believed that our will can be broken by the blackmail of intervention of foreign troops. We do not want this, but we are prepared to defeat it, should it take place. Our conviction is objective and our will is firm. Let it not be believed either that our fronts and the Salvadoran people can be easily deceived and manipulated in their desires for peace in order to turn the dialogue into an instrument for the benefit of the military strategy of counterinsurgency, as Duarte wants to do.

Blood has not been shed in vain. The people's aspirations should be satisfied and the objectives for which it has been fighting for decades should be achieved. Things cannot remain how and where they were prior to the war, or where they now are.

Within this framework, the goal of the FMLN and the FDR is that, through dialogue, we will reach an overall solution to the conflict that will recover and strengthen national independence, ensure the people's rights to self-determination, social justice, a respect for human rights, and the reorganization of power that will truly guarantee the majority interests of the working people.

In order to clearly state our position to the national and international political and social forces, we hereby present the FMLN-FDR principles, elements of analysis, political positions, and fundamental objectives in the dialogue process. Nevertheless, it must be clarified that none of these proposals, if considered in a separate way, can be taken as a specific negotiation proposal. We understand that the criteria on the gradualism and links between some topics within a framework of reciprocal guarantees for the parties involved must be maintained in every negotiation process that seriously intends to reach a political solution. In this sense, we maintain in force—although open to discussion—the political logic of the proposal we presented on 30 November 1984 in Ayagualo.

Fundmental Contents of Our Position

1. The causes that originated and justify our revolutionary popular war are not only still in force, but have also become more evident and deeper. The dialogue process cannot ignore this reality and not discuss it.

2. An objective and undeniable situation of duality of powers exists and is expressed in political, demographic, military, and territorial terms.

3. We are a political-military force that is advancing and growing. We are sure we will achieve victory. We seek dialogue and the negotiated solution

because we want to close the path to greater levels of intervention in our fatherland, rescue national independence, and avoid a greater social cost to our people.

4. Democracy cannot be achieved without independence. The U.S. intervention in our country must end in order to achieve peace. Therefore, the process of dialogue and negotiation must resolve this essential process.

5. The government is an interlocutor in the dialogue because it is the belligerent counterpart and not because it is legitimate. The past electoral processes are an integral part of the counterinsurgency plan and they lack any validity. As long as there is no independence and the elections have been controlled by the same genocidal and repressive Armed Forces that are now totally subordinate to the U.S. Government, we do not accept the government's legitimacy.

6. In the present conditions, none of the parties can seek, through the dialogue, the unilateral surrender or disarmament of the other and much less propose it as a precondition as the government unrealistically proposes in its peace proposal.

7. We do not recognize the country's constitution because the process used to draft it and that served as its foundation is vitiated. It seeks to generalize the existing unjust economic, social, and political order and to cover up the U.S. counterinsurgency plan we are defeating.

A new constitution will stem from the liberation and self-determination that the Salvadorans will achieve. This constitution will institutionalize a just and free society.

8. A negotiated peace through dialogue must include the formation of a provisional government with broad participation including the FDR-FMLN, while maintaining the FMLN's armed power, as well as the sectors that make up the present government and the maintenance of its Armed Forces. This provisional government would solve pending problems including the existence of two armies and would create the conditions that allow the Salvadoran people to democratically and freely decide the country's future path through truly free elections. We are not demanding the disarmament of the Armed forces or the resignation of the present government. Instead, we are demanding that they join the process and the mechanisms that the peace accord will create. The counterpart cannot either demand the disarmament of the FMLN or try to exclude the FDR and the FMLN from participating in the provisional government. The fact that the FMLN maintains its weapons is the main guarantee that the people's interests will be respected and the working people's wishes will come true.

9. The idea of the humanization [of the conflict] assumes that the war will continue. The true humanization of the conflict can only be reached through a just overall political solution. The idea that the weapons will be gradually silenced only through successive humanization agreements is false.

10. We will strive at all times to carry out a dialogue for an overall nego-

tiated solution. Consequently, we reject that the Duarte government continues to use the dialogue as a maneuver in favor of Reagan's policy against the Salvadoran people and its aggression and blackmail against Nicaragua.

11. The sabotage of the war economy is a strategic weapon of the people and the FMLN. It is negotiable in exchange for the government and its Armed Forces relinquishing equally strategic weapons.

12. The Duarte government dumps on the working people a large share of the costs of its war in addition to receiving a great deal of U.S. Government aid. Although the revolutionary war is basically financed by the people, the FMLN claims the right to impose war taxes on the big landowners and capitalists who are cooperating with the repression and are guilty of social injustice. We will discuss this issue. We are prepared to negotiate it if the government and its Armed Forces are prepared to give up Reagan's financing.

13. Although in many cases they are nonexistent and in no cases could a comparison be made between the alleged logistical supplies to the FMLN from abroad with the regime's supplies, we are willing to accept controls to eliminate them if the Army also stops receiving supplies of weapons and materiel from the United States.

14. We maintain our proposal for an overall solution that we took to Ayagualo as a basis for an overall political solution.

15. Dialogue should be serious, public, and opened to the participation of all sectors of the nation.

16. The dialogue as an effort for a political solution requires a mediation which, to contribute to that effort, must maintain a . . . conduct of respect for the equal rights of both sides. It also requires a small group of witnesses acceptable to both sides.

El Salvador, November 1985 [Signed] FMLN General Command. Commanders Joaquín Villalobos, Leonel González, Jorge Shafick Handal, Roberto Roca, Fernan Cienfuegos

Bibliography and Resources*

SELECTED BIBLIOGRAPHY

Philip Agee, *Whitepaper Whitewash: The CIA and El Salvador* (New York: Deep Cover Books, 1981).

T.D. Allman, "Rising to Rebellion," *Harper's* (New York), March 1981.

Stephen E. Ambrose, *Rise to Globalism: American Foreign Policy, 1938–1980* (Pelican History of the United States, vol. 8., Robert A. Divine, ed.) (Harmondsworth, England: Penguin Books, 1980).

Americas Watch, *With Friends Like These: The Americas Watch Report on Human Rights and U. S. Policy in Latin America* (New York: Vintage Books, 1985).

Thomas P. Anderson, *Matanza: El Salvador's Communist Revolt of 1932* (Lincoln: Univ. of Nebraska Press, 1971).

Robert Armstrong and Janet Shenk, *El Salvador: The Face of Revolution* (Boston: South End Press, 1982).

Cynthia Arnson, "Cold War in the Caribbean," *Inquiry* (San Francisco), December 10, 1979.

Manilio Argueta, *One Day of Life* (New York: Vintage Books, 1983).

Enrique A. Baloyra, *El Salvador in Transition* (Chapel Hill: University of North Carolina Press, 1982).

Richard J. Barnet, *Intervention and Revolution: America's Confrontation with Insurgent Movements Around the World* (New York: New American Library, 1968).

———, *Real Security: Restoring American Power in a Dangerous Decade* (New York: Simon and Schuster, 1981).

Joseph Baylen, "Sandino: Patriot or Bandit?" *Hispanic-American Historical Review* (Durham, N.C.), 31, August 1951.

* The Editors gratefully acknowledge the assistance of Professor Susan Besse of the City College of New York in preparing this select bibliography. For a broader bibliographical and resource list on Central America, see Susan Besse and Marvin E. Gettleman, eds., "Central America: Teaching and Resource Guide," FACHRES/NY (c/o Department of Social Sciences, Polytechnic University, 333 Jay Street, Brooklyn, NY 11201).

Philip Berryman, *Inside Central America: The Essential Facts Past and Present on El Salvador, Nicaragua, Honduras, Guatemala and Costa Rica* (New York: Pantheon Books, 1985).

Morris Jo Blachman, William M. LeoGrande and Kenneth E. Sharpe, eds., *Confronting Revolution: Security Through Diplomacy in Central America* (New York: Pantheon, 1986).

Raymond Bonner, "The Agony of El Salvador," *New York Times Magazine,* February 22, 1981.

Raymond Bonner, *Weakness and Deceit: U.S. Policy and El Salvador* (New York: Times Books, 1984).

James R. Brockman, *The Word Remains: A Life of Oscar Romero* (Maryknoll, N.Y.: Orbis Books, 1982).

David Browning, *El Salvador: Landscape and Society* (London: Clarendon/Oxford University Press, 1971).

Marco V. Carías, *Análisis sobre el Conflicto entre Honduras y El Salvador* (Tegucigalpa, Honduras: Universidad Nacional Autónoma, 1969).

James Chace, *Solvency: The Price of Survival: An Essay on American Foreign Policy* (New York: Random House, 1981).

Roy A. Childs, Jr., "El Salvador: The Roots of Conflict," *Libertarian Review* (Washington, D.C.), 10, No. 1, April 1981.

Noam Chomsky, *Turning the Tide: U.S. Intervention in Central America and the Struggle for Peace* (Boston: South End Press, 1985).

Shirley Christian, *Nicaragua: Revolution in the Family* (New York: Random House, 1985).

Charles Clements, M.D., *Witness to War* (New York: Bantam Books, 1984).

Alexander Cockburn and James Ridgeway, "El Salvador: Reagan's War," *Village Voice* (New York), March 4, 1981.

Joshua Cohen and Joel Rogers, *The Rules of the Game: Constraints and Opportunites for the Central America* [Nonintervention] *Movement* (Boston: South End Press, 1986).

Committee to Protect Journalists, *Repression of Journalists in El Salvador and Guatemala* (New York: The Committee, 1981).

Marc Cooper, "Can Duarte Last Two More Years?" *The Nation,* 142, May 24, 1986.

————, "Whitewashing Duarte: U.S. Reporting on El Salvador," *NACLA Report on the Americas,* 20: 1 (January/March, 1986).

Abel Cuenca, *El Salvador: Una Democracía Cafetalera* (Mexico City: ARR-Centro Editorial, 1932).

Roque Dalton, *Clandestine Poems* (San Francisco: Solidarity Publications, 1985).

————, *Miguel Marmol: Los Sucesos de 1932 en El Salvador* (San José, Costa Rica: Editorial Universitaria Centroamericana, 1972).

Karen De Young, "White Hand of Terror: How the Peace Was Lost in El Salvador," *Mother Jones* (San Francisco), June 1981.

Joan Didion, *Salvador* (New York: Simon & Schuster, 1983).

José Napoleón Duarte (with Dianna Page), *Duarte: My Story* (New York: Putnams, 1986).

James Dunkerley, *The Long War: Dictatorship and Revolution in El Salvador* (New York: Schocken Books, 1983).

Robert V. Elam, "Appeal to Arms: The Army and Politics in El Salvador, 1931–1964" (Ph.D. thesis, University of New Mexico, 1968).

El Salvador: Another Vietnam—a film by Catalyst Media available from Icarus Films, 200 Park Ave. South, New York, N.Y. 10003

Plácido Erdozain, *Archbishop Romero: Martyr of Salvador* (Maryknoll, N.Y.: Orbis Books, 1981).

Richard R. Fagen, *The Nicaraguan Revolution: A Personal Report* (Washington, D.C.: Institute for Policy Studies, 1981).

James Fallows, *National Defense* (New York: Random House, 1981).

Roger Fontaine, Cleto DiGiovanni, Jr., and Alexander Kruger, "Castro's Specter," *Washington Quarterly,* Autumn 1980.

Jonathan Fried, Marvin Gettleman, Deborah Levenson, Nancy Peckenham, eds., *Guatemala in Rebellion: Unfinished History* (New York: Grove Press, 1983).

John Gerassi, *The Great Fear in Latin America* (New York: Macmillan, 1965).

Renny Golden and Michael McConnell, *Sanctuary: The New Underground Railroad* (Maryknoll, N.Y.: Orbis Books, 1986).

E. O. Guerrant, "The Recognition of El Salvador in 1934: An Alteration in the Foreign Policy of the United States," *The Historian* (Wichita, Kansas) 6, Autumn 1943.

Gustavo Gutiérrez, *A Theology of Liberation* (Maryknoll, N.Y.: Orbis Books, 1977).

Edward S. Herman and Frank Brodhead, *Demonstration Elections: U.S.-Staged Elections in the Dominican Republic, Vietnam, and El Salvador* (Boston: South End Press, 1984).

Fred Kaplan, *Dubious Specter: A Skeptical Look at the Soviet Nuclear Threat* (Washington, D.C.: Institute for Policy Studies, 1980).

George F. Kennan, "Cease This Madness," *The Atlantic* (Boston), January 1981.

Michael T. Klare and Cynthia Arnson, *Supplying Repression: U.S. Support for Authoritarian Regimes Abroad* (Washington, D.C.: Institute for Policy Studies, 1981).

Stewart Klepper, "The United States in El Salvador," *CovertAction Information Bulletin* (Washington, D.C.), April 1981.

Lawyers Committee for International Human Rights, *El Salvador's Other Victims: The War on the Displaced* (New York: Lawyers Committee, 1984).

David Lena, "Análisis de una Dictatura Fascista Latino-Americana: Maximiliano Hernández Martínez," *La Universidad* (San Salvador), 94, September–October 1969.

Penny Lernoux, *Cry of the People: United States Involvement in the Rise of Fascism, Torture, and Murder and the Persecution of the Catholic Church in Latin America* (New York: Doubleday, 1980).

Michael McClintock, *The American Connection.* Vol. 1: *State Terror and Popular Resistance in El Salvador* (London: Zed Press, 1985).

Alejandro D. Marroquín, *Latin America and the Caribbean: A Handbook,* Claudio Véliz, ed. (Belfast, Ireland: Anthony Blound, 1968).

Percy F. Martin, *Salvador of the Twentieth Century* (London: Edward Arnold, 1911).

Ignacio Martín-Baro, *Acción e ideologia: Psicologia Social desde Centroamérica* (San Salvador: UCA Editores, 1983).

John D. Martz, *Central America: The Crisis and the Challenge* (Chapel Hill: University of North Carolina Press, 1959).

Rafael Menjivar, *El Salvador: El Eslabón Mas Pequeño* (Costa Rica: Editorial Universitaria Centroamericana, 1980).

Segundo Montes, *Estudio sobre Estratificación Social en El Salvador* (San Salvador: n.p., 1979).

Tommie Sue Montgomery, *Revolution in El Salvador,* 2d ed. (Boulder: Westview Press, 1986).

Dana G. Munro, *The Five Republics of Central America: Their Political and Economic Development and Their Relations with the United States* (New York: Oxford University Press, 1918).

———, *Intervention and Dollar Diplomacy in the Caribbean, 1900–1921* (Princeton, N.J.: Princeton University Press, 1964).

National Lawyers Guild, *Guatemala: Repression and Resistance* (NLG, 1980).

North American Congress on Latin America (NACLA), "El Salvador: Why Revolution?" (New York: *NACLA Report,* January–February 1981); "El Salvador: A Revolution Brews" (*NACLA Report,* March–April 1981); "Central America: No Road Back" (*NACLA Report,* May–June 1981). "Duarte: Prisoner of War" (January–February 1986). *Guatemala* (New York: NACLA, 1981).

Michael Parenti, *Inventing Reality: the Politics of the Mass Media* (New York: St. Martin's Press, 1968).

Franklin D. Parker, *The Central American Republics* (London: Oxford University Press, 1964).

James Petras, *Class, State and Power in the Third World: With Case Studies of Class Conflict in Latin America* [with A. Eugene Havens, Morris H. Morley, and Peter De Witt], (Montclair, N.J.: Allanheld, Osmun, 1981).

James Petras and Maurice Zeitlin, eds., *Latin America: Reform or Revolution?* Political Perspectives, Marvin E. Gettleman, ed. (New York: Fawcett: 1968).

David R. Raynolds, *Rapid Development in Small Economies: The Example of El Salvador* (New York: Praeger, 1967).

J. Fred Rippy, *Latin America: A Modern History,* Revised ed. University of Michigan, History of the Modern World, Allan Nevins and Howard M. Ehrmann, eds. (Ann Arbor: University of Michigan Press, 1968).

O. Rodríguez [pseud.?] "The Uprising in Salvador," *The Communist* (New York) 11, March 1932.

Oscar A. Romero, *La Voz de los Sin Voz* [edited by Ricardo Cardenal, Ignacio Martin-Baro and Jon Sobrino] (San Salvador: UCA Editores, 1980).

Philip Russell, *El Salvador in Crisis* (Austin: Colorado River Press, 1984).

William O. Scroggs, *Filibusters and Financiers: The Story of William Walker and His Associates* (New York: Macmillan, 1916).

Edward R. F. Sheehan, "The 'Clean' War [in El Salvador]," *New York Review of Books,* 33, June 26, 1986.

Daniel and Ester Slutsky, "El Salvador: Estructura de la Explotación Cafetalera," *Estudios Sociales Centro-Americanos* (San José, Costa Rica), 1, May–August 1971.

Jon Sobrino, *Mons. Romero: Veradero Profeta* (Managua: Instituto Historico Centroamericano, 1981).

U.S. Central Intelligence Agency, Foreign Broadcast Information Service, *Daily Reports* (Latin American Series, 1962–   ), daily.

Rafael Guidos Vejar, *El Ascenso de Militarismo en El Salvador* (San Salvador: UCA Editores, 1980).

Alastair White, *El Salvador* (Nations of the Modern World), (London: Ernest Benn, 1973).

William Appleman Williams, *Empire as a Way of Life* (New York: Oxford University Press, 1980).

Everett A. Wilson, "The Crisis of National Integration in El Salvador, 1919–1935" (Ph.D. thesis, Stanford University, 1969).

Ralph Lee Woodward, *Central America: A Nation Divided,* 2d ed. (New York: Oxford University Press, 1985).

Alan Wolfe, *The Rise and Fall of the "Soviet Threat": Domestic Sources of the Cold War Consensus* (Washington, D.C.: Institute for Policy Studies, 1980).

RESOURCES

Some Organizations Concerned about El Salvador and U.S. Foreign Policy *

Ad Hoc Committee of Scholars/El Salvador, 21 Washington Place, Box 138, New York, NY 10003

American Friends Service Committee, 1501 Cherry Street, Philadelphia, PA 19102

Americans for Democratic Action, 1411 K Street NW, Washington, DC 20005

Americas Watch, 33 West 44th Street, New York, NY 10036

Amnesty International, 304 West 58th Street, New York, NY 10019

Campus Outreach Committee, Mobilization for Survival, 135 West 4th Street, New York, NY 10012

Center for Defense Information, 122 Maryland Avenue, NE, Washington, DC 20002

Clergy and Laity Concerned, 198 Broadway, New York, NY 10007

Coalition for a New Foreign and Military Policy, 120 Maryland Avenue, NE, Washington, DC 20002

COMADRES [Committee of Mothers and Relatives of Political Prisoners, Disappeared, and Assassinated of El Salvador/Monsignor "Oscar Arnulfo Romero"], Box 21129, Washington, DC 20009-0799

Committee for Medical Aid to El Salvador, Box 384, Planetarium Station, New York, NY 10042

Committee for Non-Intervention in Central America, Box 20391, New York, NY 10025

Committee in Solidarity with the People of El Salvador [CISPES], 853 Broadway, New York, NY 10003

Communist Party USA, 253 West 23rd Street, New York, NY 10011

Council on Hemispheric Affairs, 30 Fifth Avenue, New York, NY 10011

Democratic Socialists of America, 853 Broadway, New York, NY 10003

Educators Committee on Central America, Box 873, Times Square Station, New York, NY 10108

Ecumenical Program for Inter-American Communication and Action [EPICA], 1470 Irving Street, NW, Washington, DC 20010

* For a fuller listing, see *Directory of Central America Organizations* [in the U.S.], Central America Resource Center, Box 2327, Austin, TX 78768.

FACHRES/CA [Faculty Committee for Human Rights in El Salvador and Central America], 613 Eshleman Hall, University of California/Berkeley, Berkeley CA 94720

Fellowship of Reconciliation, Box 271, Nyack, NY 10960

Friends Committee on National Legislation, 245 Second Street, NE, Washington, DC 20002

Institute for Policy Studies, 1901 Q Street, NW, Washington, DC 20009

Interreligious Task Force on El Salvador, 1747 Connecticut Avenue, NW, Washington, DC 20009

Labor Committee in Support of Democracy & Human Rights in El Salvador, c/o Joint Headwear Board, ACTWU [American Clothing and Textile Workers Union], 99 University Place, 9th floor, New York, NY, 10003

Mobilization for Survival, 3601 Locust Walk, Philadelphia, PA 19104

National Council of Churches (Human Rights Office), 475 Riverside Drive, New York, NY 10027

National Lawyers Guild, 853 Broadway, New York, NY 10003

National Network in Solidarity with the Nicaraguan People, 2025 Eye Street NW, #402, Washington, DC 20006

National Network in Solidarity with the People of Guatemala (NISGUA), 930 F Street NW, Suite 720, Washington, DC 20004

North American Congress on Latin America (NACLA), 151 West 19th Street, New York, NY 10011

OXFAM America, 115 Broadway, Boston, MA 02116

RESIST, 38 Union Square, Somerville, MA 02143

SANE, 514 C Street NE, Washington, DC 20002

War Resisters League, 339 Lafayette Street, New York, NY 10012

Washington Office on Latin America, 110 Maryland Avenue, NE, Washington, DC 20002

SELECTED PUBLICATIONS WITH RELEVANT COVERAGE OF CENTRAL AMERICA AND U.S. POLICY

Caribbean Review, Florida International University, Miami, FL 33199; quarterly.

Central America Bulletin, Box 4797, Berkeley, CA 94707

Central America Report, Inforpress Centroamericana, 9a Calle "A" 3-56, Zona 1, Cuidad de Guatemala [Guatemala City], Guatemala, Centro America

Christianity and Crisis, 537 West 121st Street, New York, NY 10027; bimonthly.

ECA/Estudios Centroamericanos, the leading publication on events in El Salvador. Published monthly by the Center de distribucion, Central American University, Apartado postal (06), 668 San Salvador, El Salvador, Central America. Should be supplemented by the weekly *Proceso,* published at the same distinguished Jesuit-run University in El Salvador.

El Salvador Alert (Monthly organizing newsletter of CISPES), Box 50139, Washington, DC 20004

FBIS/Daily Reports (Foreign Broadcast Information Service, a branch of the U.S. Central Intelligence Agency, provides these daily reports in English of monitored radio broadcasts, including commercial stations as well as rebel transmitters). Volume 6, each day, covers Latin America, including a segment on Central America. Invaluable source, used extensively in this volume.

Guardian, 33 West 17th Street, New York, NY 10003; weekly.

Inquiry, 747 Front Street, San Francisco, CA 94111; monthly.

In These Times, 1300 West Belmont, Chicago IL 60557; weekly.

JPRS (U.S. Department of Commerce, Joint Publications Research Series, *Translations*) offers selections from newspapers, periodicals, documents, etc., from all over the world, including Central America.

Latin American Perspectives, Box 792, Riverside CA 92502; quarterly.

Latin America Weekly Report and *Latin America Regional Report,* 90–93 Cowcross Street, London EC1M 6BL, England.

Maryknoll Magazine, Maryknoll, NY 10545; monthly.

Monthly Review, 62 West 14th Street, New York, NY 10011; monthly.

Mother Jones, 625 Third Street, San Francisco, CA 94107; monthly.

NACLA Report, 151 West 19th Street, New York, NY 10011; bimonthly.

The Nation, 72 Fifth Avenue, New York, NY 10011; weekly.

The New Republic, 1220 19th Street, NW, Washington, DC 20036; weekly.

The Progressive, 408 West Gorham, Madison, WI 53703; monthly.

Socialist Review, 4228 Telegraph Avenue, Oakland, CA 94609; bimonthly.

Washington Office on Latin America, *Newsletter,* 110 Maryland Avenue, NE, Washington, DC 20002; monthly.

Index

This is a selective index containing significant names and subjects that cannot be readily found in the table of contents. —Editors

SHOWSTOPPERS!

THE
SURPRISING
BACKSTAGE STORIES OF
BROADWAY'S
MOST REMARKABLE SONGS

GERALD NACHMAN

DISCARD

CHICAGO
REVIEW
PRESS

An A Cappella Book

Published by Chicago Review Press Incorporated
814 North Franklin Street
Chicago, Illinois 60610
ISBN 978-1-61373-102-4

Library of Congress Cataloging-in-Publication Data
Names: Nachman, Gerald, author.
Title: Showstoppers! : the surprising backstage stories of Broadway's most
    remarkable songs / Gerald Nachman.
Description: First edition. | Chicago : Chicago Review Press, 2016. |
    Includes bibliographical references and index.
Identifiers: LCCN 2016012969 (print) | LCCN 2016013216 (ebook) | ISBN
    9781613731024 (trade paper) | ISBN 9781613731048 (adobe pdf) | ISBN
    9781613731055 (epub) | ISBN 9781613731031 (kindle)
Subjects: LCSH: Musicals—New York (State)—New York—History and criticism.
Classification: LCC ML1711.8.N3 N33 2016 (print) | LCC ML1711.8.N3 (ebook) |
    DDC 782.1/4097471—dc23
LC record available at http://lccn.loc.gov/2016012969

A list of permissions for the lyrics quoted in this book can be found on pages 361–363.

Cover design: Rebecca Lown
Cover images: Photofest
Interior design: Jonathan Hahn
Interior images: Photofest (except where noted)

Printed in the United States of America
5 4 3 2 1